UNCOMMON VALOR ON IWO JIMA

UNCOMMON VALOR ON IWO JIMA

The Story of the Medal of Honor
Recipients in the Marine Corps'
Bloodiest Battle of World War II

James H. Hallas

STACKPOLE
BOOKS

Published by Stackpole Books
An imprint of Globe Pequot
Trade Division of The Rowman & Littlefield Publishing Group, Inc.
4501 Forbes Boulevard, Suite 200, Lanham, Maryland 20706
www.rowman.com

Distributed by National Book Network

Printed in the United States of America

10   9   8   7   6   5   4   3   2   1

Cover design by Wendy A. Reynolds

Library of Congress Cataloging-in-Publication Data
Names: Hallas, James H., author.
Title: Uncommon valor on Iwo Jima : the story of the Medal of Honor
    recipients in the Marine Corps' bloodiest battle of World War II / James
    H. Hallas.
Other titles: Story of the Medal of Honor recipients in the Marine Corps'
    bloodiest battle of World War II
Description: Mechanicsburg, PA : Stackpole Books, [2016] | Includes
    bibliographical references and index.
Identifiers: LCCN 2015047355 | ISBN 9780811717953
Subjects: LCSH: Iwo Jima, Battle of, Japan, 1945. | Marines—United
    States—Biography. | United States. Marine Corps—Biography. | Medal of
    Honor.
Classification: LCC D767.99.I9 H34 2016 | DDC 940.54/2528—dc23 LC record
available at http://lccn.loc.gov/2015047355

CONTENTS

MAP KEY

1) Lt. (jg) Rufus Geddie Herring
LCI(G)–449
February 17, 1945

2) Sgt. Darrell S. Cole
23rd Marines, 4th Marine Division
February 19, 1945

3) Cpl. Tony Stein
28th Marines, 5th Marine Division
February 19, 1945

4) Gunnery Sgt. John Basilone
27th Marines, 5th Marine Division
February 19, 1945

5) Lt. Col Justice M. Chambers
25th Marines, 4h Marine Division
February 19–22, 1945

6) PFC Jacklyn H. Lucas
26th Marines, 5th Marine Division
February 20, 1945

7) Capt. Robert Hugo Dunlap
26th Marines, 5th Marine Division
February 20–21, 1945

8) PFC Donald Jack Ruhl
28th Marines, 5th Marine Division
February 19–21, 1945

9) Sgt. Ross F. Gray
25th Marines, 4th Marine Division
February 21, 1945

10) Capt. Joseph J. McCarthy
24th Marines, 4th Marine Division
February 21, 1945

11) Cpl. Hershel W. Williams
21st Marines, 3rd Marine Division
February 23, 1945

12) PFC Douglas T. Jacobson
23rd Marines, 4th Marine Division
February 26, 1945

13) Pvt. Wilson D. Watson
9th Marines, 3rd Marine Division
February 26–27, 1945

14) Gunnery Sgt. William G. Walsh
27th Marines, 5th Marine Division
February 27, 1945

15) Pharmacist's Mate 1st Class John H. Willis
27th Marines, 5th Marine Division
February 28, 1945

16) Cpl. Charles J. Berry
26th Marines, 5th Marine Division
March 3, 1945

17) Sgt. William G. Harrell
28th Marines, 5th Marine Division
March 3, 1945

18) PFC William R. Caddy
26th Marines, 5th Marine Division
March 3, 1945

19) Pharmacist's Mate 2nd Class George E. Wahlen
26th Marines, 5th Marine Division
March 3, 1945

20) Pharmacist's Mate 3rd Class Jack Williams
28th Marines, 5th Marine Division
March 3, 1945

21) 2nd Lieutenant John H. Leims
9th Marines, 3rd Marine Division
March 7, 1945

22) 1st Lt. Jack Lummus
27th Marines, 5th Marine Division
March 8, 1945

23) PFC James D. LaBelle
27th Marines, 5th Marine Division
March 8, 1945

24) Platoon Sgt. Joseph R. Julian
27th Marines, 5th Marine Division
March 9, 1945

25) Pvt. George Phillips
28th Marines, 5th Marine Division
March 14, 1945

26) Pvt. Franklin E. Sigler
26th Marines, 5th Marine Division
March 14, 1945

27) Pharmacist's Mate 1st Class Francis J. Pierce
24th Marines, 4th Marine Division
March 15–16, 1945

28) 1st Lt. Harry L. Martin
5th Pioneer Battalion, 5th Marine Division
March 26, 1945

INTRODUCTION

Capt. Donald Beck was at his wits' end. It was February 23, D+4 on Iwo Jima, and all morning he had watched helplessly as his company bled itself out in futile efforts to break through a cordon of Japanese pillboxes protecting the island's centermost airfield. Frustrated and out of ideas, he gathered his noncoms in the protection of a large shell hole and asked for suggestions. No one seemed to have the solution to their problem. In some desperation, Beck looked at his last surviving flamethrower operator, an undersized kid from rural West Virginia, and asked if he could do something with his flamethrower.

Trying to swallow his fear, twenty-one-year-old Willie Williams replied, "I'll try."

Williams then proceeded to crawl out and destroy seven pillboxes in a four-hour rampage that would earn him the Medal of Honor. No one could understand how he managed to survive—least of all Williams himself—but he did.

It would be the rare American who failed to recognize the iconic flag raising on Iwo Jima's Mount Suribachi. A moment frozen in time, captured by AP photographer Joseph Rosenthal, the image stands as a stirring symbol of American determination and fighting spirit. Large measures of both those qualities were needed on Iwo Jima, targeted

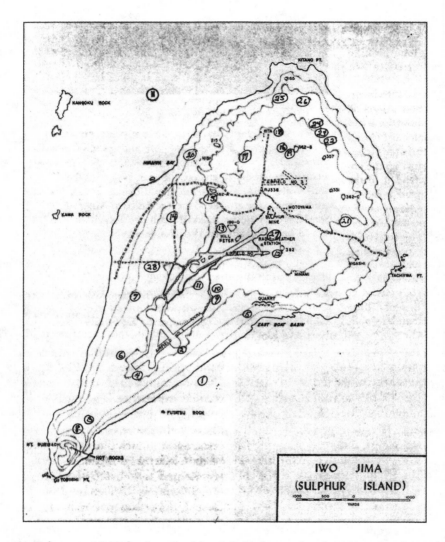

in February 1945 for its valuable airfields located only 660 miles from Tokyo. Fighting from holes, caves, tunnels, and pillboxes dug into the volcanic ash and the island's sandstone core, the 22,000-man Japanese garrison fought nearly to the last man, inflicting terrible casualties on assaulting U.S. Marines.

"About the beach in the morning lay the dead," wrote *Time* magazine correspondent Robert Sherrod of the landing on February 19,

1945. "They had died with the greatest possible violence. Nowhere in the Pacific have I seen such badly mangled bodies."

It would not get any easier. Over a period of thirty-six days, three Marine divisions—the 3rd, 4th, and 5th—suffered over 24,000 casualties, including over 7,000 killed. It was the bloodiest battle in the history of the U.S. Marine Corps, and the only major Pacific battle where a U.S. landing force suffered more casualties than it inflicted. Decades later, veterans of the battle referred to themselves as "Iwo Jima survivors." It was that bad.

"Victory was never in doubt," observed Maj. Gen. Graves Erskine immediately following the battle. "Its cost was. What was in doubt, in all our minds, was whether there would be any of us left to dedicate our cemetery at the end, or whether the last Marine would die knocking out the last Japanese gun and gunner."

As Adm. Chester Nimitz was to say, "Among the Americans who served on Iwo Island, uncommon valor was a common virtue." In fact, Iwo Jima was the most highly decorated single engagement in U.S. history. Twenty-seven Medals of Honor were awarded for actions that took place in just over a month of combat. Twenty-two went to Marines and five went to sailors. The first was earned on February 17, 1945, two days before the Marines landed on Iwo's black sand beaches, by a navy lieutenant commanding a boat too small to have a name. The last was awarded for an action that took place ten days after the island had been officially—if prematurely—declared secure. Thirteen of the awards were posthumous.

A Marine who had previously received the Medal of Honor for heroism on Guadalcanal nearly two and a half years earlier was also among the dead, killed within hours of the landing on the first day. His name was John Basilone. Already a national hero at the time of his death, Sergeant Basilone was one of over 200 Marines and sailors awarded the Navy Cross for heroic actions on Iwo Jima—an astonishing number. The citations for those Navy Cross medals—an award second only to the Medal of Honor—portray a record of heroism and self-sacrifice that is almost beyond comprehension. Almost any one of the actions described in that official record could just as easily have warranted the Medal of Honor.

Add to this the countless acts of heroism on Iwo Jima that went unreported and unrewarded as the fighting men concentrated on the dirty job at hand, witnesses were killed or wounded, or exceptional acts of courage were taken as simply a matter of course. "They died so fast," said a company commander. "You'd see a man do something almost unbelievable and a minute later you'd see him die." What is surprising, perhaps, is that there were "only" twenty-seven Medal of Honor awards, and not ten times that number.

The recipients themselves knew this to be true. When asked, they almost invariably said they did nothing special; that other men showed equal bravery and received no recognition; that combat is a team effort; that they were just lucky to have been singled out; and that they wear the medal on behalf of their buddies and for the real heroes—the men who never made it home. All of that may be true, but none of it changes what they did.

Today, the heroes of Iwo Jima have been largely forgotten. Age has done what Japanese bullets could not. As of this writing, only one Iwo Jima Medal of Honor recipient—Hershel Williams, known to his Marine buddies as "Willie"—survives. Some recipients—particularly those who died in action—were never much celebrated outside their own hometowns to begin with. Others, who were more widely known at the time, have since faded from popular memory. Their numbers included high school dropouts, a former professional football player, a onetime milkman's assistant, farm kids, a youngster who hoped to one day become a doctor, a tool and die maker, a couple of kids who dreamed of playing professional baseball, even a lawyer. They deserve to be remembered.

These are their stories.

CHAPTER ONE

Opening Bell

Saturday, February 17 (D–2), dawned clear off Iwo Jima. The seas rolled with a slight swell, while the low ceiling and intermittent squalls of the previous day had lifted, promising good visibility for aerial target spotters.

As the sun emerged on the eastern horizon, sailors aboard the great naval armada gathered offshore saw Mount Suribachi beginning to take shape, looming 550 feet over the southern tip of the pork chop–shaped land mass. The entire island was only 4.5 miles long and 2–5 miles wide at its broadest, a miserable place reeking of rotten eggs from the sulfur fumes wafting from cracks in the heated rock. To Suribachi's right stretched the two miles of beach where the 4th and 5th Marine Divisions were scheduled to land forty-eight hours later, hedged in on the right by rising cliffs that held the threat of enfilade. Black volcanic sand rose in a series of terraces behind the beaches to Iwo's airfields and an ominous interior, where 22,000 Japanese waited in pillboxes, blockhouses, tunnels, and holes, or sweltered in underground caverns carved from the soft rock.

It was for this forsaken hunk of rock and ash—dubbed "Sulfur Island" by its defenders, by virtue of its noxious emanations—that 495 ships crewed by thousands of sailors and carrying 70,000 U.S.

Marines had crossed seemingly endless miles of ocean. The horizon was crowded with ships: hulking battleships dedicated to shore bombardment, agile destroyers, cruisers and aircraft carriers, and a multitude of smaller craft, each with a task to perform in that most intricate of military dances—an amphibious landing on a defended shore.

The preliminaries for that dance had already begun in the form of days of air and naval bombardment. Now some new participants were about to take the floor before the main event. Aboard the battleship *Tennessee*, modernized and back in action after being damaged in the Japanese attack on Pearl Harbor over three years before, *Harper's* correspondent John P. Marquand learned there was to be "a diversion" later that morning. "We're going to reconnoiter the beach with small craft," an officer told the fifty-one-year-old writer. "And the LCIs [Landing Craft Infantry] will strafe the terraces with rockets."

By now the sun had broken through the cloud ceiling and the sea was almost blue, observed Marquand. "The heavy ships had formed a line, firing methodically," he recalled. "Two destroyers edged their way past us and took position nearer shore." The LCIs appeared, dwarfed by the big warships.

"Where are they going in those things?" he asked.

"They are going to see what there is along the beach," came the reply.

"Eight or ten LCIs—it was difficult to count them—were passing among the battleships, with their crews at their battle stations," wrote Marquand afterward. "They were small vessels that had never been designed for heavy combat. They had been built only to carry infantry ashore, but in the Pacific they were being put to all sorts of other uses—as messenger ships to do odd jobs for the fleet, as gunboats, and as rocket ships. Each had a round tower amidships where the commanding officer stood. Each had open platforms with light automatic guns, and now they were also fitted with brackets for rockets. They were high and narrow, about a hundred feet [long] overall, dabbed with orange and green paint in jungle camouflage. They were a long way from jungle shores, however, as they moved toward the beach of Iwo Jima." Strapped into kapok life jackets, peering out from under their steel helmets, the crews seemed motionless at their stations.

Afterward one of the LCI crewmen told Marquand, "If we looked so still, it was because we were scared to death. But then everyone had told us there was nothing to be scared of. They told us the Japs never bothered to fire at LCIs."

LT. (JG) RUFUS GEDDIE HERRING

LCI(G)-449
February 17, 1945

Rufus Geddie Herring. U.S. Navy

Among the unprepossessing vessels John Marquand observed plowing toward Iwo's dark shore was LCI(G)-449—a landing craft converted into a gunboat, hence the "G"—commanded by Rufus Geddie Herring, a slender, rather low-key twenty-four-year-old reserve lieutenant (jg) from tiny Roseboro, North Carolina. The "Rufus" was a mere formality—a nod to his paternal grandfather. Family and friends all called him Geddie, which was his mother's maiden name.

Three years before finding himself in command of a gunboat off Iwo Jima, Geddie Herring had been pursuing a degree in economics at peaceful Davidson College, a liberal arts school founded by Presbyterians in 1837, 140 miles northwest of the Herring homestead in rural Roseboro. As the son of one of the more prominent families in the eastern part of the state, Geddie and an older brother had grown up in considerable affluence. Their imposing residence is still considered the finest example of a grand Classic Revival house in Sampson County, complete with paneled staircase, inlaid floors, and columned entrance. The house was built in 1912 for their wealthy father, Troy Isaac Herring, whose lumber company was one of the largest businesses in that part of the state. The patriarch of the family was also involved in banking, along with a variety of civic and social endeavors that included the building of Roseboro's Methodist Church. Troy Herring had succumbed to heart failure in 1935 at the age of only fifty-two, but the family retained its social and economic stature. Geddie intended to put his degree to good use by following in his father's entrepreneurial footsteps, but the outbreak of war put that ambition on hold, at least temporarily

Herring joined the U.S. Naval Reserves in April 1942 after receiving his Bachelor of Science degree in economics. He attended Midshipman School in New York City, and was commissioned with the rank of ensign. He subsequently received diesel engine instruction at the University of Illinois, followed by orders to the Amphibious Training Base at Solomons, Maryland. He must have been an astute student, for in August 1943 he received his own command— not particularly glamorous, perhaps, but his: the newly built landing craft USS LCI(L)-449. Too small to boast a name, having only a number, 449 was just over 160 feet long, with a 23-foot beam and a maximum speed of 16 knots. As a landing craft, the LCI was crewed by four officers and twenty-four enlisted men, and could carry nearly two hundred troops.

Herring and his crew soon found themselves on the vast Pacific, where the American counterattack against Japanese expansion was building powerful momentum in early 1944. Between February and July 1944, Herring's LCI participated in the invasions of Kwajalein, Saipan, Tinian, and Guam, her skipper performing competently enough to earn a promotion to lieutenant (jg) in March.

Meanwhile, the art and tools of amphibious landings, including the role of Herring's LCI, had been steadily evolving. By the time of the Marianas campaign in June, 449's designation had been changed from LCI(L), translated as Landing Craft Infantry (Large), to LCI(G)-449, or Landing Craft Infantry (Gunboat). Instead of troops, she was now to carry heavier firepower. Her five 20mm guns were replaced with two

40mm guns, four 20mm guns, six .50-caliber machine guns, and ten MK7 rocket launchers. Located along the sides, the 4.5-inch rockets could be triggered electronically to provide salvos of close-in fire support for troops assaulting a beach. The additional weaponry required more hands, and the crew was expanded to five officers and sixty-five enlisted men. In this new role, LCI(G)-449 took part in the capture and occupation of Saipan, Guam, and Tinian in the summer of 1944. Having participated in four landings without harm, morale was high on the LCI. Veteran crewmembers told newly arrived youngsters not to worry. The 449 was a lucky ship.

LCI(G)-449, Rufus Herring's command. Armed with 40mm and 20mm guns and carrying rockets, the gunboat was intended for close support during landing operations. At Iwo, the boat got a little too close. U.S. Navy

Despite the "gunboat" designation, Herring's command was downright puny in comparison to the other warships now gathered off Iwo's shores, but the planners had found a role for LCI(G)-449 and her crew. Their job on the morning of February 17 was to move in close to the shore and use their guns to protect Underwater Demolition Teams (UDT) reconnoitering the landing area. With the assault on Iwo Jima scheduled for February 19, the UDT swimmers had been directed to make a last-minute survey of the waters just off the beaches, searching for mines and other obstacles that might interfere with the landing. The swimmers would disembark from small craft 500 yards offshore. Close-in protection would be provided by Herring's LCI(G) and six other LCI gunboats armed with 20mm and 40mm guns. The LCIs were also to fire rocket salvos at the shore in an effort to distract enemy defenders while the swimmers did their work. The gunboats would set off at 1000.

Wooden-hulled minesweepers were already at work offshore shortly after 0800. As the minesweepers came under fire from Japanese coastal batteries, the cruiser USS *Pensacola* sallied forth to retaliate, boldly approaching to within 1,500 yards of Iwo's northeastern shore. It turned out to be too close. At about 0935 a Japanese gun crew dropped a 150mm shell fifty yards short of the ship, then proceeded to put six shells into the cruiser in the space of about three minutes. Seventeen officers and men were killed, including the ship's executive officer; 120 men were wounded, the combat information center was knocked out, and the ship was hulled in several places.

The incident did not bode well for the waiting LCIs. The *Pensacola* boasted armor up to four inches thick. The only armor on LCI(G)-449 was two inches of plastic splinter protection on the gun turrets, conning tower, and pilot house. That plastic would be about as much protection as a stick of butter in the event of a direct hit from a 150mm shell.

The small landing craft carrying the UDT swimmers approached Iwo's shoreline in a staggered formation. The LCI gunboats 457, 441, 449, 438, 474, 450, and 473 followed, plowing along abreast at 9 knots. The symmetry of their formation, and their location behind the boats racing forward with the UDT teams, persuaded the Japanese that the actual invasion was underway. Shortly before 1100, as the gunboats passed the 1,500-yard line, crews noticed geysers of water erupting around them and realized they were under fire.

"At first, we thought that the shell splashes between us and the beach were shots from our own ships falling short," recalled Lt. (jg) Matthew J. Reichl, commanding LCI(G)-474, "but as these splashes walked up towards the gunboats on our port hand and then swung over to us, we realized that it was return fire from Jap shore batteries. This fire was coming from both the northern and southern flanks of the beach. We immediately commenced heavy 40mm and 20mm strafing while maneuvering as radically as possible in our small area attempting to avoid hits."

The LCIs found themselves ridiculously outgunned. The water roiled as enemy fire rained down on the boats from both flanks—artillery, large mortars, 37mm, 25mm, and machine-gun bullets—as the Japanese sought to turn back what they mistakenly believed to be a landing attempt. To the shock of U.S. gunnery officers responsible for softening up enemy defenses before the landing, much of the fire directed at the LCIs came from heretofore unknown and unsuspected positions. Their premature disclosure would prove a boon to Marines who landed two days later—had they remained unidentified, these guns would have added immeasurably to the havoc wreaked on the actual landing—but the LCIs, now within 1,000 yards of the base of Mount Suribachi, were about to pay a high price for that intelligence.

Three boats—LCI(G)s 474, 450, and 473—were hit almost simultaneously at 1055. LCI-474 took ten heavy-caliber hits in eight minutes, knocking out all seven guns, flooding four compartments and starting fires. LCI-450 received two hits in the starboard forward head, followed two minutes later by two more hits on the port side, then one in the captain's cabin. Several crewmen were wounded. LCI-474 was hit by a 5- or 6-inch shell on the starboard side at 1055, wounding over a dozen men and starting a fire that was extinguished in about three minutes. Those hits were quickly followed by three more shells that flooded the engine room and left the gunboat dead in the water. The accuracy of the fire was greatly enhanced by ranging buoys the enemy had placed offshore. The buoys had been spotted earlier, but inexplicably no action had been taken to remove or destroy them.

John Marquand got a close-up look at the devastation when one of the LCI(G)s came alongside the *Tennessee*. "There was blood on the main deck, making widening pools as she rolled in the sluggish sea," he wrote. "A dead man on a gun platform was covered by a blanket. The decks were littered with wounded. They were being strapped on wire stretchers and passed up to us over the side."

Herring's 449, assigned to cover UDT swimmers off Yellow Beach 1, escaped the initial battering at 1055—narrowly eluding at least one near miss—but the respite was only momentary. At 1058, a Japanese shell slammed into 449's bow just aft of the 40mm splinter shield. Aboard LCI(G)-457, which had problems of its own, Seaman 3rd Class Wally Exum looked to his left as he heard a loud explosion and saw the hit on 449. "I saw two men flying through the air," he recalled. Then 449's 40mm ammunition began to explode. Exum looked at his own 40mm crew and said, rather unnecessarily, "I think we're in for it!"

The two men Exum saw blown in the air were twenty-six-year-old Seaman 1st Class John Flook and Ensign Fredrick S. Cooper, the bow gunnery officer and a former high school teacher from Orange, Iowa. As 449 continued toward the beach, Cooper was spotted floating in the water, either dead or unconscious. His body was never recovered. Of Flook, only a leg remained.

Seaman 1st Class Bruce Hallet was serving as pointer on the bow 40mm cannon when the shell hit. "There were seven of us on the bow and only two of us came out alive," he recalled. "Both of us were wounded. All I can recall was looking through my gun sight and focusing in—we were a thousand yards from the beach, relatively close." He had just begun firing on what he took to be Japanese machine-gun emplacements. "I fired in on three of them and the next thing I know I was enveloped in a wall of flame," he recalled. "That's the first thing I can remember, I thought I would be burned alive. I was scared to death. There were just flames all the way around me." Next thing Hallet knew, he was out of the gun tub and lying semiconscious on the very point of the bow. How he got there, he had no idea.

Seaman 1st Class Lawrence Bozarth was less fortunate; his head had been blown off. Hallet saw Bozarth's body lying next to a gaping six-foot hole where Ensign Cooper had been stationed. Another survivor, Boatswain's Mate Frank Blow, recalled there seemed to be bodies everywhere. The gun captain, Gunner's Mate 3rd Class Chuck Banko, was knocked unconscious and came to his senses hanging upside down on the ladder leading down to the well deck.

At the conn, Herring barely had time to register the first hit when 449 found itself in even deeper trouble. At 1103 the gunboat was hit again, this time on the portside 40mm. The gun crew was virtually wiped out. A sailor coming topside to help the wounded had the top of his head cleaved off. Another man was sheared in half. Others lay dead by the gun or on the deck. One lucky sailor survived when his life jacket caught on a rail, preventing him from being blown over the side. Another sailor pulled him back on board and slapped out the fire on his life vest. Gunner's Mate 3rd Class Howard Schoenleben, who had been manning the starboard 40mm, was less fortunate. The blast nearly sliced off his whole right shoulder, exposing his beating heart. A pharmacist's mate administered morphine, but Schoenleben quickly expired.

Up on the bridge, Herring maintained his crippled ship's position in the line of LCIs. The situation was highly confused. His ship was on fire in places, and messages to the pilothouse below were not being acknowledged. Unknown to Herring, the second shell had also riddled the pilothouse, killing or wounding everyone inside. One man was later found still seated—headless—in his chair behind the radio.

Herring and a mixed group of officers and enlisted men crowded the bridge as he worked to keep 449 on course. The group included Herring's executive officer, Bryon Yarbrough, and two signalmen; a navy photographer, Leo McGrath, who had volunteered to go along and take pictures of the UDT sweep; and two observers, Lt. (jg) Leo Yates from the UDT teams and twenty-two-year-old Marine corporal Edward Brockmeyer of Severna Park, Maryland, who had been commended less than a year earlier for personally knocking out a Japanese pillbox on Saipan. The son of a grocer, Brockmeyer was one of five boys in the service; his younger brother had been killed at Salerno earlier in the war. The gunboat's deck log recorded the sequence of events beginning with the first hit on 449:

> 1058—Received shell of undetermined size on the bow aft of the 40mm splinter shield with the resulting casualties: Two men killed, two men missing, both were blown off of the bow; and three men wounded.
>
> 1103—Received shell of undetermined size on the port side 40mm with casualties unknown.
>
> 1104—Received a shell of undetermined size on the starboard side of the conning tower with unknown number of casualties.

Herring was still fruitlessly attempting to raise the pilothouse when the third hit—a Japanese mortar shell—exploded on the starboard side of the conning tower. While the ship's deck log subsequently recorded the three hits on the gunboat as taking place over a period of about six minutes, Herring's recollection was that they followed each other in rapid succession. "It all happened in forty-five seconds," he recalled of the sequence of events. "The first shell hit our forward gun and killed that entire crew. The second shell took out the other forward gun and killed that crew. The third shell hit the bridge. There were seven of us up there and everyone was killed but me."

In fact, they weren't all dead, but considering the carnage, it certainly seemed that way. Brockmeyer, Yarbrough, Yates, and navy photographer McGrath were all killed instantly—Yates eviscerated, slumped in a pile of his own guts; the rest mostly blown to pieces. The two signalmen were also badly injured, one of them fatally.

Herring was blown out of the conning tower and landed on the deck below, bleeding heavily from multiple wounds. One arm was shattered at the elbow. A large shell fragment protruded from the torn flesh and muscle. One of his legs was broken. His command was a wreck. Almost every man topside was now dead or wounded. Both his

40mm guns and all but one of his 20mm guns were out of action. Fire had broken out on board; the ship was wallowing out of control and in danger of sinking. "The ship was foundering and we were heading straight for the beach," he recalled. "I looked out and there wasn't a soul standing. The covers on the ammunition were burning and there were bodies everywhere, with some on fire."

Aboard LCI(G)-471, Ensign L. M. Hermes Jr. examined 449 as the vessel passed by to the starboard. "It was badly damaged and smoking—only one person was topside and he was staggering towards the fantail," he recalled. "I have later wondered if this was Lieutenant Herring, who won the Medal of Honor for saving his LCI(G)."

Despite his severe wounds, Herring struggled to pull himself together. "My first thought was, 'You SOBs, you had your chance and you didn't get me and you're not going to get me now,'" he said later. Somehow he managed to drag himself to the blood-spattered pilot-house. "There were fourteen crew members below deck and some-body had to try to save them," he explained.

Inside the pilothouse, Herring found Ensign Robert W. Duvall, who had been badly wounded but was still trying his best to steer the ship. Fighting to remain conscious, Herring established communication with the engine room, regaining control of the ship. Topside, a sailor continued to fire toward shore with the lone remaining 20mm gun. As Herring's strength waned, the blood-soaked skipper struggled to remain upright by sheer force of will.

Meanwhile, frantic radio calls revealed that 449 wasn't the only vessel in distress. 471 asked, "Where do we go" for medical help? Engines had been knocked out on 441, and the LCI was dead in the water. 457 appeared to be sinking fast. 469 took multiple hits and was flooding. 438's bow gun had been blown away. 459 was anchored, on fire, and needed a tow to survive. 466 was in the same terrible condition. 473 had been riddled with nearly 200 holes in the hull and was on fire.

By now, even Herring's stubbornness could not compensate for his loss of blood. He had regained control of his ship, but it was obvious he could not continue as he started to drift in and out of consciousness. Clinging to the bow, Seaman 1st Class Bruce Hallet groggily charted the course of events from the time the first shell hit. "The ship was blown up enough that we had to stop our coverage of the Underwater Demolition swimmers," he recalled. "Our skipper, Lieutenant Herring, was wounded at this time. He got us all together again and we went back in again! And we got hit more and *he* was hit again. We had to stop again, stop our combat action and withdraw again, re-form . . . he took us in a third time. And we covered the swimmers. We finally had to leave because every gun on the vessel was out of commission. We had one 20mm weapon left firing, that's all we had. We were just shot to hell."

Dead and wounded on the deck of one of the LCI gunboats damaged while supporting the UDT teams on February 17, 1945, at Iwo Jima. U.S. Navy

Of the seven officers aboard, only the engineering officer, Ensign L. W. Bedell, had not been killed or wounded. He now assumed command. Boatswain's Mate Frank Blow took the wheel and turned the stricken ship out to sea in hopes of finding assistance. At 1130 the gunboat—its deck littered with dead and wounded and fragments of bodies—hove to on the port side of a destroyer-minesweeper, which sent over a small boat with a doctor and several corpsmen to give medical assistance. At 1135 the gunboat got underway at one-third speed and proceeded to fleet minelayer USS *Terror*. Serving as a tender to the minesweeping operation, *Terror* now found itself pressed into service as a casualty evacuation vessel for the small craft seeking help. Over a period of about forty-five minutes, twelve gunboats—both the original seven and five others that rushed in for support as boats were damaged—were hit. One was sunk. Total casualties were forty-seven dead, with three missing and presumed dead, and another 148 wounded. Ironically, the UDT teams, who arguably had the more dangerous mission that morning, lost only one swimmer killed during their reconnaissance.

LCI(G)-449 had been hit before the crew could fire its complement of rockets toward shore. Now the survivors had to hurriedly dump the starboard-side rockets overboard before *Terror* would allow the gunboat to come alongside. Several doctors, corpsmen, and volunteers came aboard to help transfer the wounded and dead aboard the ship. It was now noon.

Though severely injured and weak from loss of blood, Herring was still alive, having propped himself up against a pile of empty shell casings in a last determined effort before finally relinquishing command. At 1346 he was brought aboard *Terror*, along with nineteen other wounded officers and men. They were followed shortly by the dead, some of whom had been blown to pieces. The dying wasn't over yet. At 1630 Signalman Carl Park, who had been at the conn with Herring when the mortar hit, succumbed to his wounds. Gunner's Mate 3rd Class Ralph Owens died the following afternoon, bringing the number of 449's dead to twenty-one.

"We put the dead in body bags made out of real heavy canvas," remembered James Bush, a water tender serving aboard USS *Terror*. "We sewed a 35-pound practice shell between their feet. We had a board rigged up like a heavy piece of plywood. . . . We had the flag over the body in the canvas, and we'd go through the whole service and they'd say 'Now we commend this body to the deep,' and we'd pick up the board and the body would slide straight out and down into the water. It would disappear in a hurry."

USS *Terror* remained off Iwo Jima until the afternoon of February 19. By that time, the carnage ashore made the bloodshed of February 17 look like a minor skirmish. *Terror* headed for the Marianas. "There were so many wounded that we had them in our bunks," said Bush. On February 21, *Terror* transferred the casualties on board to an army hospital on Saipan. Herring was eventually transferred to a hospital back in the States.

Herring's war was over, though his recuperation would take months. His ship, the little LCI(G)-449, was still afloat, battered but repairable. A summation of battle damage noted: "Conn shot away, gyro and magnetic compasses destroyed. May be able to return to duty if parts can be found." Efforts were also underway to verify the actions of February 17. Lt. J. J. Mittleton, who went aboard 449 with nineteen sailors to relieve the survivors, compiled the action report for that terrifying half hour off Iwo's beaches. In terse, official prose, he observed:

> In less than one minute, three hits started two serious fires, left the ship temporarily out of control, disabled all 40mm guns and wounded nineteen (19) men, five of the latter suffering critical injuries. The Commanding Officer, Lieutenant (JG) R. G. HERRING, USNR, had suffered multiple wounds and was in critical condition, rapidly losing strength from severe bleeding, but continued to fight his ship. . . . The pilot house not answering orders from the conn, the Captain went to the pilot house, assigned a replacement for his helmsman, conned the ship and directed the care of the wounded from there. All officers except the Engineer were either missing, killed or wounded.

Secretary of the Navy James Forrestal presents the Medal of Honor to Lieutenant (jg) Herring on September 5, 1945, in Washington, D.C. From left center to right center: Mrs. Susan Geddie Herring (Lt. Herring's mother), Mrs. L. Geddie (his aunt), and Mr. L. Geddie (his uncle). U.S. Navy

On September 5, 1945, accompanied by his mother, aunt, and uncle, a smiling Rufus Geddie Herring was awarded the Medal of Honor by Secretary of the Navy James E. Forrestal. His was the only Medal of Honor to be awarded to an LCI sailor during World War II. Also honored at the ceremony at the Navy Department in Washington, D.C., were eight other naval officers, commanders of other craft in LCI action off Iwo Jima, who received the Navy Cross. The secretary also presented the Navy Unit Commendation to LCI(G) Group 8. A wire service account of the ceremony observed with cool brevity that "Herring was twice critically wounded by enemy fire which disabled many of his guns, set his ship afire, and killed most of his officers. Recovering consciousness the second time, he took over the helm and carried on until relief was obtained."

Herring recovered from his wounds and remained in the navy until 1947, when he was retired for disability with the rank of lieutenant commander. That same year he married Virginia Lee Higgs, a navy nurse from Parkersburg, West Virginia, who had served seventeen months in the Pacific Theater as a lieutenant. They returned to Herring's home-town of Roseboro, where he joined his older brother, Troy, as partner in the lumber business. In 1949, he opened a retail furniture business, and in 1957, now the father of two boys and a girl ranging in age from two to seven years, he started a Purina Feed Mill and hatching-egg operation partnership. In 1979 he sold his interest to a Pennsylvania corporation and worked for them until 1982, when he retired.

He was active in the community, serving as mayor in 1948–49, and was a Sampson County Board of Education member from 1952 to 1962. In 1996, the governor of North Carolina honored him with the Order of the Long Leaf Pine, the state's highest award for public ser-vice. Critically ill with cancer, Herring was unable to travel to the cap-ital to receive the award, so the capital came to him. Dignitaries, family, and friends packed the small chapel at Duke Hospital in Durham for a brief ceremony. Herring attended the ceremony in a wheelchair, assisted by hospital staff and his grandson, Geddie II. Neatly dressed in blue-and-green-plaid pajamas and a blue-and-white-striped robe, he wore around his neck—probably for the last time—the Medal of Honor presented to him by President Harry Truman fifty years before. Ever the hometown boy, he expressed his great pride at being a North Carolinian. "He was a life-long resident of Roseboro, except for the time he went to college and World War II; he lived, died and he was buried in Roseboro," his oldest son, Max Herring, observed later. "He even declined the offer to be buried in Arlington National Cemetery to lay in repose in Roseboro."

Herring died of lung cancer on January 31, 1996, at the age of seventy-four and is buried in Roseboro Cemetery. A family member later remarked that Herring never had much to say about his heroics off Iwo Jima. Over two decades after that bloody morning, however, he did offer an observation on the medal to Robert Patterson, an 82nd Airborne Division paratrooper who had just been awarded his own Medal of Honor for heroism in Vietnam. "Young man, let me tell you something right now," Herring quietly told the young airborne trooper. "It will be much harder to wear that ribbon than it was to earn it." Recalling that conversation some twenty-five years later, Patterson observed, "Geddie was right. Scarcely a day goes by that I don't think of the responsibilities of this medal."

If the UDT mission had the unforeseen benefit of prompting the enemy to prematurely reveal his hidden guns, it also produced a serious miscalculation. An examination of the sand off the beaches seemed to indicate it would support vehicles surging ashore in the upcoming amphibious assault. In fact, the coarse black volcanic cinders were like loose grain; the stuff would bog down both men and vehicles, adding enormously to the difficulty of getting inland.

Planners had divided the 3,500 yards of shoreline extending from Suribachi to the Eastern Boat Basin on the right into 500-yard segments coded by color, from left to right: Green, Red 1 and 2, Yellow 1 and 2, and Blue 1 and 2. The 5th Marine Division would land over the three beaches on the left; the 4th Marine Division would land on the three beaches to the right. If all went according to plan, there would be 8,000 men on the beach within the first hour, 30,000 by nightfall. The 4th Division was a veteran outfit, having participated in combat at Roi-Namur, Saipan, and Tinian. The 5th Division had never fought together as a unit, but contained a large number of combat veterans, many of them culled from the disbanded Paramarine and Marine Raider outfits. The Marines were told it would take an estimated three to five days of fighting to secure the island. Some of them may even have believed it.

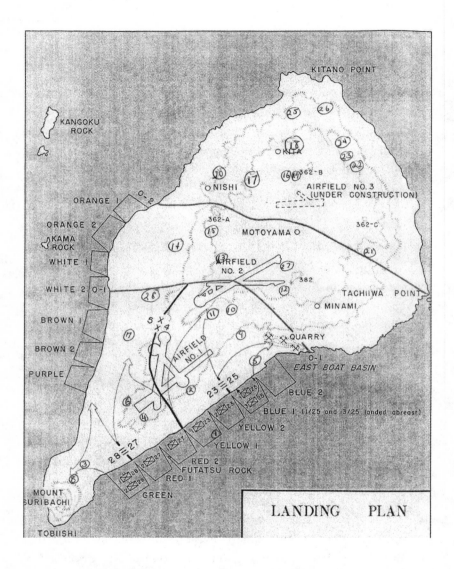

The assault troops were up and starting breakfast at about 0300, reveille in the crowded troop compartments consisting of "no bugle call," recalled Pvt. Allen R. Matthews, "but the turning on of lights and the cry, 'Hit the deck! Hit the deck!'" Breakfast consisted of the traditional steak and eggs. There were the usual jokes about being fattened up for the slaughter, but the laughter was a bit forced. The food was eaten standing up. Many men found themselves with little appetite.

The transports were in position by 0630. The bombardment began ten minutes later. At 0645 Adm. Kelly Turner ordered, "Land the Landing Force," and Marines began the process of boarding their amtracs. Many descended to the lower decks of LSTs to board the amphibious tractors, waiting in clouds of exhaust for the bow doors to open and disgorge them into the sea. Others, less fortunate, had to climb over the side and down cargo nets to the bobbing tractors. "The water was rough, and we were tossed and slammed against the side of the ship while climbing down the nets to the landing craft," recalled twenty-three-year-old Cpl. Edward D. Burow, a veteran of Guadalcanal. "Many men were injured trying to jump down into the landing craft. I remember most of the Marines were violently sick from the motion of the landing craft bouncing in the rough sea, and the black, noxious fumes from the engines that just made matters worse. I remember thinking that this was a hell of a way for some of us to spend the last moments of our lives, throwing up and violently ill."

The first three waves were boated and circling at the Line of Departure, two miles offshore, by 0815. At 0830 the Central Control Vessel dipped her pennant and the first wave of armored amtracs headed for Iwo's smoking shore, followed by a second wave of LVTs carrying 1,360 assault troops. Eight more waves began to form up behind them, scheduled to land at five-minute intervals. On the inside ramp of one landing craft, the last thing the occupants would see before it crashed down on the beach, someone had painted, "Too Late to Worry."

The first armored amtank hit the sand at Red Beach 1 at 0859, one minute ahead of schedule. Four minutes later, about 1,000 yards to the right, the tractors carrying twenty-four-year-old Sgt. Darrell S. Cole and his fellow Marines in B Company, 1st Battalion, 23rd Marines, nosed ashore on Yellow 1.

SGT. DARRELL S. COLE

23rd Marines, 4th Marine Division

February 19, 1945

Darrell S. Cole USMC

Somewhere along the line, someone with a gift for alliteration hung a title on Darrell Samuel Cole. They dubbed him the "Fighting Field Music."

The nickname may have been the brainchild of a clever newspaper correspondent or a public relations man looking to grab the imagination of the civilians at home. But in Cole's case, the title, though perhaps a bit melodramatic, was also appropriate. He was a fighter by nature; he was a field music by decree of the United States Marine Corps.

Born July 20, 1920, in Flat River (now Park Hills), Missouri, about fifty-five miles south of St. Louis, Darrell Cole was one of twelve children of Samuel and Magdalena Williams Cole. Sam Cole supported his hungry brood working as a railroader in a lead mine. Darrell was still a sophomore in high school when his father was seriously injured in a mining accident. With so many children to support, Sam told Darrell he needed to go to work. If he wanted to stay in high school, that was fine, but he would have to find a night job.

Undaunted, Darrell landed a job as the high school janitor. He also somehow found time to serve as editor of the yearbook, as a member of the band, and as a singer in the chorus; ran the mile on the track team; and served as an officer in student government—a schedule that brought him to school at 7 A.M. and kept him there until 9 P.M. Outside of school, he sang in the Esther Baptist Church choir, was interested in photography, and enjoyed hunting and the outdoors.

The youngster with a grin that could light up a room is remembered as an especially gifted musician, playing the French horn in high school. "He was a very talented person," recalled Darrell's nephew Vincent Cole years later. "Musically he could play five or six instruments. I can remember him sitting on the front porch of Grandma and Grandpa's house making music, playing the guitar."

Cole graduated from the high school in nearby Esther (now also part of Park Hills) in 1938 and immediately joined the Civilian Conservation Corps (CCC). He followed his year in the CCC with a stint as a salesman in Kansas, then relocated to Detroit, where he worked as a truck driver. He was a bellhop at Fordson Hotel in Dearborn, and then a shop clerk. "I was a footloose vagabond," he admitted later. "I have tried my hand at doing nearly everything, and succeeded at nothing. Simply because it never held any interest enough for me to continue it."

Eventually the footloose vagabond found work as a skiver machine operator for a company specializing in the manufacture of engine gaskets. But something seems to have been missing from his life. In a diary he kept at the time, he observed, "I have suddenly looked at life and decided I was making a lot of money but I wasn't accomplishing much." On August 25, 1941, less than four months before Pearl Harbor, he and some pals joined the Marine Corps Reserve for the duration of the national emergency.

Blond and blue-eyed, standing nearly six-foot-two and weighing in at 172 pounds, he looked the personification of the "fighting Marine." But, to Cole's dismay, the Marine Corps took more notice of his musical abilities. After boot camp at Parris Island, he was assigned to Field Music School to become a bugler. Cole detested the assignment. He had joined the Marines to fight, not to blow into a bugle, he declared. But the Marines weren't interested in what their new recruit wanted. The Corps needed buglers.

In August 1942, Cole and his bugle landed on Guadalcanal with the 1st Marine Division. "For one month and a half, we ate Jap rice with the husk on it, and it was full of little white worms," he wrote. The Marines were subjected to constant air attacks. "It wasn't any fun lying in a hole watching those bastards drop eggs on you, and you can't do nothing about it," he observed. One bombing attack nearly obliterated Cole's foxhole. "It caved the dirt in on my legs and arms," he recalled. "I got out o.k. Picked up a chunk of shrapnel big as my head out of the hole with me."

Undaunted, the young field music continued to agitate for a more direct combat role because he "didn't see enough action." When a regular machine gunner in his outfit—Company H, 2nd Battalion, 1st Marines—was wounded, he got his wish. Filling in as a gunner, he earned praise from his commanding officer, but shedding the field music albatross wasn't going to be easily accomplished. Immediately following the campaign, he submitted a request to join Weapons Company. His request was turned down "due to a shortage of field musics."

Life on the personal side wasn't going much better. "I came back and found my girl almost married to a guy in the army, as most of the boys did," he noted in his journal. "She did at least wait until I got back. Most didn't." As for his service overseas, he observed, without any especial malice, that the returning Marines didn't get much in the way of accolades back home. "Some people appreciate it all; most just take it for granted," he wrote.

Cole returned to the United States on February 2, 1943. The following month he was reassigned to the 23rd Marines, 4th Marine Division, again as a field music. "He was a tall, lanky kid," recalled Cole's tentmate, Bill Lee Herman. "He was older than the rest of us. He knew his way around. It was good to have guys like him with us because they settled us down. We were a rough group. Guys like him knew what it was all about."

Again Cole requested reassignment to line duty and again he was turned down. On a happier note, on Christmas Eve 1943 Field Music Cole married Margaret Belle Willett in San Diego. Their honeymoon was brief. Less than a month later, the 4th Marine Division shipped out for the Marshall Islands campaign. Compared to what was to come, the Marshall Islands fight was relatively easy. The Japanese atolls of Roi and Namur were seized quickly, and casualties were few. Cole's best friend, Pvt. Bill Glazier, recalled that the field music approached him on the return voyage from Roi-Namur with larceny on his mind. "Bill," he said, "our artillery chest [the chest where the spare machine-gun parts were kept] is down there in the storeroom. Let's go down there—get permission to go down there—and load it with fruit cocktail from the navy."

Glazier thought this was a great idea. "Well, we went down there and we loaded cases into the artillery chest," he recalled, "and we got back to Maui and the first thing we did, we went up and got that artillery chest. Well, they were going to have a shakedown inspection because so much stuff was stolen off the docks, that we went down there and [found] we had stuff like canned corn and green beans— nothing that you could really eat. We had to bury it behind our tent to get rid of the evidence."

Four months later, Cole was in action again when the 4th Marine Division landed on Saipan. As casualties mounted, Cole, by now recognized as an experienced combat veteran despite his field music rating, was assigned to lead a machine-gun section. When his squad leader was killed, Cole, though wounded, took command of the entire squad. "He was hit, but he went back to the aid station and returned to action," recalled B Company commanding officer Capt. William Weinstein. "I really don't remember how long he was gone or what the type of wound it was." Cole's performance earned him the Bronze Star for "his resolute leadership, indomitable fighting spirit and tenacious determination in the face of terrific opposition."

Cole could also be reckless, particularly in his quest for souvenirs. "I remember on Saipan," recalled Bill Glazier, "we were resting up for a few days before we went to Tinian. We walked over to where there was sort of a cliff. And Darrell said, 'Boy, there's a place that no one has looked for souvenirs.' So we got a rope and lowered him down where he could look into a little overhang there. Which was a very very dumb thing to do really in retrospect."

Other expeditions were more fruitful. Scavenging through a Japanese supply dump, the Marines found three bugles. Ever the musician, Cole proceeded to teach a buddy, Cpl. Thomas Bayly, how to play. Bayly was making good progress when an officer came along and threatened to make him a bugler. "I said I didn't want to be a bugler because everyone hated them because they got you up," recalled Bayly. "Cole said, 'Why do you think I wanted out of it so much?'"

Emerging from the Marianas campaign with a Bronze Star and Purple Heart, Cole requested a change of warrant for the third time. He pointed to his experience and combat record, stating he felt he would be more valuable to the Marine Corps as a line Marine. At long last, his wish was granted. The powers-that-be redesignated him as corporal "line." In November, he was promoted to sergeant. "He was a happy-go-lucky guy," recalled Sgt. Kenneth Phillips, who served in the same company. "If there was a crowd, he'd be in the middle of it. He was very outgoing . . . always laughing and cutting up."

On February 19, 1945, the 4th Marine Division stood off Iwo Jima with Sgt. Darrell S. Cole finally—officially—in the combat infantry role he had so avidly sought. Waiting aboard ship, he and Sgt. Peter J. Zocchi watched the naval bombardment of the island. "There were rookies and they were saying things like, 'We're going to kick the hell out of them. We're going to run them right off that rock.' Guys like Cole and me, we knew better," recalled Zocchi.

Cole's unit—B Company, 1st Battalion, 23rd Marines—landed on the far left of the 4th Marine Division over Yellow Beach 1, directly opposite Motoyama Airfield No. 1. The first waves poured ashore through ankle-deep volcanic ash shortly after 0900, encountering surprisingly little fire. Just ahead, about a hundred yards inland, lay the first of a pair of terraces paralleling the shore. Beyond the first terrace lay open ground for another 100 yards, then another terrace, then more open ground leading to the airfield.

Coming ashore with the third wave, Cole led his machine-gun section up to the first terrace. Reports during the first half hour after

*U.S. Marines hit the beach and charge over a dune on Iwo Jima in
the Volcano Islands on February 19, 1945, the start of one of the
deadliest battles of the war against Japan. USMC*

landing indicated that both of the 4th Division's Battalion Landing
Teams (BLTs) were progressing inland under increasing mortar and
machine-gun fire, and were beginning to encounter pillboxes within
their zones. At 0930, BLT 1 reported its forward elements "250 yards
inland, and continuing slowly."

"Then the Japs came to life," noted division historian Carl W. Proehl.
"From the sand dunes, machine guns began to chatter. Dual-purpose
guns on the edge of the airfield were depressed to deliver plunging fire
on the advancing Marines." Zocchi recalled, "They let us land one, two,
three and even four waves, and then they hit us, and believe me they
kicked the hell out of us."

Indicative of the volume of fire directed at the Marines was the
fate of twenty-five-year-old Capt. John Kalen, commanding officer of
A Company, which landed alongside Cole's outfit on Yellow Beach 1.
Seeing his radioman hit a few yards ahead of him, Kalen went out after
the man and was himself shot. Unable to reach him because of the
heavy fire, his men watched in frustrated agony for forty-five minutes

as Kalen lay there, just out of reach, his life ebbing away. When they finally got to him, he was dead.

The most immediate problem was a deep band of defensive positions manned by the Japanese 10th Independent Anti-Tank Battalion and the 309th Infantry Battalion. On one 500-yard stretch blocking access to the airfield, Marines later counted no fewer than fifty pillboxes, along with two blockhouses and a multitude of tank traps and infantry trenches. "Ahead of us were literally dozens of pillboxes and many blockhouses," recalled Capt. LaVerne Wagner, a company commander with the 23rd Marines. "In fact you couldn't move twenty-five yards in any direction without running into some kind of position."

"The whole beach had pillboxes and was mined," recalled Bill Glazier, who came in about five minutes after Cole in the succeeding wave. "They were ready for us. It was very difficult to see these pillboxes. It was just like being in a field of loose cinders with that volcanic ash. They were well camouflaged."

Members of the 1st Battalion, 23rd Marines—Darrell Cole's battalion—burrow in the volcanic sand on the beach of Iwo Jima, as fellow soldiers unload supplies and equipment from landing vessels, despite the heavy rain of artillery fire from enemy positions in the background. USMC

As Cole's section moved up the first terrace, they ran into a pair of Japanese pillboxes. "I saw Cole set up a light machine gun to fire on the pillbox," recalled Lt. Francis T. Brahaney, soon to be seriously wounded on the beach. "And then [I saw] him take hand grenades and throw them himself into the installations."

Cole knocked out both enemy positions and headed for the second terrace fronting the airfield. Well dug in, enemy troops on the plateau beyond the terrace poured devastating fire on any Marines attempting to advance. A call went out for tank support. "All you could do is hug the ground and dig like a dog," recalled a 4th Marine Division veteran.

By now, Cole was down to one machine gun. He turned it on a pillbox—one of three—holding up the assault. "It was about twenty-five yards away from his right front," recalled Platoon Sgt. Clarence "Hank" Harron. "The enemy at this time started throwing knee mortars, shells and grenades out of their positions and down the slopes toward our men." The return fire wounded Cole's gun crew and put the weapon out of action.

Cole took cover by Sergeant Zocchi. Now armed only with a phosphorus grenade and a .38-caliber revolver given to him earlier by his friend Bill Glazier, he remained determined to break out of the killing ground along the beachhead. "I remember we got pinned down by this pillbox," Zocchi recalled years later. "Darrell kept saying 'We've got to get out of here.' I told him 'Keep your head down. Don't be a hero. We'll get help soon.' The next thing I knew he was gone. Then I saw him running through this fire around the pillbox and throwing a grenade in it. I lost track of him after that."

When his first assault failed to silence the most troublesome pillbox, Cole returned for more grenades. Again he tortuously worked his way into a position to attack the pillbox and again the enemy gun remained in action after his grenades exploded. Incredibly, Cole insisted on trying yet again. "He was off to my right," recalled Harron. "He was calling for grenades. I pulled them off my belt and gave them to a man and told him to 'get them to Cole because he's doing a job.'

He went back over that rise and when he didn't come back I knew something had happened."

Out beyond Harron's view, Cole had once again worked around to the rear of the enemy position. This time his aim was true. The grenades exploded in the pillbox, silencing the machine gun. But as he stood at the entrance to the pillbox, a wounded Japanese inside dropped a grenade at his feet. The explosion killed Cole outright.

Cole's tenacious attack, however, had destroyed the key pillbox of the three. His platoon managed to knock out the remaining two and the assault moved forward past Cole's body and on toward Airfield No. 1. "He made it possible for us to get off the beach," recalled Harron. "If it had not been for Darrell Cole, a lot more people would have died out there trying to get off that beach."

Back at the beach, Bill Glazier heard his friend had been killed. Glazier slogged through the cinders to where the body lay, just to make sure. The Japanese grenade had done its work well. "It was instant death for him," recalled Glazier.

On April 17, 1947, two years after his actions on Iwo Jima, Darrell Cole's posthumous Medal of Honor was presented to his wife. Sergeant Cole was initially buried in the 4th Marine Division Cemetery on Iwo Jima. After the war, at his father's request, his remains were brought home and interred in Park View Cemetery near Farmington, Missouri. A bust of the hero was dedicated at Mineral Area College in Flat River in 1985. His Medal of Honor and other memorabilia were placed on display in the college library.

On October 12, 2000, the heroic sergeant was once again in the news when the USS *Cole*, an Aegis guided-missile destroyer named in his honor, was damaged in a terrorist suicide attack while at port in Yemen. Seventeen sailors died. The ship was repaired and returned to duty, living up to its motto, "The Determined Warrior." The motto is appropriate in many ways, observed Vincent Cole, not the least of which was because of his uncle's tenacity in combat. "He was determined to do what his country asked for—and more," remarked Cole.

"I'm telling you this was my fourth operation and I'm no coward," observed Sgt. Pete Zocchi. "I was wounded on Saipan . . . but I stayed with my men. But I'm telling you I was scared all of the time. I'm sure Cole was too. Hell, we all were. But Cole just did it and a lot of guys like him did it out there."

While Darrell Cole's division attempted to punch a hole through enemy defenses blocking the way to Motoyama Airfield No. 1, the 5th Marine Division was pouring ashore in the shadow of Mount Suribachi just to the south. Capt. Gerald Russell landed on Red Beach 1 with the third wave. "[W]hen we got out [of the landing craft], I kept yelling to the troops, 'Get off the beach! Get off the beach! Get up on the high ground!' And of course they were trying to climb up that soft volcanic sand. It was extremely difficult. You'd go up, and you'd go sliding back, and already there were a lot of casualties. There was firing on the beach, not the heavy volume that came later, but there was firing."

Slogging through ankle-deep volcanic sand, the Marines met light resistance until they were about 300 yards inland, when a deluge of mortar and artillery fire descended on the crowded beachhead. Enemy machine gunners firing from well-hidden bunkers cut down the exposed Marines. Men attempting to dig in for cover found the loose volcanic sand sifting back into the hole as fast as they could shovel it out. One Marine recalled it was like trying to dig a hole in a wheat bin. "Death was all around me," recalled Cpl. Bill ("Dave") Davenport. "Dead Marines were scattered in great violence from the beach to the first terrace. Moving forward, I could see another group that had been chopped down on their charge to the second terrace. All I could see was three kinds of Marines. The dead. The wounded. The frightened. And I was one of the frightened."

The 28th Marines, charged with cutting across the narrow neck of the island and isolating Mount Suribachi, struggled forward at great cost. Farthest to the left, tasked with protecting the open flank, the men of A Company, 1st Battalion, 28th Marines, faced Mount Suribachi. Among them was a former paratrooper from Dayton, Ohio, named Tony Stein.

CPL. TONY STEIN

28th Marines, 5th Marine Division
February 19, 1945

Tony Stein USMC

Tony Stein was a tough guy long before he ever set foot on Iwo Jima.

Anthony Michael Stein—he preferred to be called "Tony"—came from Dayton, Ohio's north side, the son of Steve and Rose Stein, German-speaking immigrants from Yugoslavia. Steve worked in a local foundry as a molder. Born September 30, 1921, Tony was a good-looking boy with curly hair, gray eyes, and the restlessness of youth. His older sister, Theresa, remembered him as a boy who knew no fear. He would dive from the highest spots into Dayton's Mad River and loved sports of all kinds, emerging as a natural leader among the neighborhood youths. "He always planned things because he had more guts," said Theresa. "It never occurred to him to be afraid." She remembered going to a local swimming pool with him once. Tony was just a little kid, but "[he] went right up and dived off the highest board," she said. "I couldn't let this wee little kid show me up, so I did it too. I hit my head on the bottom and split my cap."

By 1930 the Stein marriage had foundered. Steve remarried and found work as a caretaker on a private estate. The children—eight-year-old Tony and thirteen-year-old Theresa—stayed with Rose in their house on Kiser Street. Tony attended Webster and McGuffey elementary schools in Dayton before going on to Kiser High School, just down the street from his house. But school was not his first interest; he dropped out of Kiser High before finishing the ninth grade.

Times were hard, but somehow Tony always seemed to be able to make money, recalled his sister. He worked as a pinboy in a bowling alley and as a golf caddy, then learned toolmaking at a machine shop at Dayton's Patterson Field. He also did a brief hitch with the Civilian Conservation Corps, toiling in a lumber camp, and worked on construction before finally settling into a job as an apprentice tool and die maker at the Delco Products plant in Dayton. "He took after his father who could make anything," recalled Theresa.

Some indication that Tony Stein was more than just average occurred in 1940, when he leapt into the Mad River to save the life of a drowning boy—a feat duly noted in the Dayton newspapers. He also devoted many of his off-hours to amateur boxing and was adept enough in the ring to win Dayton's Golden Glove championship in February 1942, fighting at 128 pounds. Ironically, if given a choice, Stein would not even have been in Dayton that winter. He had wanted to enlist in the Marine Corps right after Pearl Harbor, but his occupation as a tool and die maker was considered essential to the war effort. The exemption came as a relief to his mother, but in September 1942 his occupation was dropped from the essentials list. On September 22 Tony enlisted in the Marines.

Stein completed boot camp in San Diego and—ever the daredevil—promptly volunteered for the Paramarines. He broke his leg on his first parachute jump, recalled his sister, but remained unfazed. "Oh, he was fearless!" she said. "He didn't know the meaning of the word fear." When his leg mended, he finished his parachute training, then shipped overseas with the 3rd Parachute Battalion. He saw limited combat in the closing days of the Guadalcanal operation, but later participated in the Bougainville campaign and the seizure of Vella Lavella. On Bougainville, he served as a runner, carrying messages back and forth. He also developed a reputation as a sniper exterminator. "The snipers could hide everything but their eyes," he explained. "They couldn't shoot with them covered, so I just waited 'til one raised his head and then I let fly with a burst before he could fire." He was credited with killing five snipers on Bougainville, dropping one of them nearly at his company commander's feet.

The specialized Paramarines and Marine Raiders were disbanded after the Bougainville campaign, and Stein returned to the United States in early 1944. To the surprise of his family, the scrawny youth who had left Dayton in 1942 showed up in the old neighborhood that June as a fully grown, well-muscled, 190-pound man. But he seemed restless. "He couldn't wait to get back into action," observed his sister. He would get his wish. Like many of the veteran Paramarines, Stein was assigned to the 5th Marine Division, then organizing at Camp Pendleton. "He was a tough little guy," recalled PFC John Armendariz. "He had a big panther tattooed on his arm—something that none of us did in those days . . . big tattoos like that."

Stein was promoted to corporal and made an assistant squad leader. He also found time for romance, marrying Joan Stominger, an employee at Patterson Field in Dayton, on July 21, 1944. The couple enjoyed a three-day honeymoon in San Diego before the 5th Marine Division left for Hawaii. Stein wasn't concerned about the orders. He was one of those rare men who actually liked combat. "He's a tough one, that Tony," observed his mother, who also confessed she would have been happier had her son remained exempt from military service.

And on the next campaign, Stein would have a surprise for the Japanese—a .30-caliber machine gun salvaged from a wrecked aircraft and modified for infantry use. The special weapon was the brainchild of Sgt. Mel Grevich of the 28th Marines, put together in an effort to come up with a fast-firing machine gun that could be handled by one man. The standard M1919A2 .30-caliber machine gun was heavy and had a rate of fire of about 500 rounds per minute. The lighter aircraft-mounted ANM2 could spit out up to 1,300 rounds per minute. By fitting the gun with an M1 Garand buttstock, a BAR bipod, a BAR rear sight, and a fabricated trigger, Grevich produced a weapon with a devastating rate of fire that was light enough—it weighed 25 pounds with a 100-round belt of ammunition—to be handled by one Marine in an infantry assault. The ingenious sergeant turned out six of the guns—nicknamed "Stingers"—while the division was at Hawaii. Five of them stayed with Grevich's own 3rd Battalion. The sixth somehow found its way into the hands of Tony Stein in A Company.

Just how Stein—who had served with Grevich in the 3rd Parachute Battalion—acquired his Stinger isn't clear, but his platoon leader, 2nd Lt. Alma Sonne, offered a clue. According to Lieutenant Sonne, "One day, while we were still at the Hawaiian base, Stein approached me and said he had a friend who could get us three of these machine guns from an F4U fighter plane that had crashed on the airfield, for the sum of two fifths of whiskey. . . . Well, I got the booze he asked for and received two weeks special duty for Stein to fix the guns. I think he enjoyed his time very well and when I noticed him walking down the company street, he seemed to stagger more than usual. I determined that the booze had been meant for him, but it turned out to be a good investment nevertheless."

Sonne also recalled that Stein seemed resigned to the idea that he would not survive the division's upcoming battle. "Tony was a happy-go-lucky fellow and in my private talks with him, he had told me that problems he had at home didn't offer any incentive for him to return and that he didn't expect to live through the operation," remarked Sonne. If Stein offered any details on the nature of those "problems," Sonne did not record them.

On February 19, 1945, the 5th Marine Division landed on Iwo Jima. Stein came ashore at Green Beach at 0912 in the fourth wave with 2nd Platoon, Able Company, 1st Battalion, 28th Marines. His platoon debarked on the extreme left flank of the landing beach in the shadow of Mount Suribachi, the 550-foot extinct volcano that would be the scene of the famous flag raising four days later. The battalion attack plan was simple. Baker Company and Charlie Company were to drive straight forward 700 yards across Iwo's narrow neck to the western beaches, isolating Mount Suribachi. A Company, commanded by Denver native Aaron C. Wilkins, would guard the left flank of the assault, facing Suribachi, with its right flank maintaining contact with B Company. When the 2nd Battalion came ashore shortly after 0930, A Company would join B and C Companies in the push for the western shoreline.

The 28th Marines, including Don Ruhl and Tony Stein,
came ashore in the shadow of Mount Suribachi. USMC

By 1035, a few B Company men reached the far shore, but casualties had been high and the battalion was badly disorganized. Large numbers of bypassed Japanese continued to resist from a belt of sand-covered pillboxes and bunkers, many of them protruding only a few feet above the surface and barely distinguishable from the surrounding terrain. As the 2nd Battalion came ashore, Wilkins was told to take Able Company and his men and start mopping up the bypassed Japanese positions.

Draped with belted .30-caliber ammo and lugging his Stinger, Stein pushed out ahead, eager to get at a pillbox he had spotted. He had lost his helmet aboard ship before landing, but that didn't make him any more cautious. Teaming up with twenty-two-year-old Sgt. Merritt M. Savage, a one-time Arizona plumber turned demolitions expert, and Cpl. Frederick J. Tabert, a former CCC quarry worker from Pasco, Washington, Stein took the pillbox's gun port under fire with the Stinger. As a swarm of slugs from the fast-firing Stinger forced the Japanese away from the aperture, Savage closed in and blew up the pillbox. Backed by Stein, Savage proceeded to make frontal attacks on two more pillboxes, knocking them out with hand grenades and killing seven Japanese with his pistol.

Pinned down on the third terrace by a Japanese machine gun, Lieutenant Sonne saw Stein firing the Stinger toward Mount Suribachi. "I saw his assistant shot and Tony carrying him back out of gunfire range," recalled Sonne; "then picking up a box of ammunition, he went back to his gun position. He was wearing a baseball cap because someone had stolen his helmet. I talked to him about it earlier and he remarked that the baseball cap would distinguish him from everybody else."

Over the course of the next several hours, Stein was the sparkplug in A Company's attack, knocking out nine other strongpoints. He was later credited with killing at least twenty of the enemy in the first hour alone. His method of locating the well-camouflaged positions was near suicidal. He would stand up until he was shot at, then turn the Stinger on the source of the fire. Twice the weapon was knocked from his hands by enemy fire. Twice he retrieved it. Unable to reduce one particularly obstinate pillbox with his Stinger, he directed the fire of a half-track on the position until it went silent.

One problem with the Stinger was its voracious appetite for ammunition. "The bad part about it was that it used to shoot 1100 rounds a minute so he went through an ammo belt '*harrumph*,' that fast," recalled PFC John Armendariz. "He kept the enemy down, no doubt about that, but oh God, he would have to run back to the beach to get more belts of ammo. He wanted someone to go with him back to the beach but nobody wanted to run back with him."

Stein had to make eight separate trips back to the beach to obtain more ammo for the weapon as the assault progressed. Already helmetless, he shed his boondockers and ran back barefoot through the heavy shellfire to make better progress in the shifting ash. "He would do that a number of times and each time he did that he would get one of the guys that was wounded but still walking and drag him along down with him and leave them on the beach," said Armendariz. "He did this about ten times that I know of." Returning with belts of ammo draped over his shoulders, Stein would pick up the Stinger and look for new victims. One by one, the Japanese pillboxes were reduced to tombs for their occupants.

"I believe that Tony's actions on the beach that day saved my life and the lives of many of my men," said Lieutenant Sonne years later. "He was brave as well as foolhardy. Later on, that first day, he asked me if he could be detached from the platoon and help some of the adjacent units. I told him to go ahead. Stories of his heroic deeds spread all over the island. I found out later that he had been wounded and had been sent back to the battalion aid station." The historian of the 5th Marine Division later observed, "In battle, no man can be singled out as having been 'first' to fight or as having been solely responsible for the success of an attack, but one man in Company A, 28th Marines, came as close, perhaps, as any man can come to fulfilling these impossible conditions. He was Corporal Tony Stein."

On his last trip up from the beach, Stein was hit in the shoulder with a spray of mortar fragments. Captain Wilkins ordered him back to the beach for medical evacuation, but Stein refused. He stayed for the rest of the day. That evening, as his platoon pulled back to consolidate their line for the night, he covered the withdrawal with the Stinger. Only then did Stein finally give in to his shoulder wound. Slogging back to the beach, he boarded a landing craft out to a hospital ship. It appeared that Iwo Jima was over for him. But as tough fighting continued over the next week, Stein chafed at being away from his unit.

Anyone who knew Tony Stein could have predicted what happened next. He climbed onto a craft bound for Iwo.

He rejoined his platoon on March 1, just as it was about to tackle one of the most infamous positions on Iwo Jima: Hill 362A. "About ten minutes before moving out, Tony Stein came moseying up the road, approached me and said he was reporting in from the aid station where he had been treated for wounds," recalled Lieutenant Sonne. "He asked me what his orders were and [Platoon] Sergeant Enoch Shoultz interrupted and said, 'Come with me, Tony, and I will fill you in as we go.'"

The highest point on the western side of the island, Hill 362A was the backbone of Japanese defense in the sector. "Its sharp, barren edges were chopped up with caves, and concrete pillboxes and blockhouses dotted its nearly vertical cliffs," observed the 5th Marine Division historian. The base was surrounded by jagged, rocky outcrops commanding all approaches to the hill. "The fighting was very intense and there had been many casualties," observed Sonne. "In trying to gain some kind of fire superiority, I had watched other commanders place machine gunners in position to fire to the front and all were killed before firing more than a few shots."

Now, in an effort to break the position, 1st Battalion sent A Company around the right shoulder of the hill into a draw, while B circled around the other side. "When 'H' hour came, I hadn't had time to organize my platoon and make a plan of attack," said Sonne, "and everyone was yelling to 'move out,' and so we made our attack under these conditions. Of course, all confusion broke loose at the onset."

The assault quickly came apart. B Company's captain was shot through the neck and the attack bogged down. A Company came under mortar and sniper fire. A mortar round fatally wounded Captain Wilkins—the last of the battalion's original company commanders—and killed two other Marines outright. Sonne's platoon sergeant, Enoch Shoultz, a tall, good-looking career Marine from Sunnyside, Alabama, threw together an eighteen-man assault group and led it forward. One of the eighteen Marines was Tony Stein, just back with the unit. The men moved cautiously forward into the broken ground. Sonne had great regard for Shoultz, but the sergeant's effort was in vain. Waiting Japanese let them in, then opened up with rifle and machine-gun fire. The survivors scrambled back to the dubious safety of the A Company line.

"The fire was so intense that some of the men came back, and I found myself in a large shell crater with about six of my men, about two hundred yards ahead of the front line," recalled Sonne. "We were completely pinned down and couldn't go forward nor backward." Among the survivors sheltering in the crater was Cpl. Ben L. Green Jr., a former Paramarine from Louisiana who had celebrated his twenty-fourth birthday just the day before, and who had gone out with Shoultz and Stein in the effort to knock out the enemy guns. Green told Sonne that Shoultz and Stein had been caught in a crossfire from Japanese machine guns out in the ravine to their front. Both were dead.

Tony Stein's body was recovered by Graves Registration a week later and interred in plot 5, row 6, grave 1107, of the 5th Marine Division Cemetery on Iwo Jima. His Medal of Honor, awarded in recognition of his exploits on the first day of the assault, was presented by Adm. Richard Pennoyer to Stein's twenty-four-year-old widow on February 19, 1946, one year to the day after the Iwo Jima landings. The ceremony took place at the Ohio Statehouse in the presence of the governor. A photo of the presentation shows Joan Stein looking both proud and resolved as the blue-and-white-starred ribbon is fastened around her neck.

Tony Stein's remains were returned home to Dayton a week before Christmas 1948. It was a cold, wintry day as the train pulled into the station. The mayor declared a three-day tribute to the hero. The casket was first brought to Stein's childhood home on Kiser Street. Later, carried from the living room of the modest house, the casket was drawn through the streets of North Dayton on an ammunition trailer, past flags at half-staff. Tony's mother was there, and his wife, along with many friends and crowds of spectators. The casket was transported to Our Lady of Rosary Church for a solemn high requiem mass, followed by burial in Dayton's Calvary Cemetery overlooking the Miami River on the city's south side.

Speaking to reporters, Rose Stein tried to make them understand what had driven her son. "Tony always had to be doing things, hard things," she explained. "That's why he just had to be in the Marines. He wanted to see if he could do it."

While Tony Stein's regiment pushed toward Iwo's western shore in an effort to isolate Mount Suribachi on the morning of February 19, the 27th Marines had landed over the Red Beaches on the right of the 28th Marines. Their job was to drive across the lower end of Airfield No. 1 and then turn north. Cpl. Mike Vinich of Hudson, Wyoming, came ashore over Red Beach 1. As the front ramp of his landing craft dropped open, a blast of small-arms fire dropped two Marines in front of him. Vinich scrambled out onto the sand and began crawling up the first terrace, following one of his buddies, Cpl. Barney Bernard. "What does it look like, Barney?" Vinich yelled as Bernard reached the top. Bernard lifted his head to look over the edge and a bullet smashed into his forehead. He dropped face-first and slid back in the loose ash, killed instantly.

Machine-gun, mortar, and artillery fire ripped into the Marines struggling to get inland. "They just tore us apart," recalled PFC Robert Butinel, who landed with the 27th Marines. "My buddies were hit all around me. It was a massacre, and it wasn't just my platoon either; it was both divisions on the entire island." Among the dead was a national hero—a Medal of Honor recipient who could have avoided Iwo Jima had he wished.

GUNNERY SGT. JOHN BASILONE

27th Marines, 5th Marine Division
February 19, 1945

John Basilone USMC

The landing was only hours old when word began to circulate among disbelieving Marines clinging to isolated shell holes and ruined enemy pillboxes amid the rain of enemy fire: "John Basilone is dead." If anyone still needed a reminder of the peril, this was it—for if Gunnery Sgt. John Basilone could be killed, then no one was immune to sudden death.

When "Manila John" Basilone joined the 5th Marine Division in January 1944, he was already a national hero, entitled to wear the starred ribbon of the Medal of Honor, his face familiar to millions of Americans from newspaper and magazine photos. He could have sat out the war basking in public adulation. Instead, he ended up wading to his death through the volcanic ash of Iwo Jima. And he was there by choice.

Born November 4, 1916, in Buffalo, New York, Johnny Basilone grew up with ten brothers and sisters in a two-bedroom duplex on the wrong side of the tracks in Raritan, New Jersey. His father, Salvatore, was a tailor who had emigrated from Italy in 1902 in search of a better life. "Dad worked seventy hours a week as a tailor in his own business in Somerville to put food on the table," recalled John's younger sister, Mary. "Once he made our family doctor a fancy overcoat in return for John and me to have our tonsils out. Counting my grandmother, he had thirteen mouths to feed."

Friends later recalled Johnny as a good-natured cut-up, a jug-eared mop-top who wasn't above stealing apples or saving himself a dime by sneaking into the downtown movie theater. "People often ask me what kind of person Johnny was when he was growing up," said Mary Basilone. "I tell them he was a happy-go-lucky kid who wanted to sing opera. He had a twinkle in his eye that the nuns at our school loved. . . . [H]e knew all the operas and he'd sing them to my mother while she was cooking."

Not much of a student, and with the Basilone family facing hard times, John quit school at age fifteen after finishing the eighth grade at St. Bernard's parochial. The nuns might have enjoyed the twinkle in his eye, but the departure of the high-spirited youth with the wide grin probably came as something of a relief. Johnny Basilone had tended to resist the discipline of the classroom and his lowest marks were always in "conduct." His eighth-grade yearbook listed his hobby as "chewing gum," his life's ambition to be "an opera singer," and his current status as "the most talkative boy" in his class.

Freed from academia, Basilone found work as a caddy at the Raritan Valley Country Club for forty cents a day. When winter arrived, he got a job working on a laundry truck—then lost it when the boss caught him napping on a pile of clothes. One night in 1934, sitting around the family dinner table, he announced, "I'm joining the army." The decision changed his life. During a three-year hitch that took him to the Philippines, he fell in love with Manila and the girls and the good times in the bars along Dewey Boulevard. Along the way, he did some middleweight boxing and became an expert in the workings of the .30-caliber water-cooled Browning heavy machine gun.

When his enlistment was up in 1938, Basilone returned to Raritan, where he worked for a year as a laborer at the Calco Chemical plant. He then moved in with his sister in Reisterstown, Maryland, and got a job installing propane gas tanks. Bored silly, in July 1940 he quit his job and enlisted in the Marine Corps, with the idea that he would get back to his beloved Manila more quickly with the Marines. Tough guy that he was, he couldn't bring himself to tell his mother he had reenlisted—his father had to break the news for him, his sister recalled.

A return to Manila was not to be, but Basilone's incessant tales about his previous tour of duty in the Philippines quickly earned him the nickname "Manila John" among his Marine buddies. "You would have thought he was the mayor of Manila," remarked one Marine of Basilone's nostalgic stories. By 1942 when the 1st Marine Division landed on Guadalcanal, Basilone was serving as a sergeant in the heavy weapons company of the 7th Marines. He was very good at his job. "He was absolutely a genius with machine guns," recalled fellow Marine Richard Greer.

Left on Samoa during the initial Marine landing on Guadalcanal, Basilone's regiment did not come ashore until September 18. The situation on Guadalcanal was still very much in doubt, and the 4,262 men in the 7th Marines were almost immediately engaged in heavy fighting. Despite the American reinforcement, Japanese pressure on the Marine line continued, and Henderson Field, the crucial island airstrip, remained vulnerable. The night of October 24, Basilone's machine gunners were placed in defensive positions on Edson's Ridge, screening the inland side of Henderson Field. Manila John was in charge of fourteen men and four .30-caliber machine guns in support of Company C in the center of the American line. Earlier that same day, a Japanese officer had been spotted examining the Marine positions through binoculars. Everybody knew it was only a matter of time before the ridge came under attack.

A drenching rain pelted down as darkness closed over Marine positions on October 24. Basilone's Marines were wet, but their guns and ammunition were dry, well sheltered by the ponchos of men who knew a working weapon was more important than a comfortable Marine. Basilone sat barefooted in his muddy foxhole, having kicked off his boondockers because his feet had been wet for weeks and they "itched like hell," he said later. At 2130 a Marine outpost phoned in from the sopping jungle beyond the perimeter. "Colonel," whispered an apprehensive Marine to Battalion Commander Lewis B. "Chesty" Puller. "There are about 3,000 Japs between me and you."

Enemy probes began at about 2200. Then, about an hour after midnight, the 9th Company of the 3rd Battalion of the Japanese 29th Regiment charged out of the soaking jungle directly toward "Manila John" Basilone's machine guns. "When the first wave came at us, the ground just rattled!" recalled Basilone. "We kept firing and drove them back, but our ammunition was getting low so I left the guns and started running to the next outfit to get some more."

Despite the toll exacted by Marine guns, the enemy attacks continued. A slight incline in front of Basilone's position forced the Japanese to expose themselves as they attempted to knock out the machine guns. With that small advantage, the Marines piled up the enemy dead. But as the hours wore on, the enemy's numbers began to tell. One of the Marine machine-gun sections suddenly went silent. A runner ducked into Basilone's gun pit. "They got the guns on the right," he informed Basilone.

Basilone realized the enemy attack would pour through the hole left by the now silent machine-gun position if something wasn't done quickly. "I took off up the trail to see what had happened," recalled Basilone. "I found [Pvt. Cecil H.] Evans there. He had a rifle by him and was screaming at the Japs to come!" Aside from the defiant Evans, there wasn't much to stop the Japanese. Both machine guns were inoperable and it was only a matter of time before the Japanese rolled through. Hustling back to his own position, Basilone grabbed a water-cooled machine gun—90 pounds of gun and tripod—and shouted to two Marines, "Follow me!" As they scrambled back to the over-run position, they bumped into a group of about eight Japanese. The Marines mowed them down in a wild melee, and kept going.

Setting up in the abandoned pit, the new crew opened up with their gun, while Basilone went to work on the two inoperable weapons. One gun had been ruined; the other was jammed. He worked by feel in the darkness. "Bullets were smacking into the sandbags," he recalled. The rain had stopped, and in the lulls as he worked, he could hear the *thwack thwack* as the Japanese cut the barbed wire out front.

He finally managed to clear the gun, fed in a new belt of ammo, and opened up to his front. The other crew fed ammo to the guns while Basilone fired. "The Japs were still coming at us and I rolled over from one gun to the other, firing them as fast as they could be loaded," he recalled.

"The ammunition belts were in bad shape from being dragged on the ground. I had to scrape mud out of the receiver. They kept coming and we kept firing. We all thought our end had come. Some Japs would sneak through the lines and behind us. It got pretty bad because I'd have to stop firing every once in a while and shoot one behind me with my pistol." As the bodies heaped up, Basilone's men crept out front to roll the corpses down the slope and clear their fields of fire.

Ammunition again began to run low. "I'm going back for ammo," Basilone told his crew. With Japanese filtering through everywhere, Basilone, still shoeless, headed back to an ammunition point 150 yards to the rear, where he grabbed six belts of ammo, draped the 14-pound belts over his shoulders, and struggled back to the muddy gun pit on the ridge. "That lousy last 100 yards," he said later. "I thought it would never end!"

Eight separate Japanese attacks were made against the American line before the fighting tapered off at about 0700 on October 25. In the morning, the legendary Col. Chesty Puller came across Basilone lying in a foxhole with thirty-eight dead Japanese strewn around, almost at arm's length. They didn't come much tougher than Puller, but even he was impressed. "Nice work," he remarked. An estimated 1,200 Japanese were killed in the assault on the 7th Marines that night. "At dawn our guns were burned out," observed Basilone. "Altogether we got rid of 26,000 rounds. After that, I discovered I was hungry, so I went to the CP to see about getting chow. All we could get was crackers and jam."

PFC Nash Phillips, who lost a hand fighting alongside Basilone during the night, was surprised when the sergeant materialized beside him at the aid tent early that morning. "He was barefooted and his eyes were red as fire," remembered Nash. "His face was dirty black from gunfire and lack of sleep. His shirtsleeves were rolled up to his shoulders. He had a .45 tucked into the waistband of his trousers. He'd just dropped by to see how I was making out—me and the others in the section. I'll never forget him."

Wet, muddy, and exhausted, the kid from the wrong side of the tracks found he was the hero of the hour. His courage and tenacity had kept his machine guns operating, "contributing in large measure to the virtual annihilation of a Japanese regiment," noted his subsequent citation. In recognition of his actions, Basilone received the Medal of Honor from Gen. A. A. Vandegrift on June 23, 1943, in Australia. His machine-gun company expressed their admiration by collecting $200 to buy the former laundry truck worker a watch. "I am very happy, for the other day I received the Congressional Medal of Honor, the highest award you can get in the armed forces," the sergeant wrote to his parents.

Returning to the United States in September, Johnny Basilone was greeted as a national hero. Raritan held "Basilone Day" on September 19 and presented him with a $500 bond. He spent several months touring the country on a war bond drive. Curly-haired, personable, and quick with a boyish grin, he was a photographer's dream.

He hated it.

"I felt pretty embarrassed every time I spoke," he admitted later. A lieutenant assigned to escort the hero during the tour recalled asking him if he owned a set of dress blues. "What d'ya think I am, lieutenant," Basilone retorted, "a Navy Yard Marine?"

Though not comfortable with his celebrity, the fawning movie stars, and the pop of the flashbulbs, Basilone's tour raised $1.4 million in war bond pledges. "After about six months of tours and speeches, I found myself doing guard duty at Washington, D.C. Navy Yard," Basilone said later. Once again, he was bored. "Washington was a pleasant place," he admitted. "But I wasn't very happy. I wanted to get back to the machine guns. I felt out of things."

The Marine Corps offered to make him an officer and let him spend the rest of the war in Washington, but Basilone had endured enough. He was just a "plain Marine," he said. He wanted to get back into the war. "I ain't no officer, and I ain't no museum piece," he remarked. "I belong back with my outfit." He reiterated that his great ambition was to be present at Manila's recapture. "I kept thinking of how awful it would be if some Marines made a landing on Dewey Boulevard and Manila John Basilone wasn't among them," he observed slyly.

The Marine Corps turned down his repeated requests to rejoin a line outfit. But Basilone persisted, and finally, in late 1944, the Corps relented. Gunnery Sgt. John Basilone joined a machine-gun platoon of the 27th Marines, 5th Marine Division. "We tried to keep him from going," recalled his brother Carlo. "I said, 'Johnny, it's a miracle you got out of Guadalcanal.' I had a hunch Johnny wasn't coming back. He knew it too. But he still went. He wasn't afraid."

Fellow Marines who expected a brawny giant capable of firing heavy machine guns off hand were surprised to find that the heroic sergeant was only five feet eight and a half inches tall, weighing in at 158 pounds, an unpretentious sort who spoke with the "dems" and "doses" of his Jersey grade-school education. He also sported two tattoos: one on the upper right arm incongruously (considering his New Jersey background) depicted the head and shoulders of a full-blown Wild West girl in blue and red; the left depicted a sword plunged into a human heart, all entwined with stars and flowers and a ribbon reading, "Death before Dishonor." He didn't make much of his Medal of Honor, but his fame had benefits—especially on liberty. "When you went out with him, everyone paid for your drinks," recalled Sgt. Clinton Watters. "We walked out of places and left them on the table. You just couldn't drink them all."

Cpl. William D. Lansford recalled the first time he saw Basilone in one of Camp Pendleton's slop chutes, describing him as "a jug-eared young gunny who wore his cap sideways, drank beer with the gusto of a millionaire guzzling champagne and laughed so infectiously that you couldn't help liking him on sight." Asked about his future plans, Basilone indicated to *Leatherneck Magazine* that he intended to return to civilian life after the war. "I've got a girl back east and, thanks to the people of my hometown, Raritan, N.J., I have enough money invested in war bonds to get a start in civilian life as soon as the shooting is over," he remarked. "It'll either be a restaurant or a farm. I haven't decided which."

The "girl back east," whoever she was, was in for a surprise. Basilone's eye was caught by a female Marine, Sgt. Lena Riggi, who worked as a cook at Camp Pendleton. Three years older than Basilone, the daughter of Italian immigrants who operated a small farm in Portland, Oregon, Riggi did not seem impressed with her admirer, but Basilone persisted. "He was very attentive," recalled one of Riggi's friends. They were married July 10, 1944, at St. Mary's Church in Oceanside. They honeymooned at the Riggi family onion farm in Portland. Basilone happily talked about a future that included buying a ten-bedroom house and putting "a kid in each room." Thirty-two days later, the 5th Marine Division received its orders. The division was shipping out. Their destination was Hawaii, and then, five months later, Iwo Jima. From Pearl Harbor, Basilone sent his mother a photo of himself in uniform with the note, "Tell Pop his son is still tough."

Just how tough was witnessed by PFC Chuck Tatum on the beach at Iwo Jima, the morning of D-Day, February 19. Tatum, who had never been in combat before, was huddled in the sand debating what to do next as enemy fire rained down all around, when he noticed "a lone Marine walking back and forth on the shore among hundreds of prone figures, kicking asses, shouting his profane displeasure and demanding, 'Move out! Get your butts off the beach!'" It was Manila John Basilone.

Basilone and the executive officer of the 27th Marines made their way toward Tatum, booting the huddled men and shouting, "Move out! Move out! Get the fuck off the beach you dumb sons-of-bitches." Basilone directed Tatum and his machine gun toward a reinforced-concrete blockhouse to their front. A field piece concealed in the fortification was firing down the beach to their right. Basilone coordinated the assault on the structure. As Tatum covered them with fire from his

Get off the beach! John Basilone got his men inland, but was killed at Airfield No. 1.
USMC

machine gun, other Marines got close enough to toss demolitions into the blockhouse; then a flamethrower operator stuck his nozzle through an aperture and cut loose.

Eighteen-year-old Tatum suddenly realized that Basilone was standing over him, releasing the machine gun from the tripod. "Get the belt and follow me," he screamed in Tatum's ear. The youngster followed Basilone at a run to the top of the blockhouse, just as a knot of burning Japanese scrambled out the rear entrance. Holding the machine gun by its "Basilone Bail" (a specially adapted handle the gunny had devised for the barrel of the weapon to make it easier to use), Manila John mowed them down. "It was a mercy killing," observed Tatum.

Ninety-three minutes after coming ashore, Basilone's small group found itself on the runway of Airfield No. 1, about 500 yards in from the landing beach and less than halfway across the narrow neck of the island. Coming under heavy fire on the open runway, the Marines started to fall back. Basilone told them to dig in and hold their ground. "I'll go back for more men," he said. He disappeared in the direction of the beach.

Not half an hour later, Tatum lifted his head to see a small knot of Marines heading toward the runway with Basilone in the lead. They were seventy-five yards from his shell hole when a Japanese mortar shell plummeted down, knocking them to the ground like so many rag dolls. The shell exploded at Basilone's feet, sending metal tearing into his groin, neck, and left arm. His brother's fears had been realized: Johnny Basilone's luck had finally run out. If not killed instantly, he died within minutes.

At about noon, the executive officer of the 2nd Battalion, 26th Marines saw Basilone's close friend, CWO John Daniels. "Gunnery Sergeant Basilone is laying dead at the end of the first airstrip," he told him. Daniels went out to the runway and found Basilone there with three other C Company Marines cut down by mortar fire. The dead gunny was just "a thin, pallid kid," recalled Cpl. Bill Lansford, who wasn't entirely convinced at first that it was really Basilone lying there. "His helmet was half off and he lay face up, arched over his combat pack, with his jacket torn back and his mouth open. He looked incredibly thin, like an undernourished kid with his hands near his stomach as though it hurt," observed Lansford.

Over the next few hours, word filtered along the line. Basilone was dead. They couldn't believe it, recalled Tatum. But it was true. A graves registration detail pulled Basilone's poncho from his backpack and wrapped him in it, and the hero of Guadalcanal eventually joined the growing line of dead Marines awaiting burial in Iwo's black volcanic sand. Lena Basilone got the bad news on March 7, her thirty-second birthday; she had to be sedated. She lived until 1999, never remarrying. "It's sad what happened," Basilone's brother Carlo said years later. "I told Johnny to stay home, after all he went through, but that wasn't enough. I always had a feeling he wasn't going to come home."

For his actions in the first hour and a half of the Iwo Jima assault, Gunnery Sgt. John Basilone was awarded a posthumous Navy Cross. He was the only enlisted Marine in World War II to receive the nation's two highest awards for valor, and to this day his memory as a fighting Marine is revered and held up as an example in the Corps. Following the war, his remains were removed from the 5th Marine Division cemetery on Iwo Jima and reinterred at Arlington National Cemetery, where he rests today in section 12-384 under a simple marble marker engraved with a rendering of the Medal of Honor.

Marines would again walk the streets of Manila. But John Basilone would not be among them.

One of the toughest fights of the day—on a day when all the fights were tough—was taking place on the 4th Marine Division's right, where the 25th Marines had been charged with seizing a key piece of rocky high ground known simply as "The Quarry." Enemy guns dug into the dominating height poured fire down on the beaches. Efforts to neutralize the strongpoint from the air and by naval gunfire had little effect; in many cases, it did more harm than good. "The Quarry had guns sticking out of it, and the friendly fire damage was about the worst I ever seen," recalled Cpl. Glenn Buzzard, a 4th Division machine gunner. "They were trying to get at them guns, and they'd call in an air strike and our kids would just roll dead off them hills because the planes hit short."

Sgt. Albert J. Oulette landed below the Quarry with L Company, 3rd Battalion, 25th Marines. "The place was a mass of confusion, men were being blown to pieces or wounded by the shrapnel, and running in that ash was like running in a wheat bin," he recalled. "When the day was out, our battalion was down to 150 men out of over 900. My company was down to twenty-six. When we seized the Quarry, we took seventeen casualties. Twelve were my men. My platoon was now down to nine men and all we had captured was less than one mile of area."

Perhaps the least surprised by these developments was the 3rd Battalion commander Lt. Col. "Jumping Joe" Chambers. Iwo Jima was Chambers's fourth battle, but he had been uneasy ever since learning his battalion's mission and the terrain his men would face trying to get off the beach. Now events were proving his fears were well founded.

LT. COL. JUSTICE M. CHAMBERS

25th Marines, 4th Marine Division
February 19–22, 1945

Justice Chambers USMC

Under normal circumstances, colonels are not supposed to get shot on the battlefield—that is more typically the misfortune of privates, noncoms, and junior officers. But "Jumping Joe" Chambers was no ordinary colonel, and Iwo Jima was certainly no normal circumstance.

Justice Marion Chambers was born on February 2, 1908, in Huntington, West Virginia, one of four children of Arthur and Dixie Chambers. In Huntington, he recalled years later, "you either had money or you didn't. We didn't." Arthur was a salesman, first in groceries and later in furniture. Justice, better known to family and friends as "Joe," attended local schools and was active in Boy Scouts. He played some football at Marshall College in Huntington, subsequently making a brief stop at George Washington University before finally earning a law degree at National University. At the same time, he held down a job in the Office of Personnel and Business Administration in the U.S. Department of Agriculture.

While a student, Chambers enlisted in the Naval Reserve in 1928, enticed, he said later, by the prospect of the supposed perks. "I was working for the federal government and somebody told me that I could get two extra weeks' vacation with pay as military leave," he confessed later. A seasick vacation on a World War I destroyer convinced him of his error, but when he tried to extract himself from his commitment, he was told he had signed up for four years and that's what he would have to serve. There was only one option: he could transfer into the Marine Corps Reserve. "What are the Marines?" he responded.

Chambers suffered through two years as a naval reservist before being honorably discharged on June 25, 1930. The very next day he enlisted in the Marine Corps Reserve as a private, later joking that "you could really get seasick in a small boat bobbing around reef lines." It turned out to be the right choice. He found he liked the company and studied hard in an effort to get ahead. Two years later the weekend warrior received a second lieutenant's commission. His life was progressing in other ways as well. On Christmas Day 1932, he married Johanna Maria Schmutzer, described as "a pretty Canadian miss of English and Austrian parents, from Montreal," who was working at the time as secretary to the president of the U.S. Chamber of Commerce in Washington.

His civilian career also seemed promising—he rose to become chief of the Division of Administration, U.S. Maritime Commission—but the call of the military proved more alluring. Promoted to captain in early 1938, he requested active duty later that same year. His request was denied, but in 1940 he was called to active duty with the rest of the Marine Corps Reserve. When war came, he was serving as a company commander with the 5th Marines, and in the spring of 1942 he joined the 1st Raider Battalion. Promoted to major in May 1942, he shipped out for the Pacific that summer.

The former government bureaucrat turned out to be one of those men who just can't stand by and watch while other men act. He was a leader, a doer. "I . . . found early on that you weren't going to get very far if you simply told the men what to do," he said later. "You had to do it with them." Standing six feet two inches tall, rawboned and hoarse-voiced, he was, someone once said, "as tough as a 50-cent steak." His nickname "Jumping Joe" derived from his bounding stride. He could be loud and profane when things went wrong and needed correction, but he also possessed a ready smile and the full devotion of his men, who knew the real thing when they saw it.

Chambers first saw combat on August 7, 1942, landing on Tulagi in command of Company D, 1st Raider Battalion. He didn't last very long. A mortar shell drove fragments into his left thigh and both arms just as he was getting started. He was never sure if it was a Japanese mortar or friendly fire that cut him down. "We were after a Jap machine gun nest which I had spotted," he remembered, "and were using our own mortars when a shell exploded in the air about ten feet from us. The Japs were [also] using mortars, so it could have been a shell from either."

Chambers was lying in the battalion aid station early the next morning when an enemy counterattack threatened to overrun the area. "When morning came the firing started and we were right in between," he recalled. "My arms were in splints and I rolled to the ground to get out of the line of the firing. And then we managed to evacuate the wounded." Chambers took charge, saw that the wounded were removed to a safer area, and directed the defense of the station itself. He was later awarded a Silver Star for his actions.

Sent back to the United States for treatment of his wounds, Chambers was promoted to lieutenant colonel in March 1943. When the 25th Marines formed that summer as part of the 4th Marine Division, he was given command of the 3rd Battalion. In January 1944 he participated in the invasion of Roi-Namur in the Marshall Islands. That campaign was followed in June by the invasion of Saipan and Tinian. In the course of the fighting there, Chambers was blown to the ground in an explosion, knocked unconscious by blast concussion. He was taken back to an aid station, but returned to his outfit the next morning. His handling of his battalion during the campaign earned him the Legion of Merit. His concussion earned him a second Purple Heart.

Meanwhile, inspired by their commanding officer's rigorous training regimen, his men had taken to calling themselves "Chambers Raiders"—a sobriquet outsiders immediately bastardized to the "Chamber Maids." But no one could deny that Chambers was a tough character. "He reminded you of a pirate as he stalked about, except that he is a strapping big fellow," wrote a *Leatherneck* correspondent. "On his hip was a .38-caliber pistol, carried in a specially made snap draw holster. From under his armpit peeked another pistol, a .45, and dangling from his belt he carried a wicked looking knife that had been cut down from a bayonet on Tulagi."

By now the "Raiders," having endured Chambers's personal training regimen, considered themselves about the roughest, toughest outfit in the Marine Corps. "He spoke of mental conditioning, and at first we thought it was just a pat phrase to explain a lot of unnecessary hardships," recalled one of the battalion officers. "But he showed us what it meant. The battalion would never have made it through the first two days at Iwo if it hadn't been for Chambers's training. On that we all agreed."

February 1945 found Chambers Raiders aboard ship, headed for Iwo Jima. While still at sea, the battalion celebrated Jumpin' Joe's thirty-seventh birthday. Somewhere someone had managed to find a birthday card for an eight-year-old. With a blithe disregard for basic math, well-wishers drew a "3" in front of the "8" and added irreverent salutations such as "Grandpa, what long hair you have" and "Too old for combat." Someone of a more delicate mindset wrote, "Very best wishes. Sincerely, yours."

Best wishes couldn't hurt on Iwo. Directed to lead his battalion against the rocky cliffs along the East Boat Basin, Chambers knew his Marines were in for a rough time. In addition to facing the rugged terrain to their front, they also would be on the extreme right flank of the landing, completely open to enemy fire from that direction, "an unpleasant prospect in any operation," wrote Chambers later, "but in this case, one which looked like organizational suicide." Combat veterans in the battalion—and there were many—were not deceived by assurances of a quick and easy campaign. Some took to calling themselves the "Ghouls of the 3rd Battalion" and one anonymous wag even went so far as to pen some verse to be sung to Chopin's "Funeral March":

> We are the ghouls of the Third Battalion.
> One thousand men and one Italian.
> We waded through swamps:
> The earth we learned to hug.
> And all we got was a goddamn dizzy bug.
> But ten thousand dollars went home to the folks.
> But won't they be happy; won't they be surprised.
> When ten thousand dollars go home to the folks!

The "one Italian" was Capt. Sam Pitetti of Rillton, Pennsylvania, a popular company commander who had been a student at Washington and Jefferson College in Pennsylvania when the war started. Within hours of landing on Iwo, he would be dead.

On February 19 Chambers led his battalion ashore on Blue Beach 2. The 3rd Battalion's objective the first day was to get on top of the cliff-like "quarries" just inland from the beach. To his surprise, things were relatively quiet the first half hour or so after landing, he recalled. But as his men slogged over the terraces rising from the beach, the Japanese opened up with a vengeance. "It [the terrace] was about 30 to 40 feet wide and I know as we went across the first terrace, the fire from automatic weapons was coming from all over," Chambers said. "You could have lit it on the stuff going by."

Casualties piled up quickly. As Chambers continued forward, he saw a Marine lying in a shell crater. "He was alive, but his guts were all hanging out," recalled Chambers. "He had no chance in the world to live." Chambers paused and injected the Marine with about half a pack of his morphine syrettes—probably more than enough to kill him, but

Marines hit the beach on February 19, 1945. USMC

he didn't think it mattered much at that point. "I saw no reason to leave him there suffering," he observed years later.

It was only about 0830, but heavy casualties were already threatening the momentum of the assault as Chambers set up his command post in a shell crater on Blue Beach. Much of the fire was coming from a fortified cliff area beyond his battalion's objective. "What I was concerned about at that point was what was going to happen if we couldn't move and get to the quarries and get on top of them," Chambers remembered. By noon it had become imperative to seize the high ground to the northeast, where Japanese guns were cutting the Marines on the beach to pieces and taking a toll among the amtracs churning toward shore.

Working out of his shell crater, Chambers radioed Lt. Col. Lewis Hudson, commanding the 2nd Battalion, which had landed in reserve. "For God's sake, get a company up there," he pleaded, referring to the high ground to the northeast. Hudson said he had a company in position. "All right, if you don't get up on that high ground, I'm never going to get up on those quarries today," replied Chambers. He told Hudson he planned to jump off and attack the quarries at 1600. "I haven't got much left, but we're going to try and get up there," he said.

Now Chambers radioed Maj. Clark Stevens at regimental head-quarters, asking for fire support. "Starting at 1530 I want to hit the top of the quarries and 200 or 300 yards in back of them," he told Stevens. "I need everything we can put in there. I need a naval vessel concentrating its fire in there. I'd like to get an air strike in there if we can get it and I don't give a damn if you come right at us. It's going to be tougher than hell getting up on there."

By this time, Chambers's battalion had already been badly hurt. K Company had lost all eight of its officers; Company L had lost five officers and I Company had lost six. Company L had been reduced from 240 men to eighteen effectives in the rifle platoons; the 3rd Battalion itself was reduced to 150 effectives. Chambers ordered Capt. Jim Headley to organize K and L Companies for the assault on the quarries. Headley stood up in a hail of fire, moving around, getting the men together. Chambers picked up the radio and screamed at him, "Goddammit, do you want to get killed? Get down!" Headley calmly radioed back that he had to get the men organized, then proceeded to ignore Chambers. Headley got his men off at 1600. Within half an hour, by sliding around to the north almost down to the ocean side of the quarry area, he succeeded in getting twenty-six men to the top of the high ground. Headley's small force suffered seventeen more casualties in the fight that followed, but managed to hold on. "It was beginning to get dark and I reported that we were on top of the quarries with a few men and I needed troops," recalled Chambers.

"If the Japs counterattack, they're going to run us right off of there and I haven't got anything to put there," he told Stevens by radio.

"We'll get you some," said Stevens.

He was as good as his word. Later that night a company arrived to reinforce the small force on top of the quarries. "Once I got that company up there, for the first time, I began to feel pretty good," said Chambers.

Meanwhile the night had turned miserable. It was cold, the wind had whipped up, and by midnight a steady, almost sleet-like rain was falling. "We had tried to dig into the side of this crater," said Chambers. "We had sort of a half-assed shelter in there. I was ready to see if I could catch a little shut-eye." There weren't many enemy probes that night, but the noise never seemed to stop. "If you take all the fireworks you ever saw anywhere on the Fourth of July and multiply it by about fifty times, you get some idea of what was going on," he remarked. "That whole island seemed to be on fire."

In the morning he moved his command post right up against the quarries. He didn't have a lot left to command. In his morning report, the battalion listed 22 officers and 500 men as casualties. Some explanation of how the Japanese had survived the preliminary bombardment lay in a tunnel near Chambers's command post. Some Marines ventured in to investigate and couldn't find the end of it, with all of its side passages and levels. "It just branched off and went all over hell's half acre," remarked Chambers. Fortunately, there didn't seem to be any Japanese inside now.

Though not subjected to mass counterattacks, infiltrators were a constant threat to the Marines. On his second night ashore, Chambers went looking for his K Company people. "I saw a figure alongside a bush who I thought was a Marine," he recalled. "He was about fifteen or twenty yards away, and I hollered, 'Hey, Mac, have you seen Breck?' I saw his right hand hit the top of his helmet and I realized he was a Jap arming a grenade. I had my .38 in my hand and I let fly. I hit him before he could even throw because he went right down and the grenade went off on top of him. But that scared the hell out of all of us."

Over the next couple of days, Chambers's battalion stayed in place, held in reserve—or what passed for reserve on Iwo Jima. The 3rd Marine Division came ashore and attempted to straighten the line alongside, so the 25th Regiment could continue its push. The initial effort failed. "I saw one squad move out and men just dropping like flies, both officers and men," remembered Chambers. In his area, part of the holdup was a piece of Japanese-held high ground known as Charlie Dog Ridge. On the afternoon of February 22, a rocket platoon came forward and dumped 124 rockets on the Japanese. The barrage stunned the defenders. "In a matter of two or three minutes the debris, crap, dust and smoke started settling on Charlie Dog Ridge and there was any number of Nips wandering around in plain sight," remembered Chambers. "We had all of our automatic weapons and everything up there and the boys didn't need any command to open fire, boy. They just cut loose and had a turkey shoot."

A Marine moves forward under fire. USMC

As he stood watching, Chambers saw his air-liaison officer walking around in the open. He had already lost two air liaisons and he didn't want to lose a third. He pointed a finger at the youngster. "Son, you'd better learn to keep down or you'll get yourself shot," he warned. The words were no sooner out of his mouth when there was a sudden burst of fire. Chambers had just an instant to mentally classify the weapon as a Japanese light machine gun when a slug slammed into his upper left chest, knocking him to the ground. The shot may have come from the machine gun or from an enemy sniper; he was never sure. "Be this as it may, I got hit hard," he recalled. "I went down and started fading in and out. I don't remember too much about it except the frothy blood gushing out of my mouth and in my own mind I was gone." Sure he was dying, he gasped out for someone to tell his family he loved them.

"Then somebody started kicking the hell out of my feet," recalled Chambers. It was his friend, now second in command, Capt. Jim Headley. He and Headley went back a long way; it was Headley who had taken over for Chambers when Chambers was blown up on Saipan. "Get up, you lazy bastard," urged Headley in an effort to keep Chambers conscious. "You were hurt worse on Tulagi."

But Jumping Joe wasn't going anywhere under his own power. "The corpsman probably saved my life because this was a sucking wound, and he packed the point of exit with bandages," he said later. "It went down through the lungs and knocked out a block of ribs and a couple of the transverse processes of the spine. . . . Somehow they got a stretcher, put me on it and crawled me out. We were under fire. They started giving me albumen and blood in both veins before snaking me out on the ground." On the beach, Dr. Michael Keleher looked at the injury. "Colonel, they're going to take you out to the ship," he said. "If they've got plenty of whole blood and plenty of oxygen, you've got a 50–50 chance of living."

Despite that less than cheery assessment, Chambers survived the quick hop out to the *Ozark*, a converted minelayer, and the voyage to a hospital on Guam. He was subsequently transferred to Hawaii, and then to the United States for more medical attention. Lucky just to be alive, he was told it was a near miracle that he hadn't been left paralyzed by his injury. Meanwhile, his dogged efforts to seize the key high ground off Blue Beach 2 on February 19—a success that averted a potential disaster on the right flank of the invasion force—had earned him a recommendation for the Medal of Honor. The recommendation was knocked down to the Navy Cross, which was awarded to Chambers on August 31, 1945, by Marine Corps commandant Gen. A. A. Vandegrift.

But Chambers's actions on Iwo Jima, and their crucial impact on the landing, continued to fuel feelings that a higher decoration was warranted. Col. James Taul, executive officer of the 3rd Battalion on Iwo, wrote that Chambers's actions had been key to the seizure of the beachhead, adding, "It is my firm opinion that had the high ground not been promptly seized on D-day, the subsequent operations ashore would have been severely threatened." A review by the Navy

*Five years after the war, President Harry S. Truman
decorates Col. Justice M. Chambers with the Medal of
Honor as Secretary of Defense George C. Marshall (left)
and members of the colonel's family look on. Department
of Defense*

Department's Board of Review for Decorations and Medals initially
upheld the award of the Navy Cross. However, after a third review by
the board, the award was upgraded to the Medal of Honor. The medal
was presented by President Truman on November 1, 1950, more than
five years after the war. Among those in attendance were the hero's
twin baby boys, one of whom grabbed the paper the president was
holding as he read his remarks, while the other attempted to abscond
with the handkerchief in the president's breast pocket as movie cam-
eras ground and flash bulbs popped.

By then, Chambers was a civilian again. Declared incapacitated
for service due to his wounds, he retired from active duty with the
rank of colonel. He went on to become assistant chairman of the Fed-
eral Personnel Council and a staff advisor to the U.S. Senate Armed
Services Committee. He also worked with the Federal Civil Defense
Administration and was deputy director of the Office of Emergency
Planning from 1962 to 1964. He subsequently served as president of
J. M. Chambers Co., Inc., a consulting firm, before retiring in 1973.

On a more personal level, his first marriage ended in divorce after the war, but he later remarried. His second wife, Barbara, once remarked that the things her husband valued most in his life were his service with the Marines, the ties with the men he had served along-side, and his family. Third in his heart after Marines and family, she joked, were his beloved Washington Redskins.

Justice Chambers died at Bethesda Naval Hospital on July 20, 1982, after suffering a stroke. He was survived by his wife, a daughter, and four sons, one of whom was then serving as a major in the Marine Corps. The man once described as tougher than a fifty-cent steak was buried with full military honors in Arlington National Cemetery, plot 6-5813-A-9.

In a memoir written before his death, he talked about trying to get off the beaches at Iwo Jima—not about his own courage, but of the courage of the men he commanded. "Heroism was commonplace, no longer awe-inspiring or even surprising," he wrote, "There was Sergeant Manuel Martinez of Moses, N.M., who walked erect into a cave full of trapped Nipponese. Blasting them with his automatic rifle, Martinez killed fifteen, but escaped without a scratch. Then there was Private Delbert Maupin, a kid from Hannibal, Mo., who threw himself on a grenade to save his squad leader who didn't see it fall into their midst." He spoke too of his battalion's attack into the murderous fire pouring down on them from the rocky cliffs above East Boat Basin at Blue Beach 2. "Heroes in that initial drive were a dime a dozen," he said.

Capt. Jim Headley, who assumed command of the shot-up 3rd Battalion after Chambers was evacuated, would forever remember both the courage of the Marines and the horrific casualties. By the end of the Iwo Jima campaign, over 750 of the 916 men who had come ashore with the battalion on February 19 were either dead, wounded, or missing. "They died so fast," said Headley. "You'd see a man do something almost unbelievable and a minute later you'd see him die."

In a letter to the commandant of the Marine Corps in late 1945, Chambers reflected on what serving with such men meant to him. "Just boiling it down to language which I can perhaps use best," he wrote simply, "I am proud to have been one of you."

CHAPTER TWO

Round I

Day two on Iwo Jima dawned cold and miserable with a light rain falling. Enemy fire had persisted through the night, depriving all but the most exhausted Marines of sleep. In the 5th Marine Division sector, Mount Suribachi, isolated but not conquered, loomed over the 28th Marines in the gathering light. The division's two other regiments faced north toward the airfields—their whole reason for being there.

Morning finally ended hours of agony for one unlucky Marine in Sgt. Alfred R. Stone's platoon of the 27th Marines. The man had been moving from one hole to another at about sundown when a machine gun from somewhere out front opened up. A bullet hit a BAR magazine in the Marine's cartridge belt. "It shattered and went on through his lower abdomen," recalled Stone. "A corpsman got him into a shell hole and worked on him as well as he could. We could not take him back to the east beach and transfer him to a hospital ship because of the heavy artillery and mortar fire that came in all night. He died in the corpsman's foxhole just before sunrise the next morning."

The attack north toward the airfields got underway at 0830. Stone's platoon caught a break, ordered to stay in their foxholes as men of the 1st Battalion, 26th Marines, moved through them to assault the bands of trenches and pillboxes manned by an invisible enemy. As Japanese fire picked up, Stone heard one of the Marines singing:

> Oh what a beautiful morning
> Oh what a beautiful day
> I've got a God-awful feeling
> That everything's coming our way!

Among the Marines moving into the attack that morning was seventeen-year-old Jacklyn Lucas. Brash and reckless, blessed with a teenager's sense of immortality, Lucas was about to become the youngest man to earn the Medal of Honor during World War II.

PFC JACKLYN H. LUCAS

26th Marines, 5th Marine Division
February 20, 1945

Jacklyn Lucas USMC

Among the thousands of Marines burrowing into Iwo Jima's black volcanic sand on the afternoon of February 19 was a happy-go-lucky youngster carried on Marine Corps rolls as PFC Jacklyn Harrell Lucas. Jack Lucas should not have been on Iwo Jima. In fact, he should not even have been in the Marine Corps; he had celebrated his seventeenth birthday only five days before. But that didn't bother Lucas. Digging in as bullets and shells whipped the sand, the cocky youngster assured his buddies, "I'm right where I want to be."

Born on Valentine's Day 1928 in Plymouth, North Carolina, Jack Lucas had wanted to be a Marine ever since his Uncle Frank gave him a Marine garrison cap when he was only six years old. By his own admission, Jack was a troublesome child. His father, a tobacco farmer, died of cancer in 1939, leaving a vacuum the already headstrong boy found difficult to deal with. "I was kind of shattered to lose my father," he admitted later. "I guess I just resented a lot of things and that loss. I was a mean kid." His attitude was not improved by the subsequent arrival of a much-despised stepfather into the Lucas family fold.

Unable to control the boy, his mother packed him off to Edwards Military Academy. It didn't help much. Discipline had never been one of Jack Lucas's strong suits, though he found he liked the structure of military life, within certain limits. When war broke out, the head-strong thirteen-year-old promptly tried to enlist in the Marines, but couldn't hoodwink the recruiter. In 1942, now a grizzled fourteen years old, standing five feet eight inches tall and looking full-grown at about 185 pounds, Lucas tried again. He told his mother he was going to claim he was seventeen and sign her name on the permission papers. She could stop him, but sooner or later he'd find a way into the service, he said. For once, he found an unlikely ally in his stepfather, who presumably viewed Jack's departure into the military machine as a personal godsend. Jack's mother reluctantly agreed she would not stand in his way, so long as Jack promised he would finish school after his enlistment expired.

Equipped with his forged paperwork, Lucas proceeded down to the recruiting station in Norfolk, Virginia, on August 6, 1942, and finagled his way into the Marine Corps. As might be expected, Marine Corps discipline agreed with Lucas only insofar as it coincided with his personal desires. He excelled in boot camp, but proved to be a poor "back of the lines" Marine. His attitude didn't improve when his commanding officer discovered he was underage and took steps to keep him well away from combat. Assigned to drive a trash truck for the 6th Base Depot, a rear-area supply facility in Hawaii, the frustrated youngster was in constant trouble for brawling and other infractions, accumulating over five months of brig time. One of the more notable incidents occurred when he was caught in possession of a stolen truck and several cases of beer, then tried to slug it out with a military policeman. That piece of ill-advised bravado earned him a thirty-day stint in the brig. If nothing else, the punishment gave him plenty of leisure time to admire the recently acquired USMC bulldog tattoo now adorning his right bicep.

Determined to get into combat, Lucas made his way down to the docks at Pearl Harbor in early January 1945 to see his cousin, PFC Sam Lucas, who was shipping out with the 5th Marine Division for Iwo Jima. Jack found his cousin aboard the USS *Deuel* with C Company, 1st Battalion, 26th Marines. The two visited until dark, when Sam suggested Jack had better be getting back ashore.

"I'm not going ashore," replied Jack. "I'm going wherever this ship is going."

His cousin and buddies kept him hidden until they were well out to sea, when Lucas finally revealed himself to Sam's company commander, Capt. Robert H. Dunlap. Back in Hawaii, Lucas's outfit was in the process of listing him as a deserter. By revealing himself, Lucas avoided that charge. For his part, Dunlap, a veteran Paramarine, was happy to get the combat-hungry youngster for his C Company. "I had eighteen-inch biceps in those days," observed Lucas. "I was so muscled up I could run through a brick wall." When one of the C Company Marines came down with appendicitis and was taken off the ship at Saipan, Lucas appropriated the man's M1 and other gear and filled his slot on one of Dunlap's fire teams.

The invasion of Iwo Jima began five days after Jack Lucas's seventeenth birthday. Coming off guard duty in the ship's hold at 0400 hours, he missed out on the best part of the traditional steak and eggs breakfast. "By the time I got to eat, eggs were all that remained," he recalled. He was not afraid, but he had taken one precaution. The day before, he had stuck a note in his wallet asking the finder to send it to Mrs. Radford Jones in Bellhaven, North Carolina, adding, "That is my mother."

Held in division reserve, his adopted battalion landed at 1500 hours under heavy fire. "My coxswain was in a hurry to offload us and depart," recalled Lucas. "The boat was in fairly deep water for a landing, and when I stepped off the ramp, I sank into the sea up to my chin." Struggling up onto the beach, he made a less than heroic picture, he admitted later. His borrowed fatigue pants, too big to begin with and now soaking wet, flopped down over his feet, "making me look like Charlie Chaplin." Lucas took out his combat knife and cut off both pants legs just below the knee. "I could see small arms fire hitting the ground in front of me and I imagined a Japanese soldier specifically aiming for me," he recalled. There were dead Marines and wrecked equipment everywhere.

The battalion moved up off the beach and headed inland. "We did not see many Japanese that first day, but our battalion's casualties were heavy," said Lucas. As darkness fell at around 1845, his fire team began digging in for the night, trying to enlarge a shell hole in the sifting volcanic ash. Flares hung over the battlefield and shells continued to crash down on the crowded Marine beachhead. "Shells were flying, people were being blown apart, and bullets were everywhere," recalled Lucas. "They made hash of us." He found himself feeling more vengeful than afraid. "I was just as anxious as ever to kill as many Japs as I could kill," he observed.

The following morning Lucas's battalion joined in the push toward Motoyama Airfield No. 1. Mortar shells rained down from unseen Japanese. Watching helplessly as an adjacent outfit got chewed up in the barrage, Lucas lost a bit of his bravado. "I could see the guys getting all torn to pieces," he recalled. "I thought, 'Boy, I hope they don't shift that fire over here.'"

In addition to Lucas, his four-man fire team consisted of PFC Riley E. Gilbert of Texas, PFC Malvin B. Hagevik of Wisconsin, and PFC Allan Crowson of Arkansas. A former Paramarine, nineteen-year-old Crowson carried the team's BAR, while the other three were armed with M1 rifles. They were still alive and moving forward at around noon when word came to hold up. Hagevik, the oldest of the group at twenty-four, led Lucas, Gilbert, and Crowson into the shelter of a nearby trench. "There were two 20-foot-long trenches, running parallel to each other, approximately four feet apart," recalled Lucas. The four Marines were in a line—Hagevik first, then Lucas, followed by Crowson with the BAR, and then Gilbert. Gilbert decided to check out the trench to their front. He jumped in, landing directly on a Japanese soldier. As Gilbert scrambled back to the fire team, nearly a dozen Japanese suddenly stood up in the second trench, practically at arm's length from the startled fire team. The Marines cut loose from the hip—if he had tried to raise his rifle to his shoulder, said Lucas, the muzzle "would have been in the other fellow's mouth." The firefight was brutal and confused. "Nobody said nothing," recalled Lucas. "It wasn't no social hour."

Lucas gunned down one Japanese, then shot another in the forehead. "I saw the blood spurt from his head as he stared at me," he remembered. "Then my rifle jammed. I was looking down at my rifle trying to get the damned thing unjammed, and when I did, I saw the grenade."

A Japanese grenade had landed between him and Crowson, who was standing just to his right. "Grenade!" Lucas shouted, pushing Crowson aside. He fell to his knees, ramming the bean can–sized device as far as he could into the loose sand with his rifle butt. Suddenly a second grenade materialized next to the first. In the split mini-second that followed, Lucas realized that if the grenades went off among them, he and his three buddies would be killed or wounded. Falling forward, he grabbed the second grenade with his right hand, pulled it underneath his body and pushed it as far as he could into the volcanic ash.

He felt someone run across his back and had just enough time to think, "Luke, you're gonna die." Then there was a deafening explosion and he was blown into the air and onto his back. "Blood poured out of my mouth and I couldn't move," he recalled. "I knew I was dying." He prayed, "God save me."

God did save Jack Lucas. By some miracle or slipshod Japanese manufacturing, only one of the grenades had gone off. Somewhat deadened by the loose sand, it grievously wounded the seventeen-year-old, but didn't kill him. That same volcanic ash, deeply embedded in his wounds, helped staunch the bleeding. And finally, his own grenades—six of them draped across his chest for quick access—deflected the metal fragments from his heart.

Lucas sprawled on his back, helplessly looking skyward, his ears ringing. Fragments had punctured his right lung and been driven into his thigh, neck, chin, and head. His riddled right arm was twisted so far under him he thought it had been blown off. "Barely audible above the escalating ringing in my ears was the sound of my team finishing off the enemy," he said later. "My mind struggled to process the muffled noises, but everything sounded as though I were underwater." His clothes were in shreds and his backpack had been blown off. "I raised my head as much as possible and saw blood spewing from my chest and thigh," he remembered. Blood filled his mouth and throat. Still conscious, he kept moving his left hand in hopes of attracting someone's attention. "That was the only thing I could move," he said.

In the confusion, and thinking Lucas was dead, Crowson and the others had moved on. Fortunately for Lucas, another Marine stumbled

Dead Japanese lie in a trench. Jacklyn Lucas nearly died in a similar trench. "Nobody said nothing," he recalled of the point-blank firefight. "It wasn't no social hour." Associated Press

upon him as he feebly waved his hand, saw that he was still alive—if only barely—and shouted for a corpsman. "My right eye was blown out of its socket and lying on my cheek until the corpsman put it back," said Lucas. As he worked, yet another Japanese soldier popped up from a tunnel and prepared to throw a grenade at them. The corpsman snatched up his carbine and shot the man.

Rushed back to the beach on a stretcher, Lucas had one more scare when someone covered him with a poncho to protect him from the elements. "Oh Lord, I'm dead," he thought before drifting off in a morphine-induced stupor. But Lucas was still breathing—albeit with a tube down his throat—when he finally arrived aboard an LST and then the hospital ship *Samaritan*. "Maybe he was too damned young and too damned tough to die," marveled a surgeon. Doctors at the naval hospital at Guam even managed to save Lucas's mangled right arm.

In addition to a partially crippled arm, Lucas was left with over 200 bits of metal in his body, much of it too close to his heart, spine, and other vital organs to be safely removed. Postwar X-rays showed forty-five holes in his upper thigh alone. His X-rays, he joked years later, looked like a starry sky at night. A newspaper reporter could not help but notice that "his fingers stick out at funny angles when he tries to salute."

Eight months and twenty-two operations after he was carried off Iwo Jima, Jack Lucas went to the White House to receive the Medal of Honor from President Truman. He was the youngest serviceman to receive the Medal of Honor in any conflict since the Civil War. The day was so hot that three members of the Marine honor guard passed out during the forty-minute ceremony for fourteen recipients. While going to shake Lucas's hand, Truman inadvertently hit the hero's still painful wounds. "It hurt, but I tried not to wince," recalled Lucas. Then, as he was prone to do, Truman told Lucas he'd rather have the Medal of Honor than be president of the United States. "Sir," replied the still irrepressible youngster, "I'll swap with you."

Suddenly famous, Lucas received thousands of letters from admirers following the award ceremony at the White House. He appeared in a parade down New York's Fifth Avenue, accompanying Adm. Chester Nimitz. "I never really thought of myself as a hero, period, but they chose to decorate me," he said. "Then I was cocky after all that fanfare. It really blew my mind, women jumping on me and kissing me and half-dragging me out of the automobile. I loved it. I was popular. I got engaged four times. I was really hitting my stride, see?"

Discharged from the Marine Corps, which decided to overlook his numerous transgressions, Lucas went back and completed high school. He then attended a series of colleges on a hit-or-miss basis, finally earning a business degree from High Point University in North Carolina in 1956. In the meantime, in 1952 he had acquired a wife. Their high-profile wedding ceremony was performed on a national television program, *The Bride and Groom Show*. In 1954 a son, Luis, was born.

Unfortunately, the years after the war were not entirely kind to Jack Lucas. He was just too restless. He worked for the Veterans Administration, opened then closed a drive-in restaurant, and dabbled in real estate. Unable to settle down in a job he liked, he finally obtained a commission in the army in 1961. But the peacetime army didn't agree with him either. He drank too much and brawled with other officers. Finally, in 1965, after Captain Lucas took on three lieutenants in a fight, the army decided it had suffered enough. Lucas was placed on inactive reserve and given an honorable discharge.

A civilian again, Lucas started a meat company in California. The business did well, though his marriage did not. His first wife divorced him after discovering he had taken up with another woman. Lucas married his second wife, Erlene, a divorcee from Texas, in 1966, and moved to Maryland, where he opened another meat business. The business turned into a gold mine. He and Erlene lived in an eleven-room mansion, drove "his" and "hers" Lincoln Continentals, and owned a pet chimpanzee that strolled around the house in a dress. But unknown to Lucas, Erlene, who kept the company books, was siphoning tens of thousands of dollars from the business. When he finally discovered the losses in 1973, he threatened to cut her and her nineteen-year-old daughter from her previous marriage out of his will.

Instead of remorse, Erlene decided to have Lucas killed. Her daughter's husband, who worked for Lucas in the meat company, arranged for a killer to dispose of the former Marine. The plan was to drug Lucas, then shoot him with his own gun, making his death appear a suicide. But the hired "killer" was actually an undercover state police officer. On June 27, 1977, the day of the scheduled "murder," Erlene and her son-in-law were arrested.

But by the time the trial rolled around, Jack and Erlene had reconciled. "I didn't want our own children, aged eleven and nine, to have a mother in prison," Lucas said later. "That would be worse than anything." Lucas sat at the defense table with Erlene, holding her hand, as she pleaded guilty to a charge of soliciting to commit murder. He asked the court for leniency for his wife. The court agreed. Erlene and her son-in-law received ten-year suspended sentences.

Predictably, the reconciliation did not last. He and Erlene eventually went their separate ways. His run of bad luck continued as he also found himself with serious tax problems. The IRS descended on him, claiming he owned $55,000 in unpaid taxes, a debt that more than doubled with penalties and interest, and continued to grow when Lucas could not pay up. He lost his business and his home. The IRS even garnisheed his $800-a-month disability checks.

Destitute, Lucas and his eighteen-year-old son moved into a mobile home, where they lived without electricity, phone, or running water. When he tried to recover some of his possessions from his former home, he was arrested for trespassing and carrying a concealed weapon. "You see your whole life unravel, everything taken away," he remarked emptily. "I've thought about killing myself." As if he didn't already have enough trouble, the mobile home burned down. Lucas salvaged his Medal of Honor from the ashes, though the ribbon had been burned off. He moved into a garage and then set up camp in a tent on a farm rented by a friend in Maryland. "I had one outstanding year in my life," he told a newspaper reporter on the fortieth anniversary of the battle for Iwo Jima, "and I have been jinxed ever since."

Six months later, Lucas made the headlines again. In August 1985 he was arrested when Maryland State Police raided the farm and found ninety marijuana plants, which they valued at $90,000. "They think I'm a big wheel in a dope racket," said Lucas. "I don't smoke it or raise it. I knew the stuff was there on the farm, but I couldn't run up to my friend and tell him not to grow it. He did a lot of things for me." Later he conceded ruefully, "I was dumb as a box of rocks to set up house-keeping in a field of pot."

In the end, the state showed more compassion than the IRS. Citing his "heroic service to his country," the state declined to prosecute Lucas. The publicity also brought some help for the embattled hero. The Veterans Administration intervened with the IRS in an effort to resolve the tax problem. Lucas moved to Mississippi, remarried, and managed to pull his life together. In his later years he was the guest of presidents and undertook numerous speaking engagements for veterans groups and social and civic organizations.

The medal remained the crowning achievement of his life—and perhaps his greatest burden as well. "I don't want to embarrass the Medal of Honor," he said some years ago, then added candidly, "When I got my medal, they didn't say 'Jack Lucas, you've got to be a saint from now on. You've got to be on guard every moment.' . . . . I know I've never grown any wings."

Hospitalized with leukemia, Jack Lucas died on June 5, 2008, after directing doctors to remove a dialysis machine. As his final moments approached, his wife Ruby was by his side. "I said, 'Jack, you know you're dying,'" she recalled. "He just raised his head off the pillow. He said, 'I ain't dead yet.' Just as plain as day. . . . That's Jack Lucas. He wanted to get the last word in." He was laid to rest at Highland Cemetery in Hattiesburg, Mississippi.

In 1995, on the fiftieth anniversary of the battle, Jack Lucas was asked about his decision to fall on the enemy grenades. Why? Why volunteer for almost certain death? "Better for one Marine to go down than all four," he said simply. "It wasn't for us to decide who's going to survive this damn thing."

While Jack Lucas lay terribly wounded in an abandoned Japanese trench, Capt. Robert Dunlap led the rest of C Company north into the relatively open ground west of Airfield No. 1. Among them were the survivors of Lucas's fire team, all three of whom would soon be wounded themselves—Crowson so severely that he spent eighteen months in the hospital. A former Paramarine, the short-statured Dunlap didn't look particularly imposing, but outward appearances were deceiving. Bobby Dunlap was about as tough and savvy as they come.

This morning, advancing with little cover under excellent observation from Japanese artillery and mortar spotters, both those qualities would be needed in abundance.

CAPT. ROBERT HUGO DUNLAP

26th Marines, 5th Marine Division
February 20–21, 1945

Robert Dunlap USMC

Bobby Dunlap was built for speed. He ran the dash in high school and used his quick-footedness in college to make All-Conference as a running back. But it wasn't speed that earned him the Medal of Honor in the shifting sands of Iwo Jima—it was his tenacity.

Robert Hugo Dunlap—everybody called him "Bobby"—was born October 19, 1920, in Abingdon, Illinois, to Guy William and Leona

Smith Dunlap. His father, a veteran of World War I, was a dairy farmer whose family had first homesteaded in the area in 1837. Bobby was the oldest of their three children, followed by a sister and a brother.

Bobby attended school in rural Abington, graduating from high school there in 1938 as salutatorian of a class of thirty-two students. His father, a graduate of the University of Illinois, had been an outstanding athlete in his youth, and he encouraged the boy to be competitive. Bobby did not disappoint. During high school, he was active in football and basketball, and ran track. He also enjoyed acting in theater productions. After graduation, he went on to nearby Monmouth College, where he continued to excel in athletics while majoring in economics and business administration and minoring in mathematics.

His cousin, Jim Stockdale, who himself would one day wear a Medal of Honor earned for his actions as a prisoner of war in Vietnam, recalled, "He was three and a half years older than I, and thus my idol in high school and college sports." There was plenty to emulate. Standing five feet six inches tall and weighing in at 148 pounds, Dunlap was a tenacious competitor on the athletic field and a bright mind in the classroom. "A dash man at track, he tried for four years to break the Knox County, Illinois, dash record set by his father in 1905 at 'ten flat'—almost Olympic time in those years," recalled Stockdale. "My mother was his high school teacher for a while and she always said that Bobby had a marvelous mind. She was also his drama coach and he was good at that, too."

During his senior year at Monmouth, Dunlap served as treasurer of the student body. Described in his college yearbook as the "biggest little man on campus" and "a little man with a big heart," he earned three varsity letters in football, two in track, and one in basketball. Though short, he was very muscular through the legs and torso, and he played football well enough to attract the attention of the Philadelphia Eagles, who invited the college senior to try out for the team.

With a war underway, the Eagles never had a chance. "I don't think we're taking the war seriously enough on campus," Dunlap publicly

*Robert Dunlap, "the biggest little man on campus," as a senior
at Monmouth College. Courtesy of Monmouth College*

chided his classmates. "I think fellows should attempt to get in shape
to meet the physical requirements of our democracy." He wasted little time living up to those words. On March 5, 1942, he enlisted in
the Marine Corps after former University of Iowa quarterback and
Heisman Trophy winner Nile Kinnick visited the campus seeking
recruits for officer training. "Most of the athletes, over sixty of us, went
to see the [Marine] recruiter," Dunlap recalled. "He then came to the
campus to talk to us. We had decided that we would enter the service
together and serve together, but I was the only one to pass the physical
at that time."

Allowed to take early graduation in order to enter the service, Dunlap received his commission as a second lieutenant on July 18, 1942,
at Quantico, Virginia, despite complaints from a drill sergeant that he
bounced when he walked because his legs were so short in proportion
to his body. Gold bars in hand, Dunlap promptly requested parachute
training, mostly because of the higher pay, he admitted later. The extra
money would help him pay off his college loans, assuming he survived.
In October he arrived at Camp Gillespie in San Diego, California, to
attend parachutist training school. He passed the demanding course
without difficulty. "A physical marvel, he broke obstacle course records
all over the Marine Corps," observed Stockdale.

Earning his wings on November 23, Dunlap was assigned to the
3rd Parachute Battalion. He was promoted to first lieutenant in April

1943. Overseas duty quickly followed, with Dunlap seeing action with the Paramarines on Vella Lavella and Bougainville. Years later, reflecting on his first combat, Dunlap said the thing that worried him most was that "I wasn't sure I could shoot at anybody. I didn't think I could kill anybody."

When the time came, Dunlap found that his instinct for survival was stronger than any moral qualms. Taken under fire by a Japanese machine gun in the Bougainville jungle, he rolled directly into the firing lane as the gun paused, squinted down the barrel of his rifle, and shot the operator through the head. "The first opportunity came and it was either him or me," he observed of his first close kill. "Not a one would surrender. It was them or us."

The former athlete was awarded a Letter of Commendation for his actions on Bougainville on December 9, 1943. When his platoon was pinned down by a Japanese machine gun, Dunlap exposed himself to the heavy fire and managed to rally his depleted platoon, maneuver it into position, and reoccupy lost ground. His commanding officer felt compelled to make note of the seeming contradiction between Dunlap's personalities in and out of combat. "Apparently a very quiet, retiring personality, this officer demonstrated outstanding qualities of battlefield leadership," remarked the commanding officer. "Skilled, courageous and tenacious in adversity."

Following the decision to break up so-called elite units such as the Raiders and Paramarines, Dunlap returned to the States in March 1944 and joined the 5th Marine Division, then forming at Camp Pendleton. First assigned as a machine-gun platoon leader, he was subsequently promoted to captain. By the time the division came ashore at Iwo Jima, Dunlap had command of Company C, 1st Battalion, 26th Marines.

Dunlap, lugging the treasured Johnson rifle of his paratrooper days, brought C Company in over Red Beach 1 the afternoon of D-day. The beach was clogged with men and equipment, and under steady enemy artillery fire. "I stopped in a hole and there were eight holes in my pack," remembered C Company machine gunner PFC Oliver Taylor.

Marines of the 5th Division inch their way up a slope on Red Beach No. 1 toward Suribachi as the smoke of the battle drifts about them on February 19, 1945. USMC

"I wasn't scared until I saw that." Such was the intensity of enemy shellfire that, by day's end, the 1st Battalion had lost all of its officers with the exception of two second lieutenants and Dunlap himself. "The exact word that told all . . . was 'carnage,'" Dunlap said years later. Rather than join the useless congestion on the beach—little more than a stationary bulls-eye for Japanese gunners—Dunlap led his men 200 yards inland. "I thought, 'If I'm going to get men killed, I'm not going to do it sitting here on the beach,'" he recalled of his decision. "'I want them accomplishing something.'" Seeing Dunlap's company moving through, many strays from other units got up out of the sand and joined him. By evening Dunlap figured he had a mixed bag of perhaps as many as 400 or 500 Marines under his command.

The morning of February 20, Charlie Company jumped off as part of the multibattalion push northward by the 26th and 27th

Marines, parallel to Airfield No. 1. The C Company Marines suffered most heavily from well-directed enemy mortar and artillery barrages, but also had to deal with belts of pillboxes and land mines blocking the way north. The enemy fortifications in this area were typically about fifteen feet square, made of reinforced concrete and covered with sand, recalled Dunlap. The embrasures were seven or eight inches high and about two feet wide. Some of the positions were empty, but others contained as many as a couple of dozen Japanese. Dunlap brought his machine guns forward and told them to concentrate their fire on the narrow openings in the enemy blockhouses, forcing the occupants to keep their heads down. Assisted by flame-throwing tanks, Marine riflemen and demolitions teams then took the fortifications on one by one. In approximately an hour and a half by Dunlap's estimate, C Company killed about 300 Japanese, pushing steadily forward until they found themselves well in advance of adjacent Marine units.

As he paused with C Company's flanks hanging out in the wind, Dunlap realized he had managed to punch through the center of a major defense belt and was now past the actual airfield. To his front stretched an open area of rolling hills that ended about 400 yards away in a cliff face pocked with Japanese defensive positions. Enemy artillery dug into this high ground was raising hell, with the growing congestion on the beach and units trying to move inland. His own men were also falling victim to the enemy artillery fire as they paused in the scant cover of the black sand hills. "I wanted to see where all this enemy fire was coming from because we were getting so darn much," recalled Dunlap. "The Japs were concealed in caves, pillboxes, and bunkers. We couldn't see them and we were really catching hell."

Dunlap realized there was only one solution to his problem. He needed to get someone far enough forward to spot the specific enemy positions, and call in Marine artillery and naval gunfire to knock them out. The question was how. He was still mulling his options when one of his Marines blurted, "Look at that Jap!"

"That Jap" was an enemy soldier who had suddenly risen up out of the ground about 100 yards in front of the Marines and was now strolling slowly inland, angling off to the right, apparently unaware of the watching Americans.

Dunlap had a sudden—some might say crazy—idea. "Don't shoot!" he yelled to his Marines. Getting up from the sand, he walked after the Japanese soldier, dragging his Johnson rifle in a similar fashion, in hopes any enemy troops watching would mistake him for a comrade in arms. "My medal [citation] says I crawled. . . . There's no way to crawl [that distance] without getting killed, so I walked just like the Japanese," he recalled.

The charade worked. Dunlap made his way nearly 200 yards beyond his own lines, at one point passing so close to a Japanese pillbox he could hear the occupants talking inside. Finally, topping a low rise just in front of the heavily defended cliff face, he almost literally stumbled into an artillery battery manned by about thirty Japanese. "I got out there in front and I walked until I got right at the base of the cliff," he said. "There I saw three big artillery pieces that looked like they were big enough to tear all of us apart. I was close enough that I could have hit them with hand grenades. I saw a lot of Japs beside each gun."

He had little time to absorb the scene. "All of a sudden the Japs realized who I was," he recalled. Presumably more startled than Dunlap, the Japanese opened fire with everything they had. Dunlap turned and ran. "I got back running and diving. I'd dive into a bomb crater . . . and then look for my next hole, [then] I'd zigzag, dive. The Japs were on me all the time," he remembered.

Dodging enemy bullets and at least two grenades lobbed at him from one of the still-active pillboxes, it took Dunlap an hour and a half to make it back to the low sand hill where his company waited. He immediately got on the radio and called in artillery fire on the enemy battery he had spotted at the base of the cliff. Meanwhile, the advance of adjacent units had stalled in the face of intense enemy artillery and mortar fire, leaving C Company hanging out about 200 yards in front of the general assault. With the situation not likely to improve in the immediate future, battalion ordered Dunlap to fall back some 500 yards.

The Marines pulled back—all except Bobby Dunlap. Armed with his voice-powered radio, he moved into a shell hole on a low hill well in advance of the main line and began to call artillery fire down on the Japanese. There was no shortage of targets. To his immediate front was the enemy-held cliff line; to his left were scores of Japanese pillboxes and defense works; to his right rose a large enemy-occupied hill. As his efforts showed results, runners arrived with several field telephones, and he was joined by a small crew of radiomen.

An observer calls in fire. Capt. Bobby Dunlap spent two days in a shell hole beyond the front lines calling in artillery on Japanese positions. USMC

Standing on a shelf at the forward edge of the crater, his head sticking just over the edge, Dunlap directed fire on cave after cave. Japanese to his left popped away with mortars in an effort to eradicate this nuisance; enemy artillery fire repeatedly knocked out his phone lines, but Dunlap and his team stuck to their post. "My men were the greatest," he remarked. "They did everything they knew how to do, well."

It is indicative of the magnitude of the enemy defenses that the spotting party's efforts continued through the next day and night, and into the following day. Dunlap manned his vantage point, going virtually without sleep, smoking endless cigarettes during the daylight hours when the glow would not betray him, occasionally choking down a square of a chocolate D-bar for nourishment. Death loomed constantly as the enemy tried to knock out his small outpost. At least six large-caliber shells landed on his position, recalled Dunlap. He survived, though a shell killed one of his sergeants. Eventually Dunlap found himself directing two battalions of artillery, naval gunfire from the USS *New York*, and sixteen planes, in the effort to break the Japanese defense system.

Some small indication of his success can be found in 5th Marine Division records: "The naval gunfire officer with the 1stBn, 26th Marines, fired on enemy guns in three instances," observed one report. "On one occasion he reported that a company commander adjusted a ship's fire on a Jap emplacement and silenced the gun. The company commander started the adjustment on a second gun position but was able to turn it over to the ship for direct fire. The second emplacement was also silenced."

Japanese return fire gradually began to diminish under the constant pounding, and Dunlap was finally able to leave his home in the shell hole for a temporary respite in reserve. The hiatus was short-lived. On the evening of February 26, C Company was ordered forward. Once again, Dunlap moved out beyond the lines, venturing over a hill in an effort to pinpoint the source of enemy artillery fire on his unit. Seeing four or five Japanese manning machine guns, he paused to shoot them before running back over the hill. This time he didn't quite make it. An enemy rifleman in a pillbox shot him through the left hip. Knocked to the ground and unable to move his legs, Dunlap was rescued by litter bearers who ventured out under machine-gun fire, loaded him onto a stretcher, and lugged him past his C Company Marines, back toward the beach.

"The proudest moment I ever had was when they carried me off Iwo Jima on a stretcher," recalled Dunlap. "Over 100 men got out of their foxholes and saluted me by presenting arms while shells were falling all around." Dunlap lost his composure in the face of this spontaneous tribute. "I bawled like a baby," he admitted.

Dunlap was aboard the hospital ship *Samaritan* headed for a hospital on Saipan when he got the first indication that he had been recommended for a decoration. Weeks later, now at the Great Lakes Naval Hospital, he was officially informed he had been recommended for the Medal of Honor. "I was asked if I wanted to go to Washington to receive it, but I told them that I wasn't physically able to travel in a full body cast," he remarked sardonically. "I had also been hit in the left eye and was wearing a patch." Though Dunlap subsequently dismissed his war injuries as "a Hollywood wound," the Japanese bullet left him in a body cast for nine months. Paralyzed from the waist down, he eventually regained the use of his legs, but the aftereffects of his wound would remain with him the rest of his life. He considered himself fortunate to even be alive. "I was lucky," he remarked. "God was with me. He had to have been."

Robert Dunlap is awarded the Medal of Honor by President Truman on December 18, 1945, after being released from the naval hospital. He never fully recovered from his wounds. USMC

On December 14, 1945, finally released from his plaster prison, Dunlap married his college sweetheart, Mary Louise Frantz, whom he had met at a school dance before the war. "I've never been more nervous in my life," he confessed, as a naval chaplain performed the wedding ceremony at Great Lakes Naval Hospital. Four days later, with his new bride looking proudly on, he received the Medal of Honor from President Truman in a ceremony at the White House. The citation made note of his tenacious vigil and skillful direction of "a smashing bombardment against the almost impregnable Japanese positions despite numerous obstacles and heavy Marine casualties."

Years later, now an old man, Dunlap expressed mixed feelings about the wisdom of his actions on Iwo Jima. "What I did was really great—but stupid in a way, too," he observed. "I am proud of it," he said of the Medal of Honor. "But I am prouder yet of the men who were with me. . . . My battalion, 1/26th Marines, was awarded the Presidential Unit Citation for our part in taking Iwo Jima. Sadly, our casualty rate was terrible. They got most of us," he observed, his voice cracking. "I'll never forget those boys. I can still see their faces."

Dunlap retired from the Marine Corps in 1946. "I just didn't heal and I had trouble walking," he remarked. Following a brief stint with the Veterans Administration in Chicago, he returned to Monmouth and took up farming. He and Mary also began a family, eventually becoming parents to one daughter and a son. In 1947 a representative from Paramount Pictures came along and offered him $20,000 for his story—a considerable amount of money at the time. Dunlap declined. The moviemakers could never show Iwo Jima's true brutality, he explained; he simply could not bring himself to be a part of some idealized Hollywood portrayal of those terrible days. "I never heard him even mention being in the service," remarked an acquaintance upon learning of Dunlap's record.

Dunlap stuck to farming for the next fifteen years, until his war injuries began taking such a physical toll that he realized he could not continue. He then took a job with Warren High School near Monmouth, where he taught mathematics and coached football, basketball, and track for the next nineteen years, retiring in 1982. A fellow teacher observed that he was more than an aging war hero; the former Marine with the ready grin was an inspiration in everyday life. "[He] taught me how to be kind, tolerant . . . to laugh at myself. . . . Bobby spread joy [and] awoke a positive spirit deep within me," wrote the teacher.

Dunlap liked to refer to himself self-deprecatingly as "a simple ordinary kind of fellow . . . 100 centimeters around the waist, 100 around the chest and 100 around the golf course," but he was far from ordinary. He coached the Warren Football team to a state championship. He also helped coach a YMCA swim team and Little League. He was a member of the Coldbrook Christian Church, where he served as a deacon and was involved with Bible school. He was a member of the Monmouth Rotary Club and was named a Paul Harris Fellow. In 1986 Dunlap was inducted into the M-Club Hall of Fame at Monmouth College. By an odd twist, his cousin, Jim Stockdale, who had so admired him as a boy, went on to become a Navy pilot and was awarded the Medal of Honor for his heroism as a POW during the Vietnam War—the only time in history cousins have shared that honor. Of his years following the war, Dunlap once remarked, "I thank God, not only for saving my life, but in my case for doing so much more."

By late 1999, Dunlap was in poor health. He had suffered two strokes, and was unable to walk and had difficulty talking. Due to his health, he was unable to accept an invitation to the annual Marine Corps Birthday Ball in Washington. Learning of Dunlap's condition, Marines of the Inspector-Instruction staff in Peoria brought the birthday party to him, conducting a color guard ceremony at his house and sharing birthday cake with the ailing hero and his wife, Mary Louise. The strokes left Dunlap unable to speak, "but the sparkle in his eyes and the smile on his face said it all," observed 1st Sgt. Sergio J. Estrada.

Bobby Dunlap passed away on March 24, 2000, from heart failure brought on by pneumonia, fifty-five years after his exploits on Iwo Jima. He was seventy-nine. The country church where services were held in rural Coldbrook was scarcely big enough to accommodate all those who turned out to pay tribute. A public-address system and chairs had to be set up in the basement for the large crowd. A friend and fellow Marine drove all night to be sure Dunlap had a new Marine uniform to be buried in. Others secured all new ribbons and decorations. A Marine Corps unit from Peoria provided full military honors for Dunlap at the church and at Warren County Memorial Park Cemetery, where he was laid to rest. His grave is marked by a simple bronze plaque with a rendition of the Medal of Honor above his name, and dates of birth and death along with the notation "PURPLE HEART" below, in recognition of the agonizing wound that plagued him for the remainder of his life.

From his youth, Bobby Dunlap was known for his "big heart" and giving, caring nature, said friends. One of his boyhood friends, Gene Josefson, later remarked that Dunlap was the perfect example of the citizen soldier. "He came back and went back to living the way he did before," observed Josefson. "He never forgot he had friends back in the old days that are still friends."

Years after Iwo Jima, the Medal of Honor recipient, former Paramarine, and standout athlete typically preferred to turn the spotlight on his Marines. "My men were the greatest," he remarked. "I had good officers. I had the best fighting men you ever saw—I pulled my poncho over my head a number of times and cried like a baby. I was scared; it upset me to lose anybody."

"He was an American veteran," said his wife, Mary Louise, after Dunlap's death in 2000. "He thought the American people were worth fighting for."

While two of the 5th Marine Division's three regiments began to press the attack to the north, the 28th Marines, commanded by Col.

Harry "The Horse" Liversedge, faced south toward Mount Suribachi, now cut off from the rest of the island by the success of the American landing. Japanese Gen. Tadamichi Kuribayashi had anticipated this development and organized Suribachi—codenamed "Hotrocks" by the Marines—as an independent defense sector. Looming 550 feet over the plain and defended by 2,000 troops under the command of fifty-six-year-old Col. Kanehiko Atsuchi, the height was valuable real estate, in that it dominated Iwo's eight square miles of volcanic ash rubble. General Kuribayashi hoped Suribachi could hold out for at least ten days, pounding away at the landing area with its own guns and serving as eyes for his artillery to the north. The volcanic cone was riddled with caves, tunnels, and underground galleries, the sides infested with reinforced pillboxes, mortar, and sniper pits overlooking the approaches. Just getting to the height would be problematic; the base was protected by a belt of more than seventy concrete blockhouses, pillboxes, and a maze of trenches tucked amongst the scrub and stubble.

The 2nd Battalion had taken a crack at Suribachi on D-day, but was forced to relinquish its minor gains at day's end. On D+1 Colonel Liversedge—who, by an odd coincidence, came from Volcano, California—added his 3rd Battalion to the effort against the Japanese cordon. Even with help from tanks, the two battalions gained less than 200 yards by sunset, losing twenty-nine men killed and 124 wounded, roughly one Marine for every yard of ground. "I never seen so many caves and bunkers," recalled Corporal Chuck Lindberg, a flamethrower operator. "Every bunker was attached to another one, and they'd go by one connector on down fifteen feet, and then someone would come up behind and shoot you in the back." In the morning they would try again.

It was in this rat's nest of pillboxes and entrenchments on the third day of the battle that PFC Donald J. Ruhl earned the only Medal of Honor awarded to a Marine from the state of Montana during World War II.

PFC DONALD JACK RUHL

28th Marines, 5th Marine Division
February 19–21, 1945

Donald Ruhl USMC

Before Iwo Jima, most of the forty-six men of the 3rd Platoon, Company E, 2nd Battalion, 28th Marines would have described PFC Don Ruhl as a monumental pain in the ass. Maybe it was Ruhl's cowboy background herding cattle near his home in Joliet, Montana, before the war, but the twenty-one-year-old PFC had an independent streak that tended to rub up against the military status quo, and earned him a reputation as a bit of a malcontent.

Born July 2, 1923, at Columbus, Montana, Donald J. Ruhl—the "J" stood for "Jack"—was the second of John and Edith Ruhl's four children. John Ruhl had served in a machine-gun battalion with the American Expeditionary Forces in France during World War I, before returning to farm life and working as a blacksmith in the sparsely populated ranch country around Columbus. Educated in Columbus grammar schools, Don went on to attend Joliet High School, where he was a standout athlete and entertained hopes of one day playing major league baseball. That may have been an unlikely dream, but he showed enough promise as a youth to win a spot on the competitive Laurel Oil Refinery team.

During high school, the brown-haired, blue-eyed Ruhl worked as a general farmhand on a 400-acre spread owned by Lowell Gibson of Joliet. His pay was $15 a week and room and board. Shortly before graduating from high school in 1942, he found work as a laboratory assistant for the Independent Refining Company of Laurel at a respectable $32 a week. For fun and relaxation, he took to the outdoors and hunted small game with his 12-gauge shotgun.

Ruhl's younger brother Clyde remembered him as a hard worker and a good hand with horses. Don also had a tendency to be a bit of an "operator." Once, when a large gasoline tank sprang a leak, Don sopped up the fuel, poured it into jugs, and sold them for twenty-five cents each. "It had water in it, so when they pulled their old Model T's away and drove off, you could hear them backfire," chuckled Clyde. "He was always into something."

On September 12, 1942, Ruhl enlisted in the Marine Corps Reserve in Butte. He trained at San Diego, qualifying as a sharpshooter and combat swimmer. Always athletic, the five-foot eleven-inch, 147-pound Montanan boxed and played baseball and basketball. In keeping with his devil-may-care attitude, he also volunteered for parachute training. After earning his wings, he was promoted to private first class and assigned to the 3rd Parachute Battalion at Camp Elliot. In March 1943 he shipped out for New Caledonia as a member of a 60mm mortar crew, and later that year participated in the Bougainville campaign, which apparently did little to satisfy his thirst for action.

Cpl. John B. Lyttle, who was a tentmate with Ruhl on Vella Lavella where the parachutists were running security for the fighter strip and PT-boat base, remembered an incident that, in retrospect, seemed strangely prescient. "I remember D. J. reading the *Leatherneck Magazine* that told about a Marine that had saved his buddies by rolling on two grenades and surviving," he recalled. "Ruhl made the remark that 'I bet that made his folks at home feel good and proud of him.' I tried to talk him out of this type of foolishness but I guess I didn't make my point. Ruhl was from Greybull, Wyoming on the Big Horn River and spent his summer tending the family sheep in the high country, so he was a very private guy."

In September 1944, following the breakup of the parachute battalions, Ruhl was assigned as a rifleman to Company E, 28th Marines, 5th

Marine Division. Cpl. Richard "Dick" Wheeler, who served with Ruhl in the 3rd Platoon, remembered the twenty-one-year-old westerner as the one "confirmed rebel" in an otherwise well-disciplined platoon. The former parachutist tended to balk at orders he considered unreasonable, and sometimes made trouble for himself by trying to ignore them. As a mark of personal independence, he preferred a baseball-type fatigue cap to his helmet, wearing the latter only at the insistence of his squad leader, and maintained that brushing one's teeth only helped to wear them down. He didn't seem to care if others approved of him or not. "He was a character," remarked PFC Grady Dyce. "Don would just wear everyone out."

Ruhl's new platoon was a mixed bag of veterans and newcomers. Some of the men had come from hospitals, having recovered from wounds suffered in previous campaigns; some came from guard units; there was a handful of former Marine Raiders and paratroopers, along with men fresh from boot camp. The oldest man in the outfit was Cpl. Everett M. Lavelle of Bellingham, Washington, a career Marine in his thirties. The youngest was eighteen-year-old PFC James A. ("Chick") Robeson, coincidentally also a native of Washington State.

The platoon was commanded by a twenty-three-year-old Texan, 1st Lt. John K. Wells. A serious man with a deep interest in the art of warfare, he got along with the men and was well thought of. He did show an occasional flair for the theatrical, once declaring, "Give me fifty men who aren't afraid to die and I can take *any* position."—a pronouncement that caused some consternation among the forty-six Marines of the 3rd Platoon, who presumed they were likely to be among the fifty in question.

Don Ruhl shared his platoon commander's craving for action. He was impatient to get into combat and chafed at the monotonous routine of training. "His attitude earned him the platoon's criticism from time to time, but he seemed to feel that he shouldn't be judged until he'd been tested on the battlefield," remembered Wheeler.

The platoon's opportunity arrived on February 19, 1945, when E Company, designated as battalion reserve, landed on Iwo in the ninth wave. Clambering up the terraces, the company moved inland and dug in, all too aware of the hostile eyes on Suribachi looming to their left. "We must have presented clear targets to the Japanese on the volcano, but only a few bullets snapped through our ranks and we were able to keep going," remembered Wheeler.

From their vantage point, they could see small groups of Marines from the 1st Battalion moving against one pillbox after another in the push across Iwo's 700-yard-wide neck. The pillboxes had an uncanny tendency to come back to life after the initial assault passed by, so the Marines following along in their wake began making sure "dead men" were really dead. "We watched as each new group would shoot the same Japanese so many times that I thought that only their clothes held them together," recalled Wells. "Soon a mixture of dead, wounded and live Japanese and Marines lay scattered across the island."

The call for Wells's platoon came later in the afternoon. He was ordered to follow up behind the 1st Battalion, which had been badly shot up and disorganized in the course of pushing across the island neck. The platoon moved out under persistent small-arms and artillery fire, in what Wells described as "a column of bunches" with him in the lead, proceeding through a brushy area laced with anti-tank ditches that seemed to be crowded with 1st Battalion wounded. Wells was having trouble keeping in touch with his noncoms, when Ruhl suddenly materialized and volunteered to act as runner. "Let me work with you, Lieutenant," said the former platoon malcontent. Ordinarily, Wells had little need for a runner, but now Ruhl was the answer to an unspoken prayer, and the lieutenant quickly agreed. With Ruhl tagging along to be available if needed, Wells got the platoon to the western shoreline as operations began to wind down for the day. He set up his men with their backs to the ocean, facing the way they had come. Out beyond the center of his line loomed a huge concrete blockhouse they had bypassed on the way in. Wells had been uneasy about the blockhouse from the moment he first saw it, but had been told to leave it be. Now the hulking fortification came to life as the Japanese hiding inside opened a set of steel doors and began firing a field piece toward the landing beaches.

Accompanied by Ruhl, Wells ventured out into the scrub to see what was going on. Wells carried a Thompson submachine gun, while Ruhl toted his M1 rifle with fixed bayonet. The lieutenant noticed that Ruhl had already discarded his much-despised helmet in favor of a fatigue cap. "Ruhl wanted action," recalled Wells. "He soon got it."

They made their way up to the blockhouse to find it already under attack by a platoon from the 1st Battalion. Dogged by a machine gun firing from the top of the fortification, the attackers swung around and managed to quiet the weapon. A Marine dashed forward with a shaped charge. Clambering to the top of the mound, he scraped off a section of sand, placed the charge, and ran for cover. The charge drove a hole down through the concrete interior. Before anyone could take advantage, the machine gun up top started firing again, knocking down a number of Marines. The attackers patiently flanked the gun and knocked it out again. Wells saw another Marine scramble to the top and drop a thermite grenade into the hole blown earlier.

"Only seconds after the thermite grenade dropped in, things started happening," recalled Wells. "Ruhl and I were standing by the big concrete door when suddenly the door flew open and a billow of dense white smoke came out. At the bottom of the smoke I saw little Japanese feet. The Japanese were bent over. Each man was holding onto a piece of equipment of the man in front of him. They were that close together. At least two or three were carrying hand grenades but no rifles or other weapons."

Wells ripped off an entire 30-round magazine from his Thompson and knocked down six or eight Japanese. Hit by the heavy .45-caliber slugs, "They fell like sacks of potatoes thrown from a truck," said Wells. In the excitement, he wasn't sure Ruhl got off a single round; "He may have," remarked Wells. One of the Japanese he had knocked down was trying to get to his feet. Ruhl rushed forward and drove his bayonet into the man. Wells looked up to see a grenade arch out of the gathering darkness toward Ruhl. "Look out! Grenade!" he shouted. Ruhl hit the deck and the grenade exploded harmlessly. Wells went charging into the underbrush in search of the grenade thrower, but came up empty.

The day's events and shoot-out at the bunker persuaded 3rd Platoon that maybe Ruhl was not all empty bravado. "Criticized in training for his discontent and rebelliousness, he had let us know he intended to 'show us' when he got into combat," observed Wheeler. "And he'd made a good start."

Ruhl continued his "start" the next morning as the platoon made its way back through the scrub to get into position for the push on Suribachi. Enemy artillery shells rained down. The Japanese antitank ditches they had passed through the day before were filled to overflowing with a mix of dead, dying, wounded, and live Marines. "Enemy artillery, pounding the earth around us, herded us there like cattle," recalled Wells. "To make room in the ditches they . . . stacked the dead and covered them with ponchos. If the dead or near-dead were out of the ditch and in the open, they laid there."

Burial teams identify the dead before they are interred in the division cemeteries. USMC

As they rounded a bend in the ditch, they came upon a Marine sitting in plain view of the enemy. "Congealed blood covered the upper part of his body, and I could hardly see his eyes peering through the blood," recalled Wells. "His eyes had the look of a man in shock. An enemy machine gun was still kicking dirt over him and us."

Ruhl asked 1st Sgt. John Daskalakis for permission to go out after the man. Daskalakis thought it was too dangerous; Ruhl persisted until Daskalakis gave in. "He jumped out of the tank trap we were in," recalled Daskalakis, "ran through a tremendous volume of mortar and machine-gun fire, and made it to the wounded man's side. Then he half dragged and half carried him back."

Apparently developing a proprietary interest in the wounded man, Ruhl proposed to take him the short distance to the beach where he would have a chance to be evacuated. Worried about losing more men on such mercy missions, Wells turned him down in no uncertain terms, but when he turned around again, Ruhl, the casualty, and two other Marines were gone. Ruhl returned, but, as Wells had feared, the other two did not. "I did nothing to Ruhl, who was already condemning himself," remarked Wells.

The platoon spent the rest of the day taking its position in the line facing Suribachi. As the others dug in under the malevolent height, Ruhl ventured out to explore an abandoned antiaircraft gun emplacement just beyond the platoon perimeter. Finding a tunnel, he crawled inside, lighting his way with matches. Fortunately there were no live Japanese lying in wait, but he did find a considerable amount of enemy equipment, including some white woolen Japanese navy blankets, which he lugged back for his appreciative platoon to wrap up in as temperatures began to drop.

Wells was concerned about the antiaircraft emplacement, viewing it as a potential assembly point for any Japanese effort to overrun his line after dark. His dilemma was solved when Ruhl volunteered to go out and man the abandoned position overnight. "He knew it needed to be done," recalled Wells. "His volunteering was nearly suicidal. He could not stop the attack, and he would possibly be killed. He could sound the alarm that the attack was underway. With this time gap we could move the reserve to help him or wherever the enemy attack looked to be strongest."

Ruhl seemed surprisingly nonchalant about the danger. "It was like playing cowboys and Indians for him," observed PFC Grady Dyce. Dick Wheeler had a slightly different take on Ruhl's actions. "Ruhl seemed intent on making us eat the critical words we had spoken about his independence and hardheadedness in training," noted Wheeler.

Ruhl's luck held out and the Japanese never came. As the sky began to lighten with dawn, the platoon gathered itself for a frontal assault on the Japanese defense belt around Suribachi. Wells, who was the furthest thing from being a coward, was not optimistic. The ground in front of his platoon was almost flat. Naval gunfire had stripped the shrubbery away from the base of Mount Suribachi, revealing rings of interlocking concrete pillboxes, blockhouses, and connecting trenches. "They were strung like beads around an old lady's wrinkled neck," wrote Wells years later. Over the phone he received orders to attack a large fortification directly ahead of him. A preattack bombardment slammed in, probably with negligible effect on the well-entrenched Japanese, thought Wells. When it ceased, he jumped up, waved the platoon forward with his tommy gun, and trotted toward Mount Suribachi. He had never felt so alone in his life.

In fact, the hard-charging lieutenant was not alone. Trotting alongside were sergeants Ernest Thomas and Henry O. Hansen, and his self-anointed runner Don Ruhl, with the rest of the platoon close behind. Despite coming under machine-gun fire, they made the first fifty yards relatively unscathed. "The enemy pillboxes and blockhouses had slits to fire through, but they remained closed," recalled Wells. "We ran on past the slits." The four of them were not more than ten or fifteen feet from a large blockhouse on their right, and about the same distance from a good-sized pillbox with a damaged roof a little to their left. Ruhl and Hansen trotted ahead toward a trench joining the two fortifications.

A former Marine paratrooper from Somerville, Massachusetts, Hansen had been in the Corps for seven years, having joined up before the war at the age of eighteen. A slender, clean-cut youngster, known to his buddies as "Harry" or "Hank," Hansen "had a way of looking natty even in fatigue clothes," remarked a fellow Marine.

Twenty-three-year-old Sgt. Kenneth D. Midkiff of Pax, West Virginia, recalled what happened next. "Ruhl moved up behind a Jap bunker and Hansen followed him," said Midkiff. "They called for more grenades and we threw them the grenades. Ruhl got up on the bunker and Hansen went up after him." But when the two reached the top of the bunker and looked over the back, they recoiled in shock. A trench system on the other side was swarming with Japanese. "They must have almost bumped heads with the Japanese, because they jerked back fast," recalled Wells, who had paused to check on the rest of his platoon.

Falling prone in the sand, Ruhl and Hansen opened fire on the crowded trench. Looking toward them, Wells saw an object arch through the air and land between the two men. Midkiff heard Ruhl shout, "Hansen! Grenade!" Before Hansen could react, Ruhl shoved him aside and threw himself on top of the charge.

"We heard the muffled explosion," recalled Wells. "From the power and shock of the explosion I saw Ruhl's body rise into the air, then flop back."

Hansen recoiled down the slope of the pillbox. Spattered with blood and bits of flesh, he reached up and grabbed Ruhl's foot, intending to drag him back down. "One of Ruhl's shoulders fell back," remembered Wells. "It looked disconnected from his body and I could see a great cavity that was once his chest."

"Leave him alone," he yelled to Hansen. "He's dead."

With the Japanese only yards away, Wells beckoned a couple of BAR men forward. The ensuing melee around the trenches and blockhouse involved grenades, small arms, and flamethrowers. The Japanese were cleared out, but it cost the Marines dearly. The platoon suffered seventeen casualties—Wells himself was badly wounded in the legs—

but miraculously only four dead. Among the latter was PFC Donald J. Ruhl, the platoon troublemaker and malcontent, who gave his life to save a fellow Marine.

On January 12, 1947, Don Ruhl's parents accepted his posthumous Medal of Honor at their home in Greybull, Wyoming, where they had moved after Don went into the service. Their son's remains were returned to the United States two years after the war. Services were held in the Greybull Presbyterian Church on April 12, 1948. "The Rev. W. R. Marvin officiated at the service and was assisted by Leonard C. Purkey, Post No. 3305, Veterans of Foreign Wars," reported the *Billings Gazette*. "Ellis Caldwell and William Jones sang two hymns, 'Be Thou Near' and 'Never Alone,' and the former sang 'The Lord's Prayer.' Mrs. A. J. Pederson was accompanist." Burial was in Greybull's Hillside Cemetery. A news item noted that the hero was survived by his parents; two brothers, Sgt. Robert J. Ruhl of Bolling Field, Washington, D.C., and Clyde Ruhl of Laramie; and a sister, Frances Ruhl of Greybull.

In later years, Don Ruhl's Medal of Honor became the focus of an unusual controversy. Sometime after the death of her husband in 1955, Don's mother donated the medal to the Marine Corps Reserve Center in Billings for display, expressing the hope that it might serve as an inspiration to others. When the building was being renovated during the late 1970s, the medal disappeared, along with the original citation signed by President Truman. Its whereabouts remained a mystery until 1995, when a collector/historian spotted the medal in the hands of a private collector. The collector claimed he had obtained the medal from the Department of the Navy in 1982, after learning it had been sent from Billings to Washington, D.C., three years earlier. Armed with a letter purportedly signed by Don's second brother, Robert, who had since died, the collector gained possession of the medal, ostensibly for display in a museum. The collector resisted repeated suggestions that the medal be returned to the Reserve Center in Billings. However, after the FBI expressed an interest in the matter, he finally acquiesced. In June 2001, the medal and the original citation signed by President

Truman belatedly showed up unannounced in a Federal Express package at the Reserve Center in Billings.

As it turned out, Don Ruhl's sacrifice on Iwo Jima bought Hank Hansen only a few more days of life. He was among the Marines who raised the first flag on Mount Suribachi on February 23—the one that preceded the flag raising immortalized by Joe Rosenthal's famous photo—but he did not live to see any acclaim. A week later, as his unit fought its way north, Hansen was moving toward a ridge when someone yelled to him to be careful, the position was under heavy small-arms fire. "You worry too much!" Hansen shouted back. An instant later, as he moved around the side of a large boulder, he was killed by a burst of machine-gun fire. He was twenty-five years old.

On February 21, the 4th and 5th Marine divisions attacked north toward the upper reaches of Motoyama Airfield No. 1. The assault jumped off at 0810.

Pvt. Allen R. Matthews recalled that the attack got away almost lazily, the men getting up out of their holes, toying with their helmets, or checking the actions of their rifles. "It was a fascinating spectacle to me, for it shattered every conception I had of an attack's being a dashing, furious charge. The line formed with almost slow-motion clarity and the troops, for the first time facing toward the ridge, walked slowly forward, some crouching as they moved, others standing upright," he observed. Someone shouted, "Don't bunch up! Keep contact! The guide is right!"

As the Marines emerged into the open, Japanese artillery fire began to fall on them. Then enemy machine guns opened up from concealed pillboxes and caves to the front. "Groups of men from my platoon lay in shallow holes or flat against the ground in front of me," recalled Matthews. "Along the right was a terrace wall not more than two feet high, and just below it lay a dead Marine. . . . [H]is skin had a purplish tinge, and swarms of the great blue-green flies clung hungrily about his throat, forehead, and mouth."

As the advance stalled, a soft-spoken Alabaman—a man about as far from the stereotypical tough-talking Marine as one could imagine—got up out of the dirt and went after the Japanese in a one-man rampage.

SGT. ROSS F. GRAY

25th Marines, 4th Marine Division
February 21, 1945

Ross Gray USMC

Ross Franklin Gray wasn't a big man physically. When he joined the Marine Corps in 1942, his record indicates he stood five feet ten inches tall and tipped the scales at only 120 pounds. Shy, soft-spoken, and deeply religious—back home in West Blocton, Alabama, he had been a lay preacher and deacon in the Methodist Church—he didn't drink, smoke, or swear. "He was kind of quiet, the best I remember about him," recalled his cousin Mary Lippett. "He was just kind of a quiet person."

The Grays were a hardworking, God-fearing family. Patriarch Benjamin Franklin Gray had left his home in Mississippi at the age of nine, walking alone to Alabama to live with an aunt. A carpenter by trade, he is remembered by family members for his ingenuity, having once patented a device for removing boll weevils from cotton. Benjamin married West Blocton native Carrie Wood in 1907 at the town's Ada Chapel. Their first child, daughter Willowdean, was born in 1909. She was followed by eight siblings, including Ross Franklin (number six), who arrived on August 1, 1920. "They weren't boisterous people," recalled family friend Bill Murphy, who grew up eight or nine miles from the Gray homestead. "They were hardworking, good people."

Located in "dry" Bibb County, the Blocton area had once been a center of coal production, but by the 1930s and the Great Depression, the industry had declined and the huge coke furnaces were being used as shelters by hobos and other transients. Ross, known to his family simply as "R. F.," attended local elementary schools, then went on to Centerville High School, where he played football and basketball. After-school hours were spent working part-time for his father as a carpenter, and hunting and fishing. His high school education concluded in 1939 after his junior year, when he left to go to work for his father full-time.

The Grays were Southern Methodists. They were "fairly much" religious, remembered Mary Lippett, "but Ross was the most. He got to going to the Wesleyan Methodists and he liked them. . . . He was a preacher before he went into the service. Real religious. He'd preach at different churches."

Though it seems out of character considering his religious bent, the twenty-one-year-old Alabaman enlisted in the Marine Corps Reserve on July 22, 1942, in Birmingham. He took his recruit train-ing at Parris Island, then went to New River, North Carolina, and was subsequently assigned to the 23rd Marines, 4th Marine Division. Promoted to private first class in April 1943, he was transferred to Company A, 1st Battalion, 25th Marines a month later. In a letter home to "Mother and Daddy" on October 1, 1943, from Camp Pendleton, Gray provided a simple code he would use in his letters to let them know where he was headed once his outfit shipped out. Training had intensified and the company was spending a lot of time in the field, he wrote. "We have been given combat jackets, they are real nice. We do not have any lights here except for a few candles and a lantern. I made a lamp out of a bottle and a rope for a wick the other night and now almost every tent has one. We are getting in some new men and we will be at full strength before long. . . . I am busy all day and at night I study the Bible. I have just read the book of John and Joshua and am almost through with Judges. There are only three of us in the tent, and I have a lantern so I have enough light."

As his letter reveals, military service did not diminish Gray's deep commitment to his religion. At night, before turning in, he would read his Bible for half an hour, recalled veterans of his outfit. Sundays, he would drop by the tents of other men who attended church and invite them to go along. He wasn't pushy about it; he didn't force his deeply held beliefs on anyone. Neither did anyone seem to feel his convictions should be a target of ridicule. "He probably was the best liked man in his outfit," wrote USMC combat correspondent Sgt. Bill Hengen. The other Marines called him "Preacher."

The 4th Marine Division went overseas in January 1944 and took part in the seizure of Roi-Namur. The following March, Gray was promoted to corporal. When the division landed on Saipan on June 15, 1944, he was serving as company carpenter. His normal duties did not require him to be in the front lines, apparently out of deference to his religious training and beliefs, though he hadn't claimed to be a conscientious objector when he enlisted. The Marines had taken heavy casualties during the landing, but by July 6, three weeks into the battle, the shattered Japanese units were fleeing toward the northern end of the island. While organized resistance was crumbling, it was still treacherous going. "Here Japanese soldiers could remain concealed in the caves until Marines attempted to approach; then, suddenly they would open with devastating bursts," recalled Maj. Carl W. Hoffman.

Among the Marines advancing warily through the warren of cliffs and caves was one of Gray's best friends in the company, a twenty-one-year-old Polish-American kid, Sgt. Stanley A. Maheski. The fact that Maheski had been raised Catholic and Gray was a dyed-in-the-wool Methodist didn't affect their friendship one iota. The son of a coal miner from Indiana, Pennsylvania, Maheski had joined the Marines in late 1942 and was now a rifle squad leader with A Company. On July 6, Maheski's squad was ambushed by some Japanese diehards with a machine gun. Maheski shouted for the other men to pull back, but stayed behind to cover their withdrawal, firing on the enemy with his rifle. The squad got out, but Maheski was killed.

Maheski's death had a dramatic effect on Ross Gray, who heretofore seems to have been content to serve in a supporting role to the front-line Marines. It changed him. Maybe he got mad. Maybe the experience steeled his resolve. Maybe he decided he should contribute more directly to the fighting. Maybe he came to realize more deeply "what it was all about, that he was fighting for his country and for his family and people," remarked Mary Lippett years later.

Whatever the case, he put down his carpenter's tools and headed for the front lines. On Tinian he volunteered to handle a BAR and fought with his platoon throughout the campaign. In August he was promoted to sergeant. He then attended the 4th Marine Division Mine and Booby Trap School, which offered instruction in how to lay minefields, reconnaissance of enemy minefields, and disarming and removing mines and booby-traps. That training would prove invaluable during his company's next campaign: Iwo Jima.

On February 19, the 1st Battalion, 25th Marines landed in the first wave at Blue Beach 1. The battalion, with A Company on the left, managed to scratch its way forward 300 yards in the first half hour, but at high cost. Among those killed was Gray's platoon commander. The situation was chaotic, recalled Cpl. Robert T. Webster Jr., who, like Gray, came ashore with Able Company. A veteran machine gunner who had been wounded on the first day at Saipan the previous June, Webster led his squad through artillery and mortar fire to the shelter of a large shell hole, losing one man wounded along the way. They set up their machine gun facing Airfield No. 1, the flat expanse of the runway clearly visible just ahead.

Things began to go bad for the squad almost immediately. Webster's number-one gunner looked out over the machine gun and was promptly shot through the forehead. As Webster tried to drag the dead man back into the hole, he was hit in the back of the helmet by a bullet that traveled around the inside of the steel pot and exited the side without drawing blood, though it "did just about jerk my head off," he recalled. "I was lying at the top edge of the shell hole looking over the edge when I saw a Jap run toward the airstrip. I took aim with my rifle and fired. Just as I fired a shell landed right in the middle of our shell hole."

Webster felt as if he had been slammed into the ground with a two-by-four. When he collected his senses, he became aware of screaming from the bottom of the hole. The screams came from two mortally wounded Marines, rolling around in agony. One was missing a leg. "And there was another guy there and he had his stomach blown out," recalled Webster. "They were rolling around in the bottom of the hole and there were several around the side that had been hit, but they were just laying there dead." Two other Marines lay dead within arm's length, one on either side of him.

Only Webster and one other man from his squad had survived, and Webster had been seriously wounded all along his right side. The other Marine called from the other side of the hole, "Can you move?" Webster said he could. The other Marine yelled, "Let's get the hell out of here." He helped Webster back to the beach where the veteran corporal was put on a landing craft and taken off the island. He would spend the next few months in naval hospitals; his war was over.

Ross Gray was more fortunate. He survived the carnage of the landing, but the next day was little better as the battalion slugged inland toward the northern end of Motoyama Airfield No. 1, directly into General Kuribayashi's main defense line. The morning of D+2, Gray's A Company platoon—or what was left of it after two days of bitter fighting—attacked northeast into broken terrain past the end of the airfield's main runway. Wrote Lt. Col. Whitman S. Bartley, "The entire area was a weird looking mass of cliffs, ravines, gorges, crevices and ledges. Jumbled rock, worn stubble of small trees, jagged ridges and chasms all sprawled about completely within this macabre setting. The Japanese were deeply entrenched in hundreds of excellently constructed positions. From blockhouses, bunkers, pillboxes, caves and camouflaged tanks, enemy guns jutted defiantly. Every possible approach to the north was contested by weapons with well-integrated fields of fire."

Japanese resistance was ferocious. Gray's battalion found enemy infantrymen dug into a spider's web of emplacements connected by covered communication trenches and fronted by minefields. Speaking of the Japanese positions in general, a 4th Marine Division lieutenant wrote, "There was no cover from enemy fire. Japs deep in reinforced concrete pillboxes laid down interlocking bands of fire that cut whole companies to ribbons. Camouflage hid all the enemy installations. The high ground on every side was honeycombed with layer after layer of Jap emplacements, blockhouses, dugouts and observation posts. Their observation was perfect; whenever the Marines made a move, the Japs watched every step, and when the moment came, their mortars, rockets, machine guns and artillery—long ago zeroed in—would smother the area in a murderous blanket of fire."

By 0930 the 1st Battalion had already lost seventy-five men killed or wounded, and was going nowhere. Death was no respecter of rank. The battalion commander, forty-one-year-old Lt. Col. Hollis U. Mustain of Escondido, California, was killed by a mortar or artillery round when he came forward in an effort to get the assault moving. As word passed down the line that "the Old Man got it," the battalion stubbornly resumed its attempt to break through the fortified line.

Casualties had thrust Gray into the role of acting platoon sergeant. Now, as the platoon edged cautiously forward, a sudden barrage of hand grenades rained down on them. One Marine was killed; another was wounded. Gray pulled the platoon back, moving from one knot of men to another under enemy small-arms fire, to be sure everyone got the word. Satisfied that everyone was at least momentarily out of grenade range, if not out of danger, he turned his attention back toward the enemy. Where the grenade-throwers were hidden in the jumbled rocks was anybody's guess, but as Gray studied the ground, he did discern the low silhouette of a camouflaged pillbox situated in a shallow ravine about thirty yards to his front.

That, at least, gave him an identifiable objective. Gray looked and pondered, and then he acted. Falling back on his specialized training, he went after the minefield first. Creeping forward under enemy fire, he carefully probed for mines, somehow managing to clear a path all the way to one of the enemy communications trenches without getting shot. This bit of daring brought him within throwing distance of the pillbox. Making his way back through the minefield to his waiting platoon, he told them he was going to take out the pillbox. He needed three volunteers to provide covering fire.

A demolitions team takes care of an enemy pillbox. USMC

Gray and his three volunteers commandeered twelve satchel charges—each consisting of up to twenty pounds of explosives packed into a canvas bag and equipped with a fuse—from the battalion ammo dump, and lugged them back to the waiting platoon. "Pray for me," said Gray. Putting his rifle aside, he picked up one of the satchel charges and headed back out toward the Japanese communications trench and the entrance to the pillbox. His three volunteers took up position and gave him what covering fire they could as Gray picked his way forward. Finally within range of the pillbox, he armed the satchel charge and hurled it at the Japanese position. There was a deafening blast as the charge exploded, sealing the entrance.

It wasn't enough. As Gray crawled back toward his men, the enemy machine gun opened up again. Gray grabbed another satchel charge. Again he made his way out through the lane he had cleared in the minefield. He paused to arm the charge, then heaved it at the firing slot in the pillbox. This time the blast demolished the gun and the pillbox went silent. Once more, Gray returned through the minefield, somehow still unscathed.

Despite his success, the destruction of the pillbox seemed to have only a marginal effect on the rain of enemy fire directed at the platoon. The Marines spotted another pillbox out to their front. Again Gray ventured out into the unknown, leaving his personal weapon behind and creeping forward with a heavy satchel charge tucked alongside his body. He did not go unnoticed. Now keenly alert to the threat, the Japanese showered him with hand grenades. Most were off the mark, but one well-thrown grenade exploded practically within arm's length of him. The blast blew off Gray's helmet, but he miraculously escaped injury. His platoon watched anxiously as "the Preacher" doggedly closed in on the second enemy pillbox. Finally near enough, he heaved the satchel charge; there was a thumping blast and the position went silent.

Gray reappeared from the killing field, but only to obtain more satchel charges. He had spotted more enemy positions and was determined to knock them out. He returned a fourth time, then a fifth and a sixth, blasting emplacement after emplacement. When it was over, the Japanese defensive line in front of his platoon had been broken. Twenty-five dead Japanese, a machine gun, and a small field piece were found in the first two positions Gray demolished. How many of the enemy perished in the others was never determined. Gray himself walked away from his exploits, shaken by the grenade blast, but unwounded.

Over the next few days the Marines continued their efforts to battle their way north. As casualties mounted, combat efficiency declined. The Japanese defense showed little sign of weakening. "Most assault battalions that came ashore on D-day had been in the front lines for three days and nights of grueling, nerve shattering action," wrote an officer of the first three days of battle. "Troops of these units had little chance to rest or sleep, and their diet consisted solely of K rations and water, occasionally supplemented by unheated C rations." Periodic cold drizzling rains did little to improve conditions.

By February 27, Gray's battalion and four others were slugging it out with powerful, mutually supporting enemy positions east of the airfield. Gray's Able Company and Company C were ready to move out at 0800 on D+8, but problems with the adjacent unit forced a delay until 1500 when Able moved out, supported by tanks. The first 150 yards lay across an open area, which exposed the Marines to a rain of enemy fire. Two of the Shermans were knocked out by antitank guns and a third was crippled. Heavy machine-gun fire raked the Marine line, rendering the positions along the high ground untenable. At 1715 the battalion commander ordered Company A to fall back to the line held the previous night.

Ross Gray didn't make it. Severely wounded by an exploding Japanese shell, he was one of more than a dozen casualties in A Company. Despite terrible injuries that left him unable to speak, Gray paused while being carried out on a litter, reaching into a pocket for a small booklet with the names of the men in his unit. He indicated where each of the men was located by pointing to his name and position. Only then did he allow himself to be evacuated. The last his men saw of him was when he somehow managed to raise himself up on the stretcher and feebly wave good-bye.

Sgt. Ross Gray died of his wounds that same day and was buried in the 4th Marine Division Cemetery on Iwo Jima. Among his personal effects was found a Bible. Inside, Gray had underlined a verse from 2 Timothy:

> I have fought the good fight.
> I have finished my course.
> I have kept the faith.

Gray's sister, Lorene, received the government telegram back home in West Blocton. It fell to her to walk to her parents' home to tell them that "R. F." had been killed. Meanwhile, the paperwork recommending Gray for the Medal of Honor for his one-man assault on multiple enemy pillboxes on February 21 was wending its way through the military bureaucracy. The award was approved and the medal was presented to Benjamin Gray by Rear Adm. A. S. Merrill on April 16, 1946, in a ceremony held on the Centerville High School football field. Among those in attendance was Alabama Governor Chauncy Sparks. Sadly, Carrie Gray, who had seen four of her sons go off to war, did not live to see the honor Ross had earned. She died at the age of sixty-two, less than three months after Ross was killed on Iwo Jima. Benjamin outlived her by twenty-one years, dying at the venerable age of eighty-seven. Both are buried in West Blocton's Ada Chapel Cemetery.

Ross Gray's remains were returned to Alabama in the spring of 1948 and interred next to his mother near the chapel where he once preached. By then the war had been over for nearly three years, and the event merited only a small item in the Birmingham newspapers. Ross Gray wouldn't have cared. "He was just kind of a quiet person," observed his cousin Mary Lippett. "He was just a person that we all loved."

Not far from the scene of Ross Gray's one-man war on the morning of February 21, a taciturn former firefighter from Chicago, Capt. Joseph J. McCarthy, found his company—G Company, 2nd Battalion, 24th Marines—caught up in a similar warren of bunkers and pillboxes. McCarthy's men had been in reserve when the push got started that morning, but were ordered into the attack just before 1100 hours. In short order, McCarthy found his company being cut to pieces. Like Ross Gray, he decided to do something about it personally.

CAPT. JOSEPH J. MCCARTHY

24th Marines, 4th Marine Division
February 21, 1945

Joe McCarthy
USMC

Fifteen days after landing on Iwo Jima, Capt. Joe McCarthy lay on a stretcher, his six-foot four-inch, 240-pound frame shredded by a Japanese mortar blast. A chaplain was giving him last rites.

"Joe," said the chaplain, "you're going to die."

Shot full of morphine and bleeding heavily from numerous holes, the captain still managed to take issue with the suggestion that he might actually be on his way to the 4th Marine Division cemetery.

"I'm not going to die," retorted McCarthy.

It was typical Joe McCarthy. He'd die when he was damn good and ready, and not a moment before.

Joseph Jeremiah McCarthy was born "back of the yards" at 26th Street and Normal Avenue on Chicago's tough South Side, on August 10, 1912, the youngest of Lawrence and Katherine McCarthy's six children. Lawrence supported their impressive brood by working as a teamster, but by 1920 he had disappeared from the scene, and Katherine McCarthy had married labor foreman William Hart, who was about seven years her junior. Always a big kid, Joe attended Englewood High School, where he was an all-city first baseman on the baseball team, an all-state lineman in football, and an outstanding swimmer. After leaving school, he went to work as a laborer for the People's Gas Light and Coke Company. He worked his way up to serviceman, but he craved more excitement than the utility company could provide. As a boy, he had thrilled to the sight of fire horses charging out of the barn near his home, as firefighters rushed to emergency calls. That fascination had stuck with him through the years, and in 1938 he joined the Chicago Fire Department and was assigned to Hook and Ladder Company 11. His chosen profession certainly was anything but boring. "That was the busiest truck company in the world and it still is," he observed years later. "We would make 1,800 to 1,900 runs a year."

McCarthy was also active in the Marine Corps Reserve, having joined up in early 1933 after the regulars turned him down for a "physical defect"—a problem with his molars. By late 1940 when his reserve unit was called up as war loomed on the horizon, McCarthy was a twenty-eight-year-old first sergeant, and a problem with one's molars was no longer an issue of any great importance. By January 1941, Sergeant McCarthy had been named "Chief" of the fire department at the Marine base in San Diego. He also acquired a wife, marrying twenty-nine-year-old Mildred G. Young, who moved to Chicago from Ironwood, Michigan, to work at the Marshall Field department store.

After briefly returning to Hook and Ladder Company No. 11, McCarthy went back into the Marines the day after Pearl Harbor, regaining his first sergeant's stripes. The powers-that-be saw potential in the blunt-talking Chicago fireman, and he eventually ended up at Officers Candidate School in Quantico, Virginia. Upon graduation as a newly minted lieutenant, he was assigned to the 4th Marine Division. Superior officers sometimes winced at McCarthy's direct manner, but the husky, red-faced Irishman—known to his men variously as "Big Mac," "Black Mac," "Gus," or "Joe"—wasn't one to play politics or suffer any qualms about stating the truth as he saw it. "I don't like malarkey or bullshit," he declared, and he meant it. Promoted to captain, McCarthy was given command of G Company, 2nd Battalion, 24th Marines. Though old for a company commander, he proved to be a leader in the Marine mold. "Mac doesn't tell you where to go," remarked one of his men later. "He takes you there."

Capt. Joe McCarthy receives the Purple Heart after Saipan. USMC

Any doubters became converts during the bitter combat the 4th Marine Division experienced on Saipan. On July 4, while in a defensive position, McCarthy's company was taken under intense enemy rifle and machine-gun fire. An officer was hit. Two corpsmen that went to the officer's aid were shot in quick succession. "Hearing the cries of the wounded, Captain McCarthy, without hesitation or regard for his own safety, left his covered position and, under intense enemy fire, went to the aid of the wounded," noted his citation for the Silver Star. "Upon reaching them, he found one of the corpsmen still alive and started to carry him to safety. While so doing, the wounded man was shot through the head and died in Captain McCarthy's arms."

Then came Iwo. Years later, G Company PFC Pete Santoro described the landing. "I saw a boatload of Marines take a direct hit," he recalled. "Bodies were flying all over. My heart went *boom boom boom.* You're ready to go in, but you see somebody right beside you get blown up." Held as part of the division reserve, McCarthy's battalion didn't come in at Yellow Beach 2 until 1650, taking over for the 2nd Battalion, 23rd Marines, which had been badly shot up during the landing and push toward Airfield No. 1. The newcomers quickly organized and headed inland almost 700 yards to take over the front line. There were dead Marines everywhere. "They fouled up Iwo Jima by sending in too many people," remarked McCarthy in retrospect. "No matter where the Japanese fired, they were going to hit someone." Experiencing his first operation, machine gunner PFC Jack Snyder recalled, "It was horrible just trying to get off the beach. We were under cross fire from artillery, mortars and small arms fire."

The following day McCarthy's company was placed on the right of the battalion push. Swinging from west to north, Fox and George moved rapidly across the northeast–southwest airstrip against heavy enemy resistance from bunkers, pillboxes, and high-velocity 47mm guns in covered emplacements. "Tanks could not be used after the first hour due to the character of the terrain and mined approaches thereto," noted the battalion special action report. "Progress was slow but steady." After a night on the receiving end of heavy mortar, rocket, artillery, and small-arms fire, the 2nd Battalion jumped off the next morning at 0810, again with George Company on the right and Fox on the left. The assault was preceded by air, naval gunfire, artillery, and an 81mm mortar preparation placed on suspected close-in enemy positions.

The assault companies bogged down in a wide swath of enemy pillboxes and entrenchments. "The wild terrain resembled, with its hundreds of bomb craters, the surface of the moon," wrote the division historian of this general area. "The ash was ankle-deep, and when the wind blew, it pelted the men's faces like buckshot. The Japs had converted every dune into a bunker from which the muzzles of the machine guns and anti-tank weapons jutted defiantly." Fighting was point blank, recalled company commander Capt. LaVerne W. Wagner. "We were chasing the Japs down trenches, and they were chasing us," he said. "Grenade duels took place everywhere. More often than not, we found ourselves in the rear of Jap pillboxes, which were still doing business on the other side."

Again, tanks could not be used initially because of terrain and mined areas. Faced with uninterrupted machine-gun fire and an enemy high-velocity 47mm gun, McCarthy's Marines made little progress. "We had been suffering heavy casualties from fortified positions and bunkers which seemed to be all over our front," recalled the company executive officer, 1st Lt. Roy Christensen. "Our right assault platoon was pinned down around noon, and we seemed to be almost at our wits' end in trying to effect an advance of even a few yards. The entire area was also subjected to intermittent large caliber mortar and artillery fire and we were in direct line of sight from one or two high velocity guns." The platoon leader of the right assault platoon had been wounded and evacuated the day before, and the platoon was "a little shaky from the terrific pounding," noted the exec.

McCarthy lost patience. He put Lieutenant Christensen in charge of the command post and went up to get the platoon moving. "He took one flamethrower, three demolitions men, and a squad from the reserve platoon and moved out," recalled the exec. "He learned that there were at least three pillboxes to the right front, and at least seventy-five yards away, on a ridge line."

McCarthy beckoned to his flamethrower/demolitions team. "Let's go!" he shouted. "Let's get it!"

"I saw Captain McCarthy get up and run across the open and exposed terrain," recalled a Marine. "It was a miracle he was not hit, as fire was now coming from both flanks as well as to the front." McCarthy recalled, "Even though I was thirty-two back then, I could run like a deer, and I think that's why they didn't kill me. . . . I had all those young punks. They called me the old man. But they couldn't keep up with me running like hell."

Charging forward over seventy-five yards of bullet-swept terrain, McCarthy threw himself to the ground in front of the first enemy position. Rapidly pulling the pins from three grenades, he threw them into the pillbox in quick succession. There were muffled screams from inside.

"There were six or seven of us with my captain, McCarthy," recalled PFC Pete Santoro. "I'm behind, trailing a guy, and I said, 'Wait a minute.' There was this big hill they were going around. I thought: I'm going to go over the top; I'm going to see what the fuck's on the other side. So I get over this bank and look down on the entrance to one of those sulfur mines. Two Japs were lying there, crawling, so I put a shot in each one from up above. Then McCarthy shows up. He doesn't see me up there, and then, *bing, bing, bing*, he says, 'I got them. I got them.' I was waiting for some more to come out. He spoiled it all. He didn't know they weren't alive. He just saw them and shot."

McCarthy's attention was still focused on the pillbox. Three of his men had been hit in the charge across the open ground, but the flame-thrower man had survived. A whoosh of flame roasted any possible remaining defenders; then the demolitions men placed a charge and destroyed the smoking ruin.

Accompanied by his demolitions team and still under intense fire, McCarthy headed toward a second pillbox. The demolitions men maneuvered into position, placed a charge, and blew the strongpoint apart. As he entered the shattered remains of the pillbox, McCarthy saw a Japanese taking aim at Sgt. Thomas F. McCarthy (no relation). "I saw a Jap soldier raise his rifle and point it at me," recalled the sergeant. "Captain McCarthy then moved to the side of the pillbox and, as the Jap moved out to get a good shot at me, Captain McCarthy grabbed the Jap's rifle, wrenched it out of his hands, and shot him with it."

Intent on exploiting the narrow breach he had created in the enemy defenses, McCarthy gathered the rest of his company—now totaling only three officers and 112 men, including a gunnery sergeant and a corporal acting as platoon leaders—and pressed the attack, swarming up onto the high ground beyond. They took it, though Pete Santoro didn't get to enjoy the victory. "As we went to take more high ground I found the entrance to another tunnel," he remembered. "I fired a rifle grenade but it fell short so I fired my last one. As I started to move in, I was shot in the back." The bullet shattered an eight-round clip on his ammo belt, driving a spray of brass fragments into Santoro's back. "It felt like I was hit with a sledgehammer," he recalled. Unable to move his legs, Santoro was evacuated. Fortunately, he regained use of his legs, though doctors never did get all the debris out of him. "My wife was pulling that stuff out with tweezers for years afterwards," remarked Santoro.

"I was scared all the time," McCarthy recalled years later. "Any man tells you he wasn't scared was an imbecile. But you dealt with it." He did what he did, he said, because "it had to be done, and you can't just tell the boys what to do—you have to show them, and lead them. And if they believe in you, they can do anything in the world."

McCarthy's near-suicidal assault contributed materially to breaking the enemy defense belt protecting Airfield No. 2, but the campaign was far from over. On D+10 (March 1), after another week of fighting, G Company was thrown into the effort to seize Hill 382, located just 250 yards northeast of the east–west runway of Airfield No. 2. The highest point on the island after Suribachi, the hill was heavily defended. "The top of the hill, surmounted by the stark remains of a Japanese radar station, was hollowed out and rebuilt to contain field pieces and anti-tank weapons," reported Lt. Col. Whitman S. Bartley in a study of the action. "Each of these concrete gun housings was in turn protected by as many as ten supporting machine gun emplacements. The rest of the hill was honeycombed with the same elaborate tunnels that character-ized other major installations on the island. In addition crevices and ridges crisscrossed the entire surrounding area. Light and medium tanks armed with 57mm and 47mm guns, parked well back in these crevices, commanded the length of the main (northeast–southwest) runway of the airfield and approaches from the southwest."

Hill 382 where Doug Jacobson earned his Medal of Honor during fierce combat on February 26, 1945. USMC

Elements of the division had been trying to secure Hill 382 since February 26. Casualties had been horrendous. The Marines had been on the hill a number of times, but could not retain possession. Now the 2nd Battalion and G Company were going to have a turn.

Commanding the adjacent Fox Company, Capt. Walt Ridlon, a twenty-five-year-old New Englander who four years earlier was studying economics at Tufts University, had been watching his men get shot to pieces as they tried to get up the hill. "The sonsabitchin' Nips are doing their goddamned best to make this the worst day of my life," he told his platoon sergeant as they hugged the slope in an effort to escape the torrent of fire. Ridlon got McCarthy on the field phone. "What will we do, Joe?" he asked as the two debated their options.

"I guess we'd better attack," McCarthy replied.

"Hill 382 . . . we went up there five times," McCarthy remembered. "They chased us off each time. The sixth time I said *that's enough.*"

Ridlon's Fox Company, aided by the G Company Marines, finally wrested the top of the hill away from the Japanese, and this time they were there to stay. "Flame throwers, bazookas and grenades were used in close combat, and assault squads exposed themselves to intense and accurate small-arms fire as they blasted cave entrances in a systematic yard-by-yard advance," reported Bartley. Six hours into the fight, Ridlon sent a message to the battalion command post at the foot of the slope: "Almost to the high ground!" Half an hour later, the radio crackled again as Ridlon reported, "Fox Company on top of radar hill." Later he admitted of the hill, "You barely know it's there. But when we climbed it, it was higher than anything I ever saw."

G Company was also there. By late afternoon McCarthy's outfit held a line running across the center of the hill, after tough fighting that included the destruction of two enemy tanks dug in as stationary pillboxes. Battalion estimated 150 Japanese had been killed during the assault, but it would take yet another day to firmly secure the position. Night brought little respite. "Hand grenade fights and hand to hand fights with the enemy frequent," reported battalion. "The enemy filtered out of recesses in the hill in front, into and behind the Marines' positions. Two Marines received saber cuts in hand to hand fighting." Assault squads were still blowing cave entrances and using flamethrowers on remaining points of resistance the following day, but the Japanese grip had been broken. G Company hadn't done it alone, but it had played a key role in the success. "You've got to give the old boy credit," observed McCarthy's exec. "When we took that hill, old Mac was going up with his men or die in the attempt."

A lot of Marines did die in the attempt. The battalion clinging to the top of Hill 382 was a mere shadow of its former self—G and F Companies had been decimated, and E Company had been virtually wiped out. Among the G Company dead was Sgt. George L. Barlow of Verbank, New York, who went after an enemy hand grenade that landed among a five-man machine-gun squad after dark that first night. Barlow blocked the grenade explosion, saving the squad, but bled to death from his wounds.

McCarthy himself lasted only a few more days. On D+15, his luck ran out when an enemy mortar blast drove metal fragments into his neck, head, and back as he directed an attack on enemy machine-gun positions. "It felt like a red hot poker," he recalled. A corpsman cut away

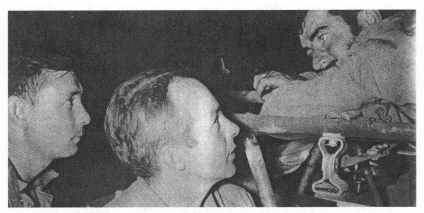

Joe McCarthy (on stretcher) at a field hospital on Iwo Jima. He was given last rites, but managed to survive his wounds. Leatherneck Magazine

his clothing and shot him full of morphine, but it looked bad. "I didn't think about dying until they were getting ready to operate," observed McCarthy. "I heard them say, 'Get a priest.' I said, 'I'm not going to die.'" The priest gave McCarthy last rites anyway. "The chaplain was giving me the last rites," McCarthy recalled years later. "He says, 'Joe, you're going to die.'" McCarthy retorted, "I'm not going to die." He didn't die, though he underwent three operations for the removal of shrapnel and lost some hearing in his left ear. He would carry pieces of Japanese metal in his body for the rest of his life.

McCarthy was back in the United States attending a transport quartermaster school at Camp Elliott, California, when he was notified on September 18 that he was to receive the Medal of Honor for leading the breakthrough of the Japanese defense belt on February 21. The medal was presented during a multiple awards ceremony on the south lawn at the White House on October 5, 1945. McCarthy's wife was not in attendance—their marriage had failed to survive their four-year separation. McCarthy, brash as ever and not at all intimidated by a mere president of the United States, dragged Truman over to meet his mother. Catherine gave the president a hug and a kiss. "That's the nicest thing that's happened to me in weeks," confessed a pleased Truman.

Returning to Chicago, McCarthy was asked by then-mayor Ed Kelly if he could handle an important job for the city. "I can handle anything," replied McCarthy in typical fashion. The job was to set up the city's fire and rescue operation, which McCarthy did. He also met and married his second wife, Anita, who was six years his junior. Anita encouraged him to attend DePaul University in Chicago, where he earned a degree in commerce. He remained with the Chicago Fire Department, eventually attaining the rank of chief of fire and rescue operations. He retired in 1973.

The old warrior also remained in the Marine Corps Reserve, retiring after more than thirty-seven years of service. "I loved it," he admitted years later, by then an old man. "I loved the Corps." A fighter to the end, he tried twice to reactivate his commission during the Korean War, but the Corps declined.

The McCarthys spent their later years summering in Wisconsin and spending winters at their condominium in Delray Beach, Florida. McCarthy often spoke to high school students and other groups on his love of country. He attended 4th Division reunions, where he also often spoke. "When he talked," remarked a former Marine, "you felt like reenlisting." One time, after McCarthy gave a talk at a Wisconsin high school, an educator casually referred to the students as "children." McCarthy bristled. "Wait a minute," he protested. "These aren't children. They're seventeen and eighteen years old. That's how old they were in the Pacific—those Marines, those kids." He went into Iwo with 254 men, he said later. "On D-day plus three they gave me ninety replacements and I ended up with seven men in my company," he remembered. "Boy did I love those kids. They asked nothing and they gave a lot."

In 1949 he drove from Maine to North Carolina, stopping along the way to visit the families of G Company Marines who had not survived Iwo Jima. "I just wanted them to know that someone thought a lot of their sons," he explained. "I wanted them to have something more than a letter from the Marine Corps or the Navy Department." He made a point of attending 4th Marine Division reunions, where emotions could run deep. "One guy, no arm," he recalled. "One guy—part of his head shot away. As soon as I walked up, he put his arms around me and said, 'You never let us down.'"

Anita passed away in the late 1970s. The couple had no children. McCarthy soldiered on, raising and lowering the flag on the grounds of his Florida home every day. He enjoyed listening to military marches on the stereo, and always stood at attention when the "Marine Corps Hymn" sounded. A guest noted that visitors were expected to do the same.

An interviewer visiting in the early 1980s noted that McCarthy, a devout Catholic, kept a statue of St. Jude, the patron saint of impossible causes, on his lawn. "Why St. Jude?" asked the visitor. "Because I'm an impossible cause," replied the old man. "And so are you, my friend. We all are."

Joe McCarthy, holder of the Medal of Honor, Silver Star, and three Purple Hearts, the only active firefighter to receive the Medal of Honor in World War II, died of heart disease at the age of eighty-three on June 15, 1996, in Delray Beach. He is buried beside his beloved Anita at Arlington National Cemetery.

McCarthy suffered a stroke in the mid–1990s and had a little trouble talking and writing in his last years. But he never forgot his Marines. "I had the greatest company that God ever created," he said years after the war. "George Company, 2nd Battalion, 24th Marines. I loved my Marines. *My Marines.* They never let me down. They *never* let me down."

As the 4th and 5th Marine Divisions struggled northward into a jungle of stone on February 21, it had already become clear that more troops would be needed. Early in the morning, the 21st Marines, waiting aboard ship in reserve with the rest of the 3rd Marine Division, was told to prepare to go ashore. The V Amphibious Corps advised 4th Marine Division commander Maj. Gen. Clifton Cates that the regiment would be coming in on the Yellow beaches beginning at 1130.

"Assign assembly area your zone," directed V Corps commander Gen. Harry Schmidt. "Will be released to you on your request to assist if required in capture of Airfield Number 2."

Veterans of Bougainville and Guam, the 21st Marines landed amid a logjam of swamped landing craft, burned-out tanks, smashed trucks, and a horrific litter of dead Marines and parts of dead Marines—arms, legs, headless torsos, and unidentifiable viscera strewn along the beach and black-sand slopes. Scores of wounded waited on the beach for evacuation. By 1700 all three battalions were ashore and in assembly areas near the edge of Airfield No. 1. General Cates wasted no time assigning a mission to the newcomers: the following day they were to relieve the badly shot-up 23rd Marines, which had suffered over a thousand casualties since landing on February 19. Their objective would be what a Marine historian later described as "an intricate network of mutually supporting pillboxes emplaced on high ground between Airfields 1 and 2." The description, couched in professional understatement, didn't begin to convey the nightmare that lay ahead. Their only option was frontal assault. The attack that first day gained only fifty to seventy-five yards. Fighting the following day wasn't going much better. Then a frustrated captain asked Cpl. Woody Williams, a twenty-one-year-old flamethrower operator from West Virginia, if he could do something about the pillboxes holding up his company.

CPL. HERSHEL W. WILLIAMS

21st Marines, 3rd Marine Division
February 23, 1945

Hershel Williams
USMC

When Hershel Woodrow ("Woody") Williams was fifteen years old, he hitched a lift from a man driving a convertible. It was very nearly his last ride on earth. As Williams pleaded with the driver to slow down, the man heedlessly accelerated until finally he missed a sharp curve and hit a pole. Thrown from the car, Williams came to his senses to find most of his clothes torn off and his body a mass of scrapes and cuts, but, by some act of God, still alive and in relatively one piece.

It may have been the first miracle in his young life, but it was not to be the last.

Born October 2, 1923, on a dairy farm in Quiet Dell, West Virginia, Williams was the youngest of five children (six other siblings had died during the 1918 flu epidemic). "I got all the hand-me-downs," he joked later. Before he was even old enough to go to school, he was helping out on the farm. "My job was to get out to the barn around 5 A.M. with a bucket of soapy water so I could wash the cows' teats before the others got there," he observed. "We milked thirty to thirty-five cows on a sixty-eight acre farm." When he got a little older, he helped out with deliveries, jumping off the running board of his father's pickup truck to leave milk on doorsteps and pick up the empties for refill.

His father died of heart trouble when Woody was only nine years old, and tough times became even tougher for the Williams family. Woody's early education was in a two-room schoolhouse in Quiet Dell. "[Y]ou'd go from first to fourth grade in one room and then from fifth to eighth in the other," he said. High school was in Fairmont, about seven miles from the family farm. "Any sports or extracurricular activity was completely out of the picture for us," he recalled. "There was too much to do at home."

He later described himself as "a bashful, shy country boy," but as an adolescent his don't-give-a-damn attitude seems to have created a few disciplinary issues. He was, in his own words, "headed for reform school." He quit East Fairmont High School in his junior year—apparently much to the relief of school officials—and followed his older brother into the Civilian Conservation Corps (CCC). "He was making about twenty-one dollars a month," recalled Williams. "That was a lot of money then, so I decided I wanted to do the same thing." He was working on fence lines in Montana when word came of the Japanese attack on Pearl Harbor. "On December 8, 1941, everyone was called out of the barracks and we were shocked to find out that Pearl Harbor had been bombed," he remembered "We were told that we could go directly into the army or we could request our release from the CCC so we could go home and join whichever of the services we wished."

A lot of the other CCC men went immediately into the army, but Williams, still months shy of his eighteenth birthday, had his heart set on the Marine Corps. None of his family had ever served in the military, but when Williams was twelve or thirteen years old, a couple of Marines from Quiet Dell—farm boys who had signed up for a six-year hitch, figuring military life would be preferable to hoeing corn or baling hay—would occasionally come home on leave. The visiting leathernecks thoroughly impressed all the local youngsters with their snappy dress blues and confident attitude. "We kids would hang around and go with them wherever they would let us," Williams remembered. "They'd tell us these great big wild stories, probably most of them not true." The experience left a lasting impression on Williams and he was determined to join the Marines.

Unfortunately, the fates seemed to decree otherwise. Discharged from the CCC, Williams went home, only to find that his mother would not sign a waiver for him to get into the service at age seventeen. He waited around until his eighteenth birthday, killing time with a variety of odd jobs, then headed down to the Marine recruiting station in Fairmont. The recruiter took one look at him as he handed over his paperwork and said, "We can't take you."

"How come?" said Williams.

"You're not tall enough," said the recruiter. The height requirement for the Marines was five feet eight inches. Woody was five feet six inches tall and weighed in at about 135 pounds.

Williams worked for a while in a steel mill in Sharon, Pennsylvania, and also drove a taxi, but his disappointment was not to last long. By early 1943, the need for men had persuaded the Marines to relax the height requirement and "begin taking little runts like me." The recruiter had kept his paperwork; he got in touch with Williams, and in

May Woody found himself on a train bound for California. He received recruit training in San Diego, followed by tank/infantry instruction at Camp Elliot. "Right from that moment my life began to change," he said later. "Marine boot camp, with its rigid discipline, taught me for the first time to respect authority." It was tough, he admitted. "[Sometimes] I thought I might not get through it, but I never thought about quitting. They could kill me, but I wasn't going to quit."

Sent overseas in December as a replacement, he was assigned to the 21st Marines, 3rd Marine Division. He arrived on Guadalcanal as the division was wrapping up the Bougainville campaign. The division returned to Guadalcanal and began a new regimen of training. Originally a BAR man, Williams was now sent to flamethrower/demolition school. Apparently no one saw any illogic in saddling a 135-pound self-described "runt" with a 72-pound flamethrower. "They picked the dumbest guys in the outfit to make flamethrowers," he joked years later. In July 1944, Williams participated in the assault on Guam. There wasn't much need for flamethrowers during the campaign, so he trudged along as a rifleman. In an ironic twist of fate, the Marine who took over the BAR when Williams went into flamethrowers was killed during the fighting. "We had a banzai one night and they overran his outpost and got him," said Williams.

By the time of the Iwo Jima campaign, Williams—known to his buddies as "Willie"—was a corporal with a special weapons section, trained to take out enemy pillboxes and fortifications. Since the 4th and 5th Marine Divisions were making the initial assault, with the 3rd Division in reserve, most of the men in Williams's outfit figured they had lucked out. Two Marine divisions should be perfectly adequate to clean up a limited area like Iwo Jima. According to scuttlebutt circulated at briefings, they'd float around offshore four or five days, and then go back to Guam. "They told us, 'You will probably never get off ship,'" recalled Williams.

The scuttlebutt was wrong. As casualties mounted and progress slowed to a crawl, the call went out for more troops. The 21st Marines were first boated on February 20, but there was no room on the beachhead to land them. They went round and round in the choppy seas hour after miserable hour, getting soaked to the skin. Williams had never been seasick before, but his immunity ended off Iwo Jima. "I don't know if I got seasick because of the waves or because somebody puked on me. But everybody was puking," he recalled. They bobbed around all day before finally returning to the ships. "They gave us some food and everyone collapsed and slept wherever they were," remembered Williams, who had been particularly nervous about the day's maneuver. He had never learned to swim, and was so loaded down with gear that he knew he wouldn't have a chance if he fell into the water while getting on or off the landing craft.

The following day they were ordered back into the boats, and this time they went ashore. The destruction was shocking. "Just a

Wrecked vehicles litter an Iwo Jima beach. Coming ashore later, Woody Williams's outfit was shocked at the scene of death and destruction on the beaches. USMC

bunch of wrecked stuff scattered on the beach," observed Williams. "You couldn't hardly get through the stuff that was on the beach . . . things blown up and buried into the sand. Lots of bodies . . . lots of dead Marines around." There was no cover. It was almost impossible to walk in the shifting volcanic sand, and every time he tried to dig a hole, the sides slid in. The only decent cover was the big shell holes that had been blasted in the sand. "There'd be six or ten guys in each crater," he recalled.

Assigned to support the 4th Marine Division, the 21st Marines were directed to pass through the badly shot-up 23rd Marine Regiment and continue the attack at 0815 on February 22. Williams's battalion had a tough time getting across the eastern part of Airfield No. 1 that morning. Aside from an occasional shell hole, there was simply no cover. "We lost an awful lot of Marines just getting across the airfield," he recalled. "There were bodies everywhere, absolutely stacked up like cordwood, just unbelievable." They got across, but the following day brought a different kind of trouble as the battalion ran up against a cordon of pillboxes protecting Airfield No. 2, just to the north. Williams later heard there were as many as 800 pillboxes and fortifications, in an area approximately 1,000 yards wide and 200 yards deep, blocking their way north. It didn't look good. "The Japs were madder than the devil that we got across that [first] airstrip and they were really throwing it at us," said one of the men, Cpl. Darol "Lefty" Lee.

"We were too busy in our own little realm to pay any attention to what anybody else was doing," recalled Williams. "But suddenly Marines around me started jumping up and firing their weapons into the air, screaming and yelling and that kind of stuff, and I really thought everybody had lost their mind there for a second. I couldn't figure out what was going on." Williams looked south and saw that the American flag had been raised on Mount Suribachi. "So I jumped up and started doing the same dumb thing they were doing," he laughed.

The Marines could use a little encouragement. Williams had seen combat on Guam, including terrifying banzai attacks, but he had never seen anything like this. "We were drawing constant fire and much of the time we were in the open as we tried to advance slightly uphill against the Japanese who were in reinforced concrete pillboxes," he recalled. "Now these pillboxes were reinforced concrete covered over with sand and you could drop a bomb or artillery or whatever on top of that thing—there was three or four foot of sand on top of it—it would blow a lot of sand around but it certainly wouldn't penetrate the pillbox." The Japanese had dug shallow trenches between the pillboxes, enabling them to crawl from one to the other and escape grazing fire. Tanks were having trouble getting off the treacherous beaches and the infantry couldn't break through without help. "Every time we'd charge, they'd knock us back," said Williams. His special weapons team had taken especially heavy losses over two days. "I had a team of six flamethrowers and six demolitions men and it was no time before all my flamethrowers were gone, either killed or wounded," he recalled.

"The Japs were everywhere," said Sgt. Lyman D. Southwell, a squad leader from Denver, Colorado. "Fire came from sand piles, ditches, tunnels, pillboxes everywhere. I never thought I would get out alive." The C Company platoon, commanded by twenty-four-year-old 2nd Lt. Howard Chambers, lost five men in the first minutes of the morning attack, and suffered several more casualties among the rough, sandy ridges over the next six hours. Chambers's actions that day would materially assist in a significant breakthrough and earn him a Silver Star medal, but things didn't look particularly promising at that moment.

As the afternoon dragged on with no progress against the Japanese defense belt, twenty-eight-year-old Capt. Donald Beck, now commanding HQ Company, gathered his NCOs and officers in a large shell hole for a conference. "We only had a couple of officers left," recalled Williams, who, though only a lowly corporal, gained admission by virtue of his position as head of HQ Company's special-weapons section. Beck was no combat neophyte—he had won a Silver Star on Guam for his coolness during a Japanese banzai attack—but now he was clearly frustrated. His outfit was taking heavy casualties and getting nowhere. "He was looking for ideas," recalled Williams. "How do we do this thing? What can we do to make progress and not get people killed?" No one seemed to have an answer. The captain looked at Williams. "Do you think you can knock out some of those pillboxes with a flamethrower?" he asked.

Covered by riflemen, a flamethrower operator burns out a sand-covered pillbox. Woody Williams knocked out seven of these pillboxes in one afternoon. USMC

Having seen his men practically annihilated, Williams knew his chances were not good. "I figured, what the hell, I might as well join them wherever they were," he said later.

"I'll try," he told Beck.

His outwardly calm appearance was belied by the butterflies in his stomach, but Williams resolved to do what he could. "I had six full flamethrowers. . . . I took two automatic riflemen and two riflemen for cover and one of my men to help carry demolitions." Accompanied by Cpl. Allan Tripp, a demolitionist from Salt Lake City, Utah, Williams moved on up toward the no-man's-land between the Marines and the line of pillboxes. "I was scared to death," he admitted. "I was shaking in my boots." Their initial target was a trio of Japanese pillboxes about 100 yards beyond C Company's forward positions. "We could see them as we left our front lines and began to crawl forward," Williams recalled.

"The center pillbox was my main objective because it was the one really giving us fits."

The covering party—two riflemen and two BAR men—fanned out to the left and right to provide support. Williams and Tripp moved on past them, Williams laboring under his 72-pound flamethrower. The twin tanks contained a four-gallon mix of high-octane gasoline and diesel fuel, propelled by compressed air in a third tank atop the other two. Tripp lugged his M-1 rifle and a pole charge, basically a stick or pole with a 20-pound satchel charge tied to the end.

"I began crawling out through the sand dunes," recalled Williams. "I didn't jump and run, or charge, or anything. I just crawled as close as I could crawl." His goal was to get to within twenty or thirty yards of the closest pillbox and then "roll" a burst of flame through the aperture. "You'd roll it along the ground," he explained. "It would roll fifteen or twenty yards. Just a huge ball of flame." The burst of flame, which reached about 3500 degrees Fahrenheit, not only burned whatever it hit; in the confined space of a pillbox, it would also suck all the oxygen out of the air, asphyxiating anyone who wasn't incinerated.

Williams and Tripp crabbed their way to the cover of a shell hole and paused to confer. The pillbox Williams had his eye on was now within about fifty yards—still too far for the flamethrower. Getting Tripp's assurance that he would be right behind him with the pole charge, Williams squirmed out of the hole and into a shallow trench. Machine-gun bullets tore up the ground in front of him. From behind and to the left, a BAR opened up with a long burst at the firing slot of the pillbox. Lifting his head out of the dirt to check on his progress, Williams was shocked to see a Japanese soldier suddenly rise out of the ground less than twenty feet away, his head and shoulders emerging from a lidded oil drum buried in the sand. As the man started to raise his rifle to fire toward the Marine lines, he noticed Williams lying there staring at him. "Then we were looking at each other, and I could see the surprise in his eyes," remembered Williams. "We were that close."

Before the Japanese had a chance to do anything but look astonished, Williams squeezed the triggers on his flamethrower and incinerated him. That eliminated one threat, but stirred up the occupants of the pillbox, who turned their Nambu machine gun on Williams. "When the Japanese saw us coming, they really opened up," he recalled. "I could hear the bullets ricocheting off the back of the flamethrower. I was trying to get to it and I couldn't. Every time I would start, he'd get too close for comfort and I'd back out."

Williams clawed at the sand, propelling himself backward. He made it back to the shell hole, landing almost on top of Tripp, who was just ahead of him. As they considered their options, a bazooka man fired a rocket at the center pillbox. Williams saw it hit just below and to the left of the firing slit. "Some of the white smoke from the explosion was sucked into the concrete opening and I noticed a wisp of it curling out the center top of the pillbox," he observed. "This told me that there was an opening of some kind on top so I decided that our only chance was to work around the pillboxes and attack the center one from the rear."

Crawling out again, Williams and Tripp worked slowly from one bit of cover to another, finally slipping around to the blind side of the center pillbox, which was situated only fifteen to thirty yards from the pillboxes on either flank. "It was buried deep in the side of a hill," recalled Williams. Tripp covered Williams as he crept up the mound of sand covering the pillbox. As he had guessed, there was a 4-inch air vent on top, just large enough to accommodate the flamethrower nozzle. Williams stuck the nozzle into the vent and shot a long burst of flame down the tube and into the room below. When he stopped, the stench of oily smoke and seared flesh wafted back up the pipe. "Somebody said there were seventeen in there," he remembered. "I don't know. I have no idea. But I got that one. Knocked that one out." Tripp shoved his pole charge in the smoking ruin and blew it up.

Williams dropped the empty flamethrower, and he and Tripp crawled back to the waiting platoon. Williams picked up another flamethrower and strapped it on. This time, he went after the pillbox on the right. Again making the terrifying crawl out into no-man's-land, he worked within range of the pillbox and rolled a ball of flame through the firing slot. The gun stopped firing.

Stripped of its sand covering, a Japanese pillbox lies exposed. USMC

Again dropping his tanks and making his way back to the other Marines without getting shot, Williams picked up another flame-thrower and headed out after the third pillbox. Accompanied by Cpl. Alex Schlager, the twenty-six-year-old son of Russian immigrants who had settled in Torrington, Wyoming, he paused in a shell hole to look things over. The two men noticed that a shallow trench angled off in the general direction of the pillbox, meandering left, which would put the pillbox more to his right. Part of the network dug by the Japanese to link the pillboxes, the trench was only twelve or fifteen inches deep.

Williams decided to make a quick dash for the trench and use its shelter to crawl closer to the pillbox. Schlager would follow with the pole charge. They gathered themselves, then Williams bolted for the trench. To his horror, as Schlager came up over the edge of the hole, a bullet hit him in the front of the helmet, knocking the Wyoming Marine back into the crater. Williams scuttled back to the shell hole. "I was sure he was gone," he remembered. He found Schlager lying on his back. His eyes were rolling, but Williams couldn't see any blood. "Are you all right?" he asked as Schlager started to come around.

"Yeah, I think so," Schlager replied groggily. He took his helmet off and found he had experienced a miracle. The bullet had penetrated the front of his helmet and instead of continuing into his head, had traveled around the helmet between the steel pot and the fiber liner and exited the rear.

Schlager pulled himself together and they made a second, successful sprint for the ditch. Again, as Williams got closer to the pillbox, he felt bullets glancing off the tanks on his back. This time, instead of trying to back away, he crawled forward as fast as he could manage. The decision probably saved his life, for as he got within flamethrower range of the pillbox, he found himself in a dead zone where the Japanese couldn't depress the machine gun far enough to hit him. Williams pointed the flamethrower nozzle at the aperture and rolled a ball of flame into the pillbox. The gun went abruptly silent.

Over the next four hours, the West Virginian knocked out seven Japanese pillboxes, returning to his own lines only to retrieve recharged flamethrowers. He went through six flamethrowers in the course of the assault. Later, he could remember only bits and pieces of that long afternoon. He attributed this combat amnesia to his great fear. "Much of that day, I have no memory of," he said. "It was wiped clean. Fear is what caused that memory to disappear."

One incident he did vividly remember. Creeping to within thirty yards of yet another pillbox, keeping his face pressed to the ground as bullets kicked up the sand around him, he finally picked up his head to see a chilling sight. Three helmeted Japanese soldiers in mustard-col- ored uniforms and carrying bayoneted rifles had emerged from behind the pillbox and were charging toward him through the loose volcanic sand. Later Williams speculated the enemy infantrymen had run out of ammunition, but it is more likely that they had left protected positions in an effort to catch him before he could burn out the pillbox.

Williams raised the gun nozzle on his flamethrower and squeezed the triggers. "I'll never forget the looks on their faces when the fire hit them," he recalled. "It didn't bowl them over. It just stopped them. It was as if the whole thing were happening in slow motion. When the flame hit, it just went right on through. One great big 'puff' that paralyzed them. Petrified them. They stopped dead in their tracks and just fell over."

Though the image would remain with him for life, Williams didn't pause to ponder the scene. Crawling forward, he sent a second blast of flame through the slit of the pillbox, incinerating the occupants and silencing the chattering machine gun. At this point, Williams admitted, his mind shut down, though his actions did not. "I can remember being wet with perspiration late in the afternoon and coming back for the last flamethrower," he said later. "I didn't think that I'd ever make it back up that trench. I reached the point where I had to get down on my stomach and begin wiggling in the sand again. I remember being tremendously tired. Exhausted. But I don't remember attacking any of the pillboxes after the third one."

But others did see and remember. "[Woody] moved right up to those pillboxes," recalled Southwell. "He got up to within a dozen yards of the first one, emptied his flamethrower and came back for another. He had cover, but we couldn't give him a lot because we had one hell of a day and were so low on ammo. And everyone had to hug the ground so we didn't have such good fighting."

Over the course of the afternoon, Williams knocked out four more enemy pillboxes and killed at least twenty-one Japanese—probably a conservative estimate. "Willie had a hell of a time with one bunker," recalled PFC George Schwarz, who helped provide covering fire. "He used two or three flame throwers on it before he finished the job."

Despite a hurricane of enemy fire, he remained untouched. "You almost have to be automated," said Williams. "The mortars are going off, people are firing weapons. Just everything's going on. Things are blowing up around you. It's very chaotic."

"It was a major miracle that Williams lived, but he did," remarked a Marine Corps combat correspondent later. "Two riflemen trying to cover him during his attack were less fortunate: they were killed." Cpl. William Naro remembered a group of Japanese, some wielding swords, who charged the Marines. Schlager hit one twenty feet away, but the Japanese just lurched and kept coming. Schlager hit him again in the chest and the man buckled but continued to stagger forward before a third bullet finally put him down. Two other Japanese went after Lt. Howard Chambers, who killed them with two rounds from his .45 pistol. In retrospect, Williams was as surprised as anyone that he survived the afternoon. "They never touched me," he observed in some disbelief years after. "I have no answers for that except that somebody up there [pointing heavenward] was taking care of that situation."

Williams continued to live a charmed life over succeeding days. Just how charmed is indicated by the fact that by March 5, Company C numbered a mere seventeen survivors from the approximately 270 Marines that had initially landed on Iwo Jima. That night, a group of half-trained replacements arrived. "They brought in a whole group of new Marines, straight from the States," recalled Williams. "They had very little training. They didn't know what a flamethrower was. They didn't know how to operate a machine gun. They just didn't know a whole lot of anything." Williams and the handful of veterans spent most of the night giving the newcomers a crash course in survival, in hopes of at least giving them a chance to avoid being killed straight out of the box.

C Company attacked the next morning at about daylight, heading for "a kind of a rise" or "knoll" out to the front, recalled Williams. "They were firing mortars at us," he remarked, but there wasn't so much in the way of small-arms fire. The Marines would run forward a ways, hit the deck, then get up and run again. During one of the stops, Williams found shelter in a small hole. It was big enough to shelter his torso, but his legs were exposed. As he lay there waiting for a lull in the fire, a shell fragment hit him in the left leg. He yelled for a corpsman. "And he jerked the metal out of me and he handed it to me," recalled Williams. Then he sprinkled some sulfa powder on the wound and applied a pressure bandage. "I'm gonna give you a tag and send you back," he told Williams

"I'm not going back," retorted Williams.

The corpsman tagged him anyway and moved on. As soon as he was gone, Williams tore the tag off and limped along with the attack. Lying nearby, as Williams argued with the corpsman, was his best friend, Cpl. Vernon Waters, a big Montanan whom Williams had known since boot camp. The two of them were "closer than brothers," remarked Williams. Back before Iwo, the two had made a pact. When Williams went into the service, his fiancée, Ruby, had given him a small ring to remember her by. Waters also had a ring, a fairly large affair with a lake scene engraved on it, given to him by his father. The men agreed that if either of them were killed, the other would retrieve his ring and return it to his family, even though both were well aware that removing personal items from the dead was strictly forbidden. Now, as Waters got up to run forward, a mortar shell came down almost directly on him.

"Of course I ran to him, but he was already gone," said Williams. He saw the ring on Waters's index finger and remembered their pact. After a brief struggle, and with the help of some spit, he managed to work the ring off his friend's finger. He put the ring in his pocket, then noticed the glaring white spot where the ring had been on Vernon's finger. Fearing someone would realize he had taken the ring, Williams took some volcanic ash, spit on it, and smeared it over the white spot before moving on.

Williams gimped along for another three weeks, and was one of the few original members of his outfit to walk off Iwo under his own power when they finally left at the end of March. Back on Guam the following month, he noticed that certain parties seemed to be taking an inordinate interest in his actions of February 23. When he asked why, he was told it was for the division's history. In fact, the accounts were being compiled to support a recommendation for the Medal of Honor. "I had never heard of the Medal of Honor," he remarked. "I didn't know what that meant." Finally, one day Williams was called in by the powers-that-be and asked if he was ready to go home. "Very funny," retorted Williams, who thought he was the butt of a not particularly humorous joke.

President Truman congratulates Hershel Williams during the Medal of Honor awards ceremony on the White House lawn.
USMC

But it was no joke. On October 5, 1945, Sgt. Hershel Woodrow Williams found himself on the White House lawn receiving the Medal of Honor from President Harry S. Truman. The man who wiped out seven enemy pillboxes with a flamethrower was so nervous that he had to walk forward on his toes to keep his legs from shaking. "I was very frightened at the time," he admitted. "It was difficult to believe this was happening to me." Noticing that Williams had the shakes, Truman put a reassuring hand on the former dairy farmer's shoulder and said—as he was to say many times on these occasions—"I would rather have this medal than be president."

The next morning, Williams and ten other medal recipients reported to the office of Marine Corps commandant Gen. A. A. Vandegrift. If meeting the president had been nerve-wracking, remarked Williams, facing the commandant was "like reporting to God." The men were called in alphabetically, one by one. When Williams's turn came, he went in, marveling at the thick carpet on the floor. He didn't hear much of what the general was saying until Vandegrift—himself a medal recipient for his actions on Guadalcanal earlier in the war—admonished him, "That medal does not belong to you. It belongs to all of those Marines who did not get to come home. And don't ever do anything that would tarnish that medal."

Williams later found that Vandegrift had not said that to any of the others: "He said different things to different people." But the words hit home for Williams, who knew painfully well that two Marines had been killed trying to protect him while he attacked the pillboxes. He never even knew their names. "It really belongs to them," he said of the medal many times afterward, echoing General Vandegrift's words. "I'm just a caretaker of it." Later, Williams mused further, "I was always confident I would not die, but I kept wondering why I was permitted to live when so many of my buddies didn't." He accepted the medal on their behalf, but not without a sense of bewilderment. "They made it possible for me to be there," he remarked. "I still couldn't understand, 'Why me?'"

That January, he and Ruby, now married, borrowed a car from a friend and drove out to tiny Floyd, Montana, located in wheat country up by the Canadian border, to see Vernon Waters's family. Williams brought the ring he had taken from his friend's finger on Iwo Jima and kept safe through the rest of the war, and—as promised—gave it to Vernon's father. "You would have thought that I was delivering the greatest diamond that ever existed," he said of their appreciation.

After his discharge, Williams began a career with the Veterans Administration. When he retired in 1979 after thirty-three years of service, he was contract officer in charge of fourteen field offices. He and Ruby had two daughters. Following his retirement, they focused on raising Morgan horses on their farm in Ona, West Virginia.

In the meantime, the formerly unreligious Williams experienced a life-changing revelation when he found God. Shepherded by Ruby, his family had attended church for years, but Williams always stayed home. The town he grew up in as a boy had no church, and he had no religious background. "I didn't go. I didn't need it," he said. "Tough guys don't need God, we think."

But one Sunday in 1961, he reluctantly agreed to accompany his family to church and the experience changed his life forever. The preacher talked about sacrifice—something Williams had experienced in its rawest form. "I'd had men who gave their lives to protect me," he said. Now he felt the true meaning of Christ's sacrifice. "I stopped the sermon and asked the preacher to pray with me," he recalled. He joined the Methodist Church, eventually becoming a lay speaker.

As for Iwo Jima and the Medal of Honor, he admitted that, looking back, "it's like a dream," and once again he spoke of the men who died to keep him alive, as he did what had to be done. "When I get to heaven," he added, "one of my first questions to God will be: 'Why me?'"

CHAPTER THREE

Into the Hills

By the morning of February 26, one-third of Iwo Jima was in American hands. After six days of intense combat, the Marines had lost 1,605 men killed and 5,496 wounded, and had logged 657 cases of combat fatigue, for a total of 7,758 casualties—a number that was probably on the conservative side. By now it was clear, even to the most naïve private, that V Amphibious Corps commander Maj. Gen. Harry Schmidt's prediction that Iwo would be seized within ten days was a pipe dream of major proportions.

"By the morning of the sixth day, casualties were so horrendous I didn't recognize many faces at all," recalled Cpl. James Dugan, serving with the 27th Marines. "For every yard we moved, we seemed to leave a body. The fighting was so intense, it wasn't like graves registration could come up and take care of the dead. We were getting killed beside the dead. Nobody could move. The tanks would run over the decomposing bodies. . . . The stench was unimaginable."

There was to be no respite. With Suribachi captured, full focus on D+5 turned to the drive north. The point of the spear consisted of the 26th Marines on the left, the 24th Marines on the right, and the 21st Marines in the center. Blocking their way, as they were about to learn in the worst fashion possible, was General Kuribayashi's main defensive belt, a lethal warren of caves, pillboxes, blockhouses, and interlocking fields of fire laid down by an invisible enemy. The effort to break through quickly broke down into a series of uncoordinated individual small-unit brawls. Even tanks were of little help, falling victim to mines and well-concealed high-velocity direct-fire weapons. The network of carefully planned strongpoints held up the Marines for two weeks and cost them thousands of casualties, gaining dark fame as "the Meat Grinder."

"The hopes we had of a quick victory melted away slowly," recalled war correspondent Robert Sherrod, who visited the 24th Marines on February 24. "One day it seemed that only a few more days would be required, the next day it seemed that surely a break would come somewhere; a week later our progress was still being measured 50 yards, 100 yards, 300 yards, at a time. Kuribayashi never gave the order of the battle-ending banzai attack. His men stayed in their tunnels and their mole hills to the deathly end, and we had to go in and dig them out or burn [them] out or seal them in. There was nothing else for us to do."

On February 26, the 3rd Battalion, 24th Marines moved out to attack Hill 382, a natural fortress on the eastern side of Motoyama Airfield No. 2. Among those joining the assault was a big-boned youngster from Port Washington, New York, now participating in his third campaign. His name was Doug Jacobson. "By the time we got to Iwo, I'd been through three landings," he said years later. "I was no virgin to battle. But this one wasn't in the books."

PFC DOUGLAS T. JACOBSON

23rd Marines, 4th Marine Division
February 26, 1945

In the early 1940s, the citizens of Port Washington, Long Island, would have thought you were addled if you suggested there would be talk one day of naming an elementary school after Douglas Thomas Jacobson. There was nothing malicious about it; the boy just didn't seem like the

Douglas Jacobson USMC

type of person to earn such an honor. Even Doug himself would have conceded he was an unlikely candidate for such recognition.

Doug Jacobson was born November 25, 1925, in Rochester, New York, to Hans and Hannah Jacobson. The family subsequently moved to Port Washington, on the north shore of Long Island. The village, part of the town of North Hempstead, was home to the largest sandbank east of the Mississippi River (its sand was used in the concrete that went into construction of the Empire State Building) and served as F. Scott Fitzgerald's model for East Egg in his legendary novel *The Great Gatsby*. The solidly middle-class Jacobson family was considerably less glamorous than Jay Gatsby and his associates. Doug's parents were naturalized citizens: Hans, a carpenter, had been born in Norway, and Hannah was originally from Sweden.

An only son, "Jake" worked as a draftsman for his father, and as a lifeguard and swimming instructor during the summer on Long Island's beaches. He also seems to have displayed a bit of a wild streak growing up in "the Port." Friends recalled that he was always joking around or playing tricks on people. One memorable incident involved an inebriated young Jacobson driving a car into the side of the Port Washington police station. Luckily, the officer on duty knew Jacobson and reportedly went easy on him, but not everyone was so forgiving. "I'm sure there were a lot of people who were not real fond of little Doug Jacobson," remarked Jacobson's wife, Joan, years later.

Considering his reputation, it probably came as no surprise to the neighborhood when Jacobson dropped out of the eleventh grade to join the service. Enlisting turned out to be more of an ordeal than he might have expected. Though he had played blocking back on the high school football team and worked as a lifeguard at the local beach, both the army and navy recruiters told him he was too fat. Finally, in January

1943 he stormed into the Marine recruiting station and announced, "I'm here to sign up!"

"Okay, get in the other room and take your clothes off," said the recruiter. "You're pudgy, but maybe we can get you by."

Accepted and sent off to Parris Island, the new recruit dropped the excess weight, but failed to qualify with the rifle, finally squeaking by on his second attempt by a mere four points. Subsequent training proved him more adept with the BAR and bazooka. He became a demolitions expert and fought in the Marshalls and on Saipan and Tinian with the 4th Marine Division. He was commended in division orders "for excellent performance of duties as a Browning automatic rifleman while serving with a rifle company during action against enemy Japanese forces on Saipan, Marianas Island from June 15, to June 28, 1944." By the time he hit Iwo Jima, the pudgy kid in the recruiting station was just a distant memory. Now he was a combat veteran who had long since proved his worth and was about to prove it again.

"Not many of us had slept," Jacobson recalled years later of the morning of the landing. "When you're going ashore in the morning, who can sleep?" Offered a breakfast choice of steak and eggs, turkey with mashed potatoes, or ham, the young veteran chose the infamous S.O.S., creamed beef on toast. "That, I knew, would stay with me," he remarked.

Hours later, Jacobson's landing craft was headed toward the billowing smoke that marked Iwo. His outfit, the 3rd Battalion, 23rd Marines, had been held in regimental reserve during the initial landings, but the assault battalions—the 1st and the 2nd—had run into trouble ashore. At 1300 hours twenty-seven-year-old Maj. James S. Scales was ordered to land his 3rd Battalion along Beach Yellow I, move inland about 200 yards, and support the 2nd Battalion's attack.

"The coxswain had the LCVP wide open," Jacobson recalled. "We crouched down, hoping we would get ashore in one piece. One Marine was in the bow. His job was to tell how close we were to the beach because when you hit a beach everything and everyone was thrown forward." In another LCVP, Cpl. Ed Burow, also coming ashore with L Company, was scared to death and just hoping he would have a chance to fight. "I remember a guy next to me tugged on my sleeve and pointed to the guy driving the landing craft," he recalled. "The driver was above us and could see everything happening on the beach, and his eyes must have been as big as headlights. Just looking at him scared me even more."

Five hundred yards. Three hundred. Many of the Marines in Jacobson's landing craft prayed; others just tried to crouch as low as possible. A projectile of some sort slammed into the ramp, then the LCVP struck ground. "The ramp stayed up," recalled Jacobson. "Everyone yelled at the coxswain, 'Drop the ramp! Drop the ramp!' He tried, but it was stuck. About five Marines stood back and then lurched forward, batting the door with their shoulders and *blam*, the ramp was down and out we went."

Jacobson ran out into ankle-deep water. "Well, I thought, not bad considering the times I'd been waist-deep," he joked darkly. As he slogged through the cloying ash and up the terraces, shells slammed down onto the beachhead. "Suddenly the air was full of *zing zing* and an explosion or two," remembered Jacobson. "We couldn't see much because of the smoke. Every few minutes there would be an explosion, followed by 'Corpsman! Corpsman!'"

Stunned by the carnage and the amount of enemy fire coming in, Jacobson heard someone yell, "What the hell did the first ten waves do?"

Someone hollered back, "Die, you dumb bastard!"

Jacobson recalled, "There was only one beach we could land on and they had us zeroed in. They threw everything at us. They fired down from the mountain, from the cliffs. Bullets came from three directions."

Not far from Jacobson, Ed Burow was also trying to run inland through the volcanic ash. "My first sight was machine gun tracer fire crossing in front of us, and I thought at that second not a single man would live for more than a minute under such fire," he recalled. "We followed Lieutenant [William] Sheffield forward, but we got only a few steps before his head was blown off and his brains flew back onto all of us running just behind him. I didn't stop to pause for reflection: I just wanted to get off that beach and find cover."

Major Scales, who less than five years earlier had been studying for a degree in commerce at the University of North Carolina at Chapel Hill, could hardly believe his eyes. "That beach was unbelievable, almost indescribable," he said. The area was crowded with Marines, and "every round was getting four or five" of them. "When the ramp of the landing craft went down I said, 'Oh Lord,'" he recalled. "It was wall-to-wall dead men. . . . A lot of the men were new to combat and this intense bombardment just paralyzed them. . . . It was a terrible, terrible situation."

At about 1430, with the battalion still stuck on the beach, Scales was ordered to pass through the 1st Battalion to continue the attack across the airfield. Scales admitted that a few of the stunned men had to be "kicked in the butt." He even went so far as to brandish his .45 as he struggled to get his disorganized unit off the beach. The battalion's difficulties were alluded to in its subsequent special action report on that first day: "Due to considerable casualties, disorganization, and difficulty in locating front lines of LT-1 and adjacent units, the passage of lines was not completed until about 1700." The battalion finally dug in for the night along the edge of Airfield No. 1.

"When we got up to that airfield you could look straight across to the dunes and so forth on the other side," recalled Cpl. Robert Perrin. "[It] just looked like sand dunes." Probably few men slept that night. "I don't remember much about that night except that we looked out over the airfield continually trying to see movement," said Pvt. Clayton Chipman. "We expected a banzai charge which, of course, [General] Kuribayashi didn't believe in. He believed in a defense at depth and extracting the most due that he could out of the Marines."

Jacobson's company attacked across the airfield through mortar and small-arms fire the next day, then turned north toward Airfield No.

2 and the enemy-held high ground. Casualties in the battalion were heavy as the Marines tackled well-concealed pillboxes and blockhouses and came under artillery and mortar fire. "Minefields were everywhere," recalled Jacobson. "We moved about fifty yards ahead of the tanks looking for tank mines. You stuck a bayonet in the ground feeling for them. All of a sudden this tank behind us blew up. The turret blasted off, the tank flew into the air. We went down like bowling pins. The blast killed a couple of the guys I was with. Our company commander yelled, 'Hey, what the hell happened?!' We found out. They buried aerial torpedoes five feet deep. They were setting them off electrically. They had a guy there sitting behind a rock with the wires and a battery just waiting for us."

Five days after coming ashore, the battalion crossed the east–west runway of Airfield No. 2 and came up against Hill 382 about 250 yards east of the airstrip. The highest point on Iwo after Suribachi, the hill was surmounted by the twisted remains of a Japanese radar tower that now looked like a badly vandalized baseball backstop. The hill itself was a jumbled mess of rocks and crevices honeycombed with tunnels, concrete emplacements with field pieces and antitank weapons, and numerous machine-gun revetments. "Four tanks, buried to their turrets, commanded natural routes of approach," reported the division historian. "Antitank guns peered down every crevice. Three 75mm AA guns, with their muzzles depressed, looked down the throats of the Marines. Twelve twin-mount guns, four heavy machine guns and numerous Nambu and Lewis-type machine guns were scattered throughout. In addition, there were at least 20 pillboxes and an uncounted number of caves, some of them several tiers deep."

The first effort to take the height jumped off on February 25. Coming out of corps reserve, Jacobson's division traded considerable casualties for limited gains. Among the casualties was the commanding officer of the 3rd Battalion, 24th Marines, Lt. Col. Alexander A. Vandegrift, son of the commandant, who was badly wounded in both legs by an exploding mortar shell. The attack failed. At 0800 the following

The rugged southwest slopes of Hill 382 where Doug Jacobson embarked on a one-man rampage on February 26. USMC

day, Jacobson's battalion jumped off under clear skies in another effort to seize Hill 382. "The approach to it was like being in a gully with maybe seventy-five yards of flat, and then Hill 382 went up, real rugged, and then behind was a concave wall or cliff," recalled Pvt. Clayton Chipman. Committed on the regiment's right, the 3rd Battalion moved doggedly into the enemy fields of fire, pushing through the rocky rubble toward the hill's forward defenses. Casualties mounted. "We had to advance through narrow pathways in the rock, which made it impossible to know if there were Japs above you or around the corner," recalled Cpl. Ed Burow. "Jap snipers were hidden in every crevice, and I thought I was going to die a hundred times."

As he worked forward with the others, Jacobson saw a bazooka man cut down by enemy fire. Later he would have some trouble explaining what he did next—or why: It was a question of survival; it was what he had been trained to do; he was just doing his job; the only way off that damn hill was to kill every Japanese defender. Maybe it was just impulse. Whatever the reason, Jacobson picked up the dead man's launcher and rockets and set out after a 20mm antiaircraft gun that had been depressed to fire on the attacking Marines. Ordinarily used to defend against low-flying aircraft, the 20mm—an 800-pound machine cannon—had a range of nearly 5,500 yards and a muzzle velocity of 2,720 feet per second, and was capable of firing high-explosive, tracer, or armor-piercing ammunition at the rate of 120 rounds per minute. Depressed for use as a ground weapon, it was a killer.

A 25mm antiaircraft gun used for ground fire overlooks the open approaches to Japanese defenses in the north. USMC

Stalking to within bazooka range of the machine cannon, Jacobson sighted down the tube and sent a rocket whooshing into the position. The gun and its crew went up with a blast. Next was an enemy machine-gun position. Shoving another rocket into the tube, Jacobson set the electrical contacts and went after the chattering machine gun. He destroyed that gun, then another, scrambling over the hillside, loading and firing the two-man bazooka by himself. His efforts sprang his platoon loose, but only momentarily. The Marines inched forward, only to butt up against a strongpoint built around a concrete blockhouse. Again Jacobson made his way forward and managed to knock out the blockhouse without getting himself killed. He then added another pillbox to his score, sidling up to the embrasure and slinging a demolition charge through the firing slit. The pillbox shuddered as the charge blew, killing the five-man crew inside. The next victims of Jacobson's one-man rampage were the occupants of a series of earth-covered rifle emplacements. Armed with his rifle and grenades, Jacobson took them on one by one. In a matter of minutes he reduced six of the rifle pits, killing ten Japanese.

Blasted to near oblivion, Hill 382 is finally conquered. USMC

Jacobson had already lived longer than could reasonably be expected, but he continued to press his luck. Having punched a hole through the outer defenses in his own sector, he now strayed over into the zone of the adjacent assault company, where he knocked out yet another pillbox. Then a dug-in Japanese tank caught his attention. The tank was firing away at an American Sherman trying to support the Marine assault from the base of the hill. Jacobson worked his way close to the tank and sent a bazooka round smashing into the turret, killing the crew. When yet another blockhouse stopped the advance of his adopted company, Jacobson crawled up to the fortification and killed the occupants.

It was later estimated that Jacobson's one-man assault had lasted no more than an hour. During that hectic period, he knocked out sixteen enemy positions and killed approximately seventy-five of the enemy without suffering any serious injury of his own. His rampage opened a gap in Hill 382's defenses and allowed the Marines to get through, though they were pushed back down later in the afternoon. The hill would be the scene of heavy fighting for days to come.

Looking back on that morning, Jacobson seemed surprised at his own actions. "I don't know how I did it," he remarked. "I had one thing in mind: getting my ass off that hill." Years later, he admitted to his wife, "I didn't even think about it at the time because your adrenaline is pumping so hard. It's kill or be killed. You charge ahead and do what you have to do."

It says something, perhaps, about medals that Jacobson's exploits on Iwo Jima first earned him a recommendation for the Silver Star. As this recommendation made its way through channels, Division attached the comment, "For his extraordinary heroism and the result of damage inflicted, it is believed that the Navy Cross medal is more appropriate." As that recommendation moved still further along, a high officer observed, "It appears from these very brief statements, that Jacobson was a very outstanding performer with his rocket launcher and that he may have been one of the leading single outstanding fighting Marines of the war. In justice to him and considering that he may be more highly recognized than by the award of the Navy Cross medal, a more complete investigation of this case is desired. . . . Whether or not investigation leads to higher award, it is believed that Jacobson should have a more complete statement of his exploits made a part of his official record."

That investigation led to the conclusion that Doug Jacobson's heroics on February 26, 1945, merited the Medal of Honor. The decoration was presented on October 5, 1945, at the White House. The ceremony was followed the next day by a parade in his honor down Port Washington's Main Street and a reception at the local Manhasset Bay Yacht

President Truman presents the Medal of Honor to Doug Jacobson during ceremonies on the White House lawn on October 5, 1945. After the war Jacobson was named the "outstanding living Marine enlisted man of World War II." USMC

Club. A panel of top newspapermen and combat veterans subsequently named Jacobson "the outstanding living Marine enlisted man of World War II." The selection was based on a comparison of records to determine the enlisted Marine Medal of Honor recipient whose combat record most closely resembled that of Sgt. Alvin York, the most famous hero of the American Expeditionary Forces in World War I.

Discharged from the service, Jacobson found civilian life not much to his liking. "The jobs turned out to be either $20-a-week office-boy jobs or being a salesman in order to wave the medal in a customer's face and dare him not to buy the product," he told a reporter later. He took a job with the Veterans Administration in Washington, D.C., but stayed only four months. In April 1946 he walked into the Marine recruiting office and signed up for three years. "I like the service better," he said simply, when asked what prompted his speedy exit from civilian life.

Doug Jacobson spent the next twenty years in the Marine Corps, with one more brief stab at civilian life from 1949 to 1952. He saw duty in China, graduated from officer candidate school, served during the Korean War, did a hitch with a helicopter squadron during the Vietnam War, and rose to the rank of major. His first marriage, to a hometown Port Washington girl, produced three daughters but eventually ended in divorce. He married his second wife, Joan, an elementary school teacher, in 1962, shortly before shipping out to Vietnam. She was surprised when they received an invitation to President John F. Kennedy's inauguration, a courtesy extended to all Medal of Honor recipients. "I had no idea what the Medal of Honor was," she admitted. "I had never heard of it. I came from this little town in northern California. I was pretty naïve."

A former Marine enlisted man remembered seeing Jacobson, then a captain in command of a company, at Camp Lejeune. "He was a real 'salt,'" recalled the Marine years later. "He had a sawed-off pool cue that he used as a walking stick/staff . . . and had a German shepherd dog that he would bring to the company area with him. He would double-park behind the company area and the Camp Lejeune MPs would come and park his Volkswagen convertible in the parking lot for him. . . . The [Medal of Honor] had its perks in those days!"

Friend and former Marine Clyde Prier described Jacobson as "a good-natured guy who would give you the shirt off his back. He was that typical Marine. He treated everyone like a long lost buddy." He never made a big deal about being awarded the Medal of Honor, added Prier. "He said he didn't think he deserved it . . . that he was just a kid doing what any other Marine would have done."

As Jacobson was preparing to retire in 1967, his commanding officer decided there was some unfinished business at hand—business that extended all the way back to 1942. "During my last month in the service, in 1967, the old man told me I was among the few majors in the Marines who did not have a high school diploma and asked me to consider taking the general equivalency diploma test," recalled

Jacobson. "After seeking the help of two of my captains, I returned the test and got my diploma."

After retiring from the military, Jacobson lived in New Jersey and sold real estate. The family moved to Florida in 1987. "He was always available to go anywhere to talk to veterans groups," said Joan. "He traveled all over the United States, speaking at Legion posts and VFW posts. Doug was a great reader, at least four or five books a week. . . . He was quite a golfer too. He started playing when he was ten years old and played ever since." And though his military career was over, he never removed his Marine rings, wearing them even when sleeping. "He was always ready," remarked Joan.

Douglas Jacobson died on August 20, 2000, at a hospital in Port Charlotte, Florida, at the age of seventy-four. The cause of death was pneumonia and congestive heart failure. He left his wife Joan, three daughters by his first marriage, and two grandchildren. His ashes were interred at Arlington National Cemetery. "He was a good friend and just a common, ordinary guy," recalled a fellow veteran. "He never flaunted his medals. We all knew he had them, but he never used them."

As the 4th Marine Division spent its life's blood on the rocky slopes of Hill 382, the 3rd Division was leaving a litter of dead Marines and knocked-out tanks along the flat, open runways of Motoyama Airfield No. 2 in its effort to reach the higher ground to the north. On Sunday, February 24, the 3rd Battalion, 21st Marines, did the near unimaginable: the Marines made a mad dash across the open ground and, despite heavy losses, gained a foothold on the slope at the northern edge of the airstrip.

Among the survivors was PFC Cecil ("Bub") Harvey. "I just ran as fast as I could run and the shells were popping all around me and the machine guns were bursting," he recalled. "It was just wild; everything was going on at once." Harvey ran up a small embankment on the other side of the airfield and almost fell into a Japanese machine-gun nest. Firing his BAR, he tumbled backward down the slope and took cover in a hole.

Suddenly, a wave of Japanese erupted out of a gully and charged into the Marines clinging to the slope. Harvey looked up to see a Japanese swinging a saber at a nearby Marine. "The Marine reached out and grabbed it with his bare hand and took it away from the Jap," remembered Harvey. "He then killed the Jap and came over and fell in our hole. His hand was badly damaged." Harvey saw another Marine take a bayonet through the collarbone as he fought hand-to-hand on the slope, but the Marine managed to kill his attacker. When the melee finally ended, the Marines had killed about fifty Japanese and remained in possession of the slope. By 1820, the companies were busily digging in with orders to hold at all costs. Success, however, had come at a high cost and it was decided to relieve the 21st Marines with the 9th Marines. The newcomers passed through under heavy fire the next morning. Among them was a largely uneducated private who had grown up in the American South, the product of a hardscrabble upbringing as a sharecropper's son. His name was Wilson Douglas Watson, and the next couple of days would change his life, perhaps not for the better.

PVT. WILSON D. WATSON

9th Marines, 3rd Marine Division
February 26–27, 1945

In February 1963 newspapers throughout the country carried an item about a forty-one-year-old U.S. Army private who was sitting in an Arkansas jail on a potential desertion charge. The aging soldier's name was Wilson Douglas Watson, and the reason his predicament made national news was simple: eighteen years earlier, then a United States Marine, he had been awarded the

Wilson D. Watson USMC

Medal of Honor for an act of almost suicidal heroism on Iwo Jima.

Doug Watson was born on February 16, 1921, in Tuscumbia, Alabama, the fourth child and third son of Charlie and Ada Watson, whose brood would eventually grow to nearly a dozen children. Charlie Watson farmed and worked as a laborer in a sawmill, but it was not an easy life, and children were expected to pitch in at an early age. Doug, a quiet unassuming boy and somewhat of a loner, later recalled that he started working in the sawmill at the age of eleven. One of his other childhood memories was going coon hunting with his father. His schooling ended with the seventh grade.

In 1938 Charlie Watson moved the family to a farm in Tyronza, Arkansas, in the state's rural northeast. The local economy had originally depended largely on timber, but as the trees were harvested the land was opened to farming, with cotton being the main crop. But by the time the Watsons arrived, the Tyronza area had seen some hard times. A flood in 1927 had caused a great deal of damage. The flood was followed by the stock market crash in 1929, and then by a severe drought that lingered for two years. The Bank of Tyronza failed in 1930, and many of the small farmers lost their land. The bulk of the acreage ended up in the hands of a few investors who rented it out to sharecroppers and tenant farmers such as Charlie Watson. On the 1940 census form, the forty-one-year-old Watson noted he was "working on own account." He had worked twenty-six weeks the previous year and made $100, he stated, to support a household consisting of his forty-year-old wife, Ada, and six sons ranging in age from eleven months to eighteen years.

Doug toiled alongside his father and brothers until the summer of 1942, when he traveled 120 miles to Little Rock and enlisted in the Marine Corps just one day after the 1st Marine Division landed on Guadalcanal. After completing basic training at the Marine Corps Recruit Depot in San Diego, he was deployed overseas on January 24, 1943, and saw combat at the Battle of Piva River at Bougainville and the invasion of Guam as an automatic rifleman with Company G, 2nd Battalion, 9th Marines, 3rd Division. Men who served with Watson recall him as small and wiry—about five feet eight inches tall and maybe 140 pounds—and soft-spoken with a pronounced Arkansas drawl. He was considered an outstanding BAR man.

Watson celebrated his twenty-third birthday at sea on February 16, only three days before the U.S. landing on Iwo Jima. As his battalion came ashore on February 24 in an effort to make up for some of the horrendous casualties already suffered by the V Amphibious Corps, there was considerable doubt he would celebrate a twenty-fourth birthday. "We were scattered across the airfield that night [Airfield No.1]," recalled Sgt. Jay Strode Jerome, who came ashore with the 1st Battalion, "and the Japs were shelling us with rockets. First squad of our platoon was practically all wiped out that night." It was a portent of things to come.

V Amphibious Corps needed to drive the enemy from the high ground in the center of Iwo Jima to open up the western beaches to supply ships. Unfortunately, the only option was frontal assault, and the Japanese had cunningly located their main-line defenses to take every advantage of the central plateau's dominating position. Watson's battalion, located on the far left of the 9th Marines, faced a line of fortified bluffs extending north from the western end of Motoyama Airfield No. 2. To get to the bluffs—and at the enemy—the Marines would have to cross the open runways. To help them get through the killing zone, the battalion was assigned twenty-six medium tanks.

Passing through the 21st Marines at 0930, the assault jumped off after a forty-five-minute artillery barrage. "The tanks drew heavy mortar fire which resulted in many casualties in the accompanying infantry; then they were subjected to fast, accurate cannon fire," reported 1st Lt. Robert A. Aurthur. A Weasel speeding across the airfield to evacuate the wounded took a direct hit, and men riding in the attached trailer leaped out with their clothes on fire. Nine tanks were knocked out, though the survivors persevered and managed to destroy a number of enemy installations, including three heavy guns.

For the infantry, the advance to the high ground was a nightmare. "The Ninth faced a heavy curtain of small-arms fire from exceptionally well-concealed positions—so well-concealed, in fact, that the men were unable to locate the source of the fire until within 25 yards of the emplacements," reported the regimental historian. "Areas in defilade to one enemy automatic weapon were covered by others and they presented a difficult problem to the attacking Marines. In addition, enemy mortar, artillery, and rocket fire was well zeroed in on all approaches to his position. . . . Jap snipers and machine-gunners shot hot sheets of steel at the infantry men as they advanced from shell hole to shell hole. When a man so much as exposed a hand, he drew fire."

Twenty-six-year-old Capt. Francis "Dutch" Fagan, a former Phi Beta Kappa and Beloit College football star, got G Company across the airfield, keeping the attack moving. Fagan had received the Navy Cross on Guam for rallying his men and stemming a Japanese breakthrough. His actions before Hill 382, where he "continuously exposed himself to intense machine gun, antitank, grenade and mortar barrages as he directed the sustained fire of his automatic weapons against heavily fortified pillboxes which he personally located and driving his tanks relentlessly forward . . . mak[ing] slow but steady progress toward the fanatically defended ridge position," would earn him a second Navy Cross, though Fagan would not live to receive the award.

Reaching the bluffs, the attack deteriorated into what one witness described as "rock fighting—fierce localized struggles for mounds of tumbled boulders, for 100-foot, craggy ridges, for sharp chasms and twisting gullies." By 1400, the assault was at a stalemate. An effort to bypass the Japanese center of resistance in front of the 2nd Battalion by driving forward with the 3rd Battalion just to the right came to naught as the Japanese responded with a torrent of fire. Both company commanders in the assault were killed within minutes. As casualties rapidly mounted, there were signs of disorganization, and some ground that had been seized was given up.

Watson's company clung to its foothold among the trenches and smoldering pillboxes on the rising ground north of Airfield No. 2, and tried to recoup for a renewed effort the following day. Among the walking wounded was Dutch Fagan, who had been shot in the shoulder but refused to be evacuated. He remained in command, aided by his exec, 1st Lt. Paul F. McLellan of Lantry, South Dakota. G Company spent a long sleepless night within arm's length of the Japanese lurking among the rocks. The next morning, at 0800, after a forty-five-minute artillery barrage, they were at it again.

Once again the brunt of the fighting fell on the 1st and 2nd Battalions. Gains were slight, even with the help of naval gunfire on suspected enemy mortar and machine-gun positions. Watson and his comrades were hit hard from the start, struggling forward a mere fifteen yards. As his squad sought cover from an unseen machine gun, Watson spotted the source of the fire. It was a pillbox. Blending in with the terrain, the structure barely cleared the ground just to his front and slightly to the right. A machine gun was firing from the slotted aperture.

Watson knew what had to be done. Half crawling, half running, he scrambled through the rubble and around to the flank of the pillbox where he was out of the direct line of fire. He loosed a burst from his BAR at the aperture, in an effort to keep the enemy machine gunners down. Continuing to chip away at the opening with short bursts from his BAR, he edged closer and closer, until he was finally near enough to almost smell the Japanese inside. Putting down the BAR, he took out a grenade, pulled the pin, leaned over and shoved it into the slot. The explosion killed four Japanese soldiers inside and took out two machine guns, as Watson dove into a gully past the sprawled bodies of two Marines who had been less quick, or perhaps less lucky.

Watson was not the only one closing with the enemy. By ones and twos, G Company went after the bunkers and pillboxes that had been killing them. Dutch Fagan was leading an attack on another pillbox when he was hit for the second time in two days, this time struck down by machine-gun fire. Badly wounded, the Wisconsin native was hauled away to the rear. Lieutenant McLellan took over the company.

Two Marines edge carefully toward the crest of a ridge. It was places like this where Doug Watson was credited with killing sixty Japanese, and where Gunny "Red" Walsh lost his life. USMC

Casualties continued to mount as G Company scratched away at the dug-in enemy. One Marine who pressed his luck too far was PFC Donald W. Day of Madison, Wisconsin, who persistently braved the withering fire to carry messages to the units fighting on the slope. Another Marine asked Day why he kept exposing himself—it was literally suicidal. "I don't seem to think about the danger," he replied. Soon after, he was shot in the back. The wound was fatal.

The noncoms trying to keep the attack going also suffered heavily. Gunnery Sgt. Jacob J. Rozenberg was killed. S/Sgt. George T. Jennings, normally a demolitions man, took over a platoon after its lieutenant was killed. He and his men managed to seize a prominent cluster of rocks where he set up an observation post and radioed back firing data for the mortars.

Seeing one of his inexperienced replacements struggling with a jammed BAR, Jennings ran over to help him and was shot in the chest. He died before help arrived.

It wasn't completely one-sided. Over in F Company, 1st Lt. Felix A. Endico went after a Japanese tank dug in among the rocks. "The tank was buttoned up, its long gun barrel pointing at the American positions," wrote a Marine combat correspondent. Endico climbed out of his shell hole and managed to put two grenades down the tank's gun barrel, knocking it out. He then noticed the swarm of bullets directed toward him. "So I beat it back to my hole," he remarked.

Doug Watson was also still in the fight. Around sunset, acting on orders from McLellan, the Arkansas sharecropper hefted his BAR and set out after another pillbox that had been raising hell with the assault. Again, he managed to get close enough to the aperture to shove a grenade inside. As it exploded, he scrambled around to the rear of the pillbox just as two surviving Japanese bolted from the exit. He gunned them both down with a burst from his BAR. Nightfall found G Company and the rest of the 2nd Battalion still clinging to a tenuous foothold on the rocky slope. "All day long the 9th battled to gain the high ground that blocked its way, but by nightfall there had been no significant gain," observed a Marine Corps monograph on the fighting.

Weather the next morning, February 27, was fair but overcast. Offshore, Dutch Fagan died of his wounds and was buried at sea. He left a wife and young son in Wisconsin. On the northern edge of Motoyama Airfield No. 2, the 9th Marines resumed the attack, making slight gains. "[The 2nd Battalion] moved in waves across the open ground behind a heavy barrage," wrote a Marine combat correspondent. "Enemy mortar shells fell smack among our men, as they went forward. Gaps appeared in our ranks. Our men ran and stumbled, falling over jagged rocks and diving from one shell hole to the next. Smoke and powdered rock filled the air, all but obscuring our view. The noise was deafening."

"You just keep going," observed G Company's new commanding officer, Paul McLellan, in retrospect. "You think about the danger. You can't help but think about it, but you have a job to do and you just keep moving forward." But the Japanese were also growing weary. The break came that afternoon. At 1250, after a ten-minute barrage by division and corps artillery, both the 1st and 2nd Battalions struck out in a coordinated attack. Stunned by the massed artillery fire, the Japanese defenders were slow to react. The fighting was hand-to-hand. "Grenades popped and flamethrowers spurted liquid fire," wrote a Marine later. "The Japs rushed from behind stones and were cut down. There was an enemy emplacement every ten yards hiding a machine gun. The sulfuric dust whipped up by the struggle jammed our weapons. Many men had to work their automatic rifle bolts by hand. A corporal, rushed by a knot of Japs, couldn't even get his bolt working manually. He grabbed the front of his weapon and used the stock as a club, bashing out the brains of the first Jap to reach him." The others were cut down by a burst of fire from the Marine's companion.

A flamethrower operator of Company E, 2nd Battalion, 9th Marines runs under fire on Iwo Jima. USMC

Watson's platoon made it to within about twenty yards of the crest of the ridge when another flurry of Japanese fire sent them scrambling for cover. But Watson had had enough. The crest was within reach and he wasn't about to stop. Firing his BAR from the hip, he continued up the hill under fierce mortar and machine-gun fire. Somehow, trailed by his loader, he made it to the crest and looked over. After days of battling an often-invisible enemy, the scene below was a rifleman's dream. The reverse slope was swarming with Japanese gathering to push the Marines back off the hill. Spotting Watson, the Japanese opened fire and started up after him. Behind the two lone Marines, the rest of G Company was still trying to fight its way the last few dozen yards to the crest. Whether they would get there in time—or even get there at all—was far from certain.

Watson raised his BAR and started shooting. Looking back on it later, he said he was "running on adrenaline," and that what he did was almost a reflexive response. "The only thing on my mind was that if you don't get those Japs, they are going to kill all of us," Watson said. "You just act, you don't think."

The magazine capacity for a Browning Automatic Rifle is twenty rounds. Firing short bursts, Watson ran through one magazine, dropped it, slammed in another, and ran that one dry as well. Shoot, drop magazine, insert new magazine, shoot, drop magazine . . . sticking doggedly to the crest, Watson kept the milling Japanese at bay for fifteen long minutes, often standing upright to get a clear field of fire. Finally, the rest of his platoon clambered up to the crest, their added firepower driving the Japanese to ground. By the time the reinforcements arrived, Watson had just two rounds left for his BAR. He was subsequently credited with killing approximately sixty Japanese.

Still the Japanese weren't finished. "A fierce hand-to-hand fight took place in gun pits and at the small entranceways to the Jap caverns," wrote a Marine combat correspondent. Though hit in the shoulder with fragments from a mortar round that landed only twenty yards away, Watson fought on for another half hour until an officer ordered him off the ridge to obtain medical treatment. "When it was all over and the other Marines came running up to him, one of them said, 'Get down Watson! We've got to get a corpsman up here to patch you up,'" recalled Carl Hurst, who got to know Watson in the 1960s. "He said he didn't even know that he had been hit until he looked down and saw blood was spurting everywhere. He had not felt a thing."

With the bluff seized, the 2nd Battalion was able to move forward almost 1,700 yards—a huge distance compared to previous days when gains were measured almost in inches. Watson was sent back to have his wounds treated. They proved to be relatively minor. Forty-eight hours later he was back with G Company, but his combat days were coming to a close. On March 1, the 9th Marines tangled with the better part of an enemy infantry battalion supported by tanks in an area just east of Motoyama Village. "The Japs fought from well-concealed caves dug deep into rock, and from large bunkers, each protected by rifle pits and deep holes dug straight down into the earth to the depth of 15 to 40 feet," reported the regimental historian. On March 2, during an assault on this position, Watson was shot through the neck. This time there was no coming back after a quick patch job. The wound required his evacuation from the island.

Watson was on Guam when he learned he was to be awarded the Medal of Honor for his actions on February 26 and 27. Dutch Fagan had also been recommended for the Medal of Honor for his handling of G Company in the assault on the high ground north of Motoyama Airfield No. 2. For reasons that are hard to understand, that award was knocked down to the Navy Cross—Fagan's second. Lt. Paul McLellan, who took over G Company after Fagan was hit, and who was himself severely wounded on March 15, was also awarded the Navy Cross.

Doug Watson received the Medal of Honor in a ceremony on October 5, 1945, at the White House. None of his relatives could attend, as his family received notice of the ceremony too late. "Our parents were real proud of him," recalled his brother Kenneth. "It was pretty remarkable what he did, and to be so young. He never bragged about it, though. He just said it was something he had to do." His hometown of Earle, Arkansas—population 1,900—threw a big parade to welcome the hero home. "They even brought down the Budweiser Clydesdales from St. Louis," recalled another brother, Paul. Newspaper headlines trumpeted, "Killer of 60 Japs Welcomed Home." At a crowded reception in the local high school auditorium, attended by the governor, among other dignitaries, Watson was presented with a 12-gauge shotgun as a token of the town's esteem. "I guess I grew up with a gun," he remarked, apparently uncertain about how to respond to all the attention. He later lost the shotgun in a card game. It was, perhaps, an early indication that whatever it is that prompts a man to hold off swarms of enemy soldiers with a BAR virtually alone does not necessarily mesh well with the expectations of his civilian admirers.

Discharged from the Marines, the Arkansas farm boy found himself at loose ends. He went back into the service within a few months, this time enlisting in the Army Air Corps. "The crop's in, so I've signed up for another two-year hitch to start with," he remarked when reporters asked for comment. A year later, a newspaper reported: "Army Pvt. Wilson D. Watson of Earle, Ark., winner of a Congressional Medal of Honor, has been assigned to the army food service school here [Columbus, Ga.] to learn to be a cook." If the reporter found anything odd about a Medal of Honor recipient training to be an army cook, he held his tongue.

By about 1961, Watson was serving as a mess hall cook at Fort Rucker, Alabama, and had a wife and son in Marked Tree, Arkansas. "He was quiet, unassuming and something of a loner," recalled Carl Hurst, who had charge of the mess hall storeroom. "He certainly did not fit the image of a hero." As far as Hurst could see, the aging GI "wouldn't hurt a flea." Watson had also become a heavy drinker. "Every payday he would disappear for three or four days," remarked Hurst. "It was kind of a joke in the company. They would laugh and say, 'Well, Watson's gone again, but he'll be back when he runs out of money.' He made private first class once, but got busted the next day for being AWOL."

In February 1963 Watson was arrested in Marion, Arkansas, after being absent without leave from his unit since October. Jailer Robert Warren, who had gone to school with Watson when they were young, said Watson told him he had been trying to obtain a discharge from the army, but was "getting the run around" on his application. "He told me they had his records messed up," said Warren. "He said they were just passing him around and he had got tired of it all and just drove off." Interviewed in his cell, Watson seemed unimpressed with the uproar, saying he "just got fed up with the Army" and left. "I just got tired of messing with them," he said without elaboration. "I don't know what they are going to do. All I want is out."

The story of "the hero arrested for desertion" hit newspapers across the country. News accounts reported that Watson had been taken to the Fort Sill, Oklahoma, hospital for "rest and consultation." He was subsequently transferred to Walter Reed Army Hospital. "He seems like a heck of a nice guy who just got in over his head with personal problems," remarked a Fort Sill information officer. "We hope to get everything ironed out." Reporters also noted that an emergency loan had been arranged to help Watson's wife with financial difficulties.

In the end, everything was indeed "ironed out." Watson returned to duty, finally retiring from the army as a staff sergeant in 1966. He returned to the family farm in Arkansas and later served from 1969 to 1972 as the game warden in Clarkesville. In 1992, a forty-three-year-old out-of-wedlock daughter, the result of a two-year relationship he had while in the service at Lowry Air Force Base in Colorado, contacted him. Put up for adoption by her mother, the woman had spent thirty years seeking her natural parents. Watson, who had recently suffered a heart attack and who still carried twenty-seven pieces of mortar shell in his body, professed to be delighted by the reunion. "It's hard to explain. But I've never felt better in my life," he said.

Doug Watson died on December 19, 1994, and is buried in Russell Cemetery in his hometown of Russellville. He was survived by his wife, a son, two daughters, and eight brothers. Ironically, his grave marker, which bears an engraving of the Medal of Honor, lists his final branch of service, the U.S. Army, along with "World War II" and "Korea." There is no reference to the Marine Corps or Iwo Jima.

Though Watson hit some rough spots after the war, what he did that one day on Iwo Jima earned him enough respect for a lifetime. But he refused to think of himself as a hero. Years later, now in the destructive grip of alcohol, he was approached by a young soldier at Fort Rucker who had learned of his Medal of Honor. Watson admitted he had received the medal, but insisted he was no hero. The young soldier would have done the same thing in his place, he said. "Look," he added, "there were probably a hundred Marines there that day that deserve this medal more than me, but the right people did not see them."

Not everyone agreed. As jailer Robert Warren observed to reporters while watching over the AWOL GI in an Arkansas cell in 1963, despite all Watson's troubles, "I guess he was about as big a hero as you can get."

While the 3rd Division battled its way across Airfield No. 2 and the high ground beyond, the 5th Division was engaged on the left. Fighting on February 26 yielded about 300 yards and brought the front to within about 1,000 yards of Hill 362A. The hill turned out to be the western anchor of the enemy's main cross-island defenses. Dominating the division's route of advance north, 362A became a critical objective. But first the Marines would have to get there. On February 27, the 3rd Battalion, 27th Marines came in on the division right. The battalion faced the most commanding terrain in the division area. Its progress—or lack of it—would largely determine the progress of the division as a whole.

GUNNERY SGT. WILLIAM G. WALSH

27th Marines, 5th Marine Division
February 27, 1945

William "Red" Walsh USMC

On D+8 the 27th Marines lost Red Walsh in the jungle of stone around Hill 362A.

"Red" was Gunnery Sgt. William Gary Walsh, a former Marine Raider who had joined the 5th Marine Division after participating in the Northern Solomons campaign in 1943. "He was a pretty good sergeant," recalled Sgt. Dean Voight, another former Raider assigned to the same platoon. "Strict, but fair. Honest . . . tough. . . . He let you know he was in charge. He wouldn't take nuthin' from nobody."

Most accounts state that Red Walsh was born in Roxbury, Massachusetts, on April 7, 1922, but his true background was a bit more complicated. He was actually born in Maine, apparently to a single or abandoned mother. According to Walsh family descendants, the infant, whose real name was William Gary, was placed in the care of his grandmother. When she became too ill to look after the boy, she gave him to her close friend, Mary Walsh, who lived in Roxbury. The timing is unclear, but by 1930 the grandmother had apparently died and William was listed in census records as the "adopted" son of Mary Walsh.

Mary herself had seen more than her share of tragedy. Emigrating from Ireland in 1898, she married Irish-born Dennis Walsh, a Boston fireman. The couple had two daughters, and Mary was pregnant with a third child in late 1915 when Dennis was killed fighting a fire in downtown Boston four days before Christmas. Walsh and another fireman died when the burning building collapsed; a third firefighter somehow survived. A month later Mary gave birth to a son. She named the boy Dennis after his father.

Luckily for her family, the widow Mary Walsh proved to be a very resilient woman. "You talk about work ethic!" marveled her great-nephew, Michael J. Murphy, years later. "She worked as a housekeeper and a cook"; she took in boarders and was a waitress. "They used to go up to Winnipesauke [New Hampshire] during the summer. She was a cook in the mansions, the old, old Yankee money," related Murphy. And with all of that responsibility, she still took in young William Gary as her own son.

The family called the youngster "Billy," but to the kids on the neighborhood ball field he was "Red" by virtue of his sandy red hair. "I know he was quite athletic," remarked Murphy. "He was a baseball player. And I think he worked for a trucking company at one time." If not for the war, Red probably would have ended up in the Boston Fire Department like Mary's husband before him. "I kind of think if Billy had come back [from the war] he would have been brought into that," speculated Murphy.

The year 1941 saw Red playing catcher on the Dorgan Athletic Club baseball team from Dorchester. A soft-spoken youngster, he was remembered as a solid player—"the guy who handled pitchers with that easy way of his," remarked a sportswriter covering the team. Then came Pearl Harbor. That same night, eighteen-year-old Red Walsh and the entire Dorgan baseball team trooped down to the Federal Building in Boston to be on hand when the recruiting offices opened the next morning. They slept on the hard benches and on the floor, and they were first in line when the Marine sergeants showed up Monday morning.

After boot camp at Parris Island and advanced training at Camp Lejeune, Walsh shipped out to Samoa, part of a buildup intended to fend off a feared Japanese attack. Those fears proved unfounded. Looking for more immediate action, Walsh volunteered for the Raiders. He joined the 3rd Raider Battalion and served with that outfit during the Bougainville campaign. Returning to the United States when the Raider battalions were disbanded, Walsh attended noncommissioned officers school. He was promoted to platoon sergeant and assigned to the 5th Marine Division, drawing a billet with G Company, 27th Marines. One of the men he asked to come aboard was fellow Raider Dean Voight, a veteran of the famous Carlson Raid on Makin Island. "He was a platoon sergeant and I was a buck sergeant and he wanted me in his platoon," remembered Voight.

Physically, Walsh was of medium height, about five feet seven inches tall, "light build, but ornery" with "reddish sandy hair," a "feisty little Irishman" who "just liked it rough and ready so that's why he had signed up for the Raider Battalion," recalled Voight. Walsh also had what Voight considered a rather amusing idiosyncrasy. Somewhere along the line, probably playing baseball, he had lost a front tooth, which had been replaced with a dental plate—"a big tooth he kept sticking out every time he'd get excited or nervous," recalled Voight with a laugh. "Then he'd pop it back in. He'd pop it out when he would get excited."

The sergeant also found time for romance. Prior to shipping over-seas again, he hastily married twenty-two-year-old Mary Louise Pen-rod, a member of the Marine Corps Women's Reserve. Mary's father was a chemist with International Harvester in Wisconsin, but the fact that she wasn't Irish Catholic prompted a "big blowout" in the Walsh family, according to Red's great-nephew, Michael J. Murphy. "My great grandmother went through the roof," remarked Murphy. "Typical Boston Irish family. My grandmother and great aunt never spoke about it. It was a taboo subject."

Walsh soon had more immediate concerns as his platoon entered the maelstrom of Iwo Jima. The fighting was ferocious. Even combat veterans were taken aback. "Iwo Jima was as close to hell as you could get," recalled Voight, "I can't even begin to describe it to you. It was always hot—active gunfire all the time and explosions going off. People getting killed right and left."

On February 27, G Company was thrown into the fight for a low ridge guarding the approach to Hill 362A, a key to the Japanese defenses north of Motoyama Airfield No. 2.

The 3rd Battalion was directed to move up into position before dawn and launch the attack at 0800. Any hopes the Marines might have had for a reasonably quiet night were soon erased. Shortly after midnight a terrific mortar and artillery barrage slammed down on the battalion as it tried to get some fitful sleep in scattered craters and holes. Buried in volcanic rubble, men clawed their way free, shaking and praying as the shelling went on and on. A shard of metal struck one man in the helmet, penetrating the steel and lodging in his skull. Unable to remove the shell fragment, his buddies dumped sulfa on him and wrapped his head, helmet and all, in bandages. A lieutenant was blown out of his hole and left lying unconscious on the open ground. Another blast shredded a sergeant. His foxhole buddy lifted the non-com's head, only to hear his dying gurgles. For two hours, mortar shells and artillery rounds worked the Marines over before finally shifting away to other targets.

Two Marines pass by an upright rifle marking the body of a comrade. USMC

As the battalion evacuated its casualties, runners began moving through, telling the company commanders to get their people saddled up and ready to move. The three companies—G, H, and I—stumbled forward in the dark over the 500 yards to the assembly point, passing the scattered corpses of 3rd Division Marines killed in earlier attacks.

There was no talking. Now and again a flare popped overhead and the men froze in place. They arrived just before dawn in front of the low ridge blocking the way to Hill 362A.

With the assault scheduled for 0800, G Company waited, their apprehension tempered by the satisfaction of watching as their own artillery punished the ridge only fifty yards away. Corps and divisional artillery and naval gunfire raised curtains of smoke and dust. Just before the infantry moved out, truck-mounted launchers from the 3rd Rocket Detachment plastered the area with a barrage of 4.5-inch rockets, followed by a final softening up from carrier planes roaring in low over the blasted hills to hit the Japanese defenders with bombs and rockets.

As the planes pulled out, the G Company Marines rose out of their holes in a frontal assault. "Let's move! Move out!" shouted Walsh, loping forward at a crouch. Any lingering hopes that the artillery had broken enemy resistance were quickly and cruelly put to rest. The Marines made it up onto the slope and were promptly hit by point-blank fire from three directions. The survivors recoiled and took what cover they could find.

In an effort to keep the assault moving, Walsh gathered up a group of men and led them around toward the right. The movement met heavy fire, and the Marines went to ground in a line of shallow trenches below the crest. Again Walsh reorganized his men. "Hell, we can't stay here!" he shouted, as Japanese bullets probed for them. "Let's hit the sons-a-bitches again!" Once more the Marines charged for the crest, only to run into a hail of grenades from Japanese dug in on the reverse slope. Walsh and a handful of survivors rolled into a hole below the top of the ridge, trying to catch their breath and regroup.

Firing his machine gun at caves and rock grottos along the face of the ridge, twenty-three-year-old Cpl. Robert J. Gjerness, a former Marine Raider and farm laborer from Minnesota, couldn't see much of the Japanese besides the occasional flash of a hand contributing to the rain of grenades pelting down on the Marines below. The attack was clearly in serious trouble. The assault troops were pinned down and there weren't enough able-bodied men to get the growing number of wounded out. Gjerness could see Gunny Walsh in a hole only about fifteen feet from the top of the hill. Some of the survivors periodically scrambled back to get out from under the grenades, but Walsh apparently had wounded men in the hole with him. He would not leave them. As grenades rolled in on him, Walsh pitched them back out in what was the most incredible display of courage Gjerness had ever seen.

Sgt. Dean Voight had taken cover nearby. "I was repairing a BAR for one of my men who had trouble with it and I happened to be sitting right below, and I looked up and I see this Jap coming across up on the cliff," recalled Voight. "And I grabbed my rifle, 'cause I see he had a hand grenade in his hand—it was a potato masher, an old type stick hand grenade. And he was getting ready to throw and I shot him. Now I don't know whether I killed him, but I do know he went down and threw the grenade."

The grenade landed among the knot of Marines huddled with Walsh. "Grenade! Grenade!" someone yelled. Without a word that anyone could hear, Red Walsh spontaneously rolled over on the grenade as it exploded. He died there in the trench. "He jumped on the grenade to save his squad but he didn't quite make it. Most of them were killed too," recalled Voight. While clearly proud of his friend, Voight, who was himself severely wounded on Iwo Jima later in the campaign, was not surprised by his actions. "He was protective of his men," remarked Voight. "It was the one thing we had instilled in us because without them you've got nothing."

Forced off the slope, the Marines reorganized and tried again. This time they made it to the crest to stay, the exhausted G Company survivors looking out at Hill 362A looming up only a few hundred yards away. Gunny Walsh's poncho-covered body was eventually lugged down the ridge and interred in the 5th Marine Division cemetery on Iwo Jima. He had died only a few weeks before his twenty-third birthday. After the war his remains were returned to the United States. On April 20, 1948, the one-time star baseball catcher was interred at Arlington National Cemetery.

The Secretary of the Navy presented Red's Medal of Honor to his young widow on February 8, 1946, in Washington, D.C. Also attending the ceremony were Mary Walsh, Red's sister, his young nephew, and his widow's parents. In later years, Red's widow dropped from sight and the Walsh descendants were unsure what happened to her. "I don't think they ever saw her after that—after Washington," said Murphy, who once made some unsuccessful efforts to track her down. Whatever the case, at some point Red's widow gave his Medal of Honor to the Walsh family. It has since passed into the possession of a great-nephew who served in the Marines during the First Gulf War.

Interestingly, the Walsh family would be back in the news within a few years after the medal presentation. While Red was in the Marines, his older brother, Dennis—the boy Mary Walsh named after her fireman husband—had been undergoing novitiate training as a Franciscan priest, taking the name Cormac. When the Korean War broke out, Cormac Walsh joined the U.S. Army as a chaplain and was sent to Korea, where he accumulated four Silver Stars and a Presidential Citation for aiding wounded soldiers while under heavy fire, making him the most highly decorated chaplain of the war. In 1955, Cormac was selected as Chaplain of the Year. He and his mother were received by President Eisenhower, an occasion that also gave them the opportunity to visit Red's grave in Arlington National Cemetery. Cormac went on to become a highly regarded prison chaplain at Dannemora State Prison in Clinton, New York. He died in 1977, following his mother by less than ten years.

"If you go downtown in Boston there's a plaque to my great grandfather [the firefighter]," observes Michael Murphy. "My uncle—William Gary Walsh—he has an American Legion Post named after him and a ballpark in Dorchester. And my Uncle Cormac has a bridge named after him. It's quite the family."

But it's Red Walsh the Marines remember. "Yeah, he was a good boy," remarked Dean Voight sixty years after the war. "There's no argument there."

Marines weren't the only Americans in harm's way on Iwo Jima. Sailors were also on the firing line, charged with ministering to the wounded. The Marine Corps had no medical service of its own—medical treatment was provided by U.S. Navy personnel. Indistinguishable from Marines except for their medical bags, they were pharmacist's mates and hospital apprentices, collectively referred to as "corpsmen." To the Marine infantryman, most were simply "Doc." Out of combat, these navy men were often ribbed by cocky young Marines about being members of a "lesser service." There was no ribbing on Iwo Jima. Many a Marine would leave Iwo Jima alive by the grace of God and a corpsman who risked death to run out under fire to tie off a traumatic amputation, clamp a spurting artery, or try to keep a gut-shot kid alive long enough to reach an aid station. As casualties passed the 7,000 mark the first week of the battle, their days became a horrific blur of spilled guts, shattered limbs, and blood. And still they continued. Their dedication was beyond reproach.

"I had a medical kit on each shoulder," recalled Pharmacist's Mate 2nd Class Stanley Dabrowski. "In the left pouch we carried all our battle dressings, sulfa powder, burn dressings. In the right pouch were morphine syrettes, tags, iodine pencils, ammonia inhalants, hemostats and scalpels, and other assorted equipment. . . . The first thing you had to do was assess the casualty. Almost certainly they had immediately gone into shock. Combating shock and hemorrhage were the first priorities. We used tourniquets and hemostats. There were so many cases where there were traumatic amputations—no arm or both legs. And then there were abdominal injuries—torn-out intestinal tracts. Often I was beside myself trying to decide what to do with these people."

As the 3rd Battalion, 27th Marines, struggled toward Hill 362A, the battalion's chief medical officer, navy lieutenant James Vedder, followed behind with his group of corpsmen, establishing an aid station in an abandoned Japanese revetment on the edge of Airfield No. 2.

The battalion had suffered serious casualties on the approaches to Hill 362A on D+8—including Sgt. Red Walsh, who was now beyond the ministrations of a corpsman—but these were just a prelude to the bitter resistance that lay ahead. Following Walsh's death, the remnants of G Company had managed to fight their way to the top of the ridge and stay there. By day's end the 27th Marines had gained some 500 yards, penetrating into the heart of the enemy defense belt. Now they waited in the shadow of Hill 362A. Among them was a sailor from Tennessee who hoped one day to become a doctor.

PHARMACIST'S MATE 1ST CLASS JOHN H. WILLIS

27th Marines, 5th Marine Division
February 28, 1945

*John Harlan Willis
U.S. Navy*

John Harlan Willis set two goals for himself as a young man coming of age along the banks of the Duck River in Maury County, Tennessee. One was to become a doctor. The other was to marry Winfrey Morel.

Born June 10, 1921, in Columbia, Tennessee, sixty miles south of Nashville, John Willis was one of twelve children of John and Margaret (Harlan) Willis. "He came from a big family and had a hard time growing up as a boy," recalled Winfrey Morel, whose father worked a farm in the area. Willis met Winfrey at Columbia Central High School and quickly decided she was the girl for him. "I used to get so aggravated at him because he'd tell the other boys, 'Don't you date her because I'm going to marry her someday.' And that was the farthest thing from my mind," laughed Winfrey.

Though he was an excellent student, John Harlan's homelife left much to be desired. Around his junior year in high school, fed up with the constant friction with his father, Willis moved in with his beloved grandfather, who, as Winfrey later said, "adored the ground he walked on last week." Willis was a big, well-muscled youngster, "strong as an ox," but he had little time for school sports or other extracurricular activities, recalled Winfrey. He spent most of his time working at the local grocery store. "He'd get up and go down there and open up and clean up and get everything ready for the store to open up at eight o'clock," said Winfrey. "And then he'd go to school and come back in the afternoon and work till five. . . . He'd cut up some, but basically he was serious-minded about his work and everything. He knew what he wanted to do."

What John Willis wanted to do, besides marry Winfrey Morel, was to become a doctor. He had no money to pay for college, but he had a plan. He'd get his start in the navy. "He was hell-bent on coming out and being a doctor," remarked Winfrey. "That was his whole goal from the day he went in the navy. That's what he wanted to do."

Graduating from high school in 1940, Willis enlisted in the navy and was accepted for training as a hospital corpsman. Conscientious and dedicated, he served at various naval hospitals on the East Coast, receiving high praise from his superiors. Then came Pearl Harbor. Now a pharmacist's mate 3rd class, Willis wanted nothing more than to get out of the stateside hospitals and into the action overseas. "He wanted to get overseas so bad and they wouldn't turn him loose," recalled Winfrey. The soft-spoken youngster who wanted to be a doctor was too good at his job; none of his superiors wanted to lose him. But Willis was nothing if not persistent. He was finally accepted for service with the Paramarines. As it turned out, the Paramarines and Raider battalions were disbanded about the time he finished his combat training, and Willis, like many of the members of those elite units, was sent to the newly formed 5th Marine Division.

Meanwhile he and Winfrey—or "Pete," as she was known to her friends—had been in constant contact, writing to one another almost every day. In 1944, while Willis was stationed in California, she traveled out to join him and they were married on June 25. Their time together as man and wife was brief. John's outfit, the 3rd Battalion,

27th Marines, shipped out to Hawaii later that summer, and Winfrey returned to Columbia. February found Willis's battalion standing off Iwo Jima. Writing to Winfrey at about this time, he confided, "Having you to love me and to want me back home is really a great source of peace of mind and also it will make me be especially careful while on the beach. . . . I love you with all my heart Dearest and am really looking forward to our life together soon."

Leading the battalion medical personnel was Lt. James S. Vedder, a thirty-two-year-old surgeon from Marshfield, Wisconsin. In addition to a chief pharmacist's mate and assistant battalion surgeon, Vedder had forty-eight navy corpsmen and sixteen Marine litter bearers under his command. "I had assigned twenty-four of the more experienced corpsmen to the three combat companies that formed the spearhead of our battalion," he recalled. "As a result, eight corpsmen were available in each of these companies to render expert first aid to the Marines immediately after a man received an injury. Pharmacist Mates 1st Class Bokousky, Willis, and Thronson were the senior men respectively in G, H, and I Companies." The other twenty-four corpsmen would work from the battalion aid station. The litter bearers were all Marine privates who had been inducted into the service only a few months before. All were eighteen years old and each one's name began with the letter "B," which led Vedder to assume they had been assigned en bloc from some boot camp in the United States.

Vedder felt concern about the young, inexperienced litter bearers, who would be among those in the greatest danger as they carried out the wounded, but he had no reservations about Willis and the other two pharmacist's mates he had assigned to lead the corpsmen serving with the assault companies. Willis struck him as "a fine young southern gentleman. . . . His full round face and curly brown hair made him appear much too young to be a member of this Marine expeditionary force." But Vedder knew Willis was tougher than he looked. "His tough internal fiber belied these external appearances . . . " Vedder observed.

"He could hold his own with his hard-bitten comrades and still be liked and respected by these front line troops."

Later Vedder remembered Willis raising only one concern as they prepared to land on Iwo. The previous day, the corpsmen had been issued small bottles of medicinal brandy for the wounded—a hoard that had become a matter of great interest to certain alcohol-deprived Marine officers. At their final meeting before landing, Willis raised his hand in response to Vedder's call for any questions or concerns. "Since the brandy was passed out yesterday, my company officers have been bugging me to turn it over to them," reported Willis, obviously looking for some authority to deal with the badgering.

"Navy regulations and the colonel say you are to keep it and to dole it out to the wounded only," replied Vedder.

Willis gave Vedder a relieved smile and said, "Thanks, Dr. Vedder."

By the last day of February, that conversation seemed a lifetime ago, and the unauthorized disposal of medicinal brandy had become a minor concern to officers and corpsmen alike. Desperate fighting had brought the Marines within reach of Hill 362A, but the cost to Willis's company had been high. The steady stream of casualties included H Company commanding officer Capt. Ralph Hall, killed the night of the landing when a Japanese shell landed in the hole that served as company headquarters, and killed or wounded all the occupants.

A corpsman, either Willis or someone in his small medical detachment, attempted to save the captain, but it was no use. Lt. Richard Johnstone cradled Hall, a former Paramarine and veteran of Bougainville, in his arms as the corpsman tried to get a plasma transfusion started. The captain was in great pain, badly burned, and bleeding in dozens of places. "Johnny," whispered Hall, looking up at Johnstone, "this is rough." Then he closed his eyes and died. Also killed by the shell were a radioman, two runners, and H Company's executive officer, Capt. Robert McCahill, who had been literally obliterated in the blast. The corpsmen and Marines could find no trace of his body.

There were more horrors the next day as H Company attacked across the open ground of Airfield No. 2. One Marine was decapitated by a shell as he ran, his headless body continuing for several steps before collapsing. Another man in the stream of wounded had no face. Captain Hall's replacement, Lt. Russell Hewitt, lasted less than two days before an explosion practically blew off his foot. D+2 had also been bad. Cpl. Billy Cagle, hit by a mortar fragment, remembered stumbling to an enormous shell crater where one of Willis's men, Pharmacist's Mate 3rd Class Jack G. Cupp, knelt surrounded by at least ten broken, bleeding men. Intent on his work, Cupp never looked up. Cagle surveyed the scene for a moment, then thought, "I'm not hit bad enough to be here." He made his way back to his squad, where one of his buddies patched him up as best he could. Meanwhile, shellfire blocked the evacuation route to the battalion aid station. Willis radioed Vedder to say he needed help immediately to get the wounded out. Vedder personally led three litter teams up to H Company, found Willis, and took out three wounded men unable to walk out under their own power.

On February 28, H Company attacked on the battalion right, in the effort to seize Hill 362A. The large flat-topped mound was more than just a hill; it was a fortress. The Japanese had dug a warren of tunnels—some virtual highways—connecting subterranean assembly areas, hospitals, and storehouses, and allowing the sheltered movement of troops from one area to another. The near-vertical sides were studded with concrete blockhouses, pillboxes, bunkers, and caves. A necklace of rocky outcroppings around the base, in combination with steep-sided ravines and gullies, made tank support nearly impossible. It was against this bastion that the 3rd Battalion attacked the morning of February 28, getting up out of their holes at 0815 and starting forward over 200 yards of bare, rolling ground.

The Marines immediately came under heavy—and extremely accurate—rifle fire. Twelve men went down in three minutes, eleven of them shot through the head. Vedder moved his aid station forward at 1300 hours, picking through the broken terrain amid a litter of Japanese

Sketch of Hill 362A, made by the 31st U.S. Naval Construction Battalion. Dotted lines show the underground Japanese tunnel system. U.S. Navy/USMC

corpses, bloated dead horses, and smashed artillery. He was surprised to see that many of the dead Japanese sported luxuriant black beards. Setting up shop in a bowl-like depression just west of the lower slopes of Hill 362A, he was soon treating a stream of casualties, including the captain of I Company, who had been fatally concussed by an exploding shell. As Vedder had feared, corpsmen and litter bearers attempting to retrieve the wounded proved especially vulnerable. A weeping private, just back from trying to pick up one of Willis's wounded, confronted Dr. Vedder at the 3rd Battalion aid station. "Brautigen, Blaunch, and myself went up the hill to get a guy from H Company," he sobbed. "Just as we picked up the litter, a machine gun opened up. Everybody got shot dead except me."

Willis lasted through the morning, but shortly after 1400 he was hit in the shoulder by shell fragments. Ordered off the hill, he had the wound dressed at the aid station. Then, obviously knowing how badly he was needed on the firing line, he headed back toward Hill 362A. The day before, dashing off a quick note to Winfrey, he tried to be reassuring. "I know you must be worried, but there is really no need for it as I am confident that as long as I live and think right, me and all my corpsmen will come through all right," he wrote.

Doc Vedder was much less sanguine. His corpsmen and litter bearers were getting shot down as fast as he could send them forward. He finally contacted regiment and asked for riflemen to accompany the medical personnel. "Doc, we have nobody to spare," an officer told him.

"We've got to get help in getting new casualties out."

"There won't be any fresh casualties," the officer replied. The battalion was going to be pulled back from the hill, he told Vedder.

Arriving back at Hill 362A with his bandaged shoulder, Willis found plenty of work waiting for him. The fighting was at arm's length. Marines clung to the rocky outcroppings under a shower of enemy grenades. A Marine, his legs shattered by a grenade blast, dragged himself into a shell crater. Willis went to help. He flopped into the hole to find a second wounded man sheltering there as well. Willis went to work on the wounded Marines, but the Japanese on the higher ground had already singled them out.

Joining in with his carbine in a futile effort to suppress the torrent of fire coming from above, Platoon Sgt. David J. Moses, a twenty-six-year-old mortar man from Wheeling, West Virginia, saw a grenade plummet into the hole with Willis. The corpsman grabbed it and threw it out. It exploded among the rocks as Willis turned back to his patients. Marine riflemen continued to fire at the enemy, unseen except for a flash of movement now and again, followed by the slow arc of a grenade falling from above. Moses saw another grenade plunk down into Willis's shell hole. Again Willis scooped it up and tossed it out.

Word began to pass among the Marines, sent down from Lt. Charles McCumby, H Company's third commander since the landing: "Fall back!" Men began to leapfrog back from shell hole to shell hole, dragging the wounded. The dead were left. Still in the shell hole with the two wounded Marines, Willis was in trouble. Refusing to abandon his patients, he had already lived longer than he could have expected. But the Japanese were relentless. Grenades continued to rain down on the three men. Again and again, Willis managed to throw them out or bat them aside before they exploded. According to the official report, he survived eight grenades in all, though it seems unlikely that anyone on the scene was in a position to keep an accurate count. Whatever the number—six, or eight, or twenty-eight—there were too many. As yet another grenade fell into the shell hole, Willis grabbed for it too late. It exploded in his hand, killing everyone in the crater.

Witnesses were stunned. By now they were accustomed to violent death, but this was something different. Willis's best friend, Pharmacist's Mate 2nd Class Harvey M. Prince, showed up at the battalion aid station to relay the news to Dr. Vedder. Prince was crying. "How can I tell his wife about his death?" he sobbed. "He could have saved himself after the first grenade landed by pulling back and abandoning his patients. As it turns out, all three of them are dead anyway."

"You know Willis could not have done that," replied Vedder. "He could never have lived with himself afterwards."

Lucy Sparkman shared an apartment with Winfrey Willis, who had returned to Tennessee after John shipped out. "I remember the day Winfrey got a letter that John Harlan Willis, her husband, had been killed on Iwo Jima," Sparkman recalled. "The letter came from a buddy who was there and saw it happen. She knew it was true, but there was a period of waiting to get the news from the War Department that his death was official." Winfrey was seven months pregnant when the news arrived.

A few weeks later, Winfrey Willis gave birth to a son, John Harlan Willis Jr. By then Iwo Jima had been secured and her husband's body was lying in the 5th Marine Division cemetery. Meanwhile, Dr. James Vedder recommended Willis for the Medal of Honor. The following year, carrying her son, Winfrey traveled to Washington with John's sister and grandfather, and accepted the medal from Secretary of the Navy James Forrestal.

Winfrey had a difficult time coming to terms with John's death. She found herself brooding, reading and rereading his old letters to her. Her grief was becoming obsessive, incapacitating. One day her family doctor came over to the house and told her to get the letters together. "You're going to go crazy if you don't quit reading those things," he told her. "The only way to stop you from reading them is to burn them up." They went out into the backyard, found a bare spot, and burned all of the letters. "In a way I was glad they were gone and in another way I was sorry they were burned," she said sixty years later. "I know I would have lost my mind. Because there was something about that bundle of letters that just drew me back like a magnet."

Mrs. Winfrey Willis, widow of John Harlan Willis, receives her husband's posthumous Medal of Honor from Secretary of the Navy James Forrestal at a ceremony on December 3, 1945. U.S. Navy

Winfrey did move on with her life. In July 1946, she married Kenneth B. Duke, managing editor for the *Columbia Daily Herald*, whom she met at the presentation of the Medal of Honor. They subsequently had a son together. She attended Draughons Junior Business College, and upon graduating worked for the state of Tennessee until retirement, after which she sold insurance to the Tennessee National Guard under the name of Duke Insurance Agency. Kenneth Duke passed away in 1962. In 1986, Winfrey married Arnold R. Willis (no known relation), who preceded her in death in 1990.

Following the war, John Willis's body was returned to Tennessee. He is buried in Rose Hill Cemetery in Columbia. In 1965, Winfrey loaned the Medal of Honor and some of her husband's personal effects, including his dog tags and uniform and the flag that draped his casket, to the Tennessee State Library for display at the Women's Building at the State Fairgrounds. In October a fire ravaged the fairgrounds, destroying everything she had loaned. "It just wasn't meant for me to have them, I guess," said Winfrey.

There are many memorials to John Willis, including a commemorative stone on the north side of the bridge named for him on Highway 31 in Columbia. In 1956, the navy named a ship in his honor, the USS *John Willis*. Winfrey attended the launching, appeared at over forty ship's reunions, and served as the ship's "mother" for over three decades. For years she also tried to keep a wreath of flowers on the monument in Columbia, making the trip from her home in Nashville once in the spring and once every fall. Winfrey spent her last years in Florida, where her sons also lived. She passed away peacefully on October 20, 2013, at the age of ninety-one. Her ashes were interred at Rose Hill Cemetery with her beloved John Harlan.

Years after John's death, Winfrey recalled him with deep affection, remembering his ambition to one day become a doctor. "He would have made a good one," she observed. "He was real dedicated and thorough about what he did in everything—I don't care what he was doing. That was his nature, to do the best at everything he can."

CHAPTER FOUR

A Shower of Stars

Progress was being made. Slow, painful, expensive, but progress all the same. Casualties in the 5th Marine Division alone had hit the 4,000 mark by the end of February. There was a long way to go before inevitable victory, but there were indications that Japanese resources— both in manpower and materiel—were reaching the breaking point. While fierce fighting continued in the push to the north, the western beaches had been opened to supply ships; the naval evacuation hospital and army field hospital were both in operation near the northern end of Airfield No. 1; roads were being graded; tank parks, water points, supply depots, repair shops, showers, and even post offices were sprouting up behind the front.

The big picture gains were less evident to the Marine infantry involved in close combat with a largely unseen enemy amid the tortured landscape of upheaved stone that characterized the northern end of the island. A 5th Marine Division intelligence officer recalled: "Volcanic eruption has littered the whole northern end of the island with outcrops of sandstone and loose rock. . . . Our troops obtained cover only by defilade or by piling loose rocks on the surface to form rock-revetted positions. A series of irregularly eroded crisscrossed gorges with precipitous sides resulted in a series of compartments of various shapes . . . the compartments were lined with a labyrinth of natural and artificial caves which covered the approaches from all directions. Fields of fire were usually limited to 25 yards."

Five members of the 5th Marine Division would earn the Medal of Honor in close combat on Iwo Jima in a single day, March 3. The first two actions took place in the early morning hours as enemy infiltrators emerged from holes and caves amid the jungle of stone, with one object in mind: to kill Marines.

CPL. CHARLES J. BERRY

26th Marines, 5th Marine Division
March 3, 1945

Charles Berry USMC

On July 20, 1960, a U.S. destroyer lay to off the island of Iwo Jima, her flag at half-mast and her crew bowed in prayer for a United States Marine they had never met. The name of the ship was the USS *Charles Berry* and the man so honored had been dead for over fifteen years.

Charles Joseph Berry was born July 10, 1923, in Lorain, Ohio—a gritty industrial city on the shores of Lake Erie about thirty miles west of Cleveland—the only child of Carl and Caroline Berry. Like so many other men in the region, Carl Berry labored in Lorain's steel mills. It was tough work. "They were working charging cranes in the open hearth," recalled lifelong resident Jim Mahoney. "The heat was there, temperatures were hot, they put in long days. . . . South Lorain meant work, work, work, and tough, strong guys. Barrel-chested men, strong, muscular guys."

Chuck, as his friends called him, earned a reputation in school as a standout athlete and tough competitor. The blue-eyed six-footer played football at Clearview High and was a three-year member of the track team; he captained the team in the spring of 1941, his senior year.

Summers he spent toiling in the fiery Lorain steel mills. His best friend from those days was Steve Baksa, whose own father worked in the mills as a pipefitter. He recalled Berry as an upbeat youngster who was well liked by his classmates. "[He] was always smiling and you couldn't help liking him," remarked Baksa.

After graduating from Clearview High School, Berry went to work as a truck driver for a moving company, but this was only a brief interlude. On October 1, 1941, he and Baksa enlisted in the Marines. Berry was eighteen years old. Within a year, Baksa was headed overseas with the 1st Marine Division, never to see his friend again. The athletic Berry's military career took a somewhat different turn—at least initially. After basic training at Parris Island, he was assigned to the Transport Battalion, Post Service Detachment, at Quantico. Among the perks of that billet, he made the cut to play end for the Quantico Marines football team, which competed against college and service squads. However, Berry was not going to be satisfied with twiddling his thumbs stateside, even if he did get to play football with the very competitive Quantico squad. "One gung ho Marine," according to his buddies, he volunteered for Paramarine training, and by January 1943, now a private first class, he was enrolled in the rigorous jump school program at New River, North Carolina. Volunteers for the Paramarines were required to be unmarried, and the standards of physical fitness were so high that 40 percent failed the training course. Fitness was presumably no problem for the athletic Berry, who earned his jump wings in short order. In March he sailed to join the 1st Parachute Battalion, then refitting on New Caledonia after suffering heavy casualties in the fighting on Guadalcanal the previous year.

It was during a baseball game on New Caledonia that Berry ran into fellow Lorainer PFC Joe Magazzine, also serving in the 1st Parachute Battalion. Coming up to bat, Magazzine worked a walk, then did a double take when he came face-to-face with the first baseman. "Doggone it, you look familiar!" he exclaimed. "Where are you from, Mac?" Berry said he was from Lorain, Ohio. "You've got to be kidding!" said

Magazzine. "I'm from Lorain!" Upon hearing his name, Berry said, "Yeah, I remember you. I played football against you when I was a sophomore." Magazzine had played for Lorain High School, while Berry played for Clearview. "My parents knew his parents," recalled Magazzine. "My dad ran a little tavern where his mom and dad used to come in." Though they didn't know it, Berry and Magazzine would serve together all the way to Iwo Jima and—for Joe Magazzine, at least—their relationship would last more than six decades.

In November, Berry and Magazzine headed into combat as the 1st Parachute Battalion landed at Empress Augusta Bay during the invasion of Bougainville in the Northern Solomons. By November 26, the landing force had secured its beachhead, but the Japanese 23rd Infantry Regiment continued to hold the high ground to the northeast. I Amphibious Corps decided to send the 1st Parachute Battalion and a company of Marine Raiders around behind the Japanese. The combined parachutist/Raider force landed just before dawn on November 28 near Koiari, ten miles to the east of the U.S. beachhead. They were greeted by a Japanese officer who strolled down to the beach and attempted to strike up a conversation, apparently thinking the Marines were friendly reinforcements. He recognized his mistake too late, but the Marines discovered they too had made a mistake: they had landed in the middle of a large enemy-held supply dump.

Japanese forces responded quickly to the incursion, bottling up the raiding party in its limited beachhead where the Marines were subjected to continuous fire from mortars, machine guns, and rifles. By noon, the situation was so bad the landing party requested evacuation, but efforts to get boats in later that afternoon were driven off by enemy fire. As night fell and the landing party's ammunition began to run low, U.S. destroyers closed on the beach, providing covering fire for the rescue boats. "The Navy shelled the beach and eventually we were rescued at eleven that night," said Magazzine. The raiding party lost seventeen killed, seven missing, and ninety-seven wounded, nearly 20 percent of its strength, but Berry and Magazzine got out unscathed.

As it turned out, Bougainville was the last hurrah for the 1st Parachute Battalion. Following the campaign, the powers-that-be decided there would be little practical need for parachutists in the Pacific Theater, so the battalions were broken up and the men reassigned to conventional units. Berry returned to the United States following the disbandment of the parachutists. Enjoying a thirty-day furlough in Lorain, he and Joe Magazzine and another former Paramarine, PFC Alex Vanche, were written up in the local newspaper, complete with a photo of the three returning heroes. They remarked to the news reporter on the novelty of being able to walk down the streets without having to watch for enemy snipers or dig holes to avoid enemy fire.

Those dangers were not far distant, however. Like so many other former Paramarines, Berry, now a corporal, was among the veterans sent to the newly formed 5th Marine Division. He and Magazzine were assigned to G Company, 3rd Battalion, 26th Marines, Berry as a machine gunner and Magazzine with the company mortars. Commanded by Capt. Richard "Dick" Cook, also a former Paramarine, the outfit soon became known as "Goat Company," a tribute to Cook's grueling regimen of training hikes in the hills around Hawaii's Camp Tarawa. Like most of the other companies, Goat included a large proportion of veterans, so though the division itself was new, there was considerable combat experience among the men in the ranks.

The 26th Marines spent most of D-day at Iwo Jima aboard ship, waiting in reserve, but when they finally came ashore late in the afternoon, they found bedlam. "When we landed on Iwo, we had guys blown up all around us," recalled Milton Flynt, a corporal in Berry's battalion. "The incoming was so intense. We would crawl from shell crater to shell crater, and arms and legs would fly past. I remember that. I remember seeing the dismembered bodies of my fellow Marines, lying dead, half covered in volcanic ash, blown to hell."

Over the next several days the regiment participated in the push to the north, helping to overrun Airfield No. 1 and the rocky steppes

A U.S. Marine firing his Browning M1917 machine gun at the Japanese. USMC

beyond, leaving a litter of dead and wounded in their wake. Even for those with prior combat experience, Iwo Jima was a nightmare beyond reckoning. "We were seasoned veterans compared to many of the guys," recalled Magazzine, who was hit in the arm the first day, but soon returned to the outfit. "We tried to help them the best we could, but we were scared too."

The misery continued on March 2 as Berry's machine-gun squad picked its way through the warren of ridges and gorges dominated by Japanese-held Hill 362B. Dozers were called in to cut new roads, allowing tanks to come forward. The Marines made gains, but took heavy casualties in the process. Among them was Joe Magazzine, whose shoulder was shattered by shrapnel. This time there was no coming back; he was evacuated from the line and eventually ended up in a naval hospital on Guam.

As darkness fell over the lines, the survivors dug in. Berry and the two men in his machine-gun crew scraped out a hole along one of the gorges meandering through the area, and settled in for the night. Most Marines found it impossible to actually dig a foxhole in the rocky ground—the shifting volcanic ash of the beach area was well behind them. They had to be content with finding a natural depression and piling up some rocks around the edge for protection. With Japanese lurking all through the area, the men set up watches and tried to get some fitful sleep. Firing along the line testified to the presence of infiltrators. Sentries caught glimpses of shadowy figures darting among the rocks.

Sometime after midnight, one of the Marines nudged Berry and whispered, "Here come the fuckin' Nips."

The Japanese had located them as well. Time suddenly stood still as a grenade rolled in among the three Marines. There was a scramble and Berry fell on the grenade as it exploded, smothering the deadly spray of metal fragments with his own body. "He dove on it to stop the shrapnel from hitting the other guys," said Joe Magazzine. "He died later at the aid station."

Carl and Caroline Berry accepted the Medal of Honor on behalf of their only son on December 7, 1945, the fourth anniversary of the Japanese attack on Pearl Harbor. Although Marine commandant A. A. Vandegrift invited them to travel to Washington for the presentation, the Berrys decided against making the trip. The medal was presented at their home in Lorain.

Charles Berry's remains were brought home to the United States aboard the army transport ship USS *Walter W. Schwenk* in 1948, one of 3,295 war dead returned to their still-grieving families. He was interred at Elmwood Cemetery, only a half mile from the playing fields at Lorain's Clearview High School. For many years, his grave was marked only by a nondescript flat stone, often obscured by grass and weeds. In 2005 local veterans groups spearheaded a drive to provide a more suitable memorial, replacing the original stone with a two-foot marble marker. "Hopefully people will see it when they pass through and stop," observed a member of the Lorain Veterans Council.

In 1959 a U.S. Navy destroyer was named in Berry's honor. Mrs. Berry attended the christening in New Orleans. As an honorary crewmember, she maintained a connection with the ship over the years, writing many letters to those serving aboard. Clearview High School dedicated the Charles Berry Memorial Library in 1956; the school also created an annual Charles Berry Citizenship Award. In

February 1988, Lorain erected signs at the city limits noting that the city was the birthplace of Medal of Honor recipient Charles J. Berry. The city's bascule bridge was also named in his honor, in a ceremony on Veterans Day in 1988.

Joe Magazzine recovered from his wounds and returned to Lorain, where he went into the used car business. His survival remained a mystery to him. "We got fifty-three free years from the Lord," he mused, reminiscing on the anniversary of the battle in 1998. He saw Berry's parents many times after the war. "One Memorial Day, his mother came up, crying," he recalled. "I asked her why, and she said, 'He saved all those boys' lives and I never heard from any of them.'" Magazzine had an explanation. "I told her they probably all got killed later in the campaign or she would have heard from them—and they probably did," he observed. "The only way anybody survived that island was to get hurt bad enough to get carried off."

Caroline Berry died in 1971 at the age of sixty-six. Carl Berry followed her in 1981 at the age of seventy-five. He was the last survivor of the family. Today they lie alongside their heroic son in Lorain's Elmwood Cemetery. Before his death, Carl Berry entrusted his son's medals to the care of Joe Magazzine, who subsequently arranged to have the decorations placed on permanent display at the Lorain Public Library; it was his hope that they might provide an inspiration to the many young people who use the facility. The medals remain on view there today in the local history section on the second floor, a reminder of a local boy who died for his buddies.

Years later, Magazzine, now an old man, still got a lump in his throat talking about his friend's death. "Everybody's got a hero—somebody in sports or something," he observed. "But people today have their values mixed up; they've got the wrong heroes. Chuck's still my hero. . . . He was one gung ho Marine. It's not any guy that will do something like that."

On March 1, the 28th Marines came north from Suribachi to take over the assault on Hill 362A from the 27th Marines. An early morning attack by the 1st and 2nd Battalions carried the crest, but as the division historian wrote, "[T]he Marines on top found themselves staring over the brink of an eighty-foot cliff into a rocky draw. Securing the reverse slope of 362 was going to be rougher than the attack against the forward slope." Hoping to break the stalemate, Company A moved around the right shoulder of the hill and into the draw, while B Company maneuvered around to the left. Grenades and point-blank small-arms fire stopped the advance cold. Among the dead was A Company commanding officer Capt. Aaron G. Wilkins, the last original company commander in the battalion, who fell victim to a mortar blast. Another casualty, cut down by a machine gun, was Tony Stein, who had just returned to the company and whose previous actions during his first day on Iwo would be recognized—posthumously now—with the Medal of Honor.

The assault had better success the following day. With the help of an armored dozer, a platoon of Sherman tanks got in behind Hill 362A and blasted visible positions on the reverse slope. At the same time, Marines from the 2nd Battalion charged across the open draw. They got up on the next ridge and hung on under fire from both front and rear. The 1st Battalion also made progress. A Company, now under the command of Capt. Russell J. Parsons following the death of Captain Wilkins the day before, took up position along a low ridge beyond Hill 362A and dug in. As night fell, Japanese—some bypassed in the day's attack, others bent on infiltrating Marine lines—began to emerge. In the early morning hours, one such group encountered a twenty-two-year-old sergeant from Texas named Bill Harrell.

SGT. WILLIAM G. HARRELL

28th Marines, 5th Marine Division
March 3, 1945

William Harrell USMC

The temperature was dropping noticeably the evening of March 2 as Sgt. Bill Harrell settled into his foxhole. A light rain had been falling during the day, and the bottom of the hole was wet and uncomfortable. But Harrell, the son of a Texas Border Patrol agent, was a pretty tough character—and, in any case, a little rain was the least of his worries.

If life's paths went the way hopeful humans intended, twenty-two-year-old Bill Harrell would not have been huddling in a cold, wet hole on Iwo Jima; he would have been high above that blasted chunk of rock and ash. Born June 26, 1922, in Rio Grande City, along the Texas–Mexico border, William George Harrell was the third of Roy and Hazel Harrell's three children, following older brother Dick and sister Virginia. His father had served in the cavalry in World War I, then briefly as a Texas Ranger before signing on as a border patrol agent because the pay was better. Patrolling the Mexican border had its dangers and Roy Harrell "had a reputation for shootouts with banditos and bootleggers," according to accounts. One such incident was documented in a 1920s newspaper story, which reported, "Guadalupe Garcia, confessed murderer of 'Slim' Billings, La Feria constable, was killed Friday night in a gunfight with Roy Harrell, a border patrol officer with headquarters in Mercedes. Garcia was hit six times by bullets from a high-powered rifle after he opened fire on the officer when Harrell called to him to halt."

Roy died in 1931 of a cerebral hemorrhage, leaving Hazel to support their three children. The family moved to Mercedes where, in junior high school, Bill was a member of the Boy Scouts. He shared his father's love for horses. He also enjoyed camping and hunting, and hours boating on a local lake. Summers were spent in whatever jobs were available, including ranch work. Graduating from Mercedes High School in 1939, Bill enrolled at Texas A&M University where he majored in animal husbandry, expressing an interest in the scientific breeding of horses and cattle. He chose cavalry for his ROTC requirement. His future looked bright, but a shortage of tuition money forced him to leave school in the spring of 1941. He intended to earn enough money to return, but the outbreak of war only a few months later changed that plan.

Harrell tried to enlist in the Army Air Corps, but was turned down when examiners discovered he was color-blind. He was also turned down by the navy, but he persevered. "On July 3, 1942, I voluntarily joined the Marine Corps after I had been turned down twice by the Air Corps, once by the Navy and once before by the Marine Corps," he recalled. "It seems that I was slightly color-blind. What that had to do with fighting ability, I don't know. It never has bothered me before and hasn't since."

Following boot camp, Harrell trained as an armorer at Camp Elliott, California. In February 1943, he went overseas with the 2nd Antitank Battalion attached to the 2nd Marine Division. By the time Harrell returned to the States a year later and transferred to Company A, 1st Battalion, 28th Marines, 5th Marine Division, he was a corporal. When his outfit landed on Iwo, he had been promoted to sergeant. "He was always wearing a big toothy grin," recalled a buddy, "and he was one of the most likable guys in the outfit, but he could be hard as nails when he had to. You looked in his eyes and you knew it."

A Company had taken serious losses during the 1st Battalion's push across the neck of the island on D-day: eleven men killed or fatally wounded, and thirty-six others with wounds serious enough to require evacuation. Among the first to die was a twenty-three-year-old lieutenant from Akron, Ohio, who barely managed to clear the landing craft before he was cut down by a machine gun. The next several days were somewhat less expensive, as the battalion mopped up bypassed Japanese and sent patrols around the base of Mount Suribachi. "The caves were honeycombed, connecting," Harrell said in a 1960 interview. "You'd clean one out, then another, only to find the first one was full of Japs again." Due to volcanic activity, the ground was often so hot the Marines had to use their folded ponchos as insulation in the bottom of their foxholes. "At night, we were chilled from the waist up and burning up from the bottom," Harrell said. "We used to put our C rations in the foxholes to warm them up."

Casualties continued, though at a slower pace: two KIA and five WIA on D+1; one KIA, one WIA on D+2; two KIA, nine WIA on D+3; one KIA on D+4; one WIA on D+5; two WIA on D+6; none on D+7; none on D+8; and two WIA on D+9. By Iwo standards, those losses were extraordinarily light, but that changed on March 1 when Harrell's company was thrown into the struggle for Hill 362A. By day's end the 1st Battalion had suffered ninety-three casualties, including twenty dead. A Company alone lost eight killed—including company commanding officer Capt. Aaron Wilkins—and ten wounded, most of them from gunshot wounds. The next day the assault managed to break the reverse-slope resistance on Hill 362A, cross the draw, and claw 400 yards north to seize the ridge beyond. But again, the price was high. The 1st Battalion reported another ninety-five casualties, including twenty-six dead. Harrell's company lost five men killed in action, two dead of wounds, and twenty wounded. The dead included twenty-two-year-old Cpl. Frederick J. Tabert, the former CCC quarry worker who had teamed up with Tony Stein to reduce pillboxes on D-day.

As A Company consolidated along the ridge late that same afternoon, the situation was still greatly unsettled. Bypassed Japanese remained to the rear of the line, and while the Marines held the front of the ridge, the rear slope belonged to the enemy. At 1530 the Japanese launched a counterattack against the battalion. The Marines beat it off, killing 149 of the enemy. At 1645 the Marines were busily digging in, anticipating a long night of infiltrators and local counterattacks.

Harrell and PFC Andrew Jackson ("Duke") Carter, a tall, blonde eighteen-year-old from Paducah, Texas (the so-called "Crossroads of America" just south of the Panhandle) were assigned to outpost duty beyond the company command post. The two Texans had stuck together since the landing eleven days before. Now they settled into a shallow two-man foxhole scraped into the rocky ground by the crest of the ridge. "The ridge dropped away on one side to a small ravine," recalled Harrell. The company command post was situated on lower ground at a former Japanese aid station about twenty yards behind them. Marines had found forty Japanese dead in the vicinity when they seized the area earlier in the day. In a rare occurrence, two wounded enemy soldiers were captured there, including one who was overpowered when he ran out of a cave.

As darkness fell, Harrell and Carter tried to get comfortable in their hole. "We alternated in standing hour watches that night, which was quite dark," said Carter. Sporadic mortar and artillery fire fell on the lines. An occasional flare popped overhead, painting the terrain a ghastly shimmering green. Firing broke out now and again as bypassed enemy soldiers moved down from Hill 362A in an effort to make their way north. While not conducive to getting any real sleep, the night dragged by without major incident until about an hour and a half before daylight, when Carter heard a soft scraping noise and spotted movement along the adjacent ravine. "[Harrell] was catnapping about five o'clock in the morning when I saw a number of shadowy figures coming toward our foxhole," recalled Carter. "I fired four times with my Garand rifle."

The shots brought Harrell to startled consciousness. "I grabbed my own rifle and the weird light of a slowly descending flare showed a pile of crumpled Japanese bodies not more than six feet from the foxhole," he said later. Carter recalled, "There was a period of deathly quiet. Bill and I peered into the gloom, but we couldn't see anything. We heard moans and groans, however, and we fired a few shots in the direction from which those sounds were coming."

Another flare popped overhead and drifted downward, its pale light revealing more Japanese approaching the two Texans. "I killed two close to our foxhole," recalled Harrell. "Carter fired at another and then cursed, his rifle had jammed. . . . He told me he was going back to the command post for another rifle. He slipped out of the foxhole."

Harrell peered into the night as Carter sprinted back toward the command post area. The Japanese kept coming, filtering in from the small ravine. Whenever Harrell caught sight of them, he'd throw a grenade or open fire with his carbine. By now, though, the Japanese knew exactly where he was. As he started to insert a fresh magazine into his carbine, a grenade landed in his foxhole. Harrell fumbled around for it in the bottom of the hole and managed to grab it with his left hand just as it exploded.

"It was quiet in the foxhole for a moment as I laid there tensely staring into the stench of burned explosives," remembered Harrell. "I tried to pull myself together, but couldn't. I felt a strange scratching finger on my left forearm. When I looked down I realized the finger was mine. My left hand had been blown off and was dangling by tendons and shreds of muscle, the finger touching my forearm. I realized my left thigh was also shattered and blood oozed from shrapnel wounds along my body."

Back at the command post, nineteen-year-old PFC John Armendariz saw Carter running toward him. "I need a weapon, I need a weapon!" Carter yelled.

Armendariz handed over his rifle. "What's wrong?" he asked.

"We're being attacked from the other side by a whole lot of Japanese!" yelled Carter, running back up the slope. As another flare burst, he scrambled back into the foxhole just as more Japanese loomed out of the night.

"With my good right hand I struggled with my carbine trying to insert a fresh clip of cartridges. I couldn't make it so I threw the rifle aside and drew my .45-caliber pistol from my belt," recalled Harrell. Carter got off two rounds with his salvaged Garand, then swore in helpless anger as it too jammed. As two of the enemy soldiers charged the foxhole, Carter grabbed a Japanese rifle with fixed bayonet. He had picked the rifle up the day before, intending to send it home as a souvenir. Now he shoved the rifle forward as one of the Japanese came at him, impaling the man on the bayonet. The second Japanese—who turned out to be a captain—swung a sword at the teenager. "I threw up my left arm and got a nasty cut on my hand," recalled Carter. The blade struck the back of his hand, slicing deep into the flesh by the thumb and knuckles.

Harrell aimed his .45-caliber pistol with his one good hand and fired at the Japanese officer. The heavy slug blasted through the man's forehead, dropping him in mid-stride. Harrell slumped back in the hole as he and Carter took stock. By now firefights had broken out all along the line. Carter was hurt and without a functioning weapon. Harrell was pretty sure his own wounds were fatal. In any case, he knew he wasn't going anywhere with his smashed leg. He couldn't even stand. "Duke, you still alive?" he asked Carter.

"Yeah, Sarge, I'm alive, but the bastard almost cut off my hand. What the hell do we do now?"

"Duke, I don't think I'll make it," said Harrell. "There's no use in both of us dying. Get your ass back to the CP and stay there."

Carter refused, but Harrell insisted. "There's no use both of us dying here," he said. Finally Carter crept over the edge of the hole, holding his ruined hand close to his chest. He promised Harrell he'd be back with help and another rifle. Lying in the bottom of the hole, blood leaking from a multitude of punctures and slashes, Harrell figured Carter would be lucky to get back to the command post area himself, never mind returning with a rescue party. He was on his own. And yet, he felt strangely lucid. In a statement issued to a company officer much later, Harrell observed, "Despite the blood I had lost, I felt strong. My head was clear. I kept thinking, 'Hell, Mac, you're dead. Lie down.'" Maybe the Japanese would leave him alone now.

It was not to be.

"[T]wo more Japs reached the crest of the ridge and one dropped into the foxhole and lay facing me," recalled Harrell. "The other squatted on the foxhole edge." They probably thought Harrell was dead, but soon noticed he was still breathing. "They chattered wildly for a moment. Then the one in the foxhole took a grenade, tapped it on his helmet to arm it and threw it directly at me as he leaped madly out of the foxhole," said Harrell.

Harrell shot him with his .45, then, pistol still in his hand, struggled to shovel the grenade away toward the second Japanese at the edge of the foxhole. "I guess I wasn't fast enough," he said later. "I only got it to arm's length when it exploded. It killed the Jap squatting on the side of the hole, but it also blew up my pistol and my right hand." Harrell collapsed in the hole, able to fight no more.

PFC Armendariz now heard screams coming from Harrell's foxhole: "Help me, somebody help me!" Armendariz snatched up the nearest weapon at hand, which happened to be the radioman's carbine, and scrambled up the slope toward the screams. He found Harrell lying in the hole, "a bloody mess," holding the handless stumps of his arms in the air. "I'll get you out! I'll get you out!" Armendariz assured him.

Afraid there were still live Japanese near at hand, Armendariz grabbed hold of Harrell. "I got him about halfway out and then I saw a helmet coming up on the edge of his hole there," recalled Armendariz. "So I pointed the carbine at him. When I saw the eyes, I fired." The enemy soldier's head snapped back as the slug hit him from a range of about two feet.

Moments later, as dawn streaked Iwo's sky, Carter returned with help. They found Harrell with Armendariz. Twelve dead Japanese lay sprawled around the foxhole. While Carter optimistically appropriated the Japanese officer's sword on behalf of his grievously injured buddy, the others lifted Harrell from the foxhole and helped him back to the company command post, where he received first aid. As he drifted in and out of consciousness, Harrell heard two corpsmen arguing over whose sulfa powder they would use on his multiple wounds.

"I don't give a damn whose sulfa you use," Harrell managed to interject. "Just put some on me."

He was later flown to Hawaii, and then to California for further operations. Besides losing both hands, his left thigh had been shattered by a grenade blast and he had suffered more than a hundred fragmentation wounds. He later speculated that the cauterizing effect of the explosions and the volcanic ash had combined to keep him from bleeding to death.

Nicknamed the "Two-Man Alamo" for their dogged stand, Harrell and Carter joined the long list of Iwo Jima's heroes. Carter was awarded the Navy Cross for his actions that night. Harrell was put in for the Medal of Honor, but first came months of medical attention and rehabilitation at the Mare Island Naval Hospital in California. Going into the hospital, he weighed 145 pounds. Doctors put him in a cast that weighed 155 pounds. "I stayed in that same cast from March until I came out of the hospital in June," Harrell said. "They started to call me 'Stinky.'" Harrell didn't care. "I was just happy to be alive," he admitted.

His friend, Lt. John K. Wells, who had been wounded in the push toward Mount Suribachi, visited him in the hospital. "He was laughing when I hobbled up to his bed," recalled Wells. "Harrell lay there with pillows propping him up. He held a long cigarette holder in his mouth. Ashes from his cigarette had dropped on his chest and burned small holes in his short hospital gown. The nurses and I tried to keep them from hitting his chest." Wells was not taken in by Harrell's seeming good humor. "Quickly, I saw that Sergeant Harrell's laugh was not real," he recalled. As it turned out, Harrell was most concerned about how to tell his mother he had lost both his hands. "It took all the courage I could muster . . . to sustain me at that time," Harrell later admitted. A Marine friend finally told Hazel Harrell about the extent of Bill's injuries.

Unable to shake Bill Harrell's hand,
President Truman grasps the hero's arm
above the hook replacing his right hand.
Harrell became amazingly proficient
with his hooks. USMC

It was Harrell's good fortune that a noted Philadelphia surgeon, Capt. Henry Kessler, was chief of orthopedics at the Mare Island Naval Hospital. Kessler developed a process where utilitarian "hooks" were screwed into plastic cuffs on the stumps of the amputated wrists. These were connected to cables attached to the opposite shoulder, allowing Harrell to open and close his right hook by moving his left shoulder, or use the left hook by moving the right shoulder.

On October 5, 1945, wearing his new hooks, Bill Harrell received the Medal of Honor from President Truman in a ceremony at the White House. Several other men also received their medals at the ceremony, including Greg Boyington, Woody Williams, Doug Jacobson, and others. Truman liked to tell people that he'd rather have the Medal of Honor than be president, but he didn't say that to the young Texan whose arms now ended in steel hooks. He was visibly moved as Harrell's citation was read and the sergeant came to a snappy salute. "The President gripped Harrell's right arm at the elbow and shook it warmly. "All I can say, Sergeant," said Truman, "is that this medal is small enough tribute for what you have given for your country." Truman might have been slightly less misty-eyed had he known that moments before, as the medal recipients walked in to the awards ceremony, Harrell had reached out with his hook and goosed the hero in front of him.

Harrell was discharged from the Marines on February 9, 1946. Less than two weeks later, he married Larena Anderson, a clerical worker he had met while undergoing treatment and rehabilitation at Mare Island Naval Hospital. Their son, William Carter—named after Harrell's Iwo Jima comrade—was born in 1947; a daughter, Linda Gail, followed in 1948. The proud residents of his hometown of Mercedes raised $25,000 to enable him to buy a small ranch. Another gift was a palomino stallion that he named Charlie. Harrell taught himself to ride Charlie with his hooks. "He didn't let anything stop him," his son Bill said years later.

In fact, Harrell attacked his handicap with the same fortitude he had demonstrated against the Japanese. Over time he became amazingly dexterous with his hooks. He could pick up a cigarette without crushing it, and had the dexterity to dial the phone and fire a rifle. He enjoyed guns and shot frequently at local ranges, even designing a special device to let him shoot a pistol. "He could do anything," recalled his nephew Richard Harrell. "He could drive a tractor, type on a typewriter, light a cigarette, or pick up a dime off the floor. . . . There was nothing he couldn't do."

Despite the gift of the ranch, in late 1946 Harrell moved to San Antonio to take a job with the Veterans Administration. He was named chief of prosthetic and sensory aids at the San Antonio Veterans Administration regional office in 1948. The facility provided medical services for veterans throughout south-central Texas. A better representative could not have been found.

"The event that shaped his life lasted half a night," his son observed years later. "What do you do with the rest of your life? He was 100 percent disabled and could have stayed at home and done nothing. But he didn't. . . . He used his disability to his advantage to help other veterans."

Among his creations was the "Wrambling Wrecks," a group of amputee veterans who put on charity baseball games and conducted a fishing tournament. Their fishing shack was fitted with a variety of handicap-friendly features, taken for granted today but a novelty then. "It had ramps everywhere and low sinks for people in wheelchairs," remembered nephew Richard. "There was a trapeze bar above the beds so people could pull themselves up to a sitting position."

Unfortunately, Harrell's success with the VA was not echoed at home. His marriage to Larena ended in divorce, and she took the children and moved to California, where she hoped to break into the movies. Harrell moved on, marrying Olive Cortese in 1951. They had two children together, Christine Lee and Gary Douglas. "My dad was a big hit with the kids that came over to my house after they got to know him," recalled Gary. "At first they were a little afraid of the hooks, but after a while they called him 'Captain Hook.' They'd have a lot of fun with him. He could pick up a cigarette ash in his hooks without crushing it. He could write and do just about anything you can do with your hands with those hooks." He built his own brick barbecue in the backyard; he even built his own fishing boat. "It just never seemed to him that he couldn't do anything he wanted," remarked Gary.

Gary was too young to fully appreciate the significance of his father's medal. When he did ask his father about the war, Bill would usually respond with a funny war story. "Like the one he told me about being on Iwo and 'spider traps' [hidden holes used by Japanese snipers] being all over the place," recalled Gary. "He threw a grenade in what he thought was a 'spider trap,' but it turned out to be a Japanese latrine. He got everybody nearby covered with the contents of the latrines, which didn't set well with his fellow Marines."

Tragically, Bill Harrell's story was not to have a happy ending. In the summer of 1964, Harrell remained in San Antonio while Olive and the kids visited relatives and attended the World's Fair in New

York. When they returned on August 9, Harrell failed to meet them at the airport, and no one answered the phone at home. They took a cab home, arriving at about 3:30 A.M. Nine-year-old Gary bolted out of the cab to find his father, while his mother and sister retrieved their luggage. Seconds later Gary was back to tell his mother, "Mom, there's something wrong with Dad. He's lying in the yard."

Bill Harrell lay dead, half in the yard and half in the driveway. He had been shot in the head. Nearby lay the body of Ed Zumwalt, a Korean War amputee with whom the Harrells had become friendly about a year before. He too had been shot in the head. Harrell's M1 carbine lay on the ground between them. Olive called the police, who found a third body—that of Zumwalt's wife—crumpled in a corner of the kitchen, also shot in the head. The three had apparently died in the early morning hours—a neighbor testified to having heard "several shots" at about 1:30 or 2 A.M. The coroner subsequently determined that Harrell had shot Mrs. Zumwalt in the kitchen and chased Ed Zumwalt out into the driveway, where he killed him. His final act was to turn the carbine on himself. The first shot grazed his scalp. The second shot killed him.

What no one could figure out was why. Harrell was well known as a good-natured man—generous with both time and money—and he had reportedly gone out of his way to be helpful to Zumwalt, a VA client. The Zumwalts had been frequent guests in the Harrell home. Nephew Richard, who had spent the preceding month with his aunt and uncle, said he had never seen any friction between them, nor—in response to speculation of a love triangle—any indication of hanky-panky. The three friends had been at a cookout just that afternoon. "I don't think we will ever be able to determine a motive," admitted the medical examiner. "Everyone involved is dead. There were no signs of argument in the house."

Richard and Harrell's oldest son, William, refused to believe Bill had murdered the Zumwalts. "I think someone else was there," Richard observed, talking of the incident years later.

William agreed. "It goes totally against his character," he said. Son Gary disagreed. "I think he's guilty," he told a newspaper reporter, years after the fact. "I think something happened and he just snapped."

Ironically, 1964 was also a tragic year for Bill Harrell's friend Andy Carter, who, after a stint in the U.S. Army, had settled down in the Fort Worth area and become an insurance agent. On November 14, his seventeen-year-old son, James Harrell Carter, was killed in a freak accident. According to the death certificate, "This boy fell from a parachute that had been pulled by a car to be airborne (died of fractured skull)."

Bill Harrell was buried at Fort Sam Houston National Cemetery in San Antonio, Texas.

His oldest son, Bill, and his nephew Richard both subsequently served with the Marines in Vietnam. Gary graduated from the U.S. Naval Academy and made a career of the navy. He got to do what his father was denied in 1942: fly. He flew P-3s, the navy's four-engine reconnaissance planes, eventually retiring as a commander after twenty-four years of service. His mother never remarried. She died in Florida in 2003.

Years later, attending an Iwo Jima survivors reunion, Gary Harrell reminisced about his famous father and the tragic end to a life of great courage. He recalled something an Iwo veteran once told him about visiting Bill Harrell in the hospital after he was wounded. "He said he was sitting there smiling—but there was something missing from the eyes," said Gary. "I think the guys who [survived Iwo Jima] understand that. They don't judge him."

As for the medal, "He never thought of himself as a hero," Gary said. "He said he was just a Marine doing his duty to the best of his ability."

On the morning of March 3, as corpsmen worked to keep Bill Harrell alive for the surgeons, the 26th Marines jumped off in an attack just north of the unfinished Japanese airfield Motoyama No. 3.

The assault made encouraging progress through an open area before the terrain gave way to a warren of narrow gorges and rocky outcrops concealing determined Japanese. Hand grenades and flamethrowers became the principal weapons in close-quarter combat in the nightmarish terrain. Among the attacking Marines in Company I were a veteran sergeant named Ott Farris and a nineteen-year-old kid from Massachusetts, PFC William Caddy.

PFC WILLIAM R. CADDY

26th Marines, 5th Marine Division
March 3, 1945

William Caddy USMC

Shortly after dawn on Saturday, March 3, a navy C-47 hospital plane named *Peg O' My Heart* rolled to a bumpy landing on Motoyama Airfield No. 1. *Peg O' My Heart* was the first of what would become a stream of transports, fighters, and crippled B-29s to find refuge on Iwo in the months ahead—a first small indication that Marines were not dying in vain.

March 3 was also the last day of PFC Bill Caddy's life.

Born August 8, 1925, in Quincy, Massachusetts—only eight miles south of Boston proper—William Robert Caddy probably would have enjoyed an unremarkable life, had it not been for the war. His father, New Zealand–born Harold R. Caddy, worked as an awning hanger. His mother, Hattie Blanche Caddy, had grown up in Quincy and was thirty-two years old when Bill was born. Bill was Harold and Hattie's second child, following daughter Beatrice by eight years.

Brown-haired, blue-eyed, and wiry, Bill attended local schools and was athletic enough to make the varsity baseball team at North Quincy High School. "He was sort of shy," recalled his older sister. "He liked baseball. He was very interested in baseball." His other passions were fishing and stamp collecting. "He loved to fish," remembered Beatrice. "Before he got his driver's license I had to take him every place to get fishing stuff so he could go fishing." His constant companion on these expeditions was a beagle mutt named Cindy. "She slept with Billy and went everyplace with Billy," recalled Beatrice. "She loved him."

"He was kind of an all-American boy," said Bill's niece, Marcia Morse. "He wasn't, someone said, a great student. But he was a good athlete and he loved baseball. He would hide his things in the shrubs around the house and then after he was supposed to be in school he would go practice his baseball." He also spent a lot time with his stamp collection. "Oh, God, he had so many stamps I didn't know what to do with them," recalled Beatrice.

Like so many families of the day, hard economic realities intruded on Bill's schooling. "During the Depression things were very hard on all of us," said Beatrice. "Things weren't that good." Faced with those harsh realities, Bill dropped out of high school after his sophomore year. He had worked previously as a dock boy at the local marina. Now he took a job as a helper on a milkman's truck, doing deliveries for White Brothers Milk Company, a family-owned business in Quincy since 1913. The job paid $25 a week, most of which he turned over to his mother. "My brother was a wonderful boy," said Beatrice. "Very good. Never in any trouble. Never had any problems. Very well liked."

But Caddy was only marking time until he was old enough to get into the service. "He always wanted to go into the Marines," recalled Beatrice. "And I said, 'No, no, you're not going to go into the Marines, you have to go into the army. I don't want you to go into the Marines.' And he came home all excited; he came home and said, 'I got into the Marines!'"

The eighteen-year-old was inducted into the Marine Corps on October 27, 1943. He was called to active duty less than two weeks later on November 10, the Marine Corps' birthday. He did his boot training at Parris Island. Service records noted that he was five feet seven and a half inches tall and weighed 139 pounds. There was certainly nothing wrong with his eyesight: the former milkman's helper fired a score of 305 with the service rifle to qualify as a sharpshooter.

After boot camp, Caddy received a ten-day furlough before reporting to Camp Lejeune for instruction in the 20mm antiaircraft gun. Such training would presumably prepare him for service with one of the Marine defense battalions, or duty aboard ship. Instead, upon successful completion of the course he was assigned as a rifleman to Company I, 3rd Battalion, 26th Marines in the newly formed 5th Marine Division. On July 22, 1944, his outfit left San Diego for Hawaii aboard the transport *Middleton*. "We arrived there, got off a ship; and they put us on a train that took us 65 miles north of Hilo [to] our camp, and I think we could have walked faster than the train went," recalled PFC Alfred Jennings, who served with Caddy in I Company. "It was a sugar cane train, and it moved very slow. And it took us up there, and we trained there. And it was quite a bit like Iwo Jima: lava, rock, and everything." Finally, in late January 1945, the training came to an end. Company I boarded the attack transport USS *Darke* and sailed for Iwo Jima. "Of course, we didn't know where we were going at the time until we got on board ship; then they brought out the maps and showed us and said where we were headed," observed Jennings.

The 26th Marines remained aboard ship in reserve during the initial landings. Crowded beaches and limited space inland kept the regiment afloat until afternoon, when the Marines were finally ordered into their landing craft. Not until 1730 did the regiment finish coming ashore over Red Beach 1, moving into an assembly area just south of Motoyama Airfield No. 1. "They was shelling the beach as much as the front lines," recalled Jennings.

On D+3 the 26th Marines relieved the 27th Marines in a heavy rain and found themselves in a meat grinder. Casualties were horrific— among those killed were Caddy's battalion commanding officer and the battalion operations officer, both falling victim to a single mortar shell. Twenty-two-year-old Sgt. John McCormally, an ex-farm boy from Kansas who served in Bill Caddy's platoon, wrote: "How sick I am of this. For days now, going forward, always Japs in front of you— never around you—except at night when they sneak through. Always in front of you. Japs you can't see. Japs who exist only as distant cracks of rifle fire, as screaming rocket bombs and mortar fire. That plunging, ripping, everlasting mortar fire. Big fat shells gliding noiselessly down to splatter guts and brains and volcanic ash into a ghastly mulligan stew of death. Every one of 'em must carry a mortar for a personal weapon. God! Will it ever stop?"

By day's end on February 23, D+4, Sgt. Ott C. Farris, a veteran of the 1st Parachute Battalion, had inherited command of Caddy's platoon. The tall, twenty-four-year-old Alabaman had turned down a college football scholarship in 1940 in order to join the Marines, and later earned the Silver Star on Bougainville for rescuing eight wounded men under enemy fire. "The young sergeant is doing the lieutenant's job now," observed McCormally. "The lieutenant's leg is lying in the hole where he was an hour ago." Farris directed the men to dig in for the night among the shallow gullies and low mounds of ash. "Mac, we're not going any farther tonight," he called to McCormally. "The skipper wants us to pull back there"—he pointed to an open space a hundred yards to the rear—"to straighten up the lines. Send 'em back a group at a time and have 'em dig in while it's quiet."

McCormally, whose fourteen-man squad now numbered six tired Marines, had gotten his men in position and was starting to dig in when a mortar shell fluttered down on them. "I had an instant glimpse of the gray puff of smoke with flaming petals erupting from the ground, then felt the axe-chop of iron tearing flesh and rending bone," said McCormally. "The sound was muffled by my deafness from days of shell fire."

The explosion practically blew McCormally's arm off and grievously wounded PFC Jesus Garcia, who landed on top of McCormally. "There is a great, ragged, gaping hole in his side and the blood from it is rolling down my neck," recalled McCormally. As the corpsman tended to them, Farris appeared and looked down on McCormally, who obviously was headed for either a hospital or the division cemetery. Farris chose to be optimistic. "So long, Mac," he said. "Write me a letter." Hours later, McCormally was in the hands of surgeons aboard a ship offshore. Garcia died on the beach.

Seven days later, Ott Farris and Bill Caddy were somehow still alive, but things were not looking good for the immediate future. Each day saw the remnants of their platoon reduced even further by death and wounds. By ordinary standards, the unit's casualties should have resulted in its relief, but ordinary standards did not apply on Iwo Jima. The afternoon of March 3 found Company I engaged in a slugfest with Japanese infantry burrowed into the innumerable cracks and crevices in the upheaved rock formations north of Motoyama Airfield No. 3. "I've never seen such ugly terrain in my life," recalled PFC Robert Maiden. "There were gullies and caves and trails and overhanging rock shale and you just had to go very slowly and methodically and check out everything as you moved forward."

Company I's advance came apart under murderous fire from enemy machine guns and small arms. Caddy, Farris, and a lieutenant went to ground in a shell hole in an effort to find temporary cover. They quickly found the hole both a refuge and a trap as a well-concealed sniper pinned them down. Every attempt to move out was driven back by rifle fire. Then hand grenades began to rain down as unseen Japanese tried to finish them off.

The lieutenant had crept up to the lip of the hole in an effort to spot the sniper, when a well-thrown hand grenade suddenly arced into the shell hole amidst the three Marines. They had nowhere to go and no time to go there. Caddy lurched forward and covered the grenade, absorbing the explosion with his own body. He died in Farris's arms.

Farris himself was badly concussed, but he and the lieutenant survived and ultimately managed to escape from the trap.

"First they said he was missing," recalled Beatrice Caddy. "We got a notice that he was missing in action. That's all we knew. They said on March 3rd. We didn't hear anything for, oh, a couple of months I guess. And then we heard."

The Medal of Honor was presented to Bill Caddy's mother on September 8, 1946, at ceremonies on the lawn of Quincy's Montclair School, where Bill had once been a student. The presentation was made by Rear Adm. Morton L. Deyo, commandant of the First Naval District. Among those present were the lieutenant governor of Massachusetts, the mayor of Quincy, and the United States congressman from that district. Also in attendance was Sgt. Ott C. Farris, who, thanks to Bill Caddy, had managed to survive Iwo Jima.

PFC Caddy was initially buried in the 5th Marine Division Cemetery on Iwo Jima. After the war, in 1948, with the permission of his family, he was interred in grave 81, Section C, of the U.S. National Cemetery at Honolulu, Hawaii. His flat granite stone bears a facsimile of the Medal of Honor in the upper right corner. He was the seventy-second Marine of World War II to earn the medal.

Until her death in 2008, Beatrice was caretaker of Bill's Medal of Honor, which hung proudly in a frame in her home. "It is a long time ago," she said more than sixty years after her younger brother's death, "but I think about it every single night. . . . He was like a baby to me. He was just like a baby. I really felt terrible."

The Marine Corps League in Quincy is named in Bill Caddy's honor. There is also a granite monument and park named in his memory across from nearby Wollaston Beach, not far from where Bill used to go fishing. Every year a ceremony is held at the memorial in his honor. Beatrice Caddy attended them all. "She went every year she was alive," her daughter recalled. "Never missed it. It was bitingly cold on the beach there and she was so proud. She told anybody. Anybody that would listen she would tell them the story."

Ott Farris recovered from his injuries and made a career of the Marine Corps. He fought at Pusan, the Inchon Landing, and the Battle of Seoul in Korea, and served three tours of duty in Vietnam. His decorations included two Silver Stars, one Bronze Star, and two Purple Hearts. He attained the rank of sergeant major before retiring in 1968. Through the years, he remained in touch with the Caddy family and traveled to Quincy to attend some of the ceremonies held in Bill's memory. As an old man nearing the end of his life, he observed that he thought of Caddy "often."

Sergeant Farris died in his home state of Alabama in 2010 at age eighty-nine. He was survived by two sons: his namesake Ott C. Farris Jr. and William Caddy Farris, named in honor of the young Marine from Massachusetts who made the last sixty-three years of his life possible.

While Bill Caddy's battalion fought on the left of the 26th Marines line, the 2nd Battalion was in action on the right. Accompanying F Company was a weary corpsman from Utah, George Wahlen. "I don't care how heavy the fire was and how much it was out in the open," recalled an Iwo Jima veteran years later; "if someone hollered corpsman, a corpsman came running." On March 3, 1945, a badly wounded George Wahlen couldn't run—he could no longer even walk—so he came crawling.

PHARMACIST'S MATE 2ND CLASS GEORGE E. WAHLEN

26th Marines, 5th Marine Division
March 3, 1945

George Wahlen's father discouraged him from joining the Marines. Join the navy, he advised his student son when George wanted to enlist; it's a lot safer. Wahlen took his father's advice, and three years later he found himself engaged in what was arguably the most dangerous job

George Wahlen U.S. Navy

on earth at that particular moment—combat corpsman on Iwo Jima.

Born on August 8, 1924, in Fairmont, Utah, into a family of "salt of the earth, hardworking Mormons," George Edward Wahlen was the eldest of Albert and Doris Whalen's three boys, followed three years later by twin brothers Jack and Gene. The Wahlens were small-time farmers, struggling to eke out a living from the eternally parched land west of Ogden. George supplemented the family income by catching night crawlers and selling them to fishermen, and he turned into a hard-nosed youngster who wasn't about to be pushed around. Though weighing only 110 pounds, he boxed, went out for the football team, and wrestled during his high school years. He played halfback on the Weber High School junior varsity football team during his freshman and sophomore years, but when he moved on to varsity, his size kept him sitting on the bench. Frustrated and annoyed, George marched into the coach's office, threw down his uniform, and snapped, "Give it to somebody you'll let play!" A few years later, a similar lack of patience would land him on an island called Iwo Jima.

In November 1941, Wahlen dropped out of his senior year at Weber High School in order to enroll in an aircraft engine mechanics course at Utah Agricultural College. Graduating six months later, he went to work at Hill Field near Ogden. By then the war was on, and he was anxious to do his part. His father tried to discourage him from going into the Armed Forces until the government came and took him, but George couldn't wait. In June 1943, he attempted to join the Army Air Corps because he wanted to work with planes. "Well, they said there were no vacancies," he recalled. Then somebody informed him, "The navy has planes." So Wahlen took a short walk down the induction center hallway and volunteered to be drafted into the navy.

In his innocence, Wahlen assumed the navy would take notice of his aircraft mechanics training and assign him accordingly. Instead he was sent to hospital corpsman school. "So I went to Hospital Corps School in Balboa Park [California] and there talked to a chief warrant officer who was in charge of the school," recalled Wahlen. "I told him I had been an aircraft mechanic and that I wanted to get into that field. He listened to me and told me that if I did real well in the school he would see what he could do to get me transferred."

Taking him at his word, Wahlen studied feverishly. Eight weeks later, he graduated in the top twenty-five of his class of 400 or 500 sailors. "I went and showed the warrant officer my diploma and reminded him what he had promised me," remembered Wahlen. "He kind of grinned and said, 'We need good men in the Hospital Corps.'"

So the newly minted hospital apprentice ended up in a medical ward at the naval hospital there in Balboa Park. It seemed to Wahlen—already disgruntled—that most of the medical personnel at the hospital were devoted mainly to staying well out of harm's way. He noticed that his fellow apprentice corpsmen never seemed to step up and take the tests for promotion. He asked them why. "They told me that when you got promoted they sent you with the Marines or to sea," he recalled. Wahlen was not impressed. "I remember saying that I didn't like what I was doing but at least I wanted to get paid for it. So I went and took the test and got promoted to hospital apprentice first class. The following month I got promoted to pharmacist's mate third class," he said.

His enthusiasm for Balboa was not improved by ongoing confrontations with the head nurse, who liked to intimidate uncooperative corpsmen by threatening to transfer them into the Marine Corps. That ploy wasn't going to scare Wahlen, who had already been toying with the idea of escaping stateside hospital duty by signing on with the Marines. "I had met several Marines on the ward and talked to them about the Marines," he said.

He waffled on a decision, but one day, as he was coming off a long shift, the head nurse began badgering him about emptying some bedpans. "If I tell you to do something, you better do it," she threatened. "Do you want me to send you to the Marine Corps?" Wahlen bristled. "Sister, you're not sending me anywhere," he blurted. And with that, he walked out of the ward to the master-of-arms shack and volunteered for service with the Marines. "The petty officer told me to pack my bags and be ready at 8:00 A.M. to go," he recalled. "Anyhow, I packed my bags and was there the next morning with fourteen of us going to the Marines." Not all were eager volunteers. "Eleven of them were in brig uniforms. Those uniforms were white with prisoner written on the back," observed Wahlen.

Wahlen proceeded to Camp Elliot for eight weeks of advanced medical and infantry training. "You learned medical, the firing range, infiltration courses, and that sort of thing," he said. Then it was on to Camp Pendleton, where he was assigned to F Company, 2nd Battalion, 26th Marines of the 5th Marine Division. More training followed, first at Pendleton and later at Camp Tarawa on Hawaii. "We were training for amphibious landings, combat training, and living in the field most of the time," he said.

Finally, in January 1945, the regiment filed aboard a troopship. More than three weeks later, still six months short of his twenty-first birthday, George Wahlen found himself off the shores of Iwo Jima. On February 19, the landings commenced. "We were told that our regiment was going to be in reserve so we weren't to go in initially," recalled Wahlen. "Early in the morning we got up to eat. They were telling us over the loudspeaker what was going on, on Iwo, about the landings and so on. The early landings didn't encounter a lot of opposition. When they were pretty much packed in on the beaches, the Japanese opened up with lots of artillery and mortars. About noon we got word that we were going in. In the early afternoon we boarded landing boats. We were off Iwo a ways and were going in a circle and close enough to see the island. Everybody was looking over the edge and being real concerned about what was going on. An artillery shell hit very close to us and threw water over the boat. From then on everybody stayed down."

Wahlen came ashore in ankle-deep volcanic sand, lugging his carbine, a .45 pistol, and his medical kit with battle dressings, tourniquets, a tracheotomy instrument, and serum albumin, a blood expander to give IVs. "There was only one bottle of that and it was a small bottle. We used that instead of plasma," he said.

The young corpsman's introduction to combat was quick and brutal. He was lying near his lieutenant when one of the platoon runners crawled up and said he had lost his carbine coming out of the boat. The lieutenant said, "There's plenty of dead around, go find one." Wahlen watched as the runner crawled along the beach to a dead Marine and rolled him over. "The man had been hit right between the eyes, blood all over him," remembered Wahlen. The runner blanched, but pulled the rifle away from the corpse and crawled back to them. "He was just an eighteen-year-old Marine and I remember how pale and shocked he was. It kind of gave you a feeling: We're really in a war now. It was a shocking experience."

Wahlen had come ashore harboring one great fear: that he would let his Marines down and would not be able to do his job when the time came to go out under fire to help the wounded. "I realized of all things my responsibility was to take care of these casualties when they were hit," he reminisced. "Now initially of course, on being hit, they would look for a shell hole or a foxhole or get out of the line of fire, but me as a corpsman it was my responsibility to go out and take care of them and it really bothered me to think, 'Am I really going to be able to do that?'"

On D+1, after his platoon had moved inland from the beach and started to turn north, he got his answer. His platoon leader, twenty-five-year-old Lt. Jim Cassidy of Clyde Park, Montana, left shelter to check on the men. "He had done that once or twice during the day," said Wahlen. "A sniper raised up out of a spider trap in the ground and shot him. The bullet hit him in the chest." Without even thinking, Wahlen responded. He found an innocuous purple-blue hole in the lieutenant's chest near the heart. There was no exit wound. Wahlen bandaged him up, but realized Cassidy probably wouldn't survive. "He was the first casualty I treated," he said. "He was semi-conscious and we got him evacuated right away." Wahlen's medical evaluation was sadly correct. Cassidy died aboard ship.

Wahlen's initiation continued over the next few days. Among the more horrific casualties was Platoon Sgt. Joe Malone, a former Marine Raider and veteran of Guadalcanal and Bougainville, who had taken over after Cassidy was hit. Malone was leading the platoon forward when a shell landed almost at his feet. "It blew him in the air," said Wahlen. "I wasn't too far from him and so I was to him almost immediately. It had torn off one of his legs, part of his hand, and part of his face." The face wound had peeled back skin and flesh, leaving the sergeant's teeth, gums, and cheekbone exposed. Working quickly, Wahlen cinched tourniquets on the stump of his leg and on his shattered arm, and wrapped a battle dressing around his head in an effort to staunch the bleeding face wound. "Within minutes a stretcher team came behind us and they evacuated him back to the beach," recalled Wahlen.

His next casualty quickly followed, this one a Marine who had been machine gunned and was thrashing around in agony on a small rise. "I pulled his blouse off," recalled Wahlen. "He had been hit several times in the stomach and as I pulled his jacket off, his intestines just plopped out." Wahlen took out his canteen, soaked one of his battle dressings, then held the Marine's intestines in place as he tied the dressing over the wound. He followed up with a shot of morphine. The Marine was pale but no longer writhing in pain when Wahlen left him for the litter bearers.

Wahlen followed his platoon's attack, tending to casualty after casualty—a blur of blood, spilled guts, gunshot wounds, and traumatic amputations—as the 2nd Battalion struggled forward against stiff Japanese opposition. On D+3 alone, the 2nd Battalion lost 120 men killed.

Subsequent days were no better, as Wahlen treated a seemingly endless stream of casualties. As a "Jack" (nonpracticing) Mormon, Wahlen was not an especially religious man, but he found himself praying fervently—not for his own well-being, but "for the courage to do what I needed to do." God must have been listening: on two occasions Wahlen ran out to help wounded men, only to see shells explode in the foxhole he had left only moments before.

A wounded Marine being evacuated from front lines for medical treatment, Iwo Jima, March 1945. Litter bearers and corpsmen were often singled out by the Japanese. Department of Defense

God was also apparently close by on the morning of February 26. "The Second Platoon was crossing a flat, open area about an acre in size when the Japanese waited for the right minute, then hit us with mortar and machine guns," recalled Wahlen, moving alongside with his own platoon. Turning toward the screams and cries for help, he saw as many as a dozen wounded men scattered in the open and still under artillery and mortar fire. Wahlen looked for the platoon corpsman, Eddie Monjaras, a twenty-year-old Mexican-American from Cheyenne, Wyoming, who was one of his best friends in the company, but

Monjaras was nowhere to be seen. Fearing the worst, Wahlen ran out into the killing field. "I crawled and dragged a man with a leg wound into a shell hole, wrapped him, then went out and crawled from man to man," he said. "I assessed injuries, usually by the state of their clothes and how much they were bleeding. . . . Under combat you'd do whatever you could to take care of the problem. Getting shot at and everything, you didn't want to do any more than you had to, to get the job done." Seven or eight casualties later, Wahlen came across Pharmacist's Mate 3rd Class Eddie Monjaras. Badly hit, Eddie was barely conscious; Wahlen could see his friend's intestines and vital organs and there was blood everywhere. Fighting down his emotions, he bandaged Eddie up and gave him a shot of morphine before moving on.

Over a period of about twenty minutes, Wahlen took care of a dozen or more wounded Marines, according to subsequent testimony, all the while under mortar and artillery fire. He returned to his own platoon to find them looking at him in awe, scarcely able to believe what they had just seen with their own eyes. Wahlen collapsed into a shell hole and suddenly found himself convulsed with the shakes. "I remember laying there thinking about what had happened," he said. "I was still there. I was amazed I survived. Not even scratched. How do you explain that? I've often wondered."

But the young corpsman's day was just beginning. Fox Company soon resumed the advance. Progress was good, but later in the day as the Marines pushed up yet another slope west of Airfield No. 2, machine-gun fire suddenly ripped out from the higher ground ahead. As the Marines drew back, Wahlen spotted two men lying motionless in the dirt. He crawled over to check on them, but one look told him both had been killed outright. As he turned and began crawling back down the hill, he heard a thud next to his head. "I recognized it was a grenade right before it went off," he recalled. "It felt like the whole side of my face had been blown off." The blast temporarily blinded him in the right eye and he could feel blood running down his face. Stunned with shock and pain, Wahlen lay still, trying to pull himself together and hoping he wouldn't be hit again. Finally he managed to wrap a dressing around his head and resumed an inching crawl down the hill toward his platoon.

He was making good progress when he heard a cry for a corpsman. Peering out from under his bandage, he spotted an injured Marine lying about thirty yards to his left. He began to crawl toward the man. Suddenly a hand grenade exploded near the prostrate Marine. The grenade was followed by another, and then a third. Wahlen paused and saw a Japanese emerge from a hole in the ground to throw a fourth grenade toward the wounded man. Wahlen had given his carbine away days before, having found it only got in the way when he was trying to treat casualties. He still had his .45, but no grenades. Looking around, he saw some men of his platoon sheltering farther back down the slope. "Throw me up a grenade!" he yelled.

A couple of men tossed unarmed grenades up to where he lay. Wahlen picked one up and once again began crabbing along toward the hidden enemy soldier. A Japanese grenade exploded behind him, driving metal fragments into his legs and buttocks. Wahlen kept crawling, even as two more grenades exploded nearby, wounding him yet again. He came up close to the hole where he had seen the Japanese, and saw that it was actually a cave or tunnel entrance. He pulled at the ring on his grenade. The ring broke off in his hand, leaving the pin still in place. "A lot of stuff I don't remember," he laughed years later, "but that I do." Then machine-gun fire began hitting around him.

"I can't understand why I was so calm under those circumstances, but I took my KA-BAR knife out and straightened out that pin," he said. "I then pulled the pin out and looked over at the hole where the grenades were coming from. It was about eight or nine feet across and maybe that deep. There was a Japanese soldier down there. There was an interlocking tunnel and he was right there throwing grenades out as fast as he could. I was close enough to him where I could have shot him with my .45, but there I was with an armed grenade so I let the spoon flip off, counted to three and just lobbed it right at his feet. That thing went off almost as soon as it hit the ground." Wahlen was so close that he was buffeted by the concussion of his own grenade. "I didn't even look back in there," he recalled. "I knew he was dead."

Wahlen made his way over to the wounded Marine. The man's leg had been shredded. "I tried to get him to crawl out but he could hardly move," remembered Wahlen. The Marine screamed as Wahlen applied a battle dressing to the injury. "I bandaged up his leg and about that time a Marine crawled up beside us with a stretcher," said Wahlen. "We rolled him onto the stretcher and we both crawled off that hill pulling him along on the stretcher."

Covered in blood, his face badly swollen from the enemy grenade blast, Wahlen continued to treat the wounded, peering out from under his bandage with his good left eye. Finally forced to return to the company command post to obtain more medical supplies, he ran into Fox Company commanding officer, Capt. Frank Caldwell, who spotted Wahlen's battered face. "Doc, you look pretty beat up. Get yourself down to the aid station and get yourself looked at," he ordered. Wahlen shrugged him off. "I'm not leaving, I just came back for supplies," he said, hastily stuffing medical supplies into his bag and heading back to his platoon. He knew they needed him. "When you've been with these guys, they're like family," he explained. "You don't want to let them down."

Informed that Wahlen refused to leave the line, a doctor at the forward aid station sent up a small bottle of "medicinal" brandy as a morale booster of sorts. "It rained all night, but I kept warm with the brandy and didn't go into shock," recalled Wahlen. The next day, to everyone's relief, Fox Company was temporarily pulled from the front lines. The swelling on Wahlen's face had begun to subside somewhat, and he was regaining vision in his right eye. He spent much of the day picking bits of metal from his face and legs. "The fragments from those grenades were fairly small," he observed. "But I could tell they were there because they stung like crazy." He also decided it might be prudent to write a letter to his parents. He informed them he had been slightly wounded in the butt and recalled his father's oft-repeated admonishment to "get the lead out" whenever George failed to move promptly. "Dad, now you can say it legitimately," he joked, "because I really do have lead in my butt!"

By March 2, Fox Company was back in action near Hill 362B and Nishi Ridge, north of Airfield No. 3. Wahlen went out to retrieve a Marine who had been hit in the legs with mortar fragments. As he stood up to drag the man to safety, a shell exploded behind them and knocked him sprawling. "I'll always remember the feeling, like some- one hit me in the back with a sledgehammer," he said. As he regained his senses, he became aware of an agonizing pain in his left shoulder. He seemed unable to use his left arm or hand. Fortunately, litter bear- ers were already dragging away the wounded Marine, so, at least for the moment, he had only himself to worry about. Half-paralyzed with pain, he asked a Marine to pull up his dungaree blouse and look at his shoulder. "You're all right, Doc," said the Marine. "You just got a big hole in your back." Wahlen told him to put a bandage on it and remained on the line. "It had taken a big chunk of flesh out of my shoulder and kind of numbed my arm for a while, but I did get the feeling back," he said. Many years later, he tried to explain his determi- nation to stick it out. "I guess I sometimes thought that in the future I'd hate to run across any people I'd refused to take care of," he said finally. "My big concern was doing my job. It was more important than being killed or wounded."

But Wahlen's string was running out. On March 3, Fox Company was directed to circle around Hill 362B as the battalion tried to reduce the stronghold. The company had gained about 300 yards by noon, and over the next four hours managed to get a foothold on the hill. It was not a good day for Fox Company. By day's end, the shot-up company would suffer another fifty casualties: Cpl. James W. Montgomery, shrap- nel left arm; PFC Wilbur B. Schute, gunshot, back and chest; PFC James L. Sandeen, shrapnel, legs; Sgt. Julian J. Patyk, gunshot, head; PFC Dean F. Keely, fragments, multiple; 2nd Lt. Martin L. Gelshenen, gunshot, multiple; Pharmacist's Mate 3rd Class George L. Long, gunshot, left thigh; PFC James J. Campisi, gunshot, face; PFC Alvin N. Martin, gunshot, left arm and chest . . . and so the list of dead and wounded went on and on.

By late afternoon, Wahlen was the only corpsman left on the line. Word came that there was yet another wounded man who needed help. Wahlen went out to get him. "The rest of the company was dug in and I was looking for him," he recalled. "I walked by this big shell hole and there were four or five Marines in there. And as I was walking by, a shell hit that hole." Wahlen abruptly found himself lying on the ground. Shell fragments had blown off the inside part of his boondocker and splintered the bone just above the ankle of his lower right leg. He apprehensively looked to see if his leg was still attached. It was. "I sat down and put a battle dressing on my leg and gave myself a shot of morphine," he said. "That was always the treatment to prevent the patient from going into shock. I then crawled over to take care of the Marines."

Hit by a shell, Marine dead lie in a crater. George Wahlen was responding to just such a scene on the day he was seriously wounded. USMC

Of the men in the shell hole, two were dead—one of them reduced to scattered chunks of unidentifiable flesh and viscera. Of the two survivors, one had lost both legs, and the other had one leg completely severed. Wahlen was tying tourniquets around the most seriously wounded Marine's stumps when two other corpsmen slid into the hole to help. Wahlen moved aside. Litter bearers removed the wounded Marines and promised to return for Wahlen.

As he waited in the bloody shell hole with the two dead Marines, Wahlen heard a familiar shout. About fifty yards away, someone else was hollering for a corpsman. While Wahlen had been trying to help the terribly wounded men in the shell hole, a lieutenant had come forward from headquarters to check on the situation, recalled PFC Rudy Mueller. "I'm sure they were getting all kinds of pressure about why we weren't moving faster and so forth," said Mueller. The lieutenant saw a spot out in front that seemed to offer a better perspective. "He said, 'I'm going to go out there where I can get a good view,'" recalled Mueller. "And we said, 'Don't go out there. The Japs have that zeroed in.' But he went out there anyway. And he wasn't out there two or three minutes when the Japs dropped two or three mortars in there and really chopped up his legs. . . . George was the only corpsman that was still up on the front lines with us. Somebody hollered 'corpsman!' and George started crawling. . . . He couldn't walk."

All Wahlen knew was that someone was calling for a corpsman. "I heard other guys calling for help," he recalled years later. "I tried to walk over to them, but couldn't." Trying to hold his mangled foot off the rocky ground, he made his way laboriously toward the cries for aid. Though tempted to turn back, he finally made it to the lieutenant. Wahlen bandaged the officer's wounds, gave him a shot of morphine, and the two of them inched to the cover of a nearby shell hole. Stretcher-bearers found them there about an hour later. "I was beginning to think you guys had missed the train," Wahlen joked feebly when his rescuers finally pulled him out and put him on a stretcher.

His ordeal wasn't quite over. On the way back, the litter team was taken under fire by a Japanese machine gun. The litter bearers dropped him and ran for cover. "With that shot of morphine, I felt braver than I ever had while I was in that battle," Wahlen remarked. "I remember crawling off the stretcher to go after that machine gun nest but someone else got there first." Next stop was the battalion aid station where his leg was splinted; then he was transported to a field hospital closer to shore, where he spent the night among a seeming sea of wounded lying on stretchers outside the hospital tent. The next day he was boated out to a ship, which soon transported its load of casualties to a naval hospital on Guam. He spent the next several months in a succession of naval hospitals—at Guam, Pearl Harbor, Mare Island, and Camp Pendleton—and underwent three operations to repair his foot, which stubbornly refused to heal. For a while it seemed possible he would lose the leg, but surgeons were finally able to restore proper circulation, and the limb began to mend.

He was at the naval hospital at Camp Pendleton in early September when he was called into the hospital commander's office and awarded the Navy Cross with Gold Star (double award) for his actions on Iwo Jima on February 26 and March 3. Later that month, he got orders to proceed to Washington, D.C., by air. No one told him why, but he figured it had to do with his two Navy Crosses. Though the war was over, "[t]here was a lot going on as far as raising bonds and patriotic things and I thought I would be involved in that," he remarked. "I had a couple of days so I just found me a room and stayed there until I was to report to the Navy building. When I reported in there [on October 3] a commander was pretty upset. He asked me where I had been and that they had been looking all over for me. I told him that this was my reporting date and here I was."

"Don't you know why you're here?" asked the commander.

Wahlen replied that he wasn't really sure.

"On Friday you have an appointment at the White House," said the commander. "You're going to receive the Medal of Honor."

Wahlen stared at him. "No kidding?" he said.

The officer assured him it was no joke. His two Navy Crosses had been upgraded to the nation's highest award. "I was overwhelmed," Wahlen admitted. "I couldn't believe it. It seems my parents had known ahead of time but were told not to say anything. So they were in Washington too."

The award was presented by President Harry S. Truman at the White House on October 5, 1945. A nervous George Wahlen was one of fourteen recipients that day. "Well," said Truman, trying to put the youngster at ease, "I'm glad to see a pill-pusher finally made it up here."

Wahlen remained modest. "I wonder sometimes why I got the medal," he admitted to an interviewer in 1946. "I didn't do anything more than all of the pharmacist's mates. Especially [Pharmacist's Mate 3rd Class Raymond] Long, [Pharmacist's Mate 3rd Class Algie] Mishler and [Pharmacist's Mate 1st Class Everett] Kellog. They were in platoons on both sides of mine and I could see the hell they were catching. Kellog got hit in the leg and wouldn't go back. Long got dysentery and he was in misery a lot of the time, but he wouldn't go back. [Pharmacist's Mate 2nd Class Edward] McHenry was hit and patched himself up. He wouldn't go back."

Discharged from the navy, Wahlen worked for a while as a truck driver, but it was difficult to put Iwo Jima behind him. "I had nightmares in the hospital after Iwo," he said. "I would scream in my bed. They had to put me in a private room because I would wake up the other guys. I had dreams of my platoon sergeant with his face blown away, his legs gone." The nightmares continued after he returned home and became so violent that his brothers, who shared an attic room with him, often had to protect him from harming himself. Then he met his future wife, Melba, on a blind date. The nightmares abruptly stopped when they married in 1946. Wahlen used the GI Bill to earn an associate's degree in business from Weber College and found a job as a mail handler. The money was good, but the hours were long and he wasn't particularly happy. He was also uncomfortable with the great attention he received as a Medal of Honor recipient. He was not a gregarious man; he was ill at ease speaking in public and he generally tried to avoid the many invitations he received to be the center of attention at various events.

He solved both problems by returning to the relative anonymity of military life, enlisting in the army in 1948. He spent ten years as an enlisted man, then was commissioned and spent another ten as an officer. He was in Japan during the Korean War and in South Vietnam during the Tet Offensive in 1968. He retired as a major in the Medical Service Corps. In the interim, he and Melba reared five children.

Returning to Utah after retiring from the service in 1969, Wahlen worked for the Veterans Administration for twelve years, then as a real estate appraiser, and managed to play racquetball three or four times a week. He also continued to help his buddies in need, lobbying heavily for an eighty-bed proposed nursing home to serve the 45,000 Utah veterans, then in their late sixties and older.

If Wahlen was comfortable speaking up for his buddies, he remained humble about his own past. Fifty years after Iwo Jima, he was still ill at ease in trying to articulate his heroism, or even to define himself as a hero. "Initially, I had a hard time talking about it," he admitted in an interview in 1996, offering a copy of the citation instead of his own account of his actions. "It's not something you think about doing at the time. You just do what you have to do. . . . My biggest concern was taking care of these people."

George Wahlen died on June 5, 2009, after a brief battle with lung cancer. He left behind his wife of sixty-four years, five children, twenty-seven grandchildren, and forty-two great-grandchildren. He was interred with military honors in the Memorial Gardens of the Wasatch in Ogden. He would have been pleased, family members said, to know that the Ogden Veterans Nursing Home was named in his honor following his death. "My dad was a quiet, humble man," remarked son Brock Wahlen. "He didn't want much attention."

A few years before his death, Wahlen was once again asked why a man would ignore days of wounds; why, when he could no longer walk, would he leave the safety of his shell hole and crawl fifty yards, dragging a shattered leg, to tend to yet another injured Marine.

Why?

"Because I cared for my buddies," he said simply. "It was better to die than to chicken out."

George Wahlen was the first of three corpsmen to receive the Medal of Honor for actions at Iwo Jima. The second was earned on the same day, March 3, in an action playing out on the opposite flank of the 5th Marine Division, where the 3rd Battalion, 28th Marines, was pushing up along the coast. Brought into the line only two days before, the 28th Marines had already taken heavy casualties, providing more than enough work for the H Company corpsman, a tobacco-chewing kid from Arkansas. His name was Jack Williams, but he was better known to his buddies simply as Arkie.

PHARMACIST'S MATE 3RD CLASS JACK WILLIAMS

28th Marines, 5th Marine Division
March 3, 1945

Jack Williams U.S. Navy

No one would ever mistake Jack Williams for a city boy. The slow-talking, tobacco-chewing Arkansas kid was a hillbilly through and through.

Home for Jack Williams was Harrison, in Arkansas's northwest corner, described by one visitor as "a harsh land of hardscrabble farming and timber logging." The seat of Boone County, the area had first been settled soon after the Louisiana Purchase by poor, mainly Protestant pioneers from Kentucky, Tennessee, and

North Carolina. The population to this day is largely comprised of descendants of these early settlers.

Born October 18, 1924, Jack was the only son of Bill and Daughty Williams, who was nineteen years old when Jack arrived. He was followed nearly six years later by a sister, Fern. Bill Williams eked out a living as a blacksmith, mending farm equipment and forging whatever metalwork a customer might need. He later found steadier employment with the State Highway Department. The family attended the local Methodist Church.

Friends remembered Jack as a fun-loving, easygoing youngster growing up in an era when indoor plumbing was a luxury and the uniform of the day was denim overalls. He was an enthusiastic and very competent marble shooter among the local boys, they recalled, and spent many happy hours fishing and swimming along the banks of nearby Crooked Creek.

His first schooling was at Eagle Heights Elementary School, a mile's walk from his family's modest white clapboard house. He proved to be a capable student, and after junior high school he went on to Harrison High School, a three-story brick edifice constructed in 1912. His yearbook described him as a "Future Farmer with a twinkle in his eye, a dimple in his chin, and personality plus." Like many of the boys, he took high school "ag" classes in the log agricultural building located a few yards behind the regular school. "The ag classes were very popular with the boys," observed Chris Dorman, who compiled Jack's biography years later. "Raising cattle and hogs were the primary occupations of most people in the area. Their land wasn't good for much else." Just what the school could teach lifelong farm boys about their trade was a bit of a mystery. "Most of Jack's agriculture education had to do with chewing tobacco and bad language," remarked Dorman.

During his senior year at Harrison High School, Jack worked at the local Lyric Theater, which showed the popular movies of the day, such as *New York Town* with Fred McMurray and Mary Martin, and Walt Disney's epic *Fantasia*. The films were a window to a larger world far from sleepy Harrison, where the most exciting event in recent memory was the theft of a 1941 red Chevy coupe from outside the theater one night. But that was about to change. Many local youths had already left for the war, and Jack's turn was not far off. As his high school graduation day approached, he received a notice from the local draft board to report on May 20, 1943, for a "blood test only." He was being drafted. The Selective Service allowed him to opt for the navy as a "selective volunteer."

One day later, on May 21, 1943, Jack Williams and sixty-two other members of his graduating class received their high school diplomas during commencement exercises at the new Central Elementary School. As might be expected under the circumstances, the ceremony was a highly patriotic affair; student speakers addressed topics including liberty, unity, and democracy. Wearing gray caps and gowns, each student walked across the stage as his or her name was called to shake hands with the president of the board of education and accept the diploma. By virtue of his name, Jack Williams was the last senior across the stage. Three weeks later, he climbed aboard a bus headed for the naval recruiting station in Little Rock. He went with few expectations beyond getting a look at something beyond northwestern Arkansas. "I'm just a hillbilly who wants to get away from the hills, maybe fight a few Japs and see the world," he supposedly remarked. He was sworn into the navy on June 12, 1943, at Little Rock, then put on a train headed west to California.

Williams received his seven weeks of recruit training at the naval training station in San Diego, where he was also tested for general intelligence aptitude. The navy must have seen special potential in their new recruit—or maybe it just needed corpsmen. Whatever the reason, after graduation in early August, the newly minted seaman second class was ordered to hospital corps school at Balboa Park in San Diego. Six weeks of intensive study in various medical subjects culminated in his graduation on September 17, promotion to hospital apprentice second class, and assignment to the nearby naval hospital.

Five months of changing bandages, making beds, and emptying bedpans was enough for the nineteen-year-old Williams—he asked for a new assignment. On January 31, 1944, he headed for the Field Medical School Battalion Training Center at Camp Elliot, where he would learn the infantry skills intended to help keep him alive in the field, as well as how to treat a wide variety of combat wounds as he sought to keep others alive. He finished in March with an 85 percent average in all classes. Promoted to pharmacist's mate third class, he was directed to report to the 5th Marine Division at Camp Pendleton. Williams found his new home with the 2nd Platoon, H Company, 3rd Battalion, 28th Marines.

Slow talking and easygoing, he proved to be a calm and professional corpsman. Physically, he was lean, but strong and tough as a piece of rawhide. "We called him Arkie because he was from Arkansas," recalled fellow H Company corpsman Edward McCartan. Another H Company corpsman, Ernie Lang, who became good friends with Williams, recalled his perpetual good nature; he couldn't remember Williams ever being in an angry mood. Once when they were digging a foxhole together, Lang accidentally cut open his friend's hand with a pickax. Williams simply shrugged it off. "Continuously, he was happy-go-lucky," remarked Lang, amazed that his friend didn't even seem to be annoyed by his carelessness.

Williams's drawling speech drew some good-natured ribbing, which he took in stride. In letters home, he mentioned his new nickname and spoke of the many friends he had made in the Marines. "He was a gung-ho fun-loving hillbilly when we went on liberty together," remarked one of the men. The navy "took him out of Arkansas, but couldn't take Arkansas out of him," someone remarked. Kidded for his tobacco-chewing habit, Williams laconically replied that tobacco had many medicinal qualities that he would be happy to demonstrate as soon as the opportunity arose—emphasizing his point by directing a generous stream of the brown juice at the nearest convenient target. He encouraged his cigarette-smoking friends to try a chaw, but the only one rash enough to take him up on the offer soon turned a most unhealthy-looking shade of green, much to Arkie's amusement.

Training and conditioning at Camp Pendleton continued until October when H Company boarded the U.S. Army transport (USAT) *Etolin* for Hawaii. The ship arrived at Hilo on October 19, just one day after Williams's twentieth birthday. Trucks took the new arrivals on the bumpy, 65-mile ride to Camp Tarawa, where they took up residence among the 400 acres of pyramidal tents alongside the Parker Ranch, some 1,800 feet above sea level, where training and conditioning continued. As the weeks wore on, the men began to chafe at the repetition. When would they finally be sent into combat?

That much-anticipated day was not long off. On January 22, H Company and some 1,200 other Marines sailed from Pearl Harbor aboard the USS *Lubbock*, part of an armada carrying the 5th Marine Division on the near month-long voyage to a place most of them had never heard of. After brief stops at Eniwetok and Saipan, the invasion force arrived off Iwo Jima on February 18. Despite some apprehension, morale was high. "An eighteen-year-old doesn't think too far ahead," remarked PFC John Douglas years later. The tension was more evident as H Company waited for word to board the Higgins boats the morning of the landings. "Everybody was pretty tense," recalled PFC Jim "Red" Naughton, a nineteen-year-old rifleman from Saint Charles, Illinois. "Nobody talked down in the hold while we were waiting to go. God only knew what was ahead of us, whether we were going to get wounded, killed or what it was going to be like." Finally the loudspeaker blared, "Marines, report to your debarkation stations."

"This is it," Platoon Sgt. Gene Bull told the waiting men. "Let's go."

Williams and the others started down the cargo nets into the waiting boats. "Leg over the rail and we started climbing down," remembered Naughton. "You'd like to be climbing up, but you're climbing down. You want to do anything but that. But that's what your orders are and that's what you've been trained to do. So you do it." Held in reserve for the initial landing, Williams's battalion was boated by about

0700, then spent the next five hours cutting wide circles two miles off the beaches. Finally, at noon the word came to hit the beach. They churned ashore to find a charnel house of dismembered Marines, smashed equipment, and lethal fire from an unseen enemy that immediately pinned them down among the steep terraces backing the beach. "It was like walking into a shooting gallery," said Naughton.

Despite previous threats to treat wounds with a stream of tobacco juice, about the first thing Arkie did upon landing on Iwo's fire-swept beaches with H Company was to dispose of his chaw—he didn't have enough spit left in his mouth to keep it moist. He had found cover in a shell hole with H Company Marine PFC Keith Rasmussen when the cry went up, "Corpsman! Corpsman!" Williams scrambled toward the shouts to find his first H Company casualty, PFC Knox Wilson, a blond-haired nineteen-year-old from Huntsville, Alabama, who had suffered a grievous wound in the upper left chest. Williams did what he could for the youngster, marked him for evacuation, then followed H Company inland.

The 3rd Battalion accomplished little that first day. Heavy enemy fire made movement almost impossible and it wasn't until late afternoon that the battalion was able to get on line in the center of the regiment's zone of action. By then it was too late to press an attack, and the men dug in for the night. Williams had survived a busy day, treating the many wounded. Platoon Sgt. Gene Bull, a Marine since 1939, did his best to keep the young corpsman alive, constantly admonishing him to watch himself and not take unnecessary chances. "Don't get yourself killed; you can't do us any good if you're dead," he told Williams.

Casualties continued over the next couple of days as H Company tackled the maze of pillboxes and spider holes around Mount Suribachi. Among them was PFC Keith Rasmussen, who had shared a shell hole with Williams in the moments after the landing. Arkie saw Rasmussen, who had been wounded in the hip and partially paralyzed, being helped along by PFC Conrad Taschner, who had been blinded by a mortar blast. Arkie intercepted the two, treated them as best he could, and passed them back toward the beach. Taschner subsequently regained his sight—a miracle he attributed to the prompt aid he received from Arkie Williams.

The battle to isolate Suribachi brought a steady stream of casualties. "Every day was worse," remembered one H Company Marine. The parade of dead and wounded wore on the usually easygoing Williams; he told a friend he felt as if he had treated every one of them. Nights offered little relief as infiltrators crept in among the Marines. On the third night ashore, screams arose from a forward foxhole. As Williams grabbed his medical bag and started out of the hole he shared with Sergeant Bull, the sergeant pulled him back. "We had better let these boys know you are coming or they might take you for a Nip and put a hole in that expensive uniform," he said calmly.

Bull called out to the nearest foxhole, "Arkie's gonna move up. Check your fire. Pass it on."

As the warning passed from hole to hole, Williams started out, crawling laboriously through the loose volcanic sand toward the pleas for help. The cries weakened and then stopped altogether. The Marines in the nearest foxhole heard Williams suddenly exclaim, "I can't crawl in this shit!" He rose to his feet and ran the last twenty yards to the foxhole. There were two men in the hole, both dead. One Marine's throat had been cut, his grotesquely hanging head nearly severed from his body. The other, presumably the man who had been screaming for help, had been slashed to the femur from knee to hip, bleeding out in a matter of minutes. The Japanese infiltrator who had caught them unawares was gone, disappeared into the night.

PFC John R. Douglas was more fortunate during another attack the following night. His leg shattered when an infiltrator emerged from the darkness and lobbed a grenade into his foxhole, he crawled painfully out into the open toward Arkie's position, unwilling to endanger the corpsman by calling for him. His consideration almost got him killed. Thinking Douglas was a Japanese infiltrator, Arkie's foxhole companion took a shot at him before Douglas hastily identified himself. Williams grabbed the eighteen-year-old and dragged him into his own hole, where he took care of the shattered leg before Douglas could bleed to death or die of shock. "Arkie gave me some morphine," recalled Douglas. "And then he just sat there in the hole with me. He just sat there all night with me. He just never left me. He just stayed right there." Douglas was evacuated the next morning. "He just was a hero," he said of Williams. "He's my hero."

The flag went up on Mount Suribachi on February 23 as the 28th Marines accomplished their initial mission. The morning of February 25, H Company got a reprieve of sorts as the 28th Marines was ordered into corps reserve. Casualties continued as the Marines mopped up Japanese holdouts, but losses were nowhere close to those being suffered by the 5th Division's other two regiments, trying to fight their way north through General Kuribayashi's main cross-island defense belt. Many of the Marines in the 28th Regiment thought they had done their job and the battle was pretty well done, as far as their involvement was concerned. "We thought it was over," admitted Jim Naughton ruefully. In fact, their worst ordeal was just about to begin. On February 28 the regiment was alerted to prepare to move north. The following day, the Marines were thrown into the battle for Hill 362A and Nishi Ridge, filtering through the remnants of the 27th Marines, which had been badly shot up in its efforts to subdue this western anchor of General Kuribayashi's defense line.

H Company was relatively lucky that first day. Assigned to the far left of the line, the 3rd Battalion faced somewhat easier terrain along Iwo's western shoreline than its sister battalions directly in front of Hill 362A and Nishi Ridge. The battalion gained 350 yards before heavy fire from unsecured enemy positions in the adjacent unit's zone to the right forced a halt. The following day, H Company, on the battalion right, was squeezed out of the line as the front narrowed, but the respite was brief. The 1st Battalion had been taking heavy casualties and needed help. At daybreak on March 3, H Company was shifted over to assist the 1st Battalion. At 1100, as the battalion's casualties soared while fighting for a maze of enemy emplacements in the rugged terrain, H Company was sent in to relieve B Company.

They found themselves on the wrong end of a shooting gallery. The company was almost immediately cut to pieces as the fighting degenerated into a series of isolated encounters with the dug-in Japanese, much of it hand-to-hand. PFC Red Naughton and a few Marines from 2nd Platoon found shelter on the side of a low rocky ridge. The Japanese were just on the other side and they weren't leaving. "Does anybody got any grenades?" shouted a Marine up by the crest. Naughton pulled a couple of grenades out of his dungarees and tossed them up to the other man. Then he saw an object plummeting down on him. After nearly two weeks of battle, he wasn't as alert as he might have been, and it took him an instant too long to recognize the object as a Japanese hand grenade. Before he could react, the grenade exploded next to him, almost severing his right leg. The Japanese followed the flurry of grenades with a counterattack, driving the Marines off the ridge. A couple of men dragged Naughton, stunned and bleeding, to a shallow hole not far from the base of the ridge, where they were forced to leave him as intense enemy fire drove them back another thirty yards.

Arkie Williams had already treated a dozen or more casualties as the fleeing Marines dove for cover nearby. Turning, they fired on the ridge they had just left, but without noticeable effect. One of the Marines noticed Williams. Arkie had known Naughton for a year and a half; they had shared a tent together and were good friends. Naughton had been hit, the Marine told Williams, adding, "Red is still in the hole, we couldn't move him." Another, knowing Williams's disregard for his own safety, added, "You better wait till we clear the ridge."

Williams knew Naughton might very well bleed to death out between the lines before the Japanese could be pushed back. He told the others he was going out. Dodging around rocks as Marine rifle fire passed overhead, he made it safely to Naughton's refuge. It wasn't much of a hole. More of a shallow depression in the ground, it offered very little shelter. Williams slid in, finding Naughton alive and conscious but badly wounded, his right leg a mangled mess. Naughton mumbled his thanks as Williams examined the wound. He had been standing at the bottom of the ridge, he said, rambling on with shock. The grenade had come out of nowhere. By the time he saw the grenade, it was too late; the thing exploded and slammed into him with the force of a speeding truck. Williams dug through his medical bag for a morphine syrette. "I think he gave me a shot of morphine," remembered Naughton. "I'm not positive. He was going to do other things and he straightened up a little bit." It was a fatal mistake. From somewhere beyond the hole, an unseen Japanese shot him.

"Ooohhh, I'm hit!" exclaimed Williams, clutching his lower abdomen. He collapsed next to Naughton. He pulled his dungarees down and Naughton saw three round holes in Williams's stomach and groin area. They were barely bleeding. Most of the damage was apparently internal.

Retaining his presence of mind, Williams told Naughton how to give him a shot of morphine. Naughton managed to get the needle into Williams's hip. "I'm going back," said Williams. Not wanting to be left alone, Naughton tried to talk him out of leaving. "No, stay here," he pleaded. Their buddies would come for them, he said. "They know where we are. They'll come and get us."

But Williams wasn't sure either one of them would last that long. They both needed serious medical attention. He could still move, but Naughton wasn't going anywhere unless Williams could get out and tell the stretcher-bearers to come get him. "No, I'm leaving," he said.

Despite Naughton's pleas, Williams scrambled out of the hole. Using the larger rocks as shelter, he was making his way back when he spotted another wounded Marine lying among the boulders. Though desperately wounded himself, Williams stopped to minister to the man, injecting him with morphine and sprinkling sulfa powder on his wounds. He told the Marine he would send someone after him, then got up and again started weakly toward H Company. He had taken only a couple of steps when a Japanese rifle bullet tore through his chest. Williams pitched to the ground, fatally shot.

Back by the little ridge, Naughton had been drifting in and out of consciousness. "The pain was intense," he recalled. "And I kept thinking if I had a knife I could cut that [foot] off and it wouldn't hurt so bad, which is ridiculous, but you don't know what to think." When he came to once again, it was dark. Knowing he could not last indefinitely, he risked attracting the attention of any roving Japanese and began shouting for help. He was lucky. Initially suspicious of a Japanese trick, one of Naughton's buddies, Sgt. Jack Burns, recognized his voice. "Keep talking so I can find you," called Burns.

Taking their lives in their hands, three H Company Marines crept fifty yards out into no-man's-land and located his shallow refuge. Naughton's right foot was dangling by shreds of muscle and skin, but he was still alive. The Marines loaded him onto a shelter half and lugged him out, dropping to the ground every time a flare went up. Despite getting last rites at the battalion aid station, Naughton would survive.

Still up on the line, H Company mortar man PFC John P. Lyttle found himself in a foxhole surrounded by a scattering of dead Marines and Japanese, but mostly Marines. "The legs of one body extended partially into our hole," he recalled. "The man was barefoot, lying on his face. He wore no helmet but instead a light blue 'bucket' hat was pulled down over his ears. If his feet hadn't been so large we would have figured him for a Jap, but that afternoon the body detail came by and took back a large number of these dead. When they rolled over our barefooted man, there was a hectic scramble for his .45, which he had been lying on. It was then that we realized he was one of our corpsmen, Jack Williams. . . . The bucket hat was his Navy cap dyed blue and turned down so he could wear it under his helmet."

The telegram arrived in Harrison on the evening of March 28, informing Bill and Daughty Williams that their only son had died of wounds. Two days later, Jack's obituary appeared on the front page of the *Harrison Daily Times*. Neighbors responded with cards of sympathy and platters of food in an effort to comfort the grieving family. A letter from a Marine chaplain informed the family that Jack had been "highly respected and loved by his comrades." Another letter, this one from Jack's battalion commander, assured them that Jack had performed in "a most commendable manner."

Just how commendable a manner became evident almost a year later, when the family learned that Jack would be posthumously awarded the Medal of Honor, based on the accounts of eyewitnesses and the two Marines he had treated just before he was killed. "At this time we had no officers left to witness his deeds but plenty of enlisted men who would testify to Arkie's efforts in treating his Marines, covering them with his own body even after being seriously wounded himself," said John Lyttle. "He was wounded several more times and died while trying to take care of his own wounds. Lieutenant John Leslie, who had been wounded and evacuated to Guam on D-day, returned to the company in the last week and being the only officer, gathered witnesses together and wrote a citation for Arkie."

At the family's request, the presentation was made at their home on March 8, 1946, by Capt. Arthur Ageton, who came in from New Orleans accompanied by a navy photographer and a driver. As Jack's father, sister, and two grandmothers looked on in the privacy of their five-room home on North Second Street, Captain Ageton fastened the blue ribbon of the Medal of Honor around Daughty Williams's neck.

Jack Williams's remains were brought back from Iwo Jima's 5th Marine Division Cemetery in 1948, and interred in Section 30, Grave 2375, at the national cemetery in Springfield, Missouri. His plot is marked with a simple marble stone bearing an image of the Medal of Honor. In 1980, the navy further commemorated his heroism by naming a guided-missile frigate in his honor. The Harrison Noon Lions Club also remembers Williams, awarding an annual scholarship in his name to a student attending North Arkansas College.

Red Naughton lost his right leg below the knee. Lying in a hospital bed on Guam, he dictated a letter to his mother, telling her that doctors had been forced to amputate his leg. "I'm very anxious to reassure you that I'm not worried about myself one bit," he wrote; "that I know how very lucky I am to be alive, and I'm looking forward to the day when I can be home with you for good." He eventually returned to his native Illinois, went to college, became an accountant, got married, and raised eight children. As an elderly man, he spoke about his long dead friend, Arkie Williams. "He was just an ordinary guy who you knew would do what he had to do," observed Naughton. "You know, I guess Americans are like that—we do what we have to do when we have to do it. . . . But he was a great guy—and he was gone just like that."

Bill Williams passed away in 1966. Daughty followed him in 1986. They are buried in Maplewood Cemetery in Harrison. And, if there were those who saw the easygoing, tobacco-chewing Jack Williams as an unlikely hero, his mother was not among them. Reading the official citation for her son's medal for the first time, Daughty Williams remarked simply, "It was just the sort of thing Jack would do."

CHAPTER FIVE

War of Attrition

Gen. Graves Erskine had a plan—a plan that would change the life of a young lieutenant he had never met.

By March 6, Erskine's 3rd Marine Division had bogged down in a maze of rocky hills and canyons north of Motoyama Village. Well-concealed Japanese were taking a heavy toll on his exposed Marines. Looking for a tactical solution, Erskine—a decorated veteran of World War I whose reputation for brilliance was equaled only by his notoriously abrupt and domineering manner—began to wonder if a night attack might take the enemy by surprise and open the way for a breakthrough to Iwo's northern shore. Marines typically dug in at night and stayed put—anything that moved outside the foxhole after dark was presumed to be enemy and usually was—but Erskine thought that deviating from established procedures might now work to his advantage.

Erskine's intelligence officer, Lt. Col. Howard T. Turton, was not enthusiastic about the idea, and felt strongly enough about it to risk Erskine's fearsome brusqueness and tell him so. The troops weren't trained for night fighting, he pointed out; it would be difficult to stay oriented in the warren of rock during the darkness; the terrain was too conducive to ambush. The risk was too great. "We've already been shot to pieces, and we're at the bottom of the barrel of experienced people—officers and men," added Turton.

But Erskine was not to be dissuaded. As rain began to fall, he got on the field phone to V Amphibious Corps and obtained permission to change the day's attack to 0500—an hour and a half before daylight, and two and a half hours earlier than originally scheduled. By 0320, Marines from three battalions were gathering themselves as stealthily as possible for the predawn assault.

2ND LT. JOHN H. LEIMS

9th Marines, 3rd Marine Division
March 7, 1945

John Leims USMC

Among the pawns on General Erskine's tactical chessboard in the early morning hours of March 7 was a twenty-three-year-old second lieutenant from Chicago, John Harold Leims. The son of a machinist, Jack Leims had the blond good looks of a college fraternity brother or a Boy Scout—both of which he had once been, in what must now have seemed the distant past.

In most ways, Leims wasn't much different from the thousands of other onetime college kids the Marine Corps had transformed into platoon leaders and placed in command of boys not much younger than themselves, as well as a scattering of veterans who were sometimes considerably older. While attending St. George High School, a private parochial school in Evanston, Illinois, Leims had participated in varsity football and track, and served as sports editor of the school newspaper. Graduating in 1939, he spent two and a half years of work/study at Northwestern University before leaving college to get married. When war broke out, he was working for a construction company.

He enlisted in the Marines on November 27, 1942, undergoing recruit training at San Diego. He seems to have taken the rigors of boot camp in stride. "I remember holding a rifle over my head for goofing off or something I did wrong, but you cannot train fighting men with milk toast methods," he recalled years later. Assigned to the 3rd Marine Division, he went overseas in February 1943, but missed the Bougainville campaign when he was sent back to the States in September for officer candidate training. He was commissioned a second lieutenant on March 1, 1944, at Quantico, and by summer was back with the 3rd Marine Division patrolling for Japanese holdouts on Guam. His platoon could not help but be impressed by the former enlisted man's sheer physical presence. "He was big, he was strong—a good looking son of a gun," recalled PFC Jimmy Ganopulos. "He could have been a movie star."

The newly minted lieutenant was also eager to fight. "He was always volunteering," remarked Ganopulos. "We'd come off a patrol and the Chamorros would tell us where some of the Japs were hiding and he would ask for volunteers to go out again." Perhaps despite that "let's go get 'em" attitude, he was popular with his men, running his outfit with a combination of democratic panache and "follow me" daring. "He was for the people," remarked Ganopulos. "The men loved him. They all loved him because he was right there, you know?"

Initially held in reserve at Iwo Jima, the 3rd Marine Division, which included men who had already fought in two major campaigns—Bougainville and Guam—was soon called upon as casualties soared among the 4th and 5th divisions. Leims, leading a platoon from B Company, 1st Battalion, 9th Marines, came ashore on D+3. On February 25 the platoon was thrown into what would turn out to be a three-day fight against Japanese holding Hill Peter, a 360-foot pile of rocks just north of Motoyama Airfield No. 2. Riddled with caves and tunnels, and defended by about fifty Japanese armed with automatic weapons, the hill offered the enemy a good vantage point on the Marines below. "The hill was an outstanding piece of commanding ground, having observation of the entire second airstrip and the beach," recalled Leims.

B Company, commanded by thirty-two-year-old Capt. John B. Clapp, moved through the 21st Marines in the morning to begin the assault, spearheaded by Leims's 1st Platoon and Lt. Robert F. Hagamen's 2nd Platoon, with the 3rd Platoon in reserve. The attack did not go well. "After about 150 yards advance, the company came under intense enemy mortar and machine gun fire, and was forced to hold up the attack and reorganize," observed Leims. "Enemy artillery air bursts made advance terrifically slow and by nightfall only about another 100 yards was gained."

A Marine flamethrower team works over an enemy pillbox in rough terrain. As the Marines moved north, the terrain became more and more broken. USMC

The company tried again the next morning. This time, Leims's platoon, supported by two platoons of tanks, was ordered to swing around the right flank of Hill Peter. "I called my squad leaders together," recalled Leims, "broke a match into three pieces, and had them each draw a piece to determine which squad would lead the attack." Nineteen-year-old Sgt. David H. Hockett of Greenville, Texas, pulled the short straw. Hockett's squad set out on the flanking movement at 0800 after artillery worked over the hill. Assisted by flamethrowers and bazookas, the squad knocked out three caves at the base of the hill, then worked up the slope as the rest of the platoon moved up on the flanks, supported by fire from the tanks. Infantry often didn't like to have tanks around because they drew so much fire, but Leims had nothing but praise for this bunch. "The captain in charge of the tanks didn't know the meaning of fear," he said later. "With sniper and machine gun fire hitting all around him, he'd dash to my position to see how I wanted the tanks employed, then dash back to his tank in the open."

With the help of the tanks, Hockett's squad managed to work its way nearly to the crest of the hill. As they dug in, Leims led a push up the north slope, but the advance came apart when a shell from a Japanese 75mm gun exploded among them, killing four Marines. The enemy field piece, located some 300 or 400 yards to the front, then turned its attention to the tanks with deadly efficiency, knocking out six of the Shermans in succession and forcing 1st Platoon back to a position some 75 to 100 yards from the base of the hill. Nevertheless, Leims sensed that Japanese resistance on the hill was weakening. His men had knocked out three caves, four pillboxes, and an antiaircraft gun in the course of the day, and Hockett's squad continued to hang on near the crest—albeit a bit nervously—as night fell.

Leims's intuition was right. When the assault resumed the following morning, the 2nd Platoon, now commanded by a sergeant, finally made it to the top of Hill Peter, clearing the remaining Japanese positions with flamethrowers and pole charges. Hockett's squad cut down five survivors as they attempted to flee the doomed position at the last moment. Even then, the hill was not entirely secure. "This hill was a beehive of connecting trenches and caves on top with a number of tunnels descending some three stories down," reported Leims. "It was no doubt a forward observer's headquarters for enemy artillery. Some seventy casualties, minor and fatal, were suffered in the assault of Hill Peter. Jap dead were numerous . . . and even after lines had passed on, quite a few prisoners were captured—hiding deep in their unbelievable tunnels and caves."

The casualties included Leims himself, slightly wounded by a shell fragment on February 27. He returned to duty that same day, but others were less fortunate. By March 3, as casualties among officers and men mounted—including B Company's commanding officer, Johnny Clapp—Leims found himself in command of the entire company. The survivors struggled to advance in a confused, close-quarter fight with an enemy they could rarely see. B Company machine gunner Pvt. Bob Oram, who had been sent up as a replacement, recalled that there "was no such thing as a front line. It was just a zigzag thing that, if you could kill the Japs that were able to shoot you, then you had the front line." Progress ground to a halt in the face of fierce Japanese resistance. "Day movement was held almost at a standstill," recalled Leims.

Looking for some way to break the stalemate, Gen. Graves Erskine proceeded with his plan for a predawn infantry attack, in an effort to catch the Japanese by surprise. "On the morning of the 7th at about 0230, orders were issued to C and B Companies to execute a night attack starting at 0500," Leims recalled. "Orders were to advance about 250 yards, set up a line, and be prepared to work small groups back to destroy enemy caves and emplacements by-passed during the night." Everyone knew it was a risky gamble. "We were told about the dawn attack and if you wanted to stay behind you could," recalled PFC Jimmy Ganopulos. "But I was more scared to stay behind, so we stripped off anything that would make any sound. We had complete silence, no artillery, no shots. . . . We moved up at night and waited for dawn."

Ganopulos was surprised to see Platoon Sgt. Bob Pavlovich come crawling up as they got set to move out. Pavlovich, a twenty-two-year-old veteran of Bougainville and Guam, had been hit days before and sent back to a hospital ship. "What the hell are you doing here?" Ganopulos asked incredulously. Pavlovich said he had heard the unit was getting wiped out, so he came back. "Christ, you had it made!" blurted Ganopulos. "You was on the hospital ship. You're going to get killed out here!" Pavlovich just shrugged.

Despite all fears, the attack began auspiciously. Moving out in the predawn darkness, the Marines slipped silently through Japanese terrain that had been holding them up for days. No resistance was encountered for the first fifty yards. The defenders, themselves exhausted by over two weeks of combat and not anticipating a night attack, had let down their guard. By daylight, B Company had penetrated 200 yards into the maze of fortifications that had held them up for so long. "But then it happened," reported the Marine study of the campaign. "The Japanese came suddenly to life and poured devastating fire at the Marines from all directions." Or, as Jimmy Ganopulos recalled it, "At the crack of dawn the Japanese sleeping in their holes stuck up their heads and looked around and were stretching. They saw us. That's when hell broke loose."

The company paused to consolidate its gains, sending small teams back over the route of its advance to eliminate bypassed Japanese. "Numerous caves and emplacements were blown up," reported Leims. "About six casualties were suffered during this period." By afternoon, the situation had improved to the point that Leims was ordered to continue his advance 400 yards due east toward an elevation marked on the target maps as Hill 202 Able, in an effort to contact the 21st Marines on the flank.

It proved to be one hill too far. "[The] attack moved rapidly with minor casualties until the company reached Hill 202 Able where it ran into a strong enemy defense," recalled Leims. "Heavy mortar and machine gun fire was delivered by the enemy." Two of Leims's platoon commanders were hit and the survivors were pinned down among the rocks. Among the dead was Sgt. David Hockett, who had drawn the short match at Hill Peter the week before. For three hours, the Marines fought back as best they could, but at about 1800, Leims learned that the company on his right flank was pulling back. B Company was now isolated, having lost contact with friendly units. Leims had also lost communications with the rear. Fortunately, the Japanese remained confused. "Had the Japs known our true situation, they might have come out of their defenses and overwhelmed us in one concerted attack," remarked Leims. "It was bad enough as it was, but fortunately they were still scared and puzzled over how we got up there before dawn, and they didn't attack. They just threw everything they had at us, mainly mortars and Nambus. They thought they did it in defense, but it was murder."

At 1845 the enemy launched a mortar barrage, "which caused numerous casualties," recounted Leims. The survivors were not optimistic as darkness closed in. "It was almost one of those movie-type things where you were counting out the ammunition," recalled machine gunner PFC Bill Bains. "That's what we did. We tried to figure out how much ammunition we had, how we should expend it, how many grenades we had." Leims knew he had to act or risk losing his entire company. "If we spend the night here by ourselves, we'll all be wiped out," he told his platoon sergeant. "I'm going for help."

Emerging from the shelter of the rocks, Leims ducked and dodged toward the rear and the promise of assistance. "I knew that every time I moved, it could be the last and that I'd probably die out there," he said later. "But what the hell else could I do?" Ten minutes later, miraculously unscathed, Leims stumbled into the dubious safety of the battalion command post. He pinpointed B Company's location on an aerial photo, then headed back to his beleaguered unit, dragging a field-phone wire through the gathering darkness. Again Leims zigzagged through a hail of Japanese fire, and again he survived unscathed, sprinting the last fifty yards upright in a final mad dash—a feat machine gunner Bains described as "miraculous."

Gasping from fear and exertion, he found his men hunkered down among the rocks, trying to stay alive. Most were less than enthusiastic about exposing themselves in a bid to make it back to friendly lines. "I told them I was afraid we'd be massacred if we stayed," Leims recalled. "They saw it my way. They would have followed an order, but this called for more than following orders."

"Pass the word," he shouted. "Be ready to take our wounded and pull back to the lines when I give the signal."

A Marine rifleman takes aim during close combat in the rocks of northern Iwo. USMC

By now it was completely dark. Picking up the field phone he had brought with him, Leims rang up battalion. "I'll give you map coordinates of where to deliver artillery and mortars so we can get the hell out of here," he told the officers on the other end.

Moments later, as shells screamed down in an effort to keep the Japanese at bay, the Marines began pulling back. Some carried badly wounded comrades on their backs. Among the seriously wounded was Platoon Sgt. Bob Pavlovich, who had been cut down by a mortar shell. "Jack [Leims] comes flying around the corner," Pavlovich recalled, "and he says, 'What happened?' And I said, 'I don't know about you, but I'm going to get the hell out of here.' My right arm was busted, I had shrapnel in my face and my stomach and part of it in my rear end. And I started after Jack and sort of stumbled once or twice and old Jack just picked me up and threw me over his shoulder."

Watching from nearby was Jimmy Ganopulos, who had been hit at practically the same time as his buddy Pavlovich. "I got shot in the chest and my right arm was almost half shot away and I got hit in the leg that night while I was laying there," he recalled. His situation looked grim. Out among the dark rocks he could hear Marines crying for their mothers. "All you could hear was a shot and silence," he recalled.

"Japs were killing off our wounded. I kept a .38 revolver pointed to my heart in case they came my way."

Suddenly Leims appeared out of the darkness, lugging a roll of telephone wire. "He was also wounded . . . but he grabbed Pavlovich and said he would come back for me," remembered Ganopulos. "He says, 'Greek, I'll be back for you.' I said, 'You'll never make it, Jack. . . . Let me put my arm around your cartridge belt. . . . I'll drag along . . .' And that's what I did. I don't know how far I dragged. Once I sat down, laid down, I couldn't move. My legs were gone. . . . I had two holes in my chest." Somehow they made it out—over a hundred yards back to relative safety—Pavlovich on Leims's shoulders and Ganopulos "dragging along."

For two hours, Marine mortars and small arms worked over the Japanese as the Baker Company survivors crept back from the hill. Leims went back twice more to retrieve wounded Marines left behind in the confusion of the pullout. "He was carrying wounded soldiers back getting them out of the way of the Japs. On the second carry-out, I helped him carry the guy out who was wounded, and then he went back a third time," said Pvt. Bob Oram, who was manning a machine gun on the newly established line. Leims later dismissed the idea that his actions could be considered heroic. It wasn't anything his Marines wouldn't have done for him. "They were my men, my comrades," he said the next day, "and they'd have been out there, come hell or high water, bringing me in if the situation was reversed."

By 2200 it was over. Of the sixty-five Marines who had begun the attack that morning, forty-two survived, though nearly half of those had been seriously wounded. Twenty-three had been killed. One of the miracles involved Leims's wounded runner, who had been left behind but somehow survived the night on the hill among the prowling Japanese. Searching for him the next morning, Leims found the boy being carried off on a stretcher, "weak, shaken up, but alive," he recalled.

"When the Japs came, I tried to act as dead as I could," the youngster told Leims. "My heart sounded like a trip-hammer. I was sure they could hear it pounding. I tried to hold my breath as the Nips stripped me of my canteens and cartridge belt. But I must have looked pretty dead. They kicked me into a shell hole after they had taken what they wanted."

Jimmy Ganopulos and Bob Pavlovich also survived. "When I got back and they laid me down, I couldn't even move," recalled Ganopulos. "That was it. And then the stretcher bearers came and they put me on it . . . they took about three or four steps and they had to lay down." Ganopulos still had his .38 revolver and a Samurai sword he had been lugging around. "I told them, 'Take this, take my revolver, take my Samurai sword, take everything, just get me the hell out of here, I know I'll live.' So anyway, what they did, they took the Samurai sword and they strapped it to my good leg, wrapped it and taped it on there." Then they got Ganopulos out of there. "And I still got the .38 and I still have the Samurai sword," remarked Ganopulos years later.

Leims had made it almost to the end of the campaign for Iwo Jima when he was wounded in the back by shrapnel and burned on his face and arms by white phosphorus. A year later, on June 14, 1946, in a ceremony at the White House, President Truman awarded him the Medal of Honor for his role in saving B Company from almost certain annihilation. "I was shaking in my boots worse than on any island," said Leims of the presentation, attended by his wife and parents. Also attending was Jimmy Ganopulos, who had spent nearly a year in various hospitals recovering from his wounds. Ganopulos recalled that Leims received a lot of career offers while in Washington—"they were trying to get him to come in with the FBI and all that stuff. But he wouldn't go for anything like that."

After his discharge, Leims returned to Chicago. He and his wife eventually settled in Parksville, Missouri, outside Kansas City, where they were active in their Catholic parish and raised their two adopted children. Leims held a variety of management jobs in industry, including assistant to the vice president and production manager of the Union Wire Rope Company, and then industrial relations manager of the Cramer Posture Chair Company. He served as a member of the Labor Management Council of the Kansas State Chamber of Commerce and was active in Republican politics, unsuccessfully seeking his party's nomination to run for Congress in the mid-1960s. He was also an active member of the Marine Corps League.

Jack Leims died of a heart attack on June 28, 1985, in Conroe, Texas, shortly before the much-anticipated 3rd Marine Division reunion, scheduled to be held that year in San Antonio. "He couldn't wait until he got to see us guys, you know," observed Ganopulos, "and he had a heart attack about a month before the reunion. So that sorta killed that reunion." At the time of his death, Leims was employed as a sales representative for Sentry Papers Company. He was buried with full military honors at Arlington National Cemetery.

The men he led—and the men he saved—will remember him until the day they die. "I couldn't in this world find a man better than him," said Bob Pavlovich more than sixty years after he was carried off Iwo Jima. "He stands out. Not because he won the Medal of Honor. Jack would have stood out even if he'd won nothing. Outstanding in every sense of the word. I loved the man."

The 5th Marine Division had spent March 7 trying to seize the high ground overlooking the sea in the northwestern part of the island. The Marines were near enough to practically smell the salt air, but enemy resistance remained fierce and gains were meager. Making the main effort, the 27th Marines traded heavy casualties from knee mortars, grenades, and short-range rifle fire, for a gain of only 150 yards. The regiment's orders for March 8 promised more of the same. Leading the attack for the 2nd Battalion would be Easy Company. Two days before, one of Easy's platoon leaders had finally cracked under the strain of combat. His replacement was a tall, slow-talking Texan named Jack Lummus.

1ST LT. JACK LUMMUS

27th Marines, 5th Marine Division
March 8, 1945

Andrew Lummus USMC

While stretcher-bearers were lugging Jimmy Ganopulos and his souvenir Samurai sword away from the war, twenty-nine-year-old 1st Lt. Jack Lummus found himself northeast of Motoyama Airfield No. 3, shepherding the exhausted remnants of a platoon from E Company, 27th Marines. It was D+17, nearly three weeks into the struggle for Iwo Jima. The end was in sight, but Easy Company was tired. Closing in on Kitano Point on the northernmost part of Iwo Jima, the Marines were only about 300 yards from the sea, but every hole and crevice between them and the coast seemed to contain an armed Japanese, and the going was slow. The morning of March 8 did not promise to be any better, but Lummus, a former profootball player, was no quitter. He was going to keep plugging along until he reached the goal line.

Born on October 22, 1915, on a cotton farm in Ennis, Texas, Andrew Jackson Lummus Jr. and his three sisters never had much in the way of luxuries. Jack's salvation was his prowess on the playing field. An outstanding high school athlete, he attended Texas Military College on a two-year athletic scholarship, then went to Baylor, where he majored in physical education and played end on the football team. "You'd think he wasn't mean enough to play football," recalled a teammate. "But when things got rough on the football field, he had a different personality. He would knock an opponent's block off."

At six feet four inches tall and 194 pounds, Lummus was also an outstanding center fielder on the college baseball team, compiling a .320 batting average over his four years at Baylor. He was named

All-Southwest Conference center fielder three years in a row in 1938, 1939, and 1940. A teammate remarked that Lummus "could cover more ground than a six-inch snow storm." No fly ball seemed beyond his reach. "He was so fast he didn't even look like he was moving," said one teammate, quoted in a 1965 issue of the Baylor alumni magazine. "He was one smooth runner." His coach called Lummus the "greatest center fielder in Baylor history." None of it seemed to go to his head. "He was a joy to be around," recalled teammate Jack Wilson. "He wasn't obnoxious or anything, just a good ol' country boy who liked to have fun."

In May 1941, now a college senior, Lummus signed up for the civilian flying program conducted by the Army Air Corps. Dropping out of school only weeks before graduation, he played ball for the Class D Spudders of the West Texas–New Mexico League while waiting to be called up. He finally began flight training at Hicks Field in July, but washed out of the rigorous program when he ran a wingtip into a fence while taxiing down the runway. His disappointment was mitigated by an offer to try out for the New York Giants football team. One of forty-eight players who survived the cut, Lummus played freshman end in a season that saw the Giants win first place in the league's Eastern Division. "We had three or four real excellent ends, and he was one of them," recalled fellow rookie George Franck. "He acted real sure of himself, but he could do everything he said he could. He acted like a typical Texan, a swashbuckling cowboy kind of guy."

It's likely his contract would have been picked up again, but then came December 7, 1941. The Giants were battling the Brooklyn Dodgers that afternoon when word began to circulate about the Japanese attack on Pearl Harbor. Unaware of this momentous event, the players continued the game. The Giants lost, but

Jack Lummus played for the New York Giants before joining the Marines. USMC

went on to play the Chicago Bears two weeks later in the NFL Championship game, losing in a 37–9 rout at Wrigley Field. Back home in Ennis, Lummus picked up a newspaper and came across an interview with a Marine Corps recruiter. The next morning he drove to Dallas and enlisted in the Marines. Such was his fame that the *Associated Press* sent out a wire datelined Dallas, January 31, 1942: "Jack Lummus of Ennis, former Baylor University sports star, enlisted in the Marine Corps here today and left at night for the San Diego training base."

Lummus went through boot camp at San Diego, emerging as a private. Much to his disgust, he ended up in a guard company at Mare Island, where his main contribution to the war effort was to stand at the shipyard gates checking IDs. The rapid expansion of the wartime Marine Corps and the need for officers brought his salvation. In late 1942, now a corporal, Lummus was accepted for officer-candidate training in Quantico, Virginia. He received his gold bars on December 18, finishing thirty-sixth out of a class of 255. In June, two months after completing Marine Corps Schools, he joined the Marine Raiders at Camp Pendleton, but the Raiders' days were numbered. When the elite outfit was dissolved later that same year, Lummus was reassigned to the 27th Marines, promoted to first lieutenant, and given a company.

"To me, his features were those of a classic cowpoke," recalled navy lieutenant (jg) Thomas M. Brown, assistant surgeon for the 2nd Battalion. "He was mild-mannered and very strong and had a soft slow way of speaking in a Texas drawl. He wasn't much of a talker, yet he was quite sociable. He also had a unique way of talking and grinning at the same time." Lummus dressed in dungarees like the men, but retained his old baseball cap as his personal trademark. He also sported a long corncob pipe, which he never seemed to light. The men called him "Cactus Jack," a nickname that harkened back to his baseball days.

The former ballplayer wasn't one to yell or swear at his men, but he became known as a tough taskmaster. "He showed us what we had to do for ourselves," recalled a Marine. He took his men on hard marches, twenty-six miles and sometimes as long as fifty miles, through the surrounding hills. Pvt. Don Hamilton recalled trying to keep up with Lummus's long loping stride. "To go on a hike with him, to march behind him, was to take two fast steps to his one," said Hamilton. It was indicative of Lummus's competitive nature that his unit eventually broke the twenty-mile record for Camp Pendleton, completing the hike in just under three hours.

"Jack was very competitive," noted a Marine who played sports with Lummus. Another agreed, recalling, "Jack had such a strong desire to win." But Lummus could also be solicitous of his men. A Marine recalled seeing Lummus in the mess hall one day talking with a home-sick youngster. "He put an arm around the kid's shoulder and told him to go get a second helping," remembered the Marine. While at Camp Elliott, Lummus also met champion boxer Gene Tunney, who was assisting with the training program. Tunney wanted Lummus to join his staff as a trainer, but Lummus declined. "No thanks," he told Tunney. "I joined the Marines to fight the Japanese. And that's what I'd better do." He was determined to get combat duty. "Don't worry, I'll be okay," he wrote his sister Thelma.

Tragedy brought him home to Ennis one last time in May 1944. The elder Lummus, who had lost his farm in the Depression, was working as a town constable when he was killed in an alcohol-fueled dispute with a railroad detective. The two men had known each other for a long time, but one Saturday night their kidding got out of hand and the detective shot Lummus in the stomach. While Jack was home for the funeral services, Thelma asked him what he planned to do after the war. Lummus replied that he'd probably be too old to play profes-sional ball by the time the war ended. "I've been thinking about mak-ing a career in the Marine Corps," he remarked. He also mentioned a girl he had met in California. They were serious, he admitted, and he planned to marry her if he survived the war.

Combat was drawing closer. In August the 5th Marine Division shipped out for Hawaii. By January, the Marines were at sea, bound for Iwo Jima. On Friday, February 9, only ten days before the landing,

Lummus wrote to Thelma: "It's been a long time since you heard from your long legged brother. . . . I needn't explain why I haven't written. . . . Our outfit is aboard ship and going into combat—just where and when I can't say . . . don't get excited if there is a delay because I'll write the first chance I get when we are ashore. There will be lots of work to be done before we have everything secured and little time for writing. . . . Take good care of yourself and say an extra prayer for your bud."

Ten days later he was looking out at the looming silhouette of Iwo Jima. "The day of the invasion began with an early reveille," recalled Cpl. Alfred R. Stone, who served in Lummus's battalion. "Nobody had gotten much sleep during the night. . . . The troops had been thinking about the coming invasion. Today was the day. . . . Soon we reported to the tank deck. . . . [T]he LVTs in front started their engines first. It took about thirty minutes for them all to get started and we were inhaling diesel fumes the whole time. . . . We were happy when the order came to launch boats. . . . Getting into the water, I saw it was a beautiful day. The sun was coming up and we could see the island better; it looked eerie, foreboding. . . . On order the boats began moving toward the beach. . . . Fear gripped me; some of our guys began shaking."

The 27th Marines landed on Red Beach 1. Lummus initially acted as 2nd Battalion liaison officer, maintaining communications between the battalion command post, regiment, and other units. On February 24, he wrote a brief V-mail to his mother and sisters: "Just a few words of greeting. . . . [P]lease don't worry about me—I'm O.K. and still full of vinegar. Will write again soon as I can—Love Jack"

But as the fighting dragged on, the battalion started to run out of line officers. On the morning of March 6, Lummus was summoned to battalion headquarters. The commanding officer, Maj. John Antonelli, who had served with Lummus in the Raiders and was a close friend, told him to take over Easy Company's 3rd Platoon. The platoon's original lieutenant had succumbed to battle fatigue and they needed an officer. Always a team player, Lummus was ready to go. "He was always considerate of others, more than anxious to help everybody and anybody," recalled Antonelli. "No matter what his orders were he carried them out with cheerfulness, thoroughness, and rapidity."

Lummus joined his new platoon just east of Hill 362B, captured two days before by a battalion of the 26th Marines at a cost that included two of the battalion's three company commanders. Dubbed "No Man's Land," the desolate jumble of rock reminded some men of the North Dakota Badlands. Lummus found the platoon tired, beaten down, and pretty well shot up after days of incessant combat. "A lot of us didn't know where he came from," recalled nineteen-year-old Pvt. Keith Neilson of the new lieutenant's arrival. More than a few probably didn't much care. Lummus tried to encourage the worn-out men. "We'll get things shaped up," he promised them. He started by leading by example. Everyone else was running in a crouch, recalled Cpl. Don Hamilton, but Lummus stood upright, ignoring the bullets directed his way from the ridges. "No matter where we were or how much enemy fire there was," said Cpl. Herbert J. Green, "he was always moving up and down the line giving us tips and encouragement. He used to walk straight upright on the front when everyone else was crouching or running."

But even Lummus's personal defiance couldn't do the impossible. For two days—March 6 and 7—the 2nd Battalion beat against enemy defenses, with little to show for it except lengthening casualty lists. Trying to seize Nishi Ridge, an irregular ridgeline about a quarter of a mile north of Hill 362A, the 27th Marines were facing some of the strongest enemy positions left on the island. On March 6 alone, Easy Company lost six men killed; Fox Company lost eight; and the two companies combined suffered eighty-one wounded. Nevertheless, on March 8, the 5th Marine Division was directed by V Amphibious Corps "to capture the remainder of the island." For the 27th Marines, facing a maze of interconnected caves and tunnels—the entire area heavily mined—the order was like a bad joke. The toughest ground lay in front of the 2nd Battalion, where both the forward and reverse slopes of the rocky ledges were strongly defended. E Company was in the van of the attack, with Lummus's platoon as the point of the spear. The platoon attacked at 0750 and promptly hit a wall of fire as it attempted to negotiate a gorge. "You'd raise your head," said Pvt. Keith Neilson, "and bullets would whiz by. Or mortars would come in and hit the guy beside you." The advance stalled.

Lummus got Antonelli on the field phone. "Send me tanks, Tony," he pleaded. "I need tanks."

Antonelli obliged. When the tanks had difficulty negotiating the rough terrain, Lummus and a couple of Marines went back and guided them up. Lummus ran from one knot of Marines to another. "Come on, let's get going," he exhorted. "We'll follow the tanks through the gorge." Lt. (jg) Thomas M. Brown saw the tanks rumble by his aid station. "Lummus and his men jumped out of their foxholes and followed along, firing with everything they had," he wrote later. "They were ready to go."

Aided by the big Shermans and spearheaded by the 3rd Platoon, E Company slugged forward between 100 and 150 yards during the morning. The company reported killing seventy-five Japanese in the first two hours. Lummus rode herd on the attack, pushing hard. Brown recalled, "Some of the men who survived that assault told me later that as Lummus rushed forward he ran about pounding on the tanks with the butt of his carbine to get the attention of the gunners inside so he could yell to them the positions of targets at which they must fire. He ran wildly about without concern for his own safety, bravely shouting orders, throwing rocks at anyone he thought was shirking, and always moving forward."

The attack finally bogged down in front of a Japanese position built around at least three pillboxes. The tanks got through the gauntlet, but Lummus's platoon—with no armor but their dungaree shirts—had to go to ground. Looking back, tank commander Capt. Thomas Bruns saw that the infantry had become caught up in a grenade duel at distances of only fifteen or twenty feet.

And then one man got up and started forward. Alone.

Surveying the scene from his tank, Bruns saw Lummus—carbine in one hand, a grenade in the other—head toward one of the Japanese pillboxes holding up his men. The pockets of his dungarees bulged with more grenades. Lummus loped to the shelter of a large rock a few yards from the pillbox. Crouching in the lee of the rock for a moment, he pulled the pin on the grenade, then darted out the last few yards to the pillbox and pitched the grenade through the aperture, quickly lurching back against the side of the steel and concrete structure to get out of the way. There was an explosion and Lummus jumped to the firing slot and emptied his carbine inside.

As he dashed back to his men, an enemy hand grenade exploded, knocking him down. He clambered to his feet and shouted to his platoon, "Come on out, let's move forward now!" The men no sooner started than another pillbox opened up on them. Lummus ran toward it. A Japanese grenade bounced off him and exploded, again knocking him off his feet and driving a spray of metal into his shoulder. Undeterred, he scrambled to his feet, worked quickly up to the pillbox, and heaved a grenade inside. He reappeared, waving his carbine, yelling at his men, "Let's go! Let's go!"

As the 3rd Platoon started through the ravine, still another pillbox opened fire. As the platoon went to cover, Lummus set out after the enemy gun. Edging around the side of the pillbox, staying out of the line of fire, he lobbed a grenade inside, annihilating the gun crew, before turning to rally his men. "Come on, let's dig the Japs out of their holes!" he shouted. Watching from his tank, Bruns marveled at what he had just seen. Practically single-handedly, Lummus had broken the back of the enemy position.

The platoon began combing the rocks for diehards, cleaning out spider holes, and throwing grenades into caves and crevices, as they continued to push toward the ridge barring them from the sea. "We were all doing what we were supposed to do, if you want to know the truth," recalled Keith Neilson. "He was out ahead of us pointing out where the Japanese were. That was the encouragement we needed to expose ourselves. He was not a driving force, he was in front of us."

Lummus came up to PFC Harold Pedersen and directed him to reposition his machine gun. As he moved to comply, Pederson cautioned Lummus about antipersonnel mines that had been strewn throughout the area. "Watch where you step, Lieutenant," warned Pedersen.

Lummus went off to keep the momentum going, but as he walked away from a foxhole shortly after talking to Pedersen, his luck ran out. He stepped on a mine. There was a sudden blast of noise, smoke, and dust. "He went up in the air and came down," recalled Neilson. When the smoke and dust cleared, Captain Bruns could see Lummus struggling to get up. But those nearby could see immediately that the lieutenant had suffered fatal injuries. Both legs were shattered just above the boot line. Stubs of bone protruded from his wounds. His lower body was shredded. Flesh had been stripped from under his arms by the force of the blast.

Neilson ran over to Lummus, who was still struggling futilely to lift himself up. "Don't stop now, keep going!" Lummus yelled at the horrified Marines. Neilson got down beside the stricken lieutenant, comforting him until help could arrive. "Did we take the ridge?" asked Lummus. "Yes, we did, Lieutenant," Neilson said. "He gave Lummus one of the little bottles of brandy sometimes handed out by navy medical personnel. Lummus lay there clutching the old baseball cap he'd worn under his helmet. Finally he said, "I won't play any more football."

"No," said Nielson.

Four Marines lifted Lummus onto a poncho and carried him 200 yards to the battalion aid station, where Dr. Thomas Brown was on duty. "He was still gripping his baseball cap in his hand and clenching his arms and shoulders," recalled a Marine. "He was talking a blue streak, but talking rationally." Marines came from all over to see him as he lay on the ground by the first aid station. "How do you feel?" one asked. "Fine," said Lummus, "except my legs sure hurt."

In fact, his life was leaking away. His face was gray and his blood pooled on the litter. "His right foot had been blown away," recalled Brown. "A mangled left foot hung loosely askew from the ankle joint. Only the long shinbone, the tibia, remained of his right leg. It was attached to the femur above by shreds of ligament and tendons. The flesh of the lower two-thirds of the thighs had been blown off." Shrapnel had also devastated his groin area and penetrated the abdominal cavity. "His legs were like toothpicks," recalled Corpsman Edward Jones. "His feet were gone. Spikes of bone were all that remained."

As Dr. Brown started a second bottle of plasma, Lummus opened his eyes, managed a weak grin and remarked, "Well, Doc, the New York Giants lost a mighty good end today."

Rear Adm. James Joseph "Jocko" Clark, himself one of the heroes of World War II, fastens the Medal of Honor around the neck of Mrs. Laura Francis Lummus, on Memorial Day 1946 at the Tabernacle Church in Ennis, Texas. USMC

Lummus's incredible stamina kept him alive through the litter jeep ride back to the 5th Marine Division Field Hospital, four miles to the south. There, his friend and fellow Texan Dr. Howard Stackhouse Jr. examined Lummus's injuries and realized he had no chance of survival. Lummus probably knew it. "Doc," he whispered as Stackhouse bent over him, "as one good Texan to another, looks like you're going to have a little trimming to do on me." Stackhouse had Lummus carried into surgery, though cold hard reason told him he was wasting a table.

Jack Lummus died that afternoon under the bright lights in the division's underground operating room. The next morning, while the survivors of Easy Company stirred in their newly conquered positions on the last ridge overlooking the ocean at Kitano Point, Lummus was buried in Plot 5, Row 13, Grave 1244, in the 5th Division Cemetery at the base of Mount Suribachi.

Lummus's sister Thelma was returning home from work about three weeks later when one of her neighbors stopped her. Aware that Laura Lummus was still recovering from the murder of her husband months before, Western Union had delivered the telegram to a neighbor in an effort to lessen the shock. Thelma didn't need to be told; she knew from the look on the woman's face that the worst had happened. "I just started running and crying, because I knew what she was going to tell me," she said in a 1993 *Dallas Morning News* article. It was left to her to tell her mother. "She cried, surely. But Mama did real well." A subsequent letter from Major Antonelli assured Laura that "Jack suffered very little for he didn't live long."

Fourteen months later, Laura Lummus was informed that her son had been awarded the Medal of Honor. The family couldn't afford a trip to Washington, D.C., so the ceremony was held on Memorial Day, May 30, 1946, at the Tabernacle Baptist Church in Ennis. Rear Adm. J. J. "Jocko" Clark, himself one of the great heroes of the Pacific War, presented the medal to Mrs. Lummus. The family was not entirely surprised by Jack's heroism. "He wasn't afraid of anything," recalled his sister Sue. "I don't think he thought of himself at all."

Jack Lummus's remains were brought home from the shadow of Suribachi in 1948 and interred at Myrtle Cemetery in Ennis, Texas, the dusty, hardscrabble town he had left years before to go play ball. His medal is on display at the Floyd Casey Stadium in Waco. "Jack didn't do much excess talking," his sister recalled years later. "He told you something once and you'd better listen because that was it. When he *did* tell you something, you could believe it because his word was as good as gold."

Or, as an officer who served with Lummus observed with the succinctness of a combat veteran, "He was a leader, not a director."

As casualties mounted among the front-line riflemen, losses were filled by drawing on men from the replacement battalions. In subsequent after-action reports, officer after officer complained bitterly about the lack of training these men had received. Some seemed to have little familiarity with their weapons—one newcomer didn't know enough to pull the pin before throwing a grenade at a Japanese position. An accommodating Japanese returned it to him—with the pin pulled. Too new, too slow, and too green to know what to do in combat, the replacements suffered an inordinate proportion of casualties, some of them killed so soon after joining a line unit that no one had time to learn their names. Horrified by the losses, the 27th Marines resorted to shanghaiing better-trained men from already established outfits, noting later, "This regiment found that it was much better to strip Headquarters Company and Weapons Company of all available officers and men and send them in as replacements rather than recruits." Weapons Company was especially vulnerable as its half-tracks and anti-armor capabilities were of little value as the battle progressed into the rugged north. So it was that an antitank gun crewman named Jim LaBelle found himself lugging an M1 rifle on the front lines as the battle entered its third week.

PFC JAMES D. LABELLE
27th Marines, 5th Marine Division
March 8, 1945

Jim LaBelle and his buddy, PFC William R. Smith—inevitably known as "Smitty"—were sweating out the night of March 8 in a foxhole that never seemed to be quite deep enough. The past two days had seen their regiment, the 27th Marines, taking heavy casualties from a largely unseen enemy as the Marines struggled to seize the broken high ground to their front. Nights provided little respite as Japanese infiltrators harassed the weary Marines. "They crowded right down on top of us," recalled PFC Keith Neilson. "You'd be sitting there in a foxhole and they'd come right over the edge on you."

James LaBelle USMC

The two nineteen-year-olds had taken different avenues to their present predicament. Smitty, whose widowed mother worked as a clerk in a dry goods store in the border town of Eagle Pass, Texas, had found his way to Iwo Jima courtesy of the Selective Service. LaBelle, anxious to get into the war, had volunteered for the Marines just before his eighteenth birthday. Regardless, they were both in the same boat now.

The sixth of eight children—three boys and five girls—James Dennis LaBelle was born in Columbia Heights, Minnesota, a northern suburb of Minneapolis, on November 22, 1925, to Wilfred and Therese LaBelle. The Heights was heavily Polish, but the LaBelle family was of French-Canadian ancestry on Wilfred's side and Irish on his mother's. Wilfred trained as an electrician, but by 1930 he was working as a carpenter in house construction. He was doing well enough to own his own house, which was no small thing as the country entered the grip of the Great Depression. Tragically for the family, Wilfred was killed in a head-on car collision in the summer of 1933, less than a month before his forty-second birthday, leaving Therese with their eight children ranging in age from four to about fifteen years old. Jim was only seven.

LaBelle attended local grammar schools before entering Columbia Heights High School, where he was enrolled in a vocational program focusing on wood- and metalworking. One of his best friends, Bob Probst, remembered him as a soft-spoken, unassuming teenager, "just one of the guys growing up in the Heights." During high school, LaBelle worked at a hamburger joint called Virg's on Central Avenue, recalled Probst. Though only five feet seven inches tall and 129 pounds, he starred on the school basketball and baseball teams, and boxed in the intramurals. Oddly enough, considering his penchant for active sports, his favorite hobby was raising homing pigeons. Summers he spent working as an apprentice acetylene welder for a local air conditioning company.

But none of these activities could compare with the lure of the war. Intent on getting into the service, his one distraction was his concern was for the welfare of his widowed mother and two younger sisters. He was able to put those concerns aside when his older brother Norman was labeled 4F by the draft board, which would presumably leave him available to take care of things at home. So, with the prospect of being drafted soon enough in any case, Jim finally obtained his mother's permission to join the Marines. He signed up in Minneapolis on November 18, 1943, only four days before his eighteenth birthday.

LaBelle went through boot camp at San Diego. "We really have to keep it clean around our hut or were [*sic*] sure in for hell," he wrote to his sister Virginia in January. "The sargent [*sic*] found a cigarette butt on the floor and we had bunk drill from seven thirty until eleven thirty. We made them up then made them down. They gave us two minutes to make them up and make them down. As soon as we made them up the Sarg would holler make them down. Boy we really got tired of doing that."

The youngster from "The Heights" also found himself rubbing elbows with recruits from very different backgrounds. "There's a kid above me who can't read or write and he doesn't even know how old he is," he wrote to his sister. "I tried to teach him his abcs but he can't learn them. I feel sorry for him because he can't write letters and he never gets any. Most of the guys who can't read or write are from the south. Some of them have never seen or used a telephone. They get married when they are fifteen and quit school when they want to. Some of them don't even start school."

In February, with only five days of boot camp left, LaBelle fell seriously ill and had to drop out of training. "The same day I got sick I ran the bayonet course, practiced throwing hand grenades, and had two shots in my arms. I got so sick I just had to go to sick bay," he wrote to his sister Virginia. It was pneumonia. "Out on the rifle range we had to lay on the cold ground and one night we had to march a mile back from a show in water up to our ankles and I guess that's what made me catch pneumonia," he told his sister. He spent the next month in the dispensary, grouching about being left behind as his platoon completed its training and moved on.

Finally recuperated, he finished up boot camp and went on to Camp Pendleton for advanced training. His mood was upbeat. "I'm beginning to like this life better and better," he wrote home. "If I'm still alive after the war I might stay right in the Marines." He went home soon afterward on a long-anticipated furlough. "I had sixteen letters waiting for me when I got back [to base]," he wrote. "It seemed funny to read them after I had seen all the people who wrote them when I was home."

As it turned out, all was not well at home. His mother had remarried after he left for the service and the relationship seems to have soured quickly. Adding to LaBelle's concerns, his brother Norman, whom he had expected to stay and support their mother, had gotten married, corrected his 4F status with a needed operation, and was now in the army. Deeply worried, LaBelle arranged to take his mother on as a dependent and allocated the bulk of his monthly pay to be sent to her and his two younger sisters.

On June 30, 1944, LaBelle joined Weapons Company, 27th Marines, of the newly formed 5th Marine Division, which was training at Camp Pendleton. Each of the division's three regiments had a regimental weapons company equipped with 75mm guns on half-tracks and towed 37mm guns. The gun support was originally intended as an integral antitank capability. "If you thought I was tan when I was home you ought to see me now," he wrote his sister in July. "I look just like an Indian. . . . It seems like we are out in the field more than we are at the Barracks. I don't mind it tho because I like the outdoors."

Meanwhile, the war ground on. "One of my friends in the Heights was killed in action over in France. He sure was a good kid. I can hardly believe he is dead," LaBelle advised his sister. In another, undated letter, he observed that his own initiation to combat was drawing closer. "I may as well tell you Virg that it isn't very far away that we are going to shove off," he wrote. Soon after, in August the 27th Marines sailed aboard the USS *George F. Elliott* for Hawaii and more training at Camp Tarawa on Hilo. "I thought I would drop you a few lines to let you know I am okay," he wrote Virginia on August 27. "I am on an island over here and it is really okay. I think its very pretty."

As training continued, LaBelle wrote home regularly, thanking his family for their many letters and packages, and chatting about the routine of military life. "There is a Frenchman in here named Terrell writing a letter next to me and he is one of the craziest guys I ever saw," he wrote his sister. "I laugh so much it makes my stomach hurt." In late January, in one of his last letters to his sister Virgie, he again expressed deep concern about their mother's welfare and worried that perhaps he had made a mistake in joining the Marine Corps. Then the letters stopped. The 5th Marine Division had gone to war.

The 27th Marines landed over beaches Red 1 and 2 shortly after 0900. "We went in in the third wave," recalled PFC Tom Harwell, a radioman in LaBelle's company. "And the first wave and the second wave were sitting right there with us, all of us stacked up, couldn't go anywhere on the beaches. . . . I'm in an LCVP, I got a radio jeep and a squad of us, probably ten guys in this jeep. We hit the beach and there are dead Marines everywhere, floating in the water. These guys had gone in just ten minutes before us." Harwell got the jeep off the LCVP's ramp, only to get bogged down in the loose volcanic sand. "We bailed out and got away from the jeep. . . . [W]e'd gone up and dug in this soft black sand. And about five to ten minutes later, a mortar shell hits right in the middle of the jeep. Blows the jeep all to hell."

With much of its equipment lost or bogged down, and with no marauding Japanese tanks to defend against, Weapons Company found its mission largely superfluous. Over the next two weeks, personnel were kept close at hand around regimental headquarters. However, by March 6, the regiment began using Weapons Company Marines to make up for casualties suffered in the push north. In truth, the term "push" was a bit of a misnomer; it was more of a bloody slog.

On March 7, the 27th Marines attempted to envelop high ground to its front. "Progress was slow with both flanks moving and the center pinned down," reported the regiment. "By 1030 Able Company was on the high ground and the entire line was involved in close fighting." The slog continued the next day, D+17. "Progress on the right was good but marked by hard hand-to-hand fighting," reported regiment. "The left and center of the line was pinned down all day. Units had halted and dug in by 1600."

Darkness on March 8 found LaBelle and PFC William R. ("Smitty") Smith digging in, having buddied up for the night. PFC Tom Harwell and Cpl. Rex Biggs were in another hole about fifteen feet away. Harwell, who came from a small town outside San Bernardino, California, had joined the Marines before the war at the age of sixteen. If he'd anticipated immediate service in the tropics, he was soon disappointed; the California teen spent nineteen months in Alaska before reassignment to the 27th Marines. Iwo Jima was his first combat.

Harwell's brother John—exactly a year and a half younger—had also joined the Marines and was serving in the 28th Regiment, also as a radioman. Harwell had been glad his brother was scheduled to come ashore in the later waves at Iwo, thinking it would give the kid a better chance of survival. Fate decided differently. Cpl. John V. Harwell was killed by a mortar shell shortly after coming ashore on D+1. Harwell couldn't rid himself of the feeling he should have somehow prevented his kid brother's death, though he knew that was "bullshit," he admitted; "I couldn't take care of him."

He could, however, try to take care of himself, and as his platoon called it a day on March 8, that meant digging in tight and staying alert for ever-dangerous Japanese infiltrators. There was a big rock near their position, recalled Harwell, and a machine gun dug in off to their left. "The Japs were making noise and they were down in front of us by probably 45 yards, 40, 45 yards," he recalled. "And they were either intentionally [trying] to bug us, but in any case would make a lot of noise. They were throwing grenades, but they weren't reaching us. This is at night so they're banging—of course this is a lot of it . . . keep you awake and bug you, I guess. They also had patrols out."

Earlier, Harwell had seen LaBelle and Smith working together on their foxhole. He warned them to alternate digging—one man should use his shovel while the other kept a watchful eye to the front for marauding Japanese. "I said, 'You guys dig as deep as you want to, but only one at a time dig,'" remembered Harwell. "Because you have to turn your back . . . putting the dirt in front of you to build up the bank. Most of us were two in the foxhole. One guy always looking to the front, covering your sector." In their hurry to get underground, LaBelle and Smith were violating that cardinal rule. "They didn't work for me, but they were kids and I had been around for awhile, so I kept telling them," said Harwell, who was only twenty years old himself. Now, however, things had quieted down and LaBelle and Smitty seemed to be at it again, "both down digging like hell," making their hole deeper, observed Harwell.

As Harwell had feared, this invitation to trouble did not go unanswered. It happened without warning. "These three Japs, probing the lines, get up and walk on past that rock, right up to LaBelle and Smitty's foxhole," he recalled years later. No one saw them. One of the Japanese dropped a hand grenade in the hole with the two Marines.

Caught by surprise, LaBelle scrambled to cover the grenade with his body. "The grenade damn near tore LaBelle's head off," recalled Harwell. Despite being partially shielded, Smith took a spray of fragments and slumped to the bottom of the hole, a bloody mess. He was lucky. Had LaBelle not covered the grenade he would have been killed outright too.

Apparently satisfied they had eliminated the only Marines in the immediate vicinity, the Japanese strolled past LaBelle and Smith right alongside Harwell. "I was scared shitless, but what do you do?" recalled Harwell. "I stood up with a rifle and I started shooting as soon as I got the rifle up, probably waist high." The range was point-blank. "And I went across and the first guy, I got him in the guts, I guess. He went down, moved over to the second, which the three were in a line. Moved over to the second one, I shot him and he went down. By that time I've got the rifle up to my shoulder and I got the other guy square between the horns, right in the old ring. They went down."

One of the Japanese fell into LaBelle's foxhole, landing on top of Smith. "He's hit, hurt, and he's trying to push this dead Jap off him," recalled Harwell. "In the meantime, I'm still standing up. Now I've got the rifle back down; I'm looking around for what else is going on, and I see this Jap move. I didn't get him. [So I] opened fire again." Harwell killed the man, but also managed to hit Smith through the fleshy part of the upper arm. "He was hurting so damn bad from the frag, he didn't notice that, but he did say, 'God damn, Harwell, knock it off, you're shooting me,'" remembered Harwell.

Harwell went over to see what he could do for the two youths. "And I could see no help for LaBelle," he observed. "His whole side of his face was blown away." Despite being shielded by LaBelle, Smith had been hit by multiple grenade fragments. Harwell and Biggs pulled the wounded man into the adjacent foxhole, shot him up with morphine and kept him quiet through the early morning hours. After sunrise, they got Smith back to their platoon command post, where stretcher-bearers evacuated him to the battalion aid station. He eventually ended up in a naval hospital in Hawaii, where he recovered from his wounds, and was able to return to duty with the 5th Marine Division after the Iwo Jima campaign.

Back on Iwo Jima, Harwell, Biggs, and another witness provided formal testimony to what LaBelle had done that night, "taking the grenade . . . saving Smitty in a foxhole with a grenade and all that," recalled Harwell. Their testimony was forwarded up the line with the recommendation that LaBelle be awarded the Medal of Honor. Meanwhile, back in Minneapolis, the weeks had passed without any word from LaBelle, though the papers were full of news about Iwo Jima and the high price being paid by the Marines for each square foot of the cursed place. The telegram, when it finally came, could not have been entirely unexpected. It was followed some months later by notification that Jim LaBelle was to be awarded a posthumous Medal of Honor.

The LaBelle family also heard from Jim's company commander and finally learned some of the details of his death. "James died a sudden, painless death, and a hero's death," wrote Capt. Earl G. Stearns—himself a Silver Star recipient for heroism at Tarawa earlier in the war—with pardonable circumspection. "He was on the front line defense March 8 when an enemy hand grenade was thrown into a foxhole which James was sharing with his buddies. Through his quick thinking and outstanding devotion for his fellow men, he threw his body on the grenade, which killed him, but saved the lives of his buddies."

On July 21, 1946, in a nondenominational religious ceremony attended by more than 5,000 people at the Outdoor Church of God at Powderhorn Park, Theresa LaBelle Hodge was presented with her son's Medal of Honor by Brig. Gen. William E. Riley, then director of Marine Corps Public Information. A newspaper photograph of Mrs. Hodge shows a woman who looks somber, tired, perhaps even a bit dazed. "The medal is wonderful," said Jim's sister Virgie, "but it won't bring James back and nothing could make up for all my mother went through waiting without word for twelve weeks until we got word he had been killed on Iwo Jima." Jim LaBelle's remains were returned to the United States in late 1948 and were interred in the national cemetery at Fort Snelling, Minnesota. The family later donated the medal to the Minnesota Historical Society, where it remains today, the only Medal of Honor in that institution's collections.

His hometown of Columbia Heights later honored the hero by naming a 20-acre park in his memory. His name was also carried on by his family. In May 1945, not quite three months after LaBelle was killed in action, his sister Marcella named her newborn son James Dennis Archambault. In 1957, older brother Howard followed suit, naming one of his sons James Dennis LaBelle.

About fifteen years after the war, Jim LaBelle's childhood friend, Bob Proft, happened to be painting a sign near Virg's. The old hamburger joint made him think of LaBelle and his Medal of Honor. "It struck me that I didn't know anything about what he had done," recalled Proft.

Proft ended up publishing a book listing the citations of all the Medal of Honor recipients. "It bothers me that you can talk to young people and they don't even know what the Medal of Honor is," observed Proft. "They know John Wayne. They know Rambo. Real heroes are forgotten."

Among the names listed in Proft's book is one of those real heroes, his boyhood pal Jim LaBelle, "just one of the guys," who earned the highest honor a grateful nation can bestow.

While it may not have been obvious to the Marines at the point of the spear, the unrelenting grind was bringing results. On March 7 (D+16), the 5th Division drove to within 1,500 yards of Kitano Point, the northernmost outcrop of the island. A time-lapse view of the situation map back at corps headquarters over the first week of March would have shown the 3rd and 5th divisions slowly swinging in a wide arc toward the eastern coast, pivoting on the 4th Division, which had finally seized the Meat Grinder. March 8 saw progress by all units to the north and east. On the afternoon of March 9, a patrol from the 21st Marines reached the sea north of the 4th Marine Division. The twenty-eight-man patrol washed the dirt from their faces and waded shoeless in the cool ocean water before coming under mortar fire that wounded seven men. It was also on March 9—a Friday—that Platoon Sgt. Rudy Julian earned the twenty-third Medal of Honor awarded for heroism at Iwo Jima.

PLATOON SGT. JOSEPH R. JULIAN

27th Marines, 5th Marine Division
March 9, 1945

*Joseph "Rudy" Julian
USMC*

People keep all sorts of knickknacks: family photos, flower vases, souvenirs of memorable trips. Rosalda Julian kept an object far more precious in the living room of her modest Massachusetts home. For over forty-five years, until her death in 1991, she displayed a Medal of Honor as the centerpiece of an impromptu shrine surrounded by old news clippings and photographs of her only son.

Joseph Rodolph Julian, better known to friends and family simply as "Rudy," was born April 3, 1918, in Sturbridge, Massachusetts, sixty miles southwest of Boston, to Rosalda and her husband, Adelard. Rosalda and Adelard were of French–Canadian descent, just two of the sons and daughters of an influx of job-seeking immigrants to the region during the mid-nineteenth century. The family lived in Sturbridge's Fiskdale Village, an industrial enclave of mills on the bank of the Quinebaug River. Adelard, who had served two years in the Coast Artillery immediately before World War I, was employed as a mechanic at the Snell Manufacturing Company, which produced drill bits and augurs for carpenters and woodworkers.

Rudy, their oldest child and only son, was followed two years later by sister Gloria, and two years after that by another sister, Lorraine (known to friends and family as "Julie"). Years later, they continued to remember their brother fondly. "He was a great son. Mother came first," Gloria recalled. "He was clean-cut, a nice guy, a sportsman, and never drank or smoked. He never left home until he went into the Marine Corps. . . . He loved the outdoors and fishing and hunting with his beagle dog. He never got into any trouble." He was close to his father; the two enjoyed hunting rabbits and squirrels together in the woods around Sturbridge, and even did some deer hunting in Maine. Both were also avid fishermen, plumbing the many lakes, ponds, and streams in the Sturbridge area.

The Julians were parishioners at St. Anne's Church, located on a 35-acre sanctuary operated by the Augustinians of the Assumption, not far from the Julians' Main Street home in Fiskdale. The shrine was a popular destination for the sick and infirm, who would gather during the summer months for novenas and visitations. The small white church—founded in 1883 to serve the French-speaking families who had come to work in the mills—housed a collection of crutches, braces, and other memorabilia bearing witness to those who experienced healing through the intercession of "Good St. Anne." As a youth, Rudy was an altar boy; he sang in the church choir and often accompanied Adelard to help out at the shrine. Many boys might have viewed such service as a nuisance, but Rudy didn't seem to mind. "He was always quiet and wanted to help anyone who needed assistance in any way and never seemed to lose his temper," recalled Gloria.

When he wasn't hunting or fishing, observed Julie, Rudy's favorite hobby was playing the harmonica. "He had several harmonicas, from the little metal one that he learned on by himself to those about six inches long with fancy engravings and levers to push in and out for sweeter sounds," Gloria remembered. "He was very good at playing songs by ear." They often played together. "I played the piano a little— not anywhere near great but passable for family gatherings," said Gloria. Cheerful tunes such as "You Are My Sunshine" and "Oh, Susanna" were among their favorites. "We spent many family evenings that way," she remarked.

In June 1937, Rudy graduated from Cole Trade High School in Southbridge, where he had trained as a cabinetmaker. That skill earned him a job at Southbridge's American Optical Company. The oldest optical company in the United States, the factory buildings sprawled over more than seventeen acres along Southbridge's Mechanic Street, turning out spectacles by the trainload. Rudy's job was to make cases for optometrist lens displays. He was a hard worker and well liked, observed his sisters, but when the war broke out there was no question that he would go into the service. "He was always very patriotic and carried the American flag on every occasion that called for it and with great pride," remembered Gloria. Family members recalled that he was serious about a local girl. Under other circumstances, he probably would have married her in time, had the war not intervened. He also must have had at least some sense that war was more duty than glory—his uncle had been severely gassed while serving overseas with the army during World War I and had struggled with the aftereffects on his health in subsequent years.

In January 1942 Rudy Julian enlisted in the Marine Corps Reserve and set off for recruit training at Parris Island. Standing six feet three inches tall and weighing in at about 200 pounds, he proved to be an outstanding Marine. His performance was such that, upon graduating from basic training, he was tapped to become a drill instructor. It seemed a natural job for the brother Julie described as "a Pied Piper to the kids in town—especially boys who wanted to go hunting with him and learn about guns and shooting." He managed to get home from time to time, including for sister Gloria's wedding in 1943. But as the war continued, Julian chafed at serving stateside. "He could have stayed at Parris Island as a drill instructor, but said he should go into active service because so many of the men had families and he was unmarried," recalled Gloria. "My mom begged him not to volunteer for this duty, but he was adamant about doing his duty."

As men were culled from various bases and units to fill out the new 5th Marine Division, Julian finally got his wish. In the summer of 1944, now a platoon sergeant, he was assigned to A Company, 1st Battalion, 27th Marines, at Camp Pendleton in California. His sister Julie, who had joined the women's branch of the Marines in April 1943 and been assigned as a sergeant/clerk in San Francisco, was the last family member to see him before he shipped out to Hawaii in August. They arranged to meet in Los Angeles. "He picked me up off the sidewalk and whirled me around—like he was glad to see me," she recalled nostalgically. "Again he smiled and teased me all evening about my 'stripes.'" The two took over a small piano in a café and joined in singing some old favorites. "They were old songs, 'You are My Sunshine,' 'Yellow Rose of Texas' and I think 'Pennies from Heaven,'" she recalled. "We had a good meal, lots of talk and then, of course, the end came. We had a big bear-hugging session, eye-to-eye, in tears, and said goodbye and God bless."

In mid-January, after months of training at Camp Tarawa, the 5th Division conducted a series of amphibious rehearsals. It was clear that combat was not far off. Rudy's company, commanded by Capt. John K. Hogan, a twenty-six-year-old former medical student from Iowa, embarked aboard the attack transport USS *Hansford* at Lahaina Roads, Maui, and sailed on January 27, west into the wide Pacific.

Two days out of Hawaii, battalion commanding officer Lt. Col. John A. Butler briefed his Marines on their destination: Iwo Jima. Unlike many of his men who had seen action as Raiders and Paramarines earlier in the war, Butler had yet to experience combat. A 1934 graduate of the Naval Academy, the tall, rawboned Louisianan was a career Marine who had spent most of the war assigned to the Naval Attaché office at the U.S. Embassy in the Dominican Republic. He was devoted to his wife, Denise, and three children (with another son soon on the way), but, like Rudy Julian, he itched to take a more direct role in the war. Disdaining his role as attaché, he pushed for a transfer to the Fleet Marine Force and combat. In January 1944 he was finally assigned to the 5th Marine Division, and shortly thereafter received command of the 1st Battalion, 27th Marines.

Plans for Iwo Jima called for Butler's battalion to land on the far right of the division's zone of action, with Companies B and C attacking abreast. Captain Hogan's A Company would follow in reserve. If Sergeant Julian and his comrades thought they had lucked out in being assigned a support role, they were quickly disabused of that notion as they came ashore with the fourth wave over Iwo's Red Beach 2 at about 0912. One Marine from the company had scarcely set foot on the beach when he was eviscerated in a mortar blast that left his intestines strewn in glistening cords on the black volcanic sand. Another A Company Marine, Cpl. Billy Dane Bowman, remembered looking up as a navy SBD dive bomber roaring low just offshore was hit by Japanese antiaircraft fire. The startled Marines could see the pilot slumped against his seat as the plane plummeted into the surf, narrowly missing an amtrac heading for the beach.

Scrambling up the first terrace after his platoon sergeant, eighteen-year-old PFC James Justice was shocked to see five men in tan uniforms running away from the beach. The Marines started firing. One of the Japanese fell, but the others disappeared. Over on the battalion left, a large pillbox housing a 47mm antitank gun and a heavy machine gun took the Marines under fire. A twenty-one-year-old BAR man, Pvt. Max Melville, went after it, pitching fragmentation and smoke grenades through the embrasure. Five enemy soldiers burst out. Melville raised his BAR and killed all five.

Finding that B Company had become disorganized during the landing, Lieutenant Colonel Butler directed Captain Hogan to take over Baker's sector. With Charlie on the left and Able on the right, the battalion pushed toward the southern corner of Motoyama Airfield No. 1. The two companies managed to advance west of the airfield's lower end by midafternoon and the battalion began digging in for the night. During the course of the day, the 1st Battalion had managed to claw forward 800 yards, well short of the 2,600 yards that had been anticipated. It was a precursor of things to come.

For the next week, the battalion was tasked with following up the main assault and cleaning out snipers and bypassed positions. It was not much better than being on the line. Artillery and mortars continued to inflict casualties, as did Japanese infantry holdouts. Among A Company's dead was PFC Harry Dale Hyde. On February 26 Hyde knocked out a Japanese machine-gun position holding up his platoon, then took on a second enemy stronghold located in a twelve-foot-tall observation tower. Climbing the tower, Hyde was fatally shot as he prepared to drop a grenade into the aperture.

The following day, the 27th Marines took over as the main assault force in the division sector, jumping off at 0800 following a heavy artillery barrage in an effort to neutralize Japanese positions on Hill 362A, north of Motoyama No. 2. Assigned to the center of the regimental line with Charlie on the left, Able on the right, and Baker in reserve, Butler's battalion made good progress to begin with, pushing forward 200 yards before running afoul of a series of carefully sited pillboxes and a blockhouse. Caught in an ambush, 1st Platoon was virtually annihilated, pinned down by a reinforced pillbox to its front and a withering fire from the flanks. Platoon leader 2nd Lt. Clair Voss, a former halfback on the Marquette University football team, climbed up on top of the pillbox and set off a demolitions charge, knocking it out and allowing what was left of the platoon to pull back, dragging their wounded.

The next few days were little better as the Marines struggled through what one witness described simply as a "sandstone jungle," under a hail of mortar, grenade, and small-arms fire from well-concealed Japanese. The entire area was a deathtrap with no respect to rank. On March 5, Lieutenant Colonel Butler was killed when a Japanese 47mm gun crew picked off his jeep. Butler's successor lasted four days before a booby-trapped six-inch shell blew his left arm off at the elbow. The number of A Company's dead mounted: Pvt. Richard R. Bulger on February 23; Pvt. Billy J. Birmingham on February 26; Pvt. Miguel O. Alarcon, Cpl. Elgin M. Giroir, Pvt. Donald W. Hoopes, Pvt. Charles L. Muncy, Sgt. Theo M. Lane, and Sgt. Eugene Visentin on February 27; PFC Albert J. Campbell, PFC James L. Forrister, PFC James Cederborg, PFC Edmond J. Labit, PFC Frederick M. Springer, and Pvt. Albert W. Toman on February 28; Pvt. Clinton M. Dunwiddie on March 1; PFC Earl Champlain on March 5 . . . the list went on and on, with another two men wounded for every man killed.

*A Marine lobs a grenade at a Japanese position
during the fighting in March on the northern end
of the island. USMC*

With the original platoons shot to pieces and replacements dying nearly as quickly as they could be fed into the lines, by March 9 Rudy Julian was among the few surviving noncoms that had originally come ashore with A Company eighteen days before. He could not have been optimistic about his prospects. That morning, C Company took the lead as the 1st Battalion attacked northeast of Hill 362B. The company moved 200 yards before it was forced to pull back under heavy frontal and flanking fire. Eight Marines were killed and fourteen wounded in an effort that brought no gain. Only two Marines remained in Charlie's 1st Platoon. Able Company was also stalled by a series of interlocking strongpoints, including a pair of pillboxes, two cave positions, and a web of entrenchments.

With the attack less than fifteen minutes old and already faltering, Julian scrambled to do what noncoms are supposed to do—keep things moving. Ducking low among the shattered rocks, he positioned his platoon in an effort to suppress the fire from the Japanese strongpoints. Then the man described by his sister as the "Pied Piper" of kids in his Massachusetts neighborhood took the lead. Gathering up demolition charges and loading himself down with white phosphorus grenades, he turned toward the entrenched Japanese. Maybe the twenty-five-year-old platoon sergeant had reached the point where he couldn't watch any more of his men die. Maybe he thought he could save at least a few of the fresh-faced innocents being fed into the meat grinder as replacements. Maybe he realized that what he was about to attempt was so suicidal that he couldn't ask anyone else to try. Maybe he was just plain tired. Whatever the reason, while his men laid down fire from the cover of the rocks, Rudy Julian went out after the enemy.

Crawling fifty yards through the jumble of rock—somehow avoiding being cut down by fire from the interlocking positions—the former drill instructor slowly worked his way toward the nearest of two Japanese pillboxes. The platoon poured out covering fire as Julian edged closer and closer to the pillbox, enemy return fire ricocheting among the rocks. Finally, he was there. As the platoon shifted its fire away from the targeted pillbox, Julian shoved a satchel charge into the structure, following it with white phosphorus grenades. At least two Japanese died in the blasts. As smoke poured from the aperture, five other Japanese bolted out of the pillbox into the adjoining trench system. Snatching up an M1 rifle lost or discarded during the earlier assault, Julian jumped into the trench and shot all five.

A Marine signals, adjusting the fire of a machine-gun crew on an enemy position, on March 9 during the push into Iwo's northern badlands. USMC

Slowly making his way back to the platoon, Julian replenished his stock of explosives and scarfed up a bazooka. Then he turned back to the remaining enemy strongpoints. "Your brother came back to get ammo, but before he got up he gave his canteen of water to a wounded Marine in a foxhole, picked up a bazooka, and took off," a witness told Julie Julian later. Accompanied by another Marine and loaded down with demolitions, Julian again worked slowly forward through the broken rock formations. The two Marines tackled the cave positions first, knocking them both out. Then Julian went after the last remaining pillbox. Maneuvering through the rubble, he shouldered the bazooka and fired a rocket at the strongpoint. Not satisfied, he reloaded and fired again. One after another, he put four rounds into the pillbox, completely demolishing it. "That's when they got him," a witness told Julian's sister later. As he fired the last rocket, a burst of machine-gun fire from yet another position slammed into his chest. Knocked to the ground, he died there on the rocky rubble.

In later years, Julian's sister Gloria expressed some surprise over her quiet, easygoing brother's rampage among the Japanese. "He never seemed to lose his temper, so it is difficult for me to imagine him in such a rage that he would enter that pillbox by himself," she said. "Perhaps his training as a drill instructor changed his character, but he always seemed the same when he came home on leave." Shortly after the war, two Marines who had served with Julian on Iwo Jima stopped by Sturbridge to visit his parents. "They were rather traumatized themselves and were very nearly incoherent after they spent a couple of hours with my mom and dad," recalled Gloria. "They were evidently still in rather a state of shock themselves and really upset my parents. . . . They said when Rudy saw so many of his men being killed by the Japs he seemed to become wild and just stalked ahead of everyone and marched right into the pill-box and of course was riddled with bullets."

The campaign to secure Iwo Jima was still wrapping up when the Julian family, now mourning Rudy's death, received more bad news: Rudy's cousin Rosaire, a twenty-year-old medic with the 3rd Infantry

Division, had been killed March 26 while his unit was crossing the Rhine River. Rosaire had already been wounded once at Anzio. This time his boat was hit by a German shell. His body was never recovered.

The *Worcester Sunday Telegram* took notice of Rudy Julian's death in its April 15 issue, observing that "a pre-burial solemn high mass" was celebrated for the son of Adelard and Rosalda Julian the morning of April 14 at St. Anne's Church in Fiskdale, adding, "Sergeant Julian was the first Fiskdale man to be killed in the armed forces in the current war."

The Medal of Honor was presented to Adelard and Rosalda by the Secretary of the Navy on November 15, 1945. Following the war, at the request of the family, Sergeant Julian's remains were interred at Long Island National Cemetery in Farmingdale, New York. Friends had urged them to have their son buried at Arlington National Cemetery in Virginia, but the Julians preferred a national cemetery that was closer to home. Adelard Julian died in 1957 and Rosalda followed in 1991. They are interred at St. George Cemetery in Southbridge, Massachusetts. Following Rosalda's death, Rudy's Medal of Honor passed to Julie; it remains in the proud possession of the family. Years later, Gloria expressed pride in her brother's heroism, but also regret at the price. "Had he not been so courageous, he probably would be alive today," she observed. "He was a swell guy."

Julie also recalled a peculiar incident that occurred shortly after the family received the telegram informing them of Rudy's death in action. "He had a dog, Dash, he hunted rabbits with," she remembered. "My mother told me that Dash left the house one day after they received that dreaded notice. Dash went up the hill behind the house and into the woods. He never came back. I have heard of such things as dogs sensing when their loving owners are ill. Do you suppose?"

CHAPTER SIX

Final Bell

As the battle for Iwo entered its twentieth day, the outcome was no longer in any doubt. Operating from a command post in what was left of Japanese territory on the northern tip of the island, General Kuribayashi reported to Tokyo that hundreds of American infantrymen with tanks were attacking nearby, and the level of bombing and small-arms fire was beyond description. "Before American forces landed on Iwo Jima," he continued, "there were many trees around my headquarters, but now there is not even a wisp of grass remaining. The surface of the earth has changed completely and we can see numerous holes of bombardments."

By now, the 3rd Marine Division had pretty much eradicated the enemy in its zone, while the 4th Marine Division was rooting out the last opposition in the badlands. With the eastern half of Iwo Jima relatively secure, the 5th Marine Division, facing a ridgeline running from the center of the island west to the sea, now confronted the core of die-hard resistance. Despite their hopeless situation, the Japanese survivors had lost none of their ferocity. On March 12 every artillery battalion on the island massed its fire on the enemy pocket—a total of 10,000 rounds poured down on the Japanese holdouts. An hour later, the 5th Marine Division sent two regiments into the attack against a ridgeline overlooking a gorge—soon to become known as "Bloody Gorge" or simply "The Gorge"—across its front. Two attacks netted only 30 yards at a cost of 143 officers and men killed or wounded.

Despite the horrendous casualties, the 5th Division was under tremendous pressure from the top brass to eradicate the last enemy resistance. According to one officer, V Corps commander Maj. Gen. Harry Schmidt called 5th Marine Division commanding officer, Maj. Gen. Keller E. Rockey, and told him that if his division did not advance immediately and take the approaches to the gorge, he would relieve Rockey of his command. One of Rockey's battalion commanders, tears streaming down his face, balked, saying he could no longer send his men into the attack to be killed for nothing. He was relieved of his command.

There was to be no respite.

PVT. GEORGE PHILLIPS

28th Marines, 5th Marine Division
March 14, 1945

George "Junior" Phillips USMC

It is said that time heals all wounds.

It doesn't.

More than five decades after the fighting ended on Iwo Jima, George "Junior" Phillips's foster brother still could not bring himself to talk about Junior's death in that cursed place. It did not matter that Junior was a hero; only that he would never come home.

Born July 14, 1926, at Rich Hill in western Missouri, the youngest child of Elizabeth and Isaac Phillips, George grew up in Labadie on the other side of the state, raised by his aunt and uncle, Lillian and James O'Brien. Located forty-five miles west of St. Louis, Labadie was a small rural town of a few hundred inhabitants, mostly farming families and railroad workers.

As late as 1999 a magazine writer dismissed the place as "an unincorporated settlement of about 250 humans and almost as many cats." That was something of an exaggeration, but Labadie was definitely a backwater in the 1930s.

George—known around town as Junior O'Brien—came to live with his aunt and uncle in Labadie when he was three years old. His arrival was due to tragic circumstances. His mother died in 1928, and his laborer father succumbed to pulmonary tuberculosis two years later. Their four children were taken in by various aunts and uncles. George ended up with the O'Briens, who already had two boys and a daughter of their own. The O'Briens called the little boy with the shy smile "Junie." As far as the town was concerned, Junior was an O'Brien. Once in a while there would be some reference to "George Phillips," recalled George's childhood friend, Emmett Becker, "and we thought there must be a new kid in school."

James O'Brien worked for the Missouri-Pacific Railroad on the "section" as they called it, keeping the track maintained. The O'Briens were devout, church-going people, attending the local Methodist church where Junior went to Sunday school. Lillian's obituary some years later observed, "Hers was a happy home where friends and stranger alike felt at home on entering the door."

Orphaned at an early age, Junior Phillips was raised by his aunt and uncle. Courtesy of Franklin County Historical Society

The family lived just down the hill from the Labadie school-house. "We always thought he was real lucky because he didn't have to walk a mile to the school," recalled Emmett Becker, whose father owned a farm where he and Junior would sometimes engage in spir-ited corncob wars. "I remember him as a quiet kid," he remarked. "You know, he wasn't boisterous or something like that. He was just a good old boy. He didn't cause any trouble. He wasn't a hell-raiser or anything like that."

Junior's foster sister, Edna Dutton, also described him as a quiet, even shy youngster. "His favorite holiday was Christmas—decorating the tree, opening presents and all the rest of the festivities with his young nieces and nephews," she recalled. "He also loved the outdoors and enjoyed hunting and fishing," and was active in Boy Scouts. His childhood ambition was to be a Big League ball player, and he could generally be found on the local ball field as a young boy, she remarked.

Junior attended Labadie Grade School. Emmett Becker, who was in the class behind Junior, observed that it was a small school, even by rural standards. "His class graduated three students and mine seven students," he said. Edna Dutton recalled that her foster brother loved school and received several certificates for perfect attendance. Like so many of his generation, however, Junior did not have the luxury of pursuing any higher education. He left school after the eighth grade to go to work. An old family photo shows him standing in his yard, proudly holding his eighth-grade graduation certificate, the school-house visible on the hill behind him. His hair is neatly combed and he is wearing a slightly-too-large suit in honor of the occasion.

Junior worked in the area for several Labadie farmers before land-ing a job as a painter on the Shell Oil Company pipeline. The line car-ried oil from wells in Oklahoma to refineries near St. Louis, its course taking it two or three miles east of Labadie where there was a pump station. By then Junior was turning into a young man. "I'd say he was a good six foot tall and slender," remarked Becker. "I always remember him as wearing overalls, which most of us did back in those days."

But Junior's primary attention was now on the war. His foster brother Earl had joined the army before Pearl Harbor and was only months away from combat in Europe with the 5th Armored Division. His other foster brother Arthur would soon be in the army as well. Still only seventeen years old, Junior had his heart set on the Marines. He traveled eighty-seven miles to Jefferson City to obtain a copy of his birth certificate to present to the recruiters, and on April 26, 1944, still three months short of his eighteenth birthday, he went into the Marine Corps.

He received his basic training at San Diego, then came home on a short furlough. It was the last time his aunt and uncle would ever see him. After advanced training at Camp Pendleton, he shipped out to Hawaii shortly before Christmas. He was assigned to the 27th Replacement Battalion, which was attached to the 5th Marine Division for the assault on Iwo Jima. Each of the three divisions slated for the attack was allocated two such battalions, each battalion containing 75 officers and 1,250 enlisted men. The personnel were to be used to help shore parties unload supplies during the initial landing, and would then be fed into the line units as casualties warranted.

Also assigned to the 27th Replacement Battalion, nineteen-year-old Pvt. Albert B. Knickrehm recalled arriving off Iwo among a crowd of warships, transports, and support vessels. "It was still dark and they were firing—the warships were firing shells into Iwo Jima" he said, "and the sky was lit almost like daylight and you could see the shells going through the air and the Japanese were firing the shells back whenever they could, especially out from . . . this volcano called Suribachi. . . . And it was quite an awesome sight to see for a young farm boy from Iowa who had never seen anything like that." The former Iowa farm boy observed that he and the other replacements were ready, even eager, to go into action. "We were young guys," he explained. "I was only nineteen years old. Actually, we were kind of looking forward to seeing a little action, you know. We were full of a lot of guts and we were kind of—I was kind of looking forward to that."

As the landing got underway, Phillips and the others followed the assault troops ashore and began unloading supplies and working on the beach amid exploding Japanese shells. Pvt. Bob McLanahan, a twenty-one-year-old former truck mechanic from Collinsville, Illinois, who served alongside Junior, recalled that first day as pushing endless numbers of "jeeps, tractors, artillery pieces and whatever" through the deep sand. "We worked with landing mats and munitions until dark on a dead run," he observed. When darkness fell, they were assigned to carry stretcher cases to a waiting LSM (Landing Ship Medium). "At this time the LSM had not yet been unloaded and we had stretchers stacked everywhere. The last stretcher my buddy and I carried (the last one the ship had room for) almost did us in," remarked McLanahan. Their labors were only beginning. "The next few days we fought and worked on the beach," he recalled. "Supplies were hard to get in with the sand and we must have laid thousands of landing mats."

Shore party personnel unload supplies on the beach. Both Harry Martin and George Phillips were assigned to this duty early in the campaign. USMC

Their job was no rear-echelon safe haven. Concentrated Japanese shellfire on the landing area over the first two or three days made the beach as dangerous—if not more so, at times—as the so-called front lines. "There was kind of a shelling of mortar shells and that type of thing coming, and machine gun fire coming out of Suribachi," said Knickrehm. "So it was not a safe place. Actually, [there] was never a safe place on Iwo Jima, because it was such a small island."

Meanwhile, as the days passed, the need for replacements in the combat units was becoming critical. The Marine infantry companies were being shot to pieces. Green troops fed into the line from the replacement battalions became casualties almost as soon as they arrived. Poorly trained, inexperienced, and joining units as individuals, many were killed or wounded before anyone had time to even learn their names. One battalion commander wrote later, "The casualties in those kids was horrifying. Some just sort of wandered around until they got shot or huddled in exposed places."

About a week after the landing, Junior Phillips and Bob McLanahan got their turn, two of the 292 officers and men sent as replacements to the 28th Marines. Phillips and McLanahan were assigned to Company F—or what was left of it. There seemed to be more newcomers than there were survivors. "When we met with the ones left, there were very few," McLanahan observed soberly. The company was commanded by Capt. Art Naylor, a former Paramarine, who had a tendency to express himself with football metaphors when talking with noncoms and fellow officers. F Company had achieved a reputation during training for being able to move rapidly to any given objective, but with so many new men, it was not the same outfit that had landed on February 19.

There was no time for acclimatization. The replacements had scarcely arrived when, on February 28, the regiment moved north and relieved elements of the 27th Marines. The 27th had been battling for days to seize Hill 362A, in the face of desperate enemy resistance from caves and pillboxes dug into the vertical cliffs. The newly arrived 2nd Battalion's first main objective was to reach an unimproved road that ran in front of the hill. The attack began at 0900 on March 1, and "the battalion promptly ran into heavy resistance and the most difficult terrain imaginable," according to the after-action report.

On March 2, the battalion tried something different and sent F Company around the left of Hill 362A, with tanks in support. The Marines met terrific fire from the reverse slope and suffered heavy casualties. A blockhouse built into the side of the hill raised havoc with Fox Company until gunfire finally managed to collapse the hillside above and bury the fortification. Among the dead that day was the battalion commander, Lt. Col. Chandler Johnson, killed by an exploding shell soon after leaving Fox Company's command post.

Despite the losses, by late afternoon the 2nd Battalion had fought its way past the flanks of Hill 362A and onto Nishi Ridge just beyond. The Marines dug in. After dark a large group of bypassed Japanese came down from Hill 362A and attempted to attack F Company from the rear. The Marines killed forty-seven of them. "The following morning Captain Naylor of F Company and a detail from his company found thirty of the enemy playing possum in the open ground in front of the hill and killed them with flamethrowers and small arms," reported the battalion.

After two more days of battering forward against well-entrenched Japanese determined to die in place, the 2nd Battalion was pulled out of the line. With able-bodied Marines in short supply, their rest was all too brief. On March 8, Fox Company was back in action, trying to move against a series of parallel ridges fronting Hill 165 and Kitano Point. "Again the battalion found itself fighting up hills, through cross corridors and against numerous caves and pillboxes," observed the 2nd Battalion after-action report. The 5th Division intelligence officer estimated that at least 1,000 Japanese defenders remained on the northern end of the island, and there appeared to be no shortage of weapons or ammunition. They had burrowed into the ridges like moles. When a 500-pound bomb landed at the mouth of a cave near Kitano Point, a puff of smoke blew out of a cliff face over 400 yards away. Another bomb landing at a cave entrance sent a ring of smoke and dust billowing out of firing apertures and vents over a 200-yard radius.

Bob McLanahan was part of a squad ordered to patrol down into the warren of rocky gullies to check out a grass-covered shelter. The shelter was about twenty feet square and had been built up against a steep cliff. McLanahan was not enthusiastic about going down there—and even less so when, shortly before setting off, a shell wounded the lieutenant and the sergeant who were supposed to lead the patrol. Nevertheless, he and the others made their way down a long steep path and followed a gully toward the shelter.

"We positioned ourselves," recalled McLanahan. "I remember that Wallace was to the extreme left on a shelf of the stone wall. Maddock was about two feet to my left. Just to the right rear of me was McKenna laying in a little swag. Bob, with the flamethrower, was to our right and Palmer and Ziggy were behind us near the ditch. When Bob was to light the hutch with the flamethrower, the rest of us were to move forward. Bob fired at the shelter and all heck broke loose. The entire wall in front of us opened up with fire. Never saw a Jap. Behind this stone hill they had tunneled all over with just peek holes and holes to shoot through. When the signal was to go, I raised up and took two steps to the right. Maddock did the same. Maddock was hit through the helmet and was instantly dead. Wallace to our left is dead. Bob the flamethrower was dead." McLanahan lay doggo for about an hour, then heard a guarded whisper from behind him. It was Pvt. John McKenna checking to see if he was still alive. McKenna suddenly bolted for safety, followed soon after by McLanahan, both somehow managing to dodge a hail of bullets. Two other Marines, one of them shot in the foot, also survived.

Years later, McLanahan observed soberly of combat on Iwo, "There were no good days, just some better than others." Still, the advance ground slowly forward. By March 12, the 28th Marines found themselves facing a long ridgeline running northwest–southeast across the front. The south slope of the ridgeline was fairly gradual, but cut with many small parallel draws. The top was heavily fortified with pillboxes and spider traps, and the north side dropped off in a steep cliff forty to seventy feet high, honeycombed with many caves. It was believed that this ridgeline marked the western edge of the enemy's final defensive line on northern Iwo Jima. As viewed on a map, the end appeared near, but it was not certain the Marines on the line retained the strength to finish the job. The 28th Marines were exhausted. Several companies had been reduced to the size of rifle platoons, and the survivors were fatigued to the point of dropping in their tracks. The regimental commander estimated combat efficiency at 40 percent. That assessment may have been generous. "It was running on empty," Capt. Fred Haynes, the 28th's Tactical Control Officer, said of his regiment. "It was running, what was left of it, on spirit and sheer guts alone." Because of the depleted strength of the infantry units and the bone-deep fatigue of the survivors, "it was a virtual impossibility to do more than seize the top of the ridgeline," reported the 2nd Battalion. It was finally decided that the regiment would seize the ridge and then stay in place, while adjacent units attacked across their front and down the gorge beyond the ridge to the sea.

On March 13, F and D Companies went after the ridge. It was a nightmare. "After two attempts to take an area, we were called back to the old line," recalled McLanahan. "The hill we had tried to take was covered with dead Marines. We regrouped in a gully and I must say we were beat to the ground. . . . We are kind of laying around on the rocks in this gully and I remember George Phillips made this one statement as he had a cigarette stuck to his lower lip. He said, 'If there were just some way to stop all of this killing.'" Moments later, Captain Naylor came along and stood on a rock in the ditch to address them. "By God," Naylor told them, "we are going to take that ground this time and I want you riflemen to give the others some support." He left, and a short time later the company runner came up and tried to give them some pills, apparently some kind of amphetamine. Someone knocked the pills to the ground and snapped, "If we are going to die, it won't be with pills."

McLanahan, Phillips, and the others got ready. Their corporal said he would count down. "On zero, we all take off—that means everyone." McLanahan was wondering where they would find room on the hill among all the dead Marines. There appeared to be no space left for the living. Otherwise the approach "was fairly flat ground with rocks, some a foot high, scattered all over," he remembered. The corporal gave the word and off they went.

"The minute we jumped out a Jap Nambu machine gun on our right flank and [another on] our left flank opened up," recalled McLanahan. As they crawled through the rocks on their bellies, Pvt. Elmer G. Palmer looked behind him and saw the corporal still back at the jump-off point. Lying on his side, he yelled to the corporal, "Get out here with us or I'll nail you!" The corporal jumped up to join them and immediately collapsed, hit in the leg. Phillips was off to the right, while the other four Marines remained pretty close to one another. "We [were] crawling out like snakes with constant Jap Nambus firing from both flanks, taking the tops of rocks off above our heads," recalled McLanahan. One of the Marines with McLanahan panicked and the others tried to restrain him without exposing themselves. As the attack failed, word came to pull back. Somehow they all made it. "We made it back to the starting point and to the very best of my memory, we never ever saw anyone from our company," said McLanahan. "We just assumed they were all dead or at least most of them."

It wasn't quite that bad, though it was bad enough. While Fox Company's assault had failed, Dog Company to the right struggled forward, almost literally inch by inch, and by 1620 reached the top of the ridge. At 1700 the companies were ordered to tie in their defenses for the night. Dusk found McLanahan, Phillips, and a couple of other men hunkered down on a piece of high ground. "We were laying all over the ground trying to rest up," recalled McClanahan. The Marine who had panicked during the assault on the hill had been evacuated. Staring blankly, he had nothing left. "He didn't know us or in fact anybody or anything," remarked McLanahan.

Their respite ended when a sergeant came along and pointed to McLanahan, Phillips, and privates Elmer Palmer, John McKenna and Robert E. Newton. "Stock up on ammo and grenades and follow me," he ordered. The sergeant took them over the crest and down a long slope. "The night was very dark and you could hardly see anything," remembered McLanahan. "He took us about 100 feet out on the flat ground and said, 'Dig in here.'"

The youngsters looked at the stony ground and objected, "Sarge, this is solid rock."

"I want a foxhole right here," repeated the noncom.

"The five of us ended up building a parapet with rocks, maybe ten to twelve feet in diameter and no more than one and a half feet high," recalled McLanahan. They made trips back to their former position for more ammo and grenades. The sergeant disappeared. Afterward, McLanahan couldn't remember the man's name. He later wondered if he had subconsciously blocked it from his memory "because we all thought he was way off base."

It was clear from the beginning they were in a bad spot, isolated and beyond the view of the Marines behind them. "All night we heard Japs talking and running up and down the path," observed McLanahan. "As night turned into daylight very slowly, and our rock parapet was finished, we were straining our eyes to see what kind of area we were in. Finally we see directly in front of us, about 100 feet out, a huge domed pillbox with two gun holes facing us head on. Just in front of the pillbox was a creek or gully. Everything was absolutely quiet." Though they didn't realize it, they had already been targeted by unseen Japanese. The quiet came to an abrupt end as a flurry of grenades suddenly showered down in and around their makeshift rock wall. "All at once, grenades came at us hot and heavy," said McLanahan. "I think most of the grenades were concussion type rather than fragmentation

Unable to dig in, Marines fight back from behind a rock barricade. George Phillips and his buddies had taken cover in a similar spot when a Japanese grenade landed among them. USMC

grenades. The five of us threw [back what seemed like] hundreds of grenades, or at least enough to make my right arm ache."

The exchange could not go on indefinitely. Finally—inevitably—a sputtering, sparking Japanese grenade landed among the five Marines, with no time to toss it back. Without a word, Junior Phillips smothered it. "George took the blast with his chest and two hands," recalled McLanahan. "He was killed instantly. Newton got a small hit, McKenna a small hit, Palmer a blast to his left buttocks. I being probably the closest to George did not receive any of the grenade."

Fortunately for the survivors, the Japanese grenadiers apparently decided to pull back to the big pillbox. The grenades stopped, but enemy machine guns kept the four Marines pinned down behind their meager parapet, crammed in alongside Junior's body. Their woes increased when a U.S. flame-throwing tank, with "The Torch" inscribed on the gun barrel, pulled up behind their refuge. The tankers couldn't see them and "[t]he Japs never let up enough for us to ever pop our heads out of the parapet," said McLanahan. The tank opened up on the Japanese bunker with a stream of napalm. "The hot chunks started falling on us, like burning chewing gum," recalled McLanahan. One of the Marines pulled out his poncho and they tried to cover themselves, but the chunks burned right through. The tank finally ran out of napalm and backed off, but soon returned and repeated the process all over again. "Each time the tank backed off, Nambu and rifle fire hit us constantly," recalled McLanahan.

Finally, late in the day, Newton said he was getting out. "He made a mad dash up the hill in a hail of machine gun fire and we still don't know how he made it," said McLanahan. The others waited until the sun went down and then, one by one, made their escape up the hill.

A flamethrower-equipped tank works over dug-in Japanese defenders. A tank like this created problems for Junior Phillips's buddies when they were pinned down by a machine gun. USMC

Not a shot was fired at them. "We all took different spots and when I hit the top of the ridge and over the top, I dove in a foxhole occupied by four Marines sitting in the hole with fixed bayonets," said McLanahan. "We scared each other, but I didn't get bayoneted."

Tucked in McLanahan's pocket was a note with Junior's address scribbled on it. "At that time of my life I didn't know where Labadie, Missouri, was," he said years later. "He used to talk about Hawk Point when we asked him what he did in the hills and sticks. As his body lay among us, we slipped his wallet from his rear pocket for one reason, to get his address. It said George Phillips in care of James O'Brien, Labadie, MO."

Junior's sixty-year-old uncle accepted his Medal of Honor on February 17, 1946, at a ceremony at the Methodist Church where the youngster once attended Sunday school. A Marine Corps lieutenant colonel did the honors. Photographs of Mr. O'Brien at the occasion show a broad-shouldered man with wire-rim glasses who appears to be making a concerted effort to keep his emotions in check. The crowd

Junior Phillips's uncle James O'Brien accepts his posthumous Medal of Honor from Lt. Col. M. Dobervich during ceremonies on February 17, 1946, at the Methodist Church in Labadie, Missouri. Courtesy of Franklin County Historical Society

included large numbers of veterans just home from the war. "Quite a turnout," recalled Emmett Becker. Not present was Junior's Aunt Lillian, who had passed away the preceding June, not quite three months after his death on Iwo Jima.

Initially buried in the 5th Marine Division Cemetery on Iwo Jima, Junior's remains were returned home in 1948 and interred in Labadie's Bethel Cemetery under a government marker. Some years later, Emmett Becker, by then commander of the American Legion Post in Labadie, formed a committee to erect a suitable memorial to his boyhood friend. The memorial and plaque, located at Labadie Cemetery, was dedicated in 1990. "It turned out real well," remarked Becker. "We had a little excess money, so we got a flag pole and a flag and the flag flies all the time with the light on it at nighttime. It's right along the state highway."

Among those attending the dedication ceremony was Bob McLanahan, who had survived Iwo Jima and returned home to Illinois, where he raised a family and started his own automobile sales business, McLanahan Motors. He told Emmett Becker he would never forget the young Marine who had saved his life. "Every morning when I first look in the mirror, I thank George Phillips for another day," he said. A photograph of Junior hung on the wall in McClanahan's home in Collinsville to the day he died in June 2003—nearly sixty years after that terrible morning on Iwo Jima.

Labadie, Missouri, remains a small backwater today, though the urban sprawl from St. Louis is beginning to encroach on the old rural life. But people still remember the orphan who came to live there so long ago—the kid everybody called "Junior." "You look at kids today and they're not quite nineteen or something, and you think, 'That's as far as [Junior] got,'" remarks Emmett Becker with mixed sadness and pride. "It's sad. But it's a fact of life, I guess."

The 5th Marine Division daily report characterized action along the line the morning of March 14 as light. "Activity on the front of LT26 could be heard, but was broken up by mortar fire," noted the summary. "The rest of the line was relatively quiet, although there was a lively exchange of hand grenades on the extreme left flank of 2/28 about dawn." Thus did the keepers of records make note of George "Junior" Phillips's final stand.

That same morning, at 0930, V Amphibious Corps conducted an official flag raising alongside a demolished Japanese bunker just north of Mount Suribachi. Attended by flag and general officers of the fleet and landing force, the ceremony was intended to mark the pending seizure of Iwo Jima. As the new flag went up on an eighty-foot flagpole, the flag atop Mount Suribachi was lowered. Following the ceremony, the Commander Expeditionary Troops and his staff left Iwo Jima by air. Not so fortunate was a youngster from New Jersey named Frank Sigler, one of the few remaining survivors of Fox Company, 26th Marines, still digging Japanese out of caves and pillboxes to the north.

PVT. FRANKLIN E. SIGLER

26th Marines, 5th Marine Division
March 14, 1945

Frank Sigler USMC

Nearly seventy years after World War II ended, miraculously sparing their lives, old Marines reminiscing over the days of their youth still got a laugh about how PFC Frank Sigler lost his stripe.

It was the summer of 1944 and Sigler's regiment, the 26th Marines, had been detached from the 5th Marine Division for possible use as a reserve force during the seizure of Guam.

"We got as far as Hilo, Hawaii, and the casualties at Guam hadn't been as bad as they were at Saipan so they evidently didn't need us," recalled PFC Rudy Mueller. "So we sat there in the harbor on a troopship five days while they tried to figure out were we going to Guam or were we going to stay there. And it was hot. There was no air conditioning in those things."

Hot and bored, twenty-year-old Sigler and three of his buddies—fire team leader Cpl. Jim Campisi, PFC Walt Nixon, and PFC Ed McLoughlin—were leaning on the rail idly watching Hawaiian kids swimming around the ship like fish, diving for coins the Marines tossed over the side, when it suddenly occurred to one of the intrepid group that a dip in the ocean would be awfully refreshing. "So Jim and Sigler, McLoughlin and Nixon decide they're going to go up and put on their swim trunks and jump off the fantail," recalled Mueller. "And they did. And they're swimming around there." Their fun didn't last long. "Someone on the ship called out, 'Man overboard,' and all sorts of emergency procedures took over," said Mueller. A guard yelled for the officer of the day, there was an uproar aboard ship, orders were shouted, the captain's gig was lowered, and the four delinquents were unceremoniously hauled out of the water. "When we got up to Camp Tarawa each one of them lost a stripe," chuckled Mueller. "So Sigler got busted to private, Nixon and McLoughlin to private and Campisi was broken down to private first class." Sigler probably didn't waste much time brooding. "He was a happy-go-lucky guy," observed Mueller.

Born November 6, 1924, in Montclair, New Jersey, Franklin Earl Sigler was the third child of George and Elsie Sigler, whose brood eventually totaled five boys and a girl. George was self-employed as a plumber. The family later moved to Little Falls, a town of about 5,300 souls in Passaic County, in northern Jersey. Frank went to high school there and worked for his father as a plumber's apprentice, and also at a local gas station. He was remembered mostly as a quiet youngster who liked the outdoors.

When war came, Frank's older brother Bill was already in the service, having joined the Marine Corps Reserve in Newark in 1939. His unit was mobilized in November 1940, and Bill ended up in the 11th Marines, the artillery regiment of the 1st Marine Division. He went overseas with the division in May 1942. The 11th Marines participated in the seizure of Guadalcanal in August, and at the conclusion of that campaign returned to New Zealand. A reorganization in December reassigned Bill's battalion of 155mm guns to I Amphibious Corps. But tragedy soon followed. That summer a telegram arrived at the Sigler family home in Little Falls. The news was the worst a family could receive: their son, twenty-one-year-old PFC William C. Sigler, was dead, killed on June 11, 1943, not in combat but in a jeep accident in New Zealand.

The family was devastated. Three years older than Frank, Bill was a considerate young man who had been training with his father to be a plumber prior to enlisting in the Marines. He pitched in with the volunteer fire department, and loved fixing old cars and racing speedboats. "It was the first time I had seen my father cry," recalled Frank's younger brother, Melvin. "My father didn't go to pieces when his mother passed, but when Bill died, that was it."

Adding to their worries, Frank was already gone. On March 23, 1943, he had followed in Bill's footsteps and signed on for his own set of dress blues. The eighteen-year-old recruit completed his boot training at Parris Island, and in June was assigned to the Guard Company, Marine Barracks, at the navy yard in Charleston, South Carolina. Also a member of the Guard Company at that time was Rene Gagnon, who, within a year, would gain fame as one of the five Iwo Jima flag raisers.

As members of the Guard Company, Sigler and Gagnon helped provide security at the 700-acre navy yard, a sprawling collection of dry docks, oil tanks, barracks, piers, wharfs, storehouses, and machine shops, employing almost 26,000 workers. It was monotonous duty and Sigler was presumably not unhappy when, in April 1944, as stateside units and ship detachments were stripped of personnel to help fill out the 5th Marine Division, he joined a large contingent from the Guard Company sent to Camp Pendleton. The newcomers were dispersed among the three regiments. Bound for fame on Mount Suribachi, Gagnon ended up with the 28th Marines. Sigler and a couple of others were assigned to the 3rd Platoon in Fox Company, 2nd Battalion, 26th Marines.

Eighteen-year-old Rudy Mueller, who had been with the company since March, recalled "Siggy" as being "I'd say maybe five-foot-nine, five-foot-ten. Like most of us at that time we were thin. I was just a little over six-foot and I weighed 154 when I went into the Marine Corps and when I came out in '46 I weighed 156." Mueller, whose father owned a grocery store in Louisville, Kentucky, would subsequently become quite friendly with Sigler, but for now the newcomer associated mostly with his former Guard Company pals. He had no problem fitting in. "Frank was a happy-go-lucky person who liked to play jokes on others—he had a hard time being serious about anything," recalled Mueller. "But he was always a good Marine in the field."

In July the 26th Marines boarded ship for Hawaii and their aborted role in the Guam campaign, followed by more training at Camp Tarawa up in the hills of the Big Island. Finally, in January 1945, the regiment began to board ship at Hilo for what would be the first step in their journey to Iwo Jima. Everyone knew they were headed for combat; they just didn't know where. "Going to Iwo our ships spent some time at Pearl Harbor and we had occasional liberty in Honolulu," recalled Mueller. "The big thing was to see how much beer you could drink while on liberty. They made it hard for us because all the bars limited you to two drinks and then out. On to the next bar, get in line and wait twenty-five or thirty minutes to get in and again, two drinks and out. If you were lucky, before it was time to head back to the fleet landing to get a liberty boat back to your ship, you may have seen the inside of five or six bars."

"During one of these liberties, Frank lost his cap in a bar," remembered Mueller. "Without the cap he was sure to be picked up by the

Shore Patrol or the MPs. Several of us chipped in our drinking money, hired a cab to avoid being on the streets and rode back to the fleet landing. The S.P.s there took Frank's pass away from him, and when we boarded our ship, APA #121 [*Hocking*], the Officer of the Day stopped him. Our platoon leader, Lieutenant Marty Gelshenen, had to come get him and we had to explain what had taken place. Frank did some mess duty on the ship for losing his cap."

Weeks later, as the 5th Marine Division stood to off Iwo Jima on February 19, Frank Sigler's missing cap had become a triviality. Late in the morning, Fox Company went over the side of the *Hocking*, clambering laboriously down cargo nets into the bobbing landing craft below. Waiting in reserve, they circled offshore for hours, getting seasick and hoping none of the Japanese shells sending up spouts of water around them would land in their boat. Most were grateful when the boats finally headed for shore. They soon found that they had merely gone from frying pan to fire. "First we had to move through the loose black sand (really volcanic ash/cinders from Mount Suribachi) and climb ten- to fifteen-foot terraces to reach firmer ground," recalled Mueller. "All the time we were in sight of thousands of Japs firing weapons to kill us."

Mueller clambered up a terrace and jumped into a big shell hole. There was another Marine already there, but when Mueller tried to talk to him, he realized the man was dead; a bullet had punched through one side of his helmet and out the other. "I moved out of the shell hole thinking the guy had died with a stomach full of steak and eggs from our shipboard breakfast that morning," said Mueller. Meanwhile, Fox Company had already suffered its first casualty—a gunnery sergeant wounded in the legs by a mortar blast almost as soon as he hit the beach. A fire team loaded him back into an LCVP for evacuation, kidding him that he had a "glory wound" and would soon be back in the States. The gunny was already in shock and paid no attention to them.

By dusk, Fox was digging in, apprehensively awaiting a Japanese banzai attack that never materialized. Lt. Bill Eckerson, a former

Colgate College athlete now serving as a platoon leader, remembered a Japanese somewhere out in the darkness yelling, "Marine, you die!" After a prolonged silence, he recalled, the Marines rallied with "the appropriate responses." Rudy Mueller spent the night dug into a foxhole at the end of a runway on Airfield No. 1. He had yet to fire a shot or see a Japanese. "The night passed with lots of Jap shelling of our position, but no ground attack," he recalled. "We had lived one day in combat."

Riflemen cover a flamethrower burning out a cave in terrain too rugged for tanks. USMC

On D+1, Fox began what would be a long bloody slog north. "We moved up the island going three or four hundred yards a day," observed Eckerson. Most days the gains were far less—sometimes measured in feet—and none without a price. It began slowly. Second Lt. William D. Cassidy was the first Fox Company fatality, hit in the chest by small-arms fire. PFC Donald W. Prestella was wounded by a gunshot to the neck. The following day, four more Fox Company Marines were wounded; on February 22 the casualty count was six, and on February 23 it was eleven, including Pvt. Laurence J. Walker, who was killed by multiple shrapnel wounds. On the 24th one man was killed and two wounded; the following day, seven men were hit, including 1st Lt. William D. Martt, who died of wounds aboard ship, and PFC Thomas F.

Morisak. February 26 was a veritable blood bath, with forty-two Fox Company casualties, including sixteen killed in heavy fighting west of Airfield No. 2 on the approach to Hill 362A. March 3 was even worse, with forty-nine casualties, including twenty-three dead. Among the casualties on March 3 was Frank Sigler's squad leader, Sgt. Hans G. Hirschland, who had been one of the Guard Company transfers the previous April. Hirschland, who had been wounded three days after the landing but returned to the company after a few days, was evacuated for good this time. The once happy-go-lucky Sigler took over what was left of his squad.

At 0930 on March 14, two days before the island was formally declared secure, V Amphibious Corps conducted an official flag raising attended by flag and general officers of the fleet and landing force. To the north of this brief ceremony, Frank Sigler's battalion, now down to seventy men per company, was also on the move, pushing forward against Japanese holdouts dug in among the steep, rocky crags on northern Iwo. "Enemy resistance was light on March 14, and it became evident that the Japanese had little left but machine guns, knee mortars, grenades and rifles," observed the 5th Division historian. The fact that the historian apparently considered it good news that the Japanese only had machine guns left speaks volumes for the ferocity of the campaign. Heavy casualties had sapped Marine morale; the ragged, filthy survivors could only wonder if any of them would escape the island in one piece.

"By [14] March we had lost so many men that the remains of the three rifle platoons had been consolidated into one unit under replacement Lieutenant Bill Grannell," recalled Rudy Mueller. Grannell, a second-string player on the 1943 Notre Dame championship football team, had brought up a couple of dozen new men from the 27th Replacement Draft on March 7. The twenty-three-year-old native of Denver, Colorado, took over from the two privates first class and one corporal who had been running the platoons, and quickly earned the veterans' respect by his willingness to listen to the voice of experience. Nevertheless, after another week of combat, by March 14 the weary survivors had been bogged down for two days in the face of fierce resistance. "A Jap emplacement had us stopped," explained Mueller. "Our rifles, BARs, machine guns and grenades did not damage the Japs." The terrain was too rough for tanks. "What we really needed was a 37mm piece that they could roll up there or we needed a bazooka or something like that," added Mueller. "Which we didn't have."

Mueller headed to the rear to look for more firepower. On the way, he narrowly escaped becoming the latest in a long line of Fox Company casualties when a hidden Japanese opened up on him and shot the first aid kit right off his hip. Mueller kept going, and about 150 yards back he came across his battalion commander, Maj. Amedeo Rea, and some engineers. Rea was looking for the front lines and company command posts. "They all thought I had been hit because the [iodine] bottle in the kit shattered and the medicine ran down my pants leg—it looked like blood," said Mueller. He assured them he was all right, directed Rea to the Fox Company command post, coaxed a bazooka and some shells from the engineers, and headed back to his platoon. Safely back, the shock of his narrow escape began to sink in. "So when I got up there, I wasn't ready to start running around with a bazooka," he recalled. "I just laid it down. And Frank picked it up."

Sigler gathered what was left of his squad—"a squad was thirteen men and he probably had five or six guys left there," said Mueller—and moved them into position facing the enemy gun position dug into the rocks. "He took them over to that thing and got them lined up to cover him when he was going to fire that bazooka," recalled Mueller. Accompanied by Cpl. Homer Neelly and lugging the bazooka and some rockets, Sigler set out after the Japanese position that had been holding up Fox Company for close to two days. "And he took the bazooka on up where he could get a shot at this place and he shot that thing two or three times and knocked this thing out," recalled Mueller. "From that point on, 'Siggy' aggressively went after Japs until he was wounded."

The subsequent citation for Sigler's Medal of Honor varies somewhat from Mueller's eyewitness account, noting that Sigler used grenades to knock out the first Japanese position. He "fearlessly led a bold charge against an enemy gun installation which had held up the advance of his company for several days and, reaching the position in advance of the others, assailed the emplacement with hand grenades and personally annihilated the entire crew," states the citation.

A bazooka team takes aim. Both Doug Jacobson and Frank Sigler put the bazooka to good use during their actions on Iwo Jima.
USMC

But that was not the end of it. Sigler found he had kicked over a hornets' nest. According to his citation, "As additional Japanese troops opened fire from concealed tunnels and caves above, he quickly scaled the rocks leading to the attacking guns, surprised the enemy with a furious one-man assault and, although severely wounded in the encounter, deliberately crawled back to his squad position where he steadfastly refused evacuation, persistently directing heavy gun and rocket barrages on the Japanese cave entrances. Undaunted by the merciless rain of hostile fire during the intensified action, he gallantly disregarded his own painful wounds to aid casualties, carrying three wounded squad members to safety behind the lines and returning to continue the battle with renewed determination until ordered to retire for medical treatment."

According to battalion records, Sigler's wound consisted of a gunshot to the right hand, which required his evacuation. He was lucky. Some indication of the magnitude of the resistance he faced while opening the way for his platoon is reflected in Fox Company's casualty list for the day: the company lost fourteen wounded and one man killed on March 14. By the end of the campaign, Fox and the 2nd Battalion were shadows of their former selves. Of the thirty-seven officers and 917 enlisted that came ashore with the 2nd Battalion on February 19, only ten officers and ninety-six enlisted were not battle casualties or sick by the end of the campaign. Fox Company landed on Iwo Jima with 243 officers and men, and seven navy corpsmen. When the company left Iwo Jima on March 25, of the original men, only one officer and thirteen enlisted had not been killed or wounded. One of the blessed few that walked off was Rudy Mueller.

Discharged from the hospital, Sigler rejoined the company back at Camp Tarawa in Hawaii. "When we were in California [before Iwo Jima] he hung out with those [Guard Company] guys," remarked Mueller. "But after Iwo, when we got back, there were so few of us that survived all that, the guys that came back from the hospital— he was one of them that came back from the hospital—we hung together rather than associate so much with the replacements that you know we were picking up. So I saw a lot of him and we did liberties and so forth after Iwo."

Before Sigler's return from the hospital, Mueller had been approached by Lt. Bill Grannell about Sigler's actions on March 14. "I was the guy who Lieutenant Grannell, when we came back from Iwo, he came to me and he said 'They want to put Sigler up for a medal and they need somebody to write something up on him,'" recalled Mueller "So I wrote something up. In a week to ten days Grannell came back to me and he said 'They're putting Sigler up for some higher medal, so we have to have two people who witnessed what he did.' So I gave him the name of Homer Neelly, one of our guys. So Neelly wrote up something and that was the last we heard of it."

Meanwhile, the 5th Marine Division was gearing up for the invasion of Japan, and the Iwo survivors weren't optimistic about their chances. "[Sigler] had the same feeling that all of us had [about Iwo and the coming campaign]," said Mueller. "It was a bitch, and we weren't looking forward to going to any more of them. And we were out on what was the last training problem when the word came out, they said they've dropped some kind of bomb on Japan that destroyed a whole city. And we said, 'Bullshit,' you know, it won't happen. Well then, I think we were probably out there for a week; when we came in, the guys that hadn't gone out in the field, and had access to radio and so forth, they said, they've dropped another bomb on the Japanese and it's destroyed another city and there's people that think the war's going to be over. We still didn't believe it."

But it was true. The war was soon over, and instead of invading Japan, the 26th Marines were to land at Sasebo as occupation troops. They soon boarded ship and once again had a layover at Pearl Harbor. Sigler, Mueller, and a couple of buddies decided to visit the Royal Hawaiian Hotel for some refreshments. "The place was surrounded by a chain-link fence with strands of barbed wire over the top," recalled Mueller. "Only those with proper passes could get in through a gate manned by the Shore Patrol. Since we had been there in April or May, we knew the best places to go over the fence without being seen. It was fine going in, but coming out Siggy got caught in the barbed wire, fell, cut himself in several places and lost his cap again. It was on the ground inside the fence." Mueller went back for it and as he made his way out, he too fell, tearing his pants and cutting his leg. "Two of us now had blood on our uniforms, tears in them and looked like we had been in fights," said Mueller. Back aboard ship they ended up in front of Lieutenant Grannell, but, strangely, there were no repercussions.

Frank Sigler (right) and a buddy after Iwo Jima. Sigler was on his way to Japan when he learned he was to be awarded the Medal of Honor. Courtesy of Rudy Mueller

They were at sea on their way to Japan when word came down that Sigler was to be awarded the Medal of Honor. "He did not believe them," recalled Mueller. "As soon as we landed at Sasebo, he was taken out of F Company and flown back to Washington, D.C., where Harry Truman made the award." Sigler was one of fourteen Marines and sailors awarded the Medal of Honor during ceremonies at the White House on October 5, 1945. His parents, sister, and brothers Melvin and Douglas were on hand to watch him get the decoration. Another brother, George Jr., was still on active duty with the U.S. Army. A newspaper report noted, "Private Sigler effected the release of his besieged company from enemy fire and contributed essentially to its further advance against a savagely fighting enemy." Having just arrived in the States by plane three days before, Sigler admitted he was still a little surprised at "all this fuss."

Unfortunately, the military then assigned Sigler to participate in the eighth and final war bond drive, the Victory Loan Campaign, which kicked off in Chicago on October 28 with the slogan, "They Finished Their Job—Let's Finish Ours." For an unassuming youngster like Sigler, the tour was a nightmare. "Frank was a very modest guy," remarked Mueller, who kept in touch with him after the war. "And he really didn't think—he couldn't figure out why he got the medal. And he hated that bond tour. It was the worst thing that ever happened to him. If you knew Frank, you knew that he would be the last guy to be getting up and making speeches. And he dreaded that. And he said the other thing that really got him was that everybody was patting him on the back and everybody was saying, 'Let me buy a drink.' And he said he was getting drunk before he knew what he was doing. And he cracked up and they had to take him off the tour and put him in the hospital."

President Truman presents Frank Sigler with the Medal of Honor on October 5, 1945, at the White House.
USMC

Promoted to private first class, Sigler was discharged from the Marine Corps the following June. He had been honored with a hometown parade upon his return to Little Falls—the town even presented him with a specially inscribed 12-gauge Winchester shotgun that famed aviator Wiley Post had carried with him on his flight around the world some years earlier—but the attention quickly faded. He applied for jobs with the state game warden, the VA, the Motor Vehicle Department, and others, but none of them panned out. By August 1947 he was engaged to be married and still unemployed. "I run into a lot of red tape everywhere I go," he told a newspaper reporter. "Naturally I'd like the job that pays the most money, but I'd accept almost anything." The reporter noted, "Frank is sunny and smiling despite his disappointments."

At that point his luck changed. An area newspaper published a front-page article reporting that town officials had raised $7,000 for Sigler's homecoming parade two years earlier and never given him a share of the money as they had promised. The article shamed those who deserved it, and a week later Sigler was appointed as a state fish and game warden.

Unfortunately, readjustment to civilian life came hard for Sigler. In August 1949, a nationwide news story about Medal of Honor recipients revealed that Sigler was being treated for "recurring nervous disorders" at a New Jersey VA hospital. Weekends he spent with his wife and three-month-old daughter in Little Falls, where they lived with his parents. Frank's mother, Elsie, said he had given up his first civilian job as a game warden after six months because "he was unable to adjust himself to the public." His next job, as a Passaic County court attendant, lasted two weeks. He was then offered a county detective job, she said, but was on leave at that time for further hospital treatment. Elsie Sigler said she had found it very difficult to persuade Frank to maintain his friendships. "His friends are very proud of his medal, but they don't make a big commotion about it anymore," she remarked. A comrade who had served with Sigler on Iwo Jima observed that he seemed to have developed a problem with alcohol.

In the end, Sigler managed to pull himself together and made a career with the Passaic County Sheriff's Office. He retired in 1962 and then spent ten years with a firm that built golf courses. He and his wife, Virginia Helen Seaman, enjoyed forty-seven years of marriage and had two daughters. A devoted father, he had a love for gardening and enjoyed working in his large vegetable garden, often with his girls in tow—and, in later life, with his grandsons. His daughters recalled that he always had time to play softball, ride bicycles with them, swim, take walks in the woods, and teach them respect for animals. He served as fire chief of the Great Notch Fire Department in 1952, and was a member of the Pearl River Rod and Gun Club. In 1949 he was awarded the State of New Jersey Distinguished Service Medal.

Though long active in various veterans' organizations, in later life he didn't attend many military functions. "He was always proud of what he did," recalled wife Virginia. "But it was not something he talked much about." Invited to the fifty-year celebration for the Battle of Iwo Jima, the aging hero remarked, "Give the recognition to the younger veterans." A reporter once asked him if he thought Medal of Honor recipients had been forgotten by the public. "No, I don't think so," he said. It was just that the war had been over for a long time, life moves on, and public attention turns to other matters, he mused. As for his actions on Iwo Jima, he said simply, "We were scared all of the time, but we were doing what we had to do." A point of pride for the old warrior was the graduation of his grandson, Derrick Peter, from Marine Corps boot camp at Parris Island. A news article on the two included their picture together. Such was Sigler's pride in his grandson that this picture was the only one he would give to fans.

Frank Sigler died on January 20, 1995, in a hospital at Morristown, New Jersey. He was seventy years old. At the request of his mother, he was buried near his brother Bill in Arlington National Cemetery.

Family members eulogized him as a modest man, a humble hero. "If you asked Frank what he did, he would say he was 4-F. He would never talk about it," remarked his brother Melvin. "He considered the real heroes the ones who died."

Reminiscing about his friend and the Medal of Honor decades after the war, Rudy Mueller observed, "Frank never really thought he earned anything. You know, he was that kind of guy. He was just a happy-go-lucky individual. Salt of the earth type guy, really." Added Mueller quietly, "God never created a better man than Frank Sigler. You could depend on him."

As the 5th Marine Division struggled to quash resistance in The Gorge, the 4th Division was "mopping up"—a bit of an understatement for the men involved—the last holdouts on the east coast. The division profited from a rare breakdown in Japanese discipline on the night of March 8. Capt. Samaji Inouye, a hot-headed artillery expert and superlative swordsman who commanded Japanese naval ground forces in the pocket facing the 4th Division, balked at the prospect of dying ingloriously in some obscure hole in the ground. Defying the die-in-place strategy that had cost the Marines so dearly, Inouye led the surviving navy men in a banzai attack on the 4th Division cordon. About a thousand men, armed with everything from spears to machine guns, crept toward the Marine lines and then charged to cries of "Banzai!"

The division history recorded, "From the 1st Battalion, 25th, on the right, to the 2nd Battalion, 23rd on the left, continuous waves of Japs hammered at our positions, and some broke through to command posts. Hand-to-hand fighting took place all up and down the line and in the command post of the 2nd Battalion, 23rd Marines. Many Japs carrying land mines strapped to their chests came at Marines in attempts to blow them up in a suicidal charge. Others, seeing that the attack was a failure, killed themselves with grenades. But the majority were killed by Marine riflemen who lay in their foxholes and blasted every moving object." At daylight, the Marines counted 784 Japanese bodies strewn on the ground. Among them was Captain Inouye, killed urging his men forward. Marine losses totaled 90 killed and 257 wounded.

By bringing his men out in the open to be killed in large numbers, Captain Inouye had done the Marines a service. Over the next week, the 4th Division continued to suffer casualties as riflemen eradicated the last Japanese holdouts, but organized resistance in their zone had been broken. It was during this final mopping up that a corpsman earned the last Medal of Honor to be awarded to a member of the 4th Division for Iwo Jima.

PHARMACIST'S MATE 1ST CLASS FRANCIS J. PIERCE

24th Marines, 4th Marine Division
March 15–16, 1945

Frank Pierce U.S. Navy

It is one of those odd quirks of human behavior that so many boys from America's heartland, growing up a thousand miles from the nearest salt water, feel compelled to join the navy. So it was with Frank Pierce.

Francis Junior Pierce was born December 7, 1924, in Earlville, Iowa, a forgettable whistle-stop on the Illinois Central rail line in the northeast part of the state. He was the first of Frank E. and Rose Pierce's two sons. Donald, the second born, followed three years later. Their father was a Yugoslavian-born immigrant who worked a farm just outside of town. Their mother was a native Iowan. The 1940 census taker recorded the elder Pierce's citizenship as "alien," noted that he was "working on own account," and reported that during the week before the census, he had worked a total of seventy-two hours. Young Frank loved the outdoors—one of his boyhood pleasures was hunting rabbits and other small game—but he was too restless by nature to follow his father and settle for the monotony of farm life. He figured the navy would give him the best opportunity to see a bigger world.

Pearl Harbor was yet to become a call to war when Pierce graduated from high school in June 1941. Still underage, he chafed for six months as he awaited his seventeenth birthday, when he could go into the service. "Most of my high school buddies were already in the navy," he recalled, "so it was only natural for me, I guess. I would have been in sooner, except for my age. I was sixteen when I graduated, so I had to kill six months waiting for my birthday." By coincidence, he turned seventeen on the day the Japanese attacked Pearl Harbor. Seven days later, the tall, thinly built teenager reported to the Great Lakes Training Center near Chicago for basic training. A month later he landed in Portsmouth, Virginia, for instruction as a hospital corpsman—or "bedpan commando," as the duty was sometimes derisively termed. Portsmouth offered a six- to eight-week course that emphasized the basics of medical care.

Herman E. Rabeck, who, like Pierce, eventually ended up with the 4th Marine Division, recalled the routine of hospital corps school: "We did a normal six-month course in two months. They kept us going from 8 o'clock in the morning to 9 o'clock at night. . . . We learned anything that had to do with medicine. Aboard ship you had to check the mess hall that they were taking sanitary procedures. Field lavatories, you had to oversee all that."

Pierce hadn't sought out that duty and wasn't especially happy about it. But if he was worried he would miss the "real war" emptying bedpans in some stateside naval hospital, his fears were misplaced. In March he was sent to Camp Lejeune for Marine infantry training—a sure indication he would end up in a combat outfit. Stanley E. Dabrowski, who also trained at Lejeune, recalled getting off the bus and being greeted by a very squared-away, no-nonsense corporal wearing a

"Smokey the Bear hat," duty belt, and starched shirt, all very neat. "He impressed me tremendously. . . . Everything from then on was Marine Corps. . . . We didn't even have white underwear," said Dabrowski. "Everything was green."

Marine training was no hardship for Pierce, who had spent countless hours on the farm hunting and learning how to cope in the outdoors. The "docs" went through close order drill, infiltration courses with live machine-gun fire, crawling under barbed wire, and learning hand-to-hand combat. They spent two weeks on the rifle range becoming familiar with the M1 Garand, M1 carbine, .45 pistol, machine guns, hand grenades—they even went through a bayonet course. "They had to prepare us for what we were going to face, but nobody ever told us what combat was going to be like," observed Dabrowski. Finishing up at Camp Lejeune in July 1943, Pierce was assigned to the 4th Medical Battalion of 4th Marine Division. The division was formally activated in August, and began intensive training in the rugged hills of Camp Pendleton, leading up to its baptism of fire in early 1944 in the Marshall Islands.

Pierce participated in the 4th Marine Division's landing on Roi-Namur on February 1, 1944. He saw his first combat casualties during the brief campaign, and found he could perform as expected, learning to be as quick and efficient as possible while keeping his emotions under tight control. Often he treated men he knew, but he tried to remain impersonal and to concentrate strictly on their wounds. He also disregarded conventional strictures about "noncombatants" carrying weapons. American medical personnel had learned the hard way in the early days of the war that the Japanese didn't make distinctions between combatants and noncombatants—they shot everybody. "We didn't wear the Red Cross, because those were just good targets," said Pierce. Unlike other corpsmen who were generally content with a carbine or .45 pistol for self-defense, Pierce opted for more firepower: he packed a Thompson submachine gun and he wasn't afraid to use it when the opportunity arose. He said he figured if he came at the enemy shooting, they "would have to do some ducking too," and that would make his job easier.

After Roi-Namur, Pierce participated in the invasions of Saipan and Tinian in the Marianas. "I remember there weren't many wounded at Tinian," he remarked later. "Everybody who was shot seemed to get it in the head. Those Japs could really shoot." Then, on February 19, 1945, came Iwo Jima. It was like nothing that Pierce, a veteran of three campaigns at the age of twenty, had ever experienced. "Saipan and Tinian were strictly bush league compared with Iwo Jima," he observed years later. "That place was swarming with Japs, every one of them dug in."

Pierce was one of about ten men from the 4th Medical Battalion's Company B who were attached to the 2nd Battalion, 24th Marines. The "Collecting Section," as it was called, operated out of the battalion aid station. The section helped to evacuate the wounded, supplemented aid station personnel, and filled in for corpsmen who were killed or wounded serving with rifle companies. Over the next four weeks, Pierce treated an endless stream of casualties. Somehow he managed to survive while men all around him were killed or wounded. One day, he was carrying the front end of a litter when the corpsman on the other end was killed. On another occasion, he made five nerve-wracking trips into fire-swept ground, returning each time with a wounded Marine. In an environment where life or death seemed to depend mostly on luck, Pierce exercised as much caution as he could. He carried a map and marked down the spots where he came under fire while traveling back and forth to retrieve casualties. He then planned his future routes to avoid those areas if at all possible. "I never did anything or went anywhere in combat without thinking it over and figuring a way to do it and still come out alive," he admitted.

The question was whether anybody would come out alive. E Company went through so many captains it seemed to be jinxed. Battalion couldn't seem to send replacements fast enough. A young second lieutenant, Richard Reich, who had joined the company just before

Navy doctors and corpsmen treat the wounded on the beach at Iwo Jima. USMC

the operation, found himself repeatedly in command while awaiting the arrival of yet another replacement officer. "They came so fast," he said, "I didn't even get their names." The fighting for Hill 382 during the first week of March was especially bloody. By March 8, casualties in the 2nd Battalion had been so severe that it was consolidated into two companies, Fox and George, absorbing the survivors of Easy Company. One week later, the combat efficiency of the entire 4th Marine Division was rated at only 35 percent, far below the level that would ordinarily compel a unit's withdrawal from the line.

Still, by March 15, there was hope among the front-line riflemen that the end was finally in sight. There was still plenty of opportunity to die, but organized Japanese resistance in front of the 4th Division had been largely broken—a development reflected in orders from V Amphibious Corps for the division to "mop up thoroughly" in its zone of action. That was not as simple as it sounded. Even so-called secure areas harbored individual Japanese stragglers prepared to die for their Emperor. The division history later observed that the remaining area of resistance was "studded with caves and emplacements and absolutely impenetrable to tanks and other support weapons. . . . [T]he Jap defenders fought until they were individually routed out and killed by riflemen, demolition and grenade teams, and flame throwers."

Pierce ventured into this modern version of Indian territory on the afternoon of March 15 with another corpsman and eight litter bearers to retrieve two unlucky 2nd Battalion Marines wounded in the mopping up ordered by V Amphibious Corps. Burdened down with the two casualties, they were making their way back through what passed as a secure area near Airfield No. 2, when a handful of bypassed Japanese spotted them and apparently decided they would be easy pickings. The Japanese opened fire with rifles and at least one machine gun.

Luck must have been smiling on the Americans. Pierce's fellow corpsman was hit in the initial flurry. Two of the stretcher-bearers also went down, but no one was killed. The litter party scrambled to get out of the line of fire, finding cover along an embankment just below the edge of the unimproved runway. Now saddled with five casualties, Pierce tended to the newly wounded and considered his options. There appeared to be no other Marines operating nearby, so rescue was unlikely. They would have to extricate themselves, but the only way out lay under the Japanese guns.

Pierce made his decision. "Start packing up the three men who were just hit," he told the six able-bodied litter bearers. "When I give the sign, move out on the double and head for the nearest cover on the other side of those Japs. I'll try to keep them busy." He would stay with the remaining two wounded, while the others made their break, he said. Once they were out of immediate danger, they should head for the aid station and see about sending him some help.

When they were ready, Pierce gave the sign. The litter party ran one way with their three wounded, and Pierce bolted out in the opposite direction, blasting away with his tommy gun in the general direction of the Japanese. When the magazine ran dry, he dodged around brandishing the empty weapon in an effort to divert enemy attention from the escaping wounded. An enemy machine gunner cut up the ground nearby, but Pierce managed to elude him. "I didn't really mean to get myself killed," he explained later of his duel with the Japanese machine gunner. "I knew he'd have a tough chance to nail me if I kept running across his field, even though I would be out in the open. The important thing was to guess where he'd fire next—and guess right." He managed to guess right, but it was a near thing. When a bullet is real close, it "sounds like a bullwhip," he observed years later. "I heard a few that day."

The diversion worked. The litter team escaped from the kill zone and Pierce finally dodged back behind the embankment where the remaining two wounded Marines waited. Both were conscious; one even managed a weak grin as Pierce checked his wound. But as he started to adjust the dressing, there was a rifle shot from close by and the wounded Marine was hit again. Either they had attracted the attention of yet another Japanese, or one of the ambushers with more ambition than the rest had worked around to where he could see behind the embankment. The shot, probably directed at Pierce, had hit the already wounded Marine instead.

Lying low, Pierce groped around for a rifle, then spotted a holstered .45 on the hip of the twice-wounded Marine, who had now lapsed into unconsciousness. He pulled the .45 free and crawled cautiously toward the source of the rifle shot. He didn't know just where the sniper was, but he realized the shot had come from very close range. The intruder could not be far. Stopping to peer around the side of an anemic bush, he noticed a low cave opening directly in front of him. Only about twenty yards from where his two wounded men lay, it seemed to be the only possible place of concealment. He decided to take the direct approach. "If I stood up, he'd be bound to make a motion," he explained later. That would be enough. "I was a good shot."

Pierce didn't hesitate. He got to his feet and stalked toward the opening. A helmeted figure suddenly appeared in the entrance. The Japanese had dropped to one knee and was raising a rifle. Now very close, Pierce snapped off three shots from the .45. The slugs hammered the Japanese to the ground. Pierce continued right up to the entrance, aimed carefully, and shot the now prostrate Japanese a fourth time to be sure his removal was permanent.

By now it was late afternoon and the sun was starting to go down. One of the wounded Marines by the embankment was alert, but the other man remained unconscious. No help had arrived and Pierce realized he was running out of time. Even if the two men managed to survive without further medical attention, Japanese stragglers were likely to be all over them once darkness fell. Pierce turned to the Marine who was still conscious. He propped the man up, pressed the .45 into his hand, and told him he was going to carry the other man, who was more badly hurt, out first, but that he'd be back. Though the Marine must have understood his own peril, he took the news without complaint.

Hoisting the unconscious Marine onto his back, Pierce ventured tentatively into the open. He waited for the rip of the Japanese machine gun, but there was nothing—not a shot, only silence. Gasping from the effort, he staggered along as quickly as he could under the weight of the unconscious Marine, pausing frequently to put his burden down and catch his breath before continuing. A challenge suddenly came out of the gathering darkness. They were Marines, sent out by the earlier escapees. As Pierce tried to catch his wind, the patrol leader patted him on the back and suggested it was time to call it a day.

Not yet, said Pierce. He had to go back for the other wounded man. The patrol leader tried to talk him out of it—it was nearly dark and only the Japanese moved around at night, he said—but Pierce would not be dissuaded. The patrol waited nervously while he retraced his steps to the airfield and crossed the clearing. The Marine was where he'd left him, propped up against the embankment, still alive, clutching the .45. Pierce helped him to his feet and together they stumbled back to the waiting patrol.

According to Marine combat correspondent Dan Levin, who compiled a story on the incident, enemy fire directed at Pierce during his exploit nicked his shoe, while another bullet had punctured his canteen. "The corpsman carried the [first] Marine 200 yards to safety, fell exhausted, pushed himself to his feet and started back," wrote Levin. "Five minutes later he appeared along the road again with the other wounded Marine by his side. Bullets plowed their pathway—but they made the trip safely." Compiling a report on Pierce's actions back at the battalion aid station, assistant surgeon Lt. James D. Carter noted, "Recommend highest honors."

The next morning Pierce guided a combat patrol back toward the ambush site in search of the enemy stragglers. They located some Japanese holed up in a dugout. "I don't know yet if we found them or they found us," recalled Pierce. "They had a dugout covered with sand and very hard to spot. We were right on top of it when they opened up on us. I remember tossing a firebomb into one of the openings and somebody inside tossed it right back. It was a heck of a sensation."

A Marine was hit in the exchange. As he had so many times before, Pierce ran out to render assistance, but this time his luck, already pressed too far, ran out. As he crouched over the wounded man, a rifle bullet tore a chunk of flesh out of his left shoulder. Then a hand grenade went off nearby, driving metal into his back and left leg. Another corpsman started toward them, but Pierce waved him away. Only after the wounded Marine had been carried out did Pierce accept help for his own injuries.

Frank Pierce recovered from his wounds. In addition to the Purple Heart, he was awarded the Navy Cross and the Silver Star for his actions on Iwo Jima. Discharged in December 1945, the now twenty-two-year-old veteran went home to Earlville, but could summon up no newfound enthusiasm for life on the farm. He soon headed north to Grand Rapids, Michigan, to meet a woman he had corresponded with during the war. He also had hopes of joining the Michigan State Police Department. Unfortunately, the State Police had a regulation that recruits had to be single. After meeting his wartime pen pal, Pierce decided that bachelorhood was one rule he couldn't abide by. Within a year he had married the girl and found employment as a patrolman on the Grand Rapids Police Force.

Meanwhile, unbeknownst to Pierce, wheels had been slowly turning in the military bureaucracy. Three years later, now making $3,280 a year as a motorcycle patrol officer, he received an excited telephone call from his brother back in Earlville. "Hey, you got the Medal of Honor!" his brother shouted. "We just got a letter from the Navy Department."

"I didn't believe him," Pierce admitted. "I had never heard of such a thing and the war had been over for three years. When I got that letter, I still didn't believe it until I read it two or three times."

As it turned out, Lieutenant Carter's original recommendation that Pierce be awarded the Medal of Honor had been knocked down to a Navy Cross. But after the war a review board reexamined the citations accompanying Pierce's Navy Cross and Silver Star. Impressed with the heroism demonstrated over an extended period of time, they decided to recall the two decorations and replace them with one—the Medal of Honor. Former Pharmacist's Mate 1st Class, now Patrolman Frank Pierce received the medal from President Truman at the White House on June 26, 1948. Upon his return home to Grand Rapids, he was honored with a full-scale parade. His fellow police officers gave him a watch and the townspeople presented him with a check for $2,500.

During his years on the police force, Pierce had other occasions to demonstrate his courage. In 1955 he walked into an apartment and kicked a loaded big game rifle from the grasp of a disturbed individual who had threatened to begin shooting. During a 1967 race riot, he picked up a machine gun and waded into a mob of rioters, sending them running. He decorated his office with hand grenades, mortar shells, and other military memorabilia, and served as the city's bomb disposal expert. In his spare time he was also a steeplejack and an avid hunter. Standing six-foot-one in his socks, he now weighed 196 pounds—nearly fifty pounds more than when he served with the Marines—but in other ways he hadn't changed much. "Frank is a restless person . . . a catalyst that should be in every police department," said one of his former chiefs. "But not more than one. I wouldn't want two of them." Once described as being "as abrasive as a corn cob," Pierce himself conceded that he wasn't the most accommodating of personalities. "My reputation, which in most cases is well deserved, is that I am blunt, direct, malicious, vindictive and hard to get along with," he admitted. "This has caused me problems over the years."

In the course of his career, he rose from accident investigator, motorcycle patrolman, captain in charge of the vice squad, and uniform division commander to become deputy chief of police. He was criticized in the early 1970s for using riot police to break up a group of hunger marchers, keeping them from attending a board of education meeting. He was criticized again in 1981 when he bluntly told a neighborhood meeting that citizens should arm themselves with shotguns to fight off burglars. As for the Medal of Honor, he got tired of telling the story after a time. "Somebody shot holes in my canteen and I got mad," he told a newspaper reporter. "After all, water was scarce." In a more pensive mood, he observed that despite the inspiring language of his Medal of Honor citation, he was far from fearless. In fact, he remarked, if he ever met a man who was completely fearless, "I want that man as far away as he can get because he is going to get me killed. One of the most exhilarating feelings is to know fear and be able to conquer it . . . to be scared to death yet be able to function." But when all was said and done, he added, "Becoming a hero is something accidental. You do not go out and do it. You've got to be in the right place and the right time with the right people looking on."

Pierce had two sons with his first wife, Lorraine. After her death in 1975, he married again. He had two daughters with his second wife, Madelyn. He finally retired from the police force in 1982, saying he wanted to enjoy life with his wife and children. Four years later, on December 21, 1986, he died after a long bout with cancer. He is buried in Holy Cross Cemetery in Grand Rapids. As he wished, his headstone bears a simple inscription: "He Served His Country."

The day after Frank Pierce was wounded, General Kuribayashi sent a final message to Imperial General Headquarters. "The situation is now on the brink of the last," he reported. His men had fought valiantly against overwhelming material odds and deserved the highest commendation. "I however humbly apologize to His Majesty that I have failed to live up to the expectations and have to yield this key island to the enemy after having seen many of my officers and men killed," added the general. The fall of Iwo Jima was announced to the Japanese people that same night.

The following day, men of the 5th Marine Division mopping up The Gorge closed in on a huge concrete blockhouse thought to mark General Kuribayashi's headquarters. Infantrymen spent two days chipping away at the fortification with shaped charges and 75mm guns, without success. Exasperated engineers finally planted 8,500 pounds of explosives on the massive structure and reduced it to a mound of broken concrete in a spectacular series of blasts that seemed to rock the whole island. General Kuribayashi was apparently still alive on March 23 when a last message went out to Chichi Jima: "All officers and men of Chichi Jima, goodbye." Two days later, 5th Division Marines eradicated the final fifty-square-yard pocket in The Gorge. General Kuribayashi's body was never found.

By then the 4th Marine Division was already gone, having sailed for Maui on March 19. Units of the 5th Division had begun loading on March 18 and were scheduled to shove off on March 27, leaving the 3rd Marine Division to assume patrol and defense responsibilities. The U.S. Army's 147th Infantry Regiment, which was slated to take over the defense of the island, arrived from New Caledonia on March 20.

It was over . . . except someone had neglected to tell the Japanese. Up in the rugged hills, still lurking in tunnels and caves, some 200 to 300 survivors of General Kuribayashi's garrison were quietly organizing for one last confrontation. Within two days, most of them would be dead and a thirty-four-year-old Marine first lieutenant from Bucyrus, Ohio, would be cited—posthumously—for the Medal of Honor.

1ST LT. HARRY L. MARTIN

5th Pioneer Battalion, 5th Marine Division
March 26, 1945

Harry Martin USMC

While Marine infantry battalions battled through nightmarish terrain on northern Iwo Jima in late February and into March, the southern part of the island was being transformed. The western beaches had been opened on March 2, allowing general unloading of supplies and materiel on both sides of the island. With typical efficiency, Seabees and construction troops wasted no time constructing facilities and transforming dirt tracks into highways, complete with traffic regulations. Riflemen coming back from the front lines were taken aback to find well-ordered supply depots, water points, evacuation hospitals, ammunition dumps, tank parks, and repair shops now occupying former Japanese kill zones. Airfield No. 1 was back in operation by the first week of March. Airfield No. 2, approximately in the center of the island and captured six days after the landing, was repaired and in use by March 15.

As the fighting to the north wound down and men of the combat divisions began to embark for Hawaii, the area around Airfield No. 2 blossomed into a tent city crowded with airmen, Seabees, some army units, shore party personnel, and support troops. Among the recent arrivals was the 21st Fighter Group. Consisting of the 46th, 72nd, and 531st Fighter Squadrons, and equipped with P-51 Mustangs that would fly cover for the B-29 raids on the Japanese homeland, the final elements of the group arrived on March 25, moving into tents just west of Airfield No. 2. Just to the south of the fighter group encampment, weary members of the 5th Pioneer Battalion were preparing to leave Iwo Jima with the rest of the 5th Marine Division. "Our ships are out there waiting," wrote PFC Robert L. Hurst. "Gosh, do they ever look good."

Also glad to be leaving the godforsaken rock was 1st Lt. Harry Linn Martin. A native of Bucyrus, Ohio, at age thirty-four Martin was ancient for a lieutenant. He had managed to talk his way into the Marine Corps two years earlier, mostly because he refused to take "no" for an answer. In a word, the man could be stubborn to a fault.

Former schoolmates would later describe Harry Martin as "good natured and feisty," a C-average student whose hardworking nature could not dampen an irrepressible mischievous streak. The son of a railroad worker, he could trace his lineage on his father's side back to Col. William Crawford, who had accompanied Gen. George Washington on the historic crossing of the Delaware in 1777. Despite that distinguished lineage, there was nothing pompous about Harry. He had "a merry Irish face, with red cheeks and small eyes, often crinkled up in laughter, topped by a shock of bristly, short black hair," recalled a friend. "He had a particularly strong and husky voice, even before his voice change."

Friends also remembered something else about Martin: his determination. Only five feet six inches tall and weighing in at 130 pounds, he had been one of the smallest members of the Bucyrus High School football team during the early 1920s. Despite his size and the punishment he absorbed from larger players, he never quit. "If the coach had told him to go out to the middle of the field and die to win the game he would have done it," recalled high school friend Charleton "Beanie" Myers. He was not a star and he never earned his varsity letter, but he plugged along through all four years, contributing where he could.

After graduating from high school in 1928, Martin knocked around a bit. He enrolled at Miami University (Ohio), but lasted only about a week. He hitchhiked to Texas to look for work, but soon returned. Later he enrolled at the University of Missouri, but didn't stay there either. He finally settled in at Michigan State. He worked his way through school with various jobs, including construction work on the Boulder Dam, which had gotten underway in 1931. "He borrowed money, and he paid it back by alternating periods at the Boulder Dam and school," recalled Harry's younger brother Bob.

Hard work and maturity transformed the second string football wannabe into a 185-pound fireplug of a man. His determination couldn't win him a spot on the Michigan football team, but he did earn a varsity letter as a wrestler. He also participated in mandatory ROTC training, but didn't seem particularly interested in the military. Apparently with some amusement, he wrote to a friend that the ROTC signed him up for cavalry training, though he'd never been on a horse before.

Martin graduated from Michigan State in 1935 with a bachelor of science degree in business. His first job was with Universal Credit Corporation, which hired him to repossess cars in a tough section of Toledo, Ohio. The work had its hazards. "He was hit over the head once and knocked out when he was checking a serial number," his brother recalled years later. In 1938 he transferred to a desk job in Los Angeles, but was quick to pick up and leave when an old high school buddy dropped by one day and suggested relocating to Honolulu to work on construction. By 1940 he was employed as a supervisor with a company building fuel tanks to service U.S. Navy ships. He was still there on December 7, 1941, when the Japanese attacked Pearl Harbor.

The experience may not have transformed Martin, but it gave him a singular purpose. He was determined to get into the war. And he wanted to go with the "varsity": the U.S. Marine Corps. "Harry was single-minded from then on," Bob Martin recalled. As it turned out, he needed to be single-minded. Attempting to join up in Hawaii, he was told he could not be sworn in outside the States. He left for Los Angeles and was fobbed off again, informed that he had to go to his hometown to enlist. Ohio recruiters, looking for teenaged warriors, were less than enthusiastic about a thirty-year-old volunteer. Despite the protracted runaround, Martin persisted, and finally someone decided that any man who would travel across half the country at his own expense to join the Marine Corps deserved a chance. On March 16, 1943, Harry Martin was sworn into the Marines as an enlisted man.

He trained at Parris Island before heading to Camp Lejeune, where his college degree and ROTC background earned him a shot at officer training. Commissioned as a second lieutenant on August 25, 1943, he received instruction at Quantico, then attended Engineers School at New River, North Carolina. Upon completion, he was assigned as a platoon leader with Company C, 5th Pioneer Battalion. The Pioneers were essentially a service outfit, created to meet the need for a specialized unit to conduct shore party operations during amphibious landings and provide combat-engineer support for the infantry when necessary. "I guess you could say Pioneers were the 'jack of all trades,'" remarked Pioneer Lt. Kerry Lane. "If a bridge had to be built, we built it. If demolition specialists were needed, that was us. We unloaded supplies and equipment from ships. They called on us when replacements were needed on the front line. We were a unique outfit that could do . . . and did . . . almost anything."

Martin came home to Bucyrus on leave in the summer of 1944. His brother Bob, also home on leave from the Seabees, remembered watching Harry walk down the path from the house to catch a train back to his unit in California. It was the last time they ever saw each other. Harry soon shipped out to Hawaii. Then came the landing on Iwo Jima. "H-hour was at 9 A.M. and the first waves streaked in; the day was beautiful and the surf was ideal to land assault troops," recalled PFC Robert Hurst, who came ashore with B Company. "Planes were hitting numerous Nip ammo dumps and at times it looked like part of the island was on fire. Wave after wave followed and us too—we crouched low in the landing craft and could hear bullets and mortars ringing over our heads. We finally hit the beach, no casualties so far. We got over the first bank ok and I dived in a huge crater where a mortar had hit about thirty minutes earlier. I had turned my head a little to the right and there lay a half a dozen Marines dead—all in one heap. To my left and a little to the rear was a blasted tank and a couple of dead Marines burnt to a crisp. Later I heard the first tank off the ramp was hit directly with a 75 and that was it. My lips were dry and parched and I gasped to get my breath. My heart was beating like a trip hammer."

Arriving ashore with the early waves, Martin's platoon was supposed to get supplies unloaded, organized, and inland. But with the chaos on the beach, the Pioneers spent most of that first day burrowing into the shifting volcanic ash and just trying to stay alive. "That night many of our men were killed," remembered Hurst. "An LCM had just unloaded tons of ammo about fifty yards away from our foxhole and about 2 A.M. it was hit by a Nip mortar." The ammo exploded. "It was awful," said Hurst. "[We] expected any second to be our last. Ugly pieces of sharp jagged shrapnel were falling all around us and that was when I heard a scream by someone calling a corpsman. Our warrant officer had been killed and several wounded. All this kept up until dawn. . . . Our dump finally exhausted itself and with daylight the Jap mortars stopped temporarily. There was never a night so long as this and how I thanked God it was over."

Though the beach remained jammed with smashed equipment, the Pioneers began work the next day as the infantry pushed inland. "As part of the shore party we stayed on the beach and didn't go in," recalled 2nd Lt. Robert Hansen, a platoon leader with A Company. "This was our assignment, this is what we trained for and our job was to unload landing craft that came in with ammunition, gasoline, food, whatever, and to store it on the beach in shell holes where it would be protected. The front line troops would call for supplies and send people back to pick up the different items to take up to the front lines." The Pioneers also began work on metal-matted roadways up to Airfield No. 1, so that heavy equipment could get through the shifting ash.

In a letter to his brother dated March 23, Martin mentioned he had been hit just under the chin by shrapnel about thirty minutes after coming ashore. The wound was healing well and probably wouldn't leave much of a scar, he remarked nonchalantly. The campaign had been "just a shade rough," he wrote. He had hit the beach at H-Hour plus twenty-two minutes, "and by the grace of God am alive today." The first three days had been hell, he said. After that, his men had managed to get some work done; they finally were finally able to move inland off the beach area three weeks after the landing.

As Martin noted, the Pioneers were finally released from duty with the 5th Shore Party Regiment and moved from the beaches to a bivouac area further inland. Some of the personnel were put to work in the division supply dump; a few others were sent to help out at the rapidly expanding division cemetery. However, by March 13, with casualties among front-line units soaring and manpower at a premium, the 5th Division began to send Pioneers forward to reinforce the infantry regiments. "Everybody, it seems, feels a little funny inside and no one talks much," wrote PFC Robert Hurst. "We look at each other and swallow long and hard. I can't describe this feeling, much less shake it off." Martin's C Company (less one platoon) was attached to the 28th Marines on March 17 and jumped off in the assault at 0915. "Progress was extremely slow and it was necessary to withdraw to our original positions that night," noted the battalion's after-action report.

Lt. Robert Hansen's A Company platoon relieved what was left of a company at Bloody Gorge. "This company was pretty well decimated," he recalled. "All they had left was one officer, a first lieutenant, and he had kind of a wild look in his eye." As service troops, the Pioneers were not fully prepared for close combat. Hansen remembered one of his men who stuck his head up over a rock instead of low and to the side and was promptly shot between the eyes. Four of Hurst's pals were riddled by a Nambu hidden in a cave when they neglected to take proper cover. "One boy got half his jaw shot away," observed Hurst. "Two of them got it in the lungs. Tex caught one right through the head."

Fortunately, their front-line combat experience—harsh as it was— was also relatively brief. Most of the Pioneers, including C Company, were relieved from the front lines on March 19 and sent back to their bivouac area near Airfield No. 2. Since the landing, the battalion had suffered thirty-two killed and 152 wounded. Four days later, Harry Martin sat down and wrote to his brother. Bob Martin detected an uncharacteristic note of pessimism in his brother's letter. Harry mentioned the men he had lost. "If I'm spared I will redouble my effort to make those little so and sos pay for the beating we took," he wrote. "I have a Jap rifle for you which I shall send or bring to you if I am fortunate enough to get off of here. . . . We are all so anxious to get off this place and return to our rest camp wherever that might be." Iwo Jima had finally been declared secure. However, there remained an enemy-held sector some 200 yards wide by 400 yards long that was causing considerable trouble. "Maybe we can get it in the next few days," he added hopefully.

But the enemy holdouts did not intend to wait quietly in their holes to die. In the predawn darkness of March 26, three days after Harry Martin wrote what would be his last known letter, approximately 300 surviving Japanese emerged from their caves and the gorges on northern Iwo, and moved quietly toward the unsuspecting support troops camped out by Airfield No. 2. Some of the fighter pilots had just arrived and were settling into tents along the western shore. The newcomers had no idea there was any danger from enemy ground forces. For their part, the Japanese intended no wild banzai; this was a carefully planned counterattack—a last effort to inflict as much damage and disruption as possible. Many were officers. "That they knew this was to be their last fight was evident by their dress," wrote Marine combat correspondent Keyes Beech. "Some officers, of whom there were many, wore clean white shirts; their swords were highly polished. . . . Some carried American rifles and grenades taken from dead Marines."

In addition to their own stealth and the element of surprise, the Japanese had, by coincidence, timed their attack well. Just the day before, most of the combat Marines had been directed to turn in their ammunition preparatory to embarking aboard ship. Some of the more cautious veterans retained a clip or two, but most had little ammunition immediately at hand, and some had none at all. Bob Hanson turned in his ammo with few worries. Half the Pioneers had already boarded ship on March 25 and the rest were soon to follow, so he wasn't likely to need it. "The island was secured and we were leaving the island the next day," he remarked. "I frankly didn't feel any qualms about it." Twenty-year-old PFC Sammy Bernstein, an assistant machine gunner with the battalion, was less sanguine. "We all kept a clip," he remembered. "A clip is about eight rounds. And the hell with them, we're not going to give it to them."

In the sprawling tent encampment set up by the VII Fighter Command along the western beaches just north of the Pioneers, the airmen turned in that night oblivious to any danger. Believing the island secure, no sentries were posted. The Japanese made their way down the western shore from the rugged high ground to the north and, in the early morning hours, burst into the unguarded bivouac area of the newly arrived airmen before anyone was aware they were even near. Lt. Jim Van Nada, a Mustang pilot with the 72nd Fighter Squadron, was jolted awake by hand grenades exploding next to his six-man tent. "The first one landed outside our tent shredding the back panel, and the second went off directly under my cot," he recalled. "I took a lot of shrapnel in the left leg and knee joint from that one. Our first thought was to get out of the tent which seemed to be the primary target of whoever was throwing those grenades."

Armed only with their .45 automatics, the pilots started out of the tent. Three of the men made it out, but as Van Nada reached the doorway, a grenade landed about three feet in front of him, knocking him and another pilot back into the tent. "When we came to we were lying on the tent floor bleeding from head wounds; we could now hear rifle and automatic weapon fire close by and loud shrieking voices, unmistakably Japanese," he said. He and his two tentmates barricaded themselves behind a wall of duffle bags and empty ammo boxes. It turned out to be a wise decision. The three pilots who got out of the tent were all shot: one was killed outright, one subsequently died, and the third made it back to the tent and survived. "From behind our barricade we could see the Japs running past our tent, firing their rifles and throwing grenades," recalled Van Nada. "We were hoping they were moving out of our area but the firing and yelling continued just outside our tent. I lifted the bottom of the tent flap on the side from where the voices came and saw at least six Japs entrenched in a depression in the sand about four feet outside our tent, and it didn't appear that they were planning to move out."

Dead Japanese sprawl outside a tent in the fighter-group bivouac. The attack caught many of the newly arrived airmen asleep in their tents. Department of Defense

Enemy soldiers burst into the tents, stabbing sleeping airmen in their cots and shooting or bayoneting anyone unfortunate enough to be caught in their path. "The Japs ran through those tents and just cut them up with sabers before they even knew they were being attacked," recalled PFC Sammy Bernstein. "They were slaughtered." As the Japanese continued south, they ran into the Pioneers' perimeter. The Pioneers were still dug in, preparatory to leaving the island the next day. However, unlike the airmen, the veteran unit had been keeping a watchful eye out. "I was in my foxhole guarding a field hospital when two figures approached me," recalled Pioneer Sgt. Charles A. Serio. As the two figures drew closer, Serio challenged them. "I had hardly finished challenging them when I saw they were Japs and they started running faster towards me, screaming. I tried to fire, but my rifle jammed. Lucky for me, my friend Corporal Jim Cannon jumped up and got both of them with just two shots and the two Japs fell dead in front of me."

Sammy Bernstein was dug in with his buddy, Cpl. Arthur Erdman of Tomah, Wisconsin, when they heard shouting and explosions. Erdman left their foxhole to see what the commotion was about. As Bernstein watched in helpless horror, a Japanese suddenly materialized out of the darkness and swung a sword at Erdman. "He didn't go maybe ten or fifteen feet and he was cut down by a Jap with a saber," recalled Bernstein. With scarcely a pause, the swordsman then lobbed a hand grenade into Bernstein's foxhole. Bernstein managed to get off two shots with his contraband ammo. The Japanese was now so close he fell the foxhole. Bernstein stabbed the dying man with his combat knife, all the while waiting for the grenade to go off. "I just closed my eyes and thought that was it; I figured the hand grenade was going to take us," he recalled. There was no explosion. The grenade was a dud.

Also in trouble was Lt. Bob Hanson. Sleeping in one of the cooks' tents left by the departing Pioneers, Hanson awoke to the sound of gunfire. "As I was crawling out of the tent, I got hit," he recalled. "It felt like my left foot had been blown off because I couldn't feel it. And I reached down and no, my foot was still there, so I continued to crawl out of the tent. I looked north and saw two Japanese soldiers about a hundred feet away. . . . They were reloading their weapons, I could hear the *click-clack*." Hanson had a BAR back in the tent, but he had turned in his ammunition. "I could use it for a club, but that would be the only way I could utilize it," he observed. Pressing himself close to the ground, he pulled out his KA-BAR knife. "I was afraid they were going to come my way and I knew if they did why I was probably a goner and I was determined to take at least one of them with me if I possibly could." He stayed low, waiting. The two Japanese passed him by.

Warned by the din of gunfire and explosions just to the north, Harry Martin was also awake. He wasted no time wondering what was happening. Jogging forward, he directed men into firing positions, forming a hasty defense line. His Pioneers were ready; their biggest problem was lack of ammo. Charles Serio grabbed a jeep and drove hurriedly down to the dump on the beach. He was throwing boxes of ammunition into the jeep when a supply sergeant tried to intervene. "I grabbed my rifle and leveled it at his head," recalled Serio. A major ran up demanding to know what the hell was going on. Serio told him he desperately needed the ammo because of a Japanese attack up by the airfield. He got his ammo.

Serio drove the ammunition back to Martin's defense line. The Pioneers managed to hold the marauding Japanese at bay for the moment, but several Marines had been trapped somewhere out front during the initial breakthrough. Martin could have sat tight and let them fend for themselves. He did not. Armed with his .45, he moved out into no-man's-land to locate his missing men. Japanese were roaming everywhere. Martin was hit at least twice by enemy fire, according to subsequent accounts, but he stayed on his feet, using his .45 against enemy soldiers who came directly at him. He finally located the missing Marines, who had holed up after being overrun. He led them back to the main line, which was still holding despite heavy pressure.

A new threat materialized when Japanese infiltrators took over a nearby machine-gun pit. Apparently unable to get the gun in action, they began heaving hand grenades at the beleaguered Marines. Clutching his pistol, Martin charged the pit by himself and shot all four Japanese. Though his one-man assault eliminated that particular threat, enemy pressure seemed to be building against his hastily organized defensive line. So far, the Japanese effort had been fairly disorganized, but the situation remained unclear and he feared their greater numbers could eventually overwhelm his Marines.

Maybe it was his tactical acumen, or maybe it was just his naturally aggressive personality, but Harry Martin decided to hit the Japanese before they could hit him. Shouting for his men to follow him, he did the unthinkable. He charged.

"I never saw an outfit organize so quickly," said PFC Bob Hurst. "We formed a line and spread out as skirmishers and charged in the direction of the banzai." Yelling and shooting, the Pioneers stormed forward. The Japanese recoiled, abandoning the Pioneers' area and eventually falling all the way back to the airfield perimeter. "One image I remember . . . was when a Jap came running over the crest of a little dune waving his sword at us," recalled Charles Serio. "Nothing had ever looked so big as that sword heading right for us, but I shot him in the chest. . . . He wasn't yelling 'banzai,' but something that sounded more like 'Yah! Yah! Yah!'"

Martin's bold tactic had succeeded, but the gung-ho lieutenant did not live to savor his own success. "One of the Japanese threw a grenade," remembered Bob Hanson. "It exploded near Harry and killed him."

"Lieutenant Martin had almost single-handedly destroyed several enemy positions before he was killed before my eyes," said Serio. "I saw the Jap who killed Lieutenant Martin come over a ridge about ten or fifteen feet in front of us. I yelled out to the lieutenant, but I was a split second too late. I saw the puffs of dust come out through his shirt, and he fell down dead."

Martin's counterattack pushed the Japanese back to the Fighter Command tents. Recovering from their initial surprise, groups of airmen had armed themselves and were also fighting back, going from tent to tent to check for enemy infiltrators and surviving Americans. Help was also arriving from nearby units. "The defense was getting organized up front and we could see our troops running between

*Japanese dead fill a shell hole following the early morning
counterattack on March 26, 1945. Harry Martin's heroism that
morning earned him Iwo's last Medal of Honor. Department
of Defense*

the tents," remembered Jim Van Nada. "One of our guys up front
squeezed off several rounds from a BAR right into our tent, but he
fired high and none of us was hit." The pilots yelled that they were
Americans and were soon rescued. Bob Hanson also survived, thank-
fully without having to use his KA-BAR. Sammy Bernstein, lying
in a state of shock next to the dead Japanese in his foxhole, heard
someone yelling for him: "Sam get the hell out of that foxhole. It's all
over. It's all over. Get up!"

At about 0830, three hours after it started, the Japanese attack finally
played out. In and among the blood-spattered tents lay forty-four dead
airmen. Another eighty-eight had been wounded. Seabees, shore party
personnel, and army units, including an African-American aviation
squadron, had also taken losses. "We visited the negro bivouac area
after and it was a sad sight to look onto," observed Hurst. "They lay
in huge puddles of bright red blood—arms and hands blown off by
Jap grenades. The Nips did that dirty work in the dark while the poor
negroes slept unarmed and unsuspecting."

The 5th Pioneer Battalion lost nine killed and thirty-one wounded. Among the dead was 1st Lt. Harry L. Martin, the former Bucyrus football walk-on who would never give up. He died on his parents' wedding anniversary. Later that same day, the last of the 5th Pioneer Battalion—thirty-four officers and 537 enlisted men—embarked aboard the USS *Electra* (AKA 4) and the USS *George F. Elliott* (APA 105). The following day they sailed from Iwo Jima. Decades later, Sammy Bernstein, remembering his foxhole buddy Arthur Erdman, could scarcely contain his anguish at leaving his friend behind and the injustice that he should be killed on their last day on Iwo Jima.

A board of review determined that Martin's daring and inspiring leadership had disrupted the Japanese attack and prevented an even greater loss of life in his own and adjacent platoons. That view was supported not only by witnesses, but also by the battlefield itself. The Japanese left 262 dead on the field. Of that total, 196 fell in the area of the 5th Pioneer Battalion. There was some scuttlebutt that General Kuribayashi himself had participated in the attack. If so, his body was never found.

Martin's Medal of Honor, the last of the twenty-seven earned by Marines and sailors during the battle for Iwo Jima, was presented to his parents, Ralph and Stella Martin, by Secretary of the Navy James Forrestal in Washington, D.C., on May 6, 1946. Also attending the ceremony was Marine commandant A. A. Vandegrift, Harry's brother Bob, and his sister Eleanor. A photograph of the presentation shows the secretary shaking hands with Mrs. Martin, the Medal of Honor around her neck, while Mr. Martin stands alongside. Both the Martins look as if they are determined not to cry. "Having worked so hard to get in there to do what he wanted to do, Bob and I could understand it, but it was hard on our parents," observed Eleanor years later.

In April 1948 Harry Martin's remains were returned from Iwo Jima for burial in Oakwood Cemetery in Bucyrus. Services were held at Grace Evangelical Church. The services were sparsely attended. Scarcely more than three dozen names appeared on the funeral home's register. That obscurity continued in later years. After the death of Harry's parents, the medal passed to his brother Bob, who kept it in his bureau drawer. Rarely did anyone ask to see it. In 1950, a bridge over the Sandusky River was dedicated in Harry's memory. But in 1988, when Bucyrus High School seniors were asked who Harry L. Martin was, many of them thought he was associated with a local real estate company; most of the rest guessed that he was a politician. In 1990, Bob Martin presented his brother's Medal of Honor to Bucyrus school officials for permanent display at the local high school. "I have had it here for forty-five years in a drawer," Martin said. "I think it might take on more meaning at the high school." The donation was preceded by three days of community observances. The medal was put on temporary display at City Hall where a Marine honor guard conducted hourly change-of-guard ceremonies. A military parade featuring the Parris Island Marine Band was held, followed the next day by the donation of the medal to the school Harry had graduated from sixty-two years earlier, and then by observances at Martin's grave in Oakwood Cemetery.

If the public needed an occasional reminder about Harry Martin, there were others who needed no reminding—those who, like Harry's old school chum Beanie Myers, would always remember the "un-hero-like friend who became a hero," as he put it. When he thought of heroes, remarked Meyers, he didn't think of Nathan Hale or Sergeant Alvin York; he thought of his high school classmate, Harry Martin, the mischievous kid who never quit.

"It's hard to explain what I feel," mused Eleanor Martin Abbot fifty years after the war. "I don't think my brother was better than anybody else. Harry wouldn't even have thought he did anything special. Harry would say, 'Why all the fuss? I only did my job.'"

APPENDIX

Medal of Honor Citations

SGT. JOHN BASILONE

7th Marines, 1st Marine Division

October 24–25, 1942

Rank and organization: Sergeant, U.S. Marine Corps. Born: 4 November 1916, Buffalo, New York. Accredited to: New Jersey. Citation: For extraordinary heroism and conspicuous gallantry in action against enemy Japanese forces, above and beyond the call of duty, while serving with the 1st Battalion, 7th Marines, 1st Marine Division, in the Lunga Area, Guadalcanal, Solomon Islands, on 24 and 25 October 1942. While the enemy was hammering at the Marines' defensive positions, Sergeant Basilone, in charge of two sections of heavy machine guns, fought valiantly to check the savage and determined assault. In a fierce frontal attack with the Japanese blasting his guns with grenades and mortar fire, one of Sergeant Basilone's sections, with its gun crews, was put out of action, leaving only two men able to carry on. Moving an extra gun into position, he placed it in action, then, under continual fire, repaired another and personally manned it, gallantly holding his line until replacements arrived. A little later, with ammunition critically low and the supply lines cut off, Sgt. Basilone, at great risk of his life and in the face of continued enemy attack, battled his way through hostile lines with urgently needed shells for his gunners, thereby contributing in large measure to the virtual annihilation of a Japanese regiment. His great personal valor and courageous initiative were in keeping with the highest traditions of the U.S. Naval Service.

CPL. CHARLES J. BERRY

26th Marines, 5th Marine Division
March 3, 1945

Rank and organization: Corporal, U.S. Marine Corps. Born: 10 July 1923, Lorain, Ohio. Accredited to: Ohio. Citation: For conspicuous gallantry and intrepidity at the risk of his life above and beyond the call of duty as member of a machine-gun crew, serving with the 1st Battalion, 26th Marines, 5th Marine Division, in action against enemy Japanese forces during the seizure of Iwo Jima in the Volcano Islands, on 3 March 1945. Stationed in the front lines, Corporal Berry manned his weapon with alert readiness as he maintained a constant vigil with other members of his gun crew during the hazardous night hours. When infiltrating Japanese soldiers launched a surprise attack shortly after midnight in an attempt to overrun his position, he engaged in a pitched hand grenade duel, returning the dangerous weapons with prompt and deadly accuracy until an enemy grenade landed in the foxhole. Determined to save his comrades, he unhesitatingly chose to sacrifice himself and immediately dived on the deadly missile, absorbing the shattering violence of the exploding charge in his own body and protecting the others from serious injury. Stouthearted and indomitable, Corporal Berry fearlessly yielded his own life that his fellow Marines might carry on the relentless battle against a ruthless enemy and his superb valor and unfaltering devotion to duty in the face of certain death reflect the highest credit upon himself and upon the U.S. Naval Service. He gallantly gave his life for his country.

PFC WILLIAM R. CADDY

26th Marines, 5th Marine Division
March 3, 1945

Rank and organization: Private First Class, U.S. Marine Corps Reserve. Born: 8 August 1925, Quincy, Massachusetts. Accredited to: Massachusetts. Citation: For conspicuous gallantry and intrepidity at the risk of his life above and beyond the call of duty while serving as a rifleman with Company I, 3rd Battalion, 26th Marines, 5th Marine Division, in action against enemy Japanese forces during the seizure of Iwo Jima in the Volcano Islands, 3 March 1945. Consistently aggressive, PFC Caddy boldly defied shattering Japanese machine-gun and small-arms fire to move forward with his platoon leader and another Marine during the determined advance of his company through an isolated sector and, gaining the comparative safety of a shell hole, took temporary cover with his comrades. Immediately pinned down by deadly sniper fire from a well-concealed position, he made several unsuccessful attempts to again move forward and then, joined by his platoon leader, engaged the enemy in a fierce exchange of hand grenades until a Japanese grenade fell beyond reach in the shell hole. Fearlessly disregarding all personal danger, PFC Caddy instantly dived on the deadly missile, absorbing the exploding charge in his own body and protecting the others from serious injury. Stouthearted and indomitable, he unhesitatingly yielded his own life that his fellow Marines might carry on the relentless battle against a fanatic enemy. His dauntless courage and valiant spirit of self-sacrifice in the face of certain death reflect the highest credit upon PFC Caddy and upon the U.S. Naval Service. He gallantly gave his life for his comrades.

LT. COL. JUSTICE CHAMBERS

25th Marines, 4th Marine Division
February 19–22, 1945

Rank and organization: Colonel, U.S. Marine Corps Reserve, 3rd Assault Battalion Landing Team, 25th Marines, 4th Marine Division. Place and date: On Iwo Jima, Volcano Islands from 19 to 22 February 1945. Entered service at: Washington, D.C. Born: 2 February 1908, Huntington, West Virginia. Citation: For conspicuous gallantry and intrepidity at the risk of his life above and beyond the call of duty as commanding officer of the 3rd Assault Battalion Landing Team, 25th Marines, 4th Marine Division, in action against enemy Japanese forces on Iwo Jima, Volcano Islands, from 19 to 22 February 1945. Under a furious barrage of enemy machine-gun and small-arms fire from the commanding cliffs on the right, Colonel Chambers (then lieutenant colonel) landed immediately after the initial assault waves of his battalion on D-day to find the momentum of the assault threatened by heavy casualties from withering Japanese artillery, mortar rocket, machine-gun, and rifle fire. Exposed to relentless hostile fire, he coolly reorganized his battle-weary men, inspiring them to heroic efforts by his own valor and leading them in an attack on the critical, impregnable high ground from which the enemy was pouring an increasing volume of fire directly onto troops ashore as well as amphibious craft in succeeding waves. Constantly in the front lines encouraging his men to push forward against the enemy's savage resistance, Colonel Chambers led the eight-hour battle to carry the flanking ridge top and reduce the enemy's fields of aimed fire, thus protecting the vital foothold gained. In constant defiance of hostile fire while reconnoitering the entire regimental combat team zone of action, he maintained contact with adjacent units and forwarded vital information to the regimental commander. His zealous fighting spirit undiminished despite terrific casualties and the loss of most of his key officers, he again reorganized his troops for renewed attack against the enemy's main line of resistance and was directing the fire of the rocket platoon when he fell, critically wounded. Evacuated under heavy Japanese fire, Colonel Chambers, by forceful leadership, courage, and fortitude in the face of staggering odds, was directly instrumental in insuring the success of subsequent operations of the V Amphibious Corps on Iwo Jima, thereby sustaining and enhancing the finest traditions of the U.S. Naval Service.

SGT. DARRELL S. COLE

23rd Marines, 4th Marine Division
February 19, 1945

Rank and organization: Sergeant, U.S. Marine Corps Reserve. Born: 20 July 1920, Flat River, Missouri. Entered service at: Esther, Missouri. Other Navy award: Bronze Star Medal. Citation: For conspicuous gallantry and intrepidity at the risk of his life above and beyond the call of duty while serving as leader of a machine-gun section of Company B, 1st Battalion, 23rd Marines, 4th Marine Division, in action against enemy Japanese forces during the assault on Iwo Jima in the Volcano Islands, 19 February 1945. Assailed by a tremendous volume of small-arms, mortar, and artillery fire as he advanced with one squad of his section in the initial assault wave, Sergeant Cole boldly led his men up the sloping beach toward Airfield No. 1 despite the blanketing curtain of flying shrapnel and, personally destroying with hand grenades two hostile emplacements which menaced the progress of his unit, continued to move forward until a merciless barrage of fire emanating from three Japanese pillboxes halted the advance. Instantly placing his one remaining machine gun in action, he delivered a shattering fusillade and succeeded in silencing the nearest and most threatening emplacement before his weapon jammed and the enemy, reopening fire with knee mortars and grenades, pinned down his unit for the second time. Shrewdly gauging the tactical situation and evolving a daring plan of counterattack, Sergeant Cole, armed solely with a pistol and one grenade, coolly advanced alone to the hostile pillboxes. Hurling his one grenade at the enemy in sudden, swift attack, he quickly withdrew, returned to his own lines for additional grenades, and again advanced, attacked, and withdrew. With enemy guns still active, he ran the gauntlet of slashing fire a third time to complete the total destruction of the Japanese strongpoint and the annihilation of the defending garrison in this final assault. Although instantly killed by an enemy grenade as he returned to his squad, Sergeant Cole had eliminated a formidable Japanese position, thereby enabling his company to storm the remaining fortifications, continue the advance, and seize the objective. By his dauntless initiative, unfaltering courage, and indomitable determination during a critical period of action, Sergeant Cole served as an inspiration to his comrades, and his stouthearted leadership in the face of almost certain death sustained and enhanced the highest tradition of the U.S. Naval Service. He gallantly gave his life for his country.

CAPT. ROBERT HUGO DUNLAP

26th Marines, 5th Marine Division
February 20–21, 1945

Rank and organization: Captain, U.S. Marine Corps Reserve, Company C, 1st Battalion, 26th Marines, 5th Marine Division. Place and date: On Iwo Jima, Volcano Islands, 20 and 21 February 1945. Born: 19 October 1920, Abingdon, Illinois. Entered service at: Illinois. Citation: For conspicuous gallantry and intrepidity at the risk of his life above and beyond the call of duty as commanding officer of Company C, 1st Battalion, 26th Marines, 5th Marine Division, in action against enemy Japanese forces during the seizure of Iwo Jima in the Volcano Islands, on 20 and 21 February 1945. Defying uninterrupted blasts of Japanese artillery, mortar, rifle, and machine-gun fire, Captain Dunlap led his troops in a determined advance from low ground uphill toward the steep cliffs from which the enemy poured a devastating rain of shrapnel and bullets, steadily inching forward until the tremendous volume of enemy fire from the caves located high to his front temporarily halted his progress. Determined not to yield, he crawled alone approximately 200 yards forward of his front lines, took observation at the base of the cliff fifty yards from Japanese lines, located the enemy gun positions, and returned to his own lines where he relayed the vital information to supporting artillery and naval gunfire units. Persistently disregarding his own personal safety, he then placed himself in an exposed vantage point to direct more accurately the supporting fire and, working without respite for two days and two nights under constant enemy fire, skillfully directed a smashing bombardment against the almost impregnable Japanese positions despite numerous obstacles and heavy Marine casualties. A brilliant leader, Captain Dunlap inspired his men to heroic efforts during this critical phase of the battle and by his cool decision, indomitable fighting spirit, and daring tactics in the face of fanatic opposition greatly accelerated the final decisive defeat of Japanese countermeasures in his sector and materially furthered the continued advance of his company. His great personal valor and gallant spirit of self-sacrifice throughout the bitter hostilities reflect the highest credit upon Captain Dunlap and the U.S. Naval Service.

SGT. ROSS F. GRAY

25th Marines, 4th Marine Division
February 21, 1945

Rank and organization: Sergeant, U.S. Marine Corps Reserve. Born: August 1920, Marvel Valley, Alabama. Accredited to: Alabama. Citation: For conspicuous gallantry and intrepidity at the risk of his life above and beyond the call of duty as a platoon sergeant attached to Company A, 1st Battalion, 25th Marines, 4th Marine Division, in action against enemy Japanese forces on Iwo Jima, Volcano Islands, 21 February 1945. Shrewdly gauging the tactical situation when his platoon was held up by a sudden barrage of hostile grenades while advancing toward the high ground northeast of Airfield No. 1, Sgt. Gray promptly organized the withdrawal of his men from enemy grenade range, quickly moved forward alone to reconnoiter, and discovered a heavily mined area extending along the front of a strong network of emplacements joined by covered trenches. Although assailed by furious gunfire, he cleared a path leading through the minefield to one of the fortifications, then returned to the platoon position and, informing his leader of the serious situation, volunteered to initiate an attack under cover of three fellow Marines. Alone and unarmed but carrying a huge satchel charge, he crept up on the Japanese emplacement, boldly hurled the short-fused explosive, and sealed the entrance. Instantly taken under machine-gun fire from a second entrance to the same position, he unhesitatingly braved the increasingly vicious fusillades to crawl back for another charge, returned to his objective, and blasted the second opening, thereby demolishing the position. Repeatedly covering the ground between the savagely defended enemy fortifications and his platoon area, he systematically approached, attacked, and withdrew under blanketing fire to destroy a total of six Japanese positions, more than twenty-five troops, and a quantity of vital ordnance gear and ammunition. Stouthearted and indomitable, Sergeant Gray had single-handedly overcome a strong enemy garrison and had completely disarmed a large minefield before finally rejoining his unit. By his great personal valor, daring tactics, and tenacious perseverance in the face of extreme peril, he had contributed materially to the fulfillment of his company mission. His gallant conduct throughout enhanced and sustained the highest traditions of the U.S. Naval Service.

SGT. WILLIAM G. HARRELL

28th Marines, 5th Marine Division
March 3, 1945

Rank and organization: Sergeant, U.S. Marine Corps, 1st Battalion, 28th Marines, 5th Marine Division. Place and date: Iwo Jima, Volcano Islands, 3 March 1945. Born: 26 June 1922, Rio Grande City, Texas. Entered service at: Mercedes, Texas. Citation: For conspicuous gallantry and intrepidity at the risk of his life above and beyond the call of duty as leader of an assault group attached to the 1st Battalion, 28th Marines, 5th Marine Division, during hand-to-hand combat with enemy Japanese at Iwo Jima, Volcano Islands, on 3 March 1945. Standing watch alternately with another Marine in a terrain studded with caves and ravines, Sergeant Harrell was holding a position in a perimeter defense around the company command post when Japanese troops infiltrated our lines in the early hours of dawn. Awakened by a sudden attack, he quickly opened fire with his carbine and killed two of the enemy as they emerged from a ravine in the light of a star shell burst. Unmindful of his danger as hostile grenades fell closer, he waged a fierce lone battle until an exploding missile tore off his left hand and fractured his thigh. He was vainly attempting to reload the carbine when his companion returned from the command post with another weapon. Wounded again by a Japanese who rushed the foxhole wielding a saber in the darkness, Sergeant Harrell succeeded in drawing his pistol and killing his opponent and then ordered his wounded companion to a place of safety. Exhausted by profuse bleeding but still unbeaten, he fearlessly met the challenge of two more enemy troops who charged his position and placed a grenade near his head. Killing one man with his pistol, he grasped the sputtering grenade with his good right hand, and, pushing it painfully toward the crouching soldier, saw his remaining assailant destroyed but his own hand severed in the explosion. At dawn Sergeant Harrell was evacuated from a position hedged by the bodies of twelve dead Japanese, at least five of whom he had personally destroyed in his self-sacrificing defense of the command post. His grim fortitude, exceptional valor, and indomitable fighting spirit against almost insurmountable odds reflect the highest credit upon himself and enhance the finest traditions of the U.S. Naval Service.

LT. (JG) RUFUS GEDDIE HERRING

LCI(G) 449
17 February 1945

Rank and organization: Lieutenant, U.S. Naval Reserve, LCI(G)–449. Place and date: Iwo Jima, 17 February 1945. Born: 11 June 1921,

Roseboro, North Carolina. Entered service at: North Carolina. Citation: For conspicuous gallantry and intrepidity at the risk of his life above and beyond the call of duty as commanding officer of LCI(G) 449 operating as a unit of LCI(G) Group 8, during the preinvasion attack on Iwo Jima on 17 February 1945. Boldly closing the strongly fortified shores under the devastating fire of Japanese coastal defense guns, Lieutenant (then lieutenant (jg)) Herring directed shattering barrages of 40mm and 20mm gunfire against hostile beaches until struck down by the enemy's savage counterfire which blasted the 449's heavy guns and whipped her decks into sheets of flame. Regaining consciousness despite profuse bleeding, he was again critically wounded when a Japanese mortar crashed the conning station, instantly killing or fatally wounding most of the officers and leaving the ship wallowing without navigational control. Upon recovering the second time, Lieutenant Herring resolutely climbed down to the pilothouse and, fighting against his rapidly waning strength, took over the helm, established communication with the engine room, and carried on valiantly until relief could be obtained. When no longer able to stand, he propped himself against empty shell cases and rallied his men to the aid of the wounded; he maintained position in the firing line with his 20mm guns in action in the face of sustained enemy fire, and conned his crippled ship to safety. His unwavering fortitude, aggressive perseverance, and indomitable spirit against terrific odds reflect the highest credit upon Lieutenant Herring and uphold the highest traditions of the U.S. Naval Service.

PFC DOUGLAS T. JACOBSON

23rd Marines, 4th Marine Division
February 26, 1945

Rank and organization: Private First Class, U.S. Marine Corps Reserve, 3rd Battalion, 23rd Marines, 4th Marine Division. Place and date: Iwo Jima, Volcano Islands, 26 February 1945. Born: 25

November 1925, Rochester, New York. Entered service at: New York. Citation: For conspicuous gallantry and intrepidity at the risk of his life above and beyond the call of duty while serving with the 3rd Battalion, 23rd Marines, 4th Marine Division, in combat against enemy Japanese forces during the seizure of Iwo Jima in the Volcano Islands, 26 February 1945. Promptly destroying a stubborn 20mm antiaircraft gun and its crew after assuming the duties of a bazooka man who had been killed, PFC Jacobson waged a relentless battle as his unit fought desperately toward the summit of Hill 382 in an effort to penetrate the heart of Japanese cross-island defense. Employing his weapon with ready accuracy when his platoon was halted by overwhelming enemy fire on 26 February, he first destroyed two hostile machine-gun positions, then attacked a large blockhouse, completely neutralizing the fortification before dispatching the five-man crew of a second pillbox and exploding the installation with a terrific demolitions blast. Moving steadily forward, he wiped out an earth-covered rifle emplacement and, confronted by a cluster of similar emplacements which constituted the perimeter of enemy defenses in his assigned sector, fearlessly advanced, quickly reduced all six positions to a shambles, killed ten of the enemy, and enabled our forces to occupy the strongpoint. Determined to widen the breach thus forced, he volunteered his services to an adjacent assault company, neutralized a pillbox holding up its advance, opened fire on a Japanese tank pouring a steady stream of bullets on one of our supporting tanks, and smashed the enemy tank's gun turret in a brief but furious action culminating in a single-handed assault against still another blockhouse and the subsequent neutralization of its fire power. By his dauntless skill and valor, Corporal Jacobson destroyed a total of sixteen enemy positions and annihilated approximately seventy-five Japanese, thereby contributing essentially to the success of his division's operations against this fanatically defended outpost of the Japanese Empire. His gallant conduct in the face of tremendous odds enhanced and sustained the highest traditions of the United States Naval Service.

PLATOON SGT. JOSEPH R. JULIAN
27th Marines, 5th Marine Division
March 9, 1945

Rank and organization: Platoon Sergeant, U.S. Marine Corps Reserve. Born: 3 April 1918, Sturbridge, Massachusetts. Accredited to: Massachusetts. Citation: For conspicuous gallantry and intrepidity at the risk of his life above and beyond the call of duty as a platoon sergeant serving with the 1st Battalion, 27th Marines, 5th Marine Division, in action against enemy Japanese forces during the seizure of Iwo Jima in the Volcano Islands, 9 March 1945. Determined to force a breakthrough when Japanese troops occupying trenches and fortified positions on the left front laid down a terrific machine-gun and mortar barrage in a desperate effort to halt his company's advance, Platoon Sergeant Julian quickly established his platoon's guns in strategic supporting positions, and then, acting on his own initiative, fearlessly moved forward to execute a one-man assault on the nearest pillbox. Advancing alone, he hurled deadly demolition and white phosphorus grenades into the emplacement, killing two of the enemy and driving the remaining five out into the adjoining trench system. Seizing a discarded rifle, he jumped into the trench and dispatched the five before they could make an escape. Intent on wiping out all resistance, he obtained more explosives and, accompanied by another Marine, again charged the hostile fortifications and knocked out two more cave positions. Immediately thereafter, he launched a bazooka attack unassisted, firing four rounds into the one remaining pillbox and completely destroying it before he fell, mortally wounded by a vicious burst of enemy fire. Stouthearted and indomitable, Platoon Sergeant Julian consistently disregarded all personal danger and, by his bold decision, daring tactics, and relentless fighting spirit during a critical phase of the battle, contributed materially to the continued advance of his company and to the success of his division's operations in the sustained drive toward the conquest of this fiercely defended outpost of the Japanese Empire. His outstanding valor and unfaltering spirit of self-sacrifice throughout the bitter conflict sustained and enhanced the highest traditions of the U.S. Naval Service. He gallantly gave his life for his country.

PFC JAMES D. LABELLE

27th Marines, 5th Marine Division
March 8, 1945

Rank and organization: Private First Class, U.S. Marine Corps Reserve. Born: 22 November 1926, Columbia Heights, Minnesota. Accredited to: Minnesota. Citation: For conspicuous gallantry and intrepidity at the risk of his life above and beyond the call of duty while attached to the 27th Marines, 5th Marine Division, in action against enemy Japanese forces during the seizure of Iwo Jima in the Volcano Islands, 8 March 1945. Filling a gap in the front lines during a critical phase of the battle, PFC LaBelle had dug into a foxhole with two other Marines and, grimly aware of the enemy's persistent attempts to blast a way through our lines with hand grenades, applied himself with steady concentration to maintaining a sharply vigilant watch during the hazardous night hours. Suddenly a hostile grenade landed beyond reach in his foxhole. Quickly estimating the situation, he determined to save the others if possible, shouted a warning, and instantly dived on the deadly missile, absorbing the exploding charge in his own body and thereby protecting his comrades from serious injury. Stouthearted and indomitable, he had unhesitatingly relinquished his own chance of survival that his fellow Marines might carry on the relentless fight against a fanatic enemy. His dauntless courage, cool decision, and valiant spirit of self-sacrifice in the face of certain death reflect the highest credit upon PFC LaBelle and upon the U.S. Naval Service. He gallantly gave his life in the service of his country.

2ND LT. JOHN H. LEIMS

9th Marines, 3rd Marine Division
March 7, 1945

Rank and organization: Second Lieutenant, U.S. Marine Corps Reserve, Company B, 1st Battalion, 9th Marines, 3rd Marine Division. Place and date: Iwo Jima, Volcano Islands, 7 March 1945. Born: Chicago, Illinois. Entered service at: Illinois. Citation: For conspicuous gallantry and intrepidity at the risk of his life above and beyond the call of duty as commanding officer of Company B, 1st Battalion, 9th Marines, 3rd Marine Division, in action against enemy Japanese forces on Iwo Jima in the Volcano Islands, on 7 March 1945. Launching a surprise attack against the rock-imbedded fortifications of a dominating Japanese hill position, Second Lieutenant Leims spurred his company forward with indomitable determination and, skillfully directing his assault platoons against the cave-emplaced enemy troops and heavily fortified pillboxes, succeeded in capturing the objective in the late afternoon. When it became apparent that his assault platoons were cut off in this newly won position, approximately four hundred yards forward of adjacent units and lacked all communication with the command post, he personally advanced and laid telephone lines across the isolating expanse of open, fire-swept terrain. Ordered to withdraw his command after he had joined his forward platoons, he immediately complied, adroitly effecting the withdrawal of his troops without incident. Upon arriving at the rear, he was informed that several casualties had been left at the abandoned ridge position beyond the front lines. Although suffering acutely from strain and exhaustion of battle, he instantly went forward despite darkness and the slashing fury of hostile machine-gun fire, located and carried to safety one seriously wounded Marine and then, running the gauntlet of enemy fire for the third time that night, again made his tortuous way into the bullet-riddled deathtrap and rescued another of his wounded men. A dauntless leader, concerned at all times for the welfare of his men, Second Lieutenant Leims soundly maintained the coordinated strength of his battle-wearied company under extremely difficult conditions and, by his bold tactics, sustained aggressiveness, and heroic disregard of all personal danger, contributed essentially to the success of his division's operations against this vital Japanese base. His valiant conduct in the face of fanatic opposition sustained and enhanced the highest traditions of the United States Marine Corps.

PFC JACKLYN H. LUCAS

26th Marines, 5th Marine Division
February 20, 1945

Rank and organization: Private First Class, U.S. Marine Corps Reserve, 1st Battalion, 26th Marines, 5th Marine Division. Place and date: Iwo Jima, Volcano Islands, 20 February 1945. Entered service at: Norfolk, Virginia. Born: 14 February 1928, Plymouth, North Carolina. Citation: For conspicuous gallantry and intrepidity at the risk of his life above and beyond the call of duty while serving with the 1st Battalion, 26th Marines, 5th Marine Division, during action against enemy Japanese forces on Iwo Jima, Volcano Islands, 20 February 1945. While creeping through a treacherous, twisting ravine which ran in close proximity to a fluid and uncertain front line on D–plus–1 day, PFC Lucas and three other men were suddenly ambushed by a hostile patrol which savagely attacked with rifle fire and grenades. Quick to act when the lives of the small group were endangered by two grenades which landed directly in front of them, PFC Lucas unhesitatingly hurled himself over his comrades upon one grenade and pulled the other under him, absorbing the whole blasting forces of the explosions in his own body in order to shield his companions from the concussion and murderous flying fragments. By his inspiring action and valiant spirit of self-sacrifice, he not only protected his comrades from certain injury or possible death but also enabled them to rout the Japanese patrol and continue the advance. His exceptionally courageous initiative and loyalty reflect the highest credit upon PFC Lucas and the U.S. Naval Service.

1ST LT. JACK LUMMUS

27th Marines, 5th Marine Division
March 8, 1945

Rank and organization: First Lieutenant, U.S. Marine Corps Reserve. Born: 22 October 1915, Ennis, Texas. Appointed from: Texas. Citation: For conspicuous gallantry and intrepidity at the risk of his life above and beyond the call of duty as leader of a rifle platoon attached to the 2nd Battalion, 27th Marines, 5th Marine Division, in action against enemy Japanese forces on Iwo Jima in the Volcano Islands, 8 March 1945. Resuming his assault tactics with bold decision after fighting without respite for two days and nights, First Lieutenant Lummus slowly advanced his platoon against an enemy deeply entrenched in a network of mutually supporting positions. Suddenly halted by a terrific concentration of hostile fire, he unhesitatingly moved forward of his front lines in an effort to neutralize the Japanese position. Although knocked to the ground when an enemy grenade exploded close by, he immediately recovered himself and, again moving forward despite the intensified barrage, quickly located, attacked, and destroyed the occupied emplacement. Instantly taken under fire by the garrison of a supporting pillbox and further assailed by the slashing fury of hostile rifle fire, he fell under the impact of a second enemy grenade but, courageously disregarding painful shoulder wounds, staunchly continued his heroic one-man assault and charged the second pillbox, annihilating all the occupants. Subsequently returning to his platoon position, he fearlessly traversed his lines under fire, encouraging his men to advance and directing the fire of supporting tanks against other stubbornly holding Japanese emplacements. Held up again by a devastating barrage, he again moved into the open, rushed a third heavily fortified installation, and killed the defending troops. Determined to crush all resistance, he led his men indomitably, personally attacking foxholes and spider traps with his carbine and systematically reducing the fanatic opposition until, stepping on a land mine, he sustained fatal wounds. By his outstanding valor, skilled tactics, and tenacious perseverance in the face of overwhelming odds, First Lieutenant Lummus had inspired his stouthearted Marines to continue the relentless drive northward, thereby contributing materially to the success of his regimental mission. His dauntless leadership and unwavering devotion to duty throughout sustain and enhance the highest traditions of the U.S. Naval Service. He gallantly gave his life in the service of his country.

1ST LT. HARRY L. MARTIN

5th Pioneer Battalion, 5th Marine Division
March 26, 1945

Rank and organization: First Lieutenant, U.S. Marine Corps Reserve. Born: 4 January 1911, Bucyrus, Ohio. Appointed from: Ohio. Citation: For conspicuous gallantry and intrepidity at the risk of his life above and beyond the call of duty as platoon leader attached to Company C, 5th Pioneer Battalion, 5th Marine Division, in action against enemy Japanese forces on Iwo Jima, Volcano Islands, 26 March 1945. With his sector of the 5th Pioneer Battalion bivouac area penetrated by a concentrated enemy attack launched a few minutes before dawn, First Lieutenant Martin instantly organized a firing line with the Marines nearest his foxhole and succeeded in checking momentarily the headlong rush of the Japanese. Determined to rescue several of his men trapped in positions overrun by the enemy, he defied intense hostile fire to work his way through the Japanese to the surrounded Marines. Although sustaining two severe wounds, he blasted the Japanese who attempted to intercept him, located his beleaguered men, and directed them to their own lines. When four of the infiltrating enemy took possession of an abandoned machine-gun pit and subjected his sector to a barrage of hand grenades, First Lieutenant Martin, alone and armed only with a pistol, boldly charged the hostile position and killed all of its occupants. Realizing that his few remaining comrades could not repulse another organized attack, he called to his men to follow and then charged into the midst of the strong enemy force, firing his weapon and scattering them until he fell, mortally wounded by a grenade. By his outstanding valor, indomitable fighting spirit, and tenacious determination in the face of overwhelming odds, First Lieutenant Martin permanently disrupted a coordinated Japanese attack and prevented a greater loss of life in his own and adjacent platoons. His inspiring leadership and unswerving devotion to duty reflect the highest credit upon himself and the U.S. Naval Service. He gallantly gave his life in the service of his country.

CAPT. JOSEPH J. MCCARTHY
24th Marines, 4th Marine Division
February 21, 1945

Rank and organization: Captain, U.S. Marine Corps Reserve, 2nd Battalion, 24th Marines, 4th Marine Division. Place and date: Iwo Jima, Volcano Islands, 21 February 1945. Born: 10 August 1912, Chicago, Illinois. Entered service at: Illinois. Citation: For conspicuous gallantry and intrepidity at the risk of his life above and beyond the call of duty as commanding officer of a rifle company attached to the 2nd Battalion, 24th Marines, 4th Marine Division, in action against enemy Japanese forces during the seizure of Iwo Jima, Volcano Islands, on 21 February 1945. Determined to break through the enemy's cross-island defenses, Captain McCarthy acted on his own initiative when his company advance was held up by uninterrupted Japanese rifle, machine-gun, and high-velocity 47mm fire during the approach to Motoyama Airfield No. 2. Quickly organizing a demolitions and flamethrower team to accompany his picked rifle squad, he fearlessly led the way across seventy-five yards of fire-swept ground, charged a heavily fortified pillbox on the ridge of the front and, personally hurling hand grenades into the emplacement as he directed the combined operations of his small assault group, completely destroyed the hostile installation. Spotting two Japanese soldiers attempting an escape from the shattered pillbox, he boldly stood upright in full view of the enemy and dispatched both troops before advancing to a second emplacement under greatly intensified fire and then blasted the strong fortifications with a well-planned demolitions attack. Subsequently entering the ruins, he found a Japanese taking aim at one of our men and, with alert presence of mind, jumped the enemy, disarmed and shot him with his own weapon. Then, intent on smashing through the narrow breach, he rallied the remainder of his company and pressed a full attack with furious aggressiveness until he had neutralized all resistance and captured the ridge. An inspiring leader and indomitable fighter, Captain McCarthy consistently disregarded all personal danger during the fierce conflict and, by his brilliant professional skill, daring tactics, and tenacious perseverance in the face of overwhelming odds, contributed materially to the success of his division's operations against this savagely defended outpost of the Japanese Empire. His cool decision and outstanding valor reflect the highest credit upon Captain McCarthy and enhance the finest traditions of the U.S. Naval Service.

PVT. GEORGE PHILLIPS

28th Marines, 5th Division
March 14, 1945

Rank and organization: Private, U.S. Marine Corps Reserve. Born: 14 July 1926, Rich Hill, Missouri. Entered service at: Labadie, Missouri. Accredited to: Missouri. Citation: For conspicuous gallantry and intrepidity at the risk of his life above and beyond the call of duty while serving with the 2nd Battalion, 28th Marines, 5th Marine Division, in action against enemy Japanese forces during the seizure of Iwo Jima in the Volcano Islands, on 14 March 1945. Standing the foxhole watch while other members of his squad rested after a night of bitter hand grenade fighting against infiltrating Japanese troops, Private Phillips was the only member of his unit alerted when an enemy hand grenade was tossed into their midst. Instantly shouting a warning, he unhesitatingly threw himself on the deadly missile, absorbing the shattering violence of the exploding charge in his own body and protecting his comrades from serious injury. Stouthearted and indomitable, Private Phillips willingly yielded his own life that his fellow Marines might carry on the relentless battle against a fanatic enemy. His superb valor and unfaltering spirit of self-sacrifice in the face of certain death reflect the highest credit upon himself and upon the U.S. Naval Service. He gallantly gave his life for his country.

PHARMACIST'S MATE 1ST CLASS FRANCIS J. PIERCE

24th Marines, 4th Marine Division
March 15–16, 1945

Rank and organization: Pharmacist's Mate 1st Class, U.S. Navy serving with 2nd Battalion, 24th Marines, 4th Marine Division. Place and date: Iwo Jima, 15 and 16 March 1945. Born: Earlville, Iowa. Entered service at: Iowa. Citation: For conspicuous gallantry and intrepidity at the risk of his life above and beyond the call of duty while attached to the 2nd Battalion, 24th Marines, 4th Marine Division, during the Iwo Jima campaign, 15 and 16 March 1945. Almost continuously under fire while carrying out the most dangerous volunteer assignments, Pierce gained valuable knowledge of the terrain and disposition of troops. Caught in heavy enemy rifle and machine-gun fire which wounded a corpsman and two of the eight stretcher bearers who were carrying two wounded Marines to a forward aid station on 15 March, Pierce quickly took charge of the party, carried the newly wounded men to a sheltered position, and rendered first aid. After directing the evacuation of three of the casualties, he stood in the open to draw the enemy's fire and, with his weapon blasting, enabled the litter bearers to reach cover. Turning his attention to the other two casualties, he was attempting to stop the profuse bleeding of one man when a Japanese fired from a cave less than twenty yards away and wounded his patient again. Risking his own life to save his patient, Pierce deliberately exposed himself to draw the attacker from the cave and destroyed him with the last of his ammunition. Then, lifting the wounded man to his back, he advanced unarmed through deadly rifle fire across two hundred feet of open terrain. Despite exhaustion and in the face of warnings against such a suicidal mission, he again traversed the same fire-swept path to rescue the remaining Marine. On the following morning, he led a combat patrol to the sniper nest and, while aiding a stricken Marine, was seriously wounded. Refusing aid for himself, he directed treatment for the casualty, at the same time maintaining protective fire for his comrades. Completely fearless, completely devoted to the care of his patients, Pierce inspired the entire battalion. His valor in the face of extreme peril sustains and enhances the finest traditions of the U.S. Naval Service.

PFC DONALD JACK RUHL

28th Marines, 5th Marine Division
February 19–21, 1945

Rank and organization: Private First Class, U.S. Marine Corps Reserve. Born: 2 July 1923, Columbus, Montana. Accredited to: Montana. Citation: For conspicuous gallantry and intrepidity at the risk of his life above and beyond the call of duty while serving as a rifleman in an assault platoon of Company E, 28th Marines, 5th Marine Division, in action against enemy Japanese forces on Iwo Jima, Volcano Islands, from 19 to 21 February 1945. Quick to press the advantage after eight Japanese had been driven from a blockhouse on D-day, PFC Ruhl single-handedly attacked the group, killing one of the enemy with his bayonet and another by rifle fire in his determined attempt to annihilate the escaping troops. Cool and undaunted as the fury of hostile resistance steadily increased throughout the night, he voluntarily left the shelter of his tank trap early in the morning of D-day-plus-1 and moved out under a tremendous volume of mortar and machine-gun fire to rescue a wounded Marine lying in an exposed position approximately forty yards forward of the line. Half pulling and half carrying the wounded man, he removed him to a defiladed position, called for an assistant and a stretcher and, again running the gauntlet of hostile fire, carried the casualty to an aid station some 300 yards distant on the beach. Returning to his platoon, he continued his valiant efforts, volunteering to investigate an apparently abandoned Japanese gun emplacement seventy-five yards forward of the right flank during consolidation of the front lines, and subsequently occupying the position through the night to prevent the enemy from repossessing the valuable weapon. Pushing forward in the assault against the vast network of fortifications surrounding Mt. Suribachi the following morning, he crawled with his platoon guide to the top of a Japanese bunker to bring fire to bear on enemy troops located on the far side of the bunker. Suddenly a hostile grenade landed between the two Marines. Instantly PFC Ruhl called a warning to his fellow Marine and dived on the deadly missile, absorbing the full impact of the shattering explosion in his own body and protecting all within range from the danger of flying fragments although he might easily have dropped from his position on the edge of the bunker to the ground below. An indomitable fighter, PFC Ruhl rendered heroic service toward the defeat of a ruthless enemy, and his valor, initiative, and unfaltering spirit of self-sacrifice in the face of almost certain death sustain and enhance the highest traditions of the U.S. Naval Service. He gallantly gave his life for his country.

PVT. FRANKLIN E. SIGLER

26th Marines, 5th Marine Division
March 14, 1945

Rank and organization: Private, U.S. Marine Corps Reserve, 2nd Battalion, 26th Marines, 5th Marine Division. Place and date: Iwo Jima, Volcano Islands, 14 March 1945. Born: Glen Ridge, New Jersey. Entered service at: New Jersey. Citation: For conspicuous gallantry and intrepidity at the risk of his life above and beyond the call of duty while serving with the 2nd Battalion, 26th Marines, 5th Marine Division, in action against enemy Japanese forces during the seizure of Iwo Jima in the Volcano Islands on 14 March 1945. Voluntarily taking command of his rifle squad when the leader became a casualty, Private Sigler fearlessly led a bold charge against an enemy gun installation which had held up the advance of his company for several days and, reaching the position in advance of the others, assailed the emplacement with hand grenades and personally annihilated the entire crew. As additional Japanese troops opened fire from concealed tunnels and caves above, he quickly scaled the rocks leading to the attacking guns, surprised the enemy with a furious one-man assault and, although severely wounded in the encounter, deliberately crawled back to his squad position where he steadfastly refused evacuation, persistently directing heavy-gun and rocket barrages on the Japanese cave entrances. Undaunted by the merciless rain of hostile fire during the intensified action, he gallantly disregarded his own painful wounds to aid casualties, carrying three wounded squad members to safety behind the lines and returning to continue the battle with renewed determination until ordered to retire for medical treatment. Stouthearted and indomitable in the face of extreme peril, Private Sigler, by his alert initiative, unfaltering leadership, and daring tactics in a critical situation, effected the release of his besieged company from enemy fire and contributed essentially to its further advance against a savagely fighting enemy. His superb valor, resolute fortitude, and heroic spirit of self-sacrifice throughout reflect the highest credit upon Private Sigler and the U.S. Naval Service.

CPL. TONY STEIN

28th Marines, 5th Marine Division
February 19, 1945

Rank and organization: Corporal, U.S. Marine Corps Reserve. Born: 30 September 1921, Dayton, Ohio. Accredited to: Ohio. Citation: For conspicuous gallantry and intrepidity at the risk of his life above and beyond the call of duty while serving with Company A, 1st Battalion, 28th Marines, 5th Marine Division, in action against enemy Japanese forces on Iwo Jima, in the Volcano Islands, 19 February 1945. The first man of his unit to be on station after hitting the beach in the initial assault, Corporal Stein, armed with a personally improvised aircraft-type weapon, provided rapid covering fire as the remainder of his platoon attempted to move into position. When his comrades were stalled by a concentrated machine-gun and mortar barrage, he gallantly stood upright and exposed himself to the enemy's view, thereby drawing the hostile fire to his own person and enabling him to observe the location of the furiously blazing hostile guns. Determined to neutralize the strategically placed weapons, he boldly charged the enemy pillboxes one by one and succeeded in killing twenty of the enemy during the furious single-handed assault. Cool and courageous under the merciless hail of exploding shells and bullets which fell on all sides, he continued to deliver the fire of his skillfully improvised weapon at a tremendous rate of speed which rapidly exhausted his ammunition. Undaunted, he removed his helmet and shoes to expedite his movements and ran back to the beach for additional ammunition, making a total of eight trips under intense fire and carrying or assisting a wounded man back each time. Despite the unrelenting savagery and confusion of battle, he rendered prompt assistance to his platoon whenever the unit was in position, directing the fire of a half-track against a stubborn pillbox until he had effected the ultimate destruction of the Japanese fortification. Later in the day, although his weapon was twice shot from his hands, he personally covered the withdrawal of his platoon to the company position. Stouthearted and indomitable, Corporal Stein, by his aggressive initiative, sound judgment, and unwavering devotion to duty in the face of terrific odds, contributed materially to the fulfillment of his mission, and his outstanding valor throughout the bitter hours of conflict sustains and enhances the highest traditions of the U.S. Naval Service.

PHARMACIST'S MATE 2ND CLASS GEORGE E. WAHLEN

26th Marines, 5th Marine Division
March 3, 1945

Rank and organization: Pharmacist's Mate 2nd Class, U.S. Navy, serving with 2nd Battalion, 26th Marines, 5th Marine Division. Place and date: Iwo Jima, Volcano Islands group, 3 March 1945. Born: 8 August 1924, Ogden, Utah. Entered service at: Utah. Citation: For conspicuous gallantry and intrepidity at the risk of his life above and beyond the call of duty while serving with the 2nd Battalion, 26th Marines, 5th Marine Division, during action against enemy Japanese forces on Iwo Jima in the Volcano group on 3 March 1945. Painfully wounded in the bitter action on 26 February, Wahlen remained on the battlefield, advancing well forward of the front lines to aid a wounded Marine and carrying him back to safety despite a terrific concentration of fire. Tireless in his ministrations, he consistently disregarded all danger to attend his fighting comrades as they fell under the devastating rain of shrapnel and bullets, and rendered prompt assistance to various elements of his combat group as required. When an adjacent platoon suffered heavy casualties, he defied the continuous pounding of heavy mortars and deadly fire of enemy rifles to care for the wounded, working rapidly in an area swept by constant fire and treating fourteen casualties before returning to his own platoon. Wounded again on 2 March, he gallantly refused evacuation, moving out with his company the following day in a furious assault across 600 yards of open terrain and repeatedly rendering medical aid while exposed to the blasting fury of powerful Japanese guns. Stouthearted and indomitable, he persevered in his determined efforts as his unit waged fierce battle and, unable to walk after sustaining a third agonizing wound, resolutely crawled fifty yards to administer first aid to still another fallen fighter. By his dauntless fortitude and valor, Wahlen served as a constant inspiration and contributed vitally to the high morale of his company during critical phases of this strategically important engagement. His heroic spirit of self-sacrifice in the face of overwhelming enemy fire upheld the highest traditions of the U.S. Naval Service.

GUNNERY SGT. WILLIAM G. WALSH

27th Marines, 5th Marine Division
February 27, 1945

Rank and organization: Gunnery Sergeant, U.S. Marine Corps Reserve. Born: 7 April 1922, Roxbury, Massachusetts. Accredited to: Massachusetts. Citation: For extraordinary gallantry and intrepidity at the risk of his life above and beyond the call of duty as leader of an assault platoon, attached to Company G, 3rd Battalion, 27th Marines, 5th Marine Division, in action against enemy Japanese forces at Iwo Jima, Volcano Islands, on 27 February 1945. With the advance of his company toward Hill 362 disrupted by vicious machine-gun fire from a forward position which guarded the approaches to this key enemy stronghold, Gunnery Sergeant Walsh fearlessly charged at the head of his platoon against the Japanese entrenched on the ridge above him, utterly oblivious to the unrelenting fury of hostile automatic weapons fire and hand grenades employed with fanatic desperation to smash his daring assault. Thrown back by the enemy's savage resistance, he once again led his men in a seemingly impossible attack up the steep, rocky slope, boldly defiant of the annihilating streams of bullets which saturated the area. Despite his own casualty losses and the overwhelming advantage held by the Japanese in superior numbers and dominant position, he gained the ridge's top only to be subjected to an intense barrage of hand grenades thrown by the remaining Japanese staging a suicidal last stand on the reverse slope. When one of the grenades fell in the midst of his surviving men, huddled together in a small trench, Gunnery Sergeant Walsh, in a final valiant act of complete self-sacrifice, instantly threw himself upon the deadly bomb, absorbing with his own body the full and terrific force of the explosion. Through his extraordinary initiative and inspiring valor in the face of almost certain death, he saved his comrades from injury and possible loss of life and enabled his company to seize and hold this vital enemy position. He gallantly gave his life for his country.

PVT. WILSON D. WATSON

9th Marines, 3rd Marine Division
February 26–27, 1945

Rank and organization: Private, U.S. Marine Corps Reserve, 2nd Battalion, 9th Marines, 5th Marine Division. Place and date: Iwo Jima, Volcano Islands, 26 and 27 February 1945. Born: Tuscumbia, Alabama. Entered service at: Arkansas. Citation: For conspicuous gallantry and intrepidity at the risk of his life above and beyond the call of duty as automatic rifleman serving with the 2nd Battalion, 9th Marines, 3rd Marine Division, during action against enemy Japanese forces on Iwo Jima, Volcano Islands, 26 and 27 February 1945. With his squad abruptly halted by intense fire from the enemy fortifications in the high rocky ridges and crags commanding the line of advance, Private Watson boldly rushed one pillbox and fired into the embrasure with his weapon, keeping the enemy pinned down single-handedly until he was in a position to hurl in a grenade and running to the rear of the emplacement to destroy the retreating Japanese and enable his platoon to take its objective. Again pinned down at the foot of a small hill, he dauntlessly scaled the jagged incline under fierce mortar and machine-gun barrages and with his assistant automatic rifleman charged the crest of the hill, firing from his hip. Fighting furiously against Japanese troops attacking with grenades and knee-mortars from the reverse slope, he stood fearlessly erect in his exposed position to cover the hostile entrenchments and held the hill under savage fire for fifteen minutes, killing sixty Japanese before his ammunition was exhausted and his platoon was able to join him. His courageous initiative and valiant fighting spirit against devastating odds were directly responsible for the continued advance of his platoon, and his inspiring leadership throughout this bitterly fought action reflects the highest credit upon Private Watson and the U.S. Naval Service.

CPL. HERSHEL W. WILLIAMS

21st Marines, 3rd Marine Division
February 23, 1945

Rank and organization: Corporal, U.S. Marine Corps Reserve, 21st Marines, 3rd Marine Division. Place and date: Iwo Jima, Volcano Islands, 23 February 1945. Born: 2 October 1923, Quiet Dell, West Virginia. Entered service at: West Virginia. Citation: For conspicuous gallantry and intrepidity at the risk of his life above and beyond the call of duty as demolition sergeant serving with the 21st Marines, 3rd Marine Division, in action against enemy Japanese forces on Iwo Jima, Volcano Islands, 23 February 1945. Quick to volunteer his services when our tanks were maneuvering vainly to open a lane for the infantry through the network of reinforced concrete pillboxes, buried mines, and black volcanic sands, Corporal Williams daringly went forward alone to attempt the reduction of devastating machine-gun fire from the unyielding positions. Covered only by four riflemen, he fought desperately for four hours under terrific enemy small-arms fire and repeatedly returned to his own lines to prepare demolition charges and obtain serviced flamethrowers, struggling back, frequently to the rear of hostile emplacements, to wipe out one position after another. On one occasion, he daringly mounted a pillbox to insert the nozzle of his flamethrower through the air vent, killing the occupants and silencing the gun; on another he grimly charged enemy riflemen who attempted to stop him with bayonets and destroyed them with a burst of flame from his weapon. His unyielding determination and extraordinary heroism in the face of ruthless enemy resistance were directly instrumental in neutralizing one of the most fanatically defended Japanese strongpoints encountered by his regiment and aided vitally in enabling his company to reach its objective. Corporal Williams's aggressive fighting spirit and valiant devotion to duty throughout this fiercely contested action sustain and enhance the highest traditions of the U.S. Naval Service.

PHARMACIST'S MATE 3RD CLASS JACK WILLIAMS
28th Marines, 5th Marine Division
March 3, 1945

Rank and organization: Pharmacist's Mate 3rd Class, U.S. Naval Reserve. Born: 18 October 1924, Harrison, Arkansas. Accredited to: Arkansas. Citation: For conspicuous gallantry and intrepidity at the risk of his life above and beyond the call of duty while serving with the 3rd Battalion, 28th Marines, 5th Marine Division, during the occupation of Iwo Jima, Volcano Islands, 3 March 1945. Gallantly going forward on the front lines under intense enemy small-arms fire to assist a Marine wounded in a fierce grenade battle, Williams dragged the man to a shallow depression and was kneeling, using his own body as a screen from the sustained fire as he administered first aid, when struck in the abdomen and groin three times by hostile rifle fire. Momentarily stunned, he quickly recovered and completed his ministration before applying battle dressings to his own multiple wounds. Unmindful of his own urgent need for medical attention, he remained in the perilous fire-swept area to care for another Marine casualty. Heroically completing his task despite pain and profuse bleeding, he then endeavored to make his way to the rear in search of adequate aid for himself when struck down by a Japanese sniper bullet which caused his collapse. Succumbing later as a result of his self-sacrificing service to others, Williams, by his courageous determination, unwavering fortitude, and valiant performance of duty, served as an inspiring example of heroism, in keeping with the highest traditions of the U.S. Naval Service. He gallantly gave his life for his country.

PHARMACIST'S MATE 1ST CLASS JOHN H. WILLIS

27th Marines, 5th Marine Division
February 28, 1945

Rank and organization: Pharmacist's Mate 1st Class, U.S. Navy. Born: 10 June 1921, Columbia, Tennessee. Accredited to: Tennessee. Citation: For conspicuous gallantry and intrepidity at the risk of his life above and beyond the call of duty as platoon corpsman serving with the 3rd Battalion, 27th Marines, 5th Marine Division, during operations against enemy Japanese forces on Iwo Jima, Volcano Islands, 28 February 1945. Constantly imperiled by artillery and mortar fire from strong and mutually supporting pillboxes and caves studding Hill 362 in the enemy's cross-island defenses, Pharmacist's Mate 1st Class Willis resolutely administered first aid to the many Marines wounded during the furious close-in fighting until he himself was struck by shrapnel and was ordered back to the battle-aid station. Without waiting for official medical release, he quickly returned to his company and, during a savage hand-to-hand enemy counterattack, daringly advanced to the extreme front lines under mortar and sniper fire to aid a Marine lying wounded in a shell hole. Completely unmindful of his own danger as the Japanese intensified their attack, Willis calmly continued to administer blood plasma to his patient, promptly returning the first hostile grenade which landed in the shell hole while he was working and hurling back seven more in quick succession before the ninth one exploded in his hand and instantly killed him. By his great personal valor in saving others at the sacrifice of his own life, Pharmacist's Mate 1st Class Willis inspired his companions, although terrifically outnumbered, to launch a fiercely determined attack and repulse the enemy force. His exceptional fortitude and courage in the performance of duty reflect the highest credit upon Willis and the U.S. Naval Service. He gallantly gave his life for his country.

NOTES

Sources can be found in the selected bibliography, with reference to some of the more directly pertinent material cited in the following chapter notes. I also made substantial use of census records, as well as after-action reports of the three Marine divisions involved in the seizure of Iwo Jima.

The reader will notice occasional discrepancies between official citations and witness accounts. Accounts by surviving medal recipients about their own actions sometimes vary in the telling. This demonstrates mostly that combat is confusing. Memory of specifics is certainly not enhanced by the burden of great fear, or by the passage of time. Honest witnesses may remember events differently and those charged with recording those events may err in some details. I have tried to reconcile discrepancies, according to the facts as I have been able to establish them.

INTRODUCTION

More Medals of Honor were awarded for Iwo Jima than any other Pacific Theater campaign. More than a quarter of the eighty-two Medals of Honor awarded to Marines during World War II were earned on Iwo Jima. The second largest number for a campaign was for Okinawa, with twenty-four Medals of Honor to Army, Navy, and Marine Corps recipients. It is well to remember that the Okinawa campaign lasted eight-one days (more than twice as long as Iwo Jima) and involved four Army and two Marine divisions, as opposed to the three Marine divisions (minus one regiment) at Iwo Jima. Over 200 Navy Cross awards were also authorized for Marines and sailors directly involved in the landing and ground campaign on Iwo Jima. Reading the citations, it is difficult at times to understand why some of these awards did not merit the Medal of Honor. Among the Navy Cross recipients was Pharmacist's Mate 3rd Class Byron Alfred Dary, who had previously received the Silver Star for heroism on Omaha Beach during the June 6, 1944, D-Day invasion. Unfortunately, his Navy Cross for Iwo Jima was posthumous.

CHAPTER 1

Rufus G. Herring: Account is drawn from Marquand in *Harpers*; Deck Log, LCI Group 8, Flotilla 3 at Iwo Jima; Karig; Morrison; Hallet interview; Dennis R. Blocker II, whose grandfather served aboard LCI(G)-449, has done an impressive amount of research on the ship and crew—Exum's recollection is included in that material. Lieutenant Reichl is quoted in Karig; "Herring was twice critically wounded . . . " appears in AP wire service report September 6, 1945; information and history on the Herring homestead was recorded by the State of North Carolina Division of Archives and History in 1985; Herring's own brief account of the action is quoted by Bizzell.

Darrell S. Cole: Shipboard reveille recollection appears in Matthews's *Assault*; Burows quoted in Rogers's *Marylanders*; author interviews with Bill Glazier and Kenneth Phillips; family reminiscences in October 14, 2000, *Kansas City Star* article; Cole's diary/journal and other material was kindly provided by the Stars and Stripes Museum in Bloomfield, MO. The late Joe Layden, former editor of the *Daily Journal* in St. Francois County, MO, went to great efforts to ensure that Cole was properly remembered; Layden's efforts appear in various issues of that newspaper and were also summarized in a press release by Sgt. M. D. Stover of the 9th Marine Corps District Public Affairs Branch, dated July 31, 1985. A very comprehensive story, including recollections by Zocchi, Bayly, and others, appeared in the February 19 and February 22, 1985, issues of the *Daily Journal*. Hank Harron, who provided substantiation for Cole's actions, passed away in 2002, but his widow, Enza "Holly" Harron, provided me with much of his paperwork, which proved very helpful.

Tony Stein: Census records indicate Stein's given name was Anthony; however, he went by Tony. He is carried on Marine Corps muster rolls as "Tony," and that is also the name his mother buried him under when his remains were returned from Iwo Jima. Stein is memorialized at length in Lace's *Bravest of the Brave*; a UPI wire-service report mentioned his antisniper success on Bougainville. His platoon leader Lt. Alma Sonne Jr. talks about Stein in his unpublished memoir, which can be found in the L. Tom Perry Special Collections of the Harold B. Lee Library at Brigham Young University.

There is still some confusion about "the Stinger." While Stein, a tool and die maker, is often credited with creating "the Stinger," it seems clear that the weapon was the brainchild of Sgt. Milan J. "Mel" Grevich, as is detailed in articles in the *Marine Corps Gazette* (February 1946) and *American Rifleman* (April 2006). Grevich supposedly built six Stingers. Five stayed in Grevich's 3rd Battalion and one ended up with Stein in the 1st Battalion. Grevich and Stein served together in the 3rd Parachute Battalion earlier in the war, and that may be how Stein apparently ended up with one of the six Stingers built by Grevich on Hawaii. However, Lt. Sonne indicates that Stein promised to build two Stingers (a third gun was to be used for back-up parts). Adding to the confusion, in a letter about Iwo Jima to Sonne, another A Company Marine, Cpl. John McWilliams, mentions that he and Stein "built 2 stingers at Camp Tarawa and hit the beach with them at Iwo. Joe Conte was my assistant and carried extra ammo in a bar belt. I don't remember who was Tony's assistant." If in fact A Company had two Stingers, that would seem to indicate that either two of Grevich's weapons found their way to A Company; that there were more than six built; or that Stein did in fact build two of the Stingers, either by himself or in cooperation with Grevich.

John Armendariz's recollections about Stein were recorded in the 2006 TV documentary "Shootout Iwo Jima" and in Chatfield. Stein's actions, the circumstances of his death, and the information that he actually lost his helmet aboard ship is noted by Sonne and also in Allen's *History of the 1st Battalion, 28th Marines*.

Sgt. Merritt Savage survived Iwo Jima and received the Navy Cross for his actions on February 19. He died in Nevada in 1983. Tabert was killed on March 1. Marine Corps records indicating that Stein's wounds on February 19 were due to "gunshot, right arm and neck" are apparently in error; consensus in the unit is that he was hit by mortar fragments.

John Basilone: Much has been written about John Basilone, and the majority of that is fanciful. James Brady examines the many contradictions in the Basilone "myth" in *Hero of the Pacific*, where he does a better job of pinning down the fancies than establishing the facts—which may have been a hopeless cause to begin with, the waters have been so muddied over the years. The recollections of Tatum and Lansford about Basilone's actions on Iwo Jima have the ring of truth. Marine Corps records indicate Basilone was killed by small-arms fire, but I am persuaded that is erroneous. Basilone's battalion commander, Col. Justin G. Duryea, recommended him for a second Medal of Honor for his actions on Iwo Jima, but the decoration was knocked down to a Navy Cross. Lena Basilone, by all accounts an extraordinary woman, gave her husband's $10,000 insurance payout to his family in New Jersey. The family reportedly treated her shabbily and she wanted nothing to do with them.

Justice Chambers: Glen Buzard is quoted in Smith's *Iwo Jima*; Oulette is cited in Kessler; Hruza and the Ballad of the Ghouls is from Simpson's "Iwo Jima: A Surgeon's Story," which appeared in *Leatherneck* magazine in 1990. The Paul Chambers interview with Colonel Chambers is very detailed; Jordan, *Men of Honor*; Kayser, *The Spirit of America*; AP Wire Service report November 2, 1950, on award of medal; Miller, "Builder of Rugged Marines." Donald Bittner's essay on Chambers in Muir is excellent.

CHAPTER 2

Jacklyn H. Lucas: "Oh What a Beautiful Morning" cited in Stone. Jack Lucas gave many interviews through the years about his experiences on Iwo Jima, and also maintained an online website. His postwar ups and downs were the subject of extensive newspaper coverage and are candidly treated in his book, *Indestructible*. An early autobiographical account, "Boy Marine Fought MPs, Police, Japs—and Won the Medal of Honor," appeared in the October 5, 1945, edition of *The Daily Oklahoman*. The members of Lucas's fire team—Crowson, Gilbert, and Hagevik—survived Iwo Jima, though all three were wounded later in the campaign. Jack's cousin, Sam, was also wounded. Interestingly, Lucas's wallet with his mother's address inside was salvaged from his pack on Iwo Jima and was returned to him by the Marine Corps in 1950. "Better for one Marine . . . " cited in Ruane. Lucas long wondered what had happened to the corpsman who saved him. At a 5th Marine Division reunion in 2000, he learned the corpsman had been killed two days after treating him.

Robert H. Dunlap: Unpublished interviews with Jeffery M. Taylor in "The Life of a True American Hero"; Dunlap's alma mater, Monmouth College, kindly provided me with numerous news clippings tracing his postwar years; a brief interview of Dunlap by Lance Q. Zedric in 1995 offers a couple of interesting insights, but seems to me to be generally unreliable as a factual account, due to numerous inconsistencies. Oliver Taylor is quoted by Sam Smith in "Marine Is One of 26 from Company to Survive Iwo Jima" (*Salk (IL) Valley Newspapers*, November 14, 2009); Dunlap's remarks about preparedness as a college student are cited by Rankin; Dunlap quote, "I thank God . . . " appears in the March 29, 2000, *Journal Star* (Peoria, IL). The Johnson M1941 rifle Dunlap carried on Iwo Jima was returned to him after the war and he kept the gun on his wall until his death. Due to what were described as "unfortunate circumstances within the Dunlap family," the rifle was auctioned off by a noted firearms auction house in late 2013 and was acquired by Collectors Firearms in Galesburg, IL.

Donald J. Ruhl: Lindberg as quoted in Smith's *Iwo Jima*; Allen, *The First Battalion of the 28th Marines on Iwo Jima*; Lyttle, *If I Should Die Before I Wake*. Wells and Richard Wheeler both served with Ruhl and talk about him at some length in their memoirs of Iwo Jima. Most accounts, including that of Sergeant Midkiff, refer to the device that killed Ruhl as a grenade, but Wells believed it was some sort of demolitions charge. Kenneth Midkiff's recollections were made in an interview with Marine combat correspondent Tech Sgt. Keyes Beech, whose article appeared in the April 12, 1945, *Independent Record* Helena (MT). Midkiff's recollection of what Ruhl shouted varies a bit from other accounts. He told Beech that Hansen told him Ruhl had pushed him aside as he threw himself on the grenade. Of course, Hansen himself did not live long enough to get his own account on the record. The curious story of Ruhl's medal and the reminiscences of Ruhl's brother Clyde were featured in a lengthy article by Greg Tuttle in the July 1, 2001, issue of the *Billings (MT) Gazette*. In 2010 Greybull's Hillside Cemetery was renamed the Donald J. Ruhl Memorial Cemetery.

Ross Gray: Author interviews with Mary Lippett and Bill Murphy; Hengen, "The Preacher's Persistence." Bartley on the terrain from *Amphibious Epic*; "Pray for me," is quoted in Ross. Robert Webster's experiences were detailed in an interview with the Veterans History Project. Gray's letter home dated October 1,

1943, was posted on the Internet by his great-nephew, Jeremy Gray, as part of a tribute to his great-uncle.

Joseph J. McCarthy: Many of McCarthy's reflections on Iwo Jima and subsequent life are drawn from a *Leatherneck* interview by Van Goethem. A series of very informative articles on Medal of Honor recipients appeared in an unlikely venue, *Modern Man*, during the early 1960s. The article about McCarthy by Bob Ellison, which included testimony from various witnesses, appeared in the April 1962 edition. McCarthy also received extensive press coverage after Iwo Jima in the *Chicago Sun* and *Chicago Tribune*. His remark on visiting the families of his men appeared in the February 18, 1995, *Palm Beach (FL) Post*. Pete Santoro's recollections appear in Larry Smith's interview in *Iwo Jima* and in *Iwo Jima 1945: The Marines Raise the Flag on Mount Suribachi* by Derrick Wright.

Smith cites a letter by McCarthy about the February 21 action, but at least some of the description in that letter seems to be drawn verbatim from an affidavit, which appears to have been written by McCarthy's executive officer, Lt. Roy Christensen, in support of McCarthy's Medal of Honor. Christensen's recollections also appear in an article by Jerry Trambley in the February 12, 1995, issue of the *Erie Times-News*; Jack Snyder's recollections appeared in an article by Chris Buckley in the October 30, 2007, *Pittsburgh Tribune*. Snyder said he wandered around in the dark trying to find a corpsman to help Sergeant Barlow. He found his company commander—presumably McCarthy—who told him it was too risky to get medical help up to the wounded man. "After that, the battle was pretty much of a blank," said Snyder. "When the command came to move forward, I moved forward."

McCarthy's comments on being wounded, his comment on too many men being packed onto the beaches, and his words to his men as he exhorted them to attack the pillboxes on February 21 are drawn from interviews by Eliot Kleinberg in the *Palm Beach Post*, November 11, 1992, and by *Sun Sentinel* (FL) staff writer Liz Doup, "Remembering Iwo," in the February 19, 1990, issue of that newspaper.

Lieutenant Christensen was wounded the same day as McCarthy. Of the unit's casualties he noted, "G Company landed with 254 . . . the first day. The fifth day, we got 60 replacements because we were shot up so bad. This made a total of 314 Marines. I got wounded the 15th day and, at that time, Gunnery Sgt. Flynn showed me the list. We had 32 men left; 90 percent casualties."

Hershel Woodrow Williams: As the last surviving Iwo Jima Medal of Honor recipient, Williams has been the subject of extensive oral history interviews. The two best, in my opinion, are Ed Tracy's on behalf of Pritzker Military Library, and the interview conducted by the National World War II Museum. Hirsch's compilation of recipients in *Medal of Honor* includes a vivid account of Williams's action by Bill Francois; Kayser, *The Spirit of America*; Libby Smith interview; Williams interview in May 20, 1956, *Charleston (WV) Gazette*; Williams talked about Iwo Jima and his religious awakening in an article by Brad McElhinny in the November 12, 1999, *Charleston (WV) Daily Mail*.

Being east of the Mississippi, Williams would normally have done his boot training at Parris Island, but that facility was too crowded, so recruits were being sent west.

Williams's hometown of Quiet Dell gained national notoriety in 1931 for the arrest of serial killer Harry Powers, who murdered women he contacted through advertisements in a lonely-hearts magazine. He was hanged on March 18, 1932.

Hirsch says it was Southwell who was hit in the helmet while accompanying Williams in the pillbox attack, but in subsequent oral interviews, Williams identified the Marine as Schlager. Also unclear is the order in which Williams knocked out the first three pillboxes. Williams himself admitted his memory of that afternoon is cloudy and his accounts tend to vary a bit in the details.

CHAPTER 3

Douglas T. Jacobson: Dugan quoted in Christ; Sherrod, *On to the Westward*; Joan Jacobson letter; Jacobson's personal account of landing, courtesy of Joan Jacobson; Katz's "Goliath in Greens"; *Beyond the Medal*; Kayser, *The Spirit of America*; articles in the *New York Times*, *North Port (FL) News-Press*, *Port Washington News* on Jacobson's death in August 2000.

Jacobson's landing craft was not the only one that experienced trouble with the front ramp. The 3rd Battalion special-action report noted: "Some difficulty was encountered upon landing as a result of the ramps failing to open. This necessitated going over the side and a considerable amount of heavy equipment was lost."

Jacobson is among the Marines quoted in the film documentary *Iwo Jima: Eight Square Miles of Hell* (1978), narrated by Lloyd Bridges. Unfortunately he does not go into detail about his actions on Hill 382. Scales's recollections from articles in the *Martinsville (VA) Bulletin* (May 29, 2014), the *Roanoke Times* (November 11, 2013), and *World War II* magazine, March 2005 ("Into the Meat Grinder"). Ed Burows's experiences appear in *Marylanders in World War II*; Chipman interview (Chipman was later wounded at Hill 383).

Wilson D. Watson: The account of Watson's postwar troubles is drawn from the multitude of newspaper articles about the AWOL hero that appeared around the country in 1963; a letter in the May 2005 issue of *World War II* magazine detailed Carl Hurst's recollections.

One account says Sergeant Jennings was killed when he went to help a Marine that had been hit by mortar fragments. However, Lt. Paul McLellan, who took over G Company after Captain Fagan was hit, recalls that Jennings left cover to help a new man who was trying to clear a jammed BAR. Watson's brothers' remarks appeared in an article in the *Crittenden Evening Times*. Accounts of the 2nd Battalion's struggle to seize the high ground beyond Airfield No. 2 are detailed in Henri.

William Gary Walsh: Great-nephew Mike Murphy provided a wealth of information on Walsh and his family, including newspaper articles on his baseball days. Author interview with Dean Voight, who witnessed Walsh's death. Wisconsin

Veterans Museum Research Center Transcript of an Oral History Interview with Dean S. Voight by Mark Van Ells. In 2005 the writer located a cousin of Mary Penrod Walsh. The cousin reported that Mary remarried after the war. She died in Florida in 1993 at the age of seventy and is buried in Akron, Ohio. Census records clearly indicate that William Gary was born in Maine and was subsequently adopted by Mary Walsh.

John H. Willis: Author interview with Winfrey Willis Duke; Vedder, *Surgeon on Iwo*; Veterans Oral History Project interview with Richard C. Johnstone; Stanley Dabrowski is quoted in *Battle Station Sick Bay*. On October 17, 2009, Mrs. Willis and her son John Willis Jr. were presented with a replacement Medal of Honor in a ceremony presided over by Rear Adm. Michael H. Mittelman.

CHAPTER 4

Charles J. Berry: Berry's citation says he was attached to the 1st Battalion, 26th Marines, but muster rolls for the 26th Marines indicate that he and Joe Magazzine were members of G Company. Other information is drawn from Lace, *Bravest of the Brave*. Various articles have appeared through the years in the *Lorain Journal* newspaper on Berry, Joe Magazzine's lifelong quest to gain recognition for Berry, and the eventual disposition of his medals. Magazzine's recollection of the exchange with Berry's mother appeared in the July 8, 1990, *Columbus (Ohio) Dispatch*. Baksa ended up with the 1st Marine Division after basic training and never saw Berry again. He survived the war to become principal of Clearview High School. Joe Magazzine died in Ohio in 2006.

William Harrell: Harrell has been the subject of numerous newspaper and magazine stories through the years, including Pearl's "Last Casualty of Iwo Jima." Years after Bill Harrell's death, Gary Harrell found a brief but gripping memoir by his father in his family's papers. This was published in three installments in March 2004 in the *Sun-Herald* of Venice, FL. Harrell's tragic end received widespread news coverage; Gary Harrell's recollections of his father appeared in the *Sun-Herald* series and in an article by Kimberly Hundley in an undated clipping from the *Times Record* (Wichita Falls, TX); Carter related some of his experience in the *Abilene Reporter-News* of May 13, 1945; Allen, *The First Battalion of the 28th Marines on Iwo Jima*; Wells, *Give Me Fifty Marines Not Afraid to Die*; John Armendariz's recollections were recorded for the documentary "Shootout Iwo Jima" and he is also featured in *By Dammit, We're Marines*. Carter later sent the Japanese sword to Harrell's mother while he and Harrell were in the hospital in San Francisco. "Bill deserved it more than I did," he said. Bill's father Roy had "a reputation for shootouts with banditos and 'bootleggers,'" according to *Texas Aggie Medals of Honor* by James R. Woodall.

William R. Caddy: Author interview with Caddy's sister, Beatrice Bevans, various newspaper accounts (see bibliography). I have been unable to identify the lieutenant who was in the shell hole with Caddy and Sergeant Farris.

George Wahlen: Toyn, *The Quiet Hero*. Wahlen was also the subject of a lengthy article in the February 1946 issue of *Hospital Corps Quarterly*. He told his story in various interviews including the *Salt Lake Tribune* (February 22, 1993; July 18, 1996), *Philadelphia Inquirer* (March 5, 1995), the *Hill Air Force Base Hilltop Times* (October 23, 2003); and Smith, *Iwo Jima*.

The number of Marines killed and wounded in the shell hole on March 3 is unclear. It has been variously stated as between three and five. The wounded Marine whose intestines Wahlen stuffed back earlier in the fighting survived; to his surprise, Wahlen later met him in a hospital in Pearl Harbor; he had fully expected him to die. Sgt. Joe Malone also survived his horrendous injuries, but Wahlen's friend, Eddie Monjaras, a Mexican-American from Cheyenne, Wyoming, died of his wounds on March 1. Records indicate Lieutenant Cassidy died of his wound February 21. Mueller was certain the lieutenant, who was Wahlen's last patient, would lose one or both legs, such was the extent of his injuries. Years later he encountered the man, walking with a cane, but still with both legs, at a unit reunion.

Jack Williams: Chris Dorman compiled considerable information on Jack Williams, including eyewitness accounts, for his unpublished manuscript "Jack Williams: Uncommon Valor." Red Millis loaned me the copy on file with the Marine Corps Legacy Museum in Harrison, AR (Dorman's research has since been self-published as *An Ozark Lion*). Letter to author from former corpsman Edward McCartan about Williams; DVD *Iwo Jima: The Boys of H Company*; Lyttle, *If I Should Die Before I Wake*. Knox Wilson died aboard ship on February 24 and was buried at sea. He is listed on the Tablets of the Missing. Jim Naughton returned home, earned a master's degree at the University of Chicago, and became an accountant. He died on New Year's Eve 2013 in his home state of Illinois.

CHAPTER 5

John H. Leims: Leims's recollections appear in *Two Score and Ten*; author interviews with James Ganopulos and Robert Pavlovich. Leims is also mentioned at some length in Henri, *U.S. Marines on Iwo Jima*; Kessler, *Never in Doubt*; award of the medal reported in June 15, 1946, *Chicago Tribune*. Leims was right to fear his company would be annihilated if he did not take drastic action. E Company, which also participated in the attack, reportedly came out with only seven survivors. Jimmy Ganopulos died in Pennsylvania in 2008.

Jack Lummus: Hartman, *Texas Granite* contains much information on Lummus but has some questionable material as well; a family-approved website in his honor (Jacklummus.com) also features a wealth of information on this extraordinary man, including extracts from his last letters. The Lummus family disputes Mary Hartman's claims about the extent of her relationship with Lummus, saying he had planned to marry Skipper Bookwalter, who worked in the radio industry in Los Angeles. Brown, *Battle Wounds of Iwo Jima*; Pete Wright's article on Lummus in the March 2003 issue of *Leatherneck*; Stone, *A Marine Remembers Iwo Jima*. The railroad officer who murdered Lummus's father was sentenced to ten years in prison.

Twenty-three former NFL athletes died in military service during World War II, according to the Pro Football Hall of Fame. Marine officers Jack

Chevigny, a Notre Dame back and head coach of the Chicago Cardinals, and Howard Johnson, nicknamed "Smiley," a guard for the Green Bay Packers, were also killed on Iwo Jima.

James D. LaBelle: Bob Proft's recollections were reported in the *Minneapolis Star Tribune* on January 2, 1996; Harwell's account of LaBelle's death appears in an undated oral interview with Bristol Productions of Olympia, WA. Some of LaBelle's letters home are held in the collection of the Minnesota Historical Society. The death of Wilfred LaBelle in 1933 was briefly reported in *The Evening Tribune*, Albert Lea, MN, on August 18, 1933.

Joseph R. Julian: Author correspondence with Julian's sisters, Gloria Casey and Lorraine Clem; family members also remembered Julian in a February 23, 1995, article in the *Worcester (MA) Telegram & Gazette*. Some sources list Julian as a member of C Company, but this appears to have resulted from a juxtaposition of events in the 5th Marine Division unit history. Marine Corps muster rolls for January 1945 list Julian as a platoon sergeant with A Company, 1st Battalion, 27th Marines. Billy Dane Bowman was interviewed as part of the Veterans History Project, American Folklife Center, Library of Congress, October 20, 2004. Some of his recollections and those of other A Company Marines also appear in Christ.

CHAPTER 6

George Phillips: Author interviews with Emmett Becker and Elmer G. Palmer; unpublished memoir by Robert McLanahan was provided by his daughter, Luanne Calza; the recollections of Phillips's foster sister Edna O'Brien Dutton appeared in the program for the dedication of a memorial to Phillips in Labadie in 1990; news items, copies of family obituaries, and other material was provided by Elsie Webb of the Franklin County Historical Society; Knickrehm interview. The pills mentioned by McLanahan were apparently some form of amphetamine intended to keep them going. All four of the Marines saved by Phillips survived Iwo Jima.

Franklin E. Sigler: Author interviews with Rudy Mueller and Bill Eckerson. Mueller also recorded his memories of Sigler in the Fox Company February 1995 newsletter. Other information on Sigler is drawn from newspaper articles that appeared in the *Philadelphia Star Ledger*; the comments of Sigler's mother on his postwar adjustment problems appeared in a widely published article "Where Are Heroes of Last War?" which appeared, among other places, in the *Oakland (CA) Tribune*, August 14, 1949. Records obtained by Fox Company historian Rudy Mueller indicate Sigler was wounded in the hand, which contradicts some other accounts.

Francis J. Pierce: A lengthy account of Pierce's actions appears in Parker, *Above and Beyond the Call of Duty*; Pierce was also widely quoted in articles through the years in the Detroit and Grand Rapids (MI) newspapers. Marine combat correspondent Dan Levin's article about Pierce appeared after he was awarded the Navy Cross and Silver Star, but before the Medal of Honor was approved. It varies somewhat from the account in Parker. It appears to me that Parker actually talked personally with Pierce for that story and his account is more restrained.

Harry L. Martin: Lace, *Bravest of the Brave* offers the most comprehensive biography of Martin. Eleanor Martin Abbott's comments appeared in the March 26, 1995, *Columbus (Ohio) Dispatch*; Sammy Bernstein's recollections were recorded for the documentary *Iwo Jima: 36 Days of Hell* and in an interview recorded by the Museum of World War II, Boston; Robert Hansen's experiences recounted in Gail Chatfield's *By Dammit*; Charles Serio was awarded the Silver Star for his initiative in obtaining the ammunition from the dump, and his recollections appear in *Marylanders at War*; Jim Van Nada wrote about his experiences on the 506th Fighter Group website; Robert L. Hurst's memoir was transcribed by his daughter (copy in author's possession).

SELECTED BIBLIOGRAPHY

Alexander, Joseph H., Col. *Closing In: Marines in the Seizure of Iwo Jima.* Washington, D.C.: History and Museums Division, Headquarters, U.S. Marine Corps, 1994.

Allen, Robert E. *The First Battalion of the 28th Marines on Iwo Jima.* Jefferson, NC: McFarland & Company, 1999.

Aurthur, Robert A. *The Third Marine Division.* Washington, D.C.: Infantry Journal Press, 1948.

Bartley, Lt. Col. Whitman. *Iwo Jima: Amphibious Epic.* Washington, D.C.: Historical Branch, Headquarters, U.S. Marine Corps, 1954.

Berry, Henry. *Semper Fi, Mac.* New York: Arbor House, 1982.

Bittner, Donald F. "Justice M. Chambers: An American Cincinnatus." In *The Human Tradition in the World War II Era*, edited by Malcolm Muir, 241–60. Wilmington, DE: Scholarly Resources, 2001.

Blakeney, Jane. *Heroes U.S. Marine Corps 1861–1955.* Washington, D.C.: Guthrie, 1957.

Bradley, James. *Flags of Our Fathers.* New York: Bantam Books, 2000.

Brady, James. *Hero of the Pacific: The Life of John Basilone.* Hoboken, NJ: John Wiley & Sons, 2010.

Brown, Thomas M. *Battle Wounds of Iwo Jima.* New York: Vantage Press, 2002.

Burrus, L. D. *The Ninth Marines: A History of the Ninth Marine Regiment in World War II.* Washington, D.C.: Zenger Publishing Co., 1946.

Camp, Dick. *Iwo Jima Recon.* St. Paul, MN: Zenith Press, 2007.

Caruso, Patrick F. *Nightmare on Iwo.* Annapolis, MD: Naval Institute Press, 2001.

Casad, Dede W. *Texans of Valor.* Austin, TX: Eakin Press, 1998.

Catalina, Tom, and Timothy Wallis. *Ordinary Heroes.* Zionsville, IN: Sweet Pea Press, 2002.

Chatfield, Gail. *By Dammit, We're Marines.* San Diego, CA: Methinks Publishing, 2008.

Christ, James E. *Iwo: Assault on Hell.* Chandler, AZ: Battlefield Publishing, 2010.

Clark, Johnnie M. *Gunner's Glory.* New York: Galantine Books, 2004.

Conner, Howard M. *The Spearhead: The World War II History of the 5th Marine Division*. Washington, D.C.: Historical Division, U.S. Marine Corps, 1950.

Creasing, Marc. *Heroes: U.S. Marine Corps Medal of Honor Winners*. New York: Berkley Books, 2002.

Crowder, Ray. *Iwo Jima Corpsman!* Tuscaloosa, AL: Sago Press, 1988.

Davenport, William. *D-Plus Forever*. New York: Rivercross Publishing, 1993.

Delong, Kent. *War Heroes: True Stories of Congressional Medal of Honor Recipients*. Westport, CT: Pager, 1993.

Dorman, Chris. *An Ozark Lion*. Self-published, 2014.

Garand, George W., and Truman R. Strawbridge. *History of U.S. Marine Corps Operations in World War II: Western Pacific Operations, Vol. IV*. Washington, D.C.: USMC Historical Division, 1971.

Gates, Austin, ed. *Third Marine Division's Two Score and Ten History*. Paducah, KY: Turner Publishing Company, 1992.

Hartman, Mary. *Texas Granite: Story of a World War II Hero*. Dallas: Hendricks-Long Publishing Co., 1997.

Hein, Robert D. *Soldiers of the Sea*. Annapolis, MD: United States Naval Institute, 1962.

Henri, Raymond, et al. *The U.S. Marines on Iwo Jima*. Washington, D.C.: Infantry Journal, 1945.

Herman, Jan K. *Battle Station Sick Bay: Navy Medicine in World War II*. Annapolis, MD: Naval Institute Press, 1997.

Hirsch, Phil, ed. *Fighting Marines*. New York: Pyramid Books, 1964.

——. *Medal of Honor*. New York: Pyramid Books, 1967.

Jordan, Kenneth N., Sr. *Men of Honor: Thirty-Eight Highly Decorated Marines of World War II, Korea and Vietnam*. Antigen, PA: Schaffer Military History, 1997.

Karig, Walter. *Battle Report: Victory in the Pacific*. New York: Rinehart and Company, 1949.

Kayser, Hugh F. *The Spirit of America*. Palm Springs, CA: ETC Publications, 1982.

Kessler, Lynn, ed. *Never in Doubt: Remembering Iwo Jima*. Annapolis, MD: Naval Institute Press, 1999.

Lace, David L. *Bravest of the Brave*. Galion, OH: Duvall Publishing Co., 1988.

Lucas, Jack H. *Indestructible*. Cambridge, MA: Ad Capo Books, 2006.

Lyttle, John B. *If I Should Die Before I Wake*. N.p.: Vantage Press, 2007.

Maiden, Robert F. *Return to Iwo Jima +50*. Self-published, 2000.

Manning, Robert, ed. *Above and Beyond: A History of the Medal of Honor from the Civil War to Vietnam*. Boston: Boston Publishing Company, 1985.

Masking, J. Robert. *The U.S. Marine Corps Story*. New York: McGraw Hill, 1977.

Matthews, Allen R. *The Assault*. New York: Simon and Schuster, 1947.

McKinley, E. Graham. *John Basilone Gunnery Sergeant, USMC*. Somerville, NJ: Unicoi National Somerville Chapter, n.d.

McMillan, George. *The Old Breed: A History of the First Marine Division in World War II*. Washington, D.C.: Infantry Journal Press, 1949.

McMillan, George et al. *Uncommon Valor: Marine Divisions in Action*. Washington, D.C.: Infantry Journal Press, 1946.

Michaela, Allen. *Medal of Honor: Profiles of America's Military Heroes from the Civil War to the Present.* New York: Hyperion, 2002.

Morrison, Samuel Eliot. *History of United States Naval Operations in World War II, Volume XIV: Victory in the Pacific 1945.* Boston: Little, Brown and Company, 1960.

Mozzarella, Anthony. *Iwo Jima: The Young Heroes.* Memphis, TN: Castle Books, 1989.

Murphy, Edward F. *Heroes of WWII.* New York: Galantine Books, 1990.

Newcomb, Richard. *Iwo Jima.* New York: Holt, Rinehart and Winston, 1965.

O'Donnell, Patrick K. *Into the Rising Sun.* New York: Free Press, 2002.

Overton, Richard E. *God Isn't Here.* Clearfield, UT: American Legacy Media, 2004.

Parker, William, ed. *Above And Beyond The Call Of Duty.* New York: McFadden Books, 1963.

Pearce, Harry A. *Star Shells, Condoms, & Ka-Bars.* Leadwood, KS: Leathers Publishing, 2004.

Proehl, Carl W. *The Fourth Marine Division in World War II.* Washington, D.C.: Infantry Journal Press, 1946.

Prosser, Jim, and Jerry Cutter. *I'm Staying with My Boys: The Heroic Life of Sgt. John Basilone, USMC.* Hilton Head, NC: Lightbearer Communications, 2004.

Rain, Talbot. *Remembering Iwo.* Lincoln, NE: iUniverse, 2003.

Reilly, Robin L. *American Amphibious Gunboats in World War II.* Jefferson, NC: McFarland & Company, 2013.

Rogers, Michael H., ed. *Answering Their Country's Call: Marylanders in World War II.* Baltimore, MD: Johns Hopkins University Press, 2002.

Ross, Bill D. *Iwo Jima: Legacy of Valor.* New York: Vanguard Press, 1985.

Russell, Michael. *Iwo Jima.* New York: Galantine Books, 1974.

Schott, Joseph L. *Above and Beyond.* New York: G.P. Putnam's Sons, 1963.

Scott, Jay. *America's War Heroes.* Derby, CT: Monarch Books, 1961.

———. *Marine War Heroes.* Derby, CT: Monarch Books, 1963.

Sherrod, Robert. *On to the Westward.* New York: Duel, Sloan and Pearce, 1945.

Shively, John C. *The Last Lieutenant.* New York: New American Library, 2006.

Smith, Larry. *Beyond Glory: Medal of Honor Heroes in Their Own Words.* New York: W.W. Norton & Company, 2003.

———. *Iwo Jima.* New York: W.W. Norton & Company, 2008.

St. John, Philip. *The Battle for Iwo Jima.* Paducah, KY: Turner Publishing Company, 1995.

———. *Fifth Marine Division.* Paducah, KY: Turner Publishing Company, 1991.

Stevens, Paul D. *The Congressional Medal of Honor: The Names, The Deeds.* Forest Race, CA: Sharp & Donavan Publications, 1984.

Stone, Alfred R. *A Marine Remembers Iwo Jima.* Austin, TX: Eakin Press, 2000.

Stone, John, and Jack Schiff, eds. *Fourth Marine Division.* Paducah, KY: Turner Publishing Company, 1992.

Toyn, Gary W. *The Quiet Hero.* Ogden, UT: American Legacy Media, 2006.

Vedder, James S. *Surgeon on Iwo.* Novato, CA: Presidio Press, 1984.

Wells, John Keith. *Give Me Fifty Marines Not Afraid to Die.* Quantico, VA: Marine Corps Association, 1995.

Westbrook, Jim, ed. *The Battle at Iwo Jima and the Men Who Fought There.* Paducah, KY: Turner Publishing Company, 1990.

Wheeler, Richard. *The Bloody Battle for Suribachi*. New York: Thomas Y. Crowell Company, 1965.

———. *Iwo*. New York: Lippincott & Crowell, 1980.

———. *A Special Valor: The U.S. Marines and the Pacific War*. New York: Harper & Row, 1983.

PERIODICALS

Aberle, Jessica L. "Friends Remember War Hero and Coach—Funeral of 'Bobby' Dunlap Brings Back Memories for Many." *Journal Star* (Peoria, IL), March 29, 2000.

———. "Funeral Services Set for War Hero." *Journal Star* (Peoria, IL), March 28, 2000.

Anderson, Vern. "Hero of Iwo Jima Still Comes to Aid of His Fellow Vets." *Philadelphia Inquirer*, March 5, 1995. (Wahlen)

Associated Press. "Cops: WWII Hero's Gone to Pot." *Philadelphia Daily News*, August 30, 1985. (Lucas)

———. "Heroes of Pacific." *Mansfield (OH) News-Journal*, August 14, 1949. (Lucas, Sigler, Wahlen, Pierce)

———. "Survey Shows Congressional Medal Winners in Pacific Live Quietly." *Holland (MI) Evening Sentinel*, October 25, 1962. (Lucas, Sigler, Pierce)

———. "War Hero, Feisty Cop Dies in Grand Rapids." *Detroit Free Press*, December 23, 1986. (Pierce)

Basilone, John. "I'm Glad to Get Overseas Duty." *Leatherneck Magazine*, September 1, 1944.

Batzkall, Carl V. "The Gunboats at Iwo Jima: Part I. *The Elsie Item: Official Newsletter of the USS Landing Craft, Infantry*, April 2007.

Beech, Keyes. "Montana Soldier Dies Hero's Death." *Helena (MT) Independent Record*, April 12, 1945.

Bizzell, Oscar M. "Geddie Herring, A Man to Remember." *Huckleberry (NC) Historian*, September 15, 1998.

Blocker, Dennis R., II. "My Grandpa and the LCI(G)-449 at Iwo Jima." *The Elsie Item: Official Newsletter of the USS Landing Craft, Infantry*, March 27, 2007.

Budd, Lawrence. "Lorain Hero Deserves a Better Grave." *Elyria (OH) Chronicle Telegram*, May 11, 1994. (Berry)

Casey, Matthew. "Private William Caddy: A Hero to Remember This Memorial Day." *The (Quincy, MA) Patriot Ledger*, May 30, 2011.

Casey, Michael. "Honoring Those Who Sought No Recognition." *The Bergen (NJ) Record*, May 25, 1996. (Sigler)

Clark, Carol. "Bobby Dunlap Laid to Rest." *The Register-Mail* (Galesburg, IL), March 29, 2000.

———. "Own Place in Sun at Monmouth College." *The Register-Mail* (Galesburg, IL), August 6, 1990.

Condrey, Stephen. "Red Walsh, Dorchester Ace, Won Nation's Highest Honor." *The Boston Sport-Light*, March 9, 1946.

Cox News Service. "Hard Times Stalking Iwo Jima Hero." *Wichita Eagle-Beacon*, February 19, 1985. (Lucas)

Cox, Seth Kantor. "Peacetime Troubles Dog Youngest Medal of Honor Winner." *Atlantic Journal and Constitution*, February 19, 1985.

———. "Violence Haunts an American Hero." *Atlanta Journal and Constitution*, September 9, 1985. (Jacklyn Lucas)

Crozier, Bill, and Steve Schild. "Uncommon Valor: Three Winona Marines at Iwo Jima, 1945." *Winona (MN) Post*, October 25, 2006.

Dashiell, Dick. Untitled. *Marine Corps Correspondent Dispatch*, May 17, 1945. (Hershel Williams)

Dreitzler, Bob. "Bucyrus Honors Memory of Iwo Jima Battle Hero." *The Columbus (OH) Dispatch*, July 8, 1990.

Ellison, Bob. "Yesterday's Heroes Part IV: Captain Joe McCarthy." *Modern Man*, April 1962.

Fitzpatrick, Michael C. "Monument Dedication Points to Heroism, Sacrifice of Lorain Hero Cpl. Charles Berry." *Lorain (OH) Morning Journal*, July 13, 2005.

Garbarino, Micah. "Quiet Hero." *Hilltop Times* (Annapolis, MD), October 23, 2003. (Wahlen)

Gonda, Michael. "Utah War Hero Dies at Age 84." *Deseret News* (Salt Lake City, UT), June 6, 2009. (Wahlen)

Gottlieb, Ken. "War Hero Is Honored." *Elyria (OH) Chronicle Telegram*, February 20, 1988. (Berry)

Gunn, John. "Giant of a Man: Jack Lummus." *Orange County Register* (Santa Ana, CA), July 27, 1986.

Haga, Chuck. "A Tribute to Heroes." *Minneapolis Star Tribune*, January 2, 1996. (LaBelle)

Hengen, Bill. "The Preacher's Persistence." *Leatherneck Magazine*, November 1945.

Homstad, Daniel W. "Sulphur Island's Youngest Hero." *World War II*, March 2005. (Lucas)

Hurst, Carl. "A Hero Among Us." *World War II*, July 2005. (Watson)

Jones, Charles A. "Into the Meat Grinder." *World War II*, March 2005.

Jones, D. W. "Medal of Honor: World War II Recipient Returns to PI to Watch Grandson Graduate." *The Boot*. Undated news clipping.

Katz, Kirby, "Goliath in Greens." *Leatherneck Magazine*, January 1947.

Kelly, Mike. "N.J. Veterans Describe Island's Killing Fields." *The Bergen (NJ) Record*, February 19, 1995. (Sigler)

Kirby, Robert. "Five Utahns Who Went Beyond." *The Salt Lake Tribune*, February 8, 1996. (Wahlen)

Kleinberg, Eliot. "Humble Men, High Honors: Five of America's Quiet Heroes Recall the Courageous Deeds That Earned Them the Medal of Honor." *Palm Beach (FL) Post*, November 11, 1992. (McCarthy)

Lansford, William Douglas. "The Life and Death of Manila John." *Leatherneck Magazine*, October 2002.

Layden, Joe. "Cole's Battlegrounds from Canal to Iwo." *Daily Journal* (Flat River, MO), February 22, 1985.

———. "Men Share Memories of a Hero." *Daily Journal* (Flat River, MO), February 19, 1985.

Lee, Bob. "Errant War Hero Brought to Fort Sill, Put in Hospital." *The Oklahoman*, February 16, 1963.

Leise, Cindy. "53 Free Years from the Lord." *Elyria (OH) Chronicle Telegram*, February 19, 1998.

———. "Iwo Jima Survivors to Be Honored." *Elyria (OH) Chronicle Telegram*, February 18, 2000.

Levin, Dan. "Gallantry at Iwo Brings Double Award for Earlville Corpsman." *Waterloo (IA) Daily Courier*, September 12, 1945. (Pierce)

Lucas, Jacklyn. "Boy Marine Fought MPs, Police, Japs—and Won the Medal of Honor." *The Daily Oklahoman*, October 5, 1945.

Marquand, John, "Iwo Jima Before H-Hour." *Harper's*, May 1945.

McCormally, John. "This Is How Anniversary of Battle Is Remembered." *Hutchinson (KS) News*, February 21, 1960. (Caddy)

Miller, William E. "Builder of Rugged Marines in No. 3 Civil Defense Post." *Charleston (WV) Daily Mail*, November 8, 1953.

Morgan, Martin K.A. "The Stinger." *American Rifleman*, April 2006.

Mueller, Rudolph. "Taps for Siggy." *Fox Company Scoop*, February 1995. (Sigler)

Patton, Jim. "On Display: Uncommon Valor." *Elyria (OH) Chronicle Telegram*, October 14, 1981. (Berry)

Pearl, Jack. "The Last Casualty of Iwo Jima." *Saga*, December 1964.

Pressley, Sue Anne. "Hero's Hard Luck Drug Arrest Latest in Series of Reverses." *Washington Post*, September 9, 1985. (Lucas)

———. "Maryland Drops Marijuana Charges Against World War II Hero." *Washington Post*, October 24, 1985. (Lucas)

Rankin, Jeff. "Monmouth Goes to War." *Sturdy the Band of Pioneers: Tales from Monmouth College Archives*, February 2001.

Rasdal, Dave. "Earlville Remembers Marine Who Won Medal of Honor." *Gazette* (Cedar Rapids, IA), November 5, 2007.

Richardson, Herb. "Giants of the Corps: Tony Stein." *Leatherneck Magazine*, September 1976.

Rogers, Keith. "Marine Vets Recall Iwo Jima's Horrors." *Las Vegas Review-Journal*, February 19, 2012. (Leims and Oram)

Ruane, Michael E. "Iwo Jima Survivors Marking 50th Anniversary." *Lexington (KY) Herald-Leader*, February 19, 1995. (Lucas et al.)

Russell, Gerard F. "Iwo Jima's Lessons of Sacrifice." *Worcester Telegram & Gazette*, February 23, 1995. (Julian)

Schwab, David. "Men of Courage, Men of Humility." *Newark Star-Ledger*, May 30, 1993. (Sigler)

Sherrington, Kevin. "Monumental Man." *Dallas Morning News*, January 23, 2000. (Lummus)

Simpson, Ross W. "Iwo Jima: A Surgeon's Story." *Leatherneck Magazine*, February 1990.

Smith, Bruce. "Harrell Shows Bravery in First Wave at Iwo Jima." *Brownsville (TX) Herald*, May 25, 2008.

———. "Questions Surround Shocking Death of National Hero." *Brownsville (TX) Herald*, May 25, 2008. (Harrell)

Smith, Sam. "Marine Is One of 26 from Company to Survive Iwo Jima." *Salk (IL) Valley Newspapers*, November 14, 2009. (Oliver Taylor)

Spalding, V. G. "Presenting the Stinger." *Marine Corps Gazette*, February 1946.

Stephens, Steve. "Bucyrus Man Saved Comrades, Took on Enemy, Died on Iwo Jima." *Columbus (OH) Dispatch*, March 26, 1995. (Martin)

———. "Veteran Remembers Friend Who Sacrificed Himself." *Columbus (OH) Dispatch*, March 3, 1995 (Berry)

Strong, Angela C. "Looking for Heroes." *Marines*, June 2000. (Dunlap)

Stutler, Boyd B. "In the Highest Tradition of Valor." *West Virginia Review*, March 1946.

Tatum, Charles. "Death of Manila John Basilone." *Leatherneck Magazine*, November 1988.

Thompson, Veronica. "Three Charged with Plot to Kill World War II Hero." *Washington Post*, June 29, 1977. (Lucas)

Tomlin, Gary. "War Hero's Rifle Bought by Local Shop." *Argus-Sentinel* (Abingdon, IL), March 13, 2014.

Trambley, Jerry. "Iwo Jima Has Been in Thoughts of Harborcreek Vet Every Day." *Erie (PA) Times-News*, February 12, 1995.

Tuttle, Greg. "Medal of Honor Comes Home." *Billings (MT) Gazette*, July 1, 2001.

Ullman, Victor. "Congressional Medal of Honor Award to Geo. E. Wahlen, PhM2c and Robert E. Bush, HA1c, for Heroism at Iwo Jima and Okinawa." *Hospital Corps Quarterly*, February 1946.

United Press International. "Medal of Honor Winner Arrested." *San Jose Mercury News*, August 31, 1985.

Ure, John. "Humble Hero: How Utahn Saved Lives." *Salt Lake Tribune*, July 18, 1996.

Van Goethem, Larry, "Giants of the Corps: Colonel Joseph J. McCarthy." *Leatherneck Magazine*, February 1982.

Woodcock, Richard D. "Town Honors Medal of Honor Cousins." *Medal of Honor Historical Society Annals*, September 1978. (Dunlap)

Wright, Pete. "Giants of the Corps: First Lieutenant Jack Lummus World War II Marine and Hero." *Leatherneck Magazine*, March 2003.

Yarbrough, Kristin. "County to Honor Local Heroes." *Elyria (OH) Chronicle Telegram*, March 15, 2003.

Zollo, Cathy. "Decorated Vets Attend Reunion: Medal Recipient Recalls Iwo Jima." *Wichita Falls (TX) Times Record News*, February 22, 1999. [Wahlen]

ANONYMOUS

"Amputee Kills Two, Himself." *Oklahoman*, August 10, 1964. (Harrell)

"Billy Harrell to Marry Navy Nurse." *Valley (TX) Morning Star*, February 16, 1946.

"Clearview High Dedication Will Honor Medal Winner." *Elyria (OH) Chronicle Telegram*, October 30, 1959. (Berry)

"Decorated Soldier Deserter." *Oklahoman*, February 15, 1963. (Watson)

"Dunlap, Awarded Medal of Honor, Is Dead at Age 79." *Register-Mail* (Galesburg, IL), March 25, 2000.

"Farmboy from Earle a 'One Man Regiment.'" *Crittenden Evening Times* (West Memphis, AR), November 15, 2011. (Watson)

"Father Gives Dead Son's WWII Medals to Lorain." *Elyria (OH) Chronicle Telegram*, June 28, 1974. (Berry)

"Hero Still Minus Job and Town's Gift Purse." *Newark Star-Ledger*, August 13, 1947. (Sigler)

"Manila John Basilone." *Marine Corps Gazette*, October 1963.

"Medals for Youths From Here." *New York Times*, October 6, 1945. (Jacobson, Sigler)

"Mercedes to Start Drive for Billy Harrell Ranch." *Valley (TX) Morning Star*, February 21, 1946.

"Mounts Given Ten Years in Slaying." *Lubbock (TX) Morning Avalanche*, July 15, 1944. (Lummus)

"Police Seek Motive in Triple Slaying." *Frederick (MD) News Post*, August 10, 1964.

"Ship Christening Will Bring Back Iwo Jima Memories for Area 'Doc.'" *Herald News* (Joliet, IL), June 3, 2001 (Carten on Jack Williams)

"Son Recalls Dad Who Received Medal of Honor at Iwo Jima." *Charlotte Sun-Herald*, March 3, 5, and 7, 2004. (Harrell)

"Texas Pals Stage Two-Man Alamo." *Marine Corps Chevron*, June 30, 1945.

"3 Heroes Shake in Boots; Get Honor Medal." *Chicago Daily Tribune*, June 15, 1946.

"Two-Man 'Alamo' Stands Off Jap Rushes." *Abilene Reporter News*, May 13, 1945. (Carter account)

"Vallejo Girl Becomes Bride of Armless Marine Hero." *Oakland (CA) Tribune*, February 17, 1946. (Harrell)

"War Hero Moved from Sill Hospital." *Sunday Oklahoman*, February 24, 1963. (Watson)

UNPUBLISHED

Bernstein, Sam. Oral History Interview. Natick Veterans Oral History Project. n.d. (Martin)

Bowman, Bill D. Interview. Veterans History Project, American Folklife Center, Library of Congress, October 20, 2004.

Chambers, Justice M. Oral History. Interviewed by Paul Chambers. Marine Corps Historical Center, Washington, D.C., 1978.

Chipman, Clayton. Oral History Interview. Wisconsin Veterans Museum, 1995.

Cole, Darrell S. Diary. Collection of Stars and Stripes Museum, Bloomfield, MO.

Commemorative Dedication of Monument Honoring George "Jr. O'Brien" Phillips, November 11, 1990.

Deck Log, LCI Group 8, Flotilla 3 at Iwo Jima.

Dorman, Chris. "Jack Williams: Uncommon Valor." Unpublished manuscript.

Dunlap, Robert. Interview with Major Robert H. Dunlap, USMC (ret.), by Lance Q. Zedrik, 1995.

Eckerson, William. Interview. Natick Veterans Oral History Project. n.d. (Sigler)

Hallet, Bruce M. Interview by P. J. Scott on Veterans Forum, Port Orchard, WA, May, 2011, www.veteransforum.net.

Harwell, Tom. Interview. Bristol Productions Ltd., Olympia, WA, n.d. (LaBelle)

Herman, Jan K. "Telephone Interview" with George Wahlen. U.S. Bureau of Medicine and Surgery, October 30, 1996.

Herwick, Edgar B., III. "Quincy Marine Threw Himself on Grenade to Save Fellow Marines at Iwo Jima." WGBH News, February 21, 2014.

Hurst, Robert L. "Iwo Jima Diary." Unpublished. (5th Pioneers)

Jacobson, Douglas. Unpublished account of landing on Iwo Jima, courtesy of Joan Jacobson.

Jennings, Alfred W. Oral History Interview. Veterans History Project, Library of Congress, March 17, 2007.

Johnstone, Richard C. Veterans Oral History Project interview, Natick, MA: Morse Institute Library, 2008.

Knickrehm, Albert B. Interview. Veterans History Project of the Library of Congress, May 27, 2003.

LaBelle, James. Letters. Collection of the Minnesota Historical Society.

Lummus Family. Jacklummus.com.

McLanahan, Robert. Unpublished Memoir of Iwo Jima. Author's collection.

Marine Corps History Division. Who's Who in Marine Corps History. www.tecom. usmc.mil/HD/Whos_Who.htm.

Nickell, Dr. Frank (interviewer). "Iwo Jima Veterans Tell Their Stories." Center for Regional History at Southeast Missouri State University in Cape Girardeau, MO, 2012. (Six members of L Co., 23rd Marines)

Sonne, Alma B., Jr. "Biography of Alma B. Sonne: War Years." L. Tom Perry Special Collections, Harold B. Lee Library, Brigham Young University, Provo, UT.

Stockdale, Vice Admiral James B. "IMPULSE: A Driving Force of Character." N.p., n.d. (Dunlap)

Taylor, Jeffrey M. "The Life of a True American Hero: Robert H. Dunlap." Unpublished manuscript, May 11, 1988.

Van Nada, Jim. "How I Lucked Out to Survive the Surprise Banzai Attack That Killed Eleven of My Fellow Pilots and Three Enlisted Men." www.506thfightergroup. org/Iwo%20Feb-Apr.asp.

Voight, Dean S. Transcript of Interview with Dean S. Voight, Wisconsin Veterans Museum Research Center, 1995.

Wahlen, George. "George E. Wahlen Iwo Jima Medal of Honor Story." Video interview. Weber State University, November 6, 2006.

Williams, Hershel W. Hershel Williams Interview by Ed Tracy, Pritzker Military Museum & Library, January 24, 2008.

———. Hershel "Woody" Williams, Oral history interview, National World War II Museum, November 16, 2006.

———. Hershel "Woody" Williams WWII Interview, WV Veterans Legacy Project, 2011.

———. Interview with Hershel Woody Williams by Libby Smith, July 30, 2001.

———. Interview with Iwo Jima Medal of Honor Recipient CW04 Hershel W. Williams, Marine Corps History Division.

FILM

Iwo Jima: The Boys of H Company. Stax Entertainment, 2004.

Iwo Jima: Eight Square Miles of Hell, an episode of TV Series *World War II: GI Diary*, Time-Life Television Productions, 1978

Iwo Jima: 36 Days of Hell. Timeless Media Group, 2006

Shootout: Iwo Jima: Fight to the Death. A&E Television Networks, 2006.

INDEX

Page numbers in italics indicate photographs and maps

CONTRIBUTORS

The following provided reminiscences or other material relating to the recipients: Beatrice Caddy Bevans (Caddy), Emmett Becker (Phillips), Luanne Calza (Phillips), Gloria Casey (Julian), David Reid Clark (Dunlap), Lorraine Clem (Julian), Yvonne Crumpler (Gray), Howard Davies (Hauge), John H. Duke Sr. (Willis), William Eckerson (Sigler), James Ganopulos (Leims), William Glazier (Cole), Holly Harron (Cole), Joan Jacobson (Jacobson), Mary Lippett (Gray), Edward McCartan (Jack Williams), Red Millis (Jack Williams), Rudy Mueller (Sigler, Wahlen), Bill Murphy (Gray), Mike Murphy (Walsh), Elmer G. Palmer (Phillips), Robert Pavlovich (Leims), Noreen Telisman (Walsh), Dean Voight (Walsh), Kenneth Phillips (Cole), Elsie Webb (Phillips), Winfrey Willis (Willis).

**Instrument
Flying**

Instrument Flying

THIRD EDITION

RICHARD L. TAYLOR

INTRODUCTION BY ROBERT N. BUCK,
AUTHOR OF *Weather Flying*

An Eleanor Friede Book

Macmillan Publishing Company
New York
Collier Macmillan Publishers
London

Macmillan Publishing Company
866 Third Avenue, New York, N.Y. 10022
Collier Macmillan Canada, Inc.

Library of Congress Cataloging-in-Publication Data
Taylor, Richard L.
    Instrument flying.
    "An Eleanor Friede book."
    Includes index.
    1. Instrument flying.   I. Title.
TL711.B6T39   1986   629.132'5214   85-23664
ISBN 0-02-616620-8

10   9   8   7   6

Macmillan books are available at special discounts for bulk purchases for sales promotions, premiums, fund-raising, or educational use. For details, contact:
Special Sales Director
Macmillan Publishing Company
866 Third Avenue
New York, N.Y. 10022

Designed by Jack Meserole

Printed in the United States of America

The Third Edition of *Instrument Flying* is dedicated to the five people in my immediate family who have put up with the absences from home and the unusual working hours required of an aviation author who writes from personal experience:

My wife, Nancy
our daughters, Julie and Mary Beth
our son and his wife, Rich and Karen

CONTENTS

AUTHOR'S NOTE

"THINGS are always and never the same," in the words of an anonymous philosopher who was apparently an accurate observer of the human experience. Whether the reference was to the climate, or the moods of man, is immaterial, for the more things change, the more they exhibit characteristics that have always existed.

This philosophy is certainly applicable to the rather specific subject matter of *Instrument Flying* . . . even though we have seen remarkable advances in aerodynamic, propulsive, and avionics technology, we must always consider the very basics of flight if we are to accomplish the Instrument Flying Rules (IFR) mission. After all, we go through essentially the same motions to get an airplane from here to there in the clouds as the Wright Brothers did to fly 120 feet across a sandy field.

The purpose of this third edition of *Instrument Flying* is to retain those fundamentals which continue to apply, while adding regulatory and procedural changes that affect day-to-day IFR operations in the national airspace system. In addition, I have included several chapters of new material dealing with contemporary equipment and its use. The proliferation of high-technology IFR "tools" is nothing short of stupendous, and promises to continue.

Virtually every nonfiction aviation book promotes safety of flight, whether that's a stated objective or is a subtle undertone, and *Instrument Flying* is no exception. I believe that one of the best ways to fly safely is to study and profit from the mistakes of others; with that in mind, I've included several vignettes of actual incidents that speak very eloquently of how *not* to operate as an instrument pilot. Let's understand that these recountings are not intended to pass judgment on the performance of any individuals, groups, aircraft, or equipment; the sole purpose is to illustrate the consequences of certain decisions and procedures in the conduct of IFR operations.

If you're a beginning instrument flyer, I hope this book will help you to obtain the IFR rating; for those of you already involved in instrument operations, I hope that *Instrument Flying* will be helpful in improving your IFR skills and your ability to operate more efficiently in the airspace system.

R. L. TAYLOR

September 1985

INTRODUCTION

by Robert N. Buck

THIS book is a valuable link between theory and what instrument flying is really like. It's a book to read all the way through and also one to have handy for those free moments to pick up, open anywhere, and gain a useful piece of information.

Instrument Flying is not restricted to any level of pilot experience. It will interest the person who is just beginning to think about getting an instrument rating, and it will be valuable to the experienced pilot as well.

It is difficult to dig out all the information about instrument flying. I've tried by reading stuffy technical books, the stiff FAA publications and formal study courses designed to get one through the FAA exams. And even after all this digging, there is still a long way to go to discover what it's really like—to know what's behind the scenes. Mostly this comes with experience.

Instrument Flying cuts this process short because it tells, as it teaches, all about the inside and what's behind the formal stuff. In doing this, the book gives experience as it tells. It is a welcome arrival on the instrument flying scene. I wish it had been around years ago—it would have made things a lot easier.

Richard Taylor has an excellent background in flying and in education. He has had more than thirty years' experience as a military and then a commercial pilot. Along with his practical background, he is an associate professor in the Department of Aviation at Ohio State University. The book reflects this fortunate combination as he takes us from attitude flying, which is the solid basis for flying on instruments, to the sophisticated techniques of the high-altitude airways.

The complex problems of absorbing a clearance, using the radio, and staying within the law are talked about in an easy way that will help lift the pilot from a timid, unsure position to one where he can operate like a pro. The chapters on holding patterns and instrument approaches, plus all the aspects of a flight from A to B on instruments, are extremely valuable for learning and attaining proficiency through practice.

This book is an important addition to every pilot's library. But it is not a book to leave on the shelf gathering dust; rather it will be read many times and, I'm certain, consulted time and time again to refresh your memory and settle many a friendly argument.

Instrument Flying

1

The Complete Instrument Pilot

PUT a foot-wide steel beam flat on the ground, and walk across it; a "no sweat" situation for anyone with normal balance and eyesight. Now put that steel beam between two buildings ten stories above the street, and anyone less than an experienced steel worker or a professional highwire performer would panic at the prospect of negotiating the same narrow path that presented no problem at ground level. The difference?—knowledge, experience, and practice.

Much the same reasoning applies to instrument flying; you know that you can handle your airplane when you can see the ground, but getting from here to there in IFR (Instrument Flight Rules) conditions is something else. And no matter how well you fly the machine, there's always ATC, that government monster, giving you confusing instructions, asking you to maintain cruise airspeed on an approach, clearing you to an altitude you don't want, and on and on and on. But basic principles always apply, and if you are well grounded in the "nuts and bolts" of instrument flying, there's no reason why you can't adjust to changes and involved procedures IF YOU KNOW WHAT TO EXPECT, AND HOW TO HANDLE YOURSELF IN THE IFR SYSTEM. There's nothing heartstopping about flying an airplane on instruments, nor does it take a superman to do the job well. Good instrument training plus a thorough understanding of the *total* system can make it just as easy as walking that steel beam when it's flat on the ground. When you know what you're doing, you can walk it confidently and safely ten stories high.

More than thirty years of military and civilian flying in many parts of the world, in all kinds of weather, have convinced me that once past the fundamentals, safe and efficient instrument flight is a happy combination of knowing yourself, your airplane, and the sys-

3

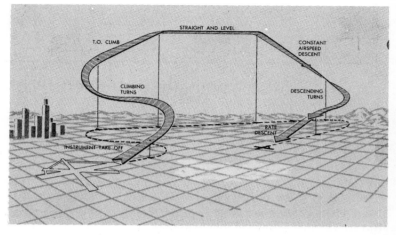

FIGURE 1 Any instrument flight, regardless of how long or how complex, is simply a series of connected basic instrument flight maneuvers.

tem. When you accept a clearance from Air Traffic Control to fly in the nation's airspace, you are considered just as qualified, just as capable as the airplane captain who flies every day. This is not to imply that controllers are so unrealistic that they expect your approaches to be as exquisitely precise as the "pros," but every IFR pilot *is* expected to conform to the same rules and procedures, because he becomes part of a *system*—a combination of parts into a whole, an orderly arrangement. The principal parts of this system, controllers and pilots, must work together if the system is to accomplish its goal of safe separation and efficient management of the thousands of instrument flights conducted every day.

The key to the whole process is knowledge; it has been proven that the average pilot can be taught to fly an airplane by referring only to the attitude instruments (indeed, it's now a required part of the practical examination for the private pilot certificate). But throw in the confusing complication of electronic navigation and rapid-fire communication, and the average pilot can come unglued . . . unless he knows what the system is all about. "You learn something every day" is a bromide perhaps more meaningful in instrument flying than in any other endeavor; for regulations, procedures, and techniques change almost daily. In my contacts with instrument pilots as an instructor, aviation educator, and professional pilot, I come across too frequent examples of "understanding gaps" which derogate pilot performance, efficiency, and sometimes compromise safety.

Several years ago I was involved in programs designed to refresh the knowledge of instrument-rated pilots and to prepare candidates for written examinations relative to IFR and ATP operations. That experience convinced me that the surface of pilot education has barely been scratched—there is a profound need to continue the training *after* a pilot obtains his instrument rating. *Instrument Flying* is intended to help put a real gouge in that surface; it has been developed with the philosophy that knowledge, added to practice and experience, will pave the way to safer and more efficient instrument flight.

This book can be used to greatest advantage as a source of information for understanding the *total* system in which we fly IFR. In addition to some basic techniques of aircraft control, you will find detailed explanations of every phase of instrument flight, from Airways to Zulu time. To help you increase the efficiency and utility of your airplane, *Instrument Flying* contains techniques and procedures for practical, legal methods of cutting down the elapsed time between point A and point B; isn't that the real reason for using an airplane in the first place?

The chapters are strung on a common thread of increased usefulness, of maximizing the dollars you spend to transport people and things through the air; chapters dealing with attitude instrument flying are not there to teach you how to fly instruments, for that is your flight instructor's job. However, you can and should use this material as a guide for practicing and polishing your flying skills. The "good" instrument pilot is the one who flies his airplane without conscious effort, conserving the major portion of his thought processes for navigation, communication, and staying at least one step ahead of the airplane at all times.

An Instrument Book with No Chapter on Weather?

When you can't beat 'em, join 'em! Robert N. Buck, now retired from his position as senior captain with Trans World Airlines, has put together the ultimate interpretation of aviation meteorology for the instrument pilot, so I defer to his work in this vital area, which has more to do with IFR operations than anything else. If you do not own a copy of *Weather Flying*, I strongly recommend that you add it to your aviation library. Seldom do we have the opportunity to share in, and profit from, the vast experience of one so eminent in his field.

Be a *Legal* Eagle

When the sands at Kitty Hawk were brushed by the skids of the bicycle-builders' airplane, when theirs was the only powered flying machine in the entire country, there was no need for rules of the air—the laws of gravity kept the brothers busy enough! But soon there were two airplanes, and then more and more and more; just like the increased traffic on rivers and roads, a burgeoning aircraft population eventually had to come under regulation and control. Safety of flight has been uppermost in the minds of rule-writers from the very beginning (check your regs—almost all of them are intended to keep us pilots from running into each other), with a secondary purpose to establish who's at fault when a no-no *does* occur.

The regulations with which we must live are therefore either restrictive or mandatory in nature, letting us know those things we may *not* do, or the things we *must* do. Although the intent remains steadfast, the language and scope of aviation regulations change constantly, as the nature of flying itself changes. It would be a fool's task to list all the rules that apply to instrument flying, because they will change before the ink on these pages is dry. The regulations (and revisions thereto) are available to all, and so the smart instrument flyer (or the smart *any*-kind-of-flyer for that matter) will subscribe to those that apply to his operations, and moreover will keep his books right up to date. For noncommercial pilots (VFR *and* IFR types) Part 91 of the Federal Aviation Regulations is a bare minimum, and the Airman's Information Manual will help you stay current in regard to changes in procedure and technique. (Jeppesen's "J-AID" combines the several parts of the regulations, all the information contained in Part I of the AIM, and a great deal of additional information you may find worthwhile . . . IFR and VFR.)

"But," you say, "I haven't time to spend going through regs and manuals—I fly good instruments, do what ATC says, keep my medical current and my nose clean." That's fine as far as it goes, but do you have the time or the resources to contend with a legal judgment against you as the result of a violation? As in any court action, ignorance of the law is never an excuse, especially when one of the very first parts of our aviation rules says that the pilot in command will, in effect, be aware of *everything* that may affect the operation of his aircraft before he even starts the engine. It takes only one small slip on your part to render yourself defenseless—there is normally no way to be involved in an accident or incident with an airplane and not be in violation of some part of the aviation regulations. Unfortunately, everyone else in the world figures that a person who can afford to own or operate an airplane can also afford a huge settlement. And after you lose all your money in a court action, the government may step in and relieve you of your flying privileges—sometimes permanently.

There's a practical side to knowing the regulations, too. With the ever-increasing variety of instrument approaches and other system options that we can put to use, the less-than-current IFR pilot will sooner or later come up against a situation that could have been avoided by knowing just what he may or may not do. Current knowledge and complete understanding make the difference between the pilot who stumbles through the airspace confused and bewildered, and the one who makes things happen for his benefit, efficiency, and safety.

The point of all this is that you *must* know the rules of the flying business, you *must* stay abreast of changes as they are effected, and it's *more* important when you are IFR. The VFR-only flyer can get by with less regulation-reading because he can always rely on the see-and-avoid rule. But when you are accepted into the IFR system, you must play in the same key as everyone else; from Ercoupes to airliners, instrument pilots must operate on a common base of regulation and control. Now that you sometimes can't see where you're going, it's comforting to know that all the other pilots up there in the clouds with you are flying by the same set of guidelines.

And what about the controllers' rules? While you can't be held responsible for knowing all the hoops they must jump through, the chances are excellent that you'll become a more understanding and system-oriented pilot once you've observed the conditions in an Air Route Traffic Control Center or Approach Control facililty. They sponsor periodic public-training sessions (usually known as "Operation Raincheck") which include an extensive tour of the facility and a series of classes aimed at developing better cooperation between controllers and pilots. The local Flight Standards Office or any handy FAA facility should have a schedule of such programs.

Your Choice of Charts

There are two popular sources of IFR charts: one is the federal government; the other is the Jeppesen Company, a commercial supplier. Both services include a wide range of publications, from SIDs to STARs and everything in between. You can purchase charts for the whole world, or only for the area in which you fly—it's entirely up to you and your pocketbook. Which service is best? That's an impossible question, because pilot preferences vary so widely. Get a sample of each, and try them—that's the only way you'll be able to decide which is best for you.

No matter what your choice, there is one common denominator: IFR charts cannot fulfill their ultimate purpose unless you know precisely what every mark thereon means. New symbols are added, airway courses are adjusted, radio frequencies are changed, so it becomes nothing short of mandatory that you keep yourself up to date with current charts, and *full* knowledge of those charts. One small, seemingly inconsequential bit of information might just save your neck some day!

Realizing the same out-of-date-before-the-ink-is-dry problem that exists with regulations, *Instrument Flying* does not include a chapter on IFR charts. On occasion, it is necessary to illustrate a particular point with symbols or numbers that are expected to remain in use indefinitely—but you must realize that you are expected to know the sometimes restrictive, sometimes permissive, sometimes directive nature of *all* the chart symbols and markings. Get *very* familiar with the legend pages supplied with your charts. Jeppesen treats this problem very thoroughly in the respective sections of their IFR chart publications. If you use the government charts, you would do well to get a copy of "Civil Use of U.S. Government Instrument

Approach Procedure Charts" (an FAA Advisory Circular), and learn it inside out.

Whenever you receive revisions to your charts, INSERT THEM RIGHT NOW, and do it yourself—don't trust anyone else, not even your spouse. Allowing three or four weeks' revision notices and new charts to pile up on your desk has two bad features: First, it's very frustrating to replace the same chart several times at one sitting, and second, anytime you're flying IFR with old charts, you're an accident looking for a place to happen. When you are inserting those revisions, pay attention to the changes that caused the revision— you'll learn a great deal about the system by noticing new procedures.

Advisory Circulars

Periodically, the FAA issues information of a non-regulatory nature in the form of Advisory Circulars. A subscription to the appropriate parts of this information system will help keep you up to date on the latest official thinking in several areas of interest. For starters, you might consider these four (each subject area is followed by the number that identifies it in the FAA system): Aircraft (20), Airmen (60), Airspace (70), Air Traffic Control and General Operations (90). Advisory Circulars can be ordered from the U.S. Government Printing Office, Washington, D.C. 20402, or any one of the government bookstores around the nation—and, saving the best for last, most of them are *free!*

That Still, Small Voice

There's really not much that can get you into serious trouble on an instrument flight except weather, and the consequences that develop around it. If your airplane is properly maintained, checked, and operated, chances are excellent that it will get you where you want to go. But sometimes, when "get-home-itis" is coming on strong, and your IFR capability is bolstering a "nothing-can-stop-me" frame of mind, listen to that still, small voice of reason that reminds you to back off and take another look at the situation. The temptation to press on in the face of bad weather has led many a pilot down the garden path; if you've worked out a Plan B to take care of non-flyable weather, you can make the decision well ahead of time, still get your business accomplished, and come back to fight another day.

There will be times when you cancel a flight only to have the weather gods make a fool of you with a beautiful day—those are the breaks of the game; but when you've left yourself no way out, and make a forced decision to take off into marginal weather that turns out *worse* than expected, you're in the wringer. If you're lucky, you may get by with a harrowing experience, and a monumental resolve never to do that again. It's a lot more comfortable to be on the ground wishing you were in the air, than to be up there, wishing you were on the ground! A professional pilot earns his pay, and the amateur earns the respect of his passengers, on those occasions when he overcomes pride with good sense and says, "The weather looks worse than I want to tackle today; we're not going by air."

Have At It!

There is no recommended order for reading *Instrument Flying;* dig right in wherever you feel your knowledge is a bit rusty, or when you come across a situation you don't understand thoroughly. Each section is functionally complete in itself, and does not depend on previous study of some other part of the book; other chapters may be consulted for more detail, and the Glossary in Chapter 2 is available for definition of terms.

Now I have your clearance; are you ready to copy? You are cleared from here to the end of the book, via twenty-one chapters packed with instrument flying information. Climb to and maintain a higher level of efficiency and safety; expect further clearance as you work through these pages and become a *complete* instrument pilot. Have a good flight!

2

The Language of Instrument Flying

PASSENGERS who listen to the radio chatter during an instrument flight probably feel as if they have been exposed to a replay of the Tower of Babel scene. The working language, the jargon, of instrument flying does get a bit sticky at times; but then, the "at work" conversation of *any* specialized occupational group will sound like glossolalia to the uneducated.

Terms, definitions, contracted phrases can pile up into a meaningless mess of initialese and confusion when you're about the business of conducting a flight under instrument conditions. When a time-saving communications short-cut comes your way and you're not sure just what you are expected to do, or a term crops up which is completely foreign, by all means *ask;* the worst thing to do is *assume* that you know what something means—you can get in trouble doing that.

There are two ways of becoming fluent in the language of instrument flying; one is to fly IFR at every opportunity and gradually pick up the jargon, and the other is to fly IFR at every opportunity and gradually pick up the jargon. But *first* know what you and they (ATC) are talking about by studying the following glossary. It's a collection of frequently used phrases, definitions, and abbreviations to help you understand what ATC is saying to you, and to improve the propriety of your electronic conversations. There are some terms which you will probably never use, but which are included to accommodate the increasing sophistication of instrument flying. Hold on to your spoon—the alphabet soup promises to get thicker and thicker. (Refer to the AIM Part I or the J-AID for a more detailed listing of aeronautical terms.)

11

Glossary

abeam   A position directly off either wingtip—a relative bearing of 90 degrees or 270 degrees.

ADF   Automatic Direction Finder: refers to the low/medium frequency radio receiver in the airplane. The ADF indicator gives the pilot a readout of the bearing from airplane to station. (Cf. relative bearing.)

affirmative   Better than "yes" because it is more easily understood.

AIRMET   An advisory of weather conditions considered potentially hazardous to light aircraft; usually high winds, low ceilings, low visibilities.

airport traffic area   A cylinder of airspace 5 miles in radius and 3,000 feet deep around and above an airport with an *operating* control tower. Exists for the protection of aircraft taking off and landing. Speed limit within this airspace is 156 knots indicated for prop-driven aircraft, 200 knots for jets, and radio contact with the tower is required.

airspeed   Velocity of an aerial machine; may be stated in a number of ways (always knots): **INDICATED** The number to which the needle points. When Approach Control says "What is your airspeed?" respond with the number of *knots* at the end of the pointer. **CALIBRATED** Pointer indication corrected for installation and instrument error. All limiting and performance speeds are quoted in terms of calibrated airspeed. **TRUE** Calibrated airspeed corrected for pressure and temperature; the actual speed of the airplane relative to undisturbed air. This is the speed used for IFR filing purposes. **APPROACH SPEED** A computed number used to determine the category (A, B, C, D) to be used for instrument approaches. It is the calibrated power-off stall speed of the aircraft at maximum landing weight in the landing configuration, multiplied by 1.3. **BASIC RULE WHEN IN FLIGHT** "Maintain thy airspeed, lest the earth arise and smite thee."

airway   Designated air route between points on the earth's surface.

ALS   Approach Lighting System: an arrangement of lights designed to provide visual guidance to a pilot breaking out of the clouds on an instrument approach. There are a number of acceptable displays; the most striking feature of a typical installation is the "ball of fire" effect from the long line of high-powered sequenced flashers cascading toward the runway.

alternate airport   A place to go if weather at the airport of intended landing goes sour. Must be part of an IFR flight plan under certain conditions.

altitude   Available in several models, including: **PRESSURE ALTITUDE** Read on the altimeter when the altimeter setting is 29.92 inches; everyone operating above 18,000 feet uses pressure altitudes. (Cf. FL.) **DENSITY ALTITUDE** Pressure altitude corrected for temperature; this is the altitude at which the airplane thinks it's flying, and the altitude upon which all performance figures are based. **INDICATED ALTITUDE** What you see on the altimeter when the current setting is placed in the window; all assigned altitudes below 18,000 feet are indicated altitudes. **ABSOLUTE ALTITUDE** Your actual height above the terrain. Used to determine decision height for Category II and III approaches, and sometimes used for over-water navigation. **RADAR ALTITUDE** Same as absolute altitude; a small radar set is used to measure height above the surface. **TRUE ALTITUDE** Your actual height above sea level.

approach category   Grouping of aircraft according to a computed speed and maximum landing weight to determine adequate airspace for maneuvering during a circling instrument approach procedure.

arc   A circle of constant radius around a VORTAC station. When a DME arc approach is specified, you will fly around the station at a fixed distance until intercepting an approach radial which will lead you to the airport.

area navigation   See RNAV.

ASR   Airport Surveillance Radar: relatively short-range radar equipment used primarily for approach control in the terminal area. May also be used as an approach aid, to vector aircraft to within one mile of a runway; however, no altitude information is available.

ATC   Air Traffic Control: any facility engaged in the direction and control of aircraft in controlled airspace; this includes Clearance Delivery, Ground Control, Tower, Approach Control, Departure Control, Air Route Traffic Control ("Center"), and Flight Service Stations.

ATIS   Automatic Terminal Information Service: a continuous broadcast of data pertinent to a specific terminal; includes weather, altimeter setting, approaches and departures in use, other instructions, and information.

back course The "other side" of an ILS Localizer course: the electronic extension of the runway centerline, proceeding in the opposite drection from the front course. Most back courses provide an additional non-precision approach for the airport, and some have glide slopes.

back course marker A range indicator similar to the outer marker, but located on the back course. Provides distance-from-the-runway information.

bearing The relative position of one object to another, stated in degrees. For instrument navigation, a bearing means the direction *toward* a non-directional beacon. All ADF approach charts show bearings TO the station; VOR instructions are always in terms of *radials*—bearings AWAY from the station.

CAVU Acronym for *C*eiling *a*nd *V*isibility *U*nlimited. Sky may be clear or scattered; visibility more than ten miles. Not an official Weather Service term.

CDI Course Deviation Indicator: in the vernacular of the everyday pilot, it's known as the left-right needle on the VOR display.

ceiling The lowest broken cloud layer not reported or forecast as "thin."

cell In conjunction with a radar advisory or report, implies a strong echo, and *usually* indicates a thunderstorm. To stay on the safe side, always consider a reported cell as a thunderstorm, and request vectors around it.

Center The ATC facility responsible for the enroute phase of IFR operations; the full name is Air Route Traffic Control Center.

circling approach Any instrument approach in which the runway to be used for landing is aligned more than 30 degrees from the final approach course, or when a normal rate of descent from the minimum IFR altitude to the runway cannot be accomplished. Clearance for such an approach will always be specific, i.e., "cleared for the runway 10R ILS approach, *circle to land* runway 15." A circling approach is *always* a non-precision approach.

clearance An authorization from ATC to proceed into or through controlled airspace. A clearance supplies, changes, or amends your limits in any one, or all three, dimensions of flight: altitude, route, and point to which you are cleared.

clearance limit An electronic fix (intersection, NDB, VOR, DME fix) beyond which you may not proceed in IFR conditions without further clearance. Never accept a clearance limit unless you receive an expect-further-clearance time.

clearance-void time The latest legal takeoff time when you have received an IFR clearance by telephone at an uncontrolled airfield.

cleared as filed A communications simplifier: means you are cleared to the destination and via the route you requested in your flight plan. Does *not* include an altitude, which must be assigned separately.

cleared direct An ATC instruction that means proceed from your present position *in a straight line* to the appropriate fix.

cleared for the approach Proceed from your present position direct to the appropriate radio facility, and execute the approach as published.

cleared for straight-in approach Proceed direct to the final approach fix and complete the approach without executing a procedure turn.

compass locator A non-directional low-frequency radio beacon co-located with the outer marker, providing a signal which you can use to navigate with ADF to the OM. Also called an "outer locator," "outer compass locator," or just plain "locator." Same as LOM.

contact approach A short-cut to a published instrument approach procedure, treated in detail in Chapter 15, "Instrument Approaches."

control zone Airspace around and above an air terminal for the protection of IFR departures and arrivals. Control zones extend from the surface to 14,500 feet MSL and are of concern only *when the airport is reporting IFR conditions.*

course A line drawn on a chart between two points, and when given a direction, is referenced to either true or magnetic north. All courses on IFR charts are *magnetic.*

cruise clearance Always implies a clearance for an approach at the destination airport, as well as important altitude and airspace limitations. See Chapter 7, "IFR Clearances," for details.

DF   Direction Finding: a disoriented IFR pilot's last resort. Most Flight Service Stations have the capability of electronically determining your bearing and supplying headings to fly to the airport. An approach aid under emergency conditions, it is one way of becoming "unlost."

DH   Decision Height: a point on the guide slope determined by the altimeter reading. Upon reaching the DH (a published height in feet above sea level), a decision must be made to either continue to a landing, or execute the missed approach procedure. Decision heights are associated *only* with precision approaches.

DME   Distance-Measuring Equipment: an airborne navigational aid which interrogates a VORTAC or VOR/DME station, and depending on the sophistication of the black box in the airplane, can provide distance, groundspeed, and time-to-station. Frequently used to identify intersections and confirm locations.

EFC   Expect Further Clearance time: always issued to holding or clearance-limited IFR flights, to provide time for controllers to clear airspace ahead in the event of communications failure.

ETA   Estimated Time of Arrival.

ETD   Estimated Time of Departure.

ETE   Estimated Time Enroute.

fan marker   A highly directional radio transmitter used to indicate distance from the runway on an approach. The radiation pattern seen from above would look like a football with pointed ends. Outer markers, middle markers, and inner markers are fan markers. Usually shortened to "marker."

final approach   That segment of an instrument approach procedure that leads from the final approach fix to the missed approach point.

FAF   Final Approach Fix: the last radio-determined position before you begin descent to the minimum altitude for an instrument approach. A report should be made when passing over the FAF inbound during an approach.

fix   A definite geographical position, determined either by crossing two bearings from radio navigation stations, or by radar observations, or by use of VOR and DME.

FL   Flight Level: term used to indicate pressure altitudes to be flown in the high-altitude route system (18,000 feet and above).

Flight Watch   The code name for contacting a specially trained Flight Service Specialist for weather information. Universal frequency is 122.0.

FSS   Flight Service Station.

glide slope   An electronic signal that provides vertical guidance during a precision approach, and that activates the horizontal needle on the ILS indicator.

GMT   Greenwich Mean Time: the standard time used throughout the IFR system; based on the time at Her Majesty's Royal Observatory in Greenwich, England. Also called "Zulu Time," but has nothing whatever to do with the position of clock hands in South Africa.

"hard" altitude   An altitude *assigned* by ATC; the actual altitude is always preceded by "climb to and maintain" or "descend to and maintain."

heading   The direction in which an aircraft is pointed, related either to true north or magnetic north. In domestic IFR operations, true headings are never used—everything is magnetic.

heavy   A term used on the air in conjunction with turbojet aircraft capable of takeoff gross weights in excess of 300,000 pounds. ("Trans-Global HEAVY 685," for example.) Controllers may not vector any other flight closer than 5 miles behind or 1,000 feet below such an aircraft, because of wake turbulence.

HAA   Height Above Airport: the number of feet above the airport's published elevation when you reach MDA on a circling approach.

HAT   Height Above Touchdown: your elevation above the touchdown zone of the runway when you reach the minimum altitude on a straight-in approach.

high altitude   Refers to routes and charts for IFR operations at and above 18,000 feet.

HIRL   High Intensity Runway Lighting: spaced evenly down either side of the runway, these lights identify the edges of the paved surface, and differ from ordinary runway lights in that the intensity can be increased or decreased to suit visibility conditions.

holding   An orderly means of "retaining" an aircraft at some specified point by circling in a racetrack pattern.

holding fix   The electronic point to which a holding aircraft returns on each circuit of the holding pattern.

hypoxia   A physiological condition arising from the lack of sufficient oxygen to perform normal functions. Suffered in varying degrees by almost everyone when flying at altitudes above 10,000 feet. (Know well thine own symptoms if thou takest thy body higher!)

ident; squawk ident   Terms used by radar controllers when requesting pilots to activate the positive identification feature of a radar transponder. Causes the signal on a radar scope to take on distinctive characteristics for instant recognition by the controller.

IFR   Stands for Instrument Flight Rules, but is used universally as a label for all instrument operations.

ILS   Instrument Landing System: a combination of electronic components which furnish information in all three dimensions (lateral, longitudinal, and vertical), designed to lead an aircraft to a missed approach point very close to the runway.

ILS Category II   A more precise system that has even lower minimums than the normal, or Category I, Instrument Landing System. Requires special certification for ground equipment, airborne receivers, and higher pilot qualifications. (ILS Category III is even *more* sophisticated.)

IM   Inner Marker: a radio transmitter identical to outer and middle markers, except for distance from the runway and signal pattern. IMs are situated between the MM and the runway, and usually transmit continuous dots (· · · · · · · · ·).

in radar contact   A controller's statement that he has positively identified your flight on radar; a polite request to "shut up"—make no position reports unless requested.

jet routes   Airways in the high altitude (18,000 feet and above) route structure, such as J50, J437, etc. Should be referred to on the air as "Jay fifty," "Jay four three seven," etc.

jet stream   A meandering river of high-speed air (sometimes 200 knots or more), generally found at high altitudes. Like smart people up North, it usually moves South in the winter.

jump   What you may want to do when all your radios and navigational equipment and instruments fail at night in a thunderstorm.

kill the rabbit   A coded request for the Tower to reduce the intensity of the RAILs (Runway Alignment Indicator Lights). Usually heard on nights when visibility is very low and pilots are being blinded by the bright lights.

kilometers   Used to quote visibility in Europe and the Far East; designed to completely confuse all pilots accustomed to distances measured in feet and miles.

knot   The expression of speed corresponding to 1 nautical mile per hour. Used universally by ATC and all foreign nations. Pilots are expected to accomplish all IFR operations in terms of knots.

LBCM   Locator at the Back Course Marker: A non-directional radio beacon co-located with the fan marker on a back course localizer approach.

LDA   Localizer-type Directional Aid: same as a localizer, but offset from the runway heading. Provides course guidance down to a point from which you can proceed to the airport by visual references.

LDIN   Lead-in Lighting System: a flashing (or distinctive) lighting system on the ground with light units in groups of at least three, positioned in a curved path to a runway threshold. They furnish directional guidance only, and should not be confused with ALS.

LOC   Localizer: the left-right information portion of an ILS; an electronic extension of the centerline of the runway.

locator   Same as Compass Locator.

LOM   Locator at the Outer Marker: same as Compass Locator.

low altitude   When referring to airway routes and charts for instrument operations, means "below 18,000 feet."

low altitude alert   A phrase used by controllers to get your attention when they observe a potentially hazardous proximity to terrain or obstructions. Usually followed by "check your altitude immediately."

maintain   What you are expected to do when assigned an altitude by ATC.

MAP   Missed Approach Point: expressed in either time or distance from the final approach fix, or as an altitude on the Glide Slope; it is the point at which a missed approach must be executed if the runway environment is not in sight.

map   Usually referred to by pilots as a "chart."

marker beacon   Same as fan marker.

marker beacon lights   Two, or sometimes three, panel-mounted lights that illuminate appropriately to indicate passage over radio range markers on an instrument approach. (Cf. OM, MM, IM.)

MCA   Minimum Crossing Altitude: indicated by an "X" flag on enroute charts when a certain altitude must be attained prior to going beyond an airway intersection.

MDA   Minimum Descent Altitude: the lowest altitude (expressed in feet above sea level) to which you may descend on a non-precision approach (one without a glide slope) if the runway environment is not in sight.

MEA   Minimum Enroute Altitude: the lowest altitude at which you can receive a satisfactory navigational signal for the appropriate segment of a federal airway.

MOA   Military Operations Area: A volume of airspace that is indicated on all aeronautical charts and is used at various times and altitudes by the military services. IFR flights are automatically cleared through or rerouted: VFR flights must use great caution when flying through these areas.

MOCA   Minimum Obstruction Clearance Altitude: guarantees terrain and obstacle clearance on the appropriate segment of a federal airway. If you should have to fly at MOCA, remember that a usable VOR signal is guaranteed only within twenty-two miles of the station.

minimum fuel   When declared to a controller, indicates that you can make it to the airport with normal handling, but that any delay may result in your declaring a full-blown low-fuel emergency.

missed approach   A procedure specified for a "go-around" if the runway environment is not in sight at the missed approach point.

MM   Middle Marker: a highly directional radio beacon located about one-half mile from the end of the runway on an ILS approach. A distance indicator, it transmits a signal of high-pitched alternate dots and dashes (· — · — · — · —). If marker beacon lights are installed in the airplane, the amber light will flash in a similar pattern. The middle marker does *not* always indicate the missed approach point.

MRA   Minimum Reception Altitude: the lowest altitude at which you will be guaranteed reception of an off-airway VOR for the purpose of identifying an intersection. Has nothing to do with communication reception.

MSA   Minimum Safe Altitude: the lowest altitude within 25 nautical miles of an approach fix that guarantees 1,000 feet obstacle clearance. Found on the approach and landing chart, it may be one altitude for all directions, or may be referenced to several sectors around the fix.

nautical mile   One minute of latitude (measured vertically on charts); all distances in IFR charts are indicated in nautical miles; all DME indicators read nautical miles.

NDB   Non-Directional Beacon: a low-frequency radio transmitter that emits a signal in all directions from the antenna. Its signal is not concentrated in any one direction, hence the term "non-directional."

negative   An emphatic, easily understood "no."

no-gyro approach   A technique used by controllers when a pilot is operating in a "partial-panel" situation . . . needle, ball, and airspeed.

no joy   A term borrowed from our military flying brothers; means "I do not see the traffic you told me about," and saves a lot of communications time.

non-precision approach   A published procedure (or surveillance radar approach) which does not provide an electronic glide slope. *All* approaches except ILS and PAR are non-precision.

NOTAM   NOtices To AirMen: information pertinent to operations in the National Airspace System. May be received via teletype, radio broadcasts, or in printed form.

obscuration   Weather condition in which the sky is hidden by rain, fog, snow, etc. The height given in such an observation is vertical visibility only; forward vision will usually be severely restricted.

OM   Outer Marker: usually the final approach fix on an ILS or localizer approach, this 75 mHz, non-tunable radio beacon is typically located 4 to 7 miles from the runway. Highly directional, its signal is transmitted in a narrow beam straight up, and is received only when directly overhead. The audible signal is a continuous series of low-pitched dashes (————) and if marker beacon lights are installed in the airplane, the blue light will flash in conjunction with the sound.

omni   Short for "Very-High-Frequency-Omnidirectional-Radio-Range," also known as VOR. "Omni" has only two syllables—don't say "om-an-ni."

outer locator   Same as LOM.

over   Used at the end of a radio transmission to indicate that a reply is expected. Quite unnecessary; if what you have said requires a reply, you'll get it anyway.

over and out   Used mostly by the Walter Mitty types who also wear helmet and goggles in a Learjet.

PAR   Precision Approach Radar: provides a precision approach based on vocal instructions given to the pilot, as the controller observes azimuth, distance, and elevation on radar. Known as GCA (Ground Controlled Approach) at military airfields. PAR is now almost non-existent in the civilian system.

parallel ILS approach   In existence at only a handful of airports, and operable only within very restrictive conditions of runway separation and radar monitoring, these approaches provide guidance to side-by-side runways simultaneously.

partial panel   Term used to describe the situation that exists when the attitude indicator and heading indicator are inoperative, or covered up with some fiendish device your flight instructor pulls from his shirt pocket. Sometimes referred to as "needle, ball, and airspeed," especially during meetings of older pilots.

precipitous terrain   Where steep and abrupt slopes exist under the final approach course, the approach chart will display a note to that effect. In addition to causing violent up and down drafts, the sudden changes in pressure can result in wild fluctuations of altimeter and airspeed indicators. Approach planners take this into account, and boost the minimum altitudes accordingly.

precision approach   An approach procedure which incorporates an electronic glide slope. In today's IFR world, there is only one in regular use, the Instrument Landing System (ILS).

prevailing visibility   The horizontal distance at which known objects can be seen through at least half the observer's horizon. It does not necessarily mean a *continuous* half of his horizon, and so can vary considerably from the actual visibility at the approach end of the runway. Other types of visibility measurement (e.g., RVR) are considered more appropriate for instrument approaches; of course the pilot's observation is the ultimate.

procedure turn A means of reversing course to line up inbound on the approach course. Generally used in non-radar situations, or when you arrive over the approach fix headed away from the airport.

procedure turn altitude Found on the profile view of the approach chart, this is your vertical limit while reversing course. You are considered in the procedure turn and must observe this altitude limit until once again on the approach course inbound.

Queen, Hangar What you call your airplane when it's in the shop more than it's in the air.

radar RAdio Detection And Ranging: pulses of electronic energy are emitted from a ground transmitter—objects which echo the energy show up on the radar scope as "blips" of bright light; the azimuth and distance, and in some cases the altitude can be measured. Airborne transponders cause a coded blip to appear on the scope.

radar altimeter An electronic device that measures the time for a radio signal to go from the aircraft antenna to the ground and return, then displays the time interval as a precise distance. Used generally for precision approaches, and is required for Category II and III ILS operations.

radar beacon The official name for a transponder.

radar contact Phrase used by controllers to indicate that a signal representing your aircraft has been identified on the radar scope.

radar-monitored approach One in which a radar operator follows the progress of an aircraft in order to provide corrections in course, and sometimes elevation. Used mostly at very congested terminals. You can request a radar-monitored approach in an emergency, or when you suspect navigational equipment malfunction.

radar service terminated A phrase used by air traffic controllers to inform a pilot that whatever radar services (including traffic advisories) he has been enjoying are hereby withdrawn.

radial A magnetic course radiating, or proceeding outward from, a VOR. Controllers *always* use the term "radial" when referencing navigation instructions to a VOR.

radio compass Same as ADF.

RAIL Runway Alignment Indicator Lights: the "ball of fire" you see running toward the runway in a fully equipped approach lighting system. Sometimes called the "rabbit."

read back What the controller says at the end of an IFR clearance. You should always read back at least altitude assignments and vector headings, and in the sequence issued.

REIL Runway End Identifier Lights: a pair of condenser discharge lights (strobes) identical to those in the RAIL system, but located on either side of the runway threshold. REILs flash simultaneously, about once a second.

relative bearing On an ADF indicator, the number of degrees the pointer is displaced *clockwise* from the nose (top index) of the aircraft. Add relative bearing to magnetic heading, and the resulting number is *always* magnetic course to the station.

report landing assured or **missed approach** When cleared for an approach to an airport with no ATC facility, you remain under protection from other IFR traffic. Should you be required to execute a missed approach, you go right back into the system for another try, or perhaps clearance to your alternate. The controller would therefore like to hear from you when "landing is assured" (runway in sight), or when you start a missed approach. He will also advise whom to contact and on what frequency.

report procedure turn A request for a report as soon as you turn away from the outbound course—call the controller at the very beginning of the procedure turn.

report procedure turn inbound When so instructed on an instrument approach, the controller wants to hear from you as soon as you are back on course, headed toward the airport.

resume normal navigation Usually follows "radar service terminated" and is your cue to intercept, stay on, or get back to the appropriate radial, airway, or course and get where you're supposed to go all by yourself.

RMI Radio Magnetic Indicator: displays aircraft heading at the top of a rotating card, with pointers tied electronically to the VOR and/ or ADF receivers. When properly tuned, the pointers indicate magnetic course to the appropriate station. The RMI is also convenient to use as a heading indicator.

RNAV　Area Navigation: an electronic system that processes information from a VOR-DME station and automatically computes the course and distance to a desired position called a "waypoint."

roger　Worldwide term to indicate complete understanding of a radio transmission. Can also be used (with appropriate volume) when answering a bartender to let everyone in earshot know that you are a pilot.

roger wilco　Means "yes, I understand and *will* comply," and is completely out of place in today's aeronautical communications. A simple "Roger" or your aircraft number does the job.

roger wilco, over and out　Be careful with the use of this phrase on the air—some enterprising musician will hear it and write a hit song.

runway environment　The runway threshold, approved lighting aids, or other markings identifiable with the runway. Having the runway environment in sight is one of the requirements for descending below DH or MDA on any approach.

RVR　Runway Visual Range: a photoelectric device called a "transmissometer" measures the visibility immediately adjacent to the runway, then computes what a pilot would see, and converts this observation to hundreds of feet. Displayed in the tower, it can be handily read to you during a tight approach, and takes precedence over all other forms of visibility measurement, except your own two eyes.

say again　Please repeat all of what you have just said.

say again all after. . . .　Please repeat everything that followed a given word or phrase—implies complete understanding of whatever came before that point in the transmission.

say again all after ATC clears. . . .　Generally used by honest pilots when they miss an entire IFR clearance.

say again, you broke up　This is a good way to "keep your cool" when you don't have *any* idea what the man said—no one can prove that the transmission *didn't* break up!

SDF　Simplified Directional Facility: an instrument approach procedure that fits on the accuracy scale between a VOR and a localizer approach. Course width may vary from 6 to 12 degrees among installations, with the final approach course offset somewhat from the runway heading.

SID   Standard Instrument Departure: a published clearance procedure designed to cut down communication time. Each SID is named and numbered and directs you to an enroute fix from which you proceed via the airways routing in your clearance.

sidestep   When approaching an airport with parallel runways very close together, the tower will occasionally clear an aircraft to "sidestep" and land on the other runway. This must always be a visual maneuver.

special VFR   An ATC clearance (sometimes called "poor man's IFR") to proceed into or out of a control zone under certain conditions.

squawk altitude   Phrase used by controllers when they want you to adjust the transponder to transmit an altitude signal.

squawk standby   When so directed, turn the transponder function switch to "standby" (or other relevant terminology), which will cause the transponder signal to disappear completely from the radar scope. Used for positive identification when the IDENT feature is inoperative or weak. Usually followed by "Squawk normal" when the controller has positive identification. "Standby" should always be selected when taxiing.

standard rate turn   A turn which results in the aircraft changing heading at the rate of 3 degrees per second. To approximate the angle of bank required, divide true airspeed (in knots) by ten and add five.

stand by   The universal reply to a question from ATC when the answer is not readily available.

STAR   Standard Terminal Arrival Route: a published route into a terminal area, with the basic aim of reducing communications between pilots and controllers. Each STAR has its own name and number; for example, "cleared via the Fountainhead Four Arrival."

star   A bright spot in the sky, often mistaken for the lights of another airplane.

stepdown fix   An intermediate point between the Final Approach Fix and the Missed Approach Point, permitting a lower altitude when it can be identified by the pilot.

stop altitude squawk   Phrase used by controllers when, for reasons of inaccuracy or internal problems, they want you to remove the altitude information from your transponder signal. Return the function switch to "Normal."

straight-in approach   A procedure which leads directly to the landing end of the runway, when that runway is aligned no more than 30 degrees from the final approach course, and a normal descent from the minimum IFR altitude can be accomplished.

TACAN   A military navigation system (TACtical Air Navigation) combined with a VOR to make a VORTAC, which supplies both azimuth and distance to DME-equipped civilian aircraft.

tally ho   Say this when you spot the traffic that Center points out to you—"Barnburner 1234 Alpha, traffic at two o'clock, four miles, eastbound"—it's a wee bit melodramatic when you answer "Tally ho!" but it sure cuts down on communication time!

TAS   True Air Speed.

TDZ   Touchdown Zone: extends 3,000 feet down the runway from the threshold; the highest elevation in the TDZ provides the point from which DH and MDA are measured for straight-in approach minimums.

track   (1) The path which an aircraft makes across the ground. When cleared direct from one point to another, that track is expected to be a straight line. (2) Parallel lengths of ferrous material secured to wooden crossties, and used for aerial navigation. Also used now and then by long lines of railroad cars.

transmissometer   The electronic visibility-sensing device which provides the basic input for RVR measurements. It is installed beside the landing runway at the approach end, and is very accurate—the next-to-the-last word in visibility measurement.

transponder   A device that responds to a coded radar pulse with a coded return, providing a distinctive display for positive radar identification.

transponder code   The specified sequence of numbers which, when selected on the transponder, provides a coded display on the radar scope.

unable   The communication code word used to indicate your inability to contact a facility; for example, "Birmingham Tower, Barnburner 1234 Alpha **unable** Approach Control on 123.8." Tower will then give you further instructions.

vector   A heading assigned by a radar controller; takes precedence over all other forms of navigation. You are expected to remain on vectored headings until advised "resume normal navigation."

verify   When used by either a controller or a pilot, means "did you really say what I think you said?"

VFR   Visual Flight Rules: conditions to which pilots are limited until they become instrument-rated. A non-specific term compared to IFR, which means "I Follow Railroads."

visibility   What you need a certain amount of in order to legally land from an instrument approach. It may be measured and reported by a ground observer, a transmissometer (RVR), or the pilot. *You* become the official visibility observer on an approach—if the runway environment is in sight at a certain point, proceeding to a landing is completely legal.

visual approach   A short-cut to a published instrument approach procedure, treated in detail in Chapter 14, "Getting Ready for an Instrument Approach."

VOR   Stands for Very high frequency Omni-directional Radio range.

What Am I Doing Here?   The question you will ask yourself in the middle of a thunderstorm.

X-ray vision   What ATC expects you to have when the controller says "the airport is at one o'clock, two miles; do you have it in sight?"

Zulu Time   A military-spawned term which is easier to say than Greenwich Mean Time; means the same thing, and is frequently shortened to "Z."

3

Attitude Instrument Flying

THE PTERODACTYL, a lizard-turned-bird with huge leather-skinned wings that soared above the swamps and marshes of prehistoric times, may well have been the first creature to experience IFR flight. According to the geological history books, the earth was frequently covered with clouds of noxious gases from the volcanoes that dotted the landscape—it's a cinch that the pterodactyls on occasion ignored their VFR-only limitations, and flew into IFR conditions. Of course no one was there to prove it, but quite likely they had an instinctive reaction to counter the sudden loss of visual clues; they were probably able to set their wings for an optimum glide speed, maintain direction with some primitive vestibular gyroscope, and keep going until they broke out of the clouds. It's just as likely that some of them didn't make it; this theory is supported by the discoveries now and then of pterodactyl remains on or just below the summits of mountain peaks!

The blind-flying capabilities of our feathered friends extends to many of the birds we know today—ducks, pigeons, geese, and others have been known to successfully navigate through the clouds to safety. Man has not fared so well, requiring some sort of help from artificial references to maintain his spatial orientation. But anyone who has flown Cubs, Airknockers, and the like knows that if things really get bad, he could always close the throttle, roll the trim all the way back, keep the turn needle centered with the rudder, and at least come out of the situation right side up.

When aviation pioneers turned their efforts to making money with airplanes, they soon realized that they would have to figure some way to overcome what appeared to be the insurmountable problem of flying all the way through clouds—halfway just wouldn't

29

do. A frightening number of our departed brothers tried it on guts and confidence, but it all boiled down to the necessity of substituting some kind of in-the-airplane instrumentation to replace the natural horizon when it disappeared. Early attempts included "playing it by ear," listening to the sound of the wind in the ample wires and stays that held those old airplanes together, watching the flutterings of pieces of cloth tied to the struts, and even Mason jars half-filled with oil that were supposed to indicate whether the airplane was banking, or in level flight.

None of these early methods worked very well, but with the advent of gyroscopic devices, a whole new world of airplane utility was introduced. When Jimmy Doolittle proved that man could take off, navigate, and land an airplane using no outside references, he introduced a system of instrument flight that we use, almost unchanged, to this very day.

Whether you took flying lessons yesterday or thirty years ago, one of the first things you learned was that when the curve of the engine cowling, or the top of the instrument panel, or some other reference showed a certain relation to the horizon, and when you had the engine wide open, the airplane would climb at a predictable airspeed and vertical speed. You learned that when, at a given airspeed, the airplane was banked until the center post of the windshield formed a particular angle with the horizon, the airplane turned at a certain rate. The substitution of a miniature airplane fastened to the instrument case and moving about a gyrostabilized bar in the same direction and to the same degree as the actual movement of the real airplane merely transfers to an artificial horizon what you used to see outside. If you set up your old familiar climb attitude with outside references and at the same time notice what you see on the attitude indicator, you can forget the outside clues, and rest assured that anytime you put the miniature airplane in the same place, with the same power setting, you're going to get the same old familiar climb performance. That, in a very small nutshell, is attitude instrument flying—basic, reliable, and really very simple to accomplish.

But the attitude indicator can't do the job alone. Although it's the heart of the system, you must refer to the other instruments to determine what is happening when you select a pitch attitude that's two nose-widths above the horizon, or a 20-degree bank, or a combination of the two. In other words, you must reason to yourself (or out loud, if it helps!), "I will place this little flying machine in the attitude that I *think* will produce a standard-rate climbing turn to the right, and then check the other gauges to see if I was right—if the needles and pointers aren't moving the way they should, I will change the attitude a bit to get the results I want." It's easy to see that if all the variables are held constant, the same attitude will give the same condition of flight every time. Now, in a manner of speaking, you *can* set your wings just like the birds, and have confidence that certain things will take place.

The Fundamentals of Attitude Control

Pitch, bank, power, and trim—the "Four Horsemen" of attitude instrument flight. When you get right down to it, there's not much you can do with an airplane except change the pitch, bank, or power, and how much you change what in which direction in concert with the others or all by itself determines what will happen. You may feel that this listing of the basics added trim unnecessarily, and left out rudder control; not so, because trim is of great importance in smoothing out your cloud-bound wanderings, and you are expected to maintain the ball in its centered position at all times in instrument flight. In general, you should always adjust pitch, bank, and power, then trim to hold the airplane in the attitude you want. The human machine is incapable of holding a constant, precise pressure for an extended period of time, but it can *recognize* that pressure and adjust trim controls until it disappears.

Now, you must become a believer. Raise your right hand, and repeat for all to hear: "I [state your name] do hereby solemnly affirm my belief in the fact that in all steady-state instrument situations [that is, any time a constant airspeed, constant altitude, or constant rate-of-change of altitude is desired], altitude shall be controlled by POWER and airspeed shall be contolled by PITCH." It's true! Believe! Go back in memory to those slow-flight exercises you went through early in your flying career—at a very-near-stall airspeed, if the altitude began to droop a bit, you didn't pull up the nose to correct, you added POWER. If the airspeed was somewhat higher than what your instructor felt was a good demonstration of slow flight, you didn't back off on the throttle, you applied BACK PRES-

SURE. And it works just as beautifully when you're under the hood or in weather—perhaps even more so than when you can see outside, because you have an exacting reference right there in front of you; it's called an "instrument panel."

When that gaggle of needles, pointers, gauges, and indicators is complete and everything's working properly, there is one instrument that must be considered THE primary one—the attitude indicator. It seems reasonable, in a context of attitude instrument flying, that the attitude *indicator* should be the most frequently consulted. It will tell you more at a glance than anything else on the panel. Changes in attitude on this instrument will be immediately reflected in the readings elsewhere—you are able to generate changes or keep them from taking place by referring to this gyroscopic manifestation of where-is-the-airplane-in-relation-to-the-horizon. Anytime it's not in the level flight attitude for the particular power setting in use, something is happening, or is about to happen. (Probably 99.9 percent of your instrument time will be spent scanning the indications of a so-called full panel, with all the instruments in working order and doing their jobs. Mechanical devices being what they are, it's possible some day to find yourself operating in a "partial panel" situation, and you should know what to do and how to handle the airplane in this condition. See Chapter 4 for details.)

Your first step in becoming a good attitude instrument pilot is to find out what the gyro horizon looks like when you *are* in normal level flight. Nearly all indicators in use today are adjustable; you should be able to move the miniature airplane up or down so that it is dead center on the artificial horizon in a straight and level, constant airspeed condition. Once you have found this attitude and adjusted the little airplane to show it, LEAVE IT THERE. This gives you a sound base from which to proceed. Now you can change the attitude as required—for a constant airspeed climb at full power, you may have to increase the pitch attitude two bar widths (raise the miniature airplane twice the thickness of its wings above the horizon bar), or perhaps you will recognize that a one-half bar width increase is required to hold altitude in a standard rate turn. Every time you make that little airplane move, the movement should be referenced to the level flight attitude as shown on the attitude indicator. (Slight adjustments for varying loads and atmospheric conditions may be required.)

Sources of qualitative information will change in various maneuvers. For example, when rolling into a standard rate turn, bank the miniature airplane until the turn needle moves to the proper indication, and then maintain the rate of turn as shown on the needle by minor changes in the bank attitude. The turn needle has become the primary source of information about rate of turn, but the attitude indicator remains stalwart in its indication of the bank required to sustain this condition. As you approach a predetermined heading, the heading indicator will tell you when to begin the roll-out, and it's back to the attitude indicator to return the airplane to level flight. When you're trying to maintain a precise rate of descent at a given airspeed (as in the final segment of a non-precision approach), the airspeed indicator tells you whether or not the attitude you have selected is the proper one, and the attitude indicator is used to make any changes that may be required. Since you believe that power controls altitude (and altitude change), when it is necessary to increase your rate of descent, you will reduce power with reference to the engine instruments, but you need the attitude indicator to maintain the pitch relationship that will keep the airspeed constant. And of course, whenever straight flight is your target, keeping the wings level with the attitude indicator (and the ball centered as always with rudder pressure) can do nothing but make the airplane fly straight ahead.

Applying the Attitude Technique

Some instrument pilots are sharper, smoother, and more precise than others—it's a fact of life, and is due partly to the physical and mental capabilities of each individual. But running through the performance of even the slowest, most plodding IFR aviator is an undeniable 1-2-3 sequence of events. Some are able to accomplish it faster than others, but you can't get away from (1) reading the instrument indications, (2) figuring out what they have to say to you, (3) doing something about it. This sequence is commonly known as cross-check, interpretation, and control.

Instrument Cross-Check

Tirades from flight instructors, grueling sessions in ground trainers, and sophisticated eye-movement studies have failed to come up with a formula for cross-checking flight instruments. In addition to the fact that the amount of time spent on any one instrument must change subtly with every change in flight condition, cross-checking seems to be a very personal matter. The number of times per minute your eyes scan the entire panel, or how long they remain on the turn needle or the heading indicator isn't really important; the essence of cross-checking lies in the *amount* of information gleaned from each sweep of the gauges. You must develop your cross-check to provide enough inputs for meaningful decisions about what to do next, if anything. It stands to reason that the more complicated the maneuver, the faster your eyes must move, especially when you are introducing a change of attitude.

There is only one way to become a proficient cross-checker; force yourself to eyeball each of the instruments, with particular emphasis on the attitude indicator (you'll be amazed at the minute changes you can detect), and practice, practice, practice. Here's where the proficiency exercises described in Chapter 21 can be a big help—without the distractions of Approach Control, with no navigational load to divert your attention, go through these maneuvers if for nothing else than to speed up your cross-check. It's a skill, and as such must be practiced regularly and methodically if it's to stay sharp.

Later on, you must begin to include navigational inputs in your cross-check. It's easy to develop instrument hypnosis, characterized by ignorance of navaid information. Pilots have been known to fly all the way to the missed approach point with great precision and beautiful timing, but at procedure turn altitude—right on course, but so concerned with maintaining an exact altitude that they forgot to descend over the Final Approach Fix!

Instrument Flying for Animal Lovers

Having detailed the concept of attitude control, there is another method which you may prefer. For reasons that will become apparent, it is recommended for those pilots whose airplanes have large, easily cleaned cabins. Known as the "Cat and Duck Method" of instrument flight, it has received much publicity and is considered to have a great deal of merit by those who have not tried it. No reports have been received from those who did try it, and none are expected. Pilots are invited to assess its merits objectively.

Basic rules for the C&D Method of instrument flight are fairly well known and are extremely simple. Here's how it's done:

1. Place a live cat on the cockpit floor; because a cat always remains upright, it can be used in lieu of a needle and ball. Merely watch to see which way the cat leans to determine if a wing is low, and if so, which one.

2. The duck is used for the instrument approach and landing. Because of the fact that any sensible duck will refuse to fly under instrument conditions, it is only necessary to hurl your duck out of the plane and follow it to the ground.

There are some limitations to the Cat and Duck Method, but by rigidly adhering to the following checklist, a degree of success will be achieved which will surely startle you, your passengers, and even an occasional tower operator.

1. Get a wide-awake cat. Most cats do not want to stand up at all. It may be necessary to carry a large dog in the cockpit to keep the cat at attention.

2. Make sure your cat is clean. Dirty cats will spend all their time washing. Trying to follow a washing cat usually results in a tight snap roll followed by an inverted spin.

3. Use old cats only. Young cats have nine lives, but old, used-up cats with only one life left have just as much to lose as you do and will be more dependable.

4. Beware of cowardly ducks. If the duck discovers that you are using the cat to stay upright, it will refuse to leave without the cat. Ducks are no better in IFR conditions than you are.

5. Be sure that the duck has good eyesight. Nearsighted ducks sometimes fail to realize that they are on the gauges and go flogging off into the nearest hill. *Very* nearsighted ducks will not realize they have been thrown out and will descend to the ground in a sitting position. This maneuver is difficult to follow in an airplane.

6. Use land-loving ducks. It is very discouraging to break out and find yourself on final for a rice paddy, particularly if there are duck hunters around. Duck hunters suffer from temporary insanity while sitting in freezing weather in the blinds and will shoot at anything that flies.

7. Choose your duck carefully. It is easy to confuse ducks with geese because many water birds look alike. While they are very competent instrument flyers, geese seldom want to go in the same direction as you. If your duck heads off for Canada or Mexico, you may be sure that you have been given the goose.

4

Partial Panel IFR

MOST of us tend to be complacent about the performance of things mechanical, especially when those things have worked properly for a long period of time. That is surely the case with most instrument pilots and their respect for the artificial horizon and directional gyro . . . "Sure, I've heard of an instrument failure now and then, but mine seems to be okay; no cause for alarm."

A spate of instrument-failure accidents in recent years has strongly suggested, however, that the average instrument pilot needs to be very aware of the potential for a gyro failure, and the *probability* of his losing control of the airplane in instrument conditions unless he's properly trained, prepared, and current. Whether the problem is caused by a malfunction of the instruments themselves, or by a failure of the vacuum/air pressure source (the most likely event), the result is the same . . . a life-threatening situation that requires seldom-practiced skills and techniques for survival. The pilot community has dubbed this unhappy circumstance "partial panel" flying.

The Heart(s) of the Problem

Up to this point, we've been coming down rather hard on the principle of "attitude flying," wherein a certain attitude coupled with a certain power setting will always produce a certain type of performance. That technique is based on the presence of a specific instrument that provides a clear and precise picture of airplane attitude in two axes . . . roll and pitch.

But when the attitude indicator fails (for whatever reason), you're playing with a different set of rules. It's not really attitude flying any more, because all you have to work with are the *reactions* of

37

pitch, power, and bank; there is no longer anything on the panel to tell you the airplane's attitude. The remaining flight instruments (turn indicator, altimeter, airspeed indicator, vertical speed, magnetic compass in a typical lightplane installation) show you what's happening, but provide no *direct* indication of how high the nose has been raised, or of how much the wings have been moved from level. Since you are now working with results only, a different technique is a *must* if you are to fly safely out of this bad situation.

The first "heart" of the partial-panel problem is the very recognition of something amiss. Of course, you can keep pushing the problem farther into the future by replacing or repairing any flight instrument that exhibits symptoms of impending failure. If an attitude indicator or directional gyro (AI and DG from now on) take forever to stabilize after engine start, or make weird, grinding noises as they wind down at the end of a flight, call in the instrument doctor and find out what's wrong. Better to spend the bucks for a new or rebuilt instrument than to put yourself through a partial-panel wringer—for *real*—on your next IFR flight.

Unfortunate but true, gyro instrument failures are likely to be rather benign in character. The usual scenario goes like this; the power source (vacuum or pressure) fails after the gyros are running at full speed, whereupon the instruments *gradually* lose their ability to tell you the truth. The AI is the prime culprit here; it will probably indicate a bank at such a slow rate that you'll follow right along with it, and by the time you realize you've been had, you've been had! This is the reason why every thorough IFR check should include a demonstration of the pilot's ability to recover safely from at least the two characteristic "critical attitudes"—a climbing turn, and a diving turn (see Exercise #12, page 321).

How to keep current on the health of your flight instruments? That's easy; just include the vacuum/pressure gauge in your normal scan of engine instruments, or install a big red light to get your attention when the value falls below an acceptable level (easier said than done, of course, but there's no good reason *not* to maintain a close watch on this Achilles' heel).

The other preventive measure is to constantly check all of the flight-instrument indications against each other. If the AI shows a bank to the right, is the DG increasing? If the DG numbers are moving to the left, is the turn needle deflected the same way? Are pitch attitude and altimeter reading consonant? Whenever instrument indications disagree, it's time to check the power source, and then prepare yourself to shift gears . . . it may well be partial-panel time.

The second "heart" of this problem is what to do after you've determined that all is not well in the flight instrument department. From now on, we're concerned only with the techniques and procedures applicable to an attitude-instrument failure in actual IFR conditions. You don't want to be there, but you *are*, and there's only one way out—fly the airplane to some place where you can see the ground, find an airport, and land safely. Keep that firmly and foremost in mind . . . if you're going to survive, you've no choice but to take command and *fly the airplane*.

Experience (*painful* experience) has shown that partial-panel operations in the clouds represent a true emergency for most pilots. There is definitely some assistance available from Air Traffic controllers (directing you to a suitable airport, toward VFR weather conditions, perhaps nothing more than an occasional "atta boy" to keep your spirits up), but if they don't know, they can't help. With that in mind, get on the horn and declare an emergency when you are placed in a partial-panel situation. There's no need to pick up the mike and scream "MAYDAY!," but be sure the controllers understand clearly that you have a real problem, and need all the help you can get. The mere mention of the word "emergency," in calm, quiet tones, will get the attention you deserve. Don't be too proud to solicit additional inputs . . . the controller might have the secret to your survival.

Problem Identified, Now What?

If, by the time you realize a problem, you've gotten yourself into an unusual attitude, the recovery procedures in Exercise #12 (page 321) will save the day; but without the AI and DG, you must change your technique a bit. Add or reduce power according to your assessment of airspeed, then center the turn indicator (needle or airplane symbol) *with aileron pressure*, and center the ball *with rudder pressure*. This will virtually guarantee a coordinated return to straight flight.

Now you must take care of the pitch attitude. If you were doing a good job of flying before "partial-panel" struck, the airplane was well trimmed, and should therefore be trying to regain the trim airspeed. You probably won't be able to sit there and wait, so an adjustment of pitch attitude is in order. With the "picture" of that attitude now invalid, it will be necessary to make an actual movement of the control wheel and evaluate the results.

Bring the altimeter into play at this point; if it is decreasing, physically move the control wheel aft a small amount—say a quarter-inch or so—and note any change in the rate at which the altimeter is moving (the vertical-speed indicator may be of some help here, but the inherent lag in its indication will likely cause you more trouble than you need). If there's no change, move the wheel aft another quarter-inch; keep this up *until the altimeter stops moving*— you are now in level flight. (Assuming that you have kept turn needle and ball centered all the while.)

Slight changes in pressure on the wheel will now permit a return to the stabilized airspeed for which the airplane was trimmed, and once achieved, *do not change the trim.* You have arrived in a known, flyable, condition, one that will get you where you need to go . . . don't upset the apple cart by changing the trim.

At this point, recognize that without direct readings of airplane attitude, the fewer the control inputs the better. So take your hands off the wheel, relegate directional control to the rudder, and altitude changes to the throttle. You'll find that gentle, steady pressure on the appropriate rudder pedal will start and maintain a shallow turn, or will hold the heading for straight flight. The turn indicator becomes primary for directional control now; keep it centered to maintain a heading, move it to left or right the proper amount to turn at standard rate.

Altitude control is vested in the throttle. Level flight implies just enough thrust being applied to keep the airplane from climbing or descending, and it stands to reason that adding power will result in a climb at the same airspeed, reducing power will set up a descent. You'll need to experiment with your airplane to find out how much power change creates a reasonable climb or descent.

In summary, when on partial panel and the airplane's under complete control, trimmed and stabilized, all heading changes will be made with rudder pressure, all altitude changes will be made with changes of thrust. It's the best way to keep from flying yourself right back into that unusual attitude you worked so hard to defeat. (You may even conclude that hands-off instrument flying works so well that you'll adopt it as your normal technique!)

Spatial disorientation is but a heartbeat away from any pilot in a partial-panel situation, especially when a really hairy unusual attitude is encountered. There will be noises and sensations you've not experienced before, and your inner ear will be undergoing gyrations that are all but guaranteed to turn you inside out. If ever you have rallied your resources to overcome inner conflicts, this is that time. Center the turn indicator, get the altitude and airspeed under control, and *cover up the AI and DG* to prevent any more distracting visual inputs. (If nothing else, isn't that the way you trained for partial-panel?)

Which Way Salvation?

Unless your partial-panel problems cropped up on a perfectly aligned final approach to an airport, you'll have to change heading occasionally to get on the ground. The magnetic compass is suddenly worth its weight in gold, but there are serious, dangerous problems involved with its use in lieu of a DG. You were taught way back in private-pilot groundschool that there is only one condition of flight in which the magnetic compass is reliable . . . straight and level, unaccelerated (no airspeed change in progress). Oh, there are methods of accounting for compass errors, but they are not suited for use in this situation.

A far more reliable and *easy* method of heading change on partial panel is the timed turn. Get good at this, and you can forget about compass errors; the so-called "whiskey compass" becomes nothing more than a device for confirmation that what you have done is correct. This technique is based on the standard-rate turn, or a heading change of three degrees per second; all turn indicators are marked to indicate when that rate of turn is achieved. If your goal is to change heading to the right thirty degrees, note the reading on the mag compass (to provide a starting and ending point), apply smooth, gentle pressure on the right rudder pedal until the turn indicator shows a standard-rate turn, and at the end of ten seconds, apply left rudder pressure to stop the turn.

It's very important that you start the *timing* when you start the *pressure* to begin the turn, and start the roll-out *pressure* when the proper time has elapsed. There's no way to do this right without practice; with the AI and DG covered, run through the proficiency exercises in Chapter 21, with emphasis on developing your roll-in and roll-out timing.

The magnetic compass must be used *only* to check heading before or after a turn. There are too many opportunities for confusion and disorientation to make it useful in any other mode. If a controller requests a turn, or if you need to change heading on your own, *always* take a few seconds to check the reading on the mag compass while it's stabilized. And when you roll out, give the compass a few seconds to settle down before taking any rash measures to correct your heading.

When only small heading changes are required, press on the rudder pedal until the needle or airplane symbol has deflected one-third of the standard-rate indication, and count the degrees of turn at one per second. Better to make two or three very small corrections and wind up where you want to be, than one huge heading change that throws everything out of kilter.

The Secret of Altitude Control

With no direct indication of airplane altitude, you'll find it rather difficult to establish consistent climbs and descents by trying to combine pitch changes and power settings. But take heart, there's a one-input way to change altitude, and it works every time.

Consider for a moment the aerodynamics of elevator trim. When your airplane is settled in level flight at a given airspeed, with all control-column pressure trimmed away and your hands off the wheel, the elevator is responsive only to changes in airspeed. If power is increased, the nose will pitch up in an attempt to maintain that trim speed, and the result is a climb—*at or very close to the airspeed for which you've trimmed*. Reduce power a bit, and the nose will drop slightly, just enough to maintain the trim speed. Voilà! A descent, with absolutely no pilot input except the power change.

Most light airplanes will respond predictably to power changes. An increase of 5 inches of manifold pressure or 500 RPM will produce roughly a 500 fpm climb; reduce power the same amount, and you can count on approximately a 500 fpm descent. These are vertical speeds that will surely suffice for getting down to approach altitude, and if you plan properly, 500 fpm will also do a creditable job of descending to minimums on an instrument approach.

Single-engine propeller-driven airplanes are particularly susceptible to yaw effects when power is changed. Bear in mind that when increasing power, you must counter the left yaw with pressure on the right rudder. How much? Just enough to keep the turn needle from moving . . . and remember that you'll need to *maintain* that right-rudder pressure throughout the higher-power operation. The opposite will be true when power is reduced. Bottom line—if you don't want the airplane to turn, use whatever rudder pressure is required to prevent that.

Some airplanes tend to climb and/or descend at airspeeds slightly different than trim speed, so once again, experiment with your airplane *before* the vacuum pump goes out, and you'll know what to expect. In any event, it's hands-off-the-wheel time again; when an altitude change is required, do it with power . . . pitch will take care of itself.

The Partial-Panel Approach

A recent informal survey of a number of "average" instrument pilots showed that almost all of them preferred an ILS approach when operating on partial panel. Sound thinking, since the ILS promises the best chance of finding the runway in bad weather . . . and when you are in a partial-panel situation, don't turn down anything that will help you get on the ground safely.

An airport equipped with ILS will more than likely have a radar approach control facility, which means that you won't have to do all the navigating yourself. Be sure the approach controller knows of your plight, and you'll probably be provided a "no-gyro" approach . . . one in which "turn right/left" and "stop turn" commands replace assignment of specific headings. Timed turns (three degrees per second) are assumed in this case, and the controller will start/ stop your turns to line you up with the final approach course for an instrument procedure, or one of the runways. Use the same steady, measured rates of roll-in and roll-out you've practiced, commencing rudder pressure on the controller's commands.

In the case of a non-precision, no-radar approach at the end of your partial-panel problem, fly the procedure exactly the way it's published, with no short-cuts. Give yourself extra time on all the segments. This is no time to be rushed; do it right the first time.

Pilots of retractables have a distinct advantage at this point, because the landing gear makes a very effective supplementary altitude control. In level flight with gear retracted, the amount of thrust is exactly that required to maintain altitude; the drag of extended wheels has the same effect as reducing power, and most light retractables will descend at about 500 fpm in this condition—again, no pitch inputs required from the pilot! In order to level off with gear extended, it's necessary only to add enough power to make up for the gear drag. How much? Whatever is required to stop the altimeter from unwinding.

In the unlikely event of a missed approach, the pilot of a retractable needs only raise the landing gear, removing drag, and the airplane will enter a climb—shallow, but a climb—with no more action than the flip of a switch. You'll also notice that because there's no power change, there's no yaw induced when entering or terminating a descent with the landing gear.

Easier Said than Done

Reading all this in the comfort of your favorite chair, in a room that you *know* isn't going to spiral into the ground, the spectre of partial-panel seems completely manageable. In the real world, however, you'll find that a completely different set of circumstances exists. Loss of your primary attitude instruments in the clouds is going to be scary, and filled with potential for a genuine catastrophe. Survival probably depends in great measure on your state of mind, and you can get rid of some of the anxiety by letting someone (probably a controller) know of your problem early on.

Preparation and practice are undeniably helpful in holding the partial-panel monster at a respectable distance. Any of the proficiency exercises in Chapter 21 will provide ample opportunity for development of your partial-panel skills. Don't be satisfied until your control of the airplane is *good*, and don't let up—stay proficient with frequent and regular practice. It's the *only* way to fly.

That "spate of instrument-failure accidents" we mentioned at the outset of this chapter seemed to focus on the Cessna 210; there were numerous instances of vacuum pump failures in these airplanes in the late 70s and early 80s. The subsequent partial-panel experiences proved catastrophic for a number of pilots, including this one, who jumped from the frying pan into the fire.

The preflight briefing indicated a significant cold front oriented northeast-to-southwest, lying across the route of the northbound flight. However, tops were reported at 10,000–12,000 feet, and the pilot elected to climb over the clouds, out of the icing and turbulence.

Just a few minutes after leveling at 12,000 feet, the pilot announced "I've lost vacuum, I'd like immmediate clearance back to Knoxville" (the departure point). Center complied right away; "cleared direct Knoxville, descend and maintain eight thousand."

A minute later, the controller had coordinated a lower altitude, and cleared the flight to 6,000 feet, but the pilot replied "we're still at twelve five." Center offered a "pilot's discretion" clearance to 6,000, and the pilot indicated that he was on his way down, didn't need any special handling, and that "everything's okay except the vacuum." In less than three minutes, the C210 had spiraled into the ground, with no survivors . . . spatial disorientation strikes again.

This pilot was acutely aware of his problem, and even though the airplane was probably on top when the vacuum failure was detected, he chose to descend through the clouds to get back to the departure airport.

Post-accident investigation revealed that clear weather existed only 50 miles to the east, ahead of the cold front. Why didn't the pilot stay above the clouds where he had a natural horizon? Why didn't he ask for more weather information, or at least proceed eastbound, where basic weather principles would suggest better conditions?

There are no answers to those questions . . . but if a similar situation ever happens to you, take a close look at *all* the options before you plunge into the clouds with less than a full instrument panel.

5

IFR Flight Plans

It's awfully nice to have the flexibility of filing or not filing a VFR flight plan, being able more or less to come and go as you please, yet having the protection of a flight plan when you want it. When the weather slides downhill, and instrument flight is necessary, the rules change, and there is no longer a choice for the pilot operating in controlled airspace. Flight plans are a way of life for instrument pilots; they're an absolute necessity for IFR in controlled airspace. Whether it's filed formally by filling out the form and handing it across the counter to the Flight Service Specialist, or filed in abbreviated form by a radio transmission to Center, you must have a flight plan on file to be legal. Use of the proper filing procedures and a full understanding of what happens when you file can save considerable time, make your IFR operations more efficient, and enable the system to serve you better.

There are several ways you can file a flight plan with a Flight Service Station—in person, by telephone, or by radio—but they share one commonality: The form on which your request is recorded is as standard as peas in a pod. Whether you file IFR three times a day or once a month, you can exhibit professionalism and save a lot of time by studying the flight plan form and using its sequence every time. You can pick up a pad or two at any Flight Service Station, and you even get a bonus—if you like to use a flight log, there's one printed on the back side of the form. That's efficiency; one piece of paper doing two jobs and making for a neater cockpit.

This flight plan form (Figure 2) is essentially the same one the FSS specialist reaches for when you call and say you would like to file a flight plan. Notice that each block on the form contains a question to which you are going to supply the answer, so there is no need to repeat the name of the item when filing. Recognizing that there will be times when you'll file without using the form, you should memorize the sequence, or carry a list of these items in the right order; a properly filed flight plan should consist of a series of numbers, abbreviations, and names—no questions, please, just the answers! Whenever you file and the specialist has to ask you to repeat something, you haven't done it right.

Get Off to a Good Start

Assuming that you have received a weather briefing, decided on a route, and are filing with FSS by telephone , you can provide the information for the first two items right off the bat by saying slowly, "This is Barnburner 1234 Alpha with an IFR flight plan." When the man on the other end of the line rejoins with "go ahead," he will have inserted your aircraft number and type of flight plan in Blocks #1 and #2. (DVFR will be discussed later in this chapter.) You've blown the quest for efficiency if you repeat these items, so charge on, beginning with Block #3.

Figure 2 Flight plan form, properly completed for the Barnburner's proposed journey from Nashville to Bowling Green. There is a flight log on the reverse side.

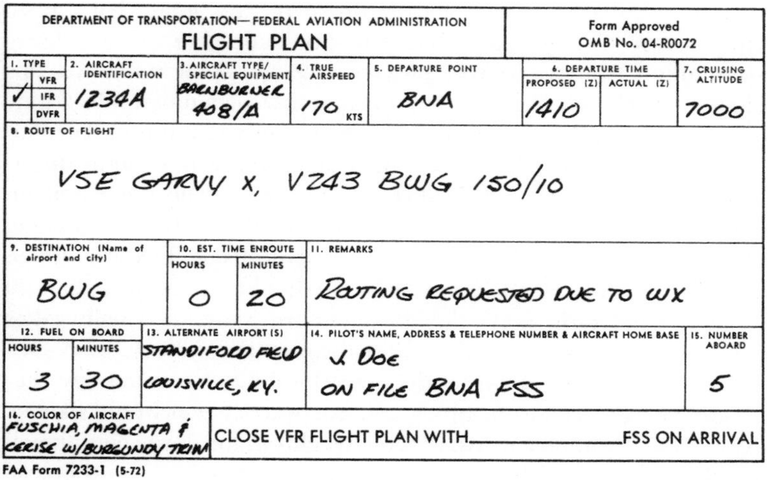
DEPARTMENT OF TRANSPORTATION— FEDERAL AVIATION ADMINISTRATION
FLIGHT PLAN
Form Approved
OMB No. 04-R0072

1. TYPE: VFR / ✓ IFR / DVFR
2. AIRCRAFT IDENTIFICATION: 1234A
3. AIRCRAFT TYPE/ SPECIAL EQUIPMENT: BARNBURNER 408/A
4. TRUE AIRSPEED: 170 KTS
5. DEPARTURE POINT: BNA
6. DEPARTURE TIME: PROPOSED (Z) 1410; ACTUAL (Z)
7. CRUISING ALTITUDE: 7000
8. ROUTE OF FLIGHT: V5E GARVY X, V243 BWG 150/10
9. DESTINATION (Name of airport and city): BWG
10. EST. TIME ENROUTE: HOURS 0; MINUTES 20
11. REMARKS: ROUTING REQUESTED DUE TO WX
12. FUEL ON BOARD: HOURS 3; MINUTES 30
13. ALTERNATE AIRPORT (S): STANDIFORD FIELD LOUISVILLE, KY.
14. PILOT'S NAME, ADDRESS & TELEPHONE NUMBER & AIRCRAFT HOME BASE: J. DOE ON FILE BNA FSS
15. NUMBER ABOARD: 5
16. COLOR OF AIRCRAFT: FUSCHIA, MAGENTA & CERISE W/BURGUNDY TRIM
CLOSE VFR FLIGHT PLAN WITH__________FSS ON ARRIVAL
FAA Form 7233-1 (5-72)

"Aircraft type" deserves some emphasis—Cessna or Piper or Beech by themselves don't tell the story, so make your description adequate. Use model numbers for most airplanes, i.e., Cessna 182, PA-28, BE-20. Everyone knows that a DC-3 is a Douglas, and nobody but Beechcraft has ever built a D-18, but who ever heard of a "Barnburner"?—it would be prudent therefore to refer to your flying machine as a specific model of Barnburner.

In this same block, an indication of special navigation equipment is requested; passed along to Center, it is vital information bearing on subsequent clearances and requests for position reports. Know which suffix applies to your airplane; if you fly several variously equipped aircraft, you might want to make a note of the suffix code:

/X   No transponder
/T   Transponder with no altitude encoding capability
/U   Transponder with altitude encoding capability
/D   DME, no transponder
/B   DME, transponder with no altitude encoding capability
/A   DME, transponder with altitude encoding capability
/C   RNAV, transponder with no altitude encoding capability
/R   RNAV, transponder with altitude encoding capability
/W   RNAV, no transponder

Moving on to Block #4, true airspeed, say only the numbers, such as "one seven zero." This figure may vary somewhat due to temperature changes aloft, but you should be able to hit it fairly accurately. Experience will provide a workable number for this block, but when in doubt, use indicated cruise airspeed plus 2 percent for each 1,000 feet above sea level, and you'll not be far off.

Block #5 should be the airport's official three-character designator (such as IND, LAX, 3G4, etc.) or the airport name if no designator has been assigned, and Block #6 should be a reasonable estimate of the time you expect to be ready for takeoff. Always given in Zulu, or Greenwich Mean Time, it should not be less than 30 minutes from right now, the time you are filing. It usually takes that long for your proposal to filter through the system, from FSS to Center and back to Ground Control or Clearance Delivery, depending on the airport facilities. If you need to get airborne sooner, explain the situation and ask FSS to expedite your clearance—they'll do all they can to help, but it is ultimately up to Center to fit you into the traffic flow. The busier the terminal, the slower this process will be, but it's worth a try. Some very busy areas (Chicago, New York, Los Angeles, for example) would like to have your request at least an hour before departure. Since you're dealing with Zulu time, know what the conversion factor is and don't ask the specialist to do your arithmetic for you—time zones and the formula for each are found on IFR enroute charts.

If it appears that you will be be able to make your proposed takeoff time, you have a responsibility to let ATC know about it; as soon as your flight plan request comes into the Center, tentative plans are made to accept it into the system. The computer will usually hold your request for an hour after the ETD, and you should amend this time if you can't possibly make it. It's simply a matter of calling FSS or Tower and asking them to revise your estimated time of departure—they'll appreciate your cooperation, and can then let someone else use the airspace they were holding for you. It's the old "golden rule" trick.

Your altitude request (Block #7) is based on a number of factors such as winds, weather, and minimum enroute altitudes, and should be decided upon before filing. You should observe the hemispheric separation rules—eastbound, request *odd* altitudes; westbound, request *even* altitudes. The key word here is "request," because an IFR flight will always be assigned an altitude by ATC. Don't argue about "maintain niner thousand" on a westbound flight; the Controller has a good reason for it, and will probably amend your clearance later on. If you are filing in the High Altitude Route Structure (18,000 feet and above), the same general rules apply until you reach FL 290 and above—altimeter errors can really build up at these levels, and so 2,000-foot separation is required. "East—odd, west—even" falls apart. (Refer to Chapter 5 in *Weather Flying* for a detailed analysis of what altitude to select with respect to the enroute weather).

Block #8 can be either delightfully succinct or unnecessarily complicated, depending on your knowledge of what you can and cannot do when planning the route for your flight. (This chapter is concerned only with the language you should use when filing the flight plan; "Preflight Planning," Chapter 6, goes into detail about airways to choose, departure routes, etc.) The route for any IFR flight, no matter how short, must be made up of three segments: departure, enroute, and arrival. You leap off from one airport (departure), navigate to some radio fix (enroute), from which you can execute an approach to another airport (arrival). If you will keep this sequence in mind as you file, it will cut down the number of words required to communicate your request to ATC.

The departure phase can consist of a SID (Standard Instrument Departure), radar vectors, direct flight to a VOR, or immediate interception of an airway (if it's reasonably close to the departure airport). So, your initial response for Block #8 should be a concise description of how you intend to get to your first fix; for example, "Briefcase Two Departure to ALB" (identifier of the first VOR), or "radar vectors to ALB," or "direct ALB," or "Victor 14 to ALB."

If you harbor a suppressed desire to drive everybody in ATC right up the walls of their windowless control rooms, make it a habit to choose the most complicated, zig-zagging routes, using all the airways on the chart. Or make it easy on yourself and the system by picking out an established route, using wherever possible just one numbered airway to get where you're going. When you reel off the enroute portion of Block #8, use the Victor airway numbers and VOR identifiers.

More often than not, one airway will do the job—for example, referring to Figure 3, consider a flight from Nashville, Tennessee (BNA), to Bowling Green, Kentucky (BWG)—Victor 5 runs straight as a die between the two airports, so why not file that way? "Victor 5 BWG" is all you need to say to tell the FSS man everything he needs to know about the departure and enroute segments. You've already mentioned the airport from which you're departing, and the next block is reserved for destination airport—the enroute portion should always wind up with the last radio fix you intend to use.

But suppose you're made aware of a line of thunderstorms along Victor 5, and you decide—very wisely—to take an eastern detour. File "Victor 5E Garvy intersection, Victor 243 BWG." Were Horace Greeley planning the flight, he would likely go west, and that's no problem, except that the airway change does not occur at a named intersection, so the flight plan should go like this: "Victor 7E, Victor 49 BWG."

In any event, make certain that the final entry in Block #8, "Route of Flight," is a *radio facility* or an easily recognized navigational fix; in case you lose communications, everyone will know exactly where you intend to go before commencing an approach to

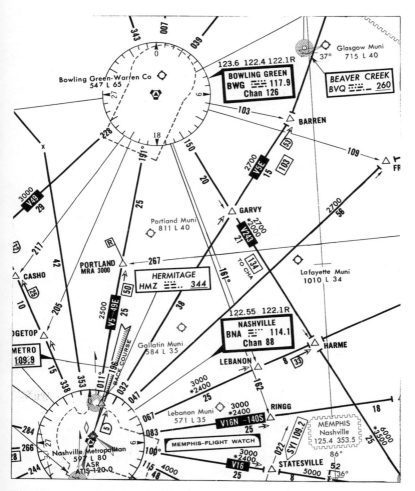

FIGURE 3 Airways and navigational facilities between Nashville, Tenn., and Bowling Green, Ky.

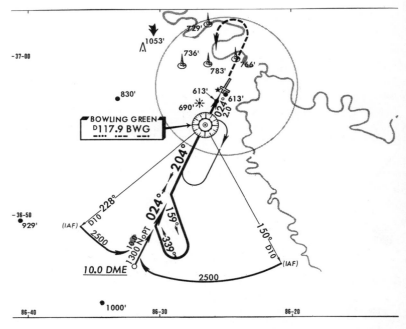

Figure 4 Bowling Green, Ky.

the airport. In Figure 4, the plan view of the VOR Runway 3 pro-
cedure for Bowling Green, it's obvious that when approaching on
Victor 5 you are nearly lined up with the final course, and the Center
Controller would most likely issue a vector to intercept the 204
radial when you were close enough. But notice that the two IAFs
(Initial Approach Fixes) are located conveniently ten miles from the
VOR on the airways leading to BWG from southwest and southeast.
Should you be approaching from these directions, it would be sensible to end the "Route of Flight"with the appropriate IAF; for
example, V5E GARVY, V243 BWG 150010 . . . which tells the computer that you'd like to begin your approach from the BWG 150
radial, 10 miles out.

There are times when it's advantageous to file direct, off-airways
routes, and your flight plan should consist of the first and last VORs
you intend using, with the identifiers of the ones in between that

will serve as checkpoints—"LVT, BWG, CCT, MWA," for example. (The restrictions that apply to off-airways flight are detailed in Chapter 6.)

Having dealt with the departure and enroute phases of filing, turn your attention to the arrival portion. For planning purposes, the enroute portion of an IFR flight terminates over a convenient IAF or the navaid itself when IAFs are not designated on the chart; the published approach procedure will get you from there to the airport. Since the Bowling Green Airport is located only a couple of miles from the VOR, your complete route of flight is covered with "Victor 5 BWG"—you'll receive an approach clearance before getting there, but in case your radios quit, ATC will know what you plan to do. If Glasgow, Kentucky (just east of BWG), were your destination, and Victor 5E did not exist, it would be proper to file "Victor 5 BWG, direct GLW." Of course, the sensible routing for such a flight would be "Victor 5E BVQ," and have it over with— Glasgow is close enough to the airway to use the NDB as a termination fix.

Destination, like point of departure, is adequately identified by the name of the airport, unless there are several terminals in the area. "Bowling Green" would suffice here, since there are no other airports with which it might be confused. Whenever the aerodrome moniker is different from the city name, it's wise to include both in Block #9, so that Approach Control vectors you to the right airport—they'll assume you want to go to Big City Municipal unless you indicate some other airport as your destination.

The reason for estimating your time enroute (Block #10) is not to see how accurately you can preplan an aerial adventure; it's something to hang your hat on when the radios fail and you're wondering when to come down from your lofty, silent perch to begin an approach. In the absence of a more relevant time, your ETE as indicated in the flight plan plus your takeoff time is the answer. (See Chapter 12, "Communications Failure.") When filing the flight plan, it is sufficient to use hours and minutes to the nearest five—just the bare numbers, no further explanation needed.

Block #11 is a catch-all, and rarely used; however, there are times when it can save you (and ATC) time and trouble. In the previous example (Nashville to Bowling Green) you elected to detour to the east because of weather. But this is not the obvious airways route between the two cities, so Center would probably clear you on Victor 5 *unless* you indicated in the Remarks block "Requested routing due to weather." Or in parts of the west where higher altitudes are required, you may wish to impose a personal limit of 10,000 feet for physiological reasons; shortstop any haggling about the route you have chosen by inserting "unable higher than 10,000" in Block #10. This is also the proper place to insert "NO SIDs/STARs" if you haven't the appropriate publications on board. Flying into Canada and some other foreign countries, you can insert the code word "ADCUS" (ADvise CUStoms) so they will be there when you arrive. Anything that bears directly on the operation of your flight can be stated in the Remarks block, but don't try to have ATC let a friend know when you'll be on the ground—that's pushing a bit!

Block #12 (fuel on board) is a "nice to know" sort of thing for Flight Service, but it has no legal significance, since *you* as a pilot in command are responsible for having the proper amount of petrol in the tanks at the start of every IFR flight. (This rule is also discussed in Chapter 6, "Preflight Planning," and is a regulation which should never, never be broken, or even bent.) Having your endurance figure on record can help Flight Service in a search and rescue situation, since it will at least give them a rough idea of how far you might have flown. This block should also be addressed with hours and minutes to the nearest five, such a "four plus four five," or "three plus two zero." Max Conrad's flight plans for his long-distance record attempts in a single-engine, four-place lightplane with more than fifty hours' fuel on board must have raised an FSS eyebrow or two!

The selection of an alternate airport (if, indeed, one is required at all) is a rather complicated process, and is treated in depth in Chapter 6, "Preflight Planning"; the concern here is the proper way to express it to Flight Service, and Block #13 needs nothing more than the identifier (or name) of the airport. If it is something other than a self-explanatory name, include the city or town nearby.

Block #14 can have legal implications if there is more than one qualified pilot on board. The name that you use to fill this space will probably be the one tagged "pilot in command" should any court action arise as a result of this flight. If you're filing for someone else and he's willing to let you use his name, that's his business;

but he should understand that the responsibility for the flight will probably be his—it's now part of the record. Initials and last names are sufficient.

Now you have a real opportunity to save time; if you haven't done it already, pick up the phone and call the Flight Service Station serving the area in which you operate most of the time. Tell them you would like to put your name, address, phone number, and home base on file. Then, even if you are filing a flight plan from as far away as Coldernell, Alaska, all you need to say when you get to Block #14 is "J. Doe, on file at Hometown Flight Service." No matter where you roam in the IFR system, this will be enough to identify you, should the occasion arise.

"Number of persons aboard" (Block #16) is requested only for the customs people on international flights, and you are not really required to furnish this information for domestic trips. (Besides, there may be times when it's nobody's business how many people are on the airplane!) But for possible rescue purposes, tell Flight Service how many souls on board—just speak the number. "Souls on Board" is often abbreviated SOB, and there will be times when you list five SOB's on your airplane and *mean* it!

"Fuschia, magenta, and cerise with burgundy trim" is a rather wild color scheme for an airplane, and the FSS man would probably figure he had a real nut on the line if you indicated that for Block #17. What they want here are the predominant aircraft colors, useful information should you alight at some location other than the one you had planned—like a mountainside, or in the desert without benefit of an airport. When you stop to think about it, "fuschia, magenta, and cerise with burgundy trim" is not so strange for an airplane with a name like "Barnburner."

All that's left to do is file the flight plan, so ring up the local FSS and in total, using the eastern detour for weather, the trip from Nashville to Bowling Green should be filed like this:

FSS: Good morning, Nashville Flight Service, Hawkshaw speaking.
YOU: Good morning, this is Barnburner 1234 Alpha with an IFR flight plan.
FSS: [*After a slight pause to write in Blocks #1 and #2*] Go ahead with your flight plan.
YOU: [*Take it from Block #3*] Barnburner four zero eight slash

alpha, one seven zero, Nashville Metro, one four one zero, seven thousand; Victor 5E Garvy intersection, Victor two four three BWG one-fifty slash one zero, Bowling Green, zero plus two zero, routing requested due to weather, three plus three zero; Standiford Field, Louisville [*or "not required" if that is the case*]; J. Doe, on file at Nashville Flight Service; five; fuschia, magenta, and cerise with burgundy trim.

FSS: [*After recovering from hysteria over that color scheme*] Roger, we'll put it on file; have a good trip.

If you have done your homework, thought out your statements, and filed the flight plan "by the numbers," the whole procedure will take about one minute; a definite time-saver for both parties, and you have invested yourself with an aura of professionalism.

Same Thing, But This Time by Radio

Filing a flight plan from the air usually results from one of two situations: You have encountered unexpected weather on a route that appeared VFR from the forecasts, or you want to have an IFR flight plan ready for the next leg of your trip. Of course, you can file a whole series of flight plans with the original FSS, and they will pass your requests to the proper people along the route. But this is not always feasible, and opens another door to the possibility of your flight plan being lost in the communications shuffle.

An Air Route Traffic Control Center is not in the business of copying flight plan requests, so unless you're really in a bind, don't bother them—take your problem to Flight Service. Once again, having gotten your mind in gear, contact the nearest FSS (it's best to use 122.1 and listen on the VOR) and when the specialist is ready, go through the names and numbers routine just as you did on the telephone. You should include the type of flight plan and your aircraft identification in the initial callup, such as "Broken Bow radio, Barnburner 1234 Alpha with an IFR flight plan, over." When he comes on the line (and it may be a minute or two if he's busy), he'll probably have his pencil poised, ready to copy—start right off with Block #3 when he says "go ahead with your flight plan." From here on, there's no difference in the filing procedure. FSS will tell you either to stand by for your clearance (if you need it shortly, he'll call Center on his direct line and probably get it in a few minutes), or he will tell you when, where, and whom to contact.

So much for getting a flight plan request into the system for a subsequent part of your trip—the other situation grows out of your need to obtain a clearance NOW! Not an emergency, but there you are, in absolutely beautiful VFR without a flight plan of any kind, and discover that your destination airport has just gone IFR. You can go from the ridiculous to the sublime, starting with a Unicom call to Irma at the FBO (Friendly Base Operator), and giving her the information to call to Flight Service. You'll be obliged to wait, remaining VFR of course, until she calls FSS, they call Center, who eventually returns the clearance to FSS, who calls Irma, who calls you back. Or you could contact FSS yourself, wait until they call the request to Center, wait until the controller decides he can accept your flight, and wait until the Flight Service Station calls you back with the clearance. By the time all this has taken place, you might as well have landed, placed the call to FSS from the phone booth, and had a cup of coffee with Irma! The same lag in communications, though not so extreme, exists when you contact Flight Service by radio, and again "waiting" is the key word—why not contact Center directly, since you are only asking for clearance into the terminal area to make an approach? (Or if you can get into the terminal area VFR, call Approach Control.)

The first job is to find the proper frequency on which to call Center; your enroute chart provides this information. Each ARTCC area of responsibility is subdivided geographically, and the chart shows the coverage of these sectors. In the general area of the symbol (Figure 5), the Walnut Ridge sector of Memphis Center has control. *Always* use the Center name, never that of the sector. Flying in the vicinity of the Walnut Ridge VOR, the proper frequency for Memphis Center is 127.4. Make your first call a short one, in case Center is busy—"Memphis Center, Barnburner 1234 Alpha." When they answer, the following dialogue might take place:

YOU: Memphis Center, Barnburner 1234 Alpha, ten miles east of Walnut Ridge, eight thousand five hundred, VFR, requesting clearance to Walnut Ridge Municipal. [*If the controller is too*

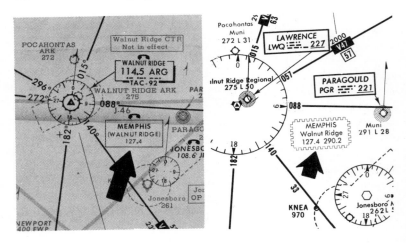

FIGURE 5   Symbols used to identify Air Route Traffic Control Center sectors (*left, Jeppesen; right, U.S.*).

busy to handle your request, he'll tell you so, and ask you to contact the nearest FSS for clearance; but more than likely, he will come back with—]

CENTER: Roger, 34 Alpha, squawk ident; are you IFR-rated and -equipped?

YOU: [*Pressing the ident button*] Affirmative.

CENTER: Barnburner 1234 Alpha, you're in radar contact, cleared from your present position direct to the Walnut Ridge VOR, descend to and maintain six thousand, say your aircraft type and true airspeed.

YOU: Barnburner 34 Alpha is cleared from present position direct to the Walnut Ridge VOR at six thousand; it's a Barnburner four zero eight, true airspeed one seven zero.

CENTER: 34 Alpha, Roger; expect a VOR Runway 27 approach at Walnut Ridge. By the way, is that the airplane with the weird paint job?

That's all there is to it; you're in the system, and can now proceed just as if you had been IFR all the way. A very efficient short-cut to the full-blown filing process, this method is much faster than going through Flight Service, although it is somewhat less preferable to filing IFR from the beginning. Don't expect this kind of service in one of the high-density terminal areas like Chicago or New York—they just don't have the time—but in less busy parts of the country, your request will almost always be granted.

And if you're not in a hurry, stop and see Irma anyway.

IFR Flight Plan to a Non-IFR Airport

There are literally thousands of small airports around the country which are used every day by general aviation pilots without the benefit of an instrument approach. Some of them lie in uncontrolled airspace, and are not subject to the IFR rules. But there are many in controlled airspace to which operations are conducted quite legally when the weather prevents VFR flight all the way. If there is an airport close by with a published procedure, you may be able to make the approach there, break it off when under the clouds, and proceed to your "little airport" destination. This is a good plan, but only under certain conditions: You must be absolutely sure that the weather will permit a safe VFR operation from the end of the published approach to the non-IFR airport; the approach used to get you down to VFR conditions should not lead to a "No Special VFR" airport if the weather is pushing visual minimums; you should be prepared to land at the IFR airport if things go down the drain.

Every bit as important as the other considerations is your responsibility to communicate to ATC your intentions as early in the flight as possible, preferably in the remarks block of your flight plan request ("will proceed VFR to Little Airport"). You'll earn the undying enmity of the controllers if you wait until you're on final approach and fitted neatly into the landing sequence to let them know that you are going to "break it off" and go to some other airport. There is usually no problem if you will just make your desires known early in the game. It's a completely legal procedure and can work to your advantage under the proper conditions; it appears underhanded and less than professional when a pilot tries to "sneak" an approach for the purpose of proceeding to a non-IFR field. Unless you will present a traffic hazard for them, ATC will go along with you, sometimes even supplying vectors to the other airport.

IFR Flight Plans from a "No-Facility" Airport

Well, here you are, back at the airport after a day's work with your clients in West Snowshoe, Montana. When you arrived this morning, the sun was shining from a clear blue sky, the weatherman promised a continuation of the same, and it looked like a perfect day. Now, preflighting the Barnburner in cold rain falling from a 500-foot overcast, you're not so sure. Besides that, the airport offices are closed—thank the gods that look out for pilots there's a telephone booth outside the hangar.

All is not lost, because there is still a way to obtain a clearance under these conditions; the only requirement is that you are able to contact someone in ATC—a Flight Service Station, or nearby Tower, or perhaps Center. If you can take off and maintain VFR while you file your flight plan and receive clearance, that's the way to do it, but it will cost you some air time (that's another way of saying *money*) as you fly around waiting for permission to enter the system.

A more efficient way to get the job done is to call the nearest FSS on the phone, explain the situation, and file a flight plan, with the additional request for a "void time" clearance. (Choose the route and altitude to the first fix with great care, because you will be entirely on your own until ATC acquires you on radar. File so as to get on an airway as soon as you can, to take advantage of the guaranteed terrain and obstacle clearance. It may be necessary to refer to a sectional chart to make sure you know the elevations along your route to the first fix.) Under these conditions, Flight Service will likely ask you to stand by, and will call your flight plan request directly to the governing Center while you wait; bear in mind that this procedure is almost always undertaken from an out-of-the-way airport, and there will probably be little if any traffic in the immediate area. When a delay is probable, Flight Service will have you call back in a few minutes, or will take your phone number and call *you* back; the latter is especially important when you have no more quarters.

If Center can handle your flight at this time, your clearance will be issued with the stipulation that you take off no later than a specified time. Your clearance will end with "void if not airborne by such-and-such a time," and you can bet that the deadline imposed by the void time will not be very far from right now! If it is too close for comfort, tell the FSS specialist and it will be revised. In anticipation of this, figure how long it will take you to board your passengers, get the bird warmed up and taxied to the runway before you call for a void time clearance. Better yet, load the people in the plane, check the engines, and *then* go to the phone booth— when you get the clearance, make like an Olympic 100-yard dasher back to the airplane.

It is important to get ready for a ten-or-fifteen-minutes-from-now void time, because Center doesn't want to hold airspace open any longer than necessary. If ATC hasn't heard from you shortly after the void time, they assume that you have taken off and suffered communications failure, and must therefore open up routes and altitudes for your entire proposed trip, just in case. This is one of those situations when a good pilot can exercise his judgment, and refuse a void time that is too close—remember that you will be taking off into IFR conditions (otherwise you wouldn't be bothered with the void time at all) and this is no time to be pushed by a pair of hands racing around a clock face. When you file your flight plan with FSS, let them know that because of the distance to the runway, or warmup problems, or whatever, you cannot possibly be off the ground in less than twenty minutes (or a reasonable length of time according to the situation). FSS will pass this on to Center, and they'll more than likely respect your problem. From the time you enter the clouds, this type of clearance is not a whit different than any other, and all the rules of IFR operations apply.

You can help yourself by anticipating the need for a "void time" clearance. Suppose that during the afternoon in beautiful downtown West Snowshoe you noticed the clouds beginning to thicken. If you suspect IFR conditions for your takeoff in the evening, call Flight Service and file your flight plan in advance, with the expectation of needing a void time. The FSS specialist may even be one step ahead of you (there's not much else to do in the Flight Service Station at West Snowshoe) and have a clearance waiting when you call.

Having received a void-time clearance, you must respect its limitations as if it meant life or death, which it might. Be sure your watch agrees with ATC time, and do all within your power to leave terra firma not one second past the appropriate mark. It's legal and proper to jump into the sky anytime between the time you receive your clearance and the void time, but very illegal and quite improper to do so later. If you can't quite cut it (and fuel-injected engines invariably choose a situation like this not to start), shut everything down, swear a lot, run through the rain to the phone booth, call Flight Service, and start all over again. It might be wise to toss a couple of quarters into the glove box of your airplane next time you fly; you never can tell when your passengers might be as broke as you are!

Restricted, Warning, Prohibited Areas, ADIZs

When it comes to flying through restricted airspace, happiness is having the word "instrument" on your pilot certificate. As long as you plan your flight on the established Victor airways, you can rest assured that ATC will not let you traverse any airspace which is also being used by artillery shells, rockets, or the annual meeting of the United States High Altitude Kite Flying Association. When you ask for a direct, off-airways routing that will cross through restricted airspace, your request will not be honored unless and until the ATC facility with which you are working has coordinated with the using agency and made certain that it will be safe for you to pass. Whether you're operating on a clearance or not, be extremely alert when in or near a Military Operations Area; especially when they're about the business of training young aerial warriors, the high speed and small profile of training aircraft makes them very difficult to see.

A PROHIBITED AREA is the most restrictive of all the limited-use airspace, and its label means exactly what it says. If it appears that an IFR clearance will take you through such airspace, it would be wise to query the Controller; get the monkey off your back. (When you're on a VFR flight, trespass of a Prohibited Area might get you an audience with somebody in the FAA, maybe even the CIA.)

IFR and ADIZs (Air Defense Identification Zones)

National security is the only purpose for establishing ADIZs, and they are primarily concerned with aircraft approaching our shores and borders from the outside in. There is a part of the Federal

Aviation Regulations set aside to describe this airspace and to lay down the laws for operating therein. Again, happiness is having an instrument rating, because your ATC clearance into or through an ADIZ takes care of all the reporting and filing requirements. There is a flight plan option (DVFR, Defense Visual Flight Rules) for pilots who wish to fly through an ADIZ without filing IFR, but once you have the rating, why not use it, whether there's a cloud in the sky or not? Of course, if you happen to be an aerial photography buff and would like to get some closeup shots of our Air Force's finest interceptors, fly out to sea a hundred miles or so, then turn around and head for shore, fast. You'll get your pictures, they'll get theirs, and in addition you will be given the opportunity to sit down for a friendly chat with representatives of several government agencies!

The ADIZ rules do not apply to any aircraft operating at less than 180 knots TAS north of 25° N. Latitude, nor west of 85° W. Longitude, unless it's a flight from Mexico to the U.S. But the same philosophy that kept you out of trouble in other types of restricted areas will work just as well here—when in doubt, file IFR, get a clearance, and you're home free. ATC knows where you are, who you are, where you're going to and coming from, and when this information is passed along to the Air Defense Command people, everybody's happy.

6

Preflight Planning

IT WAS spelled out in letters a foot high, above the door to the flight line at a military pilot training base: "PLAN YOUR FLIGHT, AND FLY YOUR PLAN!"—a good piece of advice for any pilot. When you're flying IFR, there will be diversions and changes and non-standard procedures, and on occasion ATC may require you to go rather far outside the routing or altitude or timing you had planned for the flight; but having a plan puts you in the driver's seat right from the start. When changes come up, you have at your fingertips the information you need to make a decision; go or no-go, accept a clearance or reject it, try an approach or go directly to your alternate. You're asking for trouble when you leap into the clouds knowing nothing of the enroute weather or wind, or where you can go if everything turns sour.

A Preflight Checklist

No one is going to double-check your preflight planning, so it's up to you to do it right every time. The easiest and surest way to accomplish this is to do it the same way every time—use some kind of checklist, or at least a routine information-gathering and decision-making process that leaves nothing out of the planning picture. Looking at the situation through real-world glasses, there will be many short IFR trips that don't require in-depth preparation of the sort you should go through for an extended aerial journey, especially into strange territory. However, when you form good habits, you will tend to include the critical items even though you're planning a short, uncomplicated flight.

Charts and Equipment

Like an A&P starting a 100-hour inspection without his toolbox, you will be behind the power curve right away if you try to launch the planning process without the proper equipment. It's true that weather will be the most significant factor in planning, but how can you consider alternate routes around the weather or over more hospitable terrain unless you have the charts handy? The scope of your operations and the type of flying you intend to do determines how many charts you carry around—for basic IFR work, all you need are the appropriate enroute, area, and approach and landing charts. SIDs and STARs are nice to have, especially if you frequently fly into and out of airports where they are used, since they will save you and the Controllers a great deal of time.

The equipment that you have assembled to carry with you into the air is a matter as personal as the clothes you wear—some pilots carry more gear in a Cessna 172 on a thirty-minute flight than a 747 captain needs between New York and Paris! Whatever you settle on as minimum equipment, spend a few dollars for a flight bag of some kind to keep things organized; something that will hold what you need in flight, yet will not interfere with seating or control movement in your airplane. There are a number of specially designed cases on the market that will hold a couple of approach plate binders, your enroute charts, two ham sandwiches, and a paperback novel. There are also cases available that rival steamer trunks for capacity; you have everything you'll ever need, plus a lot of stuff you'll *never* need, and the weight may put you over max gross— leave these to the big-airplane pilots, who really need all that paperwork.

In addition to the charts, you should have a time and distance computer. As your experience grows, you will be able to estimate time enroute very closely by applying an average wind component to the true airspeed of your bird, but for the sake of accuracy, use a computer—especially when the proposed flight is long enough or the headwinds strong enough to generate concern about having sufficient fuel to get where you intend to go. By all means, include a good strong flashlight and a couple of spare batteries—you never know when you might be caught out after dark, and a pack of matches or a cigarette lighter just won't do the job if the electricity quits.

Checking the Weather

Without a doubt, the biggest single factor affecting your planning for an IFR flight is the weather, but you can drive yourself right up the wall worrying about it too far in advance of your trip. The very best the weatherman can do forty-eight hours ahead is to give you a general idea of weather conditions; at twenty-four hours the forecasts become more accurate, but in most cases, you can't really obtain a good picture until just before takeoff. (Of course, this is weather information for *planning* purposes—you should always be checking a tight weather situation right up until you walk out to the airplane, and continue checking it enroute.) Always be thinking of some alternate course of action in case the weather gets worse than you can put up with; if you *must* get somewhere at a certain time, and the forecasts are filled with doom and gloom, reserve an airline seat, plan to drive, or make arrangements to go another day.

When it looks as if the weather is going to put you between a rock and a hard place, get out the instrument charts to determine whether you can make it under the freezing level with respect to the minimum IFR altitudes, or whether there is a convenient detour available. Do you have the range to make it non-stop? Does the destination airport have an approach good enough for the weather they are expecting? Don't take for granted that all ILS approaches will bring you down to 200 feet and a half mile; there are a number of them that have much higher mimimums because of terrain, and the same philosophy applies to all types of instrument approaches—check and be sure. (Chapters 3, 4, and 5 of *Weather Flying* will help you *interpret* the weather information you obtain before an IFR flight.)

Once you have decided you can get from here to there in one piece, there is another source you should consult to prevent an awkward, perhaps expensive situation. It is considered the last word in operational information (short of being there, of course) and bears the name NOTAM—governmentese for NOtices To AirMen. Whenever a radio aid goes out of service, or airport lighting systems fail, or parachute jumping is in progress (how'd you like to have a four-man star suddenly join you in the cockpit of a Cherokee?), or any one of a thousand things that could affect the operation of airplanes, it will be published as a NOTAM on the teletype circuits. It would be embarrassing indeed should you take off for Buffalo in the middle of winter with an airplane full of passengers, and find out halfway there that the only vehicles permitted on the runways today are snowplows! You can sidestep this sort of problem by asking the FSS briefer to check the NOTAMs for you while still in the planning stage.

You should be aware that there are several different types of NOTAMs, and even though you ask, you may not get all the information you need. The sleeper is the Class II NOTAM, which appears in printed form for mail distribution, and which doesn't show up in the course of a normal scan. When you request NOTAMs during a preflight briefing, the specialist looks at the end of the hourly sequence for your destination, or refers to the NOTAM summary. Unfortunately, the Class II NOTAMs don't show up on the screen, and you'll never know unless you specifically request ". . . are there any Class II NOTAMs for East Ipswich?"

An accident at a midwestern airport several years ago points up the potential importance of checking *all* the NOTAMs. Following an uneventful flight from Chicago, the light twin commenced an ILS approach, and was tracked by radar to the vicinity of the outer marker. Shortly thereafter, the airplane broke out of the low overcast in a vertical bank, struck several power lines along the main street of a small town, and crashed into a bookstore.

Pilot disorientaion? Engine failure? Instrument malfunction? We'll never know for sure, because all aboard were killed, and the airplane was completely destroyed by fire.

But an intriguing report was filed by another pilot who flew the same ILS approach an hour after the accident: "I was making an ILS coupled approach when the plane abruptly turned right and assumed a nose-down attitude. The descent rate was 2,000 fpm, and the heading changed approximately 130 degrees. I uncoupled the autopilot and hand-flew the plane to a level attitude, after losing 1,000 feet."

Now, the Class II NOTAMs become significant, because right there on the ILS approach chart is the following limitation: "AU-

TOPILOT COUPLED APPROACH NOT AUTHORIZED." The same information is included in the Class II NOTAMs for that airport.

This is the sort of *very*-nice-to-know information that is published as a Class II NOTAM. There's no evidence that the pilot of the twin requested this information, or that he noticed the restriction on the approach chart. For that matter, there's no evidence that a glitch in the ILS signal caused the accident. But there *is* a requirement (FAR 91.5) that instrument pilots become familiar with all information pertinent to a proposed flight. When in doubt (which should be always!), ASK.

Route and Altitude

At this point, you should have enough weather information to make a choice of route and altitude. Unless a detour is indicated because of meteorological mischief (weather OR winds), you should be looking for the route that will get you where you're going in the shortest possible time—this usually means the nearest thing to a straight line between departure and destination. For long trips, you should consult an IFR planning chart, which shows the airways from coast to coast and border to border. (The Jeppesen service includes such a chart, or you can purchase one from the government.) You'll generally find an airway nearly parallel to the direct route. Unless you look at the big picture, you may miss the airway that goes all the way from point A to point B; filing one airway is so much easier than a bunch of short segments, and it eases the pain for ATC, too.

Listed in the Avigation section of the Jepp charts and in the AIM are the Preferred Routes, with major terminals and the airways that ATC would like you to use when traveling betwixt and between. Preferred Routes are the fastest, most efficient way to go—not always the *shortest*, but they are ultimately the *fastest* because that's the way ATC is going to clear you, so you are better off filing the Preferred Route at the outset. (See Chapter 5, "IFR Flight Plans," for the proper way to file a devious route because of weather or limiting altitudes.)

ATC's Preferred Routes can also be used to advantage when you plan a trip to a point short of the destination terminal mentioned in the route listing—use the Preferred Route as far as you can, and you'll get better service from ATC.

Standard Instrument Departures (SIDs) are really short-range Preferred Routes, limited to the departure phase of an IFR trip, and if you frequently fly from an airport with published SIDs, you'll find it worthwhile to have these charts in your flight kit. When SIDs are in use, plan your flight accordingly, by noticing the point at which the SID injects you into the enroute structure. Your enroute planning should begin at the VOR (or other fix) specified as the end of the SID, and use the Preferred Route, if applicable, from that point to destination.

The ultimate in preflight planning, at least from a routing standpoint, would see you departing under the guidance of a SID, proceeding on your way via a Preferred Route, and winding up the flight with a Standard Terminal Arrival Route (STAR). The key is to realize that the air route structure is a huge system, and where the designers have identified channels (Preferred Routes, SIDs, and STARs) in the system, you are much better off to put yourself there as soon as possible after takeoff, and as early as possible in the terminal area. (If you don't possess SIDs or STARs, don't forget to make mention of that fact in the "Remarks" block of your flight plan. It's the best way to let ATC know of your limitations.)

When a SID isn't published, plan your departure by the most direct route that will get you to a VOR or an airway as soon as possible after takeoff. The outstanding advantage of choosing an airway, direct route, or radial to start your flight is that of definition—you know exactly which way to go in the absence of ATC instructions, or if your radios give up the ghost before you can receive further clearance.

Radar control on departure is the name of the game in IFR flying today—at most terminals, you will be picked up on the magic TV screen almost immediately after takeoff, and the controller will vector you around other traffic and onto your airway route just as expeditiously as he can. If you're not at all sure of the best way to get from the airport into the enroute structure, there's one more way you can get help: Request radar vectors to the first VOR on your route, and Departure Control will lead you by the hand.

There are parts of the country that just don't have any airways headed in the direction you want to go, or which don't connect the particular point A and B you had in mind. So why not devise your own route, direct from one VOR to the next on your intended line of flight? There are no rules against flying direct (off airways), but there are several very important limitations you must consider before undertaking such a course of action.

Right off the top, you should not file a direct IFR flight between VORs that are more than 80 nautical miles apart (this is a low-altitude limit; it's expanded to 260 miles for flights 18,000 feet above). Designed for frequency protection, the 80-mile minimum guarantees that your VOR receiver will not pick up a signal from another station on the same frequency.

Second, you must choose a flight altitude that will provide the same obstruction clearance that is automatically taken care of by airway MEAs and MOCAs—you may have to consult sectional or WAC charts or other topographic references to be sure that your off-airways route is high enough.

Third, your course must be DIRECT—in a straight line between VORs—no doglegs on this trip!

When weather is a factor (turbulence, icing, wind effects), bear in mind that these situations will almost always be at their worst when the terrain provides additional mechanical lifting action. (See *Weather Flying*, Chapter 9, for a discussion of mountain weather flying.)

At an increasing number of airports, stars are coming into use— not heavenly bodies to be wished upon or used for celestial navigation, these STARs are the acronymic way of saying Standard *Ter*minal *A*rrival *R*outes. They are just SIDs in reverse, and provide specific routings *into* the terminal area. When you are flight planning to an airport with a published STAR (the biggies may have several), end the airways portion of your route at the VOR or intersection that is the entry, or gate, to the STAR procedure. Using the STAR when you file your flight plan will save everybody time and trouble, because you won't have to be given a change of routing along the way. STARs are a near-exclusive feature of high-altitude operations.

In summary, you should consider the following order of routing priorities when planning a flight (disregarding deviations for weather):

1. The Preferred Route between departure and destination.
2. Victor airways that work out closest to a straight line between here and there.
3. A direct, off-airways route at an altitude high enough to provide *comfortable* clearance from terrain and obstructions. (1,000 feet above everything 5 miles either side of your course in the flatlands, 2,000 feet in those parts of the country that qualify as mountainous.)

Altitude

Many pilots pay surprisingly little attention to the selection of an IFR altitude, even though it plays a huge part in putting the most miles behind you for the fewest dollars, or making the difference between a miserable experience and an aesthetic adventure. Of course there are some practical limits, like the minimum enroute altitude (MEA), availability of oxygen, and the optimum performance altitude for your plane; turbulence, icing, wind and weather problems cannot be ignored, but they'll be thoroughly hashed out later.

MEAs and optimum performance altitude provide the absolute floor and probable ceiling for a non-supercharged airplane—you can't plan an IFR flight at less than MEA, and unless there's a real whopper of a tailwind, you will probably lose money by climbing above your optimum altitude. (This is usually the highest altitude at which your engine can maintain 65 percent power.) Check the route for the highest MEA—that is eventually going to become your cruise altitude. Although you can file (and be cleared at) a lower altitude before you get to that particular airway segment, ATC will move you up to the MEA at the appropriate time, so plan on it. The abnormally high MEAs will occur over the mountains, because they *must* provide 2,000 feet of obstacle clearance in those areas.

For normally aspirated (unsupercharged) engines, it sometimes comes down to a choice between less performance at high altitude and a much longer route to avoid the higher levels. There's almost always a westerly wind at altitude, so clawing your way up to 12,000 or 13,000 feet in an airplane with an optimum altitude of 7,000 is not necessarily a bad move if you're eastbound—the extra groundspeed on a long trip may easily make up for the time spent in the climb. There's only one way to decide, and that's to dig out the computer and compare the estimated time enroute for the high altitude versus a lower one. (A friend was proceeding eastbound in his non-turbo Bonanza awhile back, taking full advantage of the tailwind at 21,000 feet. An airline captain overheard one of his position reports and said for everybody on the frequency to hear, "What's a *Bonanza* doing at 21,000 feet?" My friend answered with aplomb, "Struggling!")

In general, when weather conditions are not a factor, it is probably better to file just as high as practical, at or above the appropriate MEA, and at or above the optimum altitude for your powerplant. The benefits that accrue to high flight often overcome the extra five or ten minutes spent climbing; and maybe it will put you above an icing level, or keep you out of turbulence, or treat you to groundspeeds you can brag about at the bar. And if nothing else, why not climb up above the choking brown gunk that is the rule rather than the exception over our country these days? Why not climb up into the only place left where you can see forever and, at least for a little while, treat your lungs to some really clean air? There's something to be said for the safety aspects of flying high, too. The very fact that fewer pilots use the higher levels means that there will be less people to run into at altitude; and given the usual situation of being in the clear (at least between cloud layers) when you're operating in the upper reaches of the sky, you'll have much more time to observe and react to other air traffic.

At any rate, give "high-flight" a try on your next few trips, and decide for yourself—keep records of how much time is required to climb to higher altitudes, how much fuel is burned, and the difference in elapsed times for similar wind and weather conditions. Then, compare the hard facts with your memories of the smooth, crystal-clear air up there; remember the pleasant glow you experienced when that first-time-in-an-airplane passenger became a believer after flying high with you.

Distance and Time Enroute

Now that you're settled on the route and altitude, add up the distance from departure point to the initial approach fix or the radio aid serving the destination airport. If you are not in the habit of computing time enroute, or whenever your aerial steed is an unfamiliar one, take the time to figure it out rather precisely. You'll be loading the situation in your favor, but perhaps more importantly, you will be practicing so that as your experience grows, you will be able to estimate the time very accurately with a minimum of paperwork. The basis of the computation is true airspeed, plus or minus a wind component, arriving at an average groundspeed. All three of these speeds will change during the climb, so you will have to add a time factor.

For most light, non-supercharged airplanes, a climb of less than 10,000 feet in still air will add just about five minutes to the time it would take if you were at cruise airspeed all the way. You can figure it out for your bird, but better yet, make a note of the time penalty for climbing to altitude on your next several trips, and you'll soon have a rule of thumb that will stand you in good stead.

Remember that you are asked to estimate your time enroute for only two reasons; so that you'll have enough fuel on board, and to give you and ATC a descent time should the radios fail—nobody really cares how close your estimate is on a routine trip. One thing you *don't* want to do is be ultraconservative and estimate too much time for the journey; if the radios *do* fail, you're going to hold over the destination fix until that time elapses, and if you throw in a half hour "just to be sure," you may regret it on the other end. It's no fun going round and round in a holding pattern for thirty minutes in the clouds without radios, waiting for that ETA to come up—your nerves will be tied in double knots! Be as accurate as you can, but don't spend hours working out the ETE—it's just not worth that much of your time.

Fuel Required

Disregard for fuel requirements is an open invitation for BIG trouble. There's no other situation in aviation that leaves you so frustrated, so helpless, so upset with yourself as when you realize that you haven't enough gas in the tanks to get where you're going. It's bad enough VFR, but the pressure really builds when you're on solid instruments, and it will rapidly bring you to the PMP (Point of Maximum Pucker). The most sensible way to keep from painting yourself into a gasoline corner is to observe an inviolate *one-hour* reserve fuel requirement on ALL flights, and when it appears that headwinds, holding, icing, carburetor heat, traffic delays, or route deviations are eating slowly but surely into your spare gasoline, DO SOMETHING, and do it NOW!

The fuel tanks in most light aircraft are large enough to sustain flight for four or five hours at commonly used power settings—more time than most of us care to sit in a confined space, to say nothing of the problems of human bladder capacity. It's much more comfortable to compute a reasonable maximum "time in the tanks," and vow never to fly more than 75 percent of that time. In a "four-hour" airplane, plan a pit stop at the end of three hours . . . your passengers will love you for it, and you'll never come close to running out of gas.

Whenever you are operating in IFR conditions, you must have on board enough fuel to travel from departure to destination, and have forty-five minutes of fuel remaining, based on the normal cruise fuel consumption of your airplane. Regardless of the fact that you will reduce power whenever you are in a holding pattern, the forty-five-minute requirement at *cruise power* still exists, giving you a little additional cushion in a really tight situation. But this regulation, like all the FARs, is based on a *minimum* standard, so compute the fuel you will use during taxi, takeoff, climb, and cruise at whatever power setting you intend to maintain, subtract that total from the capacity of the airplane tanks, and if the resulting number doesn't correspond to at least one hour at the cruise power setting, you will be foolish to start out on that flight. The alternatives?—plan a fuel stop, or wait for a day when the winds are a little less aggressive.

Provide yourself a solid planning figure with a little experimentation on your next short trip: Start up, taxi, take off, and climb to the highest altitude you normally use; do all this on one fuel tank (or set of tanks). When you level off, switch to a full tank and complete the flight. After landing, note the number of gallons required to top off the first tank—this figure plus the normal cruise fuel consumption rate will produce an accurate yardstick for future flights to make sure you have enough petrol.

Alternate Requirements

It's probably one of the most abused regulations in the IFR book, but treating the alternate rule lightly can get you into serious trouble. Even though Flight Service Station briefers are quite aware of the weather conditions at your destination, seldom if ever will they remind you of the need for an alternate when you are filing a flight plan; the responsibility rests only on the shoulders of the pilot. The regulation that covers IFR alternates is cumbersome, very wordy, and tends to drive pilots away from the consideration it deserves. There is a good rule of thumb that will *usually* do the job for you, and that is to get in the habit of filing an alternate for *every* IFR flight—pick the nearest airport with equal or better approach facilities within comfortable fuel range. Don't count on this procedure as an IFR panacea, but if everything goes down the drain, at least you'll have some place to go. The worst situation imaginable would see you arriving at destination in weather that prohibits a landing, with no alternate filed, followed by a radio communications failure— you don't know *where* to go, ATC doesn't have any idea where you *might* go, and the resulting traffic hysteria would certainly get you an audience with an FAA inspector, if you somehow manage to wander around through the clouds and get down safely without hitting anybody! You owe as much to the other airmen up there in the soup as you owe yourself—so always have an alternate airport planned before you climb aboard your flying machine.

Like most of the rules that govern your aviation adventures, the IFR alternate regulation is restrictive in nature, letting you know what you may *not* do; but it can be reduced to convenient operational terms by asking yourself two questions before every instrument flight:

QUESTION 1 Must I file an alternate airport?
QUESTION 2 What airport may I use for an alternate when one is required?

The answer to the first question depends on both the approach facilities available at destination and the forecast weather conditions for that terminal. If, as is usually the case, your planned destination has a published instrument approach (one the government has approved, not your personal procedure based on radio station WIFR!),

Condition	Must I File?
Destination has no approved approach procedure	Yes
Approach chart published for destination airport	No, unless weather is reported or forecast below specified minimums
Ceiling forecast or reported less than 2,000 feet above airport elevation at any time during ETA ± 1 hour	Yes
Visibility forecast or reported less than 3 miles at any time during ETA ± 1 hour	Yes

you can go on to the weather situation, which will tell you whether or not you need an alternate. But if Destination Municipal Airport has no approved procedure, stop right there—an alternate airport is automatically required; no further questions to be asked!

In a conservative effort to keep you out of trouble, the government has decreed that either one of two weather conditions at destination demand an alternate be filed in your flight plan—one concerns the ceiling, the other refers to visibility, and they both respect a two-hour time frame, from one hour *before* you expect to get there until one hour *afterwards*. Ceiling and visibility would not normally change that much for the worse during a two-hour period, and if this kind of rapid change were to take place, it would probably be adequately forecast or reported.

Here are the weather limitations about which you should be concerned: The reported or forecast CEILING (the lowest *broken* or *overcast* cloud layer) must be at least 2,000 feet above the airport elevation, and the VISIBILITY must be at least 3 miles. (The ink on the announcement of the "new" alternate rule—it was changed from the previous cumbersome regulation in the fall of 1978—was hardly dry before some clever pilot came up with an easy way to remember it: 1-2-3; 1 hour before or after your ETA, 2 thousand feet of ceiling, 3 miles visibility.) Here, in tabular form, are the basic criteria you must consider when answering the first question: Must I file an alternate?

On occasion, you will encounter a weather situation that indicates that during the two-hour time period, there will be "a chance of," or "intermittent conditions," or "brief periods" of ceiling and visibility that require an alternate on your flight plan. This problem has been hassled in the courts with little definitive guidance, so the sensible answer is always to file an alternate when there's any question about whether it will be needed—it's so much better to have a safe haven in your hip pocket, than to be forced to find one at the last minute. And how about the day when the forecast called for "clear and a million" when you filed, but now it looks like the sky has fallen at destination? That's easy—file an alternate with whomever you're talking when you discover that the bridges are burning ahead of you. Alternates aren't normally stored in the Center computer, but when you tell a controller "I'd like to add East Ipswich as an alternate," he'll get the message.

Notice that a forecast below *either one* of the conditions laid down by law (ceiling *or* visibility) requires an alternate. The complexity of the rule makes it even more sensible for you to form the habit of always filing an alternate when you're fixin' to go IFR. You'll have the comfortable feeling that comes with knowing all the bases are covered, and selecting an alternate automatically will keep you from forgetting it on those rare occasions when it's needed.

The 1-2-3 rule will force you to plan for an alternate and carry the requisite fuel, but there are situations in which forecast weather conditions meet the requirements of 91.23(b), but could still leave you out in left field. These situations are unique to high-altitude airports, and you should be aware of the potential problem when you're planning a flight into the mountains.

There are at least ten airports in the United States where all of the MDAs are greater than 2,000 feet AGL, and/or the minimum visibilities are greater than 3 miles. When operating IFR to such airports, it is possible to encounter a situation in which you wouldn't *legally* require an alternate (and therefore perhaps not carry enough fuel to get somewhere else), and find on arrival that conditions are below published minimums . . . *now* what do you do?

In addition to the airports mentioned above, there are others in the mountains that have MDAs only 100 to 300 feet below the alternate requirements. Again, only a slight worsening of weather conditions at your ETA could cause a problem.

In general, pilots should always be more diligent when planning a flight into mountainous areas (density altitude, capricious weather, survival aspects, etc.), and when planning to fly IFR, that diligence should extend to a *guarantee* of enough fuel on board to fly to an alternate . . . just in case.

QUESTION 2   What airport may I use as an alternate?

This one is not nearly so difficult to answer (it shouldn't be, with the built-in conservatism of the first question!), and it lends itself to a simple rule: If the airport you wish to use for an alternate is forecasting (at your ETA over the alternate) a ceiling of more than 800 feet, and a visibility of more than 2 miles, it's OK; go ahead and file it in block #13 of the flight plan. Since you've already covered yourself for ETA plus or minus one hour on the destination airport, the alternate must have 800 and 2 at your ETA—period. There is some mumbo-jumbo in the regulation about whether or not the alternate airport has a precision or a non-precision approach procedure, but you will be on the safe side by always using the 800 and 2 rule.

In that rare (and usually not too sensible) situation when you might want to select for an alternate an airport that has no published approach procedure, you must be able to arrive over that airport at MEA (that's the lowest enroute altitude that ATC is going to allow) in VFR conditions, make your descent, approach, and landing in VFR weather.

When choosing your alternate, make sure that you can get from destination to alternate and still have forty-five minutes' fuel (a full hour is better!) at normal cruise power—more on this later.

On page 79 are the rules to be observed when selecting an alternate airport, including the precision versus non-precision mumbo-jumbo.

Now that you have gone through all the hoops, decided that you need an alternate, and have selected an appropriate airport, forget all about those minimums—they are just for planning purposes, and have nothing whatever to do with what must exist when you get there. When you arrive at the missed approach point, only the ability to see the runway environment and being in a position for a normal landing govern your decision to continue to a landing or execute the missed-approach procedure.

Through lack of weather observation facilities or local restrictions, some airports can't be used as alternates, or require higher

Condition	May I Use This Airport as an Alternate?
No approach procedure published, but I can make it from MEA to the runway in VFR conditions	Yes
Non-precision procedure published, forecast at ETA at least 800 feet and 2 miles	Yes
Precision approach procedure published, forecast at ETA at least 600 feet and 2 miles	Yes

minimum weather conditions. Jeppesen charts include this information on the back of the sheet, and the government publications use a special symbol △ in the remarks block of the approach chart to refer you to a separate listing.

Aircraft and Instrument Preflight

A checklist within a checklist—that's the way to make sure that once you get into the air on an instrument flight, all the gauges and gadgets you need for aircraft control and navigation are doing their jobs, and doing them properly. An instrument checklist, if religiously followed every flight, will force you into two situations that can do you nothing but good. First, a preflight checklist will save your pride (ever tried to taxi away from the ramp with the airplane still tied to the ground?), and perhaps your neck; second, following a printed, orderly checklist will force you to slow down when preparing for an IFR trip. There's nothing wrong with hurrying, but there's a lot wrong with *being* hurried—the checklist will help you keep your head when all about you are losing theirs.

All the items on this instrument preflight are in-cockpit checks, except two which are of extreme importance. If you can't tell how high or how fast you are flying, you've got real troubles, so as you march diligently around kicking the tires and checking all the things you normally check, pay particular attention to these two—the static source and the pitot tube. Most static ports are stainless steel discs set flush with the aircraft skin, drilled with several small holes to admit air pressure to the static system. If any of the holes are covered, deformed, plugged with paint, wax, or dirt, don't fly until

WEATHER ANALYSIS

WEATHER
SYNOPSIS

STATION	ENROUTE WEATHER TREND		

STATION	TERMINAL FORECASTS

STATION	WINDS ALOFT FORECASTS		

LOCATION	PIREPS/SIGNIFICANT WEATHER/NOTAMS

Figure 6   Weather organizer.

you get it fixed. The pitot system plumbing must also be free of obstructions, including the cover you bought to keep ice and snow and house-hunting insects out of the tube. Even with a long red streamer with fluorescent letters warning the pilot to REMOVE BEFORE FLIGHT, the next pitot cover that is taken for a short airplane ride won't be the first one! For IFR flying, you should have a heated pitot tube, and the only completely reliable way to check its operation is to turn it on and feel the heat. (CAUTION: Let not thy sensing digits remain overlong in contact with the heated part, lest they come away medium rare!)

A general preflight item, which should become a habit so strong that you feel uneasy until it's done, is checking the fuel situation. Don't ever trust anybody but yourself to make absolutely sure there is as much gasoline in the tanks as you think there is, and that it's the grade you ordered. Gauges have been known to lie, and linemen occasionally get distracted and forget to fill the tanks on the other side of the airplane, so the last thing you should do before climbing up to the flight deck is CHECK THE TANKS. You may not always want them brim-full, but let your own two eyes gaze into the depths of the fuel cells and be sure you know how much is there. You'll realize a bonus from this last-one-before-getting-aboard check too, because you'll be certain that the fuel tank caps are replaced properly and securely (the same goes for oil dipsticks). When a lid works loose in flight (or maybe was never put on properly in the first place), you can rest assured that the low-pressure area on top of the wing will aid remarkably in the rapid depletion of the tanks. There is also the problem of what-do-I-do-now? with half the fuel supply gone and no close-by alternate.

With engine(s) running and your normally used radio equipment turned on, you should begin the operational part of the instrument checklist:

1. SUCTION AND/OR GENERATORS (ALTERNATORS)
   Check for "in-the-green" or normal load conditions.
2. ALTERNATE STATIC SOURCE VALVE OR SWITCH
   Check closed or normal. (If you haven't done so by now, open this valve in flight and record the difference in airspeed and altitude readings—they'll always be in error on the dangerous [high] side.)
3. AIRSPEED INDICATOR
   Check for normal "zero" indication. (Some never go all the way to zero.)
4. VERTICAL SPEED INDICATOR (RATE OF CLIMB)
   Check for zero reading—if it's off, you'll have to apply that correction in flight. Try tapping the case lightly to get the needle on zero. If it's way off, have it adjusted to read properly.
5. CLOCK
   Wind, and be sure that Mickey's hands are pointing to the right numbers.
6. ENGINE INSTRUMENTS
   Check them all in the green or at least moving that way. (Of course you made sure you had oil pressure on engine start.)
7. RADIO EQUIPMENT (COMMUNICATIONS AND NAVIGATION)
   Turn on everything that can be checked at this point. If there's a VOR or VOT on the airport or close by, you can check the

omni receivers and possibly DME. Tune and identify an ADF station and check for proper needle movement and relative bearing.

8. PUBLICATIONS, PERSONAL EQUIPMENT
Before you leave the chocks, check once more to be sure you have all the charts and equipment you will need.

9. ALTIMETER
Set to field elevation, then put in the altimeter setting you get from Ground Control or ATIS—if the hands move more than 75 feet either way, you have an altimeter that is outside the accepted limits of accuracy for IFR flight. If the error is less than 75 feet, don't attempt to carry the difference forward on subsequent altimeter settings—it is too easy to correct the wrong direction, and most of these small altimeter errors tend to cancel out over the duration of a flight. And if you are concerned about 75 feet being the difference between a landing and a missed-approach at destination, you're pressing your luck.

10. TURN AND BANK INDICATOR
As you taxi, check to see that the indicator shows turns in the proper direction, and that the ball moves freely in the opposite direction. If it moves in the *same* direction, call up the airport manager and thank him for banking the taxiways.

11. ATTITUDE INDICATOR (ARTIFICIAL HORIZON)
Normal taxi speeds will not affect the bank attitude of the airplane very much, but you will notice some displacement on the attitude indicator. If the bank exceeds 5° while turning on the ground, the instrument is probably unreliable for IFR flight. On those indicators that are adjustable up and down, leave the little airplane in the same place all the time—it should indicate the pitch attitude for level flight at your normal cruise airspeed.

12. MAGNETIC COMPASS
While rolling straight ahead at a steady speed, check the reading against a known magnetic heading—a taxiway which parallels a runway, for example. If your deviation card shows some error, count that in your check.

13. HEADING INDICATOR (DIRECTIONAL GYRO)
Set this to agree with the corrected reading from the mag compass and make sure the card remains stationary after you make the adjustment. DO recheck the heading indicator when you

are lined up on the runway; it's the most accurate check you can make.

14. DE-ICING AND/OR ANTI-ICING EQUIPMENT

Check for proper operation (visible check of boot inflation, load-meter check for electrical devices).

15. CARBURETOR HEAT (OR ALTERNATE AIR SOURCE FOR FUEL-INJECTED ENGINES)

Your best friend in icing conditions—check to make sure it works as it should.

16. CLEAN-UP AND SET-UP

After checking everything, and you're satisfied that the bird will fly, take a moment or two to clean up the cockpit—put away all but the charts you'll need immediately after takeoff. Before you indicate to the tower your readiness to aviate, set up your radios for the task at hand. If the weather is really tight, you'll do well to have your primary navigation receiver tuned to the approach aid for the departure airport; if anything goes wrong right after lift-off, you'll have one chore already taken care of, and can transition to the approach situation smoothly. You should also have the approach chart readily available for the same reason. Weather not too bad? Set the navigation gear on the proper frequencies and courses for your departure.

17. BEFORE-TAKEOFF CHECK

Using a printed checklist or at least one of several mnemonictype reminders, make sure all the little things are done, e.g., doors closed and locked, boost pumps on (if required), fuel on proper tank, etc. CIFFTRS is an old standard—pronounced "sifters," it reminds you to check:

Controls
Instruments
Fuel
Flaps
Trim
Runup
Seat Belts Fastened

At the proper time, open the throttles, and have a nice trip!

That's a preflight planning schedule that will keep you honest (if not busy) for any IFR situation. Change it to fit your airplane or the facilities you use, but remember that any one of these items could cause trouble if overlooked. To wrap it all up, here's the checklist in abbreviated form.

1. Charts and equipment.
2. Check weather.
3. Select route and altitude.
4. Check distance and time enroute.
5. Check fuel required.
6. Check alternate requirements.
7. Preflight aircraft and instruments.

7

IFR Clearances

THERE IS an all-encompassing rule in instrument flying, the "eleventh commandment" which says "Thou shalt not enter IFR conditions in controlled airspace without a clearance from ATC." A clearance, once accepted and acknowledged, is your authorization to proceed to a certain point, via a certain route, and at a certain altitude. With the majority of today's IFR flights under radar surveillance, the clearance becomes less a separation tool, and more a means of ensuring continued safe operation when communications fail.

Clearances must conform to aviation's three-dimensional environment and therefore must always specify (1) *a point* to which you are cleared, (2) *a route* by which you are expected to get there, and (3) *an altitude assignment.* Amendments to previously issued clearances may change any or all of these, but prior to entering IFR conditions in controlled airspace, you need all three. If the point to which you are cleared falls short of your destination airport (and this is sometimes encountered because of heavy IFR traffic), one more instruction must be added: a time to expect further clearance. The same holds true for any interruption (such as a hold) in your instrument flight.

In general, ATC will deliver clearances to you when airborne in one of three ways—the big thing here is at what time do you make your move?—when do you climb or descend or turn? Suppose Center wants you to go to a lower altitude: "Barnburner 1234 Alpha, descend to and maintain four thousand." You are expected to acknowledge the new clearance, then begin descending—there's clearly no urgency about this change of altitude. But when Center says

"Barnburner 1234 Alpha, descend IMMEDIATELY to four thousand," you'd better be on your way down even before you pick up the mike—he wants you out of your present altitude right away. When there's no traffic conflict and Center doesn't really care when you descend, you'll hear "Barnburner 1234 Alpha, descend to and maintain four thousand at pilot's discretion." Acknowledge the clearance, and when it suits your situation, start down. (It's wise to let him know when you commence the descent.)

So, when you hear:

"Descend to and maintain . . ."	Comply upon receipt.
"Descend immediately to . . ."	Do it NOW!
"Descend to . . . at pilot's discretion."	Do it when you're ready.

Copying Clearances

Time was when a pilot had to have executive-secretary shorthand skills to copy a clearance like this, delivered at machinegun speed by a ground controller with a warped sense of humor:

ATC clears Barnburner 1234 Alpha to the River City Airport via Victor 21 to the Maple intersection, Victor 418 Stone, Victor 25 West Lewis intersection, direct Elmville VOR, Victor 182 Downtown intersection direct, climb to and maintain niner thousand, cross the Hometown 23-mile DME fix at or above four thousand, cross the Smithville 120 radial at or above five thousand, cross Maple intersection at or below six thousand five hundred, expect higher altitude at Lewis intersection, contact Hometown Center on 123.8 when established on Victor 21, squawk one-one-zero-zero; read back.

There are several ways to handle a situation like this. You can develop a clearance shorthand (there are books and recordings available), or you can invest in a cockpit recorder that can be rigged not only to transcribe the clearance on magnetic tape, but to read it back to the controller in his own voice. It would almost be worth the cost of the recorder just to hear that controller try to correct himself! Or you can submerge your pride and say "ready to copy, *take it slow.*" It seems the third alternative is the best, since it will result in fewer errors, less repetition, and, more importantly, will contribute to a safer operation; both parties will have a complete understanding of all parts of the clearance; mistakes of routing, altitudes, or frequencies will stand out like an oil leak on a new paint job. Before accepting an invitation to copy a clearance at a strange airport, take a few moments to listen to other clearances, and study the chart of the local area—you will lessen the element of surprise when the controller reels off some obscure intersection or VOR station.

Pilots must somehow acknowledge receipt of a clearance before it is considered accepted. Remember that Ground Control, Clearance Delivery, Center, Flight Service Station, or any ATC facility from which you might receive a clearance is *people*, and subject to human error. If the controller really wanted you to proceed via Victor *47* to Maple intersection but cleared you down Victor *21* through force of habit, the error might go unnoticed if you acknowledge the clearance with a simple "Roger." Just like filing an IFR flight plan over the telephone or from the air, you can read back most of today's relatively simple ATC clearances with "numbers" alone. For example, when the Barnburner is cleared "to River City Airport via Victor 21, Victor 418 Elmville, maintain nine thousand, contact departure control on 123.8, squawk 4032," the readback can be simply "Barnburner 34 Alpha to River City, Victor 21, Victor 418 Elmsville, niner thousand, 123.8, 4032." And the controller knows you've agreed on the important items.

The nature of your IFR trips will have a bearing on the mechanics of copying clearances—if you frequently fly the same routes, your clearances will not deviate much from a pattern, and you'll know what to expect. But when you're trying to taxi a castering-gear taildragger in a 20-knot crosswind on solid ice, busier than a DC-3 co-pilot at gear-up time, and wishing you had another hand and foot to help, that's not the time to say "go ahead" when Ground Control has your clearance for a strange route! Tell him to "stand by," and when you have the airplane stopped and the enroute chart spread out on your lap, indicate that you are "ready to copy." Now you can devote yourself 100 percent to the business of copying the clearance correctly, noting changes in routing or altitudes as he spews them out.

And while you're at it, why not copy the clearance in soft, erasable pencil right on the chart? It gives you a record of the clearance in the handiest possible place, available for instant reference as you fly, and eliminating another piece of paper in the cramped confines of your "flight deck." You'll find plenty of blank space for this purpose on every chart. When the controller comes to "contact El Paso departure control . . . ," you know that the next item will be a communications frequency, and you can save more time by "writing" that frequency on the radio you're not using. The same technique holds good for transponder codes; when the controller speaks the numbers, "write them down" on the transponder itself. Writing on radio sets and transponders makes them the world's most expensive note pads.

Your clearance will usually come through with route and altitude just as you requested, and if you plan to fly that way again, make a note of the routing; you have probably hit on a combination that ATC will buy next time, too. But if the airways you have chosen don't fit into the computer's assessment of the traffic situation, the controller will "suggest" another route. Despite what you may on occasion feel is an attempt to see how much out of your way they can make you fly, variations from requested routes are necessary when those airways are full. It is the controllers' expression of the best they can do for you at the time.

Here's where it's good to have the enroute chart handy, to see if the suggested route is compatible with you, your airplane, and the weather. Treating the clearance as a suggestion (a strong one, yes, but still a suggestion), if you don't like the looks of it, TURN IT DOWN! It may mean a delay, but that's immensely preferable to finding yourself loaded with ice, losing altitude, and headed toward a squall line on an airway with an MEA 5,000 feet higher than you can possibly fly—all because you accepted a clearance other than the one you wanted. ALWAYS REFUSE A CLEARANCE THAT WILL FLY YOU INTO TROUBLE! This philosophy assumes your complete knowledge of existing and forecast weather conditions along the route.

Cleared as Filed

On rare occasions, you will encounter a clearance as involved as the earlier example, but more than likely you will be "cleared as filed, maintain eight thousand, contact Hometown Departure on one twenty three point eight, squawk one zero zero zero." Used more and more, "cleared as filed" takes into account the destination and routing you requested in your flight plan, and does away with all those confusing intersections and airways. It's a good idea to know what route you requested, since asking the controller "which way did I file?" can be a little embarrassing. And you'll have to ask if you're not sure, because the clearance is the only thing you have to hang your hat on if the radios quit enroute. "Cleared as filed" covers *only* destination and routing; you will always be assigned an *altitude*. It is your choice to accept or decline, but *every* IFR clearance will stipulate the height at which you are to fly.

Anytime that you change your intended route of flight after filing a flight plan, be very suspicious of "cleared as filed." Remember that there is a delay in getting a flight plan request from FSS to Center and back, and the route by which you are cleared "as filed" may be the original one. When in doubt, ask the controller to verify which route he is talking about—it may take an extra minute or two, but it might save your skin in the event of radio failure.

What'd He Say?

Perhaps the best way to learn the jargon of clearances and sharpen your copying artistry is to buy an inexpensive VHF receiver, and listen to the "big boys" at work. (Besides, it gives you another excuse to drive out to the airport on those rainy Saturday afternoons when the alternate is to move furniture or paint the living room!) Pretend you are receiving the clearances, and copy them down, using an old enroute chart for a note pad. Take heart as you listen and realize that even the most experienced professional pilots stumble over a routing now and then—if a pilot claims that he's never blown a readback, don't believe anything else he says.

And it's not always the frailties of homo sapiens that cause problems. Late one IFR afternoon, during the daily contest to see which controller could issue the longest clearance, an airline crew got the winner. There followed a long silence that was finally broken by the controller asking "Trans-Amalgamated 201, did you copy?" "You'll never believe this," said the captain, "but I think we've had a pencil failure—say again all after 'ATC clears.' "

Clearance Limits

Most of the time you will be cleared to the airport at which you intend to land, but now and then a traffic conflict will not permit enough separation to clear you all the way. If it appears the conflict can be resolved in a short time, the controller may issue a clearance with a specified limit, and it might sould like this, for a trip from Kansas City to Oklahoma City: "ATC clears Barnburner 1234 Alpha direct to the Butler VOR, climb to and maintain 5,000, expect further clearance at 37." Although a traffic conflict has prevented the controller from clearing you all the way to Oke City, he is telling you that he's willing to accept your flight in the IFR system, that he can guarantee separation to Butler, and that further clearance will be issued before you get there. The "Expect Further Clearance" time provides an emergency backup clearance if your radios (or his, for that matter) fail. Should that unlikely event occur, you would be expected to hold at Butler until thirty-seven minutes past the hour, then proceed along your route in accordance with the regulations. When there's no communications problem, controllers will issue a new clearance approximately five minutes before you arrive at a clearance limit.

As always, you have the option to accept or decline such a "short-range" clearance, but with the "we'll get you to Oklahoma City as soon as possible" implication, you're better off to accept, and trust ATC to clear you along the way. Should you turn down their offer of the short-range clearance, it is likely you will wait a considerable time until the conflict is resolved. Treat a clearance limit not as an indication of ATC snubbing your route request in favor of someone else, but as a sincere effort on their part to expedite traffic flow. If the probability of solving the aerial traffic jam is slim, Center will have you wait on the ground. With a short-range clearance, at least you're in the system, on your way, and that's far better than burning up gasoline on the ramp waiting for clearance all the way.

"Other" Clearances: VFR on Top/Special VFR/Cruise/ Approach

In the beginning, the FAA created IFR and VFR. As time went on, it became clear that these two major classifications of flying conditions could be made more flexible, and "VFR on Top" evolved as one of several ways to make the airspace more useful to more people.

There are two distinct kinds of VFR on Top. There is *VFR* VFR on Top, and there is *IFR* VFR on Top. You have probably used the VFR type, where you were able to stay above all the clouds, complied with visibility and cloud clearance regulations, and were able to take off, climb, and land in VFR conditions. Although there is some calculated risk (like an engine failure on top of an overcast with nothing but the Rocky Mountains below), this is a perfectly legal situation, and for the non-instrument-rated pilot, often the only way to get any utility out of his airplane.

The other VFR on Top is right out of the Instrument Flight Rules, and can frequently be used to advantage. It is *always* an IFR clearance, and as such, it's not something that you can do whenever you feel like it! Whether ATC actually says the words or not, VFR on Top when you're in the IFR system implies a clearance to proceed as in normal IFR conditions, but with a VFR on Top *restriction*.

Since it is a restriction, you should know the rules and conditions that apply to this type of clearance before attempting to put it to use. They are:

1. You must be *cleared* by ATC to operate "on top."
2. You must *follow the route* assigned by ATC.
3. You must *report* to ATC whenever required in accordance with IFR rules.
4. You must fly at *VFR altitudes*—eastbound, odd thousands plus 500; westbound, even thousands plus 500.
5. You are responsible (as you are at any time in VFR conditions) to see and avoid other aircraft.
6. You must be able to *maintain VFR conditions,* which means observance of all the applicable cloud-clearance and visibility regulations.

7. You should be reasonably certain you can continue your flight to destination in VFR-on-Top conditions.

So you're committed to a ball game that has two sets of rules—some IFR, some VFR. Rules 1, 2, and 3 come from the instrument book, 4, 5, and 6 are VFR-oriented, and number 7 is just plain old common sense.

When is an IFR flight plan with a VFR-on-Top restriction a good deal? Any time you have a need or desire to fly above the clouds, can maintain the altitude required to do so, and ATC is fresh out of available altitudes. But temper that need or desire with the limitations of your airplane, your passengers, and yourself; the next time a pilot gets into trouble from lack of oxygen while trying to stay VFR on Top won't be the first time.

Before you can make a rational decision about requesting VFR on Top, you should have some idea where those cloud tops are located—how high are you going to have to climb to clear all clouds by 1,000 feet? The most accurate answer is found in pilot reports (PIREPS), direct observations by the people who were there. (By the way, the more PIREPS that are made, the more complete the picture you can draw, so reciprocate by making reports of cloud tops, particularly when such information is sparse or non-existent. Early in the morning or late at night, when few other hardy souls are aloft, your reports will be of great benefit to your fellow fliers.)

The next best source of cloud heights is the Area Forecast, which will give you a general idea of the altitude at which the sky is expected to go from cloudy to clear. The information is not very specific, but it's a lot better than no information at all.

There are several situations that may prompt you to consider a VFR-on-Top clearance. Maybe there are cumulus buildups that you would like to avoid visually (ATC will allow you to deviate around them), or you might need to climb out of an icing level, or perhaps you would just rather fly high, where it's clean, clear, smooth, and cool. VFR on Top is a useful tool in your IFR kit when a higher altitude will help you, and ATC has run out of available "hard" (assigned) altitudes. If you can operate within the "on Top" rules, it is usually advantageous to seek a flight level that will reduce a headwind component or let you pick up a tailwind—that's using your knowledge to operate the airplane more efficiently.

At terminals where Special VFR is not permitted, your instrument rating can help you beat the system by obtaining a clearance to VFR on Top, then proceeding merrily on your way, especially if a full IFR clearance is not available. This situation frequently develops when a low-topped fog bank has the terminal all but shut down. CAUTION: If you leap off in below-landing-minimum weather, be sure there's a suitable airport close by to which you can go if things turn sour!

When a Controller suspects that the tops are rather high, and sees a traffic conflict developing above a certain altitude, he may clear you "to VFR on Top, if not on top at 8,000, maintain 8,000 and advise." If you're still in the clouds when you get there, or don't have the required visibility, you're stuck with that altitude until the traffic conflict is resolved or the weather conditions improve. Since you now have an assigned altitude, you also have an out if the radios fail.

If the tops of the white stuff begin to rise under you, it is your responsibility to rise with them, maintaining 1,000 feet between you and the clouds. Higher cloud tops will force a minimum increase in flight altitude of 2,000 feet to be at the proper VFR level, and it is possible that a constantly rising cloud layer will soon have you trying to operate at heights that are untenable for you or your airplane, or both. At this point, when you need all the smarts you can muster, hypoxia may be robbing you of precious judgment, and in a manner that can only be described as insidious—you don't know it's happening, and worse, you don't care! As cloud tops rise, your concern should grow; it's probably time to request a hard altitude from ATC, and nine times out of ten they will grant it. "Denver Center, Barnburner 1234 Alpha, unable to maintain VFR on Top at twelve thousand five hundred, requesting one zero thousand." And the reply will usually be "Roger, Barnburner 1234 Alpha, descend to and maintain one zero thousand, report reaching."

But the controller cannot always assign an altitude—in a sense, you forfeit some of the ATC protection when you request VFR on Top, and the controller is obliged to fit you back into the system only if it can be done without disadvantaging other flights under his control. If this happens (and it is rare), you must remain VFR on Top, either by climbing (seldom the best choice, especially if you are pushing your altitude limits at the time), or by holding as instructed until an altitude is open. Should you subsequently declare an emergency because of a fuel shortage or an impending performance or physiological problem, be prepared to explain why you didn't comply with the regulation that makes the pilot responsible for "all preflight information affecting the proposed flight." In other words, you should have known about the higher tops enroute before takeoff. Sorry, but that's the law, and it underscores your responsibility to be reasonably certain you can make it to destination in VFR-on-Top conditions before you request or accept such a clearance.

Special VFR

Special VFR is usually thought of as a crutch for VFR pilots. It's the simplest of ATC clearances, and can often be used to advantage by instrument-rated people as well. In contrast to the full-blown IFR clearance, Special VFR designates more a clearance "area" than a clearance limit, does not assign a "hard" altitude, and makes no provision for a specific route or for radio failure. You will be cleared into or out of a Control Zone, from or to a direction—north, east, southwest, etc. For example, "Barnburner 1234 Alpha is cleared out of the Fresno Control Zone to the east, maintain Special VFR conditions at or below 3,000 feet while in the Control Zone."

The heart of Special VFR is that airspace in the immediate vicinity of the airport (usually 5 miles in diameter with extensions for approach and departure paths) known as a "Control Zone." It extends from the surface to 14,500 feet MSL, and is there only for the protection of traffic executing IFR comings and goings at that airport. Since it is controlled airspace, you may not fly in a control zone without a clearance when conditions are less than VFR.

Because a lot of non-instrument-rated pilots are inconvenienced on days when the ceiling is adequate but the visibility won't creep past the $2\frac{1}{2}$-mile mark, or when they can see clear into the next county under an 800-foot cloud deck, Special VFR was developed. It is a *clearance* to proceed into or out of a control zone; the inflight visibility minimum is one mile, you must stay clear of all clouds, and respect the altitude limits specified in the clearance. (The altitude limitation is usually imposed to protect IFR operations at higher levels.) This is a "poor man's IFR clearance," available to any. pilot—instrument-rated or not—during daylight hours; after dark, an instrument rating is required, so why not request a full-blown clearance and enjoy *all* the protection of the system?

A full IFR clearance supersedes Special VFR; that is, no Specials will be issued when IFR traffic is inbound or outbound and a conflict is possible. This means that Special VFR folks face long delays getting airborne or cleared into the control zone when IFR operations are heavy. Being instrument-rated puts you into the preferential group in this situation, and filing IFR will usually produce an earlier departure or arrival. At certain airports around the country, the flow of IFR traffic is so heavy and so consistent that these terminals do not permit Special VFR operations at any time, period. Know which airports are in this group, and don't ask a controller for something he can't do.

It is at the less busy airports that Special VFR serves all pilots most beneficially. Suppose you are waiting for your clearance at West Side Airport (tower-equipped) and the minutes as well as your gasoline are wasting away because continuous IFR approaches and departures are in progress at Downtown International, 10 miles distant. If the entire area is solid IFR, settle down, cool your heels, and wait—you've no choice. But if you can depart West Side in Special VFR conditions and *very soon thereafter* fly in "regular" VFR, you may be money ahead to request a Special for departure, and be on your way. (CAUTION: You will likely have to refile your IFR flight plan, as ATC will not allow you to cancel your IFR request, take off under Special VFR conditions, then pick up the same IFR flight plan in the air.) Conversely, you can sometimes get into a smaller airport with a Special VFR clearance when there's a long waiting list for approaches at a nearby "big" terminal. If conditions are favorable, it doesn't hurt to inquire.

An inbound Special is usually not much of a problem, since you are flying toward a definite location (the airport) and various aids to navigation (radio facilities, city lights and/or landmarks, assistance from the Tower, etc.). It's the Special VFR *away from* the airport that is strewn with pitfalls for the unwary pilot; if traffic permits, you will be cleared out of the control zone, and that's as far as the controller's responsibility goes. Should the weather outside the zone prove to be worse than expected, the controller is under no mandate to let you back in, especially if he has other Specials or IFR traffic clamoring for his attention. And there you are, in IFR conditions without a clearance, can't get one, and trying to think up a good story to tell the FAA at your violation hearing!

Recognize the potential hazards of Special VFR and use it only when it can *safely* get you where you need to go. If you get in a bind and can't maintain the required conditions, don't press on, but contact ATC (Tower, Approach Control, anybody), explain the situation, and get a clearance as appropriate. Pride goeth before a fall, and when you are in an airplane, the fall usually hurteth a lot.

Cruise Clearances

Ask any ten instrument pilots to define a cruise clearance and you'll probably get ten different explanations, all the way from "maintain cruise airspeed" to "descend immediately to minimum altitude." A very useful tool of IFR operations, the cruise clearance carries a number of implications which bear on the efficiency and safety of getting to your destination, and it must be thoroughly understood to be used properly. When an ATC controller says you are "cleared to cruise," he means:

1. You are cleared DIRECT to the specified navaid.
2. You are cleared to fly at any altitude from that specified in the clearance down to the appropriate IFR minimum altitude. (A word of caution here: "appropriate IFR minimum altitude" could be MEA if you're on an airway, or the published MSA when you *know* you're within 25 miles of the approach aid. When in doubt, stay at the altitude specified in the cruise clearance, and ask the controller when it's safe to descend; under certain conditions he can provide a minimum vectoring altitude. Don't guess: Stay high, and *inquire.*)
3. You may leave the cruise altitude at your discretion for a lower altitude—your altitude clearance is for a vertical slice of airspace, described in Item #2. (If you *do* report leaving an altitude, you may not climb back up to that level without a fresh clearance to do so.)
4. You are the only *IFR* traffic at cruise altitude and below between you and the navaid.

5. You are cleared for the approach of your choice on arrival at the airport.
6. You are responsible to advise ATC (the facility will be specified in the clearance) when your landing is assured or upon missed approach, depending on the situation.

Cruise clearances were designed primarily to accommodate the final segment of an IFR flight and are generally used at locations that have no Tower or Approach Control Facility. (A cruise clearance issued before takeoff differs from a "normal" one only in the definition of altitude—see Item#2.) A very flexible instrument of traffic control, this clearance allows you to begin descent at your discretion, choose an altitude best for the situation (turbulence, headwinds, icing, inoperative cabin heaters, or other fun things), and hopefully break out of the clouds sooner than you might otherwise. When you get to the appropriate minimum altitude, and find yourself in VFR conditions, there are several ways you can complete the approach.

First, if you want the practice, go ahead with the full IFR procedure (it will take a little longer, but there's something to be said for the IFR separation this offers, plus the fact that it will keep you from getting lost or landing at the wrong airport!). The second method, if *good* VFR exists in the terminal area, is to cancel your IFR flight plan, removing you from the system (although most Approach and Center controllers will give you traffic advisories as long as their workload permits). The third and fourth possibilities are the Contact and the Visual Approaches, treated in detail in Chapter 15, "Instrument Approaches."

". . . Cleared for the Approach"

Regardless of the areas in which you fly IFR, there comes a point in every trip when the controller turns you loose and expects you to complete the published procedure entirely on your own. The phrase most commonly used for this purpose is "cleared for the so-and-so approach" and is your cue to fly the procedure as published (certain methods of short-cutting the full procedure are outlined in Chapter 15, "Instrument Approaches"). But in more and more of the real-world situations, that phrase won't be heard until you have been assigned a radar vector intended to intercept the final approach course—a definite time-saver, and one of the very good things about radar control.

But be aware of an altitude trap and the rule that was written to keep you from falling into it: Whenever you are operating on an unpublished route (as with RNAV, or when flying direct from a VOR to intercept a final approach course) or flying in accordance with a radar vector, you must maintain the last assigned altitude until a lower one is issued by ATC, or until you are on a segment of a published route or approach procedure which has a published minimum altitude. In other words, don't descend until you know (from the figures on the chart) that it's *safe* to do so.

The Last Word in Clearances

There are, we hope, no controllers who issue capricious clearances and no pilots who willfully and knowingly disregard or deviate from the provisions of an ATC clearance they've received. But controllers and pilots are humans, and as such they are subject to misunderstandings relative to what the other guy really said. As the result of several major accidents involving misunderstood clearances, the rules have been expanded to include the following proviso under the title "Compliance with ATC Clearances and Instructions": "If a pilot is uncertain of the meaning of an ATC clearance, HE SHALL IMMEDIATELY REQUEST CLARIFICATION FROM ATC." When in doubt, ask.

A South Carolina charter pilot, who talks just about as fast as he flies his old Twin Beech (that means *slowly*), found himself approaching the New York terminal area one morning at the height of the aerial rush hour. The headphones were alive with a steady stream of clearances and instructions, some of which were certainly directed toward the Twin Beech. Every time he'd try to respond, or ask about a communication, the South Carolinian would be firmly "stepped on" by some fast-talking Yankee.

Following a clearance that appeared to have some significance for his flight, our pilot waited for a break in the controller's machinegun delivery, then drawled, as only a South Carolinian can drawl, "Laguahdia Approach, this heah's Beechcraft seven foah Victah . . . was what y'all just said to me anythin' impawtant?"

Seven foah Victah got preferential treatment from that point on!

8

Communicating in the IFR System

THERE ARE a number of ways you can make your IFR communications more efficient, one of which is to get rid of the habit of prefacing every transmission with "uhhhhhh." There is no doubt some psychological theory underlying the several types of uhhh's, which range from the student pilot who truly doesn't know what to say and uses uhhh to fill a verbal void, to the 20,000-hour airline captain whose well-practiced uhhh is pitched at least two octaves below anyone else's and is his hallmark of accomplishment. There's nothing illegal, immoral, or fattening about using your own uhhh, but it takes time that can be better spent in meaningful communication. If you are a habitual uhhher and somewhat condescending about your five-second tone that will get you the best DF steer in the country, don't try it out when IFR in the New York area—by the time you've finished uhhhing, New York Approach Control will have cleared three airline flights for approaches to JFK, handed off two Bonanzas and an Apache to LaGuardia Tower, and coordinated a Civil Air Patrol search for a sailboat missing on Long Island Sound! As our terminal areas get busier, and until data link systems are in common use, it is incumbent on every pilot, and especially those using the IFR system, to become better managers of their communications.

Airborne communications problems have not escaped the attention of the wonderful world of research—someone studied it a while back with the aid of a number of in-cockpit recorders. In addition to taping the transmissions to and from the aircraft, pilot responses on the flight deck were also recorded. The researchers found that in almost every case, radioed instructions from the ground were followed by one of these phrases between pilots (listed in order of usage):

1. "What'd he say?"
2. "Was that for us?"
3. "Oh, shucks." (Cleaned up a bit so the book can retain its "G" rating.)

Practice communication management right from the start—when you turn the radio switch to the ON position, know ahead of time where the volume knob should be for normal reception. If there isn't some kind of mark on the knob, make one. On those radios provided with a manual control, adjust the squelch to a point just short of where the noise begins, and you've set up your transceiver properly for the first transmission. When Ground Control answers, adjust the volume for maximum clarity. Better yet, listen to other transmissions and adjust your radio before you talk to anyone.

Tips for Talking

Here are several things you should do (and some things you should *not* do) to improve the quality of your communications in the air:

1. Always listen to be sure the frequency is clear before starting a transmission. You will often hear just one side of a radio conversation, so take that into consideration. If Center asks somebody else a question, but he's too far away for you to hear the answer, allow a reasonable length of time before you begin. You'll probably hear Center's acknowledgment of the other pilot's answer—use that as your go-ahead signal.
2. Before you transmit to anyone at any time, know what you want to say before you press the mike button. It's not necessary to abbreviate your words as they used to do in the movies, but do compress the message so that you get your point across with a minimum number of words.
3. Don't make transmissions that are unnecessary. This should not preclude a friendly chat with the controllers when they aren't busy and exhibit a willingness to pass the time of day.

4. Don't click the mike button to acknowledge a transmission. To a controller, all clicks sound alike, and he will likely have to repeat his instructions to be sure the proper party understands. If you're too busy to acknowledge (and this is not an isolated circumstance, especially IFR), it's better to go ahead and fly the airplane in accordance with the instructions, and acknowledge a few seconds later, when you have the time.

5. If you intend to fly a lot of single-pilot IFR in busy areas, invest in a boom mike and a wheel-mounted mike switch.

6. En route, set your receiver volume so that you can hear Center's transmissions clearly. When another pilot close by blasts through your speaker at an uncomfortable level, live with it for the moment. Recognize that the loudness is the result of his proximity, or lack of communications manners—see the next item. If you turn down the volume, you may set it below the level you need to receive Center, and miss an important message.

7. Whenever you transmit, hold the mike close to your mouth, and speak in a lower-than-normal tone and volume (if the person seated next to you in the airplane can hear you talking, you're talking too loudly). This will help eliminate engine and aircraft noise, making your transmission much more readable. Most aircraft microphones "clip" the peaks of volume and pitch, and shouting just makes a bad situation worse.

8. When you're waiting in the number one spot at a crowded, busy airport and Tower clears you for immediate takeoff, and there's not time to acknowledge by radio, don't worry about it. The controller will see you starting to roll, and that's the finest acknowledgment you could give him.

9. After you have identified a VOR, turn off the audio side of the VOR receiver. The noise and occasional conversation on the omni frequency will serve only to distract you from more important business. Tune, identify, and turn off the sound.

10. Never, never sacrifice the control of your aircraft for the sake of talking on the radio. If you didn't know better, you'd sometimes think that Tower controllers were watching your take-off with binoculars, so they can ask you for your first estimate when they see you reach for the gear handle! The same philosophy applies to the required report on executing a missed approach—get the airplane on its way, and when everything is completely

under control, let somebody know of your intentions. FLY THE AIRPLANE FIRST!

Be a Conformist

You must realize that when you file and fly IFR, you become part of a *system*, highly structured and organized to provide the fastest, safest service to all comers. You cannot be denied access if you are qualified, so your task is to fit into the system as smoothly as possible, going along with the established procedures, becoming a round peg when ATC wants to fit you into a round hole—assuming that it's a *safe* hole! Communication represents a key element in the systemizing process; no matter how distinctive you like to be on the air, there's only one way to do it, and that's "by the book." There are two parts to the problem: first, knowing exactly *what* to say (and no more), and second, knowing *when* to say it.

About this matter of your aircraft identification—except for those worshippers at the altar of distinction who obtain nonstandard registration numbers, nearly all civil aircraft in the United States consist of four numbers and a letter suffix. Remember that controllers will usually be mentally juggling several aircraft call signs at once, so on your initial transmission, use just the "last three" of yours to get his attention. Suppose your full set of numbers is N1234A; say "three four Alpha" the first time, and give him the make and the rest of the call sign after you've established communications. If the controller answers with all of your numbers, you should use the full identification in subsequent transmissions. The reason? He may have another aircraft on his frequency with a similar call sign; if there are *two* Barnburners with numbers ending in 34A being worked by the same controller, confusion can reign supreme if both parties insist on acknowledging with just "three four Alpha." Use of the full identification completely eliminates this problem. However, if yours is the only one that comes close to three four Alpha, the controller will probably shorten the call sign, and then you may respond with the abbreviated number.

Clearance amendments that involve rerouting and other major changes should obviously be read back to ensure complete understanding on both sides of the electronic fence. More specifically, any clearance or instruction that involves a new heading or altitude requires a readback. "34 Alpha, turn right heading one five zero, descend to and maintain six thousand" should elicit this response from the pilot—"34 Alpha, right one five zero, cleared six thousand, leaving seven thousand."

In that last exchange (which is probably the most efficient way to accomplish that particular type of communication) notice the controller's care to place "and maintain" between "to" and "six thousand." There's good reason for this, since "to" can be easily mistaken for "two"—and the possibility of the Barnburner pilot interpreting his new altitude as "two six thousand" becomes a potential source of confusion. When controllers take pains to make *their* half of such a communication clear and unmistakable, it behooves pilots to respond in like manner. By reading back the new clearance as in the paragraph above, the controller heard exactly what he expected—the phrases and numbers he had just transmitted, and in the same order. That's *got* to be more understandable.

In addition to fostering more efficient communication, this "read-back-in-the-same-order" technique is founded in regulation and good practice: Pilots are required to acknowledge a new clearance ("cleared six thousand") and report vacating an assigned altitude ("leaving seven thousand"). So, when you are established in level flight and then cleared to climb or descend, develop the habit of responding the same way every time, as in: "Barnburner 34 Alpha is cleared niner thousand, leaving four thousand." You've acknowledged and reported in one fell swoop.

As you cruise about the airspace, you'll hear many variations on the theme of altitude reporting, such as "two point three" and "five point oh," but there's no altitude message that comes through as loud and clear as "two thousand three hundred" or "five thousand." Say it right the *first* time, and save the time it takes to "say again."

Another opportunity to streamline your IFR communications arises while you are climbing or descending to a new assigned altitude, and you are handed off to another controller. Your initial report should include altitude information, but keep in mind that the acquiring controller has been advised of your climb or descent, and is most interested in confirming where you intend to level, not where you are now. Good practice suggests that you say merely "Minneapolis, Barnburner 34 Alpha climbing (descending) eight thousand." 'Nuff said—if the controller needs to know your present altitude, he'll ask.

If, during climb or descent, you receive a new altitude clearance from the *same* controller, reply "Barnburner 34 Alpha now cleared four thousand"—no more words required to confirm the clearance.

Just as excess verbage seems to clog communications channels, pilots and controllers who are not positive and assertive often cause problems. Questions seem to beget questions: "Fort Worth, this is Barnburner 34 Alpha, did you want me to turn right to a heading of two five zero to intercept the localizer, or was it a left turn?" "Barnburner 34 Alpha, Fort Worth, did you copy right to two five zero? . . . ah, negative, that's a left turn, I say again, a *left* turn to three five zero to intercept. Did you copy?" And sometimes, more questions follow. How much better, when you're unsure, to be *assertive:* "Fort Worth, Barnburner 34 Alpha, *say again*." Elimination of questions is a good enough reason for having "say again" in the aeronautical vocabulary.

The use of radar transponders introduces an opportunity to save time, too. When a controller requests that you squawk "IDENT," you shouldn't even think about using the microphone; just press the "IDENT" button, and let the black box do the talking. There's no need to tell the controller that you have responded, for he'll see it on his scope right away, and when he informs you that you are "in radar contact," all you need reply is "Roger, 34 Alpha." The same is true of a code change; for example, ATC directs you to change your transponder to 1100, and your communication should be just that—flick the dials until the proper code appears, and wait for him to acknowledge. In those rare cases where he doesn't pick it up right away, he'll have you confirm that you have made the change; the important thing is that you didn't clutter the frequency with an unnecessary exchange at the outset.

In passing, it's interesting to note that the term "squawk" is an outgrowth of the World War II supersecret terminology that labeled the brand-new military transponders "parrots"; they replied to a coded electronic message just as the raspy-voiced green bird does. Some day when all has gone wrong, and you need an outlet for your emotions, a Center request to "squawk IDENT" provides the golden opportunity. Pick up the mike, and in the screechiest voice you can generate, make like a parrot—"IDENT! IDENT! IDENT!" (You should expect some sort of nasty reaction from ATC, but this little exercise is guaranteed to relieve your tensions.)

Say Only What's Needed

There is a standard procedure for communicating when you are handed off from one Center sector to another, or from one Center to the next. You must realize that before a controller requests that you "contact Cleveland Center now on 124.7," he has contacted the acquiring facility by telephone (all Centers and their sectors are linked by phone lines), confirmed that you are on his radar scope, and asked what frequency you should use. The subsequent sector (or Center) controller therefore knows who you are, where you're going, and really only needs confirmation of your altitude, the most important ingredient of safe separation at this point. So, when you check in with the new controller, you should say merely "Cleveland Center, Barnburner 1234 Alpha, eight thousand." If he wants to make absolutely sure, he may require you to squawk "IDENT," but he is not obligated to advise you "radar contact." You will assume that he has you on radar unless he advises otherwise—another case of the system eliminating needless conversation. If the handoff occurs while you are climbing or descending to a new assigned altitude, make this information part of your report: "Cleveland Center, Barnburner 1234 Alpha, climbing [or descending] eight thousand."

If it hasn't happened to you yet, it will—"Hometown Unicom, this is Barnburner 1234 Alpha; I'll be on the ground in ten minutes, will you call my wife and tell her to pick me up at the airport?" Followed by, "Roger, Barnburner 1234 Alpha, we'll be happy to make that call for you, but it will be long distance—this is Albuquerque Center." By switching back and forth from one radio to the other, you have transmitted on the wrong frequency! Using both radios can cause a great deal of confusion; eliminate it by using only one of your transceivers—the "other" radio should be considered a standby unit. In addition to preventing you from talking to the wrong people, this procedure takes one more monkey off your back, that of figuring out which radio is the right one to use. When you're in the IFR system, anything you can do to decrease your mental workload is good.

Play the "Numbers" Game

One of the most disturbing and time-consuming communications situations takes place on the ramp at any tower-controlled airport, where the Ground controller reels off the active runway, taxi instructions, and the altimeter setting to a departing aircraft, then hears "Barnburner 1234 Alpha, ready to taxi." Faced with this set of circumstances, the controller has no choice but to go through the whole bit again, and the needless repetitions build into frustrating numbers in the course of a day. When you get the engine started, turn on the radio, monitor Ground Control, and listen; unless you're the only airplane getting ready to go, you can copy the appropriate instructions, and when you are ready to move out, save tempers and time by saying "Barnburner 1234 Alpha, ready to taxi *with the numbers.*" (If you're on a large airport with several locations from which aircraft might taxi for takeoff, don't make Ground Control guess where you are; state your position with the original call: "Barnburner 1234 Alpha at Acme Aviation, ready to taxi with the numbers.")

When approaching for landing, the same principle applies; you can usually monitor the tower frequency from a considerable distance, learn what runway and traffic pattern is in use, and tell the Tower you "have the numbers" on the initial call, such as "Downtown Tower, Barnburner 1234 Alpha six miles northwest with the numbers, will call you on downwind for Runway 36." If the Tower controller would prefer some other pattern entry or another runway, he'll let you know. The beauty of this procedure is that he will usually only need to acknowledge your thoughtful, preplanned transmission with "Roger, 1234 Alpha," again making the most of communication time.

Both of these situations, before taxi and prior to landing, have been improved immeasurably through the ever-increasing number of ATIS (Automatic Terminal Information Service) installations across the country. As a conscientious pilot, take a few seconds to look up the ATIS frequency and get all the information before reporting "ready to taxi." There's just no excuse for Ground Control having to spend time reciting the active runway, altimeter setting, and other pertinent information when it is waiting for you on a continuous ATIS recording. It's even more important for IFR operations, since the ATIS broadcast usually includes weather, winds, and departure procedures in use. At most large terminals Ground Control doesn't have the time to cater to uninformed pilots, and will refer you back to ATIS if you call for taxi instructions without the current information. "Kennedy Ground, Barnburner 1234 Alpha at Gate 4B, taxi clearance, please" would no doubt be rejoined crisply with "34 Alpha, information Bravo is current," and he'll go on about more pressing business, leaving you to find out for yourself what information Bravo is all about.

Inbound to a busy airport, solid IFR, Center keeping you as busy as a prize bull in mating season, there's still time to tune the ATIS frequency and get yourself set for the approach segment of your flight. The busy airports don't have time to give you the good word; they expect you to be informed. Granted, it requires listening with each ear tuned to a different frequency, and ATC instructions certainly take precedence—but if you start listening to ATIS far enough out, you can pick up portions of the broadcast in between the calls from Center (use the audio switch to cut out ATIS when you hear your call sign on the primary radio), and by the time you are handed off to Approach Control, you should have the complete message.

When you're trying to obtain ATIS information as much in advance as possible, altitude always helps (another good reason for flying higher whenever you can). There's one more trick in the long-distance reception bag—adjust the squelch control, put up with the frying bacon for a couple of minutes, and you can often sort out the important parts of an ATIS broadcast much farther away from the terminal than you thought was possible. (The "test" position on a radio with automatic squelch control will sometimes get the same result.)

When the terminal weather is very good, so good that it's insignificant to instrument pilots, there will be no mention of it on the ATIS broadcast, or perhaps the simple statement, "weather is VFR." But when the meteorological situation is changing so rapidly that the controllers can't keep up with it, the ATIS will contain the words "weather will be issued by Approach Control," and you should expect to get the good (or bad) news from that facility at the appropriate time.

The law says that you will inform Approach Control or Tower

on initial contact that you have received "Information Foxtrot" (or whatever is current). To illustrate, when Center hands you off to Approach Control, you have listened to ATIS and the exchange goes like this:

CENTER: Barnburner 1234 Alpha, descend to and maintain five thousand, contact Bay Approach on one two five point three.

YOU: Roger, Barnburner 1234 Alpha cleared five thousand, leaving eight thousand. [*Unless you have some doubt concerning the facility or the frequency, there's no need to repeat that part of the clearance.*]

YOU AGAIN: Bay Approach, Barnburner 1234 Alpha descending five thousand, I have Foxtrot.

And the Bay Approach Controller will figure he's dealing with a pilot who knows which end is up.

Getting Around on the Ground

Proper communications discipline becomes more important as an airport becomes busier, and reaches its "ne plus ultra" at those terminals equipped with a Clearance Delivery facility. In addition to the requirement to listen to the ATIS broadcast, these fields insist that you have your IFR clearance before taxi. Besides the obvious rebuff you're going to get if you contact Ground Control sans clearance, consider the unruffled ease with which you can copy when you are sitting calmly on the ramp, nothing competing for your attention except getting that clearance right the first time. If you have a good strong battery (don't try this on a cold day when even the brass monkeys are heading south) and notice a long lineup at the departure end of the runway, you might consider switching on and getting your clearance before you even start the engines; if there is going to be an inordinate delay, you can save a lot of ground time on the motors. When you have filed for an immediate turnaround, it's possible to get even farther ahead of the system by contacting Clearance Delivery as you taxi in after landing.

Whether it's Clearance Delivery or Ground Control, you can help them dig your flight plan out of the heap by providing some basic information on the first call—"Washington Clearance, Barnburner 1234 Alpha, IFR to Saginaw at one zero thousand." The requested altitude and the destination give the controller something definite to look for.

Ground controllers will set you up by asking "Barnburner 1234 Alpha, I have your clearance, ready to copy?" but knowing that you are monitoring the frequency, some Clearance Deliverers will just let 'er go, ready or not! The loudspeaker suddenly comes alive with "Barnburner 1234 Alpha is cleared as filed to the Saginaw Airport, climb to one zero thousand, etc., etc., etc., read back." Remember that a Clearance Delivery facility is there to relieve congestion and you wouldn't be on the frequency unless you were ready to copy, so *be* ready; have your charts spread out to visualize route changes and all the other good practices germane to clearance copying. (See Chapter 7, "IFR Clearances.")

Now that you have your clearance and are ready to drive the Barnburner to the other end of the aerodrome for takeoff, you may face a navigation problem that is more complicated than any airborne situation. As airports have grown in size and complexity, the number of taxiways, outerbelts, innerbelts, crossovers, and switchbacks has increased to the point where you are just about ready to concede that there is no way to get to the runway from here! An old adage of the flying business applies here: When in doubt, swallow your pride and ask. Sure, the airline captain who flies into a particular airport six times a day knows the taxi routes inside out, but Ground controllers are quite aware that the "first-timer" is going to experience difficulty when he is cleared "to Runway 14 via Charlie and Mike, hold short of Juliet before crossing to the inner parallel, give way to the Shorthaul Beech 99 approaching from your right as you cross November." And Ground is more than willing to help you find your way, if you'll only ask. On a completely unfamiliar airport, the first thing to do is to break out the approach plate (or a separate taxi chart for the superlarge terminals—see Figure 7) and from the airport plan view, figure the most likely taxi route; trace it as Ground Control reads it off, and you should be able to make it on your own.

But suppose you can't find the chart, or the taxi clearance is so confusing that you don't even know which way to turn as you come off the ramp; here's where you admit to Ground Control that you are unfamiliar with the airport, and will he please give you directions? The answer may be humbling, because nine times out of ten, there just happens to be an airliner conveniently located so that you

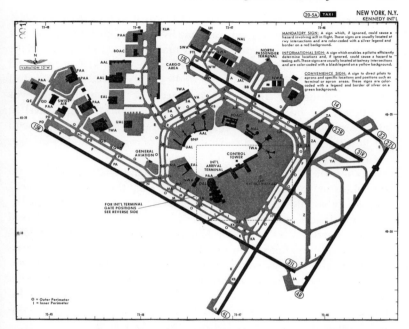

Figure 7   Taxiways and parking facilities at Kennedy International Airport, N. Y. (© 1973 Jeppesen & Co., Denver, Colo. All rights reserved. Not to be used for navigation.)

will hear (in a condescending voice), "Roger, 34 Alpha, turn right on the taxiway straight ahead of you and follow the United 747 to the active runway." So, tuck in under the tail of the big fella and it's "whither thou goest" from here to the end of the runway. Don't be chagrined, because the co-pilot is sitting up there with a road map, telling the captain which way to turn to make sure *they* are heading in the right direction.

Some air terminals are notorious for the curt manner with which their controllers operate, and others are equally famous for the complete and willing cooperation that comes from Ground Control. In either case, you certainly have a right to ask, and 'tis a far better thing to find out from them which way to turn, than to taxi onto an active runway and find yourself staring down the intakes of a just-landed DC-9.

Once you are cleared by Ground Control to the active runway, you are obligated to remain on that frequency until you arrive at the runup pad. If you want to depart momentarily to listen to ATIS, or call Unicom, be sure to check off with Ground Control, and report back. Upon arrival at the end of the runway or the end of the line, whichever comes first, it is prudent to monitor the Tower frequency for takeoff clearances and restrictions being issued to other similar type aircraft—it's another way to stay one step ahead by getting ready for the next segment of your flight before you actually get there.

When the Barnburner is the only airplane waiting to leap into the blue (or the gray, as the case may be), the switch to Tower frequency should be made just as soon as you have all the knobs, switches, levers, and handles in the proper positions for takeoff, and all you need say is "Possum Kingdom Tower, Barnburner 1234 Alpha, ready for takeoff on one four." Especially at busy airports, including the runway number helps the controller as he sorts out the departure requests. When he gets the word from Center that the system is ready to accept your flight, he'll advise "cleared for takeoff, maintain runway heading [or appropriate instructions], contact Departure Control on 124.3," and away you go.

Towers must always coordinate IFR departures with either Departure Control or Center, which means a communications lag, however slight. You can often circumvent this delay (assuming no lineup of waiting aircraft, in which case you must wait your turn) by advising Ground Control as you leave the ramp that you will be ready for takeoff when you reach the runway. This gives Tower a much more positive departure time to pass on to the other ATC facilities, and your takeoff clearance will probably be waiting for you when you switch to Tower. If you do this, don't delay getting to the runway, because a phone call will have been made informing someone else up the line that Barnburner 1234 Alpha can be off the ground in two minutes.

Position Reports—A Lost Art

One of the most pleasant sounds to filter through your speaker on an IFR flight is the phrase "in radar contact." It will usually happen right after takeoff, when Departure Control acquires you on the scope, and in most parts of the country you will continue in radar contact right down to the deck on the other end of your trip. It is comforting to know that someone down there knows who you are, where you are, and where other traffic is: but there is an additional feature that has done more to clean up the communications clutter than anything else. When you are advised that your flight is "in radar contact," what the controller politely means is "SHUT UP!" He doesn't want to hear from you, since he knows your position, groundspeed, and ETAs more accurately than you do. He doesn't want you to speak unless spoken to; as far as ATC is concerned, IFR pilots, like little children, should be seen (on radar) and not heard (on the radio).

Full-blown position reports are definitely taboo when in radar contact, but there are several other circumstances in which ATC would like to hear from you, mostly in confirmation of your actions which bear on safe separation from other IFR flights. Therefore, you should report without request when these situations exist (talk to the ATC facility with which you are in contact at the time, or as instructed):

1. Report the time and altitude reaching an assigned holding fix or clearance limit.
2. Report when leaving an assigned altitude. (Notice that a report is not required or even desired when reaching the new altitude. If ATC wants to know when you get there, they'll ask for a separate report.)
3. When you leave an assigned holding fix or clearance limit, let ATC know what time you departed.
4. On an instrument approach, you should report when you pass the Final Approach Fix inbound to the airport. ATC will always let you know to whom you should report.
5. You must report when executing a missed approach—again, you'll be told whom to call. (FLY THE AIRPLANE FIRST!)
6. If you have given ATC an estimate for a subsequent reporting point, and it appears that your estimate will be in error by more than three minutes either way, let them know.
7. You can fly at any altitude you choose (VFR altitude rules apply),

but advise ATC if you make a change when you're operating IFR with a VFR-on-Top restriction.

In an effort to streamline the ATC system, the government has cut back the number of Flight Service Stations, and has increased the area coverage of the ones that remain. For example, the Millville Flight Service Station, located between Atlantic City and Philadelphia, handles the communications for several other VORs along this very busy IFR flyway. So, if you report over Millville, Woodstown, Coyle, Atlantic City, Sea Isle, or Kenton VOR, you're going to be talking to the specialist at Millville. The chart indicates that each of these is a remote site, and if you intend to listen on the VOR frequency, it is important that you identify your position when making the initial call. The proper way to do this is to call not "Millville Radio" but perhaps "Sea Isle Radio," which lets the Specialist know on which frequency to reply. After the first call which nails down your position, you can drop the facade and use "Millville Radio," which you knew it was all along.

The widespread, almost universal coverage of enroute radar in today's ATC system makes it very unlikely that you'll have to make a full-blown position report to a Flight Service Station. But if you must do so, there is one right way to do it, and as many wrong ways as there are pilots. The correct procedure begins with the initial call: "Goodland Radio, Barnburner 1234 Alpha at Goodland with a position report, listening on the VOR, over." By starting off the exchange like this, you will have accomplished several time-saving functions—Goodland FSS knows who is calling, what you want, and the frequency on which you expect a reply. Your mention of an impending position report gives the Specialist time to pull out a blank form listing the items in the report; he inserts your aircraft identification and then tells you to "go ahead with your position." Just like filing a flight plan, there is a sequence to be followed which lets the specialist copy your report in the most efficient manner; he wants just the answers, not the questions, so compose your report in terms of numbers and names.

An easy way to remember the proper order is PTA TEN, which you should commit to memory. It makes absolutely no sense like that, but if you will line up the letters vertically, they form a mnemonic, one of the best memory joggers of all:

P Position (usually a VOR, intersection, or airway crossing).

T Time (always given in minutes past the hour when you were over the reported fix).

A Altitude.

T Type of flight plan (IFR or VFR). (On that rare occasion when Center asks you for a report, use the same format, but omit "IFR" since they already know that.)

E Estimated time of arrival at the next reporting point, again in minutes past the hour.

N Name of the next place you intend to report.

Of course, you would identify yourself as part of the report, so "Barnburner 1234 Alpha" would precede PTA TEN, and a typical IFR position report to a Flight Service Station would sound like this: "Goodland Radio, Barnburner 1234 Alpha, Goodland at four two, eight thousand, IFR, Thurman at one zero, Denver, over." A well-organized position report should not take more than ten or fifteen seconds using the PTA TEN sequence, and FSS will get it all the first time; if you've done it right, he will reply with "Roger your position, Barnburner 1234 Alpha, Goodland altimeter is two niner point seven six."

Some communications situations demand interpretation on the part of the pilot; ATC people use rather severely abbreviated phrases when time is at a premium. Such was the case one extremely busy morning when a Center controller needed confirmation of the height of a particular flight, and transmitted "Trans Global two thirty-four, say altitude." The reply came back, "altitude." In a slightly more stentorian tone, Center tried again: "Trans Global two thirty-four, say *altitude!*" Two thirty-four was still feeling frisky, and replied again, "altitude." Taking the measure of his airborne adversary and displaying more than the usual amount of savoir faire, the controller broadcast calmly, "Roger, Trans Global two thirty-four, say 'cancelling IFR.' " Only a few seconds separated that transmission from "Center, Trans Global two thirty-four is level at one zero thousand."

On occasion, and particularly at lower altitudes over mountainous terrain, you will be asked to contact another ATC facility on a new frequency, and when you dial in the proper number, nobody answers. When this happens, wait a minute, and try again. If the third attempt elicits no response, return to the previously assigned frequency and advise the controller of your plight. Nine times out of ten, the next man heard you calling, but was too busy with other traffic to answer; or perhaps you are just a bit outside the range of his transmitter.

Whatever the reason, don't go through a lengthy dissertation on what has happened, just say to the previous controller, "Memphis Center, Barnburner 1234 Alpha, *unable* Kansas City on one two three point eight." The magic word is "unable," and tells him right away of the difficulty. After advising you to "stand by," he'll call Kansas City on the phone and ask if they heard you. Sometimes the new frequency is a bad one, and you'll be assigned another—but more than likely, Memphis will ask you to try again, maybe five minutes from now, when you'll be close enough to hear Kansas City.

Don't get up tight and call over and over and over—continue on your way, and after a reasonable time, try to establish contact. Even if your radios have quit, there are iron-clad rules to follow (see Chapter 12, "Communications Failure"); of course, before you launch into those procedures, try to contact a Flight Service Station, a Tower, or any handy ATC facility.

Letters and Numbers

The International Civil Aviation Organization (ICAO) phonetic alphabet is the rulebook when it comes to proper pronunciation of both letters and numbers. Some of the letters may seem a bit unwieldy to you, but they've been chosen for their universality; theoretically, pilots fom any country in the world can make themselves understood using these phonetics. But no matter how hard they try, our Oriental brothers-in-the-airspace will change Bravo to Blavo, Foxtrot to Foxtlot, and Romeo to Lomeo. The problems transcend geographical barriers within the U.S. also; you will seldom hear a pilot from the Midwest come through with OSS-CAH, as Oscar is spelled phonetically in the book—he's bound to drawl "OSS-CURR" from now 'til the end of time. His Downeast counterpart will likewise pronounce Sierra "SEE-AIRER," and the sod-buster who calls 'em like he sees 'em will always use "LI-MAH" as in beans instead of "LEE-MAH" as in Peru.

Numbers come in for their share of abuse, too, the most easily muddled combination being "five" and "nine." To eliminate confusion entirely, the communications expert would have us use "niner," which does the job very effectively. A man who suspected his wife of hanky-pankying with an airline pilot had his suspicions confirmed when, confronting her with the evidence, he demanded to know if indeed she had been indiscreet—"I've told you niner thousand times, NEGATIVE!" she replied.

Transiting the IFR airspace can be a trying experience for those who are not familiar with "what's happening," but we all had to start somewhere. If you are not a smooth communicator, able to become part of the system with a minimum of radio conversation, buy a VHF receiver and listen to the big boys; learn the jargon of instrument flying, anticipate the instructions coming up, and play the game of thinking ahead so that you can impart the most information with the fewest words. You'll endear yourself to ATC, save time for all the other airmen who have important things to say, and brand yourself as a "pro" in the process.

9

VOR Navigation

KEEPING the needle centered enroute is a fairly simple task, and by always placing the airway course under the index, you can't go too far wrong. But when it's time for a VOR approach or a holding pattern, you've got to know what the receiver is telling you, and how to orient yourself to the desired radial.

All VOR receiver installations have this much in common. Each one is composed of (1) a Course Deviation Indicator (CDI) or in everyday language, a left-right needle; (2) a TO-FROM indicator, which solves the question of ambiguity; (3) an Omni Bearing Selector (OBS), which sets the stage for interpreting the information from the other two. When the OBS is set on a particular course, the CDI will *always* tell you whether you are on, to the left of, or to the right of the radial that the OBS setting represents. The TO-FROM indicator furnishes additional information about whether that course (the OBS setting) will take you TO or FROM the omni transmitter.

Because of this orientation to a specific course, it is imperative that you begin interpretation of what you see on the panel by getting the airplane lined up on a heading the same as, or at least close to, the course you have selected. You can do this by physically turning the plane to that heading, or more likely, by imagining yourself flying in the proper direction. When this basic condition is met, the VOR receiver indications will always tell you a true story—if you fly a heading that agrees with the course that is set into the OBS, you will proceed toward the station if the indicator shows TO, or away from the station if it shows FROM. Should the CDI be centered when heading and OBS are close together, you can be sure that you are ON that particular radial; if it's displaced to the left, you must fly left to get to the radial, or fly right if the needle lies on the other side. Unless you are turning to intercept a radial, or just entering a holding pattern, the only difference between the OBS setting and your heading should be drift correction, and it will seldom be a very large disparity. (Technically, the "true story" on the VOR indicator exists on any heading up to 90 degrees either side of the selected course, but you'll do yourself a navigational favor by always imagining the airplane's heading in agreement with the OBS. If worse comes to worst, turn the airplane until the numbers agree and proceed from there—it's better than getting completely disoriented!)

Radials, Radials, Radials

If you don't speak, read, and write the language of radials, there's no time like right now to fix it firmly in your IFR thinking, because the entire VOR navigational system is based on courses *away from the station*. There is only *one* line on the chart for each numbered radial associated with a particular VOR station; whether you are flying it outbound or inbound, holding on it or crossing it, a radial is always in the same place. The only possible complication lies in the reciprocity of the numbers—whenever you are proceeding *outbound*, your magnetic *course* (and *heading* when there's no wind) will be the same number as the *radial*; turn around and fly *inbound* and you must mentally reverse the numbers and physically reverse the OBS setting so that your course is now the reciprocal of the radial. Be that as it may, you are still flying on a *radial*—it hasn't moved or changed one iota.

Putting VOR to Work

There are four basic problems you will encounter in everyday use of VOR; whether you're holding, making an approach, or navigating enroute, a thorough knowledge of these four will enable you to handle any situation. They are:

1. Determining what course will take you *direct* to a VOR.
2. Determining your position in relation to a specific airway or radial.
3. Identifying an intersection (or crossing a particular radial).
4. Determining a wind correction angle that will keep you on course.

The first case is frequently put to use when you are cleared "from your present position DIRECT" to a VOR. The procedure is simple; after turning and identifying the station (don't *ever* forget this step!), rotate the OBS until the left-right needle is centered, and the ambiguity indicator shows TO. The number that now appears under the OBS index is your course to the station (inbound, it will always be the *reciprocal* of the radial you are on); turn to and fly that heading, adding drift correction as necessary to keep the needle centered, and that's all there is to it.

Number two starts off the same way; when you are requested to "intercept and fly outbound on the 320 radial," make certain you have the right station tuned, and select 320 on the OBS (since you are outbound, desired course and radial are one and the same). If you're not on that heading or close to it, turn to 320 degrees, to satisfy the first condition of VOR orientation. Assuming that when you received the clearance you were already northwest of the VOR, the TO-FROM indicator should settle on FROM (located somewhere else?—keep flying on a 320 heading, you'll get a FROM sooner or later!). So far, so good; now to the heart of the problem— where are you in relation to the 320 radial? If the CDI centers, you're there; and since you have turned the airplane so that your heading agrees with the OBS setting, a deflection of the needle to either side will tell you which way to turn to get on course. Needle left? Fly left, and vice versa. The same procedure applies when you're cleared to fly a radial inbound (don't forget to reverse the numbers!), except the TO-FROM meter will read TO.

Situation number three comes up frequently—when you're checking groundspeed, temporarily out of radar contact, timing a holding pattern, or when asked by ATC to report at an intersection. Reporting points are usually the well-defined crossing of two or more airways or radials. Whether you're asked to report at a charted, named intersection or when crossing a certain radial, there's a technique that will work every time. For example, if you are proceeding northwest from the Akron VOR on Victor 42E (Figure 8), and Cleveland Center requests a report passing the Crib intersection, you have a choice of either the 027 radial of Cleveland or the Chardon 285 radial as your cross-reference. The Cleveland radial seems best, because you will be closer to that station, and the bearing will be closer to a wingtip position. (Those radials indicated by arrows are

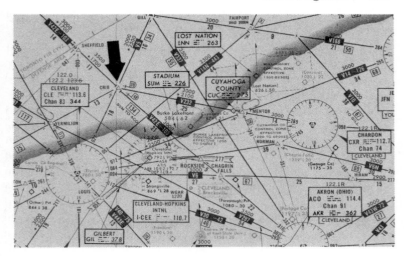

Figure 8 Navigational facilities forming the Crib intersection.

recommended, but you may use any combination you like—as long as your position is not beyond the VOR change-over point, and the angle is not less than 30 degrees.) When you tune and identify CLE, place the desired *radial* (027) in the OBS, and when the CDI centers, you have reached Crib intersection (maintaining the centerline of Victor 42E all the while, of course). Until you get to Crib, the needle will remain to the left of center, so here's the rule: When the "side" *radial* is set in the OBS, you have not arrived at the intersection as long as the CDI is deflected *toward the station*, or to the left in this case. (Prove it to yourself; before reaching Crib, mentally stop the airplane, turn it to a heading of 027 degrees— you'd have to fly *left* to get to that radial.) If you had tuned CLE and the needle came to rest on the side of the instrument *away* from the station (to the right), better let Center know about it right away—you've passed Crib.

And so to the fourth situation, the one you will use most frequently—figuring out the proper wind correction angle, or "bracketing the course." If you always take immediate corrective action when you notice the CDI drifting off center, you'll never get off course far enough to need bracketing; but a sharp turn over a VOR, or vectors to a new radial where the wind effect is unknown, may find you chasing a CDI that's off-scale.

Assuming no knowledge of the wind direction or force, the first thing to do is turn 30 degrees toward the radial, and wait for the needle to center. For example, trying to track outbound on the 360 radial (Figure 9), you find that a heading of 360 allows the airplane to drift to the right (CDI moving left). When a heading of 330 degrees puts you back on course, you have established the maximum "bracket" within which the correct heading lies—at 360, you cannot stay on course, and 330 will take you back to the radial. Now, cut the difference in half; turn to 345 degrees, and again watch the CDI— if it stays put, 345 is the correct heading. But if the needle starts

FIGURE 9   Bracketing a VOR course.

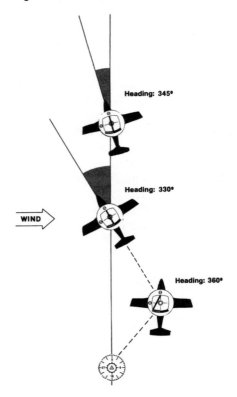

to the left again, immediately turn to 330, the heading you know will return you to course; it won't take nearly as long as the first time. Since 345 degrees has proved insufficient, take the next half-step and turn to 340 degrees; be practical, accept the nearest 5-degree increment. Before long you'll have a heading that will immobilize the CDI; this process works just as well in either direction.

This sounds like a terribly complicated, time-consuming process on paper, but in the air, it will take only a few minutes; as your experience increases, you will be able to tell roughly how much correction you'll need by observing the rate at which the CDI moves. Your target is a dead-center needle all the time—which may explain why a really good instrument pilot spends so much time checking his VOR receiver; the CDI remains so motionless, he has to make sure the set hasn't failed!

No Ident, No Good

It stands to reason that the only stations that can be used for IFR enroute operations are those that are transmitting a usable signal. The designers provided a built-in alarm system to alert you when a VOR goes off the air, when it is shut down for maintenance, or when the signal quality drops below a certain level. It's a very simple scheme, and consists of either automatic or manual removal of the station's Morse code identifier when any of these conditions exists. So, your reaction is equally uncomplicated—whenever you tune a VOR and cannot identify it, DON'T USE IT! If an explanation of the outage isn't printed on the chart nearby, let someone in ATC know of the problem. They'll check their monitoring devices and take the appropriate action.

Distance-Measuring Equipment

If your airplane is equipped with DME, you'll probably have it turned on throughout the flight, so why not use it for identifying intersections? With the CDI centered, it's merely a matter of flying up or down the radial until the charted number of miles shows up on the DME scale. Establishing yourself at an intersection with the help of DME is valid *only* when you use a station directly ahead or directly behind—authorized DME intersections are shown on the Jeppesen charts by the letter "D" and on the government charts by an open arrowhead. (Check your legend for details.) The same ahead-or-behind limitation must be observed if you intend to derive accurate groundspeed readings from your distance-measuring equipment.

VOR Accuracy Checks

The odds are probably better than even that the next trip you fly IFR will be illegal, at least from a VOR receiver standpoint. Checking VORs is one of those things that almost all pilots know about, but somehow just don't take the time to accomplish at the required intervals. According to the book, you may not fly in the IFR system unless the VOR receivers have been checked for accuracy within the preceding thirty days. Furthermore, the pilot in command is ultimately responsible for making sure this requirement has been satisfied. It matters not whether you're flying the same old airplane that you've owned for ten years, or the brand new Barnburner you rented for this one trip. You're the pilot in command, and you're the one the FAA will come looking for if they suspect a VOR malfunction is involved in a mishap.

The way to stay current is to check the receivers on every flight. The system designers have made it easy for you, by putting a ground test station (VOT) on most large airports, and designating certain spots on other fields where a nearby VOR signal can be received and used for testing. If time is running out and you are far away from either of these, there are designated airborne checkpoints (one of these, at Sulphur Springs, Texas, requires that the aircraft be positioned "over projector booth and snack bar within outdoor movie"—that's *accuracy!*), so there really is no excuse for flying with VORs that have not been checked. Look in the *Airman's Information Manual* or *Jeppesen's J-AID* for these facilities and checkpoints, and if all else fails, you may even designate your own airborne check—pick out a prominent landmark *on an airway* preferably 20 miles or more from the station, and get down low enough to fly directly overhead.

If all the electrons are behaving as they should, all these situations should result in a centered CDI when the OBS is placed on the appropriate number (radial or course). Should you have to turn the OBS more than 4 degrees either way to center the needle for ground checks, or more than 6 degrees either way for an airborne check, your set is out of tolerance, and IFR flight would be illegal.

Checking the VORs every time you fly is a fine habit to form, but all the effort and good intent will go for naught unless you make a record of what you have done. As soon as you have checked the receivers, make a note of the date, the location, the bearing error (how much you had to rotate the OBS to make the needle come to center), and affix your signature thereto. Where you maintain this record of VOR checks is immaterial, as long as *you* know where it is, because it's one of the first things the inspectors ask for when looking into the whys and wherefores of an aircraft incident. By making *some* kind of a VOR check before *every* flight, in *every* airplane, you are effectively taking yourself off *that* hook.

There is another way you can accomplish this check, but it must be placed in the last-resort category; if no other means is available within the time limits (and that's difficult to imagine—you can hardly fly for thirty days anywhere in the United States and not have been *someplace* where there was a VOR checkpoint), you may legally check one receiver against the other. Tuned to the same VOR, the OBSs may not be more than 4 degrees apart with CDIs centered— but what if the first VOR is already 10 degrees off? Treat this check as something you will do only if there's no other way, and at the earliest opportunity, check the receivers properly.

Using an HSI

The VOR system appeared in the 1950s and was hailed as the salvation of aerial navigation; after the ear-bending As and Ns of four-course low-frequency radio ranges, the simplicity of VOR seemed like an instrument pilot's Valhalla. Although the principle of VOR navigation hasn't changed over the years, the avionics people have provided better ways of displaying the information; there are rectilinear needles (which remain vertical as they move back and forth across the face of the instrument, instead of swinging from a hinge), and one manufacturer has produced a VOR/ILS display that has no needles at all . . . just bars of light that grow longer as course or glide-slope deviations get larger. But even with these much-improved displays, the pilot still must conjure up a mental image of his position relative to the VOR station or a selected radial; and that isn't always easy, especially when you're headed in the wrong direction or when a strong wind has drifted you way off course in a holding pattern.

The solution has been available for a number of years, but it has required more money, more instrument panel space, and more electricity than is associated with most light aircraft. Now, thanks to the "filter-down" concept (wherein the finer things in aeronautical life are introduced through the well-heeled military and air carrier systems, and eventually find their way into the general aviation fleet as production and technology make them less expensive), a pictorial display of the navigational situation can be installed in nearly any light aircraft intended for IFR operations. This unit is generally known as a Horizontal Situation Indicator (HSI) or Pictorial Navigation Indicator (PNI). By either name, it's the greatest thing since sliced bread for *any* instrument pilot, and especially for beginners—why not learn VOR navigation the easy way from the very start?

The Complete Picture at a Glance

In an earlier discussion of attitude instrument flying, the artificial horizon was referred to as the "heart of the system"; it deserves that definition because it shows two aircraft attitudes—pitch and roll—on one instrument. The HSI is the heart of a pictorial navigation system for the same reason . . . it provides more information at a glance than any other navigation display on the instrument panel. A typical installation (Figure 10) shows magnetic heading, desired course, TO-FROM indication, and perhaps most important, an airplane symbol on the face of the instrument so that your position relative to radial or localizer course can be *visualized* at any time. The HSI actually superimposes VOR information on the heading display; there's no need to look in one place for a left-right needle, OBS setting, and TO-FROM information, in another place for heading, and then try to put them all together in your mind's eye and hope you've interpreted everything correctly. With an HSI, your mind's eye can relax . . . because the entire navigational picture is right there in front of you. It's very much like being able to look down from a great height and watch the changes in your airplane's

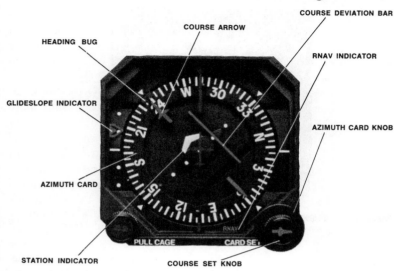

COURSE DEVIATION BAR

COURSE ARROW

HEADING BUG

RNAV INDICATOR

GLIDESLOPE INDICATOR

AZIMUTH CARD KNOB

AZIMUTH CARD

STATION INDICATOR

COURSE SET KNOB

PULL CAGE   CARD SET

Figure 10   Components of a typical HSI. (*Courtesy of Narco Avionics.*)

relationship to a course line painted on the ground; the sooner you think of it that way, the sooner your HSI will really begin to work best for you.

Enroute Use of the HSI

Just like any other navigational device, an HSI must be properly programmed. In this respect, it's no different from the traditional VOR indicator; so the pilot's first task is to set the course selector (arrowhead) to the correct number—in the example (Figure 11), a course of 120 degrees has been selected. Now the pictorial display begins to take shape; the VOR is ahead of the airplane, the course deviation bar is displaced to the right of the airplane symbol (the amount of movement is proportional to actual distance off course), and it becomes obvious that your present heading of 150 degrees will "fly" the airplane symbol to the radial on a 30-degree intercept angle. Unless you're flying into hurricane winds, the airplane and the course deviation bar will eventually come together, indicating that you are exactly on the desired course. (Whether enroute or

Figure 11   Course intercept shown on an HSI. (*Courtesy of Narco Avionics.*)

executing an approach procedure, train yourself to fly the little airplane to the course-deviation bar—think of that displaced segment of the course arrow as the line you want to be on, and fly to it. Piece of cake.) As you turn the real airplane, the azimuth ring (heading indicator) and the course selector turn, too; the entire display is constantly updated.

On course, wind correction is simply a matter of keeping the little airplane symbol centered on the course-deviation bar by means of appropriate heading changes. And when you've turned into the wind the proper number of degrees, you'll once again have a picture of the situation—the little airplane will be directly over the course-deviation bar with the wind-correction angle displayed as it really exists. The station pointer (TO-FROM indicator) will always indicate the location of the VOR—either ahead or behind—in relation to the selected course.

Even the best of the HSIs will develop a nervous needle when the aircraft approaches the VOR station, but that's a characteristic of the transmitter, not the airborne equipment. Just like other VOR displays, the heading that got you *to* the station on course will carry you *through* the confused-signal area and out the other side; so when the course-deviation bar starts its close-to-the-station shuffle, hold what you've got. Station passage is official when the TO-FROM indicator makes a complete reversal. Outbound tracking is no dif-

ferent than inbound, except that the pointer shows the station behind you.

To illustrate another of the frequently used pictorial features of
an HSI, consider an airway that changes course significantly at a
VOR. Suppose that by the time station passage is confirmed and
the new course is set up, the course-deviation bar has moved nearly
full scale to the right; a right turn is indicated, but how many
degrees? What heading will result in a course intercept within a
reasonable time and distance?

Up until now, the intercept solution has required some computation, some guesswork, or most likely, a hit-and-miss combination of the two. But the HSI changes all that to a positive navigational
technique that works when inbound or outbound; just reset the
course arrow to the new number, then turn the airplane until the
lubber line at the top of the display touches the offset portion of
the course-deviation bar. (Some HSIs don't have lubber lines quite
long enough to do this, but you can line up these two components
of the display by mentally extending the lubber line to the tip of
the offset segment.) This simple procedure puts the airplane on a
positive intercept heading (usually 45 degrees), and the display shows
precisely where you are in relation to the desired course. Sooner
or later, the deviation bar will begin to move from the fully displaced
position, and you should turn the airplane as required to keep the
lubber line and the tip of the offset bar together until the intercept
is completed. This technique is smooth, positive, and *pictorial;* it
makes the tendency to overshoot the radial a problem of the past.

Despite your diligence in keeping lubber line and bar tip together, a strong crosswind will sometimes cause the course-deviation bar to "stand off" a bit to the side. When this happens (you
have killed the drift, but are flying parallel to the desired course),
turn further into the wind the same number of degrees required to
stop the drift, and return to the original no-drift heading when the
course-deviation bar centers.

The HSI paints a beautiful navigational picture when you need
to identify an airway intersection. Having established a heading that
will maintain the enroute course, tune and identify the off-course
VOR that makes up the intersection. Then set the HSI's course
arrow on the *radial* that crosses your present course; the offset
segment displays the intersecting radial as it really is, and as the

airplane symbol "flies" across it, there will be no doubt in your mind when you've reached—or passed—the intersection.

Holding with an HSI

Let's face a fact of IFR life—a holding pattern entry flown with a non-pictorial VOR display has an element of confusion built in because you can't see where you are in relation to the holding course. On the other hand, an HSI makes holding patterns understandable. Regardless of the type of entry you elect to use, set the course arrow to the *inbound course*—the holding course—when you pass over the station the first time. The course-deviation bar will immediately display the position of that all-important holding course, and the airplane symbol will erase all doubt about where you are. When the first minute is up, merely turn the airplane back toward the holding course, complete the intercept as described earlier, and go about your business with confidence. There's no problem with so-called reverse sensing here; when the course arrow is set to a desired inbound course, the HSI will *always* display the location of that course in its correct relation to your airplane.

HSI and ILS . . . Partners in Precision

All the good things about an ILS procedure are made better when there's an HSI in your instrument panel. While it's no more accurate than any other display, it enables you to see where you are throughout the entire approach; and regardless of the amount of wind correction required to stay on the localizer, the course arrow represents the landing runway and indicates how many degrees left or right you should look to pick up the approach lights.

There's a cardinal rule to remember when setting up the HSI for an ILS or localizer approach: *Always set the course arrow on the published front course.* This rule is true for *all* localizer work, even when flying a back-course approach. Set up this way, the course-deviation bar will always display the localizer, and your position—whether flying a procedure turn or being vectored to the final approach course—will be apparent in terms of the airplane symbol's relation to the offset segment of the bar.

Whether vectored to the final approach course (the most common situation these days) or completing a procedure turn, the localizer intercept should be accomplished the same as turning onto a VOR radial; keep the lubber line directly over the tip of the course-deviation bar, and you'll arrive on the localizer automatically, with a minimum of overshoot.

Proceeding toward the marker now, the HSI display should be flown exactly as you would fly the "normal" presentation—when the bar slides left, turn left, and vice versa—but with the added safety and convenience of obtaining all the essential navigational information from one source. The glide slope indicator is activated when the localizer frequency is selected, and is interpreted the same as any other. It's always directional and always displays the location of the glide path relative to your airplane. When it moves above center, you should decrease your rate of descent; when it's on the mark, you are on the glide slope; when the indicator slips below center, you should power down and descend a little faster to regain the proper position.

A back-course localizer approach, that notorious boggler of pilots' minds, becomes crystal clear with an HSI. All you need remember is to set the *tail* of the course arrow on the published inbound back course; the offset segment of the display shows the localizer in its true relation to the airplane symbol. Thus, a back-course approach literally becomes as easy to fly as the front course, with absolutely no concern about flying "away from the needle." When properly set up for enroute, holding, or approach, the HSI's pictorial display reduces the navigational task significantly; just fly the little airplane toward the deviation bar to resolve any off-course situation.

Other Ways to Use an HSI

Even when there's no signal—VOR or ILS—being received and displayed, an HSI can be very helpful visualizing the aircraft's position. As the airplane turns, the azimuth ring turns, and the course arrow always shows you the relation between aircraft heading and desired course.

For example, when setting up for an NDB procedure, set the course arrow on the *inbound course* published for the approach. As you pass over the beacon and proceed outbound, notice that the two arrowheads—one on the ADF pointer, the other on the HSI—are pointing to the same place (the tail) on their respective dials. At the proper time, turn left or right 45 degrees to start the procedure turn. Here, once again, both arrowheads indicate the same 45 degrees from the tail position. (The HSI has convenient 45-degree "tic marks" all around the dial, so you no longer need to look at or compute procedure turn headings.) The 180-degree turn puts you on a 45-degree intercept, and the HSI's pointer will stop exactly 45 degrees from the aircraft heading. When the ADF needle is parallel to the HSI's course arrow (both indicating 45 degrees from the nose of the airplane symbols), you're on course—it's just that simple. By always setting the HSI on the *inbound course*, the relation between the two arrows is consistent, and all the computation from an NDB procedure is eliminated. This technique works just as handily when holding on an NDB.

You can also use an HSI to help orient yourself on the approach to a completely unfamiliar airport. When the course arrow is set to the number that represents the landing runway, the HSI displays a picture that can hardly be misinterpreted; you'll "see" the runway, and can plan which way to turn and how much when the field comes into sight.

On a large airport with several runways and taxiways, set your HSI in the direction of the takeoff runway before taxiing; at least, you'll be able to make a sensible determination of whether to turn left or right as you leave the ramp.

In summary, an HSI would cause that ancient Chinese philosopher to update his comment about the value of a picture: "One HSI is worth a thousand left-right needles."

10

Area Navigation (RNAV)

CROWS are not the bird-world's fastest flyers—however, in the process of exercising their legendary ability to get where they're going in straight lines, they're bound to save some time when flying from Tree A to Tree B. Instrument pilots anxious to maximize the efficiency of their airplanes should also think in terms of straight lines, but it's impossible when the primary navigational system is built on IFR routes that dogleg their way across the country. Every now and then you'll come across a situation in which there's a VOR at the departure airport and another at destination. Then an accurate, straight-line course is possible, but that's the exception, hardly the rule.

On the other hand, there are nearly one thousand VORs scattered across the United States today, so that almost anyplace you'd want to go in an airplane is on some radial of some VOR station; however, you must be *on* that radial to know where you are. Plotting two radials that cross above the destination is a big help, but it's still a blind navigational situation until you locate yourself on one of the radials and fly until the other needle centers.

The advent of the VORTAC ("TAC" refers to the military's Tactical Air Navigation system, and indicates DME capability for civilian users) and the self-explanatory VOR-DME facility means that any point within the service area of that station can be defined in terms of a radial and distance. For example, you might be located at a point 15 miles from the VORTAC on the 225° radial; the place you'd like to go might be on the 315° radial, 15 miles out (Figure 12). Any eighth grader who managed to stay awake in geometry class would recognize the triangle thus produced, and could offer a solution. When the lengths and angular relationships of two sides

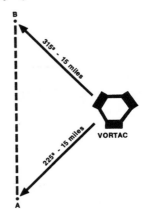

FIGURE 12 The RNAV triangle.

of a triangle are known, simple trigonometry can be used to figure out the length of the remaining side . . . and in this case, the direction of that third side with respect to magnetic north.

Voilà! But few pilots have the time (or the inclination) to consult a table of trigonometric functions and come up with the answers, especially when the airplane has moved several miles during the calculations. Why not give the job to a computer that has been programmed to figure out these triangles and come up with the right answers continuously and instantaneously? When the electronics people were able to reduce computers from the size of your living room to the size of a shoebox, area navigation became possible. Now, instead of having to fly the dogleg airways and fumble with two-VOR fixes, pilots can navigate directly to or from any point within the area served by a VOR/DME facility. Area Navigation (RNAV, for short) opens a whole new world of efficient, straight-line navigation. Look out, crows!

RNAV has introduced a new term—"waypoint"—to the aviator's vocabulary. This is the proper way of referring to those locations defined by radial and distance from a particular VORTAC. It takes the place of a "checkpoint" in other types of navigation. Since a waypoint can be placed anywhere the pilot wants it—on an airport, a Final Approach Fix, a Missed Approach Point, or a mountain (so you can stay away from it)—RNAV makes possible a navigation system with complete flexibility, a system that allows the pilot to choose the route *he* wants.

A typical RNAV installation consists of an onboard computer, a means of inserting the radial-distance information known as the "waypoint address," and a digital distance display that indicates magnetic bearing and nautical miles from the selected waypoint. An electronic interface sends the directional signal from the computer to the Course Deviation Indicator to provide steering information. From an operational standpoint, you fly RNAV exactly the same way you fly a normal VOR . . . but the LEFT-RIGHT, TO-FROM indications, the setting of the OBS, and the computer-generated range are based on a waypoint instead of a VOR station.

Nearly all RNAV manufacturers have taken advantage of the microprocessor revolution, and provide pilots with additional navigational data at the touch of a button. For example, you can call up the radial and distance from the VORTAC you're using . . . that's "raw data" (uncomputed), and it comes in handy to satisfy your own occasional curiosity as to your location, to say nothing of the easy, accurate reply to ATC when a controller asks "Where are you?" Pushing on another RNAV button will display groundspeed to or from the waypoint, and the time required to fly there.

You'll not fly with RNAV very long without noticing that the CDI has lost its "Nervous Nellie" characteristic close to the station, and that RNAV station passage is accompanied by a "soft" change of the TO-FROM indicator. These welcome changes are due in part to electronic filtering as the raw data is massaged by the computer, but more important, the steering display (left-right needle) is based on a totally different and more realistic concept than "straight" VOR . . . RNAV displays *linear deviation.*

On course (CDI centered), the RNAV and VOR presentations are identical, but the picture changes remarkably when your airplane moves to the left or right of a selected course. The VOR-only installation is limited to showing how many *degrees* you are from the selected course; RNAV presentations indicate the *distance* off course. All VOR indicators are designed with a scale of ten degrees either side of center, while most RNAVs have a scale of five nautical miles left and right.

To illustrate the difference, imagine your airplane equipped with both standard VOR and RNAV, both set up on the same station and with the same course selected on the OBS. When the airplane is 2.5 *degrees* off course, the VOR indicator will show one quarter of the ten-degree distance between center and full-scale deflection; if that same location is also 2.5 *miles* off course, the RNAV indicator will show a displacement of one-half scale.

As you continue flying straight ahead in this situation, the VOR needle will show more and more deviation, since the angle is constantly increasing . . . you are flying farther and farther from the selected radial. On the other hand, the RNAV CDI sits there steady as a rock, telling you that the course you have selected is, and remains, 2.5 miles to one side. You are flying parallel to the desired course, something that's impossible with ordinary VOR. In both cases, the TO-FROM indicator changes as you fly by the station, but with RNAV, you'll always know the displacement *distance*. This can be a very useful feature, such as when you'd like to arrive on a two-mile downwind leg at a strange airport. Set up a waypoint on the airport, fly on a parallel course to the desired side with the CDI two miles off center, and when the TO-FROM changes, you'll be at midfield on a two-mile downwind.

From the very beginning, RNAV units have incorporated a feature that lets you select a more sensitive CDI mode for RNAV approaches and other situations that require a finer display of off-course distance. Commonly called the "approach" mode, this selection changes the scale of the CDI; typically, the CDI now indicates only 2.5 miles either side of center, and small deviations from course will be easier to see. In general, the approach mode should be selected when you're approximately 20 miles from the waypoint, and should remain in that configuration throughout an RNAV approach procedure.

Putting RNAV to Work

One of the first, and most useful, applications of RNAV is for the relatively short trips from and to your home base. With a VOR-TAC located close by—or at least within reception distance after you've climbed a thousand feet or so—you can begin building a library of waypoint addresses for oft-used airports, based on the radial and distance from that nearby VORTAC. Within the RNAV equipment's range, you'll then have positive course guidance and distance information at takeoff or very shortly thereafter.

For example, a pilot based at St. Joseph, Missouri (Figure 13), who flies frequently to Trenton, Des Moines, Storm Lake, and Iowa Falls airports could plot the waypoint addresses for these locations using the St. Joseph VORTAC, and have the exact magnetic course and trip distance come up on the screen as soon as the RNAV unit acquires a usable signal from STJ. (Part of the service when you subscribe to Jeppesen's RNAV chart series is a listing of waypoint addresses for nearly every airfield in the country, but these numbers are based on the VORTAC nearest the airport, for obvious reasons.) In the language of RNAV—radial first, followed by distance in nautical miles—the waypoint addresses are: Trenton, 075062; Des Moines, 023110; Storm Lake, 347158; Iowa Falls, 018167.

For the return portion of a trip, you might draw a circle around your home airport, the radius of the circle being the working range of your RNAV equipment. Choose VORTACs in the cardinal directions on or inside this ring, and plot the waypoint addresses for your airport from these stations; now, when you're inbound and within range of one of the preselected VORTACs, load the homebase waypoint, confirm that you're getting a usable signal, and ask ATC for a clearance *direct*.

Flight planning involves nothing more than drawing a line from departure to destination and selecting waypoints at convenient intervals along the course. Figure 13, taken from one of the Jeppesen VFR RNAV charts, illustrates the method of plotting a course from St. Joseph Airport to Mason City Airport. (Always keep a "normal" IFR enroute chart handy for those times when direct flight no longer fits the traffic situation and the controller changes your clearance to a Victor airway.) Note that the waypoints are located on cardinal radials; the use of 090 or 270 (or the N-S radials when convenient) means that you have to change only one set of numbers when loading the next address. Once under way, navigation is just a matter of flying from one waypoint to the next, checking carefully to be certain that both VOR and DME units are properly tuned, that the stations are positively identified, and that the waypoint address is correct. For more affluent pilots, equipment is available that can be loaded before takeoff with the frequencies and waypoint addresses and

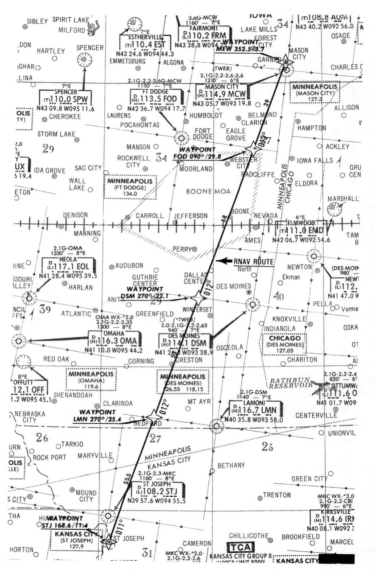

FIGURE 13 Plotting a trip with RNAV. (© 1977 Jeppesen & Co., Denver, Colo. All rights reserved. Not to be used for navigation.)

which will automatically tune the VORTACs and change the addresses as subsequent waypoints are selected. What will they think of next?

Filing an RNAV IFR Flight Plan

The suffix "R" after the aircraft type in an IFR flight plan indicates that in addition to an altitude-encoding transponder, the aircraft is equipped with an FAA-approved RNAV system. Beyond that, your flight plan for an RNAV trip is no different from one using the VOR airway system . . . except for the language used to describe the route of flight. For the trip shown in Figure 14, do the Flight Service Station Specialist a favor by letting him know that it's an RNAV flight plan, then go ahead with the waypoints you intend to use: "Direct LMN 270026, direct DSM 270022, direct FOD 090030, direct MCW." That's the only language understood by the ATC computers, and if pilots don't use it, the FSS folks have to spend their time making the route of flight readable; why not do it right the first time? In addition to waypoints selected for your convenience, include one for each turning point (if any) on your route.

Make certain that your route of flight includes at least one waypoint in each Center area you will pass through, and that such waypoints are located no more than 200 miles from the border of the previous Center's bailiwick. You should also be aware that one of the prerequisites for ATC's acceptance of a straight-line RNAV route is the capability of radar following throughout the flight; this is often the reason an RNAV direct request is turned down.

The final waypoint of the St. Joseph–Mason City trip is right on the airport. Used for convenience of illustration only, it doesn't meet the standard of good practice, which calls for the final item in "Route of Flight" to be the radio fix from which you intend to commence an instrument approach in the event of communications loss. Since Mason City has a published RNAV approach procedure (Figure 14), it would be proper to list IDYLL as the last item. If you don't subscribe to the RNAV approach procedures charts, or if your flight is bound for an airport that has no area navigation approach published, you should list on your flight plan an IAF published on a regular approach chart, or show the IAF itself—could

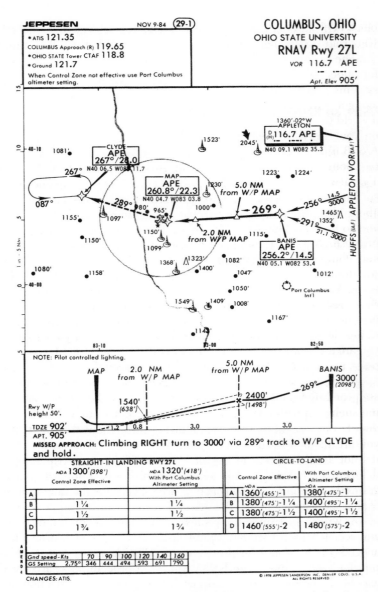

be a VOR, NDB, marker beacon, or intersection—at the end of your route of flight.

The simplicity of filing an RNAV flight plan rises to new heights for pilots with long-range navigation equipment, loosely defined as systems that provide course guidance from one point to another along a "great circle" route. (The equator is a great circle. Imagine a world globe with an equator that can be moved about until it rests on your Point A and Point B; that portion of the equator between A & B is a "great circle" route, the shortest distance between those two points. A straight line on an aeronautical chart is a *segment* of a great circle.)

You should draw a course line on your chart for information about alternate airports, fuel stops, restricted areas, obstructions, and so forth . . . the Jepp RNAV enroute charts are superb for this purpose. But as far as ATC is concerned, only Point A (departure) and Point B (destination) are important, and the computers in the Air Route Traffic Control Centers will recognize and accept such a track. You should specify any turning points on your route (such as those required to stay clear of restricted areas, for example), and include a checkpoint within 200 miles of each Center's boundary. If the destination airport's library of charts includes STARs, or if you are aware of a specific approach fix in use, file to the appropriate point instead of the airport itself.

Obviously, there are times when other traffic, "hot" restricted areas or MOAs, or local flow-management procedures will not permit such a direct flight, but it's worth a try. Even when your "RNAV direct" request is turned down, try again once airborne. Each time you are handed off to a new controller, request "RNAV direct"— it's not at all uncommon for the traffic situation to be completely different as you get closer to destination, and such a request is often granted. Why not try to wring every bit of utility and economy out of that expensive navigation equipment?

As with any off-airways journey, you are responsible for selecting and accepting an IFR altitude that guarantees proper obstacle clearance throughout the flight. With an RNAV planning chart, a Sectional or WAC chart, check terrain and obstacles along the way, and be certain that your flight altitude clears everything within 5 miles either side of course by at least 1,000 feet in the flatlands and 2,000 feet in those areas designated "mountainous." (Notice that the Jeppesen RNAV chart, Figure 13, shows a safe enroute altitude in each lat-long box.)

RNAV Approach Procedures

A significant expansion of the number of published RNAV approaches is in the cards, since the government is committed to area navigation as the system of the future (this includes inertial navigation and certain types of very-low-frequency navigation). As more aircraft are equipped with RNAV capability, it stands to reason that even the smaller airports within range of VORTAC will be IFR-qualified as the need is demonstrated.

By its very nature, an RNAV approach is always a "VOR" approach in contemporary terms. The procedure, published in chart form, will display features familiar to any instrument pilot, the only major change being the use of waypoints instead of VORs, NDBs, crossing radials, and the like (Figure 14).

The RNAV approach chart in Figure 14 is typical in most respects (minimums, designation of waypoints, missed approach, etc.) and atypical in others (it leads you to the home of the finest university aviation training program in the United States—an unabashed commercial for my academic home of almost twenty years!). Notice, however, that the initial approach fix (BANIS) stands alone in the airspace, with no procedure turn (and no holding pattern in lieu of), no feeder routes except those from the Appleton VOR (APE). What are you expected to do when you're inbound from the west?

Normally, an RNAV pilot would have to rely on vectors to BANIS from Columbus Approach Control, a procedure that involves more time than need be spent in this part of the approach. Here's where the linear deviation feature of RNAV can work to your benefit—and ATC's as well. Suppose you are approaching OSU Airport from the northwest, cleared "direct BANIS, cleared for the RNAV Runway 27L approach." Ask the controller if you may cross two miles north of BANIS for a right turn onto the final approach course; then, having received permission to do so (it will customarily be granted), fly to the left of the direct course to BANIS so that your CDI shows a two-mile displacement, and when the TO-FROM indicator reverses, turn to intercept the inbound course.

There's a cautionary note here; be certain to observe the Minimum Safe Altitude (MSA) while offset from the direct course, or *confirm* a safe maneuvering altitude with ATC. If no MSA is indicated on the chart, ask for one, *especially* if you are doing this number in a mountainous area.

Some RNAV equipment enables you to select a "cross-track" or "parallel-track" mode, in which case you can fly with the CDI centered, and be assured of a specific offset from the desired course. This feature also works admirably when conducting a circling approach, or merely setting yourself up for a properly spaced downwind leg in VFR conditions. Get to know the capabilities of your RNAV equipment, and use them to your advantage.

Good RNAV equipment is *really* good. You'll be pleased with its accuracy and delighted with the integrity of the LEFT-RIGHT display; since it is driven by computed data, the CDI doesn't respond to many of the electronic glitches that plague "raw" data and make for a nervous needle. But don't allow yourself to become complacent and overconfident so that you press on below the published RNAV Minimum Descent Altitude or into visibility situations that are well below the requirement on the approach chart. An unscheduled contact with the ground is just as unpleasant during an RNAV approach as any other.

Other Applications of RNAV

One of the nicest things to know on a non-precision approach is your distance from the Final Approach Fix—and subsequently, how far you are from the airport itself. With RNAV equipment, the distance question is answered, with considerable accuracy; you can put a waypoint on the FAF, another on the airport, and even if course guidance must officially be obtained from another source (you can use RNAV steering information to back up the primary navaid, but unless it's a published RNAV procedure, that's the best you can do), accurate range information is a great help. This is especially true in the case of an on-airport radio aid, which previously required an extension of the time outbound and a "plunge" after the procedure turn in order to guarantee reaching MDA prior to reaching the airfield; with RNAV distance working for you, all the guesswork is gone.

There's not a pilot flying today who wouldn't agree that always having an alternate airport in mind—at *any* point on *any* trip—is a good idea. The assurance of someplace to go if things turn sour is especially important at night, or in weather, or both. Enroute with RNAV, you can keep an inactive waypoint programmed for "instant alternates" throughout the flight; it takes a little extra preflight planning, but being able to push a button in time of need and have an accurate course and distance to a safe haven come up on the cockpit display . . . that's happiness.

Go back to Figure 13 for a moment, for an example of another way to put area navigation to work in a practical way when you're operating under Visual Flight Rules. Suppose that as you approach the second waypoint (DSM 270022), you find out that the Boone MOA is "hot"—in use—today. With RNAV, simply plot another waypoint that lies just outside the corner of the MOA, proceed directly to that new waypoint, and then on to Mason City. (Under IFR, of course, you would have been cleared through or around the MOA by ATC; but when the controller amends your clearance, you can suggest the shortest route, using the method just described.)

Holding at an airway intersection or an NDB is a piece of cake with RNAV. Instead of navigating on one radial while watching for the other to center, figuring out what the DME reading should be, or tying yourself in navigational knots trying to kill wind drift over an NDB, you can put a waypoint on the holding fix and fly down the proper radial until "FROM" appears; area navigation makes *every* holding fix a VOR.

Or, how about this one? You're inbound to a busy terminal, visibility barely 3 miles in summer haze, and the Tower asks you to report on a 3-mile final. Up until now, that position report has been little more than a good guess—especially at a strange airport—but with a waypoint on the airport, you can line up on a genuine final approach (merely set the OBS to the runway heading and center the needle) and let the controller know when you're *exactly* 3 miles out; that's a big help for everybody concerned. And if you want to show off a little, get *super* accurate—tell the Tower that you're "three-point-one miles on final."

11

Enroute Procedures

WHEN you're settled at your assigned altitude and have the airplane trimmed for hands-off flight, when you're through with the sometimes demanding communications of the departure phase, an IFR trip becomes largely a matter of flying from one VOR to another. An occasional traffic advisory or sector handoff may be your only contact with Center; now and then you may feel like calling the controller just to make sure he's still there. In the enroute portion, there is time to plan, check the weather ahead, and give most of your attention to flight management. On your first few flights, especially in weather all the way, you will no doubt hover over the gauges like a mother hen, but as your experience builds, you'll discover that the airplane does a very good job of flying itself. You should be more a navigator than a pilot at this point—more a manager than a manipulator. This chapter contains techniques and suggestions that should make your enroute operations less confusing, more efficient, and above all, safer. Once again, knowledge is the key—a thorough understanding of what you're doing now and what you may be doing in the miles ahead can have only one result: the making of a better instrument pilot.

First, Fly the Airplane

At the head of the list is aircraft control—without it, nothing else counts. A key element is trim, and barring rough air, you should be able to set up your airplane so that it will fly for relatively long periods of time with only gentle nudges on the controls to maintain the desired altitude and heading. Most of today's aircraft are rigged so that rudder pressure is hardly required in turns, so "feet on the floor" is not at all a bad way to fly IFR: it will help you to relax on long flights when keeping your legs in one position for extended periods can cause a distracting amount of muscle fatigue. If you have invested in a wing-leveler or autopilot, by all means use it; that takes another load off your mind, and lets you devote attention to more important things.

An automatic pilot that not only maintains straight and level flight but is also equipped with various modes of heading and altitude control is your best friend on instruments. (It's even better than a co-pilot, because it won't drink your coffee or talk back!) Study the operating manual and find out what your autopilot can do and what it can't do. Use it most of the time—you're not going to increase your instrument skills a great deal by hand-flying straight and level. At regular intervals, say, every third or fourth flight, fly the airplane manually through the departure and climb-out, and make the approach yourself so you won't lose the touch. Autopilots have been known to malfunction; no superstition implied, but they always seem to fail when they're needed most!

Like a Scalded Duck

Climbing to your assigned altitude, or moving to a new, higher level when requested by ATC should be done at the best rate of climb speed of your aircraft, with the safety-related option of climbing at a higher airspeed in VFR conditions so that you can see over the nose better. Your interest on the initial climb should be to get up there as rapidly as practical; out of the low-level turbulence, out of the icing layers, into clear air whenever possible. Your flight planning was no doubt based on the selection of an altitude as high as practical for you, the airplane, and the existing weather conditions, so get there as soon as you can. Cruise airspeed will inevitably be higher than that used for climb—since time is of the essence, spend as little of it as possible at low airspeed.

Trade Altitude for Airspeed

The low power, constant airspeed descent you use for the proficiency maneuvers should be reserved for your practice sessions under the hood—when descending in actual conditions, in the real world, the potential energy stored in the airplane as a result of climbing to altitude can be converted to airspeed on the way down. It will pay off in time saved, and that's the name of the game! The limitations to be observed are airspeed and "ear-speed," the former a function of maximum speeds for the airplane structure, the latter concerned with the rate at which you and your passengers can clear your ears. There's absolutely nothing wrong with descending at as high an airspeed as possible, as long as you stay under the never-exceed speed, and carry enough power to keep the engines warm. (Of course, if you encounter anything more than light turbulence during the descent, you must slow down to stay out of the caution range on the airspeed indicator—corrugated wings went out with Ford Trimotors!)

Advise your passengers that "we're going to a lower altitude"— never use the phrase "we're going down"; some folks interpret this as advance warning of a crash, and will try to get out of the airplane. Remind them to keep swallowing or yawning as you descend. It's far better to put up with a grumbling passenger who resents being awakened for a descent than to have him cursing you and aviation in general for the pain in his ears the rest of the day. Most people can tolerate high rates of descent if they know what's happening and what to do about it; if you have doubts, take it easy.

Most supercharged engines have manifold-pressure controllers built in, and you can come down through increasing atmospheric pressure without much concern; but normally-aspirated propeller turners are something else. Know the maximum manifold pressure for the RPM you have selected (or the limiting engine speed for fixed-pitch props) and let the pressure or RPM build up to that point, then make small throttle reductions to keep it there. You'll have longer-lasting engines, and will still be able to realize the high airspeeds that cut precious minutes from the total time. (Refer to the power chart in your aircraft handbook for maximum settings at various altitudes.)

When you have determined a comfortable rate of descent (experiment until you find the one that suits you best), divide it into the altitude that needs to be lost; this will give you the *time* required to descend. When you make an estimate of your groundspeed in the letdown, you can compute a *distance* from destination at which to request descent. In a crowded terminal area, this may be impossible because of other traffic, but plan ahead and ask—you've nothing to lose but time.

Enroute Charts Make Good Flight Logs

Your IFR route will usually be just what you requested, and maintaining a flight log is good practice; but it involves another piece of paper in the cockpit, and the most carefully-preplanned route of flight turns useless when ATC throws a change at you. Using a soft, easily-erased pencil to write your actual times of arrival and the estimates for subsequent fixes on the enroute chart puts the information you need right where you want it—in front of you, and available for quick reference (Figure 15). Put ATAs below the fix, ETAs above. (Mark down the times when you switch fuel tanks the same way.)

"In radar contact" is music to an instrument pilot's ears since it relieves him of any position-reporting responsibility; but it breeds a complacency that lurks in the shadows, waiting for the time when radar contact is lost, and you have to resume reporting. This means

FIGURE 15 The enroute chart makes a good flight log and a handy place to keep a record of fuel management.

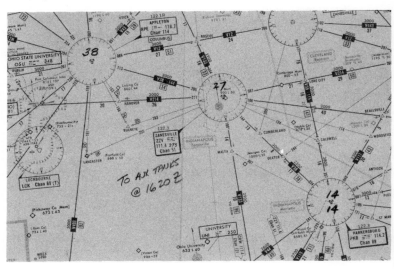

figuring ETAs, keeping some kind of a log, and making all the navigational decisions yourself. Any system of aerial navigation requires that you know where you are now, where you have been, and at what rate you are moving across the ground. To forestall utter confusion, make it a habit to record the time you pass over navaids enroute. When the day of reckoning arrives, at least you'll have some idea of *when* you were *where*—it's a place to start.

Pilot, Know Thy Fuel System!

The subject of fuel management on any flight deserves your careful attention, but it takes on greater import when you're IFR—there's not always an airport handy where you can put down to fill 'er up! Every airplane will be different in this respect, but two general rules apply to *all* flying machines: First, know what the range capabilities and fuel-burn rates are at various power settings; and second, fly by the clock—not by the indications on the fuel gauges. When you know the amount of gasoline on board at the start, and keep careful book on how much you burn, there should be no excuse for arriving at that frightening crossroads of not enough fuel for the distance you have to go. Running the tanks dry, to the point of engine stoppage, is not recommended as a continuous practice (passengers don't like to be awakened by a snorting, surging engine), but you should do it at least once for each tank under the proper conditions, keeping tab on the clock, so that you know *exactly* how long each tank will keep things going at cruise power. You may be surprised (pleasantly or unpleasantly) to discover the differences that exist between tanks; it can be twenty minutes or more on some models, and that knowledge might save your neck some day! (Chapter 6 in *Weather Flying* will add to your knowledge about fuel reserves.)

There is a plus associated with using all the fuel out of the tanks—it will keep the sumps as clean as a whistle. But remember that whatever finds its way past the fuel filter (dirt, water, bits of fuel-cell sealant) will be drawn through the engine when you try to run it on the fumes. It takes only a minute speck of dirt or a tiny crystal of ice lodged firmly in a fuel line or carburetor port or injector nozzle to shut off the power completely—you might want to limit your "dry tank" checks to conditions that will allow you to safely make like a glider.

Stand By for the Latest Change

The routing and altitude specified in your clearance are not sacred, and ATC will frequently make changes and amendments to suit the traffic situation as you proceed. It's possible that you may be asked to fly a different route, another altitude, or to hold at a designated point until a traffic conflict is resolved. You should treat any such change as a *suggestion* (just as you did when copying your clearance on the ground) and refuse *any* clearance that will fly you into trouble. This is not the sort of thing that should keep you awake at night, but remember that *you* are responsible for the safety of the flight, not the controller. Don't be unreasonable about it, but if Center asks you to fly a route or altitude that you don't like, explain the situation to them and offer an alternative. If that doesn't work and they insist, exercise your authority and fly as you think you should to stay out of trouble—and be prepared to justify your actions. (Tell the controller what you intend to do, of course.)

When ATC wants you to change altitude, they will let you know like this: "Barnburner 1234 Alpha, climb to and maintain eight thousand"—straightforward, right to the point. But you can almost always tell when a route change or a hold is coming your way, because the controller will ask, "Barnburner 1234 Alpha, I have an amendment to your clearance; ready to copy?" Your reply should be "stand by," which gives you time to break out the enroute chart so you can see if the upcoming change is compatible with the weather situation, terrain clearance, fuel remaining, and so on. With the chart spread out to cover the possibilities, you can tell the controller to "go ahead with the clearance" and visualize his new routing or holding instructions to determine if you can comply.

See How the Other Half Lives

If you haven't taken the time to visit an Air Route Traffic Control Center facility, by all means do so at your earliest convenience. In addition to gaining an appreciation of the monumental task facing the controllers, you will also come away with a firm resolve to never again put all your eggs in one basket—you will forevermore keep a careful check on what ATC is doing with you *and* with other IFR flights in your immediate vicinity. ATC is *people,* and as such, they are subject to the human errors that have plagued us all in the past, which get us into trouble today, and which will continue to cause problems in the future.

A sharp instrument pilot knows what's going on around him. Witness a situation several years ago in which a pilot felt that Approach Control was issuing vectors to the wrong airplane; after several heading changes that just didn't seem right, he said to Approach Control "you're not sure *which* airplane you have on the scope, are you?" A long, embarrassed silence followed, as Approach Control tried to sort out its targets—everything worked out all right, but whenever you have that nagging doubt, check on it. A case of mistaken identity has no place in an IFR environment; it happens *very* infrequently; but it only takes once.

A Place for Everything

Be a good housekeeper whenever you are flying, and really work at it when you're IFR. Once beyond the terminal area, put away the SID or the area chart (put them where they belong, not on the cockpit floor!) and get out the enroute chart, folded to show the route you're flying. All the charts have information on the margins that indicates the frequencies, airway numbers, courses, and distances to on-the-next-chart facilities. When you fly off one chart, put it away and get out the next one; as you approach the terminal area, you are finished with enroute information, so put the charts back in the book, and break out the paperwork you need for the approach. Find a handy spot for your navigational computer—out of the way, but always in the same place when you need it. A boom mike and a control-wheel switch will pay for themselves many times over in convenience and composure. (You can buy rigs that are truly portable and can be used in any airplane you might fly.)

Your own personal short-cuts will develop as you gain experience in the IFR system—when you've done a good job of thinking ahead and staying ahead, you may find yourself with nothing to do. But when you're tempted to sit on your thumbs, look around; there's probably something that needs to be done. Recheck the fuel situation, or find out what the weather is doing up ahead, or make a correction to get the CDI on dead center. The more frequently you take inventory, the smaller your corrections and adjustments will be, and this goes a long way toward making the enroute portion of your flight smoother, more enjoyable, and safer for all concerned.

IFR in Thunderstorm Country

"Each pilot in command shall, before beginning a flight, familiarize himself with *all available information* concerning that flight. This information *must* include, for an IFR flight, weather reports and forecasts and alternatives available if the planned flight cannot be completed." So saith paragraph 91.5 of the FARs—shortened somewhat, and with emphasis added to make this point; when a pilot obtains "all available information" and is ready to use Plan B if the original plan goes down the drain, *there is no excuse for blundering into a thunderstorm.*

Despite that, some aviators continue to disregard all the signs, fly themselves into horrible weather conditions, then fuss and fume because the controllers didn't warn them or vectored them right into the middle of a nest of nasties. The IFR pilot who is interested in living to a ripe old age must understand that *he cannot depend on ATC for weather information;* note carefully the use of the word "depend," because there's not a controller around who wouldn't help a pilot in time of need. But controllers are limited in at least two ways—the physical characteristics of their equipment, and duty priorities.

In the first case, today's ATC radar is designed for controlling air traffic, not looking for thunderstorms. Not too many years ago, you could call up the Center and get a good verbal description of the actual weather returns on radar; today, controllers look at a computer-generated radar image, which compromises some weather-seeing capabilities for the sake of better aircraft separation.

The second limitation, that of controllers' duty priorities, is clear-cut and easy to understand:

1. First priority, separation of aircraft and the issuance of radar safety advisories (low-altitude alerts and conflict alerts).

2. Second priority, other services that are required but do not involve separation of aircraft.

3. Third priority, additional service to the extent possible.

An airborne aviator has no way of assessing the limitations of the radar equipment in use, and when weather information is not proffered, we've got to assume that the controllers are busy with other duties. The message comes through loud and clear: *Pilots must not rely on ATC to keep them out of thunderstorms.*

The best way to stay safe is to avoid thunderstorms using the best detector of all—the human eye. This may mean flying low enough to see under and around the problem, or climbing until you're able to circumnavigate the buildups in the clear air above. It may also mean beating a hasty retreat—the ever-popular 180— when it appears your present course will take you into a thicket of thunderstorm-obscuring clouds. If you find yourself flying "on the gauges" in an area with thunderstorm potential, you're in the worst possible situation. Don't fly a minute longer toward possible disaster; if ATC won't give you an immediate clearance to go somewhere else, exercise your authority and *do it*! Remember that the controller's first priority is traffic separation; have faith that he'll work something out if you elect to fly in a different direction.

There's another implication in FAR 91.5 that is all too often overlooked—the meaning of the phrase "all available information." Your weather-checking responsibility doesn't end with the preflight briefing; it continues throughout the flight and includes listening to what other pilots on the frequency have to say about the weather conditions they're encountering, listening for SIGMETs and the hourly broadcasts of aviation weather on the VOR voice channels, and perhaps more important, *asking* for current weather from anyone who might know more about the situation than yourself. Good sources of weather information would include the specially trained folks in the Flight Watch stations (they are found all across the country on 122.0), a Flight Service Station that you know has weather radar, a controller whose radar might have the information you need, or another pilot along your route of flight. There's a lot of good news (or bad, depending on your point of view) available, but it's not all served up voluntarily. When in doubt, ask.

That first instrument flight all by yourself is a heady experience, the culmination of a great deal of expense and effort, perhaps an opportunity to begin realizing the benefits of utility and efficiency that may have started you down the IFR road in the first place.

Such was probably the case with a newly minted instrument pilot in the southeast, who needed to get home after a day's business on the other side of the mountains. A cold front with attendant short lines and clusters of storms lay across the route of flight; consistent with his preflight briefing, the lightning flashes in the darkened sky provided positive evidence of the weather's location as the pilot proceeded westbound in his Cessna 210.

He accepted storm-avoidance vectors from Center controllers, who made it very clear that a deviation well to the south of course would be required to get around all the storms showing on radar. About 100 miles from home, the pilot inquired into the feasibility of "going direct" (across the line of storms), was advised that several aircraft had done just that, and that a heading of 330 degrees would take him through a light spot on Center radar.

Shortly after accepting the vector, the pilot's reports of close-aboard lightning flashes and turbulence increased rapidly, and within a few minutes, his virginal IFR trip ended in disaster . . . the airplane crashed in the mountains, a victim of upset and disorientation.

A post-accident investigation of the radar pictures indeed showed a "light spot" on the controller's display; but the ATC radar *didn't* show a cyclical rise and fall pattern in this particular line of storms . . . the pilot ventured into a "soft spot" just before it turned into a very *hard* spot.

Lesson to be learned? Don't ever rely on ATC radar to select a penetration course through an organized system of thunderstorms. The very best you should expect of a controller in this situation is a vector to *avoid* the weather . . . which is precisely what ATC intended for this pilot. His decision to fly "direct," even with his own visual sightings of lightning, will never be completely understood.

There's *always* a better way to get someplace in an airplane other than through a thunderstorm . . . the risk is never worth the price that might have to be paid.

Using Airborne Weather Detectors

Here, in order of importance, are the airborne weather detection devices available to contemporary pilots:

1. The human eye
2. The Stormscope
3. Weather radar

And here, in order of importance, are the airborne weather detection devices available to contemporary pilots:

1. The human eye
2. Weather radar
3. The Stormscope

Do you get the point? For all the reasons mentioned a few paragraphs earlier, visual detection of thunderstorms will *always* be the very best way to avoid them, but the rush of avionics technology has introduced two marvelous devices that are proliferating in the general aviation fleet. Based on significantly different principles, weather radar (a generic name for the kindred products of several manufacturers), and the Stormscope (a trademarked, all-by-itself appliance) deserve explanation, for the serious instrument pilot will very likely be exposed to one or the other—or both—in the normal course of his experience. It's important for pilots to understand how these weather detectors work, because of the inherent limitations and capabilities. First, the new kid on the block—the Stormscope.

Several years ago, a certain midwestern pilot, transporting his family in their single-engine airplane, managed to blunder into a thunderstorm that nearly did them in. Badly shaken, but determined to make something worthwhile out of the encounter, the pilot set out on a quest for an affordable, lightweight thunderstorm detector that would be compatible with light airplanes, and which would help other instrument pilots avoid severe weather. He just happened to be well educated in electronics, so he left his business, returned to school to study and develop his idea, and subsequently invented the Stormscope.

The principle of the Stormscope is simple enough . . . it senses low-frequency electrical discharges that are associated with atmospheric turbulence. Each discharge sensed by the Stormscope's antenna is processed electronically, and those that bear the distinctive signature of a turbulence-producer show up as a bright green dot on a small round cockpit indicator—much like a tiny TV set with a polar grid overlay. Range can be changed at the flick of a switch, with the result that you can observe a 360-degree, 200-mile display of probable turbulence around your aircraft.

Operation of the Stormscope is as simple as its principle . . . turn it on and take a look. In the air, weather avoidance is a matter of not flying into any area where the green dots appear. Unlike radar (which only shows areas of precipitation), the Stormscope identifies areas of probable turbulence, with or without the presence of rain. A strong "generator" (most likely a full-blown thunderstorm) will usually produce a phenomenon called "radial spread," in which an elongated string of dots will grow from the storm location toward the center of the display (the airplane's location). This indicator should be a warning flag, prompting you to fly especially well clear of that area.

Although the Stormscope provides full-circle viewing (you can see problem areas to the rear, a big help when trying to decide which is the best way out of a stormy environment), your interest will most likely focus on what's ahead. To accommodate this, the controls can be adjusted to concentrate all the available green dots in the forward half of the screen—a most beneficial feature in a weather-avoidance situation.

Because it is passive in nature (no outgoing energy) and therefore neither harmful to humans or affected by buildings, mountains, or the curvature of the earth, the Stormscope is a very useful preflight weather-avoidance tool. You can power it up on the ramp, and get a good idea of turbulence to be expected, at least in the first 200 miles of your flight . . . helps eliminate surprises!

Experience based on frequent, regular observation of Stormscope indications will provide a data base for deciding how many dots, and in what concentration, are tolerable for you and your airplane. Learn to compare the Stormscope picture with actual conditions when you can see the weather, and you'll learn to evaluate and select safe weather-avoidance routes when you *can't* see the storms.

In summary, when Detector #1 (the eyeball) is rendered unusable by clouds or the dark of night, the Stormscope user who wishes to avoid severe weather need only refrain from flying where the green dots appear on the scope.

Radar, on the other hand, is hardly new . . . it's been around aviation since early in WW II, when Germany began using it to detect Allied fighter aircraft swarming off Great Britain to intercept Nazi bombers headed across the English Channel. "Radar" is an acronym which stands for RAdio Detection And Ranging; again, the modus operandi is relatively simple, in that electrical energy in the form of radio waves is transmitted by a directional (aimable) antenna, and any of that energy that strikes reflective objects is returned to the antenna (now functioning as an energy *receiver*) and displayed as a bright area on a cathode-ray tube in the cockpit. "Reflective objects" include the surface of the earth, buildings, mountains, and *raindrops*—that's the important reflector for the purpose of weather avoidance.

While this isn't the place for a detailed electronic explanation, imagine the speed of radar's outgoing radio waves slowed to a crawl; when the antenna emits a burst of energy, the transmitter portion shuts down, turns the antenna into a receiver, and waits a predetermined time for an "echo" to return. If something reflects a portion of that energy, the returning radio wave is processed electronically and shows up on the radar scope, which is overlaid with a grid to indicate direction and distance from the aircraft. If *nothing* is reflected, the radar set switches back to the transmitter mode and repeats the cycle . . . in reality, all of this happens continuously, and at a mind-boggling rate, so that an uninterrupted display is provided. It's analogous to a light bulb powered by the 60-cycle alternating current in your home; the light is blinking on and off 60 times each second as the current reverses, but it's happening so rapidly that you perceive a steady glow.

A radar antenna sweeps back and forth—left-right, left-right— usually in a 90-degree arc with the airplane position at the apex. As echos are "painted" (displayed on the scope) they remain illuminated through at least one antenna sweep so that you see a constant, updated display; the shape of an area of reflective objects is therefore easy to see.

Radar incorporates a third dimension of weather investigation; in addition to azimuth and several selections of range, the antenna can be tilted up or down as it sweeps, and can "look" for reflective objects above and below the aircraft's flight level.

Atmospheric turbulence is generally associated with high rates of rainfall and large raindrops, both of which are characteristics of most thunderstorms. Because water is very reflective of radio energy, and because a weather system producing large amounts of rainfall can normally be expected to also produce large amounts of turbulence, radar systems indicate the "severity" of echoes (in terms of potential airplane problems) in shades of green, or by using several colors.

For example, if there are no reflective objects in the "field of vision" of your radar set, the screen will be blank; but let's generate a cumulo-nimbus cloud directly ahead, a cloud that is producing light rain. This precipitation would show up as a light green echo, its shape/azimuth/range clearly defined. Imagine this cloud growing to the point at which a core of *heavier* rainfall develops within the storm. When the reflectivity of the core rainfall increases to a manufacturer-preset level, the radar displays it in a brighter green, or perhaps yellow (for CAUTION) in a multi-color system. There's usually a third level (even *brighter* green, or red—WARNING) to indicate the highest preset reflectivity.

Nearly all radar systems incorporate a feature known as "contouring," which means that when the *rate* of rainfall increases rapidly over a relatively short horizontal distance, the radar "closes its eyes" to that area. Should you be flying toward that storm mentioned earlier, and if the difference in rainfall intensity between the light rain and the core is increasing at a preset rate, the core would appear as a black hole (same as no return) on the radar scope. A pilot unaware of the significance of contouring might plunge directly into the heart of the thunderstorm, thinking he was headed for a no-rain, no-turbulence area. Surprise!

In order to call your attention to those weather systems that contain strong cores of precipitation and which therefore *must* be avoided, most radars cause contouring areas to flash on and off (in either green or red) as an additional warning. While some areas of precipitation displayed on a radar scope present no problem to most pilots in most airplanes, a "contouring" echo is all but guaranteed to rattle your teeth . . . you wouldn't like it one bit in there. The probable presence of very strong updrafts and downdrafts in close proximity to each other is the essence of life-threatening turbulence.

In the absence of very strong storms, radar will normally be capable of pointing out precipitation well in advance of the airplane, because some of the electrical energy passes through, to be reflected by another rain area up ahead. But can you imagine a big storm straight ahead that is producing so much rain that *all* of the radar's energy is reflected back to the antenna? You'd see a very bright echo, to be sure, but what you *wouldn't* see is the next big storm lurking on the other side. This characteristic is called "attenuation," and is a shortcoming of many older, less expensive units (some current-generation radars include circuitry that overcomes attenuation, or at least warns the observer of potential trouble behind the next echo). If nothing else, your knowledge of the attenuation phenomenon should make it clear that you must have some idea of the extent and severity of a weather system before putting all your weather-avoidance trust in what you see on the scope.

There is a great deal of interpretation required of the operator to extract useful, safe information from a radar display; it's much more than a turn-it-on-and-take-a-look system, because the picture changes remarkably with range selection, antenna tilt, airplane altitude and attitude, and storm characteristics. If radar is to be used with safety and efficiency, some well-founded training beyond reading the manual is required. There are frequent weather-radar classes and workshops around the country; your best source of information in this regard is the manufacturer.

Weather radar and the Stormscope are sometimes placed in a competitive posture, but any attempt at comparison soon turns into an apples-and-oranges standoff. These two weather-detection systems operate on decidedly different principles, and present entirely different pictures. The wise pilot *avoids* whatever "weather" (precipitation and/or potential turbulence) shows up on the equipment he has to work with.

By the way, the key word in that last sentence is "avoid"—the weather-detection system good enough to pick your way through a squall line, or to decide with confidence which of those storms up ahead is safe to penetrate, hasn't been built yet. There's always another route or another day; if you become a faithful follower of the weather-*avoidance* religion, your chances of becoming an old pilot increase significantly.

12

Communications
Failure

IT DOESN'T HAPPEN very often, but when it does, complete communications failure can really loosen a pilot's psychological adhesive. If your radios are going to quit, they'll probably do it when you're fighting through a cold front, carrying an inch or two of ice, and wallowing around in moderate turbulence with a rough engine. This is no time to be digging through your flight bag, trying in vain to find the communications failure rules that you *know* are in there somewhere. You had promised yourself just last week you would review and really commit to memory those few simple regulations. And now it's happened, and you don't know what to do, you're in trouble, and there is always the chance that during your confused wanderings about, you may nail an innocent victim of your procrastination and lack of good sense. The point of all this should be unmistakable: Don't put it off, but learn (or maybe relearn) the rules that govern your actions when you lose communications.

Instrument pilots should toss a very large bouquet to the regulation-writers at this point, for the communications failure procedures are clearly spelled out, with no room for error or misinterpretation. Wizards those who laid down this part of the aviation regulations. An obvious pattern of common sense is woven throughout this section of the rules; you will find that they *require* you to perform as you would instinctively, given the considerations of your safety and the well-being of other pilots sharing the airspace with you.

These rules are rather discriminating—they apply only to a failure of *communications;* when you can neither transmit nor receive on any radio, you have suffered a bona fide communications failure, and the rules spell out exactly what is to be done. If everything goes (no communications, no navigation), it's an entirely different ball game, and sorry to break the news to you, but there are no rules for this situation. You're on your own, heaven help you, break out the common sense and good luck, and here's hoping you know which way to VFR conditions. (Always insist that the Weather Depiction Chart be included in your briefing for an IFR flight; with that knowledge, at least you'll have an idea of which direction to fly.) Should ATC suspect that you have suffered radio failure, they will try to contact you on several possible communications channels; for example, the first place they will try to get through is the VOR that they figure you are using for navigation at the time. So, if you think the communications radios may have departed for some electronic Valhalla, turn up the audio side of the VOR receiver, and listen—there may be enough power left for you to hear someone trying to help you. Of course, if you can hear, common sense tells you to listen, and do what you're told.

Here's where a transponder can be worth its weight in gold (a near-literal statement, if it saves you and the airplane!). Suppose you have one enervated receiver weakly informing you of ATC's efforts to make contact following loss of your transmitter. "Barnburner 1234 Alpha, if you read me, squawk IDENT," which you do, and then hear this: "Roger, Barnburner 1234 Alpha, radar contact, turn right heading one eight zero for radar vectors to a surveillance approach at Outhouse Municipal Airport." And you would do just what he says—as long as the transponder and one receiver hold up, you've got it made; you're communicating.

There are other radio facilities on which ATC will attempt contact when your transmitter goes out, and they include Localizers, Outer Compass Locators, some NDBs, and any other navaid they think you might be able to receive. You should know that any navigational aid shown on an IFR chart (enroute, area, or approach) can carry voice signals unless the frequency is *underlined*. The essence of all this is that you should try anything you can think of when you suspect a radio failure—reset circuit breakers, check fuses, kick the panel, listen on any set available. You might even put the relief tube to your ear. If you are completely unable to establish any type of communications, don't panic, because the rules will see you safely out of your predicament.

Out of the Clouds, Out of Trouble

The first rule was written in recognition of the undeniable fact that breaking out into VFR conditions will go a long way toward solving your communications loss problem. If it happens in VFR, or if you fly into VFR conditions, it makes good sense to *stay* VFR, land as soon as practical, and let ATC know what you have done. Emphasis on that phrase "land as soon as practical"—the terrain over which you are operating has a lot to do with your decision, and as always, safe operation must be placed before anything else. If the VFR into which you have flown is a hole in the clouds with Pike's Peak sticking up in the middle, you might do well to keep right on flying.

But how about the situation when you are in IFR conditions, it's down to minimums all the way home, and as you prepare to acknowledge a clearance, the microphone falls apart in your hand? At the same time, you are hit on the head by the speaker as it falls out of the cabin roof. Friend, you have just lost communications! That reassuring voice from Center, your electronic umbilical cord to Mother Earth, has been cruelly severed, and you are on your own. What to do now? The answer is so simple: Just follow the rules. When the controller suspects after several unanswered calls that you are experiencing Marconian distress (don't forget that you should announce your problem to radar sets far and wide by squawking 7700, then 7600 on your everfaithful transponder), he is bound by the *same set of rules* to clear out some airspace for you. It's obvious that he needs to know what route you'll be flying and how far you will continue, and at what altitude. The only way to accomplish safe separation in the absence of communications is for both parties, you and ATC, to operate under a set of common and inviolate conditions—that's why *every* IFR pilot MUST know the radio failure rules inside out before he ventures into the murky mists.

It's easiest to break the problem into its basic parts; when you're IFR sans communications, you will have to decide:

1. How far you can go.
2. What route you should fly.
3. How high you should fly.

These three questions and their answers will provide the guidance that will get you safely out of trouble; the problem is whittled down to manageable dimensions with these solid guidelines. One at a time, then.

How Far Can You Go?

The first question has a most uncomplicated answer: Unless you get lucky and fly into some VFR, you're going to go all the way to the destination airport for which you filed! If your clearance at the start of the trip (or a later amendment) specified the destination airport as the clearance limit, just keep right on going; you are still cleared all the way. But suppose you accepted a short-range clearance so you could get started, and now the radios have quit short of that point. No big problem, as long as you were provided an Expect Further Clearance time. What has just happened to you is the only reason for these times being issued by ATC; in the event of a communication breakdown, the EFC is set far enough ahead to give the controller time to clear out the airspace so you can continue on your way. This leads directly into the next phase of the procedure: You will remain at the clearance limit fix (holding in a standard pattern on the course on which you approached the fix, unless there is a holding pattern depicted on the chart) until the Expect Further Clearance time rolls around, then proceed.

It should be unequivocally clear by now that any IFR pilot who accepts a "hold" without getting an EFC leaves himself wide open for a real problem. If ATC doesn't issue a time (and they very, very seldom miss on this one—it's as much for their protection as yours), DEMAND one; you're well within your rights. Picture the bewilderment on the ground and in the cockpit when the radios go out and no further clearance time has been provided; they don't know what you don't know they don't know, and it's a scramble to get everybody out of the way on all the possible routes you might take at any time.

So you were cleared all the way to destination, with no clearance limits, and the radios gave up the ghost soon after takeoff? In this situation, you will proceed to destination and hold at the appropriate altitude until your estimated time of arrival, based on the time enroute you put in your flight plan and your takeoff time, which, of course, you have forgotten. During a period of mental stress such as you will surely be experiencing following a radio failure, it may become very difficult to remember your own name, let alone what time you took off! Here's where you will be forever grateful for having formed a most useful habit—just before takeoff (before *every* takeoff, so you do it without thinking), set the red hands on your instrument panel clock, or on that 3-inch diameter, two-hundred-dollar wristwatch that does everything but compute your income tax, or write it down somewhere, but record the takeoff time. Obviously, it is also nice to remember the time enroute you filed in your flight plan.

What Route Should You Fly?

The first part of the communications rule directs you to continue to your destination, respecting any holds or clearance limits along the way; now you are faced with the question of what route to fly. Equally sensible, this part of the problem is solved in one of three possible ways: You will fly via the last assigned route, or the route ATC advised you might expect in a further clearance, or in the absence of the preceding two, the route you filed in your flight plan.

To illustrate, suppose you plan a trip from Lexington, Kentucky to Bluefield, West Virginia (Figure 16). Your flight plan requests Victor 178 to Bluefield, and your clearance comes through "as filed." If radio failure occurs anywhere along the route, you will continue on Victor 178 to the BLF VOR. So much for the first situation.

In the second case (same route, same clearance) you have just passed LOGIC intersection when Indianapolis Center comes up with this little gem: "Barnburner 1234 Alpha, you are now cleared to the TRENT intersection, maintain seven thousand and expect further clearance at 46 via direct Whitesburg, Victor 140 Bluefield, over." A couple of minutes after acknowledging this clearance, your radios give up. Combining your knowledge of the first two communications failure rules, you will hold at TRENT until forty-six minutes past the hour, then proceed to Bluefield via direct Whitesburg and Victor 140—that's the clearance ATC advised you to expect, so it takes precedence.

Back up one more time, and copy the following clearance on the ground at Lexington: "Barnburner 1234 Alpha is cleared to the

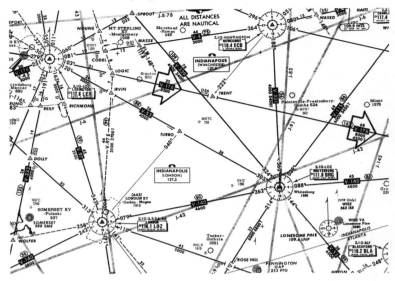

FIGURE 16　Airways and navigation facilities between Lexington, Ky., and Bluefield, W. Va. (© 1959 Jeppesen & Co., Denver, Colo. *All rights reserved. Not to be used for navigation.*)

TRENT intersection via radar vectors to Victor 178, climb to and maintain seven thousand, and expect further clearance at 28, over." The implication is that your flight cannot be cleared all the way to Bluefield at this time, but ATC is willing to get you started with a clearance as far as TRENT intersection, with the rest of the routing to follow. You accept, and as soon as Departure Control has vectored you onto Victor 178 10 miles from LOGIC, the radios die. Proceed to TRENT, hold until 28, then continue down Victor 178, in the absence of an assigned routing, without even a routing to *expect*, you'll fly just as you requested when you filed your flight plan.

ATC will frequently direct you around other traffic, or thunderstorms, or if they're not particularly busy, they will sometimes vector you right to your home drome. Should radio failure rear its ugly head at this point in an IFR flight, you will proceed directly to the fix to which you were being vectored (using your own navigational skills, of course). Good judgment once again prevails, as it would seem rather stupid to turn and fly into a thunderstorm in order to go direct to the next VOR, according to the rule; if you were advised of a storm cell 10 miles wide straight ahead, then were given vectors around it, common sense would dictate continuing the vector until you are reasonably certain you are past the storm. Don't ever let *anything* or *anybody* force you to fly through a thunderstorm. And don't worry about traffic separation if you wisely elect to continue around the storm after the radios stop radioing—you had to be in radar contact to get the vector in the first place, and the controller would probably breathe a sigh of relief, watching you exhibit some "smarts."

In summary, you will fly one of these three routes when the thread of communication snaps (they are listed in order of precedence):

1. The route you have been assigned as part of a clearance.
2. The route that ATC advised you might *expect* in a further clearance.
3. As a last resort, the route you filed in your flight plan.

(When radar vectored, proceed directly to the fix to which you were being vectored.)

How High?

Only one more question needs an answer to solve this three-dimensional problem of what to do when you realize you're talking to yourself, and that's the one regarding altitude. Your safety is the big concern here, and so the rules require you to fly at the highest, therefore the safest, of these altitudes:

1. The last assigned altitude.
2. The altitude ATC has advised you may expect in a further clearance.
3. The Minimum Enroute Altitude (MEA) for the particular airway segment in which you are operating.

To illustrate, consider the same Lexington-Bluefield trip; you are cleared "to the Bluefield Airport via Victor 178, climb to and maintain 9,000." If radio failure happens anywhere along this route, you will remain at 9,000 until reaching Bluefield (notice that there are no higher MEAs on this route), hold until your ETA, and make the approach. You are obliged to stay at 9,000 until your time runs out, then descend in the holding pattern prior to executing the approach. (By the way, in a situation like this, the approach you use is entirely up to you—anything published is legal.)

Had you requested 9,000 but ATC was unable to grant it in time for your takeoff, they might have cleared you "to the TRENT intersection, climb to 4,000 expect 9,000 after TRENT, expect further clearance at 36." You leap off the ground, climb to 4,000, and lose the radios before you reach TRENT intersection. Hold there until 36 minutes past the hour, depart TRENT climbing to 9,000, and maintain that altitude all the way to Bluefield. Again, you're above all the MEAs on the airway, and since you had been advised to expect 9,000 feet after TRENT, that's the altitude you fly.

But maybe the airways are so congested that Center can only clear you to LOGIC intersection at 4,000, gives you just an EFC time, and makes no promise of the necessary higher altitude at that time. Your task (after holding at LOGIC until the appropriate time) is to determine if there are any MEAs *higher* than your last assigned altitude of 4,000. Sure enough, there are, and it is obvious that you will need to climb to 8,000 feet for the segment between TRENT and SLINK, then descend to 6,000 for the final segment into BLF.

You are expected to fly altitudes *as published* on the enroute chart when they apply; for example, in the absence of an assigned altitude, you would fly at 3,200 feet from LEX to the Trent intersection. East-odd, west-even, and the "nearest thousand" don't count here—fly 'em like you see 'em!

Summing it up, your determination of what altitude to fly is rather simple; it's the last assigned altitude or the MEA, *whichever is higher*. If ATC has advised you to expect a higher altitude enroute, that's the one that applies. Whenever a route segment calls for an MEA higher than anything you have been assigned or advised to expect, start climbing to the higher MEA over the fix that begins that segment, and begin descending to the previous highest altitude over the fix that terminates the segment. Airway segments are indicated by the little T-bars on the airway, every enroute VOR being automatically the beginning and end of a segment. In substance, when you see a T-bar or VOR on the airway, look for a change in MEA. (When it's unsafe—because of terrain or obstructions—to start climbing at the beginning of an airway segment, the intersection will be clearly marked with a *Minimum Crossing Altitude,* requiring you to be at or above a specified level before proceeding. You'll have to shuttle upward in a racetrack holding pattern, or start climbing before reaching the intersection.)

When dealing with a communications failure situation, pilots and controllers must operate with mutual understanding of the regulations, and there's one more area in which the two parties must agree: You must not comply with the conditions of a clearance unless you are reasonably certain that ATC has received your acknowledgment. When radio failure occurs in IFR conditions, you'd best upgrade that certainty from "reasonably" to "absolutely." If you have any doubt that the man on the ground received your "roger" or your readback, proceed as if you had never heard his instructions—a clearance is considered valid only when it is acknowledged.

Here are the regulations in capsule form—when you lose two-way radio communications while in IFR conditions, you *will:*

1. Maintain VFR and land as soon as practical if the failure occurs in VFR conditions, or if VFR is encountered after the failure. (This rule is to be salted heavily with common sense and judgment.)
2. ROUTE—Continue to your destination on the last assigned route OR a route ATC has advised you may expect OR the route filed in your flight plan. On a radar vector, proceed directly to the fix.
3. DISTANCE—Proceed to the clearance limit, hold at the appropriate fix until the EFC or EAC time, then continue on your route. If the clearance limit is the destination airport, hold AT ALTITUDE until your ETA, based on takeoff time plus ETE.
4. ALTITUDE—Maintain the last assigned altitude OR the MEA, whichever is higher, OR at the prescribed fix, climb to the altitude ATC has advised you to expect. If subsequent MEAs are higher than assigned or expected altitude, climb to the higher MEA for the particular airway segment, then descend to the former highest altitude.

These rules work—don't expect to be treated like a hero at the completion of a radio-out IFR flight, because ATC knows what you will do, and makes the proper traffic adjustments ahead of you. But the rules work only if all concerned have these rules firmly established in their minds, and know how to employ them. You can bet that every traffic controller has a bound volume of the regulations and procedures within arm's reach; but they're not always that handy in an airplane. Take time now and at frequent intervals to memorize and refresh your understanding of the communications failure procedures; when it happens, it's too late to learn.

13

Holding Patterns

"THIS IS MERCURY CONTROL; we are at 'T' minus thirty minutes and holding." Remember the voice of Colonel Shorty Powers, announcing a hitch in one of the early orbital flight schedules and enriching the public vocabulary with a Space Age connotation of the word "hold"? It's about time the astronauts caught up, because holding has been with us in instrument flying for years, as an orderly way of suspending the progress of an instrument flight, either enroute or in a terminal area. Since most aircraft depend on forward movement to keep from falling out of the sky, holding really becomes a matter of flying around in circles, but not going past a predetermined point. The reasons for holding are numerous, and sometimes apparently known only to heaven and ATC. But it provides an effective, if frustrating, way to "stop" the flow of IFR flights in the face of a traffic conflict, or to slow things down when terminal operations begin to exceed the capabilities of the system.

Being cleared to hold sooner or later is just as inevitable as automatic rough over the mountains at night, and with Big Brother watching on radar, you'd best know what you're about! In B.R. (Before Radar) days, you could enter and fly a holding pattern any way you pleased, as long as you stayed within the airspace limits; but on the very first day the radar sets were plugged in, controllers observed a succession of pilots entering holding patterns, and were overwhelmed by the serpentine tracings of their entry procedures. So overwhelmed, in fact, that they were moved to call them "small intestine entries." This led to the development of an official method of holding-pattern entry.

There are basically two situations in which ATC will require a flight to hold: one during the enroute portion of a trip, the other in the terminal area, in which case you will be holding in anticipation of an instrument approach to the airport. The rules are the same for both—they differ only in the procedures you use in the event of communications failure.

No matter where or when you are instructed to hold, there is a two-step method you should use to do the job properly. Step #1, decide where the "racetrack" pattern will be located in accordance with the instructions you have received (you can do this mentally, or actually draw it on the chart). Step #2, based on the direction from which you are approaching the holding fix, determine the entry procedure you will use.

Every holding clearance must include either specifically or by implication these four components: a *holding fix*, the *direction to hold*, the *type of pattern* (standard or non-standard) and a time to *expect further clearance*. Each part of the holding instructions should be considered in turn.

The Holding Fix

ATC can clear you to hold just about any place they want to, but the holding fix will always be one you can locate electronically; it could be a VOR, an NDB, an intersection, a DME fix, or an RNAV waypoint. Most enroute holds will be at intersections or VORs along the airway, and terminal holding fixes are usually set up so that you will be in position to commence the approach when it's your turn.

Direction to Hold

Before attempting to unravel the mysteries of "which way to hold," you must understand what is meant by the holding course. For example, the Big Piney VOR has been designated the holding fix (Figure 17), and you are cleared to hold EAST of the VOR (in the absence of more specific instructions, this means you are to hold on the 090 radial). Fundamental to solving the problem is the knowledge that the *holding course* lies EAST of the fix. Remember that the *holding course* always lies in the direction you have been cleared to hold, and once in the pattern, you will fly inbound to the *holding fix* on the *holding course*, every time you come around the racetrack.

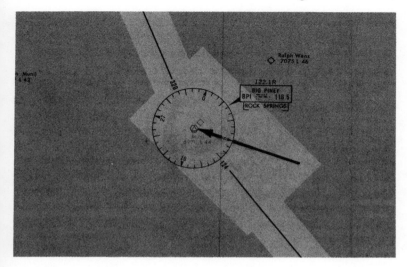

FIGURE 17   The holding course always lies in the direction you were cleared to hold.

True, you'll be flying westbound when on the holding course, but remember that "holding east" is just a means of identifying the location of the holding pattern.

Type of Pattern

With the holding fix, the holding course, and the direction to hold firmly established, determine the type of holding pattern to be flown—either standard or non-standard. For the time being, consider right turns standard, and left turns non-standard. If the controller doesn't mention the direction he wants you to turn, he expects you to execute a standard pattern, with right-hand turns. To complete Step #1, just "fly" your pencil inbound to the holding fix on the holding course, and turn in the appropriate direction. For example, to hold southwest of the Big Piney VOR in a standard pattern (Figure 18), find the holding fix and establish the holding course, "fly" inbound to the VOR on the holding course and turn right. Proceed one minute outbound, turn right again, and when

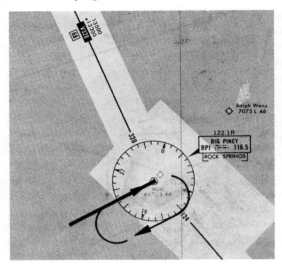

Figure 18   Standard (right turns) holding pattern southwest of Big Piney VOR.

you arrive over the VOR, you've completed one circuit of this particular holding pattern. If the controller clears you for left-hand turns, fly inbound on the same holding course, and turn left—you're still *holding* southwest of Big Piney.

Which Entry to Use?

So much for Step #1, establishing the holding pattern—now Step #2, determining the entry procedure. Fortunately, the one used most often is the easiest to accomplish. Suppose you are flying northwest at 10,000 feet on Victor 328 and are given this clearance: "Barnburner 1234 Alpha, hold southeast of Big Piney on Victor 328, maintain one zero thousand, expect further clearance at four two." If you want to copy the important numbers, do it right on the chart (Figure 19), and you'll have a permanent record of the clearance. The next thing to do is to break the clearance into its component parts:

1. The holding *fix* is the Big Piney VOR.
2. The holding *course* is Victor 328.
3. Since you will hold southeast of Big Piney on Victor 328, the holding *course* will lie southeast of the VOR on the 124 radial.
4. Absence of instructions to turn left or right implies a standard (right turns) pattern.
5. You will continue to fly at 10,000 feet while holding.
6. If you should suffer complete loss of communications before receiving further instructions, you will be expected to resume your flight at forty-two minutes after the next hour.

Now go ahead with Step #1, establishing the pattern (Figure 20). Draw (or imagine) the holding course southeast of Big Piney on Victor 328, fly your pencil inbound to the fix on the holding course, turn right to 124 degrees, and you have the proper racetrack all set up—you're holding southeast of Big Piney on Victor 328.

The Direct Entry

When you fly to the fix and turn to the outbound heading, you have accomplished a "direct" entry, which is always used when you approach the holding fix *on* the holding course. As a matter of fact,

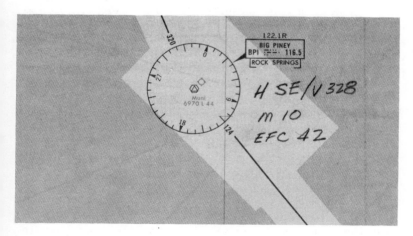

FIGURE 19   Copy your holding clearance right on the enroute chart.

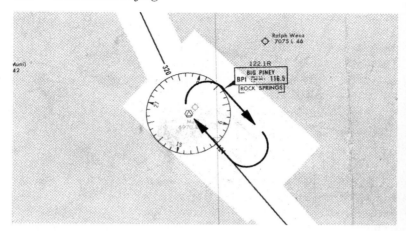

FIGURE 20   Holding in a standard pattern southeast of Big Piney VOR on Victor 328.

your approach heading can be somewhat off the holding course and the direct entry is still the proper one to use. If you draw (or imagine) a circle around the holding fix, then draw a line that lies 70 degrees from the holding course (Figure 21), a direct entry is called for any time your heading puts you in the shaded half-circle. As soon as you pass the VOR, turn right to 124 degrees, and you have entered the holding pattern. That 70-degree line is the key to determining your entry procedure. It must always be drawn (or imagined) so that it cuts across the racetrack, which you established in Step #1.

The Teardrop Entry

Keep the same holding instructions in mind (hold southeast of Big Piney VOR on Victor 328), but this time you are approaching from the west, on a heading of 080 degrees (Figure 22). Set up the racetrack again, draw the 70-degree line, and extend it thorugh the fix. While you're at it, extend the holding course through the fix as well, which divides the unshaded half of the circle into two quadrants. The smaller of the two is of concern now, since you are approaching the fix on a heading that lies within that quadrant.

When you reach the fix, a right turn to the outbound heading (124 degrees) would put you very close to the holding course, but going the wrong direction—so a procedure has been designed to get you into the holding pattern quickly, and well within the limits of the airspace set aside for you. In this entry, turn to a heading no more than 30 degrees from the holding course (which in this case would be a heading of 094 degrees), fly for one minute, turn right again until you intercept the holding course, and return to the fix. (Don't forget to reset the OBS to 304.) This is the "teardrop" entry, the name coming from the flight path described.

The Parallel Entry

The third entry is used when approaching the fix on a heading which lies in the larger of the two unshaded quadrants, and is called the "parallel" entry. Suppose you have received the same holding instructions, but you are approaching Big Piney from the north, heading 180 degrees (Figure 23). When you reach the fix, turn to

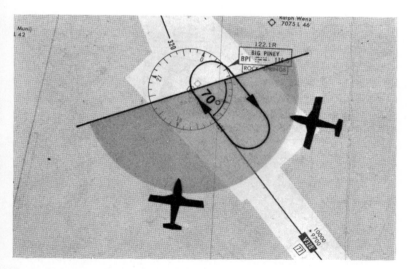

Figure 21 Approaching the holding fix on any heading within the shaded half-circle calls for a direct entry.

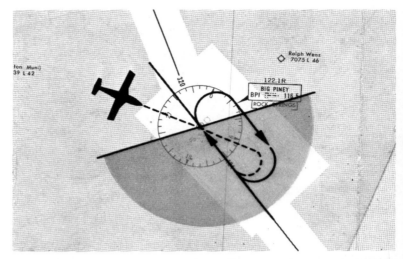

Figure 22 The teardrop entry is used whenever you are inbound in the smallest sector—turn no more than 30 degrees from the holding course.

the heading which *parallels* the holding course (in this example, a heading of 124 degrees), fly for one minute, then turn *left* until intercepting the holding course, or until you reach the fix, whichever happens first. A stiff tailwind as you turn inbound will often push you direct to the fix before you intercept the holding course.

Making It Easier

The procedures described thus far are the ones officially recommended by the FAA, and they provide a near-absolute guarantee that you will remain within holding airspace during the entry to a holding pattern. The 70-degree line and the direction of the turns were developed with adverse airspeeds and wind factors in mind, carefully calculated to take care of even the worst set of conditions. Pilots of high-performance aircraft—turboprops and turbojets operating at high altitudes where strong winds can blow them off course in short order—have legitimate concerns about drifting outside protected airspace. But for the lightplanes at lower altitudes, displace-

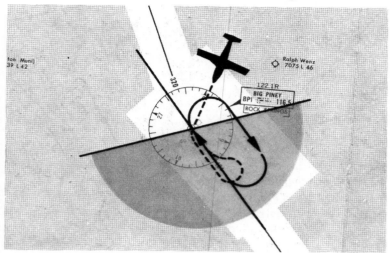

FIGURE 23 The parallel entry works when neither teardrop nor direct entry procedures apply. At station passage, turn immediately to the reciprocal of the holding course.

ment due to wind and radius of turn doesn't count for much, and a simplified holding pattern entry can be used.

To make it easier, when you arrive at the holding fix, *turn in the shorter direction to the heading that parallels the holding course.* Fly outbound for not more than one minute, proceed direct to the holding fix and start around the racetrack in the appropriate direction. (There's just one exception to "turn in the shorter direction"; when it's obvious that such a turn would place you on the side of the holding course away from the racetrack, don't do it—turn the other way. For example, the westbound aircraft in Figure 21 should turn to the *right* when reaching Big Piney VOR, even though it's the long way 'round; a left turn to 124 degrees would put the airplane on the non-holding side, where the protected airspace is considerably smaller—you're not supposed to be there while holding.)

As soon as you're squared away on the outbound leg, rotate the OBS to match the *outbound course,* and the CDI will indicate whether the holding course (where you want to go next) is to your left or right. With an HSI, put the course pointer on the *inbound* number, since the moveable course segment is always directional. During that first minute outbound, adjust your parallel heading for wind drift. A little "Kentucky windage" goes a long way here . . . 5, 10, 15 degrees into the wind, based on what you experienced while tracking toward the fix. And when you turn back toward the fix at the end of the minute, be aware of your relation to the holding course; it's quite likely that you will fly right onto it during the turn. This is a good time to put the "45-degree procedure" (page 182) to work for you.

Even though there's no regulatory basis for it, some instructors and examiners insist on the use of the FAA's entry procedures (they are *recommended*, not mandated). Prior to a flight check, a pilot who prefers the simpler entry described here (or one of his own design) should discuss his procedure with the examiner, so that there's no misunderstanding in the air. However it's accomplished, the primary concern in *anybody's* holding pattern entry is to keep the airplane close to the holding course, never more than one minute or the specified distance away from the holding fix.

Holding Pattern Limits

When you are cleared to hold, the controller assigns you a block of airspace large enough to separate you from other IFR traffic during your entry and subsequent pattern maneuvers. Airspeed limits are placed in the regulations to guarantee that aircraft entering a holding pattern will not go swooping outside the boundaries set up for them. For propeller-driven planes, the maximum speed is 175 knots indicated, and you must slow to this speed (or less) *within three minutes prior to crossing the holding fix*. Even with a strong tail wind, this maximum airspeed will see you safely through the entry and the holding pattern.

If your bird gets its "go-power" from a turbojet or two or more, you may increase the maximum speed: 200 knots up to 6,000 feet, 210 knots between 6,000 and 14,000 feet, and 230 knots above 14,000 feet (all indicated airspeeds, of course). In any event, be at or below the maximum holding speed before arrival at the fix.

There is one more variable in this airspace guarantee, and that is the angle of bank. If all aircraft observe the maximum holding airspeeds, the lateral displacement during turns will depend on how rapidly those turns are accomplished. Therefore, during the entry and while holding, you should turn at either 3 degrees per second (a standard-rate turn), 30 degrees of bank, or if you are using a flight-director system, 25 degrees of bank, whichever requires the smallest bank angle. It's easy to figure out why this rule had to be, when you consider the direct relationship between true airspeed and the angle of bank needed to generate a standard-rate turn. You can approximate the bank angle by this rule-of-thumb: Divide the true airspeed (in knots) by ten, add five, and you're pretty close to the necessary bank. Applying this to an actual situation, a jetliner flying at 600 knots TAS would have to be racked into a 65-degree bank to turn at standard rate. Although the airplanes can take it, stewardesses complained—American industry builds 2g airplanes, but not 2g bras!

It's "Four T" Time Again

Approaching Big Piney VOR and with the Barnburner slowed appropriately, the CDI will begin to dance a bit, the TO-FROM indicator starts its reversal, and when it shows FROM, two things occur simultaneously: You have arrived at the holding fix, and for reporting purposes, *you are in the holding pattern.* Note the TIME as you pass the holding fix, TURN to the outbound heading, THROTTLE back to holding airspeed, and after all this is done, TALK—you owe ATC a report of the time and altitude entering the holding pattern. There's no need to rush this report to the controller, since you're doing exactly what he expects you to, but when you are established on the outbound heading, slowed down, and everything is under control, report: "Salt Lake Center, Barnburner 1234 Alpha, Big Piney at three two [time you first crossed the fix], holding at one zero thousand."

Why slow down in the holding pattern? Because you're going to be flying around in circles for a while, and it's just not good sense to burn up more fuel than necessary. Next time you're under the hood, try several power combinations and determine a comfortable holding airspeed for your airplane—make it a trade-off between ease of handling and economy.

In the time it has taken to read this, you will have turned outbound and accomplished all Three or Four T's, so in the piece of a minute you have left before turning inbound, rotate the OBS to the holding course (304 degrees), and you are ready to turn inbound to the holding fix.

Executing standard-rate turns during the teardrop and direct entry maneuvers in a no-wind situation should put you on the holding course when you roll out of the turn toward the station. The parallel entry sets you up for a 45-degree "cut" on the inbound course, which means you will fly on this heading until the holding course is intercepted. But the gods who rule the atmosphere have seldom been known to bless pilots in holding patterns with calm winds, and the disorientation caused by zephyrian displacement can be total. An excellent clue to your position and the wind factor you're fighting shows up during the turn inbound, when your heading is 45 degrees from the holding course. (In the example, 259 degrees.) If at this point the CDI has not begun to move from its full LEFT position, *stop the turn* and hold 259 degrees until it *does* begin to move. There is obviously a westerly component to the wind, and it has drifted you east while flying the outbound leg. Should the CDI start sliding toward center while you're turning through 259 degrees, *keep turning* and you'll roll out on course. Movement of the CDI *earlier* than the 45-degree point in the turn is a signal to *increase the rate of turn* (30 degrees of bank is *plenty*) and prepare to correct for an easterly wind.

You can formulate three situations and their solutions at the 45-degree point of the inbound turn. (To make this system work, the OBS must be set on the holding course, which will cause the CDI to always be displaced toward the holding course.)

Situation (at the 45-degree point)	Solution
CDI has not moved from full left or full right (depends on direction of turn)	Roll out, fly this "45-degree" heading until CDI centers
CDI starting to move toward center	Continue turn, you should roll out on course
CDI already centered, or well on its way	Increase bank to 30 degrees, prepare to apply correction to get back on course

Timing the Holding Pattern

You are now on the threshold of the most important phase of holding pattern timing—the rules call for an inbound leg length (on the holding course) of one minute at or below 14,000 feet, and one and a half minutes above 14,000. You are given complete freedom to adjust your timing on the outbound leg so that the inbound requirement is satisfied. The moment the CDI centers on the inbound course (or when you complete the turn), start your timer and note carefully how long it takes to return to the holding fix. If it turns out to be exactly one minute, you've done it—you have hit that one-in-a-million combination of perfectly executed turns and absolutely calm winds. But suppose a minute and a half slips by before you arrive back over the VOR? You have encountered some tail wind as you flew outbound, and it's cut-and-try from here on. When you start outbound the next time, fly for only thirty seconds, head for the holding fix, and check the inbound time again; it should come out very close to one minute. There will be times when the outbound leg will be only ten, maybe twenty, seconds long; when the wind is *really* blowing, you may find yourself doing what appears to be a 360 over the fix to keep the inbound leg at the proper length. On the other hand, you might have to fly outbound for two or three minutes, depending on the wind direction and force.

Once established in a holding pattern, your only concern with respect to timing is to make certain you're on that holding course *inbound* for one minute (or ninety seconds, depending on altitude)— no more, no less. Therefore you must know where to punch the stopwatch as you turn outbound. The solution is simple: Start timing when you are abeam (directly opposite) the holding fix.

Where Is Abeam?

There are several holding situations which require different methods of determining when you are in that abeam position; the easiest is holding on a VOR, where the timing point is the TO-FROM reversal (Figure 24). Next in order of simplicity is a "square" intersection (VOR radials or a radial-ADF bearing combination crossing at or near a 90-degree angle), where you start the watch upon centering the side radial, or attaining the proper relative bearing.

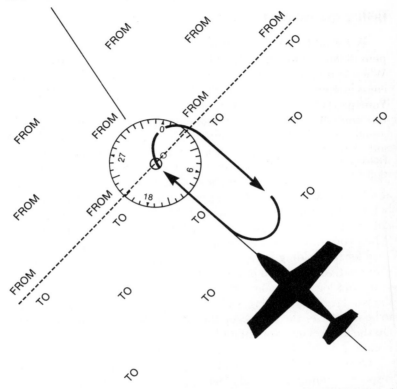

FIGURE 24   With OBS set properly, the TO-FROM indicator provides a good timing device in the holding pattern.

When the references are not close to "square," you must begin timing when you complete the turn to the outbound heading. This is also the best procedure when holding on an NDB; start timing when the outbound turn is completed.

It will likely require several circuits to nail down the exact timing, so continue experimenting until you arrive at an outbound leg length which results in exactly one minute on the holding course.

Drift Correction

A technique called "double drift" is an effective way to compensate for wind while going 'round and 'round in a holding pattern. When you have found a heading that will keep you on the holding course, correct *twice* that amount into the wind as you go outbound. Your pattern will lose its symmetry (Figure 25)—so who cares?— but you will intercept the holding course handily, and you'll stay

FIGURE 25   This is the track described by a holding aircraft using double drift to correct for wind.

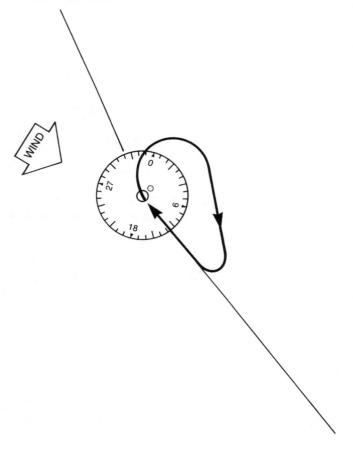

safely within the airspace reserved for you. Combine good drift correction with proper timing, and your holding patterns will be just what the doctor (ATC) ordered.

How Long to Hold?

The final portion of any holding clearance will consist of the time at which you can *expect further clearance*. Don't *ever* accept an interruption (a hold) in an IFR flight unless you receive one of these expected times; if a controller forgets it, ask him—nay, DEMAND it! You will seldom have to hold until this time, since it is purposely set far enough ahead to provide a clear route for you if your radios quit. (See Chapter 12, "Communications Failure," for details). However, you should plan to arrive over the holding fix (or at least be inbound to the fix) when the EFC time comes up on the clock. It is perfectly legal, and often necessary, to shorten the racetrack to do this. Bear in mind that a no-wind holding pattern (at or below 14,000 feet) consumes four minutes per circuit, so it is a matter of shortening the outbound leg to accomplish station passage at the proper time. Make a complete turn over the fix if your EFC is only two minutes away when you cross the fix, and be ready to go about your business on time.

Use the sometimes interminable minutes in an extended hold to listen to what's happening ahead of you. By paying attention to ATC's instructions to others in the holding pattern, you can get a good idea of whether you'll be cleared on your way or be held still longer. If your EFC is close (five minutes) and no word is forthcoming from ATC, give them a call and find out what to expect— you have a right to know, since continued holding doesn't improve your fuel situation even a little bit. You may want to divert to some less crowded route or terminal. *Any* hold should cause you to take a critical look at your fuel supply, and decide how much of what you have on board would be needed to fly out of trouble; remember that *you*, not the controller, are responsible for not running out of fuel.

An extended holding situation is a nuisance, a wearying exercise in making circles and going expensively nowhere; but sometimes it's unavoidable. When it appears that you're going to hold for a good long while and you tire of going 'round and 'round every four minutes, you might consider requesting a nonstandard, longer-legged pattern of your own. This could be done by asking for two- or three-minute legs, or by using a convenient DME fix to stretch things out a bit. If it can be done safely, ATC will usually go along with your request.

Holding with DME

"Barnburner 1234 Alpha is cleared to hold northeast of the Jack's Creek VOR, eight mile legs, maintain one three thousand, expect further clearance at one seven." This is the easiest holding pattern of all, because a DME reading replaces timing. Fly to the VOR, enter the pattern, and fly outbound until the DME reads 8; return to the holding course, fly back to the VOR, and do it all over again. It may require a bit more attention to drift correction, since you are not basing your pattern on time, and the "double-drift" method doesn't always work; but the end of the outbound leg is very clearly indicated (8 miles northeast of the VOR), and you won't have to worry about timing.

Depicted Holding Patterns

On occasion, the nice folks who figure out the whys and where-fores of instrument enroute charts eliminate Step #1 of the holding pattern procedure, by depicting the racetrack for you. Published holding patterns will be found at intersections frequently used for these "IFR merry-go-rounds." They ease the workload of controllers and pilots, because detailed holding pattern descriptions are un-necessary—if ATC clears you to hold at an intersection which sports a published pattern, the controller has only to say "hold at the so-and-so intersection," and you are expected to fly a pattern just as shown on the chart. All these are assumed to be standard as far as timing is concerned; if the controller wants you to fly longer legs, he'll let you know.

Holding on a Localizer

When the weather is really lousy, and the inbound traffic is really heavy, Approach Control may put you in a "stack," holding on the localizer at the outer marker, waiting your turn for an approach. You couldn't ask for a more easily-defined holding pattern—the fix is the marker (dah-dah-dah, flash-flash-flash, and a 180-degree swing of the ADF needle when a compass locator is installed), and the holding course is the localizer itself. Round and round you go, and each time someone breaks out of the clouds and hollers "runaway in sight," Approach Control shakes the box and moves everybody down a thousand feet.

It Happens to Everybody

Drawing a holding pattern and the proper entry on a piece of paper and actually flying it are two different things, to which every honest IFR pilot will bear witness! The first few times will likely leave you wondering where the heck you are, and fortunately there's an easy away out of this situation—when disorientation strikes, level the wings (no matter what direction you're headed), rotate the OBS until TO appears, then turn to that heading and fly to the station. On the way, orient yourself to the radial you're on, and when FROM shows up, start all over again. Should you have to do this several times in succession, don't worry—at least you're staying close to the holding fix! If you become utterly and genuinely lost, holler for help, and ATC will come to the rescue—they're perhaps more anxious than *you* are to straighten things out.

14

Getting Ready for an Instrument Approach

THERE ARE a number of instrument procedures in use today, with more just over the horizon; but before beginning *any* approach, there are several things you can do to make the entire operation easier and safer.

In the interest of constantly being one step ahead of the airplane, begin to develop your approach frame of mind when you're still many miles from the terminal area. There are clues to tell you when things are about to happen: For instance, the Center controller will clear you to a lower altitude to fit the requirements of terminal-area traffic flow; in a non-radar environment, Center will frequently hand you off to a controller at the airport, but since he doesn't have the advantage of seeing your flight on a radar scope, he'll request that you report passing an intersection or a DME fix as you fly inbound. When you reach the specified point, expect an approach clearance, or a hold, if there is traffic ahead of you. Listen to other clearances on the Approach Control frequency, and you'll have a good idea *what* to expect, and *when* to expect it.

Find out as early as you can what approach is in use at the destination, especially if it is an airport or an approach that is strange to you. If you're bound for an airfield with only one published procedure, there's no problem, but the larger terminals may have several types of approaches to three or four different runways. Chicago's O'Hare Field at one time had twenty-four procedures, plus radar approaches to eight runways!

There are several sources of approach information—at the top of the list is Automatic Terminal Information Service (ATIS), broadcast continuously on a VHF frequency listed on your approach chart. If two ATIS frequencies are given, choose the one that is *not* the localizer frequency—you'll find that the reception will be much clearer, and receivable from a greater distance. The localizer signal pattern is very directional, and is not powered for long-range transmission.

When you're headed for a non-ATIS, multiple-procedure terminal, Approach Control will usually spill the beans something like this: "Barnburner 1234 Alpha, you're in radar contact; expect vectors to the final approach course for the Runway one six VOR approach."

The Center controller can get terminal information for you, but it's a bit outside his bailiwick, and such a request really shouldn't be made unless you need to know a long way out. ATIS or Approach Control notification should give you plenty of time to get set up for the approach.

What about the airport that has no ATIS, no Approach Control, and you don't want to bother Center? Do the logical thing, and monitor the tower frequency for a while on your other radio; you'll likely find out what procedure they're using. Or ask Center if you may leave the frequency for a moment (a request almost always granted) and call the Tower, who can also give you the weather situation first hand. If there is not even a tower at Boondocks Municipal Airport, there's likely to be a Flight Service Station close by that can supply you with weather and winds, and you can make up your own mind about how to get to the runway.

As soon as you are in the terminal area, put away your enroute charts, notepads, computers, coffee jugs, and whatever else might divert your attention from the approach chart. Clean up the cockpit so that you can devote all your talents to flying the approach.

Good Practices Make Good Habits

As you study the published procedure, there is a method you should use for maximum efficiency, standardization, and safety. Done exactly the same way every time, it will soon become a habit, and will prevent missing some vital bit of information on that dark, stormy night when the engine's running rough, you're picking up a load of ice, and the gear won't go down. In a predicament like this (or any stress situation) your well-practiced system of chart study will come booming through.

Here's the way to do it: The first two items (and at this point the *only* two) to be memorized are the *first heading* and the *first altitude* of the missed approach procedure. Allow those two numbers to burn themselves into your mind, because the next item on the approach agenda is to convince yourself that you will definitely have to execute a missed approach, even though you *know* that the airport is VFR. With this attitude no major shift of mental gears is required on those very rare occasions when you are forced to pull up and go around because of weather. And what a pleasant surprise when you break out of the murk, and there is the runway, straight ahead! (It may be the wrong airport, but in lousy weather, *any* runway is beautiful!)

This leads directly to the next part of your approach preparation: What will the airport look like when you make visual contact? Approaching the home drome, you can probably handle this admirably; but an approach to a strange airport, in weather all the way to minimums, or when cleared for a circling approach to some runway other than the one on which you're lined up, can introduce considerable disorientaton. Prevent embarrassment ("Tower, this is Barnburner 1234 Alpha, if you have me in sight, *please* tell me which way to turn") by studying the airport plan view on your approach chart. Turn the chart until you're looking at the airport layout just the way you will see it when you break out of the clouds; find the landing runway, and decide which way you will turn if necessary. It's also an excellent way to make yourself aware of trees, power lines, grain elevators, high-rise apartments, and other obstructions that people insist on building in approach airspace.

Next item for the study system is the approach itself. All published procedures have one thing in common: They proceed step by step from the initial approach through various segments to the landing or missed approach, as appropriate. At this time, make a "big picture" study of the entire procedure: headings, altitudes, distances, times, etc. When you actually get into the approach, always let your mind fly one segment ahead of the airplane.

Now tune, identify, and orient yourself to the navigational aids you will use. (If you are being radar vectored to the final approach course, use this opportunity to set up all the approach aids. Your only responsibility while inbound is to follow the instructions from Approach Control.) When the weather conditions promise a tight approach, it's not a bad idea to tune two radios to the approach aid, so you can check one against the other. If the missed approach is an involved one, you would do well to set up your radio equipment so that there will be a minimum of knob-twisting when you are busy with a go-around.

After all this, you have one more number to memorize, and it's really an important one: the MDA or DH, depending on the type of approach in use. In either case it's the lowest altitude to which you may descend until the runway is visible. Picture in your mind's eye how the altimeter hands will appear when you get to that altitude, and keep it in mind. If you have a co-pilot familiar with the altimeter, have him holler when you are 100 feet above that altitude.

Approach charts are published on single pages and kept in loose-leaf binders for good reason; they are intended to be removed and placed somewhere in the cockpit for ready reference during an approach. The best possible location is in the jaws of a spring clip firmly attached to the control wheel, where you don't have to move your head to look at it. Next time you are under the hood with a well-qualified pilot in the other seat, put your approach plate on the floor between the seats; just as you begin your turn back onto the final approach course after completing a procedure turn, lower your head and look down at the chart for ten seconds, then rapidly back to the panel. This will probably induce vertigo such as you never believed could happen to you, and should convince you that the best place for the approach plate is right straight in front of you!

By the numbers, here is the approach study system:

1. Clean up the cockpit.
2. Find out what approach is in use, and place that chart where it can be easily seen.
3. Memorize the missed approach procedure (at least the first *heading* and *altitude*).
4. Convince yourself that you will have to make a missed approach.
5. Orient yourself to the airport layout as it will appear when you break out of the clouds.
6. Study the entire approach—the "big picture."
7. Set up the radio gear for the approach.
8. Memorize the DH or MDA, as appropriate.

Although it seldom happens, be ready for a missed approach every time. This includes a quick mental review of the mechanics of "going around" (for most airplanes, this means power up, pitch up [to climb attitude], flaps up, gear up), as well as an early decision concerning your intentions immediately thereafter. Remember that Tower controllers have a standard response to a missed approach report—"Roger, Barnburner 1234 Alpha, what are your intentions?" Compose your answer well ahead of time, *every* time you start an approach, and on that rare occasion when you need it, the words will come flowing forth just as if you know what you're doing.

Wind-Shear Problems

It's now accepted that when an airplane flies through a wind shear, performance is very much affected. Consider an extreme example: An airplane flying at 100 knots in a 100-knot headwind would have zero groundspeed; if the wind died suddenly, the momentum of the airplane would carry it forward, but the airspeed-groundspeed (they're now the same) would have to increase 100 knots if the original conditions are to be maintained. The heavier the airplane and/or the greater the initial airspeed, the more time is required for this acceleration to take place. (A rapid downwind turn may cause the same thing to happen.)

Whatever the span of time involved, there will be a nose-down pitch change and a net loss of altitude as the pilot tries to get back to where he was. Combine the very high mass of a heavy, fast airplane with the relatively long period of time required for a jet engine to "spool up" from a low power setting, then set up enough altitude to effect a recovery, and you've got the classic undershoot accident waiting to happen.

Fortunately, low momentum (light weights, low speeds) and the rapid acceleration characteristic of propeller-driven aircraft take the bite out of all but the worst wind-shear situations for the non-jet pilot population. However, the possibility is always there, and every now and then someone manages to ignore the indications and plants a lightplane in the approach lights or in a cornfield a mile short of the runway. Wind shear is worth knowing about and worth getting ready for, regardless of the kind of airplane you're operating.

It's true that wind shear can't be seen, but there is meteorological information available that should make knowledgeable pilots alert for the possibility of an encounter. First, whenever you've been fighting a headwind (or enjoying a tailwind) enroute, but find out that the destination airport's surface winds are calm, look out— somewhere between your present altitude and the ground, the wind is dying; second, whenever a cold front moving at 30 knots or more is going to arrive at the airport the same time you are, you should expect significant wind shear as you fly through the frontal surface; third, a warm front with a temperature difference of only 10 degrees may have potential wind-shear problems associated with it; fourth, you must expect serious wind shear encounters *anytime* there is a thunderstorm in the immediate environs of the airport.

Should you become aware of these conditions as you prepare for an instrument arrival (or a visual one, for that matter), plan to fly down the final approach a little bit faster and a little higher than normal. And most important, if the airspeed starts to bleed off (you're holding a constant pitch attitude, of course), don't hesitate to add power right now—there's nothing that will solve the problem more rapidly or positively.

Wind shear will become most noticeable on an ILS procedure, when you are attempting to descend on a fixed, electronic glide slope. If you've done your homework so that you are familiar with the airplane and know the power setting that will keep the glide slope needle centered during a normal approach, the power gauges will tell you right away that either a strong tail wind or headwind is working; more power required means more headwind, and vice versa. In either case, prepare yourself mentally for some interesting possibilities as you get close to the ground. All the warning flags should fly when you recognize the need to carry much more power than normal to stay on the glide slope at the same time as the tower is reporting the surface wind to be calm, or nearly so.

The tailwind-to-headwind shear situation (or sudden dropping off of a tailwind) introduces the opposite effects on the airplane; airspeed will increase, and the nose will tend to pitch up. Of course, the pilot responds by reducing power and lowering the nose, a combination guaranteed to produce at least a higher sink rate than before. If wind subsequently drops off at an altitude too close to the ground to allow recovery, an unplanned touchdown may well occur. Whatever the wind-shear type, the accident-prevention measures should be the same; make yourself aware of the situation, carry some extra airspeed and altitude (within reason), and at the first hint of a problem, power up and stay high.

Visual Aids to an Instrument Approach

There's a surefire way to get into serious trouble at the end of an instrument approach procedure: Look up from the instruments as soon as you see something on the ground, and continue trying to fly the airplane with visual clues only. That sort of piloting technique has probably wrapped up as many airplanes as any other single approach problem. We are taught from the very beginning to believe what we see, but at the crucial moment (at least from the point of view of an instrument pilot), our eyes play potentially hazardous tricks on us; it's well to understand the limitations of the human visual system under these conditions, and to know what to expect from the various visual aids provided to help keep you out of the treetops during the last stages of an instrument procedure. Lighting systems and other visual aids discussed here are indicated on the approach charts; you should be aware of what's available before the approach begins.

General aviation pilots (particularly those who fly light airplanes) will frequently make approaches to airfields with minimum facilities; in this case, the only visual aid is the runway itself, augmented by lighting with a variety of configurations you won't believe until you've been there. Whatever the situation, it's important to realize that the human visual system is not designed to shift rapidly from one set of clues (the instruments) to another (what you see through the windshield) and consistently and properly interpret what's really there. So, a procedure must be developed; when the runway (or runway lights) becomes visible, begin to include those clues in your crosscheck. Treat what you see out front as just another instrument indication, but give the outside clues an increasingly larger share of your scan time until the transition is complete. It only takes a few seconds, but doing it this way eliminates the possibility of making control inputs based on what you *think* you see. Even when the visibility is only half a mile, you will find that you can effect the transition from all-instrument to all-outside clues quite smoothly in the 15 seconds or so between "runway in sight" and touchdown.

Various types of approach lighting systems (ALS) have been developed and installed throughout the country—virtually all ILS runways will be so equipped—and you'll find that the light pattern, colors, distance from first light to threshold, and intensity of these visual aids may differ considerably from airport to the next. As a result, you may "see" things differently when looking at one type of installation as opposed to another—even though you are located at the same point on the approach. The key to success in this situation is to recognize that there probably will be some visual illusions and that they *must* be consciously overridden by information from the aircraft instruments—airspeed, altimeter, attitude indicator, and so on. The lights are intended to (1) make the runway environment visible as soon as possible in low-visibility conditions, (2) provide information relative to lateral displacement from the runway centerline, (3) provide information relative to the roll attitude of your aircraft. *Notice that there is no altitude information available from an approach lighting system per se;* that's why you have an altimeter. When in doubt, add at least 50 feet to the airport elevation, and resolve not to go below that number on your altimeter until there's concrete underneath the airplane.

A high-time professional pilot who had been operating in the Pacific Northwest for some years was called upon to pick up his employer late one winter night at a small, ILS-equipped airport. The cloud ceiling was very close to the Decision Height of 200 feet, but visibility was quite good under the clouds.

The Approach Lighting System was in operation, and as far as could be determined in a post-accident flight check, the localizer and glide slope signals were normal in every respect. Yet, for reasons known only to the pilot, the airplane struck the ground almost two miles from the runway threshold. The wings were level, gear down and flaps set to the position normally used during an instrument approach procedure in this airplane, suggesting that the pilot was in complete control at impact.

The most likely explanation of this accident centers on the pilot's perceived need to land (his boss was known to be a very demanding person, not very tolerant of late arrivals, to say nothing of his pilot not showing up at all), and the illusions probably produced when the airplane broke out of the low clouds. If the pilot had indeed consciously flown below the glide slope in an effort to guarantee "breakout" and landing, he would surely have noticed that the Approach Lighting System appeared much flatter and smaller (farther away) than would be expected during the final segment of a normal approach to minimums.

Even if the glide slope signal or the onboard equipment had malfunctioned, the old reliable altimeter would have saved the day for this pilot. By making a "no exceptions" decision to fly no lower than the published Decision Height, the accident could have been prevented. Of course, the boss might have thrown a fit, but the pilot would have been alive to quit his job . . . instead of losing it.

One of the toughest judgment calls in instrument operations is deciding when to commence descent to the runway on a non-precision (no glide slope) approach after the airfield has been sighted. With no lighting systems available, you'll be glad you practiced ahead of time and know the power setting and pitch attitude for a "normal" descent to a landing. Using this as a base, you can start down, using the spot-on-the-windshield technique to accomplish a safe glide path. Use power to correct when you sense the need; above all, don't go below your predetermined "minimum-minimum altitude" (runway elevation plus 50 feet) until the threshold is behind you.

There is another type of visual aid so simple that you've got to wonder why no one thought of it when the very first instrument approach procedure was developed. It's nothing more than a radio marker beacon or a DME fix at the point where a 3-degree glide slope intersects the Minimum Descent Altitude. This marks the point at which you should begin a normal descent to the runway . . . IF you have established visual contact. The VOR-DME approach in Figure 26 is typical, with the Visual Descent Point (VDP) shown in the profile view; when on final approach and at MDA, you should start down when the DME counter indicates 8.8 miles. Once again, it's extremely helpful to know ahead of time the approximate power setting needed to maintain a safe descent path.

There are two possible cases when using this visual aid: (1) arriving at the VDP with no runway in sight, (2) sighting the runway before the VDP is reached. In the first instance, get ready for a missed-approach, especially in a high-performance airplane—if you haven't spotted the runway by the time you're this close, there probably won't be time for a safe descent when the airfield does come into clear view (as you continue beyond the VDP in level

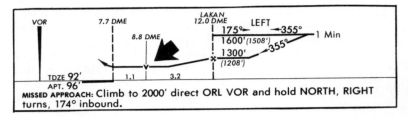

MISSED APPROACH: Climb to 2000' direct ORL VOR and hold NORTH, RIGHT turns, 174° inbound.

FIGURE 26 Visual Descent Point (VDP) shown on Jeppesen approach procedure chart. (© *1977 Jeppesen & Co., Denver, Colo. All rights reserved. Not to be used for navigation.*)

flight, the required angle of descent gets progressively steeper). In the second situation, fly up to the VDP before leaving the Minimum Descent Altitude; an early descent will produce a shallow glide path that's filled with illusions. Why upset your visual apple cart at such a crucial time? Fly to the Visual Descent Point and make a *normal* approach to the runway.

The "when to descend?" and "how fast to descend?" guesswork is eliminated by the installation of a Visual Approach Slope Indicator (VASI; pronounced "vassy"), which consists of two light sources just off the side of the runway near the approach end. (Figure 27 is a side-view schematic of a VASI installation.) When you break out of the clouds at MDA, you'll most likely see two red lights, indicating that you have not yet flown into the predetermined glide slope. As you continue the approach at MDA, the nearer light will gradually change to white, at which time you should power down and start your descent to the runway. If you adjust power to keep that color combination—red over white—in view, you will be flying along a

FIGURE 27 The Visual Approach Slope Indicator (VASI). Optical filters project white light above the lamps' centerlines, red light below.

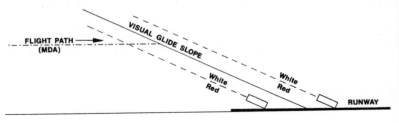

glide slope guaranteed to bring you safely across the runway threshold. The VASI glide slope is typically elevated about 3 degrees, the same as most ILS glide slopes. Should your rate of descent take you above the glide slope, you'll see two white lights; if you go below (that's a no-no!), the lights will turn red. Most important to IFR operators—don't commence the descent unless and until you see a clear red-over-white indication from the VASI lights. (At some large airports served by wide-body, jumbo jets, you may see *three* sets of VASI lights alongside the primary runway, providing two glide paths; an upper one for the big airplanes, a lower one for the little guys. The pilot's job is to fly one or the other. (To avoid wake turbulence when following a large aircraft, stay on the *upper* glide path. Interpret the lights in the same way—red over white means "you're all right.")

15

Instrument Approaches

FROM a "do what you're told" radar approach at the low end of the simplicity scale, to the Instrument Landing System where the entire job of navigation is up to you, every instrument approach is just a means to an end. When enroute navigation has brought you through the clouds to that fabled "point B," the approach charts take over to guide you to a point from which you should be able to land the airplane—it's that simple! Whenever the navaids available permit you to position yourself more accurately on the final approach segment of the procedure, that point gets closer to the runway. It will be at its maximum distance on a typical NDB (ADF) approach (because of the inherent inaccuracy of the system and the great amount of pilot navigational inputs required), moves closer with VOR, gets even better on a Localizer approach, and gets down very close to the runway with the most accurate of all, the ILS.

You may have personal opinions about the accuracy of the various types of approaches, but when it comes to precision, there is a major classification already laid down for you: ALL approaches are put into one of two general categories, precision or non-precision. (The semantics can be argued, since some of the so-called non-precision procedures lead you right down the paint stripe in the middle of the runway; but there are important implications stemming from these descriptions, basic to a complete understanding of instrument approaches.) If the installation provides electronic glide slope information, it's known as a "precision" approach; a procedure without a glide slope falls into the "non-precision" category.

For all practical purposes, the only precision approach in use today is the Instrument Landing System (ILS), in which the glide slope is displayed to the pilot in the form of a moving pointer or

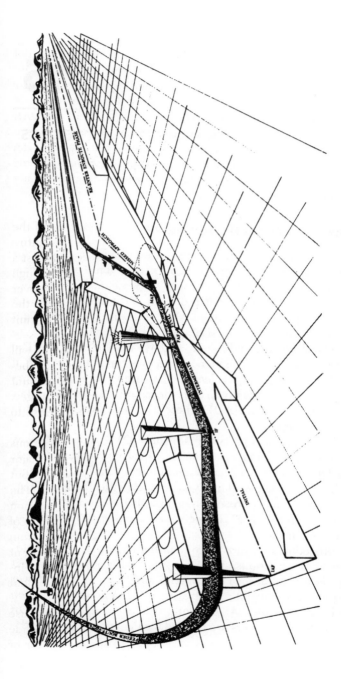

Figure 28 Segments of a typical approach procedure, showing how terrain and obstacle clearance "funnels down" toward the runway.

indicator of some sort that enables him to adjust the flight path of the airplane to conform to a prescribed path leading to the runway. There is another system that qualifies, Precision Approach Radar (PAR), but these facilities exist at only a few civil airports (three, at last count) in the United States. When it's in operation, the PAR glide slope is observed on radar and corrections are made by the pilot at the controller's direction. This means that the approach can be accomplished with only a radio receiver and basic instruments operating in the aircraft—a good deal if the weather and your navigation radios fail at the same time!

How Many Black Boxes Do You Need?

The least complicated situation would be a radar approach, for which you need only some means of receiving voice communication—no navigation gear at all. For a VOR procedure, it's obvious that at least one omni receiver is required, and an NDB approach cannot be accomplished without an ADF on board. In order to get to the Decision Height on an ILS approach, you must be able to receive the localizer, the glide slope, and two marker beacons. (The law allows you to substitute radar for the outer marker, or ADF if the system includes a compass locator. Be careful here, as locators are being phased out gradually all over the country, and with neither marker beacon, radar, nor ADF, there's no legal way to identify that point on the approach.)

Some VOR approach procedures include DME fixes that allow you to position yourself more accurately on final approach, and lower Minimum Descent Altitudes are therefore authorized; if you don't have DME, or if it's not working, you're stuck with a higher MDA. On the other hand, an approach procedure that is specifically titled "VOR-DME" requires BOTH receivers—if either is inoperative, you're out of business.

A few procedures require more than the basic navigational aids because of local conditions. They fall into two groups: those that *absolutely require* additional equipment, and those in which lower minimums are *available* for aircraft with more radio gear (or when radar service is available). At Lafayette, Indiana (Figure 29), VOR and DME or NDB receivers are needed for the approach, since the final approach fix (BATLE intersection) cannot be identified without one or the other. The VOR Runway 13 procedure at Craig Airport in Jacksonville (Figure 30) can be executed with just a VOR set on board, but you may descend 340 feet lower if you can determine the ANTIC intersection; this requires dual VOR, or VOR and DME. On a rainy, scuddy day at Jacksonville, that 340 feet could be the difference between a successful approach and a go-around. Akron-Canton's Regional Airport exhibits still another unusual situation, in that the back course approach to Runway 19 can be executed only when radar service is available (Figure 31).

With radar approach control, more often than not you will be given a vector to the final approach course, and so the procedure turn is slowly going the way of the position report. But you must know how to fly the complete approach as published, because there'll come a non-radar day when you will have to fly the whole thing by yourself. Accordingly, the first subject in this chapter is "procedure turns."

Once you've learned the basic segments of an approach procedure, and the principles underlying pilot actions at various times, you can fly any approach in the book. Each of the most-used procedures (ADF, VOR, Localizer, ILS) is discussed using this format:

Description
Setting up the radios
Initial approach
Station passage and tracking outbound
Procedure turn
Final approach

Straight-in approaches (those that lead directly to the landing runway with no maneuvering) are the first order of business, followed by circling approaches, and the next logical step when the weather is lousy, the missed approach. (In the Air Force it's a "go-around," in the Navy it's a "wave-off," and in the airlines it's "co-pilot error.")

An instrument approach doesn't have to follow the printed directions to the letter, but if you're going to take advantage of the legal short-cuts, you must know what you're doing. A pilot who accepts a contact approach but has no idea what he is expected to

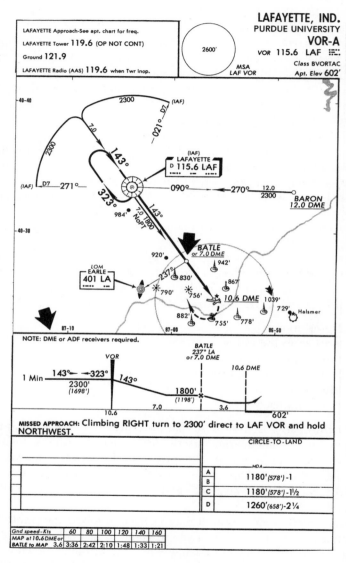

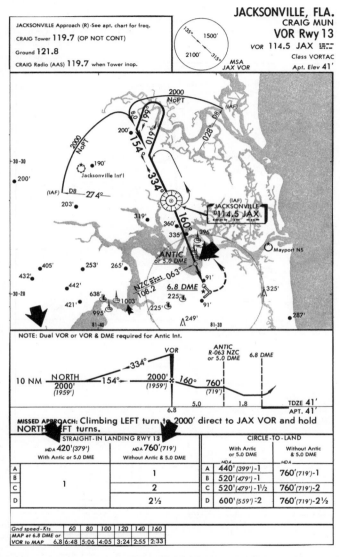

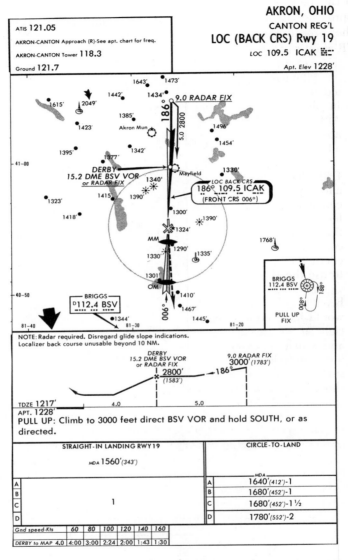

do can become a hazard in the airspace. So, contact and visual approaches are discussed, followed by radar approaches and several other procedures you should know about to make the most of your IFR abilities.

Pilot complacency, controller error, and hostile terrain make a dangerous mixture. Such was the case in a West Coast episode involving an airport that lay at the end of a long, narrow valley. Although the ILS isn't a "thread-the-needle" approach, there are ridges on either side that rise well above the initial approach altitude.

The pilot had flown the ILS on many occasions, VFR and IFR, due to his company's frequent trips between this airport and others in that part of northern California. This flight seemed completely routine on all counts, with a ceiling of several hundred feet and good visibility under the clouds. Unfortunately, as the flight approached the airport, the approach controller became confused during a hand-off from his Center counterpart, and commenced vectoring a blip that was *not* the airplane intending to use the ILS procedure.

Assuming that the pilot of the ill-fated airplane had set up his #1 nav indicator for the ILS when the vectors began, he would have noticed that he was being "vectored" well to the right of the localizer, instead of to the left, which was normal, and which *appeared* normal to the controller . . . who was unfortunately looking at another target. When the vector was issued to turn the flight around for localizer intercept, the pilot should have noticed that it was a turn *away from the localizer* . . . and toward terrain higher than his present altitude.

In due time, the controller noticed that the blip was not responding to his vectors, and inquired of the pilot if he were in fact turning to the new heading. About this time, the pilot also sensed that something was not right, questioned the vector, but it was too late; even a full-power go-around wasn't enough to clear the ridge, and the plane impacted short of the top, killing all aboard.

As always, there's something to be learned from this accident. Study each approach beforehand with a thought to what *should* happen, what the navigational indications *should* be, and stay on top of your actual position throughout the procedure . . . particularly during that portion of the approach that consists of radar vectors. (Obviously, this is especially important in those parts of the country where terrain and/or obstacles are significant.) It's called "positional awareness," and provides the foundation on which you can decide whether the controller's instructions—or your own maneuvering—is proper, safe, and adequate to get the job done.

And whenever you have even a shred of doubt about the outcome of a vector, turn, or descent, question yourself or the controller. One quick inquiry might save the day.

Practice Is a *Must*!

Pilots aren't the only egomaniacs in the world. A famous musician once said "if I practice four hours a day I am the world's greatest pianist; if I practice *eight* hours a day, I am Paderewski!" Practice improves performance in any endeavor, but it becomes more significant when you're talking about instrument flying skills.

Going 'round and 'round the flagpole at your home drome is commendable, since you'll probably make most of your down-to-minimums approaches there, but this kind of practice doesn't do much for your versatility. The time that you set aside for instrument practice (and you should do this unless you fly IFR regularly and frequently) can be more productive if you will have your instructor or safety pilot pick an instrument approach procedure at random from the chart book—give yourself a few moments to study it, using the method in Chapter 14, and then fly it. Of course you can't practice ILS or Localizer approaches this way, but if you can receive a signal from any VOR or NDB, you can use that signal to simulate an approach procedure; the local standard broadcast station is often convenient for ADF practice.

To make these exercises as realistic as possible, reset your altimeter to an indication that will put the MDA for the approach at a safe level. Under the hood, you should be concerned only with the numbers you can see—it makes no difference to you what your actual altitude is, or where the navigation signals are coming from; keeping you clear of things is your safety pilot's job. After a few of these randomly-selected-approach sessions, you'll have convinced yourself that approaches are generally the same; different altitudes, different headings, but you won't be surprised when cleared for a procedure you've never seen before.

Instrument approaches are the command performances of the flying business; the ones you make when the weather is right down on the deck are the ones you practice for, so when you have the opportunity, get under the hood and really *work*—don't bore expensive holes in the sky.

Procedure Turns

It's refreshing, in this overregulated aeronautical world, to have one instrument procedure that a pilot can legally execute just about any way he pleases. To be sure, there are limitations on the airspace you may use for a procedure turn, but by and large, how you reverse course during an instrument approach is up to you. (The real gutsy pilots could even Immelman or Split-S their way through procedure turns if it weren't for the restrictions on aerobatics in a control zone!) A procedure turn is the instrument pilot's modus operandi to get turned around and headed back the way he came, and on a specific course.

Three types of procedure turns have evolved over the years, and they are best classified in terms of their relative difficulty. (Not to imply that any one is actually harder to perform than the others, but the elapsed time from start to finish grows shorter as you move up the scale, and this means that you have to be very much on top of the entire situation when using the most rapid reversal.) The "old standard" is the 60-second procedure turn, and requires at least three minutes from the time you leave the outbound course until you're back to where you started the maneuver. The 40-second type (really just a modification of the 60-second turn) cuts the total time somewhat depending on the wind, and the fastest one of all is the 90–270—you'd better be ready for your inbound chores shortly after reversing direction. (Standard-rate turns are assumed in each case.)

These IFR turn-arounds have several things in common: They must be executed at or above a specified minimum altitude (although *maximum* and *mandatory* procedure turn altitudes are not unknown); you may not go beyond a specified limit from the approach facility as you reverse course; and your maneuvering must be accomplished on the specified side of the course. The restrictions are designed to allow plenty of room, yet keep you clear of obstacles as you turn.

The maneuvering side of the course (indicated by a barbed arrow on the U.S. charts or Jeppesen's full depiction of the turn) and the procedure turn altitude (shown on the profile view of the approach procedure) are quite variable, but the maximum distance is 10 nautical miles from the approach fix on almost every chart. And therein lies a trap for the unwary pilot who always allows himself the full 10 miles—some approaches cannot guarantee terrain or obstruction clearance for this distance, and a shorter mileage is quoted. "Nonstandard" procedure turn distances are not emphasized on approach charts, and it's easy to count on 10 miles, only to find yourself in trouble. Pay close attention to the maximum procedure turn distance on *every* approach, with airports in the mountainous sections of the country most suspect.

All three types of turns are safe procedures if you remain at or above the procedure turn altitude *until established on the approach course inbound,* when you may descend to the next lower altitude, if the published procedure permits.

The 60-Second Procedure Turn

Used by some pilots because of its simplicity and the fact that it gives you a "breather" on the inbound leg, the 60-second procedure is commenced by a standard-rate 45-degree turn away from

The 60-second procedure turn.

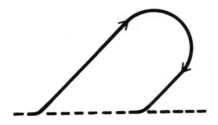

the outbound course (headings are given on the chart), and flying for one minute on the new heading. When the minute is up, turn at standard rate 180 degrees IN THE DIRECTION OPPOSITE THE FIRST TURN, or always turn AWAY FROM THE AIRPORT, whichever is easiest for you to remember. In a no-wind situation, you'll have about half a minute to fly on this heading before you reintercept the inbound course. It's a good time to refresh yourself on the MDA or DH, or your missed approach procedures, or your anticipated circling maneuvers, depending on the kind of approach you are flying. When your navigation displays show that you're approaching the inbound course, lead the turn a bit, and track to the fix.

The only timing you need worry about is the one minute outbound—when starting the procedure turn from an on-course position (which is where you should be!), activate your timing device as soon as you level the wings after the 45-degree turn. This rule also holds for those times when you find yourself *slightly* off-course on the maneuvering side—start timing when you level the wings. However, should you begin the maneuver from the *other* side of the course, you mustn't start timing until your instruments indicate that you have crossed the course.

In a situation where you have no idea of the wind conditions, the 60-second procedure turn will probably give you the best break— if there's *no* wind, it will show up as a normal 30-second trip from completion of the inbound turn to the final approach course. If the zephyrs have pushed upon the tail of your flying machine while outbound, you may need a box lunch to survive the journey back to course. And in the worst situation, a strong headwind outbound, you will see the navaids indicating course interception during the inbound turn; in this case, turn directly to the inbound heading.

Safe, simple, and sure, the 60-second reversal is a good one to use when in doubt. But don't get the idea that it's just for beginners and those who have time to spare. There are occasions when it becomes necessary to lose a lot of altitude during a procedure turn, and that full minute outbound, another in the turn, and a chunk of a minute before intercepting the inbound course can mean a couple thousand feet, even at a comfortable rate of descent.

The 40-Second Procedure Turn

Here's a way to make the procedure turn more efficient by controlling the effects of the wind, instead of accepting whatever displacement it may cause. It's a modification of the turn just discussed, and involves changes in the time outbound as well as the point at which you will reintercept the course. The 40-second turn will obviously cut down the time you spend reversing course, and can be your contribution to speeding up the flow of traffic during rush hour at the local airpatch. But it requires a little more of the pilot, since you must calculate roughly the effect of wind, apply the correction, and perhaps more importantly, be prepared to cope with the faster return to course which results—there'll be no breather after you turn inbound on this one; if properly done, you will roll out *on course,* and you must be all set to proceed with the remainder of the approach.

The 40-second turn begins the same as its 60-second brother, with a standard rate 45-degree turn away from the outbound course, and timing also starts at the same place. The duplication stops right there, because now you will add or subtract from the 40-second base figure a time factor to correct for wind. The calculation puts together the number of degrees of wind correction that was required to keep you on the outbound course, and in which direction. If your procedure turn takes you downwind, *subtract* one second for each degree of crab required on the outbound course—when turning into the wind, *add* one second for each degree. Thus, you will shorten or lengthen that first leg, and change the radius of turn as you head back for the inbound course. If this is done properly (and "properly" includes all turns made at the same rate), you should find the appropriate needles centering as you roll out on the inbound

The 40-second procedure turn.

heading, plus or minus drift correction, of course. A well done 40-second procedure turn should conclude with a smooth, sweeping standard-rate turn onto the approach course, and even if you are off a few seconds in your calculations, you will have saved some time. This is also a good one to use when there is no wind and you wouldn't mind getting on the ground a little sooner. It's a difference of only half a minute or so, but when the terminal area is saturated with IFR traffic making procedure turns, those half-minutes add up.

The 90–270 Procedure Turn

Maybe it all started with an indecisive IFR pilot not being able to make up his mind after the first 90 degrees of turn, but whatever the origin, the 90–270 will get you turned around in the minimum time, and with the minimum outbound displacement, of any of the procedure turns. You will also find it very helpful as a low-visibility approach procedure, when you are forced to fly the length of the runway, then reverse course to land. There is no timing involved, and it will work in all but the strongest winds—the key is to make your turns at a uniform rate, and to change heading a FULL 90 degrees on the first turn.

Choose carefully the point from which you begin a 90–270, because you will come back onto the inbound course not very far from where you left it. If you have more than a thousand feet to lose in the turn, you're going to be plunging earthward at a rapid rate, which will speed up the whole approach to the point where things may be happening so fast you can't keep up. Having to execute a missed approach because you started a rip-snorting 90–270 too

The 90–270 procedure turn.

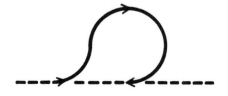

close to the fix is hardly a laudable demonstration of efficiency!

When the distance out and altitude-to-lose are compatible, start the Rapid Reverser with a 90-degree turn in the appropriate direction, and *immediately* on reaching the 90-degree point, roll smoothly into an identical angle of bank in the opposite direction. Depending on the wind condition, you will probably begin to center the nav-needles about 45 degrees from the inbound heading—keep turning, and as you roll out, you'll be "right on." Remember that the accuracy of this maneuver depends on uniform and constant rates of turn, and a 90-degree heading change at the outset—if you're holding 15 degrees of crab as you proceed outbound before starting the procedure turn, count 90 degrees from that heading, not from the course you are on. (Some pilots like heading changes of 80 degrees and 260 degrees; it's a matter of personal preference.)

Outbound Timing

No matter which of these three procedures you elect to use, you must decide how far outbound you will fly before beginning the procedure turn. Bearing on your decision will be the maximum distance allowed, the amount of altitude you have to lose, and how much time you figure you will need (or would like to have) to get squared away on the final approach course. When the weather is hovering around minimums and you want everything going for you, give yourself plenty of time. Within reason, the distance you fly outbound before beginning the procedure turn should increase as the ceiling and visibility decrease. A generally accepted figure for lightplanes is two minutes, which will supply that comfortable time pad (unless there's a terrific head wind outbound), yet keep you well within the mileage limit. Of course, you should slow down as soon as you cross the fix outbound—there's no reason for high airspeeds during the procedure turn; you'll use up more fuel, increase your radius of turn, and fly farther away from the fix. At a reasonable airspeed and two minutes outbound, you needn't worry about a 10-mile limit; a groundspeed of even 180 knots will keep you inside the envelope of airspace reserved for you as you maneuver.

No Procedure Turn, Please

There are two situations frequently encountered which preclude the use of a procedure turn. The first occurs when you are issued a radar vector that the controller states will take you to the final approach course for the appropriate instrument procedure. The second involves an approach clearance via a route on the approach chart that bears the notation "NoPT," meaning of course "No Procedure Turn." In these cases, the routing (either by vector or charted directions) will result in your intercepting the final approach course at a distance sufficient to allow you to line up and descend if required before reaching the Final Approach Fix.

A Procedure Turn Is Not the *Only* Way

When is a procedure turn *not* a procedure turn?—when it is omitted from the published approach, or replaced by some other maneuver, as at Parkersburg, West Virginia (Figure 33), where DME arcs and a lead-in heading from BELPRE intersection provide

FIGURE 32 Initial approach routes which do not require a procedure turn (NoPT). (© 1969 Jeppesen & Co., Denver, Colo. All rights reserved. Not to be used for navigation.)

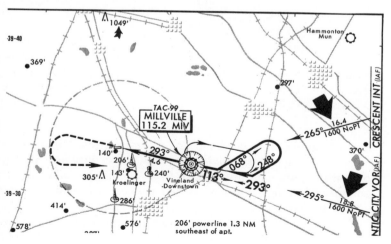

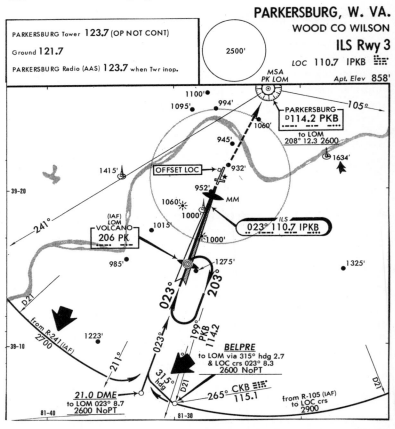

FIGURE 33 DME arcs and lead-in heading, which take the place of a procedure turn. (© 1977 Jeppesen & Co., Denver, Colo. All rights reserved. Not to be used for navigation.)

adequate guidance to get lined up on the localizer course. On occasion a holding pattern is substituted for a procedure turn; perhaps to limit the outbound distance, or to guarantee that pilots turning around will be doing so in a prescribed manner, instead of the several options available for a regular procedure turn.

One of the smoothest, least complicated procedures is the teardrop turn. (When the over-the-fix altitude gets up to 20,000 feet or so, and the rate of descent required is 5,000–6,000 feet per minute, it's called a "jet penetration.") You'll find one leading up to the localizer approach to Runway 31 at Dothan, Alabama (Figure 34). Over the VORTAC at cruise altitude and cleared for the approach, head out the 150 radial, descend to not less than 2,200 feet, and when you figure you can turn onto the localizer comfortably, do it. If you want to cut the elapsed time right down to the bone, watch the DME readout during the teardrop turn, and you can put yourself on the localizer right at the outer marker.

FIGURE 34 Approach chart for Runway 31 at Dothan, Ala., showing the teardrop turn in lieu of a procedure turn. (© 1977 Jeppesen & Co., Denver, Colo. All rights reserved. Not to be used for navigation.)

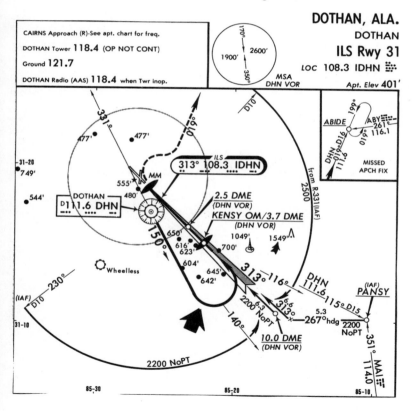

218   *Instrument Flying*

Another variation of the procedure turn is well illustrated by the VOR approach to Runway 24 at Martha's Vineyard Airport (Figure 35). On an IFR day when the airborne vacationers are swarming, you may be obliged to hold at the VOR, waiting your turn for an approach. As you move down in the stack, a question comes up regarding your actions when you are cleared for the approach: Do you execute a procedure turn or not? Take another look at the chart, and notice that the missed-approach holding pattern uses the same airspace as the charted procedure turn. The only restriction you

Figure 35   VOR approach for Runway 24 at Martha's Vineyard, Mass. (© *1977 Jeppesen & Co., Denver, Colo. All rights reserved. Not to be used for navigation.*)

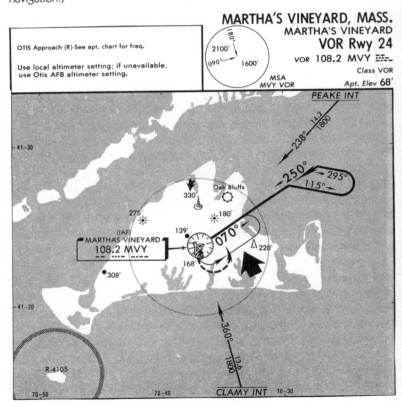

must observe here is the maximum distance of 10 miles, so be sure you stay within that limit, descend to procedure turn altitude during your final circuit of the holding pattern, and go ahead with the approach. Otis Approach Control would surely aim a word or two in your direction if they observed you making a tight turn over the station, proceeding outbound on the 070 radial, and into a beautiful procedure turn—no matter how well executed, this maneuver would be unnecessary, ill-advised, and rather thoughtless of the pilots above you in the stack. Whenever possible and practical, continue in the holding pattern when cleared for an approach IF THE HOLD-ING PATTERN AND PROCEDURE TURN ARE COINCIDENT ON THE CHART. If time versus altitude loss becomes a problem, you can always extend the outbound leg of the holding pattern for two minutes or so before turning inbound.

Referring to the *NDB* approach procedure for the Martha's Vine-yard Airport (Figure 35), it appears that the same philosophy would apply, and when cleared for the approach, continued descent in the holding pattern would be the most practical thing to do. But there's one drawback—in the profile view, "NOTE: Final Approach from EGR NDB holding pattern not authorized." With this restriction, it is incumbent on the pilot to return to the beacon when cleared for the approach, and execute a complete procedure turn.

Approaches into No-Control-Zone Airports

Notice how thick your books of approach charts have grown over the past few years? It's the result of more and more airport operators and users being able to convince the government that an instrument approach procedure is justified, and it has increased the usefulness of small airplanes many times over. The multitude of instrument-accessible landing places is certainly to be welcomed, but there is a trap of complacency that you should know about.

If an approach procedure and the airport for which it is intended meet specific requirements, a Control Zone is established for the protection of aircraft arriving and departing under IFR conditions. But many of the smaller airports, while qualifying for an instrument approach, do not meet the criteria for a Control Zone. A Transition Area is usually set up, but it doesn't do a complete job—instead of protection from the ground up throughout your approach, *you are in Controlled Airspace only during the time you are 700 feet or more above the ground!* This means that you can be cleared for an approach, fly the proper procedure, hold your track precisely and make good your timing to within a gnat's eyelash, and wind up *in uncontrolled airspace!* When the altimeter hands slide below the numbers that represent 700 feet AGL, you have gone from one world to another—from the *complete* protection of ATC to *no* protection except your own eyes.

This situation is not a fault of the system, but is the sort of thing you should know about so that you can increase your vigilance. Just because you have been cleared for the approach, don't get the mistaken idea that you are the only one who is allowed to be there. In uncontrolled airspace, the only requirements to fly VFR are 1-mile visibility and clear of clouds, so there is nothing to prevent some dedicated pilot from going out to the airport for a few touch-and-go's even though the weather is perfectly horrible. And it's not just the VFR types you have to worry about, because there could even be an intrepid soul approaching the same airport IFR—without a flight plan, a clearance, or any notification to ATC. He, too, is completely legal as long as he remains clear of controlled airspace; not necessarily smart, but legal.

There are three ways you can lessen the danger when inbound to a no-control-zone airport in IFR conditions. First, ask the Approach (or Center) controller to check for radar targets in the vicinity of the airport. Second, get on Unicom and broadcast your position and intentions as soon as you are able, continuing this broadcast in the blind as often as you think necessary. Third, get down to the MDA early and keep those eyeballs moving! Remember that the minute you descend below 700 feet AGL, you must share this uncontrolled airspace with whoever else may be using it—you're in the arena with the scud runners, obligated to see and avoid, just as you hope they are doing.

Instrument Procedures with No Final Approach Fix

The Maltese Cross symbol that appears in the profile view of most approach charts indicates the Final Approach Fix (FAF). It's the last electronic fix before beginning the descent to MDA, and is also the point at which you should begin timing for the missed-

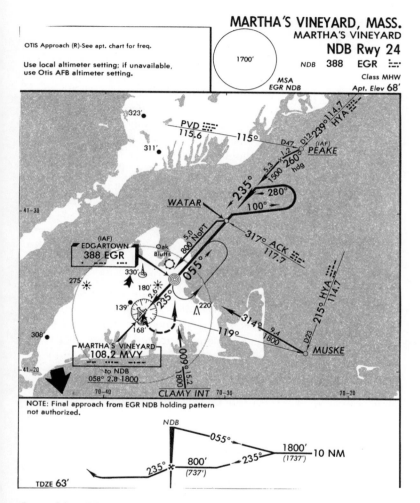

approach point. (The FAF is indicated on an ILS procedure as well, but is intended for the localizer-only approach; when flying the "full ILS," start descending when the glide slope is intercepted.)

But if you riffle through the pages of your IFR book, you'll find a number of procedures *without* a Final Approach Fix—no Maltese Cross. Almost invariably, the radio aid (VOR or NDB) will be right in the middle of the airport; you'll also find that the time-to-fly from FAF to MAP is blank. With no point from which to start the time, there's no choice but to fly at MDA until station passage . . . not all bad, because you're flying toward an increasingly accurate signal, and the missed-approach point is unmistakably clear.

Without timing and without radar service or DME to provide you with distance-from-the-airfield information, the no-FAF procedure has a built-in trap in that the outbound leg (on the way to the procedure turn) starts over the airport, not over a beacon or VOR a mile or three from the runway. The pilot who flies a normal two minutes outbound during such a procedure may find himself still letting down to MDA when he roars across the airport—or else descending at a very rapid, unsafe rate when the problem is recognized.

The solution is simple: Ask for radar distance information; set up your DME to provide it if the station is reasonably well lined up with the final approach course, use a nearby VOR radial to let you know how far to fly before turning around, or put an RNAV waypoint on the airport. In the absence of any of these, extend your outbound timing somewhat to be sure you'll have enough time to descend on the way back to the station. And as soon as it's legal (on course, inbound), head for the MDA—don't hesitate. The idea is to get down as low as possible as soon as you can do it safely. Grinding along at MDA for an extra half-minute or so is not sinful; besides, it gives you better odds on breaking out of the clouds and more time in level flight to look for the airport and make a rational decision about when to start down for the landing.

Circling Approaches

"Barnburner 1234 Alpha is cleared for the Runway 28 ILS approach, *circle to land Runway 14.*" If you operate into airports where only one approach system is installed, you can bet that you'll hear clearances similar to that one many times, since the winds don't always favor the primary runway. A circling approach increases the flexibility and utility of the airport, but like anything else, it costs something; in this case, the price is higher minimums, and some rather stringent additional requirements to keep you out of trouble while you're circling.

The criteria that make an approach a circling approach are quite straightforward; whenever the landing runway is aligned more than 30 degrees from the final approach course, or when a normal rate of descent from the minimum IFR altitude to the runway is considered impossible, a circling approach is indicated. Because either or both of these criteria cannot be met, some airports offer no straight-in minimums. This situation is indicated in the title of the approach chart; an alphabetical designator added to the title—such as NDB-A or VOR-B—means circling approaches *only.*

You may be cleared for a circling approach at the tag end of *any* published procedure, from NDB to ILS; the controller's motives are honorable, and he won't ask you to circle unless wind and weather conditions are such that landing straight-in would present a hazard. "Cleared to circle" does not mean that you are *required* to maneuver—if you have the active runway in sight in time to make a normal, straight-in landing, by all means do so; keep the Tower (or whatever ATC facility you're working with) informed, and of course, obtain the appropriate clearance.

No matter how your circling approach begins, it is going to turn into a non-precision procedure—there's no way to provide a circling glide slope for some other runway. Even if you are cleared for an ILS approach with a circling maneuver on the end, *you may not go lower than the circling Minimum Descent Altitude;* in addition, you will find no circling approaches in which the required visibility is less than one mile. The designers of the procedure must provide you with at least 300 feet vertical clearance from all obstacles in the circling area, which is the connected radii from the ends of all the airport's runways (Figure 37). When you are cleared for a circle-to-land maneuver, you should shift mental gears as you prepare for the approach, and when studying the chart, don't even look at the straight-in minimums, but let that circling MDA burn itself into your mind.

The circling area within which you are guaranteed obstacle clear-

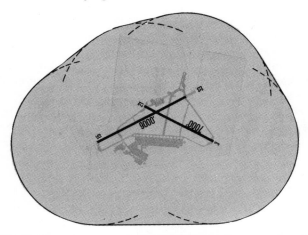

Figure 37 Circling area around a typical airport. You are guaranteed at least 300 feet of obstacle clearance within this area, the size of which varies with approach category.

Category	Speed
A	Less than 91 knots
B	91–120 knots
C	121–140 knots
D	141–165 knots
E	166 knots or more

ance (Figure 37) is based on the amount of airspace that might be required for maneuvering to a landing on any one of the airport's runways. In recognition of the smaller space required for lighter, slower airplanes, the planners came up with a series of "Approach Categories," and the MDAs and visibility requirements for each are printed on the approach procedure charts. Computation of the category for any airplane consists of determining the power-off stall speed in the landing configuration at maximum gross weight and multiplying that number by 1.3.

The legal requirements you must observe while "circling to land" in this situation are: (1) you must not descend below the circling MDA until descent is necessary for landing (usually, this means when turning base or final for the landing runway); (2) you must keep the airport in sight throughout your circling maneuver; and (3) you must remain clear of all clouds. Should you lose sight of the field because of reduced visibility or flying into a layer of scud, you are bound by law to execute an immediate missed approach.

Obviously, it would be unwise to begin circling before you have the field in sight, so fly the final approach course right down to the circling MDA; if the field doesn't show up, go around. But suppose that you have eased down to the MDA well ahead of time, and at 1 mile, the airport begins to take shape ahead of you. If you have done a good job of studying the airport layout during the preparation for the approach, you will know just how it will look, and more important, you will have decided which way you are going to circle for landing. Always check the remarks section of the approach chart before commencing a circling approach; there may be some surprises waiting for you if you maneuver where you shouldn't.

How you get lined up with the runway is completely your business, as long as you comply with the restrictions mentioned above. There are several generally-accepted patterns suggested for the low-visibility approaches (Figure 38), and it's rather difficult to imagine a situation that would require a maneuver much different than one of these. The important thing is to decide way back at the beginning of the approach what you're going to do when the field comes into view, and then stick to your plan; 1-mile visibility and only 400 or 500 feet of altitude doesn't give you much room to change your mind.

Every approved instrument approach procedure includes a set of very specific instructions for your guidance in the event you see nothing but clouds outside the airplane windows at the missed approach point. This procedure is also to be followed after an aborted circling approach, but now you will find yourself someplace other than the straight-in missed approach point. There's a special rule for a *circling* missed approach that will keep you within the allotted airspace. It says that when executing a missed approach from a circling approach situation, you will start a *climbing turn* that will take you back *over the airport* and *then* proceed with the published procedure.

The successful completion of a circling approach under really tight weather conditions depends in great measure on your ability

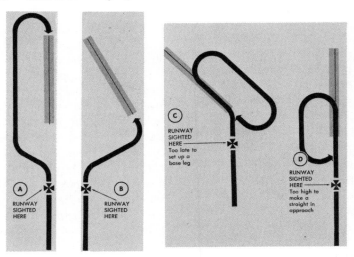

FIGURE 38 Suggested maneuvers for circling approaches in low-visibility conditions.

to maneuver your airplane in close quarters, and to do it safely. Since radius of turn increases quite rapidly with airspeed, it behooves you to slow down as you enter the final phase of the approach—when the weather is near minimums, it's a good idea to pull back on the reins a bit anyway, so that things don't happen quite so fast. Above all, don't try to bend your airplane around a tight turn to final. Remember that wind direction is probably the reason you're circling in the first place, and as you make the turn to final, the wind will be trying to blow you away from the runway— steepen the bank and pull back to tighten the turn at this low altitude in less than favorable ceiling and visibility conditions, and you just may pull yourself right into the ground. Since stall speed goes up alarmingly as you increase bank, you're setting yourself up—most stall-spin situations that close to the ground provide grist for the headline mills! If you feel uncomfortable while circling, if you get that "gut" feeling that things just aren't what they ought to be, go around and come back for another try.

When you are flying a high-performance airplane, it is possible to get into an unusual situation on a circling approach; suppose your aircraft has a computed approach speed (for Category purposes) of 89 knots, which allows you to make the approach under Category A minimums. If it is necessary to *maneuver* at an airspeed that puts you above the 91-knot maximum for this category, you should circle at the MDA prescribed for Category B—it's the circling *speed* that counts. You probably won't make your low-visibility approach with full flaps (part of "landing configuration"), so adjust the airspeed accordingly.

Here are the points you should remember about circling approaches:

1. Your circling clearance will always specify the landing runway, so you can plan ahead.
2. You must always observe an MDA on a circling approach, no matter what type of approach you started with.
3. You must remain at or above the *circling* MDA for your category until further descent is necessary for landing.
4. While maneuvering, you must keep the airport in sight and remain clear of all clouds.
5. If a missed approach becomes necessary, make a climbing turn that will take you back over the airport, *then* proceed with the published missed approach instructions.

The Side-Step Approach

At an airport equipped with close-together parallel runways, it's often convenient to have general-aviation traffic use one landing area, heavy jets the other; but it's often just as inconvenient, or operationally impossible, to install a separate ILS for each runway. To alleviate the problem, the "side-step" maneuver was developed. This provides a legal and safe procedure to fly the primary approach aid (nearly always an ILS) and, at the last minute, "side-step" to the other runway.

The MDA for such a procedure will always be somewhat higher than the Decision Height for the ILS runway, but lower than the circling minimum that would have to be used otherwise. Jepp charts list the "side-step" MDA under "Straight-in Minimum" for the *landing runway*—in other words, if the ILS is designed for Runway

23L, and you are going to side-step to 23R, look for the side-step minimum under "Straight-in 23R"; government approach charts show a separate line of minimums headed by the words "Side-Step 5R."

Controllers seldom issue side-step clearances unless ceiling and visibility are such that you'll have no difficulty finding the landing runway from a mile or so out. If you receive such a clearance and can't spot the runway of intended landing, let the controller know and he'll amend your clearance—don't try to side-step unless you have the "other" runway clearly in sight.

Short-Cuts to an Instrument Approach

When ATC gives you the "go ahead" for an instrument approach, you are cleared all the way to the missed approach point, and you're guaranteed safe separation from all other IFR aircraft while in the process of getting there, if a Control Zone exists at the airport. But an approach clearance is not ironbound; it does not mean that you must fly to the MAP in strict accordance with the published procedure. There are some very efficient ways of short-cutting the involved and time-consuming maneuvers you accomplish flying the full approach, and they're legal, safe, and sensible WHEN FULLY UNDERSTOOD AND PROPERLY PERFORMED.

All three of these short-cuts are contingent on breaking out of the clouds at some point well before the MDA or DH is reached. Be familiar with them and put them to use when you can save yourself some valuable time, and vacate a chunk of airspace for your brother airmen waiting in line behind you. ATC will be happy, too, because as soon as the controller can get you out of his electronic hair, he can let someone else in, and in general speed up the flow of traffic. This way, he gets no ulcers, doesn't beat his wife and kids when he gets home, and everybody is happier. See how far a little professionalism can go?

"Cancel My IFR"

The first method of short-cutting an approach clearance is to terminate it with a straightforward directive to ATC: "New York Center, Barnburner 1234 Alpha, cancel my IFR." This usually elicits an equally straightforward response from the ground: "Roger, Barn-burner 1234 Alpha, cancelling your IFR at one six three two." The only difference between this and any other ATC response is the tone in which it is delivered; the controller's voice will be so beau-tifully articulated, each word so perfectly pronounced that his elo-cution teacher would bust her buttons with pride. There's only one reason the controller makes his reply so clearly understood: He wants the cancellation, the time, and the aircraft number on the tape that records every radio conversation. Later, if any "discussion" of the flight were required, the evidence is right there; the world (or at least the FAA inspector) will know without a doubt that the pilot of Barnburner 1234 Alpha removed himself from the protection of the IFR system at 1632 Zulu time on the day in question.

Never, never cancel an IFR flight plan and give up all that protection unless you are absolutely sure you can get where you're going in healthy VFR conditions. ATC looks with understandable scorn on pilots who cancel IFR, then return sheepishly for a clear-ance after finding out that they can't maintain VFR. Although the people in the Center are there to help, they don't like to duplicate their efforts, and such a request is frequently answered with "call the nearest Flight Service Station and file a flight plan." Now you must go back through the system, maintaining VFR all the while, and it's going to cost you minutes on the clock, gallons on the fuel gauge, maybe a missed appointment. Anyway you look at it, an unwise IFR cancellation is spelled M-O-N-E-Y!

You must be especially cautious about cancelling after the sun ceaseth its labors for the day. The next pilot who is lulled into a false sense of "I've got it made" when he can see the rotating beacon at Destination Municipal won't be the first. He cancels, maybe even with the airport itself in sight from afar. Nothing is so reassuring as those flashes of white and green beckoning to you out of the darkness after a long trip, and the feeling of security grows as you pass over the airport, able to see the windsock and all the familiar landmarks. Now onto the final approach, and just about the time you flare, the whole world turns white; you've flown into one of those insidious shallow fog conditions. Visibility was unrestricted when you were looking straight down through the fog, lying in gossamer sheets just above the runway, but when you flatten out to land, you're looking through the fog endwise, and the visibility is something else! Not only is this situation embarrassing if you have to return to ATC for the clearance you gave up so confidently a while ago, but there is also an instinctive reaction to push the nose over when encountering suddenly lowering visibility—that close to the ground, it may be all she wrote.

"How About a Contact Approach?"

The second short-cut is very much like a Special VFR clearance, using the same basic weather and navigation criteria. Known as a "contact approach," it is unique in that it must be requested by you, the pilot, when you feel you can navigate to the airport by ground reference, thereby eliminating the need to fly the complete published procedure. It's a real time-saver—whenever you can lop a few minutes off the time you spend in the air, you're using the airplane more efficiently, and opening up the airspace for other pilots in the bargain.

Since it is a deviation from the instructions you have received, you *must* receive a clearance for a contact approach. The rest of the way to the airport, it's up to you to navigate, to look out for other aircraft, and to stay at a safe (and legal) altitude. ATC will not turn you loose unless you are safely separated from other aircraft on contact approaches, regular instrument approaches, or those operating under Special VFR clearances. The Tower will probably clear you to land on the first communication and you have just saved yourself the trouble of going to the navaid and flying the complete published procedure, which may have taken you another five to ten minutes.

The specifications for a contact approach call for you to be "reasonably certain" that you can get to the airport on your own—what happens if you are unable to maintain the 1-mile visibility clear of clouds restriction? You must let the Tower know (or Approach Control if a frequency change has not been given to you) and they will advise you to climb to the appropriate minimum altitude and continue with the published approach procedure. You are still under the protective umbrella of the IFR system, and may continue just as if you had never requested the Contact Approach in the first place.

In summary, then, the conditions for this short-cut are:

1. The *pilot* must request a contact approach.
2. ATC must come back with specific instructions, i.e., "cleared for a contact approach."
3. You must be able to maintain at least 1-mile visibility and remain clear of all clouds.
4. You must be able to navigate to the airport by means of ground reference.

As always, you are expected to avoid other aircraft whenever you are able to see them.

The Visual Approach

It is possible to cut down your time in the terminal area through the use of a third deviation from the published procedure, the visual approach. Although it accomplishes the same thing, there are significant differences from the other short-cuts; in the first place, a visual approach is almost always instigated by ATC (there's nothing wrong with your asking for one if it will speed things up). You will be radar vectored to a point at which one of two things will happen: Either you'll see the airport or you will be directed to follow another airplane, and the controller will ask you to verify that you have the other fellow or the airport in sight. More closely controlled than a contact approach, the visual approach is intended to lead you directly to the destination airport, and short-cuts the "full" approach at the discretion of ATC. The controller must know that you are in VFR conditions before issuing such a clearance—that's why he asks if you can see the airport or the airplane ahead. When it's honest-to-goodness IFR, you should expect the complete approach.

On occasion, the visual approach clearance is issued when you are behind another IFR flight approaching the same field. When the controller sees that you are 3 miles from that airplane, he will ask "Barnburner 1234 Alpha, do you have the Trans-Lunar 727 in sight, one o'clock and three miles?" When you answer "yes," he can tell you to "follow the 727, cleared for a visual approach" and your responsibility is to do just that, hoping all the while that the Trans-Lunar pilot is headed for the right airport.

With no published procedure, each visual approach is unique in terms of track and altitude. You are expected to continue toward the airport, and if the destination is tower-controlled, you may be cleared straight in, or directed to enter a normal traffic pattern. In the case of a visual approach to an *un*controlled airport, remember that you have become just another participant in VFR operations at that airport . . . use of standard VFR practices, position announcements, and *increased vigilance for other aircraft* are mandatory.

Most likely, you'll receive clearance for a visual approach while flying at an assigned altitude, probably the one indicated for the intermediate segment of a published approach procedure. When the controller clears you for "the visual," altitude management is completely in your hands, and you should descend or stay level in accordance with your assessment of weather conditions, distance from the airport, intervening obstacles, other traffic, etc.

The visual approach presents ample opportunity to cheat, since you can answer "Roger, have the airport [or Trans-Lunar] in sight" when you don't; but you're just cheating yourself, because ATC is expecting you to provide your own separation when in VFR conditions. There may be a considerable number of VFR pilots out there, milling around in the 3-mile murk (in busy metropolitan areas you can *bet* on it!). You are a definite hazard if you accept a visual approach clearance when you're not really "visual."

Here are the conditions for a visual approach clearance:

1. Usually instigated by ATC.
2. Weather minimums, basic VFR.
3. Will not be issued until you have the airport or a preceding aircraft in sight.
4. Puts the "see and avoid" monkey on *your* back where the clearance is accepted.

ATC will never ask you to cancel your IFR flight plan—after all, handling instrument traffic is their job, and they are obliged to provide all the services of the system to any pilot who operates IFR. But they sometimes make a request like this: "Barnburner 1234 Alpha, will you accept a contact (or visual) approach?" It's the controller's way of trying to tell you that a good purpose can be served by having you fly a short-cut to the full procedure. Never construe this as a goad, but make certain that you are in a position to comply with all the requirements of the situation before accepting. If this is the flight on which you promised yourself you would practice a full ILS right down to the deck, by all means tell ATC that you would prefer the complete approach. Common sense and courtesy suggest that you don't try this at Chicago O'Hare during the morning rush hour; although your request for a full approach will be granted, you will probably hear "Roger, Barnburner 1234 Alpha, cleared direct to the outer marker, climb to and maintain eight thousand, hold east on the localizer course, expect approach clearance tomorrow!"

The hazards of a visual approach are underscored rather dramatically by the sequence of events one day at a southern Michigan airport. A Skymaster, inbound from the southeast with the field in sight, requested and received a visual approach clearance when still seven miles from the airport. At about the same time, a Skylane departed for home, which lay some thirty miles southeast. The tower controller did not have the benefit of radar to help locate and separate flights in the airport traffic area.

Both pilots were advised of the other's location, heading, and intent, with no acknowledgment of sighting by either. The Skymaster pilot was a middle-experience commercial pilot, flying alone; in the right seat of the Skylane was a 4,000-hour CFII, working with an IFR student, probably under a hood.

Neither of these aircraft presents much of a head-on profile, and almost like moths drawn to a flame, they continued toward each other, one climbing, one descending, until at the very last moment, each pilot appeared to spot the other airplane. The Skylane rolled violently to its right (according to eyewitnesses), and the Skymaster rolled to its left, making a bad situation worse. There was almost time for the Skymaster pilot to realize what had happened and roll back to the right, out of trouble. But "almost" wasn't enough; the Cessnas tangled left wings, and both fell to the ground, out of control.

In this case, the pilots could have, within the limits of the rules under which they were operating, taken steps to reduce the possibility of a collision; the Skylane pilot could have stopped his climb until clear of the traffic, the Skymaster pilot could have levelled off until clear. Either pilot could have changed heading to right or left (with appropriate advice to the controllers) to resolve the head-on situation.

Isn't such an encounter a potential hazard of nearly *every* visual approach? The answer is an unequivocal "yes." The very weather conditions that spawn requests for and issuances of visual approaches (i.e., anything between 1,000 and 3 and "severe clear") place the instrument pilot right in the middle of normal, everyday VFR operations. There's no room for complacency here . . . even though you have received an "instrument approach clearance" and are operating under the Instrument Flight Rules, you are just another VFR flight when it comes to "see and avoid." *Whenever* you are able to see other aircraft, and therefore avoid them, you are expected to do just that.

Radar Approaches

"Barnburner 1234 Alpha, this is Disneyland Approach Control, turn right heading two two zero, vectors for a surveillance approach to runway one eight." Should you hear such a transmission in today's IFR world, chances are the Barnburner is either doing practice approaches or is in trouble; the use of radar for actual approaches has dropped off to just about zero. Radar "did itself in" by virtue of the very feature that promoted it not too many years ago. The fact that an aircraft—*any* aircraft—could be brought safely to earth if the pilot had basic instrument skills and one radio receiver, led many in the flying business to practice self-conducted approaches only for emergencies, such as a radar failure. But it was not in the cards, for air traffic has increased by such leaps and bounds that communications channels would be unbelievably clogged if every IFR flight had to be "talked down." A radar approach requires a lengthy and nearly continuous stream of instructions and corrections from the controller, limiting him to handling one airplane at a time— air traffic would be backed up all the way to Constantinople if all the flights coming into Kennedy Airport had to be radar-controlled.

So the tables have turned on radar. Once hailed as the best way to get from clouds to ground, it now takes a distant back seat to the cockpit-display type of approach in which one controller can point several pilots in the right direction and turn them loose, trusting to their navigational skill and keeping communications channels open for directing other flights. But like an understudy waiting in the wings for the leading lady to falter, radar is always standing by for that situation when somebody *needs* a bit of vocal assistance.

When the weather is not too much of a factor and traffic is light, controllers will be most happy to provide you with a radar approach. They realize that it is a good training exercise; as a matter of fact, it is not unusual to be asked if you will accept a radar approach, since a certain number of squares must be filled each month to keep the controllers qualified. You have an interest in the skill of the man on the other side of the radar scope (don't you want him to be *good* when it's the only way to get out of the sky?), so go along with his request whenever you can. There's not much to be gained by practicing radar approaches—you will have proved that you can do very precisely what someone else tells you to, but your instrument training time can be so much better spent on other types of approaches, the ones where all the navigational responsibility is on *your* shoulders. So, know what radar approaches are all about, and now and then go out and run through one, but consider it something you will do only when everything else has turned sour.

Precision Approach Radar (PAR)

Because of the communications problem and the availability of other types of approach procedures, *precision* facilities are available at only a handful of joint-use (civilian *and* military) airports, but nearly every Air Force Base and Naval Air Station is equipped with precision approach radar. The military services call it GCA (Ground Controlled Approach), but it's the same thing. When you are in real trouble, unable to make an approach on your own, don't hesitate to holler for the nearest GCA-equipped airbase, and put yourself in their hands. The military controllers are very adept when it comes to gathering wayward airplanes to their center-striped, edge-lighted concrete bosoms—even though weather conditions may be zero-zero, give it a try. When the controller says you're over the runway, reduce your rate of descent to about 300 feet per minute or less, hold your heading, and hope for the best—it's a lot better to blow a tire than to buy the farm. Somewhere in your mental list of good things to remember, tuck away the common military tower frequency: 126.2 is guarded by almost all of Uncle Sam's finest. If you need it, use it, and someone will probably answer.

Once you have established radio contact with the controller, he will issue vectors and altitudes that will line you up with the final approach course. At this point, you will be handed off to a Final

Controller, who is monitoring your progress in all three dimensions; altitude, azimuth, and distance. As if it weren't enough for the man on the ground to do all the *navigating* for you, he also assumes the *communication* burden when he says "Barnburner 1234 Alpha, this is your Final Controller, you are in radar contact, do not acknowledge further transmissions." What could be easier? All you have to do is to sit there and drive the machine where he tells you.

The Final Controller will provide plenty of advance notice before you reach the glide path. "Barnburner 1234 Alpha, you are seven miles from the runway, on final approach, prepare to begin descent in one mile." If you are not ready to start down, get that way, as he expects you to commence losing altitude the instant he says "begin descent." This is one of the few times in instrument flying when the vertical speed indicator earns its keep; using the controller's recommended rate of descent as a base figure (he will have provided this after you tell him your airspeed on final approach), make slight power adjustments to get on, or stay on, the glide slope.

The controller can interpret only what he sees on the scope, and when your blip moves off course, he must assume that wind is the villain, and he makes a correction accordingly. If the deviation from course is the result of your not holding the heading he has assigned, you may wind up with a double correction: one from him for "wind," and one from you as you return to the original heading. You must hold heading religiously on a radar approach—it's all the controller has to work with.

The small corrections continue, right down to the decision height, which the controller will mention at some time during the procedure. Depending on the situation, he may tell you when you are over the approach lights, and when you are over the threshold. In a non-emergency situation, you must execute a missed approach at the decision height if the runway is not in sight.

Sometime during your instrument training (which is assumed to continue forever) you should be exposed to a precision radar approach. So, fly over to Affable Air Force Base or Nice Naval Air Station, and ask if you can get a couple of precision approaches. Chances are your request will be granted, for military controllers have currency requirements, too; you will probably be limited to low approaches only—no landings allowed—but it will give you an idea of what it's like. If the day comes when you need it, you will not be a total stranger to Precision Approach Radar.

Airport Surveillance Radar (ASR)

Whereas PAR and GCA equipment is intended for use as a landing aid, ASR finds its primary function fulfilled as an *approach* control device. Not limited to the final approach area of one runway, ASR beams sweep out a considerable distance and show the controller air traffic throughout the vicinity of the airport. Coincidentally, it can also be used as a means of vectoring aircraft to the final approach course for all runways at the airport. (Some installations are limited to certain runways because of terrain features, electronic problems, etc.) ASR is a single-scope operation showing only the two dimensions of azimuth and distance; with no glide slope, it drops into the non-precision category, which means that an ASR approach will be flown to a minimum descent altitude (MDA), not a decision height (DH).

Flying a surveillance approach is much the same as precision radar, except that altitude, airspeed, rate of descent—everything except corrections in heading to maintain the final approach course— is up to the pilot. On request, the controller will compute a recommended rate of descent for you, providing a guideline, but it is always best to get down to that minimum altitude just as soon as practical; it gives you more time to look for the runway, and prevents your arriving over the airfield in solid clouds 50 feet above the ceiling, requiring a needless missed approach. Most ASR approach procedures specify a visibility minimum of one mile; but when the runway environment includes certain types of approach lighting systems, that minimum may be reduced to as little as one-half mile.

Use the same techniques for flying the airplane on a surveillance approach that you use for precision radar. It's basic instruments all the way, and as such makes a great introduction to approach work for the fledgling IFR flyer. Most terminals equipped with Approach Control radar will also be set up for surveillance approaches, and will be happy to accommodate your practice whenever traffic allows.

The No-Gyro Approach

There was a time when instrument pilots had to prove that they could turn accurately from one heading to another using only the magnetic compass. And one of the biggest reasons for that demonstration rested in the DGs of the day, prone to precessing wildly or failing altogether . . . especially those powered by venturi systems, the predecessors of today's vacuum pumps.

On occasion, however, even a modern vacuum pump gives up, and there you are—in the soup, trying to maintain a heading to follow an approach procedure, but finding it impossible because none of the numbers makes sense. Radar to the rescue again, this time with a procedure known as the "no-gyro approach," in which the controller will issue clear-cut instructions to "turn right," "turn left," and "stop turn." He's not clairvoyant, but is timing the turns so as to place you on headings compatible with the approach procedure.

If the heading indicator is not working, chances are very good that the attitude indicator is equally unreliable (most general aviation aircraft are set up with those two instruments operating on suction from the same source), so you might as well shift gears and fly partial panel for the remainder of the approach. (See "Partial Panel IFR" in Chapter 4.) You are expected to execute standard-rate turns on command. When you're lined up on the final approach course, the controller will issue a reminder that he now wants half-standard rate turns; you're proceeding into the neck of the funnel again, and heading corrections must be made on a smaller scale.

A no-gyro approach represents a great opportunity for over-controlling, but remind yourself that you are in a semi-emergency situation (out there by yourself in heavy weather on partial panel, it's a *genuine* emergency—don't hesitate to let someone know the minute you suspect instrument problems). You must settle down and fly the airplane with the finest touch you can muster. It's needle-ball-and-airspeed . . . and it's also too late to practice.

"Below Minimums" Approaches

Your military and airline brethren are prohibited by regulation from even *starting* an instrument approach when the weather at the airport is reported below their landing minimums. A different approach to the problem shows up in civilian flying rules, where the only limiting factor is visibility; if you fly down to the appropriate altitude (MDA for non-precision, DH on a precision approach) and can see the runway environment, you are within your legal rights to land the airplane. This philosophy reflects sound thinking on the part of the regulation writers, since it allows the pilot to make his own determination of visibility. And who is in a better position to decide? As long as you stay at the published minimum altitude for the approach (this height is the result of exacting computations of the lowest *safe* altitude) and sight the runway at the appropriate time, the ceiling requirement will take care of itself.

Though making an attempt is not always the smartest thing to do, you cannot be denied an approach solely because the weather is bad.

It's All Up to You

Here is where the "pilot becomes the visibility observer" law can really work in your favor. You have eased down to the MDA well ahead of the missed approach point, and when the clock tells you that you're a mile out (or the appropriate distance on the chart), you look up and see the runway lights shimmering through the fog. Is it legal to land? It certainly is, as long as you can keep the runway lights in sight the rest of the way—you have just established an official visibility observation at the runway. The airport layout often furnishes a clue to the disparity; control towers are seldom near the approach end of the runway, and the controller's visibility may indeed be only one-quarter mile, which prevents him from being able to judge conditions on the final approach course. You are in a *much* better position to decide.

There is a decided note of permissiveness in this clearance, and as such there is a very big loophole; you can press on in reported lower-than-minimum conditions, and if you do a good job of navigating, chances are at least fair that you will eventually see the airport, and be able to land. But don't forget that everything is up against the limits, and you've got to do it all right the first time. For one thing, when the visibility is such that you don't see the runway until you're right on top of it, your effective landing distance is drastically reduced. Restricted visibility is usually caused by some type of precipitation, which means that the runway will probably be wet; at worst it may be covered with ice and/or snow. The winds will invariably choose this instant to die, and the whole thing can add up to less runway than you need to touch down and bring the old bucket of bolts to a stop.

So back off and take a good long look at all the factors before you commit yourself in conditions like these. If your first approach finds you too high, too hot, and too hazardous, execute the missed approach procedure, and come back at a slower speed and mentally prepared to pick up the chips. You can't be faulted if you abide by the rules, which give you the benefit of dynamic observation.

We'll let the NTSB report set the stage for this one: "According to witnesses, the aircraft touched down about two-thirds down the length of Runway 04. Skid marks began approximately 1,000 feet from the end of the runway. These skid marks tracked the runway centerline until about the last 300 feet, when the marks began to drift slightly to the right of centerline. The aircraft then skidded off the runway and continued approximately 100 feet through a grassy overrun where the nose landing gear was sheared off. At this point the ground drops off abruptly. The aircraft, now airborne, sailed another 130 feet before striking the ground in a near-vertical attitude . . . flaps were deployed one notch, a setting normally used for short-field and soft-field takeoffs."

This accident (which killed the pilot and seriously injured his passenger) didn't involve an instrument pilot, but it illustrates the folly of a last-minute decision when a missed-approach was clearly indicated.

The pilot approached the airport in VFR conditions, but rainshowers in the terminal area obscured the field until the airplane was just one-half mile away. The controller had suggested 09 Right as the landing runway, but when the airplane came into view so close, he transmitted, "Okay, if you can make Runway 04 from that point, that's fine. If not, just keep circling and make left traffic for that runway." As previously described, the pilot touched down on Runway 04, but with a 20-knot tailwind, partial flaps, and higher-than-normal approach speed (as judged by a witness)—he didn't stand a chance.

There's a lesson here for IFR pilots, because this is the very situation that shows up not infrequently at the end of a circling approach to a strange airport. A perceived pressure to get on the ground on the first attempt, strong wind (which probably dictated the circling approach), and an unwillingness to confess and climb away for another try has resulted in embarrassment for many pilots . . . for this one, the cost was considerably greater.

Speed Adjustments During an Approach

The basic goal of Air Traffic Control in a terminal area is to provide safe separation for aircraft arriving and departing, and as the number of flying machines grows, the control problems increase accordingly. With more operations in the system every day, controllers find themselves involved in valiant efforts to sort out the speed requirements and performance limitations of a mixed bag of aircraft. At a busy airport, Approach Control is faced with funneling everything from 747s to 152s into the narrow confines of the approach corridor—speed and timing is the name of the game. A veteran railroader visiting an approach control facility noted the multitude of aircraft approaching from all directions at all speeds, flying into the "small end of the funnel" onto a single runway. He could not help comparing this operation with his own experience, in which the main line spread out into many divergent rails in the terminal, allowing trains to come to a stop on any one of a dozen or more tracks. He allowed that trying to put all those airplanes coming from every direction onto one runway was "a hell of a way to run a railroad!"

It isn't likely that we will see multi-runway airports for a long time, if ever, so we're stuck with adjusting speeds and timing to fit air traffic into the approach funnel. Controllers will cut and fit to achieve their objective, and are furnished a set of guidelines with which to do the job. You needn't know what these guidelines are, only that they exist, so that a request for a speed adjustment won't come as a complete surprise. The jets and some of the faster propeller-driven aircraft have little concern with minimum airspeeds, and are more often than not asked to *reduce* speed, but the light airplane fleet is sometimes required to add a few knots in order to fit into the schedule of approaches—that "few knots" frequently means maintaining near-cruise airspeeds to the final approach fix. Controllers are aware of the limitations of light aircraft, and would not likely ask a Musketeer pilot to maintain 160 knots, but in most of the light twins and some of the "hot" singles, these speeds are not unreasonable. In any case, you should deal with speed adjustments as *requests*—if Approach Control asks you to fly at 150 knots and there's no way the Barnburner can do it, or if you feel that such rapid passage through the air would jeopardize your performance, reject the request.

16

The NDB (ADF) Approach

AN ADF RECEIVER, adequate training and practice, and a couple of grains of common sense will outfit you splendidly for an NDB (Non-Directional Beacon) approach. (Everybody still knows what you're talking about when you refer to it as an "ADF" approach, but the official title is NDB; and rightly so, for it's the radio receiver in your airplane that is the ADF, or Automatic Direction Finder.) This procedure enables you to fly to a point on a specific course at a prescribed altitude, and from this point continue to a landing if visibility is sufficient. It's not the most accurate method of finding an airport, because it requires considerable skill and technique on the part of the pilot, but it's a lot better than no approach at all. Even with this lack of precision, a typical NDB approach will bring you to within 500 or 600 feet of the airport surface, and the visibility required for landing will be about 1 to 1½ miles.

At the heart of all ADF procedures is "relative bearing"—a term that could no doubt stand a bit of amplification. The azimuth indicator (needle) of the ADF set will always point to a number on the instrument that represents the bearing from aircraft to station, measured relative to the nose of the airplane ("0" on the ADF dial); hence the term "relative bearing." When the relative bearing is "0," the station is straight ahead; should the relative bearing turn out to be 090 degrees, the station is off the right wing tip; at 180 degrees you'd have to turn around in your seat to see the transmitter, and a relative bearing of 270 degrees puts the station off the left wing.

With this constant readout of relative bearing, the navigational task becomes one of determining whether you are on, to the left of, or to the right of a preselected course to or from the station. When you are on course, flying toward the station with no wind to push you off the track, the aircraft heading will be the same as the desired course, and the ADF will read 0 degrees relative bearing. Pass directly over the transmitter, and the needle will immediately swing to the 180 degree, or tail position; if you really want to make it easy for yourself, think of it as a 0 degree relative bearing *outbound*.

A touch of plane geometry will help you understand what happens when you intercept a course with ADF, as well as the mechanics of drift correction. Some geometrician discovered early in man's research into the properties of straight lines that whenever two of them are crossed, the opposite angles are always equal. You can put this knowledge to work on an ADF problem by thinking of the intended course (track) to the station as one straight line, the aircraft's heading the other. As long as the lines are superimposed (on course, no wind), there are no angles and no problem—but if the aircraft heading changes, the ADF needle will move, creating an angle between heading and track.

Conjure up this situation—you are on course, headed to the station, relative bearing 0 degrees. Now turn the airplane 30 degrees to the left; the ADF needle, always pointing to the station, will appear to move to the *right*, exactly 30 degrees—the opposite angles are equal. So, whenever you are *off* course and are flying at an angle to that course so as to intercept it, you'll know you are *on* course when the angles are the same. Using the same principle, you can remain on course with a drift correction that will keep the two angles equal. Using the intended track as the base, you're ON COURSE whenever the heading and relative bearing are displaced the same number of degrees. *Inbound*, heading displacement will be *opposite* that of the ADF pointer—*outbound*, heading and ADF needle will be displaced on the *same side*.

Tuning the ADF Receiver

Radio stations upon which ADF procedures are based are generally caled NDBs, for Non-Directional Beacons, which suggests that the signals from these transmitters may be received anywhere around the antenna; the signal is not concentrated, or aimed, in any particular direction. NDBs are found in the lowest frequency band on the low-frequency receiver (usually 190 to 415 KHz); the manufacturer includes two other bands, so you can listen to music, news bulletins, and ball games.

The function switch should be in the REC (receive) position whenever the set is being tuned. It may be marked ANT, for AN-Tenna, on some radios, but it means the same thing—in either case, the automatic direction-finding function is not operating until you switch to ADF. Tuning in the ADF position means that the needle will try to point to every station it receives as you turn the dial. Just like a bird dog trying to point every quail in a covey—it doesn't give you much useful information, and it's hard on the dog! Give your equipment a break by finding the proper frequency on REC or ANT, then switch to ADF, and let the needle do its thing.

With the exception of the high-powered beacons (that usually carry a transcribed weather broadcast), don't expect a usable signal until you are within 15 or 20 miles of the station. Most NDBs are intended only for approaches and are not powered for long-range reception, so don't complain to ATC about the quality of the transmitter because you can't pick it up 50 miles out. The controller will somehow get you within range before he turns you loose to navigate to the beacon.

There is only one way to make certain you have tuned the right station, and that's by listening to the Morse code identifier. A great many ADF stations are crammed into a rather narrow band of frequencies—it's easy to get a needle indication that looks OK, but it's mighty embarrassing to make an approach on the wrong station. It could also cause you to aluminum-plate a hillside, or reduce the height of a radio tower or two.

The Initial Approach

Getting to the NDB to commence the approach is a piece of cake with radar vectors, but you'll have to put on your navigator's hat when the controller clears you "from your present position direct to the beacon." Since the ADF needle always points to the station, you can turn the appropriate number of degrees to put the needle on the nose (or 0 degrees relative bearing), keep it there, and you'll wind up over the station. True, and on a windless day you'll fly directly to the station, just what ATC wants you to do. But throw in a crosswind, and the picture changes. Now instead of making good a direct line, or track, your needle-on-the-nose method will result in a curved path across the ground. This is called "homing," is done best by a specific breed of trained bird, and is not at all what is expected of you; you were cleared *direct*, and ATC would like you to go in a straight line. Leave homing to the pigeons.

In a typical situation, when you receive clearance "direct to the beacon," your heading is 360 degrees and the ADF needle is 40 degrees to the left of the nose. A left turn of 40 degrees will put the needle on 0 and the station directly ahead of you, and that's fine, as long as it lasts. But a right crosswind will eventually drift the airplane off course to the left; you maintain a heading of 320 degrees, and the needle shows the drift by moving slowly to the right. Here is a key point: Whenever the aircraft heading is the same as the desired course, and the ADF needle is off to either side, *it always tells you which way to turn to get back on track*. In this case, it indicates that your intended *track* of 320 degrees is to the *right*. The ADF needle has become a *course pointer*.

You must obviously set up a drift correction, but first get back on course (you were cleared *direct*) by turning 30 degrees to the right. When this new heading puts you on the intended course, the ADF needle (always pointing to the station) will point exactly 30 degrees to the *left* of the nose (opposite angles equal). Had you turned right 45 degrees to get on course faster, the ADF will indicate 45 degrees to the left when you are on course. The number of degrees turned is immaterial as long as you remember that a corresponding number of degrees to the *opposite* side on the ADF dial will tell you when you're on course again.

Now apply some drift correction—start with 10 degrees. As long as your heading is 330 degrees (the intended course of 320 degrees plus 10 degrees drift correction) and the ADF reads 10 degrees left, you're on course, and the drift correction is just right. By the cut-and-try method, you'll soon find a heading that will balance drift correction and wind effect—you are proceeding "direct" to the station, as cleared. (You should apply the principle of course bracketing, Chapter 9.) Drift correction is not so difficult if you will think of your situation as one in which heading and ADF needle displacement must remain balanced. If there's no wind, your heading will be the same as the desired course, and the ADF needle will read 0—no angle between the two straight lines, everything in balance.

When a 15-degree drift correction to the *left* is needed to stay on track, it will be reflected in your heading, and to balance that, your ADF should read 15 degrees to the *right;* opposite angles equal, everything in balance. A change in ADF indication (maintaining a constant heading, of course) means that your drift correction is not doing the job; if it creeps back toward the nose, you haven't enough crab, and if it goes the other way, you have overcorrected.

A directional gyro that includes some sort of heading "bug" is really a blessing, because it helps you solve the memory problem. As soon as your track to the station is determined, set the bug on that number, and you can tell at a glance how many degrees you have turned to counter the crosswind. Another glance at the ADF indicator will confirm the balanced situation or show the need for another heading change.

Station Passage and Tracking Outbound

When the ADF needle swings past the wingtip position on either side, you have passed the station. Assuming for now that a full approach procedure is required, you must track outbound on a specified course, turn around, and come back to the airport. There are a number of things to do in addition to flying the airplane, so get yourself organized.

As soon as you recognize station passage, use the Four T's: TIME, TURN, THROTTLE, TALK. Note the TIME (with a stopwatch if you have one), TURN to the outbound heading (you can make drift corrections in just a minute; the outbound *heading* is more important now), THROTTLE back to begin descent to procedure turn altitude (if you're not already there), and finally, after everything is settled down and under control, TALK; tell the controller you have passed the beacon outbound. You can make it a very brief report: "Tampa Approach, Barnburner 1234 Alpha, KAPOK outbound." He'll reply with instructions appropriate to the situation.

Now, if drift correction is required, put it in; remember that when tracking *outbound*, the ADF needle will point rearward, and the "balance" between heading and ADF indication will be on the *same side*. If the outbound course is not significantly different than your inbound track to the station and if the wind stays the same, your 10-degree drift correction will now show up on the ADF as a needle indication 10 degrees to the *right* of the tail. In other words, when the outbound *heading* is off 10 degrees to the right to correct for wind, and the ADF needle is *also* off 10 degrees to the right, you are on course. If things stay just like that, you have the proper drift correction.

To intercept a track outbound, turn to the new heading, note the position of the ADF needle relative to the *tail*. If the needle is off to the right, that's where your new track lies, and vice versa, so head that direction, with one minor change—when outbound, it's important that you get on course as soon as possible, so turn 45 degrees toward the needle right off the bat. When the ADF shows a 45-degree deflection on the *same* side, you are on track; return to the desired heading, plus drift correction if needed. Try 10 degrees, and as long as the ADF needle stays 10 degrees to the same side, everything's shipshape. If it creeps toward the tail, you've too much wind correction—if it moves away from the tail, too little. Even though your ADF dial is imprinted with "18" at the tail of the aircraft, think of it as just another "zero point," and you'll be able to handle the problem more easily.

Procedure Turn

When it's time (two minutes is a safe, practical figure in most cases), begin your procedure turn in the direction published on the chart; the headings outbound and inbound are always printed, so turn directly to the proper heading. If you started the turn on course, the ADF needle will have moved 45 degrees from the tail when you roll out on the published heading (opposite angles equal!) and once again note the time. If you miss the 45-degree indication, start the clock when you level the wings, and you'll not be far off. (By the way, have you noticed the index marks at the four 45-degree points on the face of your ADF dial? They were put there for "standard" situations like this. If your ADF dial is indexless, there's no law against painting a set yourself.)

Fly outbound for one minute (or forty seconds plus or minus wind correction if you prefer that type of procedure turn) and then turn 180 degrees in the opposite direction to intercept the final approach course. If ATC has requested that you report "procedure turn inbound," now is the time to do it. When you are on course again, the ADF needle will be 45 degrees from the nose, and it's back to a simple problem of tracking to the station. If appropriate, you may now descend below procedure turn altitude on your way to the next altitude published for the approach.

Post-Procedure Turn and the Final Approach

You've a couple of minutes to kill inbound to the station, but don't get behind the airplane. There are four things you can do here: First, compensate for wind drift—most final approach courses (from station to airport) are the same as the inbound course you are on at this point, and wind direction *generally* becomes more southerly as you descend, so anticipate it. Second, slow the airplane to approach speed, and third, configure the airplane for the final approach; gear down, flaps as required, so all you'll have to do at station passage is to reduce power to descend comfortably to minimum altitude. Fourth, recheck the DG against the magnetic compass reading (be certain you do it with wings level and airspeed constant!)—you can fly a beautiful NDB approach, with all the numbers appearing correct, and then break out of the clouds looking down the wrong runway. Remember that unlike VOR navigation, in which a centered needle means you're on the correct magnetic course regardless of heading, an NDB approach is only as good as the heading information on which it's based. If you're lucky, an approach on the wrong course will merely surprise you; if you're *un*lucky . . . well, who wants to get that intimately acquainted with a mountaintop or TV tower?

When the needle swings, note the TIME (the Missed Approach Point is always based on timing on an ADF approach, unless the beacon is located on the airport), TURN to the final approach course if necessary, THROTTLE back for descent, and when a comfortable rate of descent is established, TALK—"St. Petersburg Tower, Barnburner 1234 Alpha, KAPOK inbound." Nine times out of ten you'll be cleared for landing.

Now you're down to the nitty-gritty of the approach, and your objection is to get to the MDA as soon as practical, so that you can look for the ground. Be sure to arrive at MDA well ahead of the missed approach point—it's embarrassing and terribly inefficient to miss an approach because you didn't get down to the MDA soon enough.

Your rate of descent from final approach fix to MDA is based on the estimated ground speed for this segment, and the surface winds from the Tower are as good an input as any at this point. Your approach chart furnishes the time-distance figures (Jeppesen usually provides the required rates of descent for various ground-speeds), but it's a better practice to get down to the MDA well in advance of the missed approach point. You are guaranteed terrain and obstacle clearance for the entire final approach segment if you remain at the MDA—the sooner you can see the ground, the better off you'll be, so choose a comfortable rate of descent—one that you can handle, and one that will get you to the MDA quickly. When you get there, STAY THERE until you either see the airport or your time has elapsed. Airport in sight? Go ahead and land, in accordance with the Tower's clearance, or recommended procedures for an uncontrolled airfield.

But suppose the clock hands race around to the appointed mark, you're at MDA, and still "in the suds." Don't hesitate, *don't* go further to take a look, *do* execute the missed approach procedure NOW!

The final segment of any approach procedure is the most critical in terms of your airplane's relation to the desired course . . . you need to be *on course* if the procedure is to accomplish its objective. And, perhaps more so than approaches based on other types of radio aids, the NDB approach is laden with potential for confusion and wrong-way corrections. Until you work out a fool-proof method of analyzing the navigation indications and staying on course with no doubt about your location, don't be the least bit hesitant to make an occasional turn back to the published course to check the ADF needle deflection.

If the airplane is *on course* when you make one of these checks, the ADF needle will point to "0" of "180" (inbound or outbound tracking respectively) as soon as heading is the same as the published course . . . and you should immediately return to the former heading, since whatever drift correction you had established is evidently doing the job.

If the airplane had drifted off course, a quick check will show you which way to correct; the head of the ADF needle will *always* point toward the desired course when that course is paralleled.

A couple of these checks during the final segment, and the subsequent small corrections to keep the airplane on course, beats the socks off no checks at all, or correcting the wrong way and making a bad situation worse. You'll feel much better about your ADF work when you have the confidence that comes with sure knowledge of your position.

The Radio Magnetic Indicator (RMI)

NDB approaches fall into the shooting-fish-in-a-barrel class if you are fortunate enough to have a Radio Magnetic Indicator installed in your airplane. Fundamentally, it is a slaved gyro heading card that moves under the ADF needle. (Some installations include a second needle that points to a VOR.) Now, instead of the non-RMI presentation in which "0," or the nose of the airplane, is always at the top of the dial, the aircraft's magnetic *heading* appears under the top index; therefore the ADF needle *always* points to a number that represents the magnetic course to the station.

In the previous example, when you are cleared direct to the beacon, the ADF needle would still indicate that the station is 40 degrees to the left of the nose, but it would also show that the course to the station is 320 degrees. When you turn to the left, roll out on that heading (320 degrees), and as long as the needle stays on that number (which will also indicate a zero relative bearing), there is no drift, and you are proceeding directly to the NDB. If wind begins to drift you off course, the ADF needle will again tell you which way to turn to get back on track, but with the RMI at work for you, the correction is much easier. Use the same method of turning toward the needle, but rather than having to go through the mental calculation of balancing heading change and relative bearing, hold your into-the-wind correction until the needle once again reads 320 degrees. From here on, do whatever is necessary to keep that needle on 320 degrees, and you can rest assured that you're tracking directly to the station. (You may notice that whenever the ADF needle is on the prescribed course, it will also show a relative bearing that balances the drift correction, but you don't have to figure it out—the RMI does it for you.) Track outbound the same way, keeping the needle over the number that represents course to the station (it will be the reciprocal of your inbound track), and you will be on course. The inbound portion of the procedure turn is made much easier with an RMI; just fly on the inbound heading until the needle points to the inbound course, at which time you turn to that heading, and keep the needle where it belongs.

A less expensive version of the RMI consists of a manually-rotated compass card; with this system, it's up to you to put the aircraft heading under the index (don't forget to change it whenever you turn!). Otherwise, it is used in the same way as its electrically powered big brother.

17

The VOR Approach

BY THE VERY NATURE of the electronic equipment involved, the VOR approach climbs a rung higher on the accuracy ladder; but it still must be ranked with the non-precision procedures, since it lacks a glide slope.

The number of VOR approaches has grown steadily through the years, as the criteria for an instrument procedure are met at more and more small airports. Since an already-in-place VOR has the potential of serving several airports, you'll find that it is the most-used approach aid. The surrounding terrain has a lot to say about which airports qualify for approaches from a given VOR, as does distance. The latter will furnish some surprises though, because there are many airports located 8, 10, sometimes 12 miles from the omni—Maxton, North Carolina, used to have a VOR-DME procedure which was practically a cross-country trip in itself; the airfield is 27 miles from the VOR!

Tuning the Receiver

Tuning a VOR is as easy as falling off the bottom wing of a Stearman—it's simply a matter of making the proper numbers appear in the windows. Whether you have to turn a crank or twist knobs, make it an unfailing habit to IDENTIFY the station after tuning—it can ruin your whole day when you fly a beauty of an approach, only to run into a mountain because you didn't have the right station tuned. The FAA people are careful to separate frequencies so that you will pick up only one VOR during an approach, but don't forget Murphy's Law: "If there's a way for something to

go wrong, it will." TUNE AND IDENTIFY—a rule that will keep
you out of trouble.

So you're not a Samuel F. B. Morse—maybe the only code you
can really understand is S-O-S. Fear not, the coded identifiers are
transmitted slowly enough for you to follow them, matching what
you hear with the dots and dashes on the chart. After a while, close-
to-home stations will become familiar patterns of dits and dahs.If
you like to become constantly more professional about this flying
business, there are a number of quick-learning techniques for remembering Mr. Morse's brainstorm—for example, the VOR at
Zanesville, Ohio, is identified with ZZV, and it sings "Old-Man River, Old-Man Riv-er, this-is-a-Vee" twenty-four hours every day (—
—··, ——··, ···—). Not much of a melody, but great lyrics!

Some stations even identify themselves with a recorded voice,
saying, for example, "Indianapolis VOR." And if you want your
spirits lifted some dark, stormy night, tune in one of the VORs down
south, and let a lovely Southern FAA belle whisper the name of the
station in your ear as only a Dixie gal can do—the whole world
suddenly seems brighter!

The Initial Approach

By turning to the inbound heading and holding it, you will soon
be able to tell whether or not you are drifting, and which way—
the rate at which the CDI moves away from center gives you an
idea of how *fast* you are drifting. As soon as the needle moves, go
after it—start bracketing the course, as outlined in Chapter 9. The
secret is to recognize drift, turn to a heading to correct it, and hold
the heading until something happens. Your technique from here on
out depends on the direction and velocity of the wind; store the
correction in a corner of your memory so you can anticipate headings
and ground speeds during the approach.

Station Passage and Tracking Outbound

You've done a good job of tracking to the station when the TO-
FROM indicator reverses itself in the blink of an eye—the faster it
flips, the closer you are to the station. But even if it takes several
seconds, you have officially passed the VOR as soon as FROM ap-

pears, and it's time to proceed with the next segment of the approach.

The best way to start is with the Four T's: TIME, TURN, THROTTLE, TALK. Start your stopwatch or note the TIME, TURN to the outbound heading, THROTTLE back to slow down and descend to the procedure turn altitude, and finally, when everything's under control, TALK to the man—let ATC know that you are outbound from the VOR. Don't be in a rush to make this report; the controller knows what you are doing, since he cleared you for the approach, so get the airplane going in the right direction before you pick up the mike.

You are obliged to get on the outbound course before starting the procedure turn, so after station passage, put the right numbers on the OBS, and take a look at the CDI—it will tell you which way to turn.

You've been descending all this time, of course (gets a little like rubbing your head and patting your stomach, doesn't it?), and your target is the procedure turn altitude, on course, ready to begin the turn. A VORTAC (VOR station with distance-measuring capability) makes it a simple matter to determine your distance from the station. In the absence of DME, keep track of the time outbound.

Procedure Turn

Procedure turn altitude is a minimum to be observed until you are on course inbound, at which time you can usually descend. (Sometimes obstacles require that you stay up there all the way to the station.) During the turn, change the OBS to the inbound course. As the CDI begins to center, start your turn to the inbound course, applying drift correction as necessary. (Detailed techniques for the various types of procedure turns are found in the first section of Chapter 15, "Instrument Approaches.")

Post-Procedure Turn and Final Approach

Unless obstructions make this airspace untenable, the post-procedure-turn course to the station will be lined up with the final approach, that electronic line down which you're going to fly to the minimum altitude. Take advantage of this opportunity to really nail down the drift correction; you can get a general idea which way the air is moving as you fly this segment. You should also be slowing the airplane to approach speed, and accomplishing your "Before Landing Checklist." Having these things done early will let you focus your attention on precise flying during the final approach segment.

The closer you get to the station, the more the CDI seems to defy your efforts to keep it centered—the needle will move more frequently and rapidly, but think of this as increased accuracy (which it really is), and make the most of it with very small corrections. When the CDI begins to move, start bracketing—a few "cuts and tries" will establish a heading just right for the wind that exists. Here's where the needlechaser will rack his airplane around for 30 or 40 degrees, whereupon the CDI comes roaring back across the center and off to the right, prompting a 2g turn the other way, which then makes the needle zip to the other side—all this is happening while he is getting closer to the omni, which makes the CDI even *more* sensitive. By now, fixation has set in, and the needlechaser has lost all interest in altitude and airspeed; as if that weren't enough, Approach Control will always choose this moment to ask, "Barnburner 1234 Alpha, what are your intentions after this approach?" The reply to that question is frequently unprintable!

Over the VOR, the TO-FROM reversal will be abrupt, and it's your cue to exercise the Four T's again. You should report over the final approach fix inbound, but all you need to say is "Barnburner 1234 Alpha, VOR inbound."

The final approach segment is the climax of your short love affair with this VOR station; everything depends on your making the right moves. Your attention should be devoted to, first, keeping airspeed, altitude, and heading right where you want them; second, descending on course at a rate that will get you to the MDA well before your time runs out; third, keep track of the time elapsed so you'll know when to pull up should it become necessary; fourth, looking for the airport. Don't expect to see it, and you'll get a nice surprise when it comes into view!

Give yourself a break by getting down to the minimum altitude just as soon as practical, because you'll likely establish ground contact that much sooner. Remember that as ground speed increases, rate of descent must increase if you are to lose the same amount of altitude in a given distance.

A typical VOR approach (excluding those situations where unusual terrain features and/or distance from omni to airport require higher minimums) will bring you to the missed approach point about 300 or 400 feet above the airport elevation, and will require from ¾ to 1½ miles visibility. Keep the CDI centered, descend to MDA, fly out the time, and if the weather man cooperates, you'll find yourself all set up for a normal landing.

The VOR Approach with DME

Distance-measuring equipment (DME) adds a second dimension to the capabilities of a VOR station. Without DME, the best you can do is to locate yourself somewhere on a radial, dependent on timing to provide information relative to distance. Considering changes in wind velocity and airspeed, and the interpolation required on the time-distance tables, your position on a VOR approach is nothing but a good estimate at best. With DME, the added precision is reflected in more favorable minimums for the approach.

Approaches using DME fall into two operational categories: those in which DME provides step-down fixes and lower minimums than the VOR-only procedure, and those in which DME is an absolute requirement. In the first case (DME optional), a pilot experiencing DME loss could continue the approach, but at the higher VOR-only MDA. The second category requires *both* VOR and DME equipment, and makes no provision for pressing on if the mileage-meter falls out of the instrument panel.

Check the approach chart to determine whether the distance-measuring equipment is required, or is considered an adjunct to the procedure. The key is the inclusion of a separate set of minima for DME-equipped aircraft, indicating one MDA when you've got it, another when you don't. In the illustration (Figure 39), Category A and B aircraft are permitted to descend to 2,620 feet MSL until the 3½-mile fix is identified, then are cleared down to an MDA of 1,860 feet. If no DME is available, or is not part of the aircraft equipment, you must maintain 2,620 until reaching the missed approach point—it has in effect bought you 760 feet (and 1 mile of

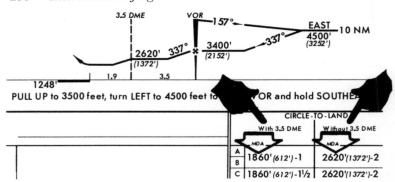

FIGURE 39 With DME available for more accurate positioning on the final approach, the MDA is considerably lower. (© *1969 Jeppesen & Co., Denver, Colo. All rights reserved. Not to be used for navigation.*)

visibility). If you frequently use such an airport, DME might pay for itself in one season by permitting landings from approaches that otherwise would have been missed.

On the other hand, a VOR-DME procedure that does not offer the option will have only one set of minimums listed—that approach *cannot be executed* unless you are equipped with *both* VOR and DME receivers, in working order (assuming that both transmitters are also operative).

Phelps-Collins Airport at Alpena, Michigan, displays still another means of putting DME to work for a more efficient approach procedure (Figure 40). Instead of maneuvering your way around a procedure turn, you could be cleared to intercept the 10-mile DME arc, to proceed around that circle until reaching the final approach course, and then fly straight in to the airport. Although it requires a bit more technique and some diligent practice before it can be accomplished smoothly, flying an arc approach can save you time and give the controller additional flexibility in spacing inbound traffic. For example, suppose you are inbound to Phelps-Collins from the west, and are instructed to proceed inbound on the 260 radial until intercepting the 10-mile arc, cleared for the VOR Runway 12 approach. Nothing different about it so far, but when the DME indicator gets close to 10, be ready to make your move. Remember that you are approaching on a 90-degree intercept heading, and things will happen rapidly when the time comes; here's where practice comes booming through in spades, where you should know what mileage lead to use for your airspeed. For groundspeeds of 150 knots or less, a lead of ½ mile should be used—in other words, start turning when the DME reads 10½ miles. As groundspeeds increase, you can compute the proper lead by using this formula: ½ percent of your GS = lead in nautical miles. A standard rate turn is assumed in both situations.

It is obvious that you must turn left 90 degrees, but don't attempt to fly in a continuous circle to keep the DME on 10—that would require your complete attention, to the detriment of all the other things that are going on. Your flight path should be a series of segments that are tangential to the arc, and it is convenient to use 20-degree heading changes as a guideline. When you complete the turn to 350 degrees, the DME should read very close to 10, and it should stay there for a short while, depending on the wind, and your airspeed. If a strong west wind appears to be drifting you toward the station, the DME may move slightly toward 9 miles, but will eventually slide back to 10 as you fly into the arc again. In a no-wind situation, you should turn to the right 20 degrees (new heading of 010 degrees) as soon as the indicator starts to move away from ten miles. Hold this heading until you once again observe the mile-

FIGURE 40 "Intercept and proceed via the 10-mile arc, cleared for the approach." Note the minimum altitude and NoPT on the arc.

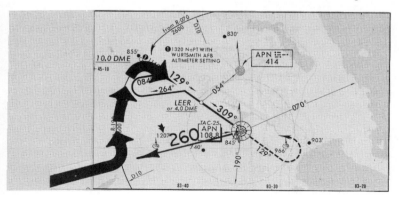

age increasing, then turn another 20 degrees to the right. Keep it up, turning farther and farther to the right to keep the DME as close to 10 as possible, until you notice the CDI beginning to center (you set the OBS on the inbound course of 129 degrees as soon as you intercepted the arc). You are on another 90-degree intercept, and should keep turning on the inbound course to center the CDI. From here on, it's just another VOR approach—fly straight down the chute to the missed approach point. A procedure turn is neither desirable nor permitted, since you are already lined up on the final approach course.

The pilot whose instrument panel sports a Radio Magnetic Indicator (RMI) with a needle slaved to the VOR instead of, or in addition to, the ADF has one more thing in his favor when he is cleared for an arc approach—it takes most of the work out of staying "in orbit." At the completion of the first 90-degree turn, the RMI will point to the right wing-tip position (or the left, depending on the situation), and will immediately begin moving toward the tail, unless you're flying head-on into a hurricane. When the RMI pointer has moved tailward 10 degrees, make your first 20-degree heading change, observing the DME to confirm that you're still close to the 10-mile arc. In a light wind, the 20-degree turn will put the RMI pointer 10 degrees ahead of the wing-tip position, and you can wait until it returns to 10 degrees behind before changing heading again.

18

The ILS Approach

THIS is the granddaddy of 'em all when it comes to getting down close to the ground! That point to which any instrument approach procedure leads you is at its "brass-tackiest" using ILS, and with the most sophisticated equipment the point can be right on the runway—a zero-zero approach. Special authorization for airport, airplane, and pilot is required for Category II and III (reduced minimums) ILS approaches, but the "normal" procedure, available to all adequately equipped aircraft and any instrument-rated pilot, allows landings from a Decision Height of 200 feet if visibility is ½ mile or better. CAUTION: This is the typical situation—some approaches have DH's somewhat higher than 200 feet, and visibility minimums greater than a half-mile, so check each approach chart you use and know what you're getting into!

In strict legalese, an ILS approach may be conducted only if all four electronic components of the system are operating and receivable in the aircraft. These four—localizer, glide slope, outer marker, and middle marker (defined in Chapter 2, "The Language of Instrument Flying")—are supplemented by the Approach Lighting System (ALS). The important thing to understand is that you may not descend to "full ILS" minimums if your aircraft is not equipped with all the black boxes, or if all of them aren't black-boxing properly, or if the transmitters on the ground are out of business. The localizer is the backbone of the ILS; when it's inoperative, you might as well request some other procedure—without a localizer to line you up with the runway, the approach is impossible.

Lack of an approach lighting system raises the minimums a bit, losing (or not having) an outer marker receiver bites even deeper, and no glide slope capability really takes a toll on how low you may descend. Without a glide slope, you are automatically pushed into the "non-precision approach" category, which will raise the minimums significantly.

Flying the Localizer

It's the same receiver and the same indicator (the CDI) you use for VOR navigation, but some important electronic changes take place when you select a localizer frequency. First, the CDI becomes more sensitive, since the localizer course is only about 5 degrees wide—this means that the needle moves much more rapidly and the displacements are much larger. (It's roughly four times as sensitive as it was when tuned to a VOR.) Second, the omni bearing selector (OBS) with which you select VOR courses for navigation is cut out of the system; the CDI is now responsive only to a left-of-course or right-of-course signal, or a blend of the two, which gives you an on-course indication. (Even though the OBS is inoperative, it's a good idea to set it on the localizer course as a reminder of the track you want to maintain on the approach.)

The instrument designers made it easy for you when they set up the left-right needle—if the CDI *points* to the left, you should *fly* to the left to get back on centerline. When it moves off to the right, turn to the right; it's really that simple. The CDI will always show you which way to turn to get back on course as you are *flying toward the runway on the front course* (during a normal approach), or *away from the runway on the back course* (executing a missed approach). You will always fly *toward* the needle on an ILS approach (Figure 41). (Check pages 130–31 for the technique of using an HSI for ILS work.)

Tuning the ILS Receivers

Since you are about to make use of a *system* of navaids, there is more than one receiver involved. First, set up the localizer frequency on the VOR receiver, and listen for the identification; it will always be three letters in Morse code, preceded by the letter "I" (· ·). So, the localizer at Los Angeles is I-LAX, at Minneapolis it's I-MSP, and so on.

When the localizer frequency is selected (always an odd tenth,

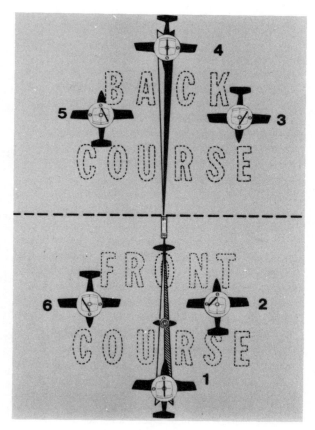

FIGURE 41 Whenever the heading is the same (or nearly the same) as the front course of the localizer, a correction toward the needle will return the aircraft to the centerline (Aircraft #2 and #5). When headed in the opposite direction (Aircraft #3 and #6), the pilot must turn away from the CDI to get back on course. Aircraft #1 and #4 show "on course" indications.

such as 109.1, .3, .5, .7, .9, etc.), it will automatically tune the glide slope receiver, a completely separate unit. Since there is no way you can identify it aurally, don't worry about it. If you are reasonably well lined up for the approach, the localizer and glide slope needles will come alive when the frequency is selected. Don't panic if the needles refuse to budge when you're approaching from the side; the ILS signals are somewhat directional in nature, and are not very strong except on the approach course, where they are intended to be used.

Tuning the next navaid is not really tuning at all, because the 75 MHz marker beacon receiver is a single-frequency, non-tuneable radio. *Every* outer marker, *every* middle marker, transmits a signal on 75 MHz, the only difference being in the pattern; the OM sends out continuous dashes (----), while the MM transmits alternate dots and dashes (·-·-·-). So make sure that the receiver is turned on, and the volume turned up. (Check the blue [OM] and amber [MM] marker beacon lights if you have them—they are not required, but help you identify these markers as you pass overhead.)

Although not a requirement or official component of the ILS, you will find compass locators (LOM) installed at many airports. (Some controllers call them "Outer Compass Locators.") The LOM is really just a low-powered NDB sited at the same place as the OM, providing navigational guidance to the OM (that's why it's called a "locator"). It also serves as an additional indication of *passing* the outer marker, and you may legally substitute your ADF receiver for the marker beacon receiver to comply with the "four components" rule. (A radar position is also acceptable.) The compass locator is tuneable, with a frequency (from 190 to 415 KHz) printed on the chart, and with a Morse code identifier. It's usually the first two letters of the localizer's three-letter identification; hence, the LOM at Los Angeles (LAX) will probably be LA, at Minneapolis (MSP) it will be MS.

Initial Approach

A terminal with enough traffic to justify an Instrument Landing System will probably be radar-equipped, which means that the initial approach will consist of vectors until you are established on the localizer. Because of this, procedure turns on an ILS approach are infrequently required—but there may come a time when you have to accomplish the approach all by yourself, with no help from radar, so you should know how to do it.

Notice that the ILS Runway 27 Approach Chart for Ross Airport at Benton Harbor, Michigan (Figure 42), indicates several points from which flights are normally cleared to the LOM to begin the ILS approach. Each of these initial approach routes has its own course to the LOM, the distance, and a minimum altitude; from the MUSKY intersection, it's 093°, 27.8 NM, and the lowest safe altitude is 2,300 feet—from the South Bend VOR, the course is 001°, 21.5 NM, and no less than 2,300 feet.

Some initial approach routes are nearly lined up with the localizer course, and do not require a procedure turn. When this

FIGURE 42 Approach and landing chart for the ILS to Runway 27 at Benton Harbor, Mich. (© *1977 Jeppesen & Co., Denver, Colo. All rights reserved. Not to be used for navigation.*)

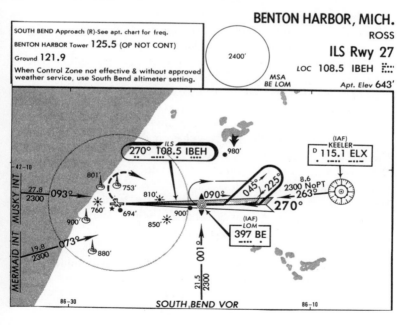

situation exists, the route will be labeled "NoPT," and you are expected to proceed as charted, straight in, with no procedure turn. An example is the route shown from Keeler VOR: notice that the minimum altitude (2,300) coincides with procedure turn altitude, and you should be ready to commence descent upon intercepting the glide slope. The controller should have you down to a compatible altitude by the time you cross Keeler, but if you need a procedure turn to lose altitude (ear problems, maybe), by all means ask for one, and chances are you'll be cleared. But don't do it without clearance, because Approach Control may have a faster aircraft right behind you! (Another situation which precludes a procedure turn is one in which you have been radar vectored to the final approach course [the localizer] and have been cleared for the approach; in this case, you're all lined up, courtesy of radar, and there's no need to turn around.)

Assume you have been cleared "from over the Musky intersection direct to the BE compass locator, descend to 4,000 feet, cleared for the ILS Runway 27 approach." You're on your own now, and after acknowledging the clearance, begin descent to 4,000 feet and track inbound to the OM via the 093° course. You should be tuning radios, cleaning up the cockpit, listening to other aircraft, and generally getting your ducks in a row for the approach. If you have two VOR receivers, tune #1 to the localizer frequency and check the identification—tune #2 to the South Bend VOR, OBS, on 001° as a cross-check. Use the same receiver for approach work every time and you'll spare yourself the embarrassment of flying the wrong needle, to say nothing of the dangers involved!

The localizer needle (CDI) will be a long time moving, since the signal is so narrow, but as you get closer to the outer marker, the CDI will begin to center, cueing you to start turning to the outbound heading of 090 degrees. With practice, you will develop the proper lead to prevent overshooting the localizer course—it's a function of airspeed, rate of turn, and wind component, and all three must be taken into consideration.

A Beechcraft Baron pilot (and his passengers) found out the hard way that an instrument pilot is expected to find his own way around the approach procedure in the absence of radar guidance. Although this accident occurred hundreds of miles from Benton Harbor, Michigan, the layout of the ILS procedure is almost identical, and will help you visualize the situation.

The Baron was approaching from the northwest (roughly a 45-degree angle to the localizer), and had been requested by the Center controller to descend rapidly from cruise altitude in order to expedite traffic flow into the airport. The pilot replied, "Okay, we'll drop it out," and he did . . . radar plots later showed 1,500 feet per minute and high airspeed, upward of 200 knots. Just a mile or so from the marker, the Center controller cleared the Baron for the ILS approach, and asked the pilot to contact the tower.

With the weather hovering at 200 feet and one mile visibility, it would seem important to take every opportunity to make the first approach a good one, but upon crossing the marker, this pilot—for reasons unknown—turned *to the right*, toward the airport. The tower controller (without radar, and expecting that the pilot would proceed eastbound for a procedure turn) asked for a report at the marker inbound, and a couple of minutes later, the pilot complied . . . "I'm at the marker, inbound."

Sounds all right—that's a little fast, but not an unreasonable amount of time for a sharp pilot in a hurry to get turned around and headed for the airport. Unfortunately, because of the high speed and the right turn, the airplane was very close to the *middle* marker, and well on its way down to Decision Height. The pilot wandered back and forth across the localizer, either completely disoriented, or perhaps looking in vain for the runway, which was now well out of sight to his left rear. The low-altitude flight continued to a point seven miles west of the airport, where the operation was brought to an abrupt halt by the guy wires of a television tower.

Lessons to be learned:

· If you can't handle an expedited approach, *turn it down.*
· When weather conditions are close to minimums, *fly the complete approach, as published.* Give yourself a chance to get it right the first time.
· Figure out well ahead of time which way you'll need to turn at the marker, and follow through with that plan when you get there.

- Whenever you are not *absolutely certain* of the meaning of a clearance, request a clarification.
- When things "just don't feel right" on an approach, they probably aren't . . . execute the missed approach procedure and come back for another try.

Station Passage and Tracking Outbound

A pilot flying a fully equipped airplane has no excuse for missing station passage at the outer marker. Think of all the indications at work for you: the most obvious will be the strident blare of the marker's continuous dashes (following which you will turn the sensitivity to "LOW," where it should have been anyway!), at the same time the blue light is doing its thing, and the ADF needle will swing from nose to tail—it's time for the Four T's.

Most controllers will descend you to procedure turn altitude well ahead of time, but if not, plan to lose half the altitude outbound, half inbound, and make your descent at a practical yet comfortable rate. Keep the welfare of your passengers in mind—for most non-pilots, a descent of more than 800–1,000 feet per minute can cause problems.

Procedure Turn

After two minutes outbound (careful, you must observe localizer back-course indications!), turn to the appropriate heading, and your procedure turn is under way. When it's time (depending on the type of procedure turn you elect), turn right to 225 degrees, which sets you up for intercepting the localizer once again. As your heading approaches 225, watch the CDI out of the corner of your eye—if it's beginning to center, continue your turn and you'll roll out on course. If at 225 it hasn't moved from the left side of the instrument, roll out on 225 and hold it until the CDI starts moving—the proper lead comes with practice. In the opposite situation, the CDI starts moving toward center during your turn inbound; obviously the result of a northerly wind component, it will require an increase in the rate of turn so that you won't overshoot the localizer and wind up doing a series of S-turns trying to get back on course.

The time from localizer interception to the outer marker is a golden opportunity to find out what heading will keep you on course; you can get a good idea of what's going on windwise right here.

Post-Procedure Turn and Final Turn

Finally inbound to the airport, the CDI is making sense again—turn left when it's off center to the left and vice versa—and it's time to configure the airplane for the final approach. As your experience, ability, and confidence increase, it is good practice to keep your airspeed somewhat higher than the final approach speed until just before intercepting the glide slope. (At large, busy terminals you will often be asked to maintain *cruise* airspeed to the outer marker, but don't do it if the resultant "too many things at once" is more than you can handle—tell Approach Control you can't comply, and let *them* handle the traffic separation problem.) By setting up the airplane in approach configuration, at approach airspeed, you will need only to reduce power a bit to establish a rate of descent that will keep the glide slope needle right where it belongs.

Still inbound to the OM, maintaining 2,300 feet, you will note the glide slope indicator begin to move from its full "UP" position; this is a good indication that you are very close to the marker. If you are carrying some extra airspeed, it's time to bleed it off—the final scene in this drama is about to commence. As soon as the glide slope needle centers, reduce power (or lower the wheels) and begin the descent, even though you have not yet crossed the marker. It's completely legal, and is an important part of the approach procedure. Check the profile view of the approach, and you'll see that if the glide slope is followed, you will cross the OM at an indicated altitude of 2,203 feet, and a glance at the altimeter will provide an accuracy check before continuing the approach; if it's way off (how much is up to you), you may have second thoughts about going ahead with the approach.

On course and on glide slope, the marker indications will be just as numerous as they were outbound, and at station passage, only two T's apply—TIME and TALK—"Benton Harbor Tower, Barnburner 1234 Alpha, marker inbound." That's all you need to say, for two reasons: First, it's merely a confirmation, since Approach Control has already called the Tower by phone and informed them that you're on the way; second, you are mighty busy flying the airplane, and you really haven't time to waste carrying on a conversation. Likewise, you shouldn't be concerned if you don't, or can't make this report until some seconds have slipped by—your primary job is controlling the airplane, setting it up as accurately as you can on the localizer and glide slope. Tower will usually come right back with clearance to land; they've been expecting you.

And down you go; down, down, down—from outer marker to runway-in-sight or missed approach can be one of the longest periods of time in a pilot's life! Slight power corrections to keep the glide slope needle centered (it's always directional; down means fly down, up means fly up) and small heading changes will correct for drift and keep the CDI centered. Don't try to "fly" these two needles— you'll inevitably chase them back and forth and up and down, and you can't win, because the needles can move faster than you can! The only technique that really works well is to plug in the CDI and glide slope as additional instruments in your cross-check. Make corrections on the *attitude* instruments to put the ILS needles where you want them to be. If the CDI slides off a bit to the right, turn to the right 5 degrees (just press the rudder a bit; don't try to bank the airplane for a 5-degree turn) and watch to see what happens— it's important to pick a corrective heading and *hold it* until you can determine the effect on the CDI. Still sliding right? Turn another 5 degrees and see what that does—when you finally get the needle centered, take out corrections in small increments with rudder only, and before long you'll have a heading that will maintain the localizer course. The same technique is used for vertical corrections, increasing or reducing power *slightly* to change your rate of descent so that you will fly back onto the glide slope.

Down, down, and down some more until, with localizer and glide slope needles centered, you see 937 feet on the altimeter. You are at the Decision Height (DH), and you can do one of two things: Either continue to a landing, or execute a missed approach. The regulation-writers, who usually play "Philadelphia lawyer" with flight rules, came up with one of their best efforts here, as far as being brief and concise and clear. "Decision Height" is very relevant nomenclature, because when you get there on a *precision* approach, you've got to make up your mind—either fish or cut bait! If the runway environment (this includes Approach Lighting System) is

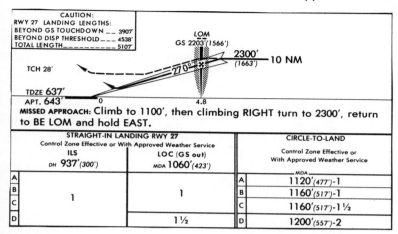

CAUTION:
RWY 27 LANDING LENGTHS:
BEYOND GS TOUCHDOWN __ 3907'
BEYOND DISP THRESHOLD ___ 4538'
TOTAL LENGTH _____ 5107'

LOM
GS 2203'(1566')

2300'
(1663') 10 NM

270°

TCH 28'

TDZE 637'
APT. 643'   0   4.8

MISSED APPROACH: Climb to 1100', then climbing RIGHT turn to 2300', return to BE LOM and hold EAST.

STRAIGHT-IN LANDING RWY 27			CIRCLE-TO-LAND
Control Zone Effective or With Approved Weather Service			Control Zone Effective or With Approved Weather Service
ILS	LOC (GS out)		
DH 937'(300')	MDA 1060'(423')		MDA
A		A	1120'(477')-1
B	1	1	B	1160'(517')-1
C		C	1160'(517')-1½
D		1½	D	1200'(557')-2

FIGURE 43 Profile view and minimums for ILS Runway 27 at Benton Harbor, Mich. (© *1977 Jeppesen & Co., Denver, Colo. All rights reserved. Not to be used for navigation.*)

visible, and if you are in a position to make a normal landing (they leave that determination to you), you may proceed to touchdown. That's the "fish" situation—but if those conditions are not met, you'll have to "cut bait"; execute the missed approach procedure.

There will be very few times when you start an ILS approach and don't complete it, for two reasons: First, the weather just doesn't get down to ILS minimums and stay there that often, and second, you will probably not be out flying when the weather is that bad. Especially in a single-engine machine, you are pulling the string out rather far in such conditions—if you should experience that increasingly rare occurrence of power failure, you've nowhere to go but down, and since the glide slope requires a rather flat approach path (it's only a 2.5- to 3-degree slope), you're going to need some power to get to the runway. Loss of that power will certainly result in a sudden and intimate meeting with terra firma at some point other than the touchdown zone on the runway.

If you spot the runway from a half-mile out (which is about where you'll be on most ILS approaches when you reach DH, but notice that the Benton Harbor procedure, Figure 42, requires *one mile* visibility), you'll more than likely be able to go the rest of the way to a landing. The law is equally clear regarding your actions if you lose sight of the airport after you go below Decision Height. You must execute an immediate missed approach—no hesitation, no hunting around for the field, get out of there, NOW! Come back for another try if you like (with ATC's blessing, of course), but don't press your luck if the runway doesn't show up at the Decision Height. (When you are cleared for the ILS approach, then to circle for landing on some other runway, you must observe *circling* minimums, which will limit you to a minimum descent altitude [MDA]. You *may not* go down to the DH, even though the Barnburner is fully equipped and all the transmitters are functioning properly. That Decision Height is a safe level for only *one* runway.)

Measured above the highest elevation in the touchdown zone of the runway (the first 3,000 feet beyond the threshold), Decision Heights are accompanied on the approach charts by another figure, called "height above touchdown" (HAT). Most ILS approaches are set up so that you will be 200 feet above the runway when you reach the decision height, but sometimes it will be considerably higher because of local terrain. For example, at Roanoke, Virginia, the DH is 615 feet above the runway, and visibility for the approach is hiked way up to 2 miles because the clouds around Roanoke are mostly cumulus granitus—full of rocks!

The Localizer Approach

Many general aviation aircraft are without glide slope receivers, and not a few airports have only a localizer transmitter installed. In addition, glide slope transmitters have been known to develop malfunctions—any of these circumstances dictate a localizer approach, which means that everything is there to help you except the vertical guidance of the glide slope. This automatically becomes a *nonprecision approach*, with attendant higher minimums. You will be limited to a Minimum Descent Altitude (MDA), and you must rely on timing for determination of the missed approach point.

A localizer approach is therefore flown very much like a VOR approach (it's up to you to begin descent at the appropriate time, get to the MDA, and determine the missed approach point all by yourself), with the increased accuracy of the localizer to line you up with the runway more precisely. The final approach fix on a localizer approach is frequently a marker or an NDB, but it can also be a VOR intersection, bearing to an off-course radio beacon, or a DME reading when that facility is located on the airport. On occasion, the approach chart carries the notation that two VORs are required—one for the localizer, one to determine the intersection making up the final approach fix. If the FAF depends on an NDB or a bearing to another nearby radio beacon, you'd also better have an ADF receiver on board!

Initial approach, procedure turn, and final approach are flown just like the full ILS, with one exception—plan to arrive at the MDA well before your time runs out, to give yourself more opportunity to look for the runway.

Controllers don't have time to ask if you have all the goodies, and will normally clear you for "the ILS approach." If your airplane does not have a glide slope receiver, it's up to you to realize that you cannot execute a precision approach, and you must look up the "Localizer Only" numbers on the chart. (You are also required to let the controller know that this approach will be "Localizer Only.") *Do not* attempt an approach down to a DH unless you are receiving a usable glide slope signal; that's really asking for trouble! And don't always assume that a localizer approach is authorized for each ILS procedure. On some approaches, the angle required for clear terrain is so extreme that the full procedure is required—no glide slope, no approach at all.

"No glide slope" applies to equipment on board the airplane as well, illustrated by the unfortunate outcome of this approach: Having purchased a used airplane on the west coast, a non-instrument pilot found himself stranded halfway home by inclement weather. He was anxious to be back for Christmas, and hired an instrument instructor to fly with him, expecting to gain some IFR instruction along the way.

The CFII was very recently qualified, the ink barely dry on his certificate, and he had zero experience in this airplane type, a Cherokee Six. Having satisfied himself that all was well with the airplane and its equipment (some avionics work had been performed as a condition of the sale in California), the instructor and his passengers departed, and the flight was unremarkable until late in the ILS approach at destination. It was long since dark, the weather was near minimums, and the last thing the

CFII remembered (he was the only survivor of the crash) was a glimpse of the approach lights just before impact. The airplane came to earth one mile short of the runway.

In a post-accident statement, the instructor described his final approach, with localizer and glide slope needles centered all the way, airspeed at a constant 90 knots, rate of descent 500 feet per minute. What he *didn't* take into account was a notation on the avionics work order; "G/S inop"—glide slope inoperative.

A failed glide slope needle will, in nearly all light-airplane installations, display a red warning flag, and go to a "centered" indication, leading an unwary pilot to conclude that he was right where he should be. Although a 500-foot-per-minute descent is a good rate for a 3-degree glide slope at 90 knots, keep in mind that the rate of descent to stay on a glide slope is dependent on *groundspeed*, not airspeed. The faster you are moving across the ground, the faster you must move vertically in order to arrive at Decision Height at the right place.

Of course, there's another facet to this accident, and it should be obvious; it would have been impossible for the airplane to strike the ground *if the pilot had not descended below Decision Height*. There is plenty to go wrong with an ILS approach to minimums (it's a lot like a golf swing!), but a steadfast refusal to go below DH *regardless of other instrument indications* unless and until the runway is clearly in sight can prevent problems like this one.

The Localizer Back-Course Approach

One statement, "a back-course approach is the same as a front-course approach without the glide slope," should suffice to explain this procedure; but because the localizer indicator (CDI) seems to work in reverse, everyone develops a hang-up about back-course approaches.

A back-course procedure always lines you up with a specific runway, and although it is not a "precision" approach, it usually offers minimums much lower than either VOR or ADF. It's up to you to determine by timing when you have reached the missed approach point, and the final approach fix is frequently an intersection rather than a marker or a compass locator. Other than that, the back-course approach is as easy and as accurate to fly as the front-course.

Initial approach and procedure turn techniques are the same as before, so this discussion begins after you have turned around and are flying toward the runway on the back course, and just before reaching the Final Approach Fix. Since completing the procedure turn or intercepting the localizer, you have been flying away from the needle to effect your course corrections. The technique of making a heading change and *holding* it until you see a change on the CDI is just as relevant as it was on the front course, and as you approach the FAF, get the airplane ready to begin descent. When the marker or intersection is passed, three "T's" apply: TIME, THROTTLE, and TALK— you owe ATC (usually the Tower) a report.

There are no approach procedures that require an unsafe rate of descent, but remember that a tail wind will necessitate going downhill somewhat faster. You might consider slowing your airplane a bit when the wind is really pushing you along, so that things don't happen so rapidly.

The LOC(BC) approach is subject to the same regulations as all the others regarding MDA, landing conditions, and missed approach procedures. If you can get to the runway using ground references and you're reasonably lined up with the runway, go ahead and land. If these conditions don't exist, or if they cannot be maintained after leaving MDA, you must "go around."

Some automatic pilot installations have a "Localizer Reverse" function, which allows George to interpret back-course signals properly during a coupled approach (that's where the autopilot does all the work and you record "IO" time in your logbook—"Interested Observer"). A less sophisticated setup permits you to flip a reversal switch on the VOR indicator so that you can fly toward the CDI or a LOC(BC) approach; if you paid for it, go ahead and use it, but don't forget to switch back to the normal function at the completion of your back-course approach, or you'll wind up in a state of complete confusion the next time you try to fly a front-course procedure. Murphy's Law again: If there's any possibility of doing something wrong, somebody will do it.

Flying a back course properly is more a state of mind than

anything else. The procedures, principles, and restrictions are not that much different than any other approach; you've just got to sit there, in firm and complete control of the airplane, and ignore the snickering from the back seats as you mumble to yourself "fly away from the needle, fly away from the needle, fly away from the needle."

19

High-Altitude IFR

THE TURBO-SUPERCHARGER, that marvelous pumper of air that makes reciprocating engines think they're running at sea level all the time, has literally boosted lightplane operation into volumes of airspace previously denied to all but the jets, turboprops, and older business aircraft powered by the big radials. Until the coming of the small, relatively inexpensive "blowers," the practical altitude limit was 10,000 feet, and most light aircraft spent so much time getting up there it was hardly worth the effort except on long trips, or when you had to cross the mountains. The single-engine ceiling of normally aspirated light twins left more than a little to be desired— in essence, when you finally got to the higher levels, there just wasn't much power left.

But now, you can "slip the surly bonds of earth" behind a supercharged engine or two, and climb into the wonderful high-altitude world of crystal-clear air. Up where altitudes change to flight levels, where the winds often move faster than a J-3 can fly, you look down from your oxygenated perch at all the murk below and wonder why you didn't do this sooner. And there's almost as much power available up here as you had at takeoff, which makes for spectacular single-engine performance in light twins. (If the fan stops on a supercharged single, you've got the same old forced-landing problem, but a heck of a lot more time to solve it!)

A wealth of benefits awaits the pilot who shells out the extra dollars to have "supercharged" lettered on the nacelles:

· Flight above most of the weather, especially that troublesome twosome, turbulence and icing.
· Much faster climb through the weather to "on top."

- The ability to see most thunderstorms and avoid them.
- Higher true airspeed at altitude.
- Much greater latitude in selecting the best altitude for winds or weather.
- You can take advantage of fantastic tail winds.
- When it's clear up there, it's *really* clear; no problem seeing other aircraft.
- Able to leap tall buildings at a single bound.
- Comparatively little traffic, and everyone else in this airspace (above 18,000 feet) is under positive control.
- The ride will almost always be smoother than at lower levels.
- If you have an obnoxious passenger on board, you can slyly unplug his oxygen hose and watch him go to sleep.
- In addition to all of this, when was the last time you flew *through* a rainbow?

And so on, with every new turbo pilot adding his own pet joys to the list. But like anything worth while, all this has a price (in addition to the cost of the equipment) that must be extracted in the form of additional pilot knowledge, new techniques to be learned, and increased vigilance. You'll have to become familiar with a whole new set of enroute charts if you're going into the high-altitude route structure, because the low-altitude paperwork won't do the job above 18,000 feet—it's like trying to take an all-interstate-highway trip with a county road map. Some new techniques will crop up, like learning how far out to request descent, or getting used to handling your high-flying bird in a high-speed descent. When you haul people to altitudes that might effect them adversely, they have a right to expect you to know all about this new environment, to be the guardian of eardrums, sinuses, and breathing apparatus. High altitudes are not necessarily dangerous, but the hazards are insidious and unforgiving.

Baby, It's Cold Outside!

There are several things that you should check more thoroughly than usual as you preflight for a high-altitude trip, and one of these is the cabin heater. On a sweltering summer day, you may look forward to the cooler air of the 5,000- to 10,000-foot levels you used before you got the turbos, but when you keep right on climbing into the teens and twenties, you won't want the fresh air vents open! Temperatures remain rather low throughout the year up there, with the OAT gauge seldom climbing above the zero mark (Fahrenheit), even in midsummer. In the wintertime, temperatures of twenty below zero are not uncommon. If the cabin heater fails, or won't start, there's no doubt that you can survive, but preoccupation with keeping yourself warm can trigger a chain reaction of inattention and forgetfulness. Besides, it's just plain uncomfortable to sit in a cold airplane—a simple preflight check of the heater saves you all the trouble. If the BTU-maker in your airplane doesn't fire up right away to full output when you ground check it, take the time to get it fixed, or plan the flight for a lower altitude—especially if you have passengers on board for their first flight. No one will walk away from an airplane with as much distaste for the whole business as the one who walks away on benumbed feet, trying to restore circulation to his frostbitten fingers, and mumbling anti-aviation epithets through blue lips.

There's nothing like a cup of steaming hot coffee to complete the settling-down process at altitude, after the autopilot has taken over the chores and you can relax for a few minutes. But if you wait until this point to open the jug, be prepared for a real surprise— nearly all thermos bottles are purposely designed with a very effective seal around the cap, and as a result you will suddenly expose boiling coffee at sea level pressure to the sharply reduced pressure of high altitude. It's a lot like pulling the plug on Old Faithful, with the painful difference of having the geyser right in your lap! No one can do a good job of flying an airplane with superhot boiling coffee all over, and there's always the chance that you may get it in your eyes—'nuff said. Remember to loosen the cap a bit on the way up so that the pressure can equalize. This is a good practice any time, even when climbing to only 5,000 feet. (If the contents of a sealed container are under pressure to start with, the opening will be even more dramatic. Consider one pilot who popped the cork on a bottle of champagne at FL 230; his airplane *still* smells like the mash room at Manischewitz!)

What You Don't Know *Can* Hurt You!

You should have a carbon monoxide (CO) indicator pasted firmly and conspicously on the instrument panel. Some pilots, especially former coal-miners, insist on carrying a live canary, but it's a good deal easier to glance at the indicator, which turns dark in the presence of CO. Until now, this may have been of concern only in the wintertime, when heater malfunctions or leaks could fill the cabin with undetectable and very poisonous CO fumes, but you'll be using the heater on nearly all high altitude flights. Have something on board to let you know when a problem exists.

Oil Is Important

Another preflight area that is not adequately served by the "kick tire, light fire" school is the oil supply. The engines are not only going to be putting out more than normal power in the turbo-boosted climb to those ever-lovin' high altitudes, they will be doing it for a longer period of time and at a relatively low airspeed. Because of this, the powerplants need all the oil specified in the aircraft manual to help dissipate the thermal energy that is the inevitable result of higher power settings. When you push the nose over at altitude, the increase in airspeed and the well-below-zero air whistling by the cylinders will improve the cooling situation, but during the climb, the oil coolers help get rid of a lot of BTU's. Give your engines a break by making sure that the oil level is right where it belongs before you turn a blade. On some installations, the oil supply for the turbo is a separate system, and must be checked—it too is responsible for heat transfer in addition to its lubrication chores.

Take Along Something to Breathe

Check the oxygen gauge for full pressure as you continue the specialized walkaround for a high-altitude flight. You should keep this system filled for a number of reasons, not the least of which is always having oxygen when you need it. How frustrating to have the capability and the smarts to climb above an area of icing or turbulence, only to be forced back down where you don't want to be because you didn't fill the oxygen bottle before takeoff! And when you *do* refill it, be very sure that nothing except *aviator's breathing oxygen* goes into the system. Anything else, even medical oxygen, contains a small amount of water vapor, which has a nasty habit of freezing in the lines, shutting off the flow completely. You may save a couple of dollars a tank buying lower grade oxygen, and lose the whole shootin' match when the system freezes shut.

One parting shot about preflighting the O₂ system: Plug in the passengers' masks and put them where they can be seen so that no one gets a big surprise when you break out the nose hoses on the way up. Some folks just don't take kindly to sticking their faces into a big plastic nose with a balloon on the end, and it's much better to find out who these people are when you're on the ground and able to reason with them. (Trying to settle down a near-panicked passenger in the back seat when your hands are full flying the airplane can be a horrendous experience.) With masks plugged in, open the valve and assure yourself that all the indicators show oxygen flow; you'll want each passenger to check his supply later on at altitude, but now is the time to make absolutely certain everything is right.

Don't Forget the Captain

The extra time spent preflighting the airplane is a complete waste if you neglect the most important system of all—YOU. The nagging cold, the slight headache, can assume monumental proportions when carried to high altitudes—not only are your aches, pains, and bad mood magnified by the environment (in an unpressurized airplane, your body is subject to probably less than half the atmospheric pressure under which it normally functions), but you will find your basic piloting and navigational skills taxed by the increased speed with which things happen. Here's the situation that really develops the "snowball" effect—less than ideal physical and/or psychological condition, coupled with high altitude effects, leads to mistakes and uncertainties, which lead to apprehension and tension, which lead to increased oxygen consumption, and on and on until the worst may happen. If you don't feel up to it, don't make the flight at all.

Given the insidious nature of hypoxia, and the fact that each individual experiences slightly different symptoms, the FAA has made arrangements with a number of military aviation facilities throughout the country to provide altitude training for civilian pilots. In a one-day course, you'll learn more about your high-altitude self than you could learn in ten years of flying. Every one of the physiological problems is fully explained and most of them are demonstrated in a carefully controlled environment. In a sense, you can "practice" getting hypoxia . . . and recognize your personal symptoms so that you'll know what to do should they ever show up in the real world. The altitude chamber courses are well done, extremely interesting, and unlike everything else in this business, inexpensive. Write to the FAA's Aeromedical people in Oklahoma City for a schedule, or get an application from the FAA office nearest you.

Make Those Turbos Work for You

Planning for a high-altitude IFR flight involves more than just picking out a convenient route, eyeballing the distance, and guestimating how long it will take. On relatively short flights, you'll discover an optimum altitude for almost any day (excepting really strong winds, icing, or turbulence), and it will probably be higher than you've been flying! With turbos providing the capability for rapid climbs, you will make money in direct proportion to your altitude, and passengers will be more comfortable in the bargain. It's amazing how people will remember the ten or fifteen minutes in smooth, clear air even though you climbed through lumpy sky for ten minutes to get them there. Common sense dictates that you shouldn't go to 15,000 feet for a fifteen-minute trip, but when you fly high, you'll be more comfortable, safer (because you will be up there where you can *see*), and remarkably close to the elapsed time of the same trip flown at lower altitudes, down in the murk where everybody else is groping along.

On the longer, more critical trips, you want those expensive air pumps to work most effectively for you, so set your sights high. Considerable advantage can be gained even without penetrating the High Altitude route structure (18,000 feet and above), especially when you are headed west. The upper air over the United States moves mostly from west to east, and sometimes at three-digit speeds— so a general rule would be to fly lower westbound, and as high as practical eastbound. It's picking out that westbound altitude that becomes tricky, since even though you may be flying upstream, the increase in true airspeed at altitude could more than make up for the head wind.

You can't go too far wrong using the 2 percent-per-1,000 feet rule of thumb to help make the altitude decision. If your airplane indicates 150 knots at 10,000 feet, you can figure on a *true* airspeed of close to 180 knots—this will hold up as long as the turbos can maintain constant power. The difference becomes quite dramatic at high altitude, where true airspeed may often be half again what the indicator shows!

Of course the price to be paid is the time you spend climbing to altitude at a high power setting and a relatively low airspeed. How far you intend to go becomes important, too—the extra knots generated by the turbos may not be justified by the many-gallons-per-hour pouring through the fuel injectors. Sometimes it becomes a matter of deciding whether to go fast for a short distance, or to give up some speed in exchange for making the trip non-stop. Remember also that turbine-boosted engines don't always have to be run wide open.

Comfort and weather conditions bear heavily on your decision, so there's really only one way to arrive at *the* altitude for an extended trip—get out your computer and weigh performance figures for several altitudes against all the other factors.

High-Altitude Charts

It's not as thrilling as breaking through the sound barrier, but when the snout of the *Turbo*Barnburner pokes through 18,000 feet, you've flown into a new world of regulations. Some major restrictions affect your operations up here, and they should be recognized in the planning phase. For example,. you *must* use the separately-published High-Altitude Enroute Charts (either U.S. or Jeppesen).

A number of differences are apparent when comparing the High-Altitude charts with their below-18,000-foot counterparts; the most striking is that a whole bunch of charts is missing—but you get your money's worth, even though there are only two pieces of paper in the mail at revision time. Because of the tremendous increase in true airspeed at high altitude, fewer checkpoints are needed, and consequently the coverage of the charts is greatly increased. Just think how far you can fly without having to refold a chart! You may also notice right away that the Jet Routes (even the name "airway" changes up here) have legs much longer than low-altitude airways.

Selection of a route in the high-altitude structure is easy—pick out the Jet Route that runs closest to a straight line between here and there, and depend on radar to get you started and stopped. Almost every high-altitude flight gets under way with vectors to a nearby VOR, or until intercepting the desired route. The same situation prevails at the other end, where you will be worked into the approach environment with the all-seeing eyes of radar. Be especially cognizant of Standard Instrument Departures (SIDs), Preferred Routes (which are published separately for high-altitude operations), and Standard Terminal Arrival Routes (STARs) when filing— you're working with the big-leaguers, and should expect to receive the same kind of ATC handling, so be prepared. When you get right down to it (beg your pardon, right *up* to it), route planning for a high-altitude flight is much easier, with fewer checkpoints and more direct legs.

Positive Control Airspace

All the airspace above 18,000 feet MSL over the entire United States is rather special in nature—it's called "Positive Control Airspace," and a better name couldn't have been chosen. ATC has an electronic tag on every flight that operates up there, which tends to keep high-speed airplanes from running into each other, and that's *got* to be good for everybody! In order to exercise this positive control, some very specific restrictions and requirements have been legislated for all who seek the advantages of flight above 18,000 feet.

In the first place, there is *absolutely no VFR allowed*—every flight within PCA must be on an instrument flight plan, with an assigned altitude. The IFR-only requirement also limits the type of pilot and airplane permitted to use the upper air, since you and your flying machine must be IFR rated and equipped. And not just normal IFR equipment either, since PCA standards must be observed: You must have an altitude-reporting transponder; when above FL 240, you need DME; and at all times within PCA you must be able to communicate with ATC on frequencies they assign. For all practical purposes, this means 360-channel capability, because you will frequently be requested to "contact the Center now on one two four point niner five," or some other 50 KHz-spaced number. (Stand by for 25-KHz spacing—*three* numbers after the decimal—it's already in use by some Centers!)

If you insist on flying VFR at high altitude, you can do it legally, but you'll have to go out over the ocean and climb to FL 600, which is the upper limit of Positive Control Airspace.

Supplemental Oxygen

An average person will begin to feel the effects of altitude at about 10,000 feet, which no doubt accounts for the long-standing recommendation for oxygen above that level. Today, you as the pilot (and your co-pilot and flight engineer if the aircraft manual requires them) may not operate an unpressurized airplane between 12,500 and 14,000 feet for more than thirty minutes without supplemental oxygen. Above 14,000 feet you must use oxygen *all* the time. This rule was not devised to *encourage* non-oxygen flights at those levels, but to *permit* them for short periods to get you over weather and high terrain. (The law requires you to provide supplemental O_2 for all occupants when flying above 15,000 feet.)

With turbos, you are on your way to heights at which some help in supplying the breath of life is necessary to function properly. And since you probably don't have an "average" person on board, why not plug into the oxygen system at, or soon after, 10,000? It gives you plenty of time to recheck the system before any physiological damage can be done, and helps acclimate you and your passengers to the environment in which you'll be operating for the next hour or so.

Make sure that everyone on board understands that he must remain on oxygen until you give the word to unmask on descent. Now open the valve and have everybody check and let you know that they are "on" as evidenced by the individual flow indicators. Most people just don't realize how quickly they can join the "blue fingernail set" without oxygen at high altitudes, so make it a practice to check your entire complement at least every fifteen minutes— they'll appreciate your concern. The effects vary with individuals, but here's what can happen at turbo altitudes without oxygen:

Feet	Hours	Effects
8,000–10,000	Over 4	Fatigue, sluggishness
10,000–15,000	2 or less	Fatigue, drowsiness, headache, poor judgment
15,000-18,000	½ or less	False sense of well being, overconfidence, faulty reasoning, narrowing of field of attention, unsteady muscle control, blurring of vision, poor memory. *You may pass out.*
Over 18,000		Above symptoms come faster, loss of muscle control, loss of judgment, loss of memory, loss of ability to think things out, no sense of time, repeated purposeless movements, fits of laughing, crying, or other emotional outbursts.

Small children represent a special liability at high altitudes in an unpressurized airplane, and very wee ones probably shouldn't be exposed at all to oxygen-requiring flight levels. Allowing passengers to sleep while at altitude can hardly be avoided, but make frequent checks of their condition.

It is absolutely mandatory that the smoking lamp be out while oxygen is in use.

Be aware that oil and oxygen make an explosive mixture under certain circumstances . . . even the oils in some cosmetics. Granted, it's a long shot, but you might give some thought to asking the gals on board to wipe off the oil-based face creams and such before they use the nose hose; there have even been instances of nasty facial burns when stick-type preparations intended to relieve chapped lips have burst into flames in the presence of pure oxygen. Why take a chance?

At the first suspicion of *any* kind of oxygen trouble, descend NOW, and do it FAST, so you can trouble-shoot at an altitude where the dangers are minimized. The pilot's well-being is more important than anyone else's, because if YOU get into difficulty, don't look for much help from a planeload of hypoxic passengers.

Flight Levels

Everyone in the upper reaches (18,000 feet MSL and above) must fly at an assigned *pressure altitude*. This means that you will set 29.92 in the window of your altimeter, and leave it there until you're once again under 18,000 feet. You are now *flying* at a certain number of feet above the 29.92 pressure *level* (which on a standard day will be at sea level), and so the vice-president in charge of names put the two together and came up with "Flight Level," the designation for assigned altitudes at and above 18,000 feet—shortened to FL 190, etc.

Altimeter Setting	Lowest Usable Flight Level
29.92 or higher	180
29.91–29.42	185
29.41–28.92	190
28.91–28.42	195
28.41–27.92	200

There are going to be times when the 29.92 level is so low (as around the center of a deep depression or "low" in the atmosphere) that 18,000 or 19,000 or maybe even 20,000 feet above it would sag down into the Low-Altitude Route structure, and would be unusable. When this happens, you will not be assigned a Flight Level unless it is safely above the low-altitude aviators. Part of your clearance when descending from high altitude will be the altimeter setting in the terminal area, and as soon as you go through 18,000 (or the lowest usable flight level), place that setting in the adjustment window, and rejoin your low-altitude brothers.

High-Altitude Weather

When you're flying high, weather avoidance doesn't amount to much, except when going through fronts or the hearts of low-pressure systems. There is the occasional problem of getting through some nasty conditions on the way up, but once you're there, most of the weather that causes trouble for pilots is below you. Having the capability to operate at the higher levels goes a long way toward all-weather flying, but some days there will be heavy icing and severe turbulence at all levels, with solid lines of thunderstorms lying across every route between here and there—these are the days when it's *much* better to "have loved not at all," than "to have loved and lost"!

Icing is not often a problem at altitude except over high mountainous terrain, because clouds that form on high are usually the cirrus type, composed of ice crystals that for the most part just bounce off the airplane. But the turbocharged engine does have one drawback in this situation—the ice crystals sometimes collect in the air intakes, partially closing off the supply, and you may experience a significant drop in manifold pressure. You'll be able to limp along at a reduced speed, but your thinking must change as you plan ahead—start checking the weather at terminals this side of where-you-originally-planned-to-go-Municipal. An alternate air source that can be selected if the intakes ice up completely will help, but you'll pay a price in reduced power. The only way to get rid of the ice is a descent to warmer altitudes, if there are any.

Turbulence associated with thunderstorms is one thing, clear air turbulence (CAT) is something else—the very visible presence of a cumulo-nimbus operating at full throttle should serve to warn you away; but CAT can claw at you invisibly, when you least expect it, and it will be the surprise of your life! Thunderstorms are rather well forecast, and there's no excuse for blundering into one. Clear air turbulence is not so easily pinned down, although the weathermen are getting better at it every day—when CAT is suspected along your route at the altitudes you wish to fly, take a long second look. When you spot thunderbumpers ahead (and from your high-altitude vantage point you can see most of them), ask for a route deviation around them—ATC is almost always willing to go along with you. When it appears that there's no way around, and the tops are out of sight, it's time to do something else—implement "Plan B." (*Always* have a "Plan B.")

The sustained high-power and rapid-climb capability provided by your turbos will stand you in good stead in an icing situation, *if you act promptly.* Two sets of circumstances usually prevail: You may be faced with getting through an icing layer while climbing to clear air or too-cold-to-freeze conditions, or you may find yourself picking up the white stuff unexpectedly in a cruise situation. In either case, the ice-producing layer is often no more than a couple of thousand feet thick (check the forecasts—sometimes there are *many* thousands of feet of icing conditions!), so your best bet is to change altitude, and do it NOW! When climbing through a relatively shallow layer, watch for the first evidence of icing—when you see it, slow down your rate of climb, let the airspeed build up, then haul back and get through it in a hurry. When encountering icing in a cruise situation, use that turbo power to get to a higher altitude as rapidly as you can. (Check *Weather Flying*, Chapter 13, for more detail.) It's unrealistic to dictate a climb in *every* icing situation, but if you go up, at least you'll have some more altitude to work with if things get worse. There are two things that are utterly useless to a pilot: altitude above and runway behind.

Fast Descents

A very large payoff of high-altitude flight comes during the descent, when you take advantage of going downhill. You stored up a lot of potential energy in the airplane by climbing, so when ATC clears you to descend, let 'er run—leave the go handles at cruise power and watch the airspeed build. Almost all turbo installations have a manifold pressure limit that is automatically controlled, so don't worry about overboost; the engines think they're still at sea level, and they love to run under those conditions. Descending at cruise power will more than likely push the airspeed indicator up into the yellow caution arc, which is quite all right unless you encounter something greater than light turbulence—if it feels uncomfortable, slow down to a safe speed. (Easy on the throttles!—prolonged descents at low power settings are bad news for engines. Keep them warm with a reasonable amount of power.)

Now you must do some calculating; groundspeed will likely increase in a high-speed descent, and you must adjust your rate of descent to arrive in the terminal area at an altitude compatible with the approach in use. It's easiest to settle on a rate of descent of 1,000 feet per minute, and let the airspeed stabilize—DME with a groundspeed readout is a big help, but in any event, estimate how fast you are moving over the ground versus your 1,000 feet-per-minute rate, and you'll have a good idea of how things are going to work out. Cruising at FL 200 and anticipating a rate of 1,000 feet per minute, you should request descent perhaps 75 miles from destination (based on a groundspeed of 3.5 miles per minute, and going to a sea-level airport.) If you are at a higher altitude, or picking up a real buster of a tail wind, you may want to start down even sooner—ATC is well acquainted with these problems, and will usually grant your request.

Ear Problems

One thousand feet per minute on the way down is an easily computable number, but sometimes it just won't get you down fast enough. Here's where you must take your passengers' welfare into consideration, because if you plunge downhill much more rapidly than that, you can bet that somebody on the airplane will leave his ears at altitude, and that hurts a lot! Fortunately, the rate of pressure increase in a descent is very gradual down to about 15,000 feet, but below this altitude, ear blocks and malfunctioning sinuses can really become a problem. If you have a limited distance in which to descend, or if tail winds are strong, do the going-downhill-fast act while you're still above 15,000 feet, and you'll be doing yourself and the people with you a big favor. When you find it necessary to limit your rate of descent, let ATC in on the secret. ANYTIME you or a passenger begins to suffer and the various ear-clearing tricks don't work, level off (advising the controller you have an ear problem on board will get you any altitude you want) and let the pressures equalize. If one of your passengers is *really* suffering, climb a few hundred feet, which will usually relieve the pain—then start down slowly, making sure he hollers, swallows, yawns, laughs, or whatever else is required to keep inner and outer ear pressures close together.

Most non-flyers, unaware of the dangers involved, will hide their discomfort behind a shield of pride, and before long the problem may solve itself, with a great deal of pain, and certainly a very black public relations eye for you and aviation in general.

Sinuses can be even worse, and you as the house doctor on the airplane should be very familiar with the Valsalva and other methods of relief, as well as knowing when *not* to use them. (Consult a qualified Aviation Medical Examiner.) Better yet, don't take yourself or anyone else to high altitudes when suffering from colds, hay fever, or other respiratory maladies.

High-Speed Approaches

If all has gone well in the descent, there's no need to slow down for the first stages of an instrument approach; in busy terminal areas, where you're being mixed with other high-speed traffic, Approach Control will usually *request* that you keep up your speed as long as possible, sometimes right up to the Final Approach Fix. No problem at all, if you're on top of the situation, meaning that you have to shift into "approach gear" very early. All the suggestions and good operating practices in Chapter 14, "Getting Ready for an Instrument Approach," apply, *in spades*. You'll undoubtedly be radar-vectored onto the final approach course, and things happen in very rapid succession—remember that you have been *requested* to maintain a high airspeed, and if you are uncomfortable, uneasy, and just don't think you can handle it, turn it down. You may be vectored through a less direct approach, but if it's better for you, don't hesitate to leave the high-speed approaches to them that wants 'em.

20

Handling IFR Emergencies

IN MY DICTIONARY, an emergency is "a sudden, unexpected event or happening; a combination of circumstances calling for swift and decided action" . . . and I think you'll agree that virtually all of the situations aviators consider "emergencies" fit that description. Probably more often than not, a pilot has advance notice of an impending problem, so the "sudden, unexpected" nature of an emergency is not always present; and while remedial action must be considered and well thought out, it shouldn't necessarily be *swift* . . . for the too-rapid movement of a control or switch or lever can often make a bad situation worse.

In the instrument environment, a pilot is subject to the very same potential emergencies as in VFR conditions, plus a couple of situations that are unique to operating in the clouds. The big difference is the *resolution* of the problem, because the IFR airplane must somehow be flown clear of visibility restrictions before it can be safely brought to earth.

The redundancy of flight instrument power (DG and attitude indicator normally driven by air, turn indicator by electricity, or vice versa) makes the likelihood of a *complete* instrument failure rather remote. In the words that follow, we assume that the pilot will always have at least the "partial panel" instruments available to control the airplane and maneuver it as required.

Yet another assumption is necessary for a sensible discussion of IFR emergencies; namely, that an instrument pilot encountering an emergency of any kind while operating in visual conditions will do whatever he can to *remain* visual until the problem is resolved. This philosophy may result in landing somewhere other than the planned destination, but remaining VFR and taking care of the problem sure beats the socks off entering or continuing in IFR conditions and compounding things.

The classification of IFR emergencies is no less difficult than it would be for any other regime of flight, because each type of aircraft has its idiosyncrasies and quirks and unique systems, to say nothing of the very apparent fact that a given situation may be perceived as a life-threatening emergency by one pilot, and a mere inconvenience by another . . . experience and preparation make the difference. However, there are some general groupings of emergency conditions that lend themselves to discussion, to wit:

- Mechanical
- Electrical
- Meteorological
- Powerplant

Before proceeding, be advised that the comments and suggestions offered for the prevention and resolution of these various emergency situations are general in nature; handling of a specific emergency must always be considered in light of the information provided by the aircraft/accessory manufacturer, and the conditions that exist at the time. Doing things "by the book" and in accord with common sense, seems a good practice.

Mechanical Emergencies

The proper operation of major aircraft systems is at issue here, so if your IFR mount is a very simple airplane in that respect, there's not much to go wrong. As speed and power and overall capabilities improve, however, it's likely that there will be more pieces of machinery on board, and that means more potential problems.

Retractable landing gear systems have become less complicated over the years, and the procedures for manual extension (and in some cases, retraction) have followed suit. If nothing else, the instrument pilot who discovers that the wheels will not operate properly is ripe for distraction from his flight-control duties, and so the first thing to do in this case is . . . *nothing*! If you've just lifted off into the clouds and the wheels won't come up, leave everything as is, and when the airplane is configured for the climb (power set, trimmed hands-off, autopilot engaged if that's your pleasure), turn your attention to the problem at hand.

Depending on the system, a fail-to-retract condition could result from a blown circuit breaker, faulty microswitches, hydraulic leak, maladjusted selector switch or lever. Frequently, recycling will solve the problem (you may have discovered this in the routine of daily flying in this airplane) . . . but what if the mechanism should jam in an unlocked condition? Your situation would be sweaty enough in VFR conditions, but why make things worse now that you are in the clouds? In general, if the landing gear fails to retract and the indications show that the wheels are down and locked, *leave them down and locked*, return and land, and take care of the problem on the ground.

On the other end of an instrument flight, a failure of the landing gear to extend creates a different kind of emergency. Now, you should do everything within reason to get the wheels down and locked, but *not while you are also trying to execute an IFR approach procedure!* Most emergency gear-extension systems require the manipulation of switches, valves, levers, etc., and most of them require more time than normal, so you'd be wise to consider breaking off the approach and asking vectors in a wide pattern (or request a holding pattern) while you get the gear down.

It's best to refer to the appropriate checklist for emergency gear extension (even in the simple systems), and if yours is a hydraulic system with inflight access to the reservoir, it's not a bad idea to carry a spare can of fluid . . . even if it's only enough to operate the system one time, it can save a lot of grief.

Gear won't go down, no matter what? Request clearance to a large airport, to take advantage of their emergency facilities, but don't expect a foamed runway . . . that procedure has largely fallen out of favor. The Pilot's Operating Handbook provides the best procedure and configuration for landing with the gear up.

Wing flap malfunctions are rare, but can be troublesome, especially for those airplanes whose size and speed cause them to depend on flaps to operate onto relatively short runways (no-flap landing distance for light airplanes is usually well within available runway length at most IFR airports).

There is little to be done when wing flaps refuse to extend, and sometimes, continued attempts to operate the system may result in flap extension on one side only . . . a situation guaranteed to test the mettle of *any* pilot! Know ahead of time what airspeed is required for a no-flap approach and landing; select a longer runway or another airport if you are really concerned about landing distance. Beware of attempting a circling approach with no flaps; you'll be maneuvering at a higher-than-normal airspeed, tempted to turn a bit tighter, and stall speed can creep up behind you and bite.

While not truly mechanical in nature, a third "system" that occasionally provides anxious moments for instrument pilots is the cabin entrance door. When closed and locked, doors are an integral part of the airplane's structure; but when unlatched, they become troublemakers of the first order.

There's perhaps as much psychological disturbance as anything else—nearly all airplanes will fly, somehow, with a door open—and the predisposition to get the offending door closed *at any cost* has resulted in more than one accident. The flat doors found on high-wing airplanes create little more than a noisy distraction when they "pop" in flight; some can be reclosed with little effort, but don't attempt reclosure *until and unless the airplane is settled down and under complete control.* Even if it can't be reclosed, there's little lost; noisy, to be sure, but you can return, land, close the door and continue . . . this time, making absolutely sure the lock is engaged!

Entrance doors on low-wing airplanes are a different story. Nearly all of them are curved to fit the top contour of the fuselage, which means that when partly open, the curved upper portion is exposed to slipstream. This may well twist the door and make it nearly impossible to close and latch. But that's not the only problem; the entrance door on a low-wing airplane opens into the area of low pressure directly above the wing (that's where the lift comes from), and is therefore *pulled* open in flight. In most cases, the unlatched door will stand open several inches, a balance between the positive pressure of forward motion and the negative pressure of the upper wing. With that relatively huge disturbance in the airstream, the tail surfaces are likely to be buffeted severely, with attendant control problems.

The pressure "stand-off" that holds the door partially open makes it very difficult to close the door; if you have a strong right-seat passenger and care to try, you *may* be able to slow the airplane and accomplish reclosure. But in most cases, it's better to fly at a comfortable speed (tail buffeting may become a factor), and land as soon as practical.

If an entrance door is going to pop open, it will most likely do so at takeoff, when aerodynamic pressures begin to work on it. There's a surprise guaranteed, but if you perceive enough runway ahead to land and stop safely, do so . . . it's much better to fix the problem on the ground than to fight it in the air.

The failure of a vacuum pump produces an emergency situation for most pilots in single-engine airplanes, in that the pilot is probably forced to operate on partial panel for the balance of the flight (see Chapter 4). There's one additional consideration here, and that's for the pilots whose single-engine airplanes are equipped with deicing boots . . . when the lone vacuum pump gives up the ghost, not only certain instruments may be inoperative, but wing and tail deicing is no longer available. That could be serious in most icing environments, and the pilot in this predicament must make *immediate* moves to get out of the ice . . . even faster than the "immediate" we recommend with boots working!

Electrical Emergencies

It may be unrealistic to expect every instrument pilot to be intimately familiar with all the systems on his airplane, but those who understand the basics of electrical power production and distribution have a leg up when a malfunction strikes. Electrical power is indeed the lifeblood of IFR operations; with plenty of electricity, navigation and communication is assured, but lose the electrons, and trouble is guaranteed. The knowledgeable instrument pilot can often spot electrical problems early enough to blunt their effects, and is able to manage the electrical system to his advantage when something goes wrong in flight.

Near the top of the electrical-emergency list would be a complete loss of *normal* electrical power . . . most likely a malfunction within the alternator or generator itself (a sheared shaft, a broken or loose belt, breakdown of regulating circuits, etc.). In any event, whatever airplane systems/accessories are using electrical power at the time will immediately begin drawing from the *emergency* power source, the battery. IFR pilots clearly need to think of the battery as an emergency power source (especially those operating single-engine airplanes), and one which has very limited capacity. The situation in which the alternator/generator has failed, and all electrical units are drawing from the battery, is a situation in which the pilot must take *immediate* steps to commence load-shedding and make plans to get on the ground ASAP.

Given the relatively small reservoir of electrical power represented by the battery, a power-source failure should be treated as if there were no way to get the dead alternator/generator back on the line; shut off everything you don't absolutely need—"load shedding"—and consider nearby airports with acceptable weather conditions, in case you can't restore normal system operation. *Then* go to the Pilot's Operating Handbook and meticulously follow the checklist procedure for alternator/generator restart; the sequence is important to keep from making a bad situation worse.

Since most of today's IFR airplanes are equipped with alternators, be aware that if there is no voltage in the system (i.e., alternator inoperative, battery charge depleted), *you will not be able to restart the alternator!* It makes sense, therefore, to include a battery-health check in your preflight routine for an IFR flight, and keep tabs on it throughout the trip.

Once electrical power is restored, it's a good idea to bring units back on line one at a time, checking the loadmeter as each is activated. *Something* caused the alternator/generator to kick off, and it would be very helpful to know if a specific electrical appliance is at the heart of the problem.

Twin engine airplanes come equipped with more elaborate emergency procedures to enable you to cope effectively with electrical-power problems; get familiar with the book, get it out of the glove box and use it religiously when the time comes.

Circuit breakers make life easier for the instrument pilot, because they readily identify and isolate electrical faults. An open ("popped") circuit breaker represents an electrical emergency only when it is ignored or misused; in the former case, by not including the CB panels in your regular scan, you might miss the loss of a critical piece of IFR equipment until the damage is done (this is particularly true with regard to electrically powered flight instruments), and in the latter case, the pilot who resets a circuit breaker more than once (or worse, physically holds it in) is bypassing the protection and is asking for trouble.

In general, it's good practice to (a) reset a popped CB *one time only*, and then only if it's protecting a system or unit essential to the continuation of the flight; (b) NEVER hold a circuit breaker to keep it from popping; that's the same as putting a penny in the fuse box in your house . . . almost guaranteed to cause more, bigger problems sooner or later; (c) some electrical systems are arranged so that certain CBs will blow only when there's a massive short . . . know which ones (if any) on your airplane fall into this category and should therefore *never* be reset.

When an electrical problem first rears its ugly head during an IFR flight, there's no assurance that it won't go "all the way," and leave you with impaired nav/comm capability. Let the controllers know early on that you have a problem, and that if you "disappear" from their headsets, you are going to continue your flight as cleared, or will divert to Airport B, or whatever the situation demands. Once again, common sense comes to the fore, but your options are more numerous when you've advised ATC of your problem and intentions.

Let's imagine that the electrical gremlins have just about done you in; you're in the clouds, far from destination, can't get out of the weather without an approach to minimums, and operating on battery power alone. Even when you're down to what seems to be the last straw, there's a lot you can do to improve your position and save the day.

First, turn off absolutely everything you don't need to survive, including lights (you *didn't* forget a flashlight with fresh batteries?!), heater, boost pumps, ventilation fan, and all radios. Yes, *all radios*. Of course, let ATC know that you are going off the air, then shut everything down, hold your heading, and turn on one VOR every five minutes or so to check your progress; save that precious electricity for the approach, when you'll need one navaid full-time.

Second, remember that transmitting requires considerably more power than receiving, so make only those calls that are absolutely necessary, and then, brutally short. If there's ever a time when clicking the mike for acknowledgment is okay, it's now . . . the controllers will understand.

Third, don't operate any electrically powered airplane systems in the normal mode if they can be operated manually. *Every* retractable has an emergency gear extension system that uses no electricity, and you can land without wing flaps if need be. At night, save the landing lights until you know that you are right on top of the runway, then turn them on and hope for the best—any light at all will be helpful at this point.

In that apparently hopeless situation of complete electrical power loss (we're talking *complete* here; no alternator/generator, no battery . . . nuthin'!), you've little choice but to head for VFR weather conditions, and hope that you have enough fuel to get there. Says a lot for good preflight planning, doesn't it!

Finally, whatever the situation, don't panic! Remember that the airplane will continue to fly quite nicely without electrical power; it's up to you to stay in control and *keep flying*, right up to the end. These three words are the most important in *any* aviation emergency . . . FLY THE AIRPLANE!

Earlier in this chapter, we mentioned the difference that experience and preparation can make in the perception of an "emergency" by various pilots. Here's a tale of woe that illustrates what can happen when an electrical *un*-emergency is allowed to take charge of a pilot's judgment and actions.

At 300 and 3, the weather was courting ILS minimums and the forecast was that it would get worse as the Comanche taxied for takeoff. Its 33-year-old pilot had accumulated 750 hours of flying time, including 76 hours of actual instruments and 47 hours in a simulator, and was now embarking on his first IFR trip in the just-bought Comanche. His instrument proficiency apparently left something to be desired, however, because during an IFR training flight six months earlier, the CFII would not endorse an instrument competency check; ". . . he was rusty on instruments, had trouble intercepting radials, and had difficulty on approaches."

The Comanche had an old horizontal-card DG, which "baffled" the pilot, according to the airplane salesman, and like many airplanes of that era, the Comanche was equipped with a generator and ammeter. The pilot had experienced a loss of electrical power on the way into Atlanta two days before, and the landing gear had to be lowered manually. Power was restored when the pilot "fiddled" with the circuit breakers; a mechanic found a malfunctioning voltage regulator, fixed it, and signed off the airplane.

Let's take stock at this point; unfamiliar airplane, questionable electrical system, at least one "baffling" primary flight instrument, very questionable IFR currency and proficiency, weather going downhill fast, but very good weather within 50 miles or so. Nevertheless, the pilot received his clearance and roared off into the clouds.

Only 12 minutes after departure, he radioed, "We'd like to go back to the airport; we're having a little, uh, alternator or generator trouble." He was immediately cleared direct to a nearby VOR in preparation for the ILS approach.

Throughout the vectoring that followed, the Comanche pilot had considerable difficulty in communicating; at one point, he said "We're alright, we're just getting a drain on our batteries; we'd like direct as possible back to the airport." When he failed to respond to four subsequent heading instructions to turn him onto the localizer course, the airplane had gotten to a point very close to the outer marker, and at an angle that made a normal intercept impossible. The controller advised of the proximity and angle, and asked if the pilot would like to "come out and try another shot at it?" "We'd like to try to shoot it," said the pilot, and those were his last words . . . the airplane struck the ground in a steep descent within one mile of the outer marker.

Investigation showed that the gyro instruments were operating at the time of impact, and that transponder signals were being received and recorded throughout the flight. That information, plus the constant strength and quality of the pilot's transmissions, leads to the conclusion that there was no electrical problem on board the Comanche.

But the pilot had recently experienced trouble with the unfamiliar electrical system, had just gotten the airplane out of the shop, and apparently convinced himself that the problem lay in the generator (or alternator . . . he wasn't sure which). With a perfectly flyable airplane, why didn't he continue eastbound toward an area of outstanding VFR weather instead of turning back into rapidly deteriorating conditions? Why, when advised of a localizer-intercept situation that would tax the skills of a pro, didn't he execute a missed-approach with his perfectly flyable airplane, and go somewhere else to land?

We don't have the benefit of answers to those questions . . . but this is a classic tale of inexperience, lack of preparation, and *failure to FLY THE AIRPLANE* in an emergency situation. If you *think* you have an emergency, you may have just manufactured one.

Lessons to be learned? Know your airplane's systems, don't take a completely strange airplane into IFR conditions, know where *better* weather exists and go there when you need to escape, and above all, when the going gets rough, FLY THE AIRPLANE!

Meteorological Emergencies

If you use your IFR capability on a regular basis, you will surely encounter some unpleasant weather during your instrument-flying career. Not just low ceilings and visibilities (they're considered routine, and the conditions for which you're trained) but *turbulence* and *structural icing* at a hazardous level. Of course, individual perceptions vary, and no matter how bad you thought it might have been, don't expect to win the "hairiest flying story" contest at the airport . . . someone will always be ready to top you

In the real world, it doesn't matter one iota where The Weather Encounter ranks; you were there, and you were concerned, and the situation required immediate attention to keep it from getting worse . . . that's an emergency in anybody's book.

The most likely place to encounter worrisome turbulence is in (God forbid!) or near an active thunderstorm; but there are other turbulence-producers that deserve just as much attention from the instrument pilot. For example, you should expect turbulence close to the ground whenever surface winds are blowing hard . . . and it will sometimes extend upward for several thousand feet, depending on the strength of the wind, roughness of the terrain, and stability of the air mass. A mountain wave condition is virtually guaranteed to produce tooth-rattling turbulence somewhere in its path. You should also learn to look for large changes in air temperature, which often signal significant wind shear activity and large amounts of turbulence.

When you have been briefed about turbulence, or have figured out for yourself that it's probably out there, prepare yourself and the airplane to handle it. Make sure that there is nothing in the cabin that can move around, because it *will*; a thermos bottle or overnight case can become an unguided missile in heavy turbulence. Make sure that you and the other occupants are really tied down; there's at least one case on record of a turbulence encounter in which a light plane pilot hit the top of his cabin so hard that a concussion resulted . . . he was barely able to get the plane safely onto the ground. Extra-tight seat belts and shoulder harnesses are a *must*.

The proper airspeed is very important; fly too fast, and you risk structural damage (perhaps failure) from gust-induced overloads, while flying too slowly may result in a gust-induced stall . . . neither is a happy situation on an IFR flight. Your Pilot's Operating Handbook provides a "Maneuvering Speed" or range of speeds for turbulence operations, but that's not enough; the airspeed indicator will probably be useless, so you must know the power setting and pitch attitude that will produce the desired speed through the air.

A good pilot always works harder in turbulence (even the garden variety) to keep his airplane on a smooth, even keel and provide the best possible ride for his passengers; but as the rides gets rougher, control inputs should soften a bit, and begin to serve more as dampers, which means a lenient but firm hand on the controls. Don't retrim, and don't make big power changes when you get into a sustained up- or down-draft; you need to be ready for a reversal of the condition. If your altitude begins to vary more than several hundred feet, let the controller know, and he'll adjust other traffic as necessary.

When the going gets so rough that you are truly concerned about maintaining control of the aircraft, you must work extra hard to prevent an upset. In addition to the obvious problems created by tumbling the gyros, and the *monumental* spatial disorientation that will surely result, you must be prepared to deal with a gross over-speed condition if the airplane is thrown beyond its beam ends, and winds up plummeting earthward under power. If yours is a fixed-gear machine, pull off the power *right away*, and execute your best partial-panel critical-attitude recovery.

The pilot of a retractable may have an advantage here; the gear can be lowered ahead of time, and may provide enough additional drag to keep the airplane from building up airspeed at such a rapid rate. Don't be concerned about the maximum gear-lowering speed at a time like this; if you are screaming earthward and nothing else seems to help, throw out the gear, and let the wheel-well doors fend for themselves!

When you've got the time (and your voice has returned!), let ATC know of your plight, and if you feel that a change of altitude or course will be helpful, request—nay, *demand* it. You'll find that controllers have plenty of respect for such requests when the reasons are made known. *Make the reasons known on the first call.*

(And don't forget to make a detailed PIREP when it's all over . . . you don't want anyone else to go through that, do you?)

An icing emergency will probably develop in a more benign manner; a few crystals form on the leading edges, then it's all white out there, and first thing you know the airspeed has dropped ten knots. A little more power, then a little more nose-up to maintain altitude, then more power . . . and when you're staggering through the air on the edge of a stall at full power, you're in deep trouble.

This is the sort of thing that feeds on itself. From just the standpoint of aerodynamic effects, each ice crystal creates drag, which requires a higher angle of attack, which exposes more surface to the airflow, which causes more icing, which decreases airspeed, and on and on and on. All the while, the propeller blades have been accumulating ice as well, reducing thrust; if the engine air intakes are restricted because of ice, the problem is multiplied. Sooner or later, your airplane will literally be unable to fly!

"Not to worry," you say, "my airplane is fully equipped for flight in known icing conditions. Paid a *bundle* for all that gear." Good investment, and it's great insurance, but don't count on it to bail you out of a bad icing situation. Somewhere out there is a weather condition that can produce more icing than all that equipment can handle. Exposure is usually the culprit, when low ceilings and cold, wet clouds force you to stay in the icing environment longer than you'd like. Deicing boots do a good job, but after a while the ice may begin to build up *behind* them, forming sharp ridges which spoil lift to a fare thee well. And of course as airspeed bleeds away and pitch attitude must increase to maintain altitude, ice begins to form on unprotected surfaces . . . drag doesn't care where it roosts.

Through all of this, you should be concerned about letting ATC know of your plight, and surely, they'll grant your request for another altitude; but do you have icing protection on your antennas? Communication systems are particularly vulnerable to severe icing encounters, since ice accumulates more readily on small-diameter objects such as wire antennas.

There is a sure way to beat the structural ice monster, but unfortunately most light airplanes aren't so equipped . . . we're talking about raw, unadulterated *power*. Power to let you climb above the icing level, or at least to an altitude where the accretion rate is less. Power to speed you out of the icing, reducing the exposure. Power to keep the angle of attack low and prevent ice from forming on unprotected airplane surfaces. If you have the power, *use it* when serious icing threatens; know where the most likely ice-free altitudes are, and go there, ASAP.

No deicing equipment, no surplus of power? You're not going to like this, but you shouldn't be there in the first place in such an airplane. In case you *do* wind up in the ice box, there are still some things you can do to make the most of a bad situation:

1. Let ATC know right away that you are encountering icing and are not equipped to handle it; confession is good for the soul, and besides, it lets the controllers begin planning ahead to accommodate you.
2. Request/demand a lower/higher altitude when you first sense trouble. It's usually better to climb, but that's not a panacea . . . your preflight briefing should have alerted you to temperatures aloft, cloud tops, etc., so that you can make a rational decision.
3. Maintain airspeed as high as practical in level flight to reduce "underbody" icing. If you decide to climb, do so with dispatch. If you decide to descend, pull out the stopper . . . what have you to lose?
4. Watch engine performance closely. Iced air intakes will shut down small engines, and will trigger the automatic alternate air systems on the larger recips . . . either way, a power loss is inevitable. If carburetor heat is required to keep the engine running, there's *another* power thief.
5. Change power frequently, rapidly and through a wide range in order to flex the prop blades and shed most of the ice they've collected. The props are your lifeline, so treat them well.
6. Choose the nearest suitable airport (in terms of facilities and weather) and request/demand clearance to be vectored there

now. The word "icing" will get the full attention of any controller in the business; tell him you're falling out of the sky, and you can have anything you need.

7. Plan ahead so that you can execute the approach procedure in the shortest possible time. Request vectors to the final approach course to save time, and advise each successive controller of your problem. Don't forget that when you *do* break out, you may not actually break out . . . the windshield will also be covered with ice; that's what side windows and credit cards are for.

8. Don't maneuver any more than absolutely necessary once the runway is in sight, and don't extend flaps for landing. An airplane coated with ice is an experimental vehicle, ready to stall/roll/sink/snap . . . you're working with an unknown quantity at this point. If it flies level, fly it onto the runway and be happy you're home.

Powerplant Emergencies

Do you recall your most recent airplane engine failure? That question can be answered emphatically by some (that unfortunate, precious few who have actually suffered such a calamity), but for nearly all of us, the reliability of today's powerplants is very much taken for granted. Otherwise, we'd not be willing to risk all on an IFR flight in a single-engine airplane.

The odds improve somewhat with a twin, if for no other reason than the second engine provides a spare source of electrical power for the nav/comm systems to complete the flight. (There will always be pilots who rail against the twin as an unnecessarily complicated machine with a horrible engine-out safety record; but training and preparation can answer the critics.)

In any event, two cases present themselves when considering IFR powerplant emergencies; *complete* engine failure, and *partial* loss of power. Single- and multi-engine procedures differ significantly, so let's take them one at a time.

The instrument pilot in clouds in a single-engine airplane has hung his hat on the continued operation of that powerplant; it not only generates the thrust to keep him airborne, but power for all of the navigation, communication, and flight instruments. A complete engine failure requires decisive, proper action, because the options are so limited.

When the only thrust-producer on board quits, your first concern *must* be to maintain airspeed. If you haven't burned the best glide speed number deep into your brain, do so right now . . . it's a life-saver. Each knot either side of the proper speed does nothing but increase the sink rate, and that will cost you precious time and altitude. Most singles, especially the high-performance models, cruise at airspeeds well above best glide speed, so if you have presence of mind, pull up the nose and *zoom* . . . trade some of that airspeed for altitude; you'll be grateful for every extra foot when you get to the bottom of the inevitable descent.

Airplanes with constant-speed props can be shifted into "overdrive" by moving the prop control to the low RPM position; in this condition, drag is reduced significantly and glide distance (or time in the air, if you choose) is increased. Time is important for developing and implementing options on the way down.

Get out a MAYDAY as soon as you're squared away, so that ATC can send the St. Bernards to the right spot, to say nothing of their ability to point out nearby airports, provide assistance with vectors, and so forth. In most such cases, you're very much on your own because of the severely limited performance of your airplane-turned-glider, but give the controllers a chance to help.

Preservation of battery power is academic at this point . . . you'll be on the ground—one way or another—long before the battery plays out. But if your ELT is wired into the airplane system, you might give some thought to shutting down electrical appliances to save as much energy as possible, especially if you have invested in an ELT with voice-transmission capabilities.

Where to glide will have to be determined on almost a minute-by-minute basis, because the "reach-ability" of airports changes constantly as you move along. It's always best to head for an airport, give it the old college try . . . you *might* make it, and if nothing else, you'll be flying in a straight line between here and there, making the search that much easier. It certainly makes sense to avoid high ground, which underscores the value of knowing the terrain over which you're operating.

Unless the weather beneath is absolutely zero-zero, you'll break out of the clouds sooner or later, and the situation has instantly reverted to a plain vanilla forced landing exercise. You haven't practiced these procedures for years? Take time to retune your forced-landing skills. (A single-engine pilot is *never* good enough at forced landings!) If the weather underneath is so bad that you must accept whatever landing site appears at the last minute, you might consider not flying IFR in such conditions (what if downtown Burbank appears at the last minute?!).

A partial power loss creates a completely different set of circumstances for the single-engine instrument pilot. Now, there's at least the hope of continuing along the way, limping to be sure, but not committed to a forced landing. You should occasionally practice flying under the hood at drastically reduced power settings, to simulate a partial power situation; you may be pleasantly surprised to find that you can remain aloft at ridiculously low airspeeds. Even if you have to settle for a slow descent, you've bought some time instead of the farm.

Make your controller aware of your plight, and then begin to trouble-shoot. Each airplane, each engine, each atmospheric condition is a bit different, and you may have to run through a lengthy litany of checks on boost pumps, fuel selectors, carb heat, throttle settings, whatever. Keep in mind that an airplane engine seldom fails without warning; the smart pilot knows what the engine gauges tell him, and includes them in his regular, frequent scan of the panel.

Multi-engine pilots certainly have the powerplant-failure odds working for them, but the price for all that capability is the additional training and skill required to keep the machine flying properly with one engine shut down. In addition to a primary concern for the proper airspeed (not less than Vyse), the twin pilot must maintain heading, get the offending engine secured, and make his plans for an approach at a nearby airport. Whenever you suffer the loss of an engine—VFR or IFR—consider yourself in an emergency situation, and *get the airplane on the ground as soon as practical.* Trying to stretch the flight to the home base (where repairs are less expensive) or the original destination (where the passengers need to be) has brought multi-engine pilots to grief more than once.

Safe engine-out IFR operations consist primarily of proper management of the airplane and its systems. You'll need to maintain a zero-sideslip attitude to get optimum performance, and that will require trimming in all axes; your attention will wander from constant control pressures, and you'll wind up fighting the airplane. Let the trim do its work.

It's good practice to shut down non-essential electrical units to reduce the load on the operating alternator/generator; check the POH for advice and guidance. Fuel management should not be a problem, unless this unpleasantness has taken place in a remote area, and you'll need some of the fuel on the dead-engine side to get out of trouble. Study and practice the crossfeed procedure well ahead of time, and *use a checklist* when you begin changing selectors and crossfeed valves; it will get mighty quiet if you make the wrong moves.

An engine-out instrument approach should be flown just like a normal one, at least in terms of airspeeds, procedure, etc. Of course, you'll want to use every opportunity to cut out excessive maneuvering, and hold up on gear extension until you are sure you can land. A single-engine go-around is hazardous at best, so choose a destination with landable weather . . . don't compound your problem.

Remember, with an engine out, airspeed is the key to your survival; *never less than Vyse until landing is assured* is a good rule of thumb. In cruise, you may have to settle for a slow rate of descent at Vyse, but it's likely that at some lower altitude, the wings will develop enough lift to maintain level flight . . . now you can reduce power a bit and save the remaining engine.

Following an unsuccessful attempt to complete the approach at his planned destination in northern Florida, the pilot of a chartered Beech E-18 elected to deliver his passengers to Gainesville. That was a good choice; with a ceiling of 400 feet and a mile and a half visibility in fog, a successful approach was all but guaranteed, the passengers could rent a car and still keep their schedule. There was an atmosphere of "hurry-up," however, as the pilot approached the outer compass locator from the northwest at a high rate of speed, cleared for the ILS for Runway 28.

Rather than proceed outbound far enough to set up a stabilized approach, this pilot—a highly experienced, retired military aviator—elected to short-cut the procedure with a modified 90-270 as soon as he crossed the marker. Predictably, the high speed turn carried the airplane well beyond the localizer course. A descent was begun on the inbound heading, even though the radar plots showed that the airplane was never established on the localizer course.

Levelling off several hundred feet above Decision Height, the pilot continued past the airport, well north of the localizer, out of sight of the runway, and still in the clouds; he reported "outer marker inbound" when the airplane was actually passing the middle marker.

And then, when the pilot decided to execute the missed approach (his best decision of the day), the trap closed. Within seconds of the "missed approach" call, tower controllers heard "I've lost an engine." After several unanswered calls from the tower, the pilot indicated that he was still there, but that his troubles were far from over . . . he couldn't get the prop feathered.

A Beech E-18 (that's one of the old-timers, with round engines up front, and the little wheel in the back) is no skyrocket on one engine in the best of circumstances; toss in a windmilling prop, and this airplane isn't likely to make *any* vertical moves.

The post-accident radar plot showed the airplane continuing westbound, at an altitude of not more than 600–700 feet above the ground (still in the clouds, of course), and finally, some seven miles west of the airport, the pilot apparently lost control; he probably encountered V_{mc} and V_{stall} at the same time. The airplane commenced a rolling, diving turn to the right, and was ripped apart by the guy wires of a large television tower. No survivors.

This was clearly a powerplant emergency, made almost irrecoverable by a propeller system that failed completely when it was needed most. The pilot seemed a victim of fate, but careful investigation turned up some intriguing facts. A filter element was completely missing from the right engine fuel system, perhaps the initial link in the engine-failure sequence. When the right engine was opened up, an uncommon amount of sludge and dirt was found in the oil screens . . . the same oil system that provides pressure for prop feathering. There had been a number of other squawks on this airplane in recent weeks regarding various mechanical problems, squawks that had not been corrected.

Finally, the autopilot was known to be inoperative . . . not that it would have saved the day, but this was a Part 135 operation, which requires either a functioning autopilot or a flesh-and-blood copilot. Could a little bit of help in that harried cockpit have made the difference when things came right down to the wire?

The moral of this story is simple and direct; when you *know* that the airplane you're about to take into instrument conditions is in less than top shape *in all respects*, you (and your passengers, through you) are assuming a terrible risk. There's always a better way . . . get a substitute aircraft, wait until the weather gets decent enough to accommodate the risk, or insist that the airplane be repaired before you go.

And since this pilot's original destination was illegal under FAR Part 135 (no weather-reporting service, weather below minimums), it wouldn't have hurt a bit to go by the rules . . . and not go at all.

21

Proficiency Exercises

IN 1974, the FAA wrote the Biennial Flight Review into the regulations, thereby requiring all pilots to demonstrate their flight proficiency at least every two years. (Air carriers and the military have had such programs for years to check the skill levels developed in intensive training and practiced in day-to-day flying.) But a lot of rust and bad habits can form in two years, and often the only time general aviation pilots find out that they are not quite as sharp as they ought to be is when they get into a bind. In most cases, nobody else knows about it, but on occasion the headlines proclaim the lack of proficiency. When you get right down to cases, is your neck less valuable in your own airplane than when you are a passenger on an airliner? You place complete faith in the man with four stripes on his sleeve because you know he must maintain a high level of competence; there's no reason why you should not demand the same of yourself when *your* hands are on the controls.

Flying, particularly instrument flying, is an art—a sophisticated skill—and unless you fly IFR regularly and frequently, you *know* that you must practice that skill to be as good as you want to be. An occasional IFR cross-country won't do the job, because a typical "real world" flight consists of following radar vectors and airways until you get into the terminal area, then some more radar vectors to the final approach course, and relatively simple navigation to the runway. When the chips are down and you are required to fly the approach all by yourself, with procedure turns, climbs, and descents to predetermined altitudes and headings, missed approaches, and no-radar navigation, your rusty techniques don't do you much good. There's only one way to be sure, to be safe, to be sharp, and that's a regular program of practice—one that will lead to precise control of the airplane almost as an afterthought, with most of your attention and thought processes devoted to staying ahead of the situation. If you're a beginner, the exercises in this chapter will help get you that way, and if you're an experienced IFR pilot, they will help keep you that way. Whether you need to use all or a selected portion of these maneuvers will depend on your particular needs, your skill level, and how often you fly on the gauges. Are you the type who likes to accept a challenge? Run through the entire series next time you're under the hood—you'll soon know whether or not you need the practice.

Exercise #1: Straight and Level Flight

It's more difficult to keep all the needles, pointers, and numbers standing still than it is to make them move in the proper direction at the proper rate. Flying straight and level, with no changes in heading or altitude or airspeed, is a great deal harder than turning, climbing, or descending, but it's not impossible, so set yourself up in level flight and adjust the little airplane on the attitude indicator so that it rests exactly on the horizon—that's your best reference for what's happening, or what's about to happen. As long as you keep the pitch attitude where it belongs, and the wings level (the ball in the turn-and-bank is assumed to be centered all the time), you will maintain straight and level flight. The altimeter will indicate immediately any climb or descent, and the directional gyro will keep you honest in the heading department. The very instant you detect any change on either of these instruments, apply corrective pressure to stop the movement, then additional pressure to return things to their proper places. The procedure is very simple, and should become an unconscious, three-step method to be used in all your instrument flying. First, cross-check the instruments (all of them, as rapidly as possible but with emphasis on the attitude indicator); then, interpret the indications so that you can decide what to do about it; third, apply control pressures to control the situation.

Straight and level flight is difficult because your task is to keep things from happening, and satisfying because it will develop a mental discipline that will carry through to other maneuvers—if you can do a good job of straight and level flight, you're well on the way to precision instrument flying. Stay at it until you can keep the needles steady, narrowing your tolerance as you progress.

Exercise #2: Standard Rate Turns

Starting from straight and level flight on a cardinal heading, practice turning at the standard rate of 3 degrees per second. The secret of smooth, accurate turns is PRESSURE; all that you should have on your mind is applying enough aileron pressure to make the miniature airplane begin to bank. A smooth, slow increase in bank attitude is what you're looking for—as long as you maintain the pressure, the airplane will continue to bank, so keep pressing until the turn needle indicates a standard rate turn. (You should know the angle of bank required for a standard rate turn at two airspeeds— cruise and approach. There's an easy rule of thumb that you can apply: Divide the *true* airspeed in knots by ten and add five. This number is the bank angle for a 3-degree/second turn. For example, cruising at 130 knots true airspeed, bank 18 degrees for a standard rate turn.) At this point, relax the bank pressure, notice the amount of bank on the attitude indicator, and make small corrections as necessary to keep it right there. As instrument indications begin to change, cross-checking becomes vitally important—you know that banking the airplane changes the distribution of lift produced by the wings, so as soon as the altimeter moves even the tiniest bit, apply a tad of back pressure to stop it.

The heading indicator should be consulted during the turn, but only with a glance, since your objective is to maintain the bank angle that will produce a standard rate turn. Don't forget about the heading completely, because you want to roll out on a certain number. You may want to experiment with this a bit, but for starters, begin the roll-out when the heading indicator passes through a number that is one-half of the number of degrees of bank from the desired heading. If your standard rate requires 20 degrees of bank, start your roll-out pressure when you are 10 degrees from the heading you want. Use the same, slow, deliberate process that got you into the turn, remembering to remove any back pressure you needed to hold altitude—as the wings return to level, the lift you redistributed in the turn will show up as a tendency to climb. A rapid, complete cross-check will help you stop the altimeter before it moves very far. As soon as the turn needle lines up with its center index, you've stopped turning, and you should go straight back to the old straight-and-level bit. If you've done it properly, you will run out of bank at the same time the heading indicator comes to rest on the sought-for number. Remember that you are maintaining constant pressure to reduce the bank attitude, which means a constantly reducing rate of turn. After a few practice turns, you should know just how much lead to use to make everything come out even. Most pilots have a strong tendency to roll out of a turn considerably faster than they roll in, so you may have to force yourself to slow down. Slow, smooth application of pressure to effect the desired change in attitude is the secret. You'll soon be making turns that will not even be noticed by your passengers when there are no outside references—this is the target you should set for yourself.

Exercise #3: Steep Turns

A safe limit in actual IFR conditions is 30 degrees of bank, but there's nothing like the ability to handle your airplane in a steep turn to build your confidence. Start your practice with enough bank to push the turn needle a little past the standard rate mark, and as your skill builds, keep it going until you can fly around confidently and smoothly in a 45-degree bank, rolling out right on the headings you desire.

There are a couple of things to watch for. Roll into the turn at a slow, deliberate rate, and as the bank angle progresses, pay more attention to the altimeter—you are changing the lift situation rapidly as the wings get farther and farther from the horizontal. A steep turn requires a great deal of back pressure, and it's not a bad idea to roll in some trim to help you maintain altitude. Your lead on the rollout headings will have to increase, too, to compensate for the faster rate of turn. When rollout time comes, use the same slow, deliberate pressure that got you into the turn. Don't forget all that back pressure and elevator trim, either.

Exercise #4: Constant Airspeed Climbs and Descents

Before you can start this one, you'll have to go back to the drawing board to discover the attitude that will produce the best rate-of-climb speed. When you have it nailed down, make a mental note of the picture you see on the attitude indicator—within the limits of available power, you can rest assured that when you apply climb power and rotate the little airplane to that predetermined position, the same airspeed will result. Next, set up an attitude and power setting for practice descents—since this is just an exercise, not an approach situation, leave gear and flaps up, reduce power to just above idle, and play with the pitch attitude until you are descending at 500 to 1,000 feet per minute at the same airspeed used for climbing. Once you've established this, remember the attitude and power setting.

Now you're ready to go to work. From straight and level flight at normal cruise, simultaneously increase the attitude to the predetermined position and smoothly add power to the climb setting. Don't worry about airspeed, it will take care of itself; but you *will* have to increase the speed of your cross-check to keep the heading indicator from wandering off to the left. Feed in whatever rudder pressure is required to maintain your original heading. Sail right on up for 1,000 feet; don't change a thing until you are within 50–100 feet of the desired altitude, when you should SMOOTHLY press the wheel forward until the little airplane rests on the horizon bar, and hold it there, rudder pressure controlling the heading. As the airspeed builds up to cruise once again, reduce power to normal and that's all there is to it! The higher the climb performance, the more you will have to lead the level-off. A rule of thumb is to lead by an amount that represents 10 percent of the climb rate—that's 50 feet when climbing at 500 feet per minute, 100 feet when the climb rate is 1,000 fpm, and so on. As soon as the altimeter hands stop where you want them, they become your primary source of pitch information.

The downhill technique is only slightly different, but of course everything works in reverse. From normal cruise, reduce power to the descent setting you worked out earlier, and hold the little airplane on the horizon bar until the airspeed approaches the proper number for descent. You'll notice a need for left rudder pressure to keep the heading constant, and as your cross-check shows the gyro numbers creeping off the mark, press with the appropriate foot. When the airplane is slowed to the speed you want, SMOOTHLY press the nose down to the attitude you set up in your test, and you're on your way. Descend 1,000 feet, but before you get to the bottom, consider the effect of both gravity and inertia resisting your attempts to level off—increase your lead by 50 feet, at which time you should begin a slow addition of power and a SMOOTH increase in pitch attitude to bring the little airplane to rest on the horizon. As in the climb, you'll have to experiment a bit to find the proper lead for your airplane, the airspeed you're working with, and your personal technique. Coordination and SMOOTH PRESSURE are the keys.

Exercise #5: Constant Rate Descents

Descending at a constant, controlled rate is useful when you must reach an MDA within a certain distance from the Final Approach Fix. The objective is to set up the descent airspeed, then control the *rate* of altitude change with power. A reasonable figure for most light aircraft on most approaches is 500 feet per minute, but a particular situation may call for a higher or lower rate of descent. Make the power changes small, keep the little airplane steady in the descent attitude, and remember how much manifold pressure or how many RPMs are required. Go down a thousand feet, and accomplish a normal level-off.

You may have noticed that 1 inch of manifold pressure or a 100-RPM change produced roughly a 100-feet-per-minute rate change in both situations. If it's more or less for your airplane, remember the figure—it will smooth out your glide slope corrections later. This is also a good time to calibrate the vertical-speed indicator, by checking the altimeter readings at the beginning and end of a fixed time period, and you'll have at least a rough idea of how much your VSI is out of calibration, if at all.

Exercise # 6: The Vertical S

This is a coordination-builder, and requires constantly changing thought patterns; you've got to start planning ahead. Like flying into a funnel without touching the sides, the Vertical S gets more demanding as you proceed. It starts with a 500-foot altitude change, next time it's only 400 feet, then down to 300, and finally 200. You'll hardly have time to make the attitude and power changes for a 100-foot dip, so be satisfied when you can go through four successive ups and downs.

Start from normal cruise and descend 500 feet at constant airspeed. When level-off time rolls around, DON'T! Keep the nose coming right on up to the climb attitude while you're adding climb power. The objective is to touch the bottom altitude and enter a climb without any change in airspeed. Talk about coordination!—this will really try your patience until you discover the right combination of altitude lead, rate of pitch and power change, and a soft touch on the rudders. During the transition from descent to climb, everything imaginable is undergoing change.

Climb back to your original altitude, *start* the level-off at the normal lead point, but *don't level off*—instead, press right over into a constant airspeed descent. You're trying to just barely brush the top altitude before starting down again. From here on, it's simply a repetition of what has gone before, but each time you bottom out, chop off 100 feet.

Exercise # 7: The Vertical S-1

If you happen to be a roller-coaster nut, and dream of the big day when you get to ride the world's wildest, one that not only goes up and down, but changes its direction of turn every time, dream no more! Your wishes have come true in the Vertical S-1, and the only disappointment will be that you won't get to see what's going on; you'll be inside, under the hood, making it happen. This is the

FIGURE 44   The Vertical S.

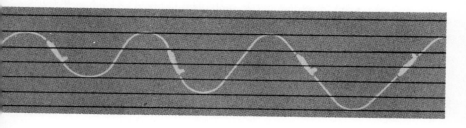

last "challenge" maneuver in the series, and when you master it, pat yourself on the back—you are doing a good job of flying your airplane on the gauges.

Start from normal cruise, but don't begin any maneuvering until you reduce airspeed to the climb/descent speed used in Exercise #4. When this is achieved, take a deep breath, and enter a descending standard rate turn. So far, much like Exercise #6, but the similarity ends when you have descended 500 feet—at this point, repeat the Vertical S "soft bounce" and enter a constant airspeed climb, *and at the same time, reverse the direction of your turn.* In other words, if you started the S-1 with a descending right turn, you should go down 500 feet, turning all the time at a standard rate, then climb 500 feet while turning to the left. When you reach the top, enter another descent and reverse the direction of turn again. Continue through the same series of altitude changes as in the Vertical S, changing the turn each time you transition from climb to descent, or descent to climb. Don't be concerned about how many degrees you turn during the exercise; the objective is to accomplish smooth, positive, and coordinated changes in aircraft attitude at the proper times. You'll have your hands full, and after a couple of times through the Vertical S-1, you may have another name for it, one that is not necessarily acceptable in mixed company.

Exercise #8: Simulated Holding Pattern

Now you can begin applying your instrument artistry to more practical matters, such as a standard holding pattern. Get squared away on a heading in straight and level flight, and at a cardinal point on the clock, simulate station passage. Using the Four Ts (Time, Turn, Throttle, Talk), enter the holding pattern by noting the *Time*, roll into a standard rate *Turn* to the right, *Throttle* back to holding power, and pretend you are *Talking* to ATC, making the required report entering a holding pattern. This procedure will form a habit that will stand you in good stead later on.

The first turn when entering the racetrack is more than just a standard rate turn, because you are also changing airspeed and are required to hold altitude precisely. You will notice that all three controls call for changes in pressure—you need a higher angle of attack because of the lift change in the turn as well as the decrease in power and airspeed; unless you decrease the bank angle, your rate of turn will pick up as airspeed goes down, and rudder pressure will be needed as you change power and bank. Roll out at the 180-degree point, and fly level for exactly one minute. Now another 180-degrees to the right, fly for one minute, and you're finished. You could go on flying in the racetrack pattern all day long, but it wouldn't prove much—you should be aiming for smooth entry technique. Try a couple of left-hand patterns for kicks.

Exercise #9: The 45-Degree Procedure Turn

When a procedure turn is required, this one comes as close to "standard" as anything else. From straight and level flight at your approach airspeed (clean airplane), roll into a standard rate 45-degree turn to the right and fly for one minute. When that time has elapsed, turn left 180 degrees—the second turn will *always* be made in the opposite direction, taking you away from the station, and helping to guarantee that wind will not blow you back toward the airport shortening the time available to line up on the final approach course.

At the completion of the 180-degree turn, maintain heading for thirty seconds, then turn left 45 degrees to put you back on course, but going in the opposite direction. That's the entire purpose of the procedure turn—to get you turned around on a specific course. Head wind or tail wind will of course change the time on that thirty-second leg when you are actually flying to an approach course, but at least this exercise will instill the principle.

For variety, try a couple of procedure turns to the other side of the course, always making the second turn in the opposite direction.

Exercise #10: The 90–270 Procedure Turn

When time is of the essence, this little gem will get you turned around *tout de suite*, and it's a good exercise in coordination. To get the most out of it, plan to make your turns greater than standard rate—use 30 degrees of bank throughout. At approach speed in straight and level flight, roll into a turn to the right, and begin the roll-out pressure as if you were going to stop the turn at the 90-degree point.

But instead of levelling the wings, keep right on going, into a 30-degree bank in the opposite direction. Continue the turn through 270 degrees, and bring the airplane back to straight and level on the reciprocal of the original heading. So that you won't develop a right-hand pattern "groove," do a few of these to the left as well. Once again, the second turn is *always* made in the opposite direction from the first.

Exercise #11: Modified Pattern B

Ask any pilot who has been through a military flying school, and he'll tell you that the Pattern B was a sort of "final exam" of instrument technique before graduating to approaches. In addition to including all of the maneuvers you have been through in the previous exercises, this one requires a good bit of planning ahead, the essence of good IFR operations.

Because of its complexity, sketch out the pattern and its instructions on a card that you can clip to the control wheel, or your knee board, or wherever you plan to put approach charts when you get to the real thing.

There is one ground rule for Pattern B that makes it a little different from the other exercises. All timing is done with reference to cardinal times on the clock, regardless of the bank attitude of the airplane. If you find yourself getting increasingly more behind, check your rate of turn, and the rate at which you are rolling into and out of turns—the whole pattern is based on precise 3-degree-per-second turns; no more, no less. Start the pattern on a north heading—this exercise is *not* a test of your ability to add and subtract!

At the end of the final leg, you are pretending that you have just arrived at the missed approach point, and unless the hood falls off, you'll still be on instruments, so execute a missed approach. The objective is to accomplish the transition from descent to climb as smoothly and rapidly as possible, with a minimum loss of altitude. Climb out for 500 feet, and take off the hood—you've been hard at

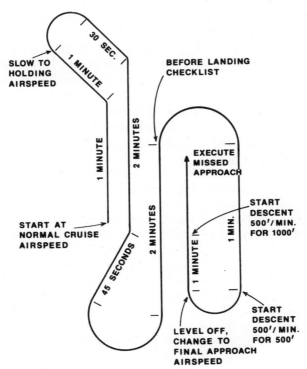

FIGURE 45 Modified Pattern B.

it for almost fifteen minutes of concentrated IFR practice, and you deserve a break.

Exercise # 12: Unusual Attitudes and Stalls

There is a purpose to be served by "unusual attitudes" practice, but it is *not* the satisfaction of your instructor's sadistic psyche. Ever since instrument flying instruction was invented, there have been CFIIs with a strong Beelzebubbian desire to devise complicated, stomach-turning, vertigo-producing attitudes that rank as truly unusual—but not necessarily useful in helping the student become a safer pilot. It is doubtful that in the course of an actual IFR flight you will allow your attention to wander completely away from the array of gauges on which your very life depends; so why should you practice recoveries from attitudes that are suddenly thrust upon you after a period of sightlessness during which the guy in the right seat has been flying the airplane? Since complete inattention is impossible to simulate as long as you can see, it is expedient for you to close your eyes while the unusual attitude is set up, but YOU should fly the airplane into the abnormal situation. You will have sensation of movement, but no idea of how much, and after a couple of turns you likely will not be able to tell which way. Under the direction of the instructor or the safety pilot, enter and roll out of turns in each direction—you may think you're doing just great, but sooner or later your inner ear and deep muscle senses will begin to fool you, and when your companion recognizes an attitude other than one required for normal instrument maneuvering, it's time for him to say, "recover."

You may have gotten yourself into a nose-low, 60-degree bank; or a wings-level, nose-high attitude. The airplane will be headed for the ground and about to go through the redline, or it could be valiantly struggling upward, ready to stall. The important part of the exercise is that YOU have flown yourself into the situation, and now it's up to you to get yourself out of it. These two attitudes, nose-low with airspeed building and nose-high with airspeed decreasing, are the themes upon which the recovery procedures are based. Allow the former to continue building and the airplane is likely to come apart if it doesn't collide with the ground first—ignore the latter and the airplane will stall, a less-than-desirable situation any time other than when you're 2 inches above the runway.

This is *not* the place for "do anything, even if it's wrong"—pull back on the wheel when you recognize the high-airspeed-if-you-don't-pull-out-of-this-dive-we'll-hit-the-ground situation, may be followed by a sharp report as the wing tips meet directly above the cabin. With this in mind, force yourself to make a thorough but rapid check of the instrument indications before you take action. There are only two basic problems, and you can experience only one at a time, so things aren't really so bad after all. And even more to your advantage, the same control is the one to reach for first in either situation—if the airspeed is high and moving higher, reduce power—immediately, rapidly, and significantly. Looking at the instruments and recognizing a near stall, your hand should instinctively go to the throttle and keep right on moving, adding power to get you out of trouble

If the wings are not level when "recover!" sounds (and they probably won't be), apply aileron pressure to get things back where they belong. The only problem yet to solve is that of pitch, which in either case should be returned to the level flight attitude; but the sequence is important, especially in a nose-low, high-airspeed situation. Unload the wings by taking out the bank before easing the nose up to the horizon—it doesn't matter quite so much in the nose-high problem, since the addition of power will probably keep you from stalling.

The ideal recovery from any unusual attitude consists of a split-second interpretation of what's going on, followed by a completely coordinated, rapid return to level flight with little loss of altitude, direction, or aplomb. It seldom works out that way, especially the problem of which controls take precedence in a particular situation. For the sake of structural integrity, organizing your thoughts, and providing guidelines, here's the order in which you should get things done when you recognize an unusual attitude (some bank will usually be present):

FIRST CASE: NOSE LOW, AIRSPEED INCREASING, STEEP BANK
1. Reduce power.
2. Level the wings.
3. Pitch attitude back to level (smooth and easy does it).

SECOND CASE: NOSE HIGH, AIRSPEED DECREASING, STEEP BANK
1. Add power (full power, if necessary).
2. Pitch attitude back to level (smooth and easy again, but it's not as critical here as in the high-speed case).
3. Level the wings.

While you're at it, run through a few stalls, while under the hood. Stalls? Under the hood? Why not?—you know that you have plenty of control over the airplane's attitude in a stall when you can see outside, and there's no difference with the blinders on. Set the power, gradually bring the nose up, keep the wings level with aileron, nail the heading indicator on the proper number with rudder pressure, and when your sturdy bird shudders and quits flying, make a normal recovery—it's just another unusual attitude. Try stalls in various aircraft configurations and power settings, and with different amounts of bank. You'll exude confidence when you can handle all these situations, and isn't it nice to know that should that one-in-a-million chance catch up with you, a stall in actual IFR conditions, you are prepared to solve the problem?